Koren Talmud Bavli

THE NOÉ EDITION

KETUBOT

Steinsaltz Center

KOREN

תלמוד בבלי

KOREN TALMUD BAVLI

THE NOÉ EDITION

כתובות

KETUBOT

Daf 2a through Daf 15b

COMMENTARY BY

Rabbi Adin Even-Israel Steinsaltz

EDITOR-IN-CHIEF

Rabbi Dr Tzvi Hersh Weinreb

SENIOR CONTENT EDITOR

Rabbi Dr Shalom Z Berger

EXECUTIVE EDITOR

Rabbi Joshua Schreier

STEINSALTZ CENTER

KOREN PUBLISHERS JERUSALEM

Supported by the Matanel Foundation

Koren Talmud Bavli, The Noe Edition
Vol. 15a: Tractate Ketubot, Daf 2a through Daf 15b
Paperback, ISBN, 978-965-7765-71-5

First Hebrew/English paperback edition, 2021

Koren Publishers Jerusalem Ltd.
PO Box 4044, Jerusalem 91040, ISRAEL
PO Box 8531, New Milford, CT 06776, USA
www.korenpub.com

Steinsaltz Center

Steinsaltz Center is the parent organization of institutions established by Rabbi Adin Even-Israel Steinsaltz

PO Box 45187, Jerusalem 91450 ISRAEL
Telephone: +972 2 646 0900, Fax +972 2 624 9454
www.steinsaltz-center.org

הִנֵּה יָמִים בָּאִים, נְאֻם אֲדֹנָי יֱהוִֹה, וְהִשְׁלַחְתִּי רָעָב בָּאָרֶץ,
לֹא־רָעָב לַלֶּחֶם וְלֹא־צָמָא לַמַּיִם, כִּי אִם־לִשְׁמֹעַ אֵת דִּבְרֵי יהוה.

Behold, days are coming – says the Lord God – I will send a hunger to the land, not a hunger for bread nor a thirst for water, but to hear the words of the Lord. (AMOS 8:11)

The Noé edition of the Koren Talmud Bavli
with the commentary of Rabbi Adin Even-Israel Steinsaltz
is dedicated to all those who open its covers
to quench their thirst for Jewish Knowledge,
in our generation of Torah renaissance.

This beautiful edition is for the young, the aged,
the novice and the savant alike,
as it unites the depth of Torah knowledge
with the best of academic scholarship.

Within its exquisite and vibrant pages,
words become worlds.

It will claim its place in the library of classics,
in the bookcases of the Beit Midrash,
the classrooms of our schools,
and in the offices of professionals and business people
who carve out precious time to grapple with its timeless wisdom.

For the Student and the Scholar

DEDICATED BY LEO AND SUE NOÉ

Steinsaltz Center

Executive Director, Steinsaltz Center

Rabbi Meni Even-Israel

Managing Editor

Rabbi Jason Rappoport

Senior Content Editor

Rabbi Dr. Shalom Z. Berger

Editors

Rabbi Joshua Amaru, *Coordinating Editor*
Rabbi Avishai Magence, *Content Curator*
Rabbi Alan Haber
Gila Hoch
Stephen Lauber
Eli Ozarowski
Avi Steinhart
Rabbi David Strauss
Rabbi Abe Y. Weschler

Copy Editors

Aliza Israel, *Coordinator*
Bracha Hermon
Ita Olesker
Debbie Ismailoff
Shira Finson
Ilana Sobel
Deena Nataf
Eliana Kurlantzick Yorav
Erica Hirsch Edvi
Nava Wieder

Language Consultants

Dr. Stephanie E. Binder, *Greek & Latin*
Rabbi Yaakov Hoffman, *Arabic*
Dr. Shai Secunda, *Persian*
Shira Shmidman, *Aramaic*

KOREN

Design & Typesetting

Dena Landowne Bailey, *Typesetting*
Tani Bayer, *Jacket Design*
Raphaël Freeman, *Design & Typography*

Images

Eliahu Misgav, *Illustration & Image Acquisition*

Introduction by the Publisher

The Talmud has sustained and inspired Jews for thousands of years. Throughout Jewish history, an elite cadre of scholars has absorbed its learning and passed it on to succeeding generations. The Talmud has been the fundamental text of our people.

Beginning in the 1960s, Rabbi Adin Even-Israel Steinsaltz שליט״א created a revolution in the history of Talmud study. His translation of the Talmud, first into modern Hebrew and then into other languages, as well the practical learning aids he added to the text, have enabled millions of people around the world to access and master the complexity and context of the world of Talmud.

It is thus a privilege to present the *Koren Talmud Bavli*, an English translation of the talmudic text with the brilliant elucidation of Rabbi Steinsaltz. The depth and breadth of his knowledge are unique in our time. His rootedness in the tradition and his reach into the world beyond it are inspirational.

Working with Rabbi Steinsaltz on this remarkable project has been not only an honor, but a great pleasure. Never shy to express an opinion, with wisdom and humor, Rabbi Steinsaltz sparkles in conversation, demonstrating his knowledge (both sacred and worldly), sharing his wide-ranging interests, and, above all, radiating his passion. I am grateful for the unique opportunity to work closely with him, and I wish him many more years of writing and teaching.

Our intentions in publishing this new edition of the Talmud are threefold. First, we seek to fully clarify the talmudic page to the reader – textually, intellectually, and graphically. Second, we seek to utilize today's most sophisticated technologies, both in print and electronic formats, to provide the reader with a comprehensive set of study tools. And third, we seek to help readers advance in their process of Talmud study.

To achieve these goals, the *Koren Talmud Bavli* is unique in a number of ways:

- The classic *tzurat hadaf* of Vilna, used by scholars since the 1800s, has been reset for great clarity, and opens from the Hebrew "front" of the book. Full *nikkud* has been added to both the talmudic text and Rashi's commentary, allowing for a more fluent reading with the correct pronunciation; the commentaries of *Tosafot* have been punctuated. Upon the advice of many English-speaking teachers of Talmud, we have separated these core pages from the translation, thereby enabling the advanced student to approach the text without the distraction of the translation. This also reduces the number of volumes in the set. At the bottom of each *daf*, there is a reference to the corresponding English pages. In addition, the Vilna edition was read against other manuscripts and older print editions, so that texts which had been removed by non-Jewish censors have been restored to their rightful place.
- The English translation, which starts on the English "front" of the book, reproduces the *menukad* Talmud text alongside the English translation (in bold) and commentary and explanation (in a lighter font). The Hebrew and Aramaic text is presented in logical paragraphs. This allows for a fluent reading of the text for the non-Hebrew or non-Aramaic reader. It also allows for the Hebrew reader to refer easily to the text alongside. Where the original text features dialogue or poetry, the English text is laid out in a manner appropriate to the genre. Each page refers to the relevant *daf*.

- Critical contextual tools surround the text and translation: personality notes, providing short biographies of the Sages; language notes, explaining foreign terms borrowed from Greek, Latin, Persian, or Arabic; and background notes, giving information essential to the understanding of the text, including history, geography, botany, archaeology, zoology, astronomy, and aspects of daily life in the talmudic era.
- Halakhic summaries provide references to the authoritative legal decisions made over the centuries by the rabbis. They explain the reasons behind each halakhic decision as well as the ruling's close connection to the Talmud and its various interpreters.
- Photographs, drawings, and other illustrations have been added throughout the text – in full color in the Standard and Electronic editions, and in black and white in the Daf Yomi edition – to visually elucidate the text.

This is not an exhaustive list of features of this edition, it merely presents an overview for the English-speaking reader who may not be familiar with the "total approach" to Talmud pioneered by Rabbi Steinsaltz.

Several professionals have helped bring this vast collaborative project to fruition. My many colleagues are noted on the Acknowledgments page, and the leadership of this project has been exceptional.

RABBI MENACHEM EVEN-ISRAEL, DIRECTOR OF THE STEINSALTZ CENTER, was the driving force behind this enterprise. With enthusiasm and energy, he formed the happy alliance with Koren and established close relationships among all involved in the work.

RABBI DR. TZVI HERSH WEINREB שליט״א, EDITOR-IN-CHIEF, brought to this project his profound knowledge of Torah, intellectual literacy of Talmud, and erudition of Western literature. It is to him that the text owes its very high standard, both in form and content, and the logical manner in which the beauty of the Talmud is presented.

RABBI JOSHUA SCHREIER, EXECUTIVE EDITOR, assembled an outstanding group of scholars, translators, editors, and proofreaders, whose standards and discipline enabled this project to proceed in a timely and highly professional manner.

RABBI MEIR HANEGBI, EDITOR OF THE HEBREW EDITION OF THE STEINSALTZ TALMUD, lent his invaluable assistance throughout the work process, supervising the reproduction of the Vilna pages.

RAPHAËL FREEMAN, EXECUTIVE EDITOR OF KOREN, created this Talmud's unique typographic design which, true to the Koren approach, is both elegant and user friendly.

It has been an enriching experience for all of us at Koren Publishers Jerusalem to work with the Steinsaltz Center to develop and produce the *Koren Talmud Bavli*. We pray that this publication will be a source of great learning and, ultimately, greater *avodat Hashem* for all Jews.

Matthew Miller, Publisher
Koren Publishers Jerusalem
Jerusalem 5772

Contents

For the vocalized Vilna Shas layout, please open as a Hebrew book.

Introduction to **Ketubot**

Ketubot is the central tractate in the order of *Nashim*. It provides clarification of most of the matters that constitute the relationship between husband and wife: Conjugal relations, mutual obligations, and monetary arrangements between them. In a general sense it addresses the entirety of marital life. Due to the abundance and variety of the topics, which branch out into many different areas of *halakha*, the early commentaries called tractate *Ketubot* the miniature Talmud or the key to the Talmud.

The marital bond is, from its inception, a sacred bond, which explains the fact that the term for betrothal is sanctification [*kiddushin*]. That bond can be terminated only by the death of one of the parties or by means of a special document, a scroll of severance. Violation of this bond by means of adultery engenders severe punishments administered both by man, i.e., execution by stoning or strangulation, and by Heaven, i.e., *karet*, besides fines and monetary penalties.

At the same time, according to *halakha*, the relationship between husband and wife within the framework of marriage is founded upon a system of mutual commitments fashioned on the basis of provisions and arrangements agreed upon by the parties. This system of arrangements is set out in a contract formulated between the husband and wife or their representatives, the marriage contract [*ketuba*]. This *ketuba* is fundamentally a written [*katuv*] contract, and is characterized in that manner because it is, for all intents and purposes, the only written document that every person requires. Since the provisions between husband and wife are articulated in the marriage contract, it is clear that the discussion in tractate *Ketubot* is fundamentally a comprehensive analysis of the marital rights and obligations.

The significance of the marriage contract is not merely as a practical apparatus regulating married life. The Sages established that marital ties not regulated by a marriage contract do not constitute marriage at all. The fundamental difference between a casual relationship, licentious relations, and marriage is contingent upon both the existence of an agreement between the parties articulating their mutual commitments for the duration of their relationship and the arrangements governing their potential separation. Any marital relationship that is not regulated by a marriage contract is tantamount to a licentious relationship.

The details of the agreement between husband and wife are like the details of any contract; both parties entering into marriage establish the provisions on the basis of which they intend to live their life together. Certain restrictions exist, as the marriage agreement, like any other agreement, cannot include stipulations that are against *halakha*, because of the principle: Anyone who stipulates a condition counter to what is written in the Torah, his condition is void. This includes stipulations that call for violation of a prohibition as well as those that abrogate obligations incumbent upon the parties by Torah law. Furthermore, over the generations, a system of permanent provisions was instituted, which constitute the standard formula of the marriage contract.

Although husband and wife can agree to abrogate certain details, or to add details and other arrangements, the standard marriage contract has a fixed configuration that establishes the guidelines for the marriage, unless additional provisions were stipulated. Analysis of these provisions, ranging from the commitments that stem from the marriage by Torah law to the various rabbinic ordinances, as well as the cases where the standard formula can be amended and the manner in which these changes are effected, constitute the primary topics of this tractate.

Most of the provisions and arrangements in the marriage contract are universally accepted. However, the Sages of the Mishna and the Gemara disputed the details: Which provisions and *halakhot* are by Torah law and which are by rabbinic law; which provisions are compulsory for all and which of them are merely customary and can be amended. Fundamentally, the conclusion reached is that there is a distinction between provisions that govern interpersonal relations, which cannot be abrogated, and monetary agreements, even those by Torah law, which can be amended or abrogated at the agreement of the two parties.

Based on Exodus 21:10, the obligations of a husband to his wife by Torah law are food, clothing, and conjugal rights. Food refers to the husband's obligation to provide sustenance to his wife according to her needs; clothing, his obligation to provide her with garments; and conjugal relations, his obligation to engage with her in sexual relations at regular intervals. Also by Torah law, the husband is entitled to nullify certain vows taken by his wife. After her death he inherits her property, although not everyone agrees that this is by Torah law. By rabbinic law, the husband is obligated to pay his wife's medical bills and to redeem her from captivity.

The Sages instituted that the wife will perform certain tasks in the home as well as contribute to supporting the family. Income that the wife earns from work, as well as any profits accrued from property belonging to her, and any lost item that she finds, belong to the husband. The Sages also instituted ordinances relating to the rights of the woman after the ties between them are severed by means of divorce or death.

One primary ordinance is the fixed sum of money identified as payment of the bill of divorce, which the husband is obligated pay his wife if he divorces her, or the heirs are obligated to pay the wife if she is widowed. For this payment, there is a distinction between a virgin, whose marriage contract is two hundred dinars, and one who is not a virgin, whose marriage contract is one hundred dinars. The husband is permitted to add to that sum any amount of money that he chooses, but he may not reduce the fixed sum. If he does, that is tantamount to nullification of the marriage contract, and the couple's relations are considered licentious and not marital relations.

The early Sages instituted that all the husband's property is liened to payment of the marriage contract. After the woman dies, the husband is obligated to bury her. After the death of the husband, the widow may continue to live in his house and be supported from his property for the duration of her widowhood. Likewise, there is a fixed condition that by the authority of the marriage contract, daughters born to the husband from this wife are supported from his property after his death, and sons born to this woman inherit the sum of her marriage contract in addition to their share in the inheritance.

This system of marital obligations and rights is typically in effect in every marriage, as even if a particular stipulation is omitted from the document, it is in effect as a stipulation of the court. However, the precise application of these provisions in different cases requires analysis. Similarly, the question arises: Which are the provisions that cannot be amended or abrogated, either due to their essence or because the Sages decreed that they cannot be changed or eliminated? And with regard to the provisions that can be amended, what is the legal way to effect this?

Marriage is based on agreement, and as such, conflict is apt to arise between the parties. Quarrels or incompatibility require intervention of the courts or halakhic authorities only if the couple decides to separate. However, there are additional conflicts that require halakhic resolution. One example is when husband and wife each accuse the other that he or she violated the provisions of the agreement. These claims can be with regard to the marriage itself, e.g., when one of the parties claims that he was misled to the extent that he would not have agreed to marry had he been privy to that information. Cases where this problem arises after betrothal and prior to marriage are discussed in tractate *Kiddushin*; cases where this problem arises after marriage belong in tractate *Ketubot*. There are additional claims with regard to fulfillment of the provisions of the agreement between the parties, where each accuses the other of failure to fulfill the obligations.

When these disputes come before the court, there are two stages to the halakhic deliberation. First, the court seeks to ascertain whether or not the claims are true. In this case, more than in any other agreement, there are various details that are difficult or impossible to ascertain. For example, if the husband claims that he discovered on the wedding night that his wife was not a virgin, there is rarely external testimony supporting either the husband's claim or the bride's counterclaim. In order to resolve the dispute, the court must rely on general determinations with regard to the credibility of the people and their claims.

The second stage involves ameliorating the situation. Based on the severity of the claims of the husband or wife, there are different manners of resolution, e.g., annulment of the marriage; mandating that the husband divorce his wife, paying her marriage contract if he was the guilty party and not paying it if she was the guilty party; or imposing fines and penalties to compel fulfillment of the terms of the *ketuba*.

All these topics, both in terms of whether certain actions are permitted or prohibited as well as with regard to the monetary ramifications of those actions, constitute the primary focus of tractate *Ketubot*. In addition, several related matters are discussed, e.g., the *halakhot* of lineage, victims of rape and seduction, and the *halakhot* of the slanderer. Typically, the Gemara addresses various tangential matters that arise in the course of discussion of these matters.

There are three general sections in this tractate: The first deals with the *halakhot* of a virgin; her marriage, as a victim of rape, and as a victim of slander. The second explores the details of the standard provisions of the marriage contract. The third discusses the *halakhot* of the wife's property and payment of the marriage contract. There are thirteen chapters in the tractate, the first five of which appear in the present volume. Typically, some address one defined issue and some address several, and some topics are discussed in several chapters.

Chapter One deals primarily with the marriage of a virgin and the credibility of the husband and the wife with regard to the claim concerning virginity.

Chapter Two deals with those cases where testimony is deemed credible from those whose testimony is typically not accepted, e.g., the testimony with regard to oneself or his relatives, or the testimony of one disqualified from testifying, such as a slave or a maidservant. The chapter also discusses the *halakhot* of a captive.

Chapter Three deals with the *halakhot* of a rapist and a seducer and analyzes the relationship between corporal and monetary punishment.

Chapter Four discusses in general the mutual rights of father and daughter, husband and wife, and specifically the *halakhot* of the slanderer. The primary provisions of the marriage contract are also explained.

Chapter Five discusses the details of the ordinances instituted with regard to the marriage contract and especially in cases where they alter the fixed provisions, either through mutual agreement or unilaterally.

Introduction to **Perek I**

This chapter deals primarily with the initial stages of marriage: The appropriate time, the marriage ceremony, and the monetary and ritual ramifications of the initial act of intercourse. Most of the questions analyzed are related to the *halakhot* of the marriage contract, specifically the marriage contract of the virgin.

The sum of the marriage contract of a virgin is two hundred dinars, and of a non-virgin, one hundred dinars. A fundamental question relates to the definition of a virgin for these purposes: Is this a medical-biological definition or is it merely a legal definition? Is a virgin a woman whose hymen is intact, a woman who never engaged in intercourse, or a woman who never married? On a related note, who are the women with the presumptive status of a virgin, and who are the women who have lost that presumptive status?

Various questions arise when a man marries a woman based on the assumption that she is a virgin and later discovers that she is not. His claim can be grounds for annulment, for reduction of the sum of the marriage contract, or for concern that the bride is forbidden to her husband as an adulteress. However, before these questions are analyzed, there is another fundamental problem: Was she or was she not a virgin when she married, and if she was not a virgin, how did she lose her virginity? Typically, there is no clear evidence or testimony in that case. There are instances where the woman admits that she was not a virgin, and there are instances where she explains the phenomenon in different ways. Therefore, it must be determined to what degree are the claims of the woman deemed credible. In what cases is the claim of the husband deemed credible, and in what cases is the claim of the wife deemed credible?

Stemming from these dilemmas, whose answers are largely dependent upon the credibility accorded to the husband's claim, another series of dilemmas is raised, not directly related to the *halakhot* of the marriage contract but related to matters of lineage. In the case of an unmarried woman who was suspected or proven to have engaged in intercourse with an unidentified man, to what degree is she deemed credible to claim that the man was of unflawed lineage and therefore she is not disqualified from marrying a priest? Likewise, if she was impregnated by an unidentified man, is she deemed credible if she says that the father of the fetus is of unflawed lineage?

These are the central issues raised in this chapter. However, in the course of clarifying them, difficulties with regard to the marriage ceremony are addressed. In addition, questions related to engaging in intercourse on Shabbat with one's virgin bride are discussed, as well as questions relating to other prohibitions.

מתני׳ בְּתוּלָה נִשֵּׂאת לְיוֹם הָרְבִיעִי, וְאַלְמָנָה לְיוֹם הַחֲמִישִׁי. שֶׁפַּעֲמַיִם בְּשַׁבָּת בָּתֵּי דִינִין יוֹשְׁבִין בָּעֲיָירוֹת: בַּיּוֹם הַשֵּׁנִי וּבַיּוֹם הַחֲמִישִׁי, שֶׁאִם הָיָה לוֹ טַעֲנַת בְּתוּלִים הָיָה מַשְׁכִּים לְבֵית דִּין.

MISHNA **A virgin**[N] **is married on Wednesday**[HN] **and a widow on Thursday.**[N] The reason for the former is **that twice a week**[N] **courts convene in the towns, on Monday and Thursday, so that if** the husband **had a claim concerning** the bride's **virginity**[N] when consummating the marriage on Wednesday night, **he would go early** the next day **to court** and make his claim.

גמ׳ אָמַר רַב יוֹסֵף אָמַר רַב יְהוּדָה אָמַר שְׁמוּאֵל: מִפְּנֵי מָה אָמְרוּ בְּתוּלָה נִשֵּׂאת לְיוֹם הָרְבִיעִי – לְפִי שֶׁשָּׁנִינוּ: הִגִּיעַ זְמַן וְלֹא נִישְּׂאוּ – אוֹכְלוֹת מִשֶּׁלּוֹ, וְאוֹכְלוֹת בִּתְרוּמָה.

GEMARA **Rav Yosef said** that **Rav Yehuda said** that **Shmuel said: Due to what reason did they say**[N] **that a virgin is married on Wednesday?** It is **because we learned** in a mishna elsewhere (57a): **If the time** that the groom designated for the wedding **arrived,** and the wedding was postponed, **and they were not married,** the brides are entitled to **eat from his** food **and,** if he is a priest, **eat *teruma*.**

יָכוֹל הִגִּיעַ זְמַן בְּאֶחָד בְּשַׁבָּת יְהֵא מַעֲלֶה לָהּ מְזוֹנוֹת – לְכָךְ שָׁנִינוּ: בְּתוּלָה נִשֵּׂאת לְיוֹם הָרְבִיעִי.

One might think that if the designated **time arrived on Sunday,** and the wedding was postponed, **he would provide her sustenance** beginning on Sunday. **Therefore, we learned: A virgin is married on Wednesday.** Until Wednesday, the designated time is not considered to have arrived, even if the original date was earlier in the week.

HALAKHA

A virgin is married on Wednesday – בְּתוּלָה נִשֵּׂאת לְיוֹם הָרְבִיעִי: In places where the courts convene only on Mondays and Thursdays, a virgin is married on Wednesday, so that if the groom has a claim concerning her virginity, he can go to court early the next day (Rambam *Sefer Nashim, Hilkhot Ishut* 10:15; *Shulḥan Arukh, Even HaEzer* 64:3).

NOTES

Virgin – בְּתוּלָה: *Tosafot* ask: Why doesn't the tractate begin with the definite article: The virgin, a style employed by the Mishna in other areas? The primary answer is that the definite article is employed only with regard to matters mentioned in the Torah, and the day set for the wedding of a virgin is a rabbinic ordinance.

Wednesday – יוֹם הָרְבִיעִי: *Tosafot* write that this indicates that the wedding is performed during the day and not on Wednesday night. This is because frequently lengthy negotiations precede the signing of the marriage contract between the parties. In addition, in the case of wedding performed at night, the wedding celebration and feast would likely extend deep into the night, (*Tiferet Yisrael*). Due to these factors, there is concern that if the wedding is performed at night, it will not be consummated that night.

The Ritva notes that use of the prefix *le*, meaning to, instead of *be*, meaning on, alludes to the fact cited later in the Gemara that the wedding is postponed to Wednesday even if the time designated for the marriage was earlier in the week. The prefix in the variant reading in the Jerusalem Talmud is the more conventional *be*.

And a widow on Thursday – וְאַלְמָנָה לְיוֹם הַחֲמִישִׁי: The mishna does not specify why a widow is married on Thursday. Some commentaries explain that the reasons cited in the Gemara for this ordinance do not apply in all cases. That the Sages were assiduous in seeing to the well-being of Jewish women (5a), ensuring that her groom will rejoice with her three days, applies only if the groom has a profession. The other reason cited there: Since the blessing of procreation was stated to man on the sixth day of Creation, is not obligatory (Ramban; Ritva).

The Ran writes that the main reason the Sages set a specific day for a wedding was for virgin brides, where there is concern that perhaps she committed adultery after betrothal and is therefore forbidden to the groom. Once that ordinance was instituted, additional reasons to establish a specific day for widows were suggested as well. However, since the primary ordinance was instituted for virgins, the Gemara does not elaborate on the ordinance instituted with regard to widows.

The Ran, in his commentary on the Rif, writes that the Sages obscured the reasons for establishing these specific days to prevent people from taking them lightly, as the reasons do not apply in all cases.

That twice a week – שֶׁפַּעֲמַיִם בְּשַׁבָּת: This ordinance that courts convene on Monday and Thursday is one of the ten ordinances instituted by Ezra (*Bava Kamma* 82a). Prior to the institution of that ordinance, no courts convened in the towns at all, and people would rely on the courts in the big cities, or convene a court ad hoc when necessary. No flexibility was displayed with regard to this ordinance in order to facilitate greater freedom in choosing a wedding day because of the significance accorded Ezra and his ordinances. There was concern that if one of his ordinances was revoked, others might follow (see Meiri).

If the husband had a claim concerning the bride's virginity – אִם הָיָה לוֹ טַעֲנַת בְּתוּלִים: The early commentaries question this reason from a variety of perspectives. For one, the Gemara in several places states that promiscuity is uncommon. Why then, did the Sages institute an ordinance due to an uncommon phenomenon?

They answer that when the Sages said that promiscuity was uncommon, they spoke with regard to specific cases, e.g., engaging in relations with one's sister's daughter or with a married woman. However, engaging in relations with a woman who is merely betrothed before marriage is sufficiently commonplace to warrant instituting the ordinance (see *Tosafot* and Rosh).

The commentaries raise an additional question with regard to the validity of the claim concerning virginity in terms of rendering the bride forbidden to him. Even if he discovered that she was not a virgin, there is a compound uncertainty with regard to whether his bride is forbidden: There is uncertainty whether she engaged in relations before betrothal, in which case she is not forbidden to him, or whether she did so after betrothal, in which case she is forbidden to him. There is additional uncertainty, as, even if she engaged in relations after betrothal, it is uncertain whether she engaged in relations of her own volition or whether she was raped, in which case she would be permitted to him. In cases of compound uncertainty with regard to a prohibition, the ruling is lenient. Therefore, the woman should be permitted in this case.

Therefore, *Tosafot* explain that the original ordinance setting the wedding of a virgin on Wednesday was instituted due to those women with regard to whom there is only one uncertainty, e.g., the wife of a priest, who is rendered forbidden to him even if she was raped, or a woman who was betrothed before she was three years and one day old, in which case it is clear that she engaged in relations after betrothal. Once the ordinance was in place, the Sages established it as the standard for all virgins.

Rashi explains that the groom's claim that the wife is not a virgin does not render her forbidden to her husband. Rather, the expectation is that once the matter is publicized in court, perhaps witnesses will come and testify that she committed volitional adultery after betrothal.

The Ritva explains that it is implausible that the Sages would institute an ordinance for the small minority of cases included in the explanation of *Tosafot*. However, if Rashi's reason is combined with theirs, that would provide sound basis for instituting the ordinance.

The Meiri cites an opinion shared by several commentaries. They explain that the hope is that when the woman stands before the court, if she is guilty, she will admit that she committed adultery. The Rashba rejects that opinion. The Meiri cites an additional consideration: There is a monetary aspect to the claim, as the groom is claiming that he agreed to a marriage contract of two hundred dinars based on the presumption that she was a virgin. After discovering that she is not a virgin, he claims that the marriage contract should be for the one hundred dinars to which a non-virgin is entitled, or even that the betrothal was a mistaken transaction and the bride is not entitled to a marriage contract at all.

Due to what reason did they say – מִפְּנֵי מָה אָמְרוּ: The commentaries go to great lengths to explain the first version of Shmuel's comments, which ties the ordinance that a virgin marry on Wednesday to the time from which the groom is duty bound to provide for his betrothed, in an attempt to explain why the Gemara thought to connect the two *halakhot*, although it was ultimately rejected.

According to the Rivash, Rav Yosef doesn't think that the claim concerning virginity is a sufficient reason to institute an ordinance, and so he wanted to explain Shmuel's position as follows: Since the Sages set a time after which the groom is obligated to provide for his betrothed, the wedding should take place on that day as well.

אָמַר רַב יוֹסֵף: מָרֵיהּ דְּאַבְרָהָם! תָּלֵי תַּנְיָא בְּדְלָא תַּנְיָא. הֵי תַּנְיָא וְהֵי לָא תַּנְיָא? הָא תַּנְיָא וְהָא תַּנְיָא! אֶלָּא: תָּלֵי תַּנְיָא דִּמְפָרֵשׁ טַעֲמָא, בִּדְתַנְיָא דְּלָא מְפָרֵשׁ טַעֲמָא!

After citing the statements above, **Rav Yosef said** in astonishment: **Lord of Abraham,**[N] Shmuel **makes** that which **is taught dependent on** that which **is not taught,** using the latter to explain the former. The Gemara asks: **Which is taught and which is not taught?** Both **this** mishna **is taught** and **that** mishna **is taught.** The Gemara answers: **Rather,** Shmuel **makes** the *halakha* that **is taught** in the mishna here, **whose reason is explicit,**[N] **dependent on** a *halakha* that **is taught** in the later mishna, **whose reason is not explicit.** Citation of the later mishna contributed nothing to the understanding of the mishna here.

אֶלָּא, אִי אִיתְּמַר הָכִי אִיתְּמַר, אָמַר רַב יְהוּדָה אָמַר שְׁמוּאֵל: מִפְּנֵי מָה אָמְרוּ בְּתוּלָה נִשֵּׂאת לְיוֹם הָרְבִיעִי – שֶׁאִם הָיָה לוֹ טַעֲנַת בְּתוּלִים הָיָה מַשְׁכִּים לְבֵית דִּין. וְתִינָּשֵׂא בְּאֶחָד בְּשַׁבָּת, שֶׁאִם הָיָה לוֹ טַעֲנַת בְּתוּלִים הָיָה מַשְׁכִּים לְבֵית דִּין. שָׁקְדוּ חֲכָמִים עַל תַּקָּנַת בְּנוֹת יִשְׂרָאֵל, שֶׁיְּהֵא טוֹרֵחַ בִּסְעוּדָה שְׁלֹשָׁה יָמִים: אֶחָד בְּשַׁבָּת וְשֵׁנִי בְּשַׁבָּת וּשְׁלִישִׁי בְּשַׁבָּת, וּבָרְבִיעִי כּוֹנְסָהּ.

Rather, if it was stated, this is how **it was stated: Rav Yehuda said** that **Shmuel said: Due to what** reason **did** the Sages in the mishna **say** that **a virgin is married on Wednesday?**[N] It is so **that if** the husband **had a claim concerning** the bride's **virginity, he would go early** the next day **to court** and make his claim. The Gemara asks: **But** if that is the reason, **let her marry on Sunday,** as then too, **if** the husband **had a claim concerning** the bride's **virginity, he would go early** the next day **to court** and make his claim. The Gemara answers: The **Sages were assiduous in seeing to the well-being of Jewish women**[N] and instituted that the wedding take place on Wednesday, **so that** the groom **would exert** himself **in** arranging **the** wedding **feast for three days:**[H] **Sunday, Monday, and Tuesday, and on Wednesday, he marries her.**

וְעַכְשָׁיו שֶׁשָּׁנִינוּ "שָׁקְדוּ", אוֹתָהּ שֶׁשָּׁנִינוּ הִגִּיעַ זְמַן וְלֹא נִישְּׂאוּ אוֹכְלוֹת מִשֶּׁלּוֹ וְאוֹכְלוֹת בִּתְרוּמָה, הִגִּיעַ זְמַן בְּאֶחָד בְּשַׁבָּת, מִתּוֹךְ שֶׁאֵינוֹ יָכוֹל לִכְנוֹס – אֵינוֹ מַעֲלֶה לָהּ מְזוֹנוֹת.

The Gemara continues: **And now that we learned** that the reason for the ruling in the mishna that a woman is married on Wednesday is that the Sages **were assiduous**[N] in this matter, then with regard to **that** *halakha,* **which we learned** in the later mishna: **If the time arrived and they were not married,** the brides are entitled to **eat from his** food **and eat** *teruma,* one may conclude: **If the time arrived on Sunday,**[H] **since** he is **unable to marry** her because he is busy preparing the wedding feast, **he is not obligated to provide her sustenance** until Wednesday.

לְפִיכָךְ, חָלָה הוּא, אוֹ שֶׁחָלְתָה הִיא, אוֹ שֶׁפֵּירְסָה נִדָּה – אֵינוֹ מַעֲלֶה לָהּ מְזוֹנוֹת.

Therefore, according to the same line of reasoning, if the husband **fell ill,**[H] **or** if the bride **fell ill, or** in a case **where she began to menstruate** [*peirsa nidda*][LN] and the wedding had to be postponed, he similarly need **not provide her sustenance** from the designated time, as he did not initiate the delay.

HALAKHA

So that the groom would exert himself in arranging the wedding feast for three days – שֶׁיְּהֵא טוֹרֵחַ בִּסְעוּדָה שְׁלֹשָׁה יָמִים: In places where the courts convene every day, a man and woman can marry on any day that he chooses, provided that he exerts himself for three days preparing the feast. Therefore, in many places it was customary for marriages to take place on Friday, after the groom had exerted himself sufficiently for the feast. However, if the bride and her family are willing to forgo the elaborate preparations, the three days apparently are not required, and that is in fact the custom (Rambam *Sefer Nashim, Hilkhot Ishut* 10:14, 19; *Shulḥan Arukh, Even HaEzer* 64:3).

If the time arrived on Sunday – הִגִּיעַ זְמַן בְּאֶחָד בְּשַׁבָּת: If a date several months after the betrothal was set for the wedding, and that date occurred, for example, on a Sunday or Friday, the groom is not required to provide for his wife from that day, since the wedding was postponed due to a rabbinic ordinance, as explained later in the Gemara (Rambam *Sefer Nashim, Hilkhot Ishut* 10:19; *Shulḥan Arukh, Even HaEzer* 56:3).

If the husband fell ill, etc. – חָלָה הוּא וכו׳: If a date was set for the wedding, and it was postponed due to unavoidable circumstances, e.g., the bride or groom fell ill or the bride began to menstruate, then the groom is not required to provide sustenance for his betrothed (Rambam *Sefer Nashim, Hilkhot Ishut* 10:19; *Shulḥan Arukh, Even HaEzer* 56:3).

LANGUAGE

Began to menstruate [*peirsa nidda*] – פֵּירְסָה נִדָּה: It is difficult to ascertain the meaning of the verb *peirsa* as it is employed here. There is a variant reading, *peirsha,* meaning separation or a discharge from the woman. Others suggest that it is taken from, or at least influenced by, the Greek ἀπόρρυσις, *aporrusis,* meaning flow or leak.

NOTES

Lord of Abraham – מָרֵיהּ דְּאַבְרָהָם: The commentaries explain Rav Yosef's powerful reaction to the statement of Shmuel in different ways. Some explain that he cited the statement as he originally heard it, and he wondered how to resolve the problem. Others explain that, as mentioned throughout the Talmud, due to illness, Rav Yosef lost his memory, and he was uncertain whether he cited the statement correctly.

The answer of the Gemara is understood in various ways, based on these explanations. According to the first explanation, the Gemara proceeds to answer Rav Yosef's question. According to the second explanation, Rav Yosef himself remembered that the statement that he cited was actually stated differently (see Rashba and Meiri).

He makes the *halakha* that is taught, whose reason is explicit – תָּלֵי תַּנְיָא דִּמְפָרֵשׁ טַעֲמָא: Although the reason isn't fully articulated in the mishna, as no explanation is provided why the marriage is on Wednesday and not Sunday, there is a reason cited: If the husband had a claim concerning the bride's virginity when consummating the marriage on Wednesday night, he would go early the next day to court and make his claim. No reason is cited in the other mishna (Ramban; Rashba).

Due to what reason did the Sages say that a virgin is married on Wednesday – מִפְּנֵי מָה אָמְרוּ בְּתוּלָה נִשֵּׂאת לְיוֹם הָרְבִיעִי: Most commentaries explain that the question is: Why did the ordinance designate Wednesday as opposed to Sunday? It is implausible to suggest that Wednesday is merely an example and the same is true for Sunday. Were that the case, the mishna should have mentioned Sunday, which is earlier in the week. According to this understanding, when the Gemara suggests: Let her marry on Sunday, it is not an additional question but rather the conclusion of the first question (Rabbi Aharon HaLevi). Others explain that the original question is: Why was Wednesday chosen and not any other day of the week? According to that explanation, there are two separate questions (Rivash; see *Shita Mekubbetzet*).

The Sages were assiduous in seeing to the well-being of Jewish women – שָׁקְדוּ חֲכָמִים עַל תַּקָּנַת בְּנוֹת יִשְׂרָאֵל: The Ramban asks: Why is this ordinance specifically attributed to the well-being of Jewish women? Don't the men rejoice as well? He explains that this ordinance is said to benefit the woman because if the husband did not prepare the feast in advance, he would be occupied with the preparations during the days of celebration, and the bride would be left alone.

The Ritva explains that the Sages sought to ensure that the groom would exert himself in arranging the wedding feast, since, as the Gemara later explains, he will be reluctant to make false accusations and have all his efforts go to waste. That is the reason his claim concerning virginity is accorded credibility.

And now that we learned that the Sages were assiduous – וְעַכְשָׁיו שֶׁשָּׁנִינוּ שָׁקְדוּ: It appears that Shmuel was referring to the *baraita* where it is stated that the Sages were assiduous in seeing to the well-being of Jewish women and ensured that the groom would exert himself in arranging the wedding feast for three days prior to the wedding. He considered that to be the primary reason for the ordinance in the mishna, and he therefore explained the mishna to mean: If the time arrived and they did not marry. An opinion cited in the *Shita Mekubbetzet* suggests that Shmuel's statement itself is a primary halakhic source, as Shmuel was one of the first *amora'im*.

With regard to the connection between the assiduousness of the Sages and the fact that the groom need not provide for his betrothed until Wednesday, Rashi explains that once the Sages instituted that the wedding must be on Wednesday, it is tantamount to circumstances beyond his control preventing him from marrying earlier in the week. Therefore, he is exempt from the obligation to provide support for his betrothed.

The Ramban explains that were Wednesday designated merely to facilitate the groom's claim concerning virginity, the bride could contend that if that is the reason for waiting until Wednesday to marry, she should not have to forgo the support to which she is entitled. However, once there is an additional reason of which she is the beneficiary, that claim is baseless and the groom is exempt.

The Ramban provides another explanation. If not for the statement of Shmuel, it could have been understood that there is a dispute between the mishna and the *baraita*. The mishna here holds that the only reason for the ordinance was the claim concerning virginity. Therefore, although the mishna stated that a virgin marries on Wednesday, the same is true for Sunday. However, according to the *baraita* with regard to the assiduousness of the Sages, a virgin marries only on Wednesday. Taken together, the reasons cited in the two sources lead to the conclusion that the *tanna* of the mishna is also of the opinion that a virgin marries specifically on Wednesday.

She began to menstruate – פֵּירְסָה נִדָּה: Based on this and other sources, the Rambam and the *ge'onim* maintain that it is actually prohibited to conduct a wedding ceremony if the status of the bride is that of a menstruating woman. Others are of the opinion that it is not prohibited, but the custom is not to do so, so that he will not be in seclusion with her while she is forbidden to him. The Meiri and others discuss this at length and tie this dispute to the fundamental dispute with regard to the nature of the wedding canopy.

וְאִיכָּא דְּבָעֵי לָהּ מִיבַּעְיָא: חָלָה הוּא מַהוּ? הָתָם טַעֲמָא מַאי – מִשּׁוּם דַּאֲנִיס, וְהָכָא נַמִי – הָא אֲנִיס. אוֹ דִּלְמָא: הָתָם אֲנִיס בְּתַקַּנְתָּא דְּתַקִּינוּ לֵיהּ רַבָּנַן, הָכָא – לָא.

And there are those **who raised it as a dilemma: If the** groom **fell ill, what is** the ruling with regard to his obligation to provide her sustenance? **There,** in the case where the designated time arrived on Sunday, **what is the reason** that he is exempt? It is **due to** the fact **that he was forced** to postpone the wedding by circumstances beyond his control. **And here too, isn't he forced** by circumstances beyond his control, and he should therefore be exempt? **Or, perhaps** there is a distinction between the cases. **There, he was forced by an ordinance that was instituted by the Sages** that a virgin marries on Wednesday, and they exempted him from providing for her until then. **However, here,** that is **not** the case. Therefore, despite the existence of circumstances beyond his control, he is not exempt from providing her sustenance due to his illness.

וְאִם תִּמְצֵי לוֹמַר חָלָה הוּא מַעֲלֶה לָהּ מְזוֹנוֹת, חָלְתָה הִיא מַהוּ? מָצֵי אָמַר לָהּ: אֲנָא הָא קָאֵימְנָא, אוֹ דִּלְמָא, מָצְיָא אָמְרָה לֵיהּ ״נִסְתַּחֲפָה שָׂדֵהוּ״?

And if you say that if he fell ill, he provides her sustenance at the time designated for the wedding, then **if she fell ill, what** is the ruling? **Can he say to her: I am standing here** prepared to wed you, and if you are not prepared, it is not my fault? **Or perhaps she can say to him that his field was inundated,**[N] i.e., her illness is tantamount to a natural disaster that befell him, and he must nevertheless provide for her.

וְאִם תִּמְצֵי לוֹמַר אָמְרָה לֵיהּ ״נִסְתַּחֲפָה שָׂדֵהוּ״, פֵּירְסָה נִדָּה מַהוּ?

And if you say that if she fell ill **she can say to him that his field was inundated,** if **she became a menstruating woman** and the wedding was postponed, **what is** the ruling? Is this too considered an unavoidable circumstance, like illness, and he must provide for her, or was this predictable?

בִּשְׁעַת וִסְתָּהּ – לָא תִּיבָּעֵי לָךְ,

If she began menstruating **at the time of her set period** [*vista*],[L] **do not raise the dilemma,**

NOTES

His field was inundated – נִסְתַּחֲפָה שָׂדֵהוּ: Based on Rashi's explanation that she is effectively saying to him that it is his misfortune that caused the postponement, the commentaries ask: Why not say when he falls ill that her misfortune caused the postponement? Some explain that since the mitzva of procreation is incumbent specifically on the husband, any delay in the wedding is attributable to his misfortune. The Ramban and others reject this.

Apparently, since he committed to marry her at a certain time, he incurs a monetary obligation. If the wedding is postponed, even due to circumstances beyond his control, it is like any case of monetary loss due to circumstances beyond one's control (Rabbi Aharon HaLevi).

LANGUAGE

Set period [*veset*] – וֶסֶת: This term is employed throughout the Talmud and midrash in the sense of anything that works on a fixed schedule. It is especially employed in reference to a woman's menstrual cycle. Many scholars attribute the word to the Greek ἔθος, *ethos*, whose principle meaning is custom or habit. However, others assert that the word, at least in its specific meaning with regard to the menstrual cycle, is connected to the Aramaic *vas*, to be sullied.

Perek **I**
Daf **2** Amud **b**

דְּלָא מָצְיָא אָמְרָה לֵיהּ ״נִסְתַּחֲפָה שָׂדֵהוּ״. כִּי תִּיבָּעֵי לָךְ – שֶׁלֹּא בִּשְׁעַת וִסְתָּהּ מַאי? כֵּיוָן דְּלָא בִּשְׁעַת וִסְתָּהּ הָוְיָא – מָצְיָא אָמְרָה לֵיהּ ״נִסְתַּחֲפָה שָׂדֵהוּ״, אוֹ דִּלְמָא, כֵּיוָן דְּאִיכָּא נָשֵׁי דְּקָא מְשַׁנְּיָא וִסְתַּיְיהוּ, כִּשְׁעַת וִסְתָּהּ דָּמֵי?

as it is clear that **she cannot say to him** that **his field was inundated.** Here, the circumstances were avoidable, and postponement of the wedding is attributable to her. **When you should raise a dilemma** is in a case where menstruation began **not at the time of her set period. What is** the ruling there? **Since it is not the time of her set period,** it is comparable to the case of her illness, and **she can say to him that his field was inundated. Or, perhaps since there are some women whose set period changes,** it is avoidable, and its legal status **is like** menstruation at **the time of her set period,** and postponement of the wedding is attributable to her.

פָּשֵׁיט רַב אַחַאי: הִגִּיעַ זְמַן וְלֹא נִישְּׂאוּ אוֹכְלוֹת מִשֶּׁלּוֹ וְאוֹכְלוֹת בִּתְרוּמָה. ״לֹא נָשְׂאוּ״ לָא קָתָנֵי, אֶלָּא ״לֹא נִישְּׂאוּ״,

Rav Aḥai resolved[N] these dilemmas through a careful reading of the mishna: **If the time arrived and they were not married,** the brides are entitled to **eat from his food and eat *teruma*. It doesn't teach:** And the grooms **didn't marry,** in the active form. **Rather,** it teaches: **And the brides were not married,**[N] in the passive form.

הֵיכִי דָּמֵי, אִי דְּקָא מְעַכְּבָן אִינְהִי – אַמַּאי אוֹכְלוֹת מִשֶּׁלּוֹ וְאוֹכְלוֹת בִּתְרוּמָה? אֶלָּא לָאו דְּאִיתְּנִיס כִּי הַאי גַּוְונָא, וְקָתָנֵי: אוֹכְלוֹת מִשֶּׁלּוֹ וְאוֹכְלוֹת בִּתְרוּמָה!

The Gemara asks: **What are the circumstances** described in the phrase: They were not married? **If the** brides **postpone** the marriage, **why do they eat from his** food **and eat *teruma*? Rather, is it not** referring to a case **where they were compelled** by circumstances beyond their control **in that manner,** e.g., the bride falling ill or beginning to menstruate, **and it teaches:** The brides **eat from his** food **and eat *teruma*,** and his bad fortune is responsible for his situation.

NOTES

Rav Aḥai resolved – פָּשֵׁיט רַב אַחַאי: *Tosafot* reject the Rashbam's opinion that this is referring to Rav Aḥai Gaon, the author of the *She'iltot*, as the *amora* Rav Ashi, who is cited in the Gemara as rejecting the resolution of Rav Aḥai, could not have rejected the statement of one who lived several centuries after his death. There are variant readings (see Meiri), who cite the rejection of the resolution of Rav Aḥai without attribution. Based on the Epistle of Rav Sherira Gaon, the reference is to Rav Aḥai of Bei Hittim, who was one of the *savora'im*, a member of the post-amoraic generation responsible for the redaction of the Talmud.

It doesn't teach: And the grooms didn't marry [*nasu*], rather: And the brides were not married [*nisu*] – לֹא נָשְׂאוּ לָא קָתָנֵי, אֶלָּא לֹא נִישְּׂאוּ: The early commentaries question how the Gemara determined that the term in the mishna is *nisu*, referring to the brides, and not *nasu*, referring to the grooms. After all, the mishna was written without vocalization. The Ritva answers, citing Rabbeinu Yitzḥak, that had the groom been the subject of the sentence, it should have said *nasa*, in the singular, as in the first clause of the mishna it says: One gives the man twelve months, in the singular. Others determined that the bride is the subject from the continuation of the mishna: The brides are entitled to eat from his food. Had the grooms been the subject, it would have continued: The brides are entitled to eat from their food. The Rashba and the Rosh explain simply that since the Gemara is a record of study conducted orally, they were aware of the correct reading.

אמר רב אשי: לעולם אימא לך: כל אונסא לא אכלה, ודקא מעכבי אינהו, ובדין הוא דאיבעי ליה למיתני "לא נשאו", ואיידי דתנא רישא בדידהי תנא נמי סיפא בדידהי.

Rav Ashi said: Actually, I will say to you:[N] **In any case of unavoidable circumstances,** whether they affect him or they affect her, **she doesn't eat** from his food, **and** the mishna is referring to a case **where** grooms **postpone the wedding. And by right,** the *tanna* **should have taught: They didn't marry,** which would have established that grooms caused the postponement. **And since** the *tanna* taught **the first clause** of the mishna cited above **in** terms of a bride: The Sages give a virgin twelve months, **it taught the latter clause in** terms of a bride. Therefore, no inference may be drawn from the formulation of the latter clause. Only if the groom postpones the wedding is he obligated to provide sustenance for the women when the time designated for the wedding arrives.

אמר רבא: ולענין גיטין אינו כן. אלמא קסבר רבא: אין אונס בגיטין.

Rava said: And although delays caused by circumstances beyond his control exempt the groom from providing support to his betrothed at the time originally designated for the wedding, with regard **to bills of divorce that is not so. Apparently, Rava maintains that unavoidable circumstances** have **no** legal standing with regard **to bills of divorce.**[NH] If one stipulated that the bill of divorce will take effect only with the fulfillment of a condition, even if that condition was fulfilled due to circumstances beyond his control, the bill of divorce takes effect.

מנא ליה לרבא הא? אילימא מהא דתנן: "הרי זה גיטיך אם לא באתי מכאן ועד שנים עשר חודש", ומת בתוך שנים עשר חודש, אינו גט. מת – הוא דאינו גט, הא חלה – הרי זה גט.

The Gemara asks: **From where does Rava learn this** principle? **If we say it is from that which we learned** in a mishna (*Gittin* 76b) with regard to one who said to his wife: **This is your bill of divorce, if I do not return from now until** the conclusion of **twelve months, and he died within** those **twelve months,**[H] the document **is not a bill of divorce.** Therefore, if she has no children from her deceased husband, the *halakhot* of levirate marriage would apply to her. The Gemara infers: If **he died,** that **is when it is not a bill of divorce,** since a divorce cannot take effect posthumously. By inference, in cases involving other circumstances beyond his control, e.g., if **he fell ill,** and therefore did not return, **it is a bill of divorce** and it takes effect. Apparently, if the reason for his failure to arrive is a circumstance beyond his control, the divorce takes effect.

ודלמא לעולם אימא לך: חלה נמי אינו גט, והיא גופא קא משמע לן: דאין גט לאחר מיתה?

The Gemara refutes that proof. **And perhaps, actually I will say to you** that in the case where **he falls ill it is also not a bill of divorce,** and the mishna cited the case of death merely as an example of circumstances beyond his control. **And** the reason **that** example **itself** was chosen is **to teach us that there is no bill of divorce posthumously.**[N] Even if the divorce is not conditional, and the husband simply states that it will take effect after he dies, it is not a valid bill of divorce.

אין גט לאחר מיתה – הא תנא ליה רישא: "הרי זה גיטיך אם מתי" "הרי זה גיטיך מחולי זה" "הרי זה גיטיך לאחר מיתה" – לא אמר כלום.

The Gemara asks: Does it come to teach that **there is no bill of divorce posthumously? Wasn't it** already **taught in the first clause** of the mishna (*Gittin* 72a) that if one on his deathbed said to his wife: **This is your bill of divorce if I die,**[H] or: **This is your bill of divorce** if I die **from this illness,** or: **This is your bill of divorce after I die, he said nothing.** The bill of divorce does not take effect after his death.

NOTES

Actually I will say to you, etc. – לעולם אימא לך וכו׳: The Meiri has a variant reading. First, the Gemara cites an unattributed response: Actually, I will say to you that in a case of unavoidable circumstances, she is not entitled to eat from his food, meaning that in a case where the circumstance came about due to the woman, he need not provide for her until the wedding. The Gemara then cites the statement of Rav Ashi: In any case of unavoidable circumstances, whether they affect him or they affect her, she doesn't eat from his food. The only case where she eats from his food prior to the wedding is when the groom made a conscious decision to postpone the wedding.

Unavoidable circumstances have no legal standing with regard to bills of divorce – אין אונס בגיטין: The early commentaries broaden the scope of this discussion and ask a more general question: In what cases do unavoidable circumstances have legal standing, so that a condition that was violated due to those circumstances is considered not to have been violated?

With regard to stipulations in monetary agreements, some maintain that unavoidable circumstances have legal standing (Rashba). Others maintain that they do not (see Rabbi Aharon HaLevi).

Others distinguish between different cases. In the case of a mutual agreement between two parties, a claim of unavoidable circumstances is not accepted in favor of one of the parties at the expense of the other. However, in a unilateral action, e.g., a gift, that claim is effective. Based on that approach, a claim of unavoidable circumstances should be effective in the case of divorce as well, as delivery of the bill of divorce is a unilateral action on the part of the husband. However, there are other reasons that the claim is not accepted in those cases.

Others distinguish between conditions that require performance of an action and conditions stipulating failure to perform an action, e.g., if I do not return. In the former case, failure to perform the action negates the transaction, regardless of the reason for that failure. However, in the latter case, since one sought to fulfill the condition and prevent the transaction from taking effect, the claim of unavoidable circumstances is effective, and his failure to fulfill the condition does not activate the transaction (see Meiri).

That there is no bill of divorce posthumously – דאין גט לאחר מיתה: The question is raised: What proof is there that the reason it is not a divorce is that there is no bill of divorce posthumously and not that there are unavoidable circumstances?

Some explain that were the intention to teach that failure to fulfill the condition due to unavoidable circumstances is not considered failure, the *tanna* should have taught the case: This is your bill of divorce from now if I did not return from now until the conclusion of twelve months, where the bill of divorce would not be posthumous. The fact that the *tanna* did not teach that case indicates that the reason the bill of divorce is void is that there is no bill of divorce posthumously.

HALAKHA

Unavoidable circumstances have no legal standing with regard to bills of divorce – אין אונס בגיטין: With regard to one who gave his wife a bill of divorce and stipulated that it will take effect only if a condition is fulfilled, if the condition remains unfulfilled due to circumstances beyond his control, the divorce takes effect because unavoidable circumstances have no legal standing with regard to bills of divorce.

The early commentaries (Rosh) rule, based on the Gemara in tractate *Gittin*, that this is the ruling only in cases involving normal circumstances beyond one's control. However, in extremely rare circumstances of that kind, even Rava would agree that the bill of divorce would not take effect.

Although the Gemara here (3a) cites an alternative version of Rava's statement, and the *halakha* is typically ruled in accordance with the latter version, the *ge'onim* and Rabbeinu Ḥananel note that in this case there are reasons for ruling in accordance with the first version. For one, the Gemara cites several sources that support the first version and are difficult according to the second. Furthermore, the discussion in the parallel Gemara in *Gittin* (34a) is according to the first version (Rambam *Sefer Nashim, Hilkhot Geirushin* 9:8; *Shulḥan Arukh, Even HaEzer* 144:1).

This is your bill of divorce…and he died within those twelve months – הרי זה גיטיך...ומת בתוך שנים עשר חדש: The Rambam rules, in accordance with the unattributed mishna, that in the case of one who gave his wife a bill of divorce and stipulated that it would take effect only if he failed to return by a specified time, and he died within that period, the divorce does not take effect. The Ra'avad, cited by Rashba and the *Tur*, rules that the divorce takes effect, in accordance with the opinion of our Rabbis, who disagree with the unattributed mishna and in accordance with the opinion of Rav (*Gittin* 72a). Based on the dispute between authorities, the ruling in the *Shulḥan Arukh* is that there is uncertainty whether or not she is divorced. Therefore, if her husband dies without children, this woman must perform *ḥalitza* and may not enter into levirate marriage (Rambam *Sefer Nashim, Hilkhot Geirushin* 9:2; *Shulḥan Arukh, Even HaEzer* 144:2).

This is your bill of divorce if I die – הרי זה גיטיך אם מתי: With regard to one who said to his wife: This is your bill of divorce if I die, the Rambam rules, in accordance with the unattributed mishna, that the divorce does not take effect. The Ra'avad rules that the divorce takes effect, in accordance with the opinion of our Rabbis. In the *Shulḥan Arukh*, the ruling of the Rambam is cited first, followed by a ruling introduced with the phrase: Some say, indicating that there is uncertainty whether or not the divorce takes effect (Rambam *Sefer Nashim, Hilkhot Geirushin* 9:12; *Shulḥan Arukh, Even HaEzer* 145:1).

דִּלְמָא לְאַפּוֹקֵי מִדְּרַבּוֹתֵינוּ? דְּתַנְיָא: וְרַבּוֹתֵינוּ הִתִּירוּהָ לְהִנָּשֵׂא, וְאָמְרִינַן: מַאן רַבּוֹתֵינוּ? אָמַר רַב יְהוּדָה אָמַר שְׁמוּאֵל: בֵּי דִינָא דְּשָׁרוּ מִשְׁחָא. סָבְרִי לָהּ כְּרַבִּי יוֹסֵי, דְּאָמַר: זְמַנּוֹ שֶׁל שְׁטָר מוֹכִיחַ עָלָיו.

The Gemara answers: **Perhaps** it was necessary for the first clause to mention specifically the case of death, **to exclude that which our Rabbis**[N] **said**[N] and not to exclude the case of one who fell ill, **as it is taught** in a *baraita*: **And our Rabbis permitted her to remarry,** in a case where he died within the twelve months that he stipulated. **And we said: Who are our Rabbis** mentioned here? **Rav Yehuda said** that **Shmuel said:** It is **the court that permitted** the **oil**[B] of gentiles for consumption. In this regard, **they hold in accordance with** the opinion of **Rabbi Yosei, who said: The time** written **in a document proves** when **it** takes effect. The fact that a certain date is written in the bill of divorce indicates that one's intention was that the divorce take effect from the day that it was written and delivered, not after his death. In any event, there is proof neither for nor against Rava's opinion from this *baraita*.

וְאֶלָּא מִסֵּיפָא: ״מֵעַכְשָׁיו אִם לֹא בָּאתִי מִכָּאן וְעַד שְׁנֵים עָשָׂר חֹדֶשׁ״ וּמֵת בְּתוֹךְ שְׁנֵים עָשָׂר חֹדֶשׁ – הֲרֵי זֶה גֵּט. מֵת – וְהוּא הַדִּין לְחָלָה.

And rather, proof may be cited from the **latter clause** of the mishna. If a man says to his wife: This is your bill of divorce **from now**[N] **if I do not return**[H] **from now until** the conclusion of **twelve months, and he died within** those **twelve months, this** document **is a bill of divorce.** This is the *halakha* in a case where **he dies,** and **the same is true** if **he fell ill.** If the divorce takes effect when his failure to return is attributable to death, the ultimate circumstance beyond his control, all the more so should it take effect if it is attributable to a less extreme circumstance.

דִּלְמָא מֵת דַּוְקָא, דְּלָא נִיחָא לֵיהּ דְּתִפּוֹל קַמֵּי יָבָם!

The Gemara rejects that proof: **Perhaps** the divorce takes effect **specifically** in the case where **he died,** because **he is not amenable** to have his wife **happen before** her *yavam*, his brother, if he had no children. However, if other circumstances beyond his control caused the condition to be fulfilled, where levirate marriage is not a consideration, his intention is that the bill of divorce will not take effect.

אֶלָּא מֵהָא: דְּהַהוּא דַּאֲמַר לְהוּ ״אִי לָא אָתֵינָא מִיכָּן וְעַד תְּלָתִין יוֹמִין לֶיהֱוֵי גִּיטָּא״. אֲתָא בְּסוֹף תְּלָתִין יוֹמִין וּפַסְקֵיהּ מַבָּרָא, אֲמַר לְהוּ: ״חֲזוּ דַּאֲתַאי, חֲזוּ דַּאֲתַאי״! אֲמַר שְׁמוּאֵל: לָאו שְׁמֵיהּ מָתְיָא.

Rather, proof may be cited **from this** case, **where a certain** man **who said to** the agents with whom he entrusted the bill of divorce: **If I do not return from now until after thirty days** have passed, **let this be a bill of divorce. He came at the end of thirty days,** before the deadline passed, **but was prevented** from crossing the river **by the ferry**[H] that was located on the other side of the river, so he did not come within the designated time. **He said to the** people across the river: **See that I have come, see that I have come. Shmuel said:** This **is not considered** to be **a return.** Apparently, even if the condition was fulfilled due to circumstances beyond his control, the condition is considered fulfilled.

BACKGROUND

The court that permitted the oil – בֵּי דִינָא דְּשָׁרוּ מִשְׁחָא: The oil of gentiles was prohibited by an ancient decree. Some assert that the decree dates back to the time of Daniel, but everyone agrees that it is one of the eighteen decrees issued during the Second Temple period. Many generations later, when the Sages became aware that the decree was not observed by a majority of the people, it was repealed. Although initially the Sages were hesitant about instituting this leniency, it was eventually adopted as normative *halakha* (see *Avoda Zara* 35b). Apparently, it was the court of the grandson of Rabbi Yehuda HaNasi, Rabbi Yehuda Nesia, which judged during the first generation of *amora'im*, that repealed the decree prohibiting the use of the oil of gentiles (see Rashi on *Avoda Zara* 35b). That is the court referred to in the Gemara by the words: And our Rabbis permitted her to marry. Some explain that any time the term our Rabbis is used, the reference is to the court of Rabbi Yehuda Nesia.

HALAKHA

From now if I do not return – מֵעַכְשָׁיו אִם לֹא בָּאתִי: With regard to one who said to his wife: This is your bill of divorce from now if I do not return within twelve months, and he dies within the twelve months, the divorce takes effect. Therefore, if her husband dies without children and the *halakhot* of levirate marriage apply, she must wait twelve months for the condition to actually be fulfilled before remarrying (Rambam *Sefer Nashim*, *Hilkhot Geirushin* 9:11; *Shulḥan Arukh*, *Even HaEzer* 144:3).

But was prevented from crossing the river by the ferry – וּפַסְקֵיהּ מַבָּרָא: With regard to one who said to his wife: This is your bill of divorce from now if I do not return within thirty days, and due to circumstances beyond his control he was unable to cross the river and complete his return, the divorce takes effect, because unavoidable circumstances have no legal standing with regard to bills of divorce (Rambam *Sefer Nashim*, *Hilkhot Geirushin* 9:8; *Shulḥan Arukh*, *Even HaEzer* 144:1).

NOTES

Our Rabbis – רַבּוֹתֵינוּ: Rabbeinu Ḥananel explains that this is an appellation for Rabbi Yehuda HaNasi, redactor of the mishna, while others explain that the reference is to his grandson, Rabbi Yehuda Nesia (Rashba).

To exclude that which our Rabbis said – לְאַפּוֹקֵי מִדְּרַבּוֹתֵינוּ: The commentaries ask: The Gemara could have learned to exclude that which our Rabbis said from the first clause of the mishna, as in the first clause, the bill of divorce is valid only if the husband said: From now, contrary to the opinion of Rabbi Yosei and our Rabbis, who hold: The time written in a document proves when it takes effect.

The Ri Migash answers that the first clause is referring to a case where no specific date was written in the document. Rather, a more general time was written, e.g., the month or the year.

The Ramban suggests the possibility that there is a distinction between the opinion of Rabbi Yosei and the opinion of our Rabbis. According to Rabbi Yosei, even if the husband explicitly said: This is your bill of divorce after my death, which is the case in the first clause of the mishna, because of the time written in the document the bill of divorce takes effect. However, our Rabbis hold that in a case where one specifically stipulated that it will take effect after death, the bill of divorce does not take effect, as he merely wrote the document to ensure that she will not be subject to levirate marriage after his death. Only in a case where one stipulated that the bill of divorce will take effect if he does not return by a specific time, and he died and did not return would the bill of divorce take effect, as in that case our Rabbis concede: The time written in a document proves when it takes effect. Therefore, the first clause does not exclude the opinion of our Rabbis.

From now – מֵעַכְשָׁיו: There is a difference between a standard bill of divorce, in which the date is written, and one in which the man giving the bill of divorce to his wife stipulates that it will take effect from now. In the standard bill of divorce, the husband's intent is that the divorce will take effect only if the condition is fulfilled. However, in the latter case, where he specifies that it will take effect from now, his intent is that the divorce will take effect; he simply stipulated a condition to void it. Therefore, even if the condition remained unfulfilled due to circumstances beyond his control, the divorce takes effect.

NOTES

Due to virtuous women and due to licentious women – משום צנועות ומשום פרוצות: Most commentaries explain that a virtuous woman is one who is concerned that perhaps there was some extenuating circumstance and she will therefore remain unmarried indefinitely, despite the fact that the failure of the husband to return was obviously due to circumstances not beyond his control and clearly the courts would permit her to remarry. In contrast, licentious women are those who remarry despite the clear impression, although it falls short of actual testimony, that the husband's failure to arrive is attributable to circumstances beyond his control (*Tosafot*; Ritva).

The Rashba writes that a licentious woman is one who, without basis, resolutely concludes that her husband's failure to arrive was not due to unavoidable circumstances, and she marries without seeking to ascertain the truth.

Rabbi Aharon HaLevi and others explain that the term licentious is a misnomer, as the court permitted them to remarry. Relative to the virtuous women, who take special precautions to avoid any possible impropriety, these women are characterized as licentious.

ודלמא אונסא דשכיח שאני, דכיון דאיבעי ליה לאתנויי ולא אתני – איהו דאפסיד אנפשיה!

The Gemara rejects that proof: **And perhaps unavoidable circumstances that are common** and could be anticipated, e.g., the ferry is located at the other side of the river, **are different, since he should have stipulated** that exception when establishing the condition, **and he did not stipulate** it, **he brought the failure** to arrive **upon himself.** Although he regrets it now, at the time his intent was that even if the condition were fulfilled due to that circumstance, the divorce would take effect. In contrast, however, if the condition is fulfilled due to an uncommon circumstance that could not have been anticipated, the divorce would not take effect.

אלא רבא סברא דנפשיה קאמר, משום צנועות ומשום פרוצות; משום צנועות, דאי אמרת לא להוי גט

Rather, Rava is stating a *halakha* based on **his own reasoning.** Circumstances beyond one's control are not a factor in determining whether or not a condition is fulfilled, and this is **due to virtuous women and due to licentious women.**[N] The Gemara articulates: There is concern **due to virtuous women** is, as, **if you said: Let it not be a bill of divorce,** if the reason that the condition was not fulfilled was due to circumstances beyond his control,

Perek **I**
Daf **3** Amud **a**

זימנין דלא אניס, וסברה דאניס, ומיעגנא ויתבה. ומשום פרוצות, דאי אמרת לא ליהוי גיטא, זימנין דאניס ואמרה לא אניס, ואזלא ומינסבא, ונמצא גט בטל ובניה ממזרים.

then **sometimes, where he was not** detained **unavoidably** but he fulfilled the condition willingly to effect the divorce, **and** the wife **thinks** that he was detained **unavoidably, she will sit deserted,** forever unable to remarry. **And** the concern **due to licentious women** is, as, **if you said: Let it not be a bill of divorce,** then **sometimes, when he was** detained **unavoidably and she thinks** that he was **not** detained **unavoidably,** she goes **and remarries. And** the result will be **that the bill of divorce is void, and her children** from the second marriage will be ***mamzerim,*** products of an adulterous relationship.

ומי איכא מידי דמדאורייתא לא להוי גט ומשום צנועות ומשום פרוצות שרינן אשת איש לעלמא?!

The Gemara questions the following premise: By Torah law, a condition that is unfulfilled due to circumstances beyond one's control is considered fulfilled, and it is merely by rabbinic ordinance that it is deemed unfulfilled: **And is there a matter**[N] **where by Torah** law **it is not a bill of divorce, but due to virtuous women and due to licentious women we permit a married woman to others?**

אין, כל דמקדש – אדעתא דרבנן מקדש, ואפקעינהו רבנן לקידושי מיניה.

The Gemara answers: **Yes,** it is within the authority of the Sages to institute an ordinance freeing the woman from the marriage, as **anyone who betroths** a woman, **betroths** her contingent **upon the agreement of the Sages,** and in certain cases, such as those mentioned above, **the Sages invalidated his betrothal**[N] retroactively.

NOTES

And is there a matter – ומי איכא מידי: The commentaries ask: Why is this difficulty not raised earlier, before the reason for Rava's opinion is analyzed? Some suggest that at that stage the thinking was that although the fact that unavoidable circumstances are halakhically significant is derived from the passage in the Torah with regard to a betrothed young woman who was raped (Deuteronomy 22:25–26), perhaps Rava holds that the claim of unavoidable circumstances is not relevant in all cases, and it has no legal standing with regard to bills of divorce. However, once it became clear that Rava holds that it is only by rabbinic law that those circumstances are ignored, and the bill of divorce is ruled effective, the question is raised: How can the Sages rule that a woman married by Torah law is divorced?

The Sages invalidated his betrothal – אפקעינהו רבנן לקידושי מיניה: This *halakha* that the Sages retroactively invalidated the betrothal is applied only in a few specific cases throughout the Talmud, and is not a panacea to be applied in every case that a problem arises, even if the problem is a severe one, e.g., a deserted wife.

Many early commentaries state that this solution is applied only in cases where there is a bill of divorce of some kind (Ramban; Rashba; Rabbi Aharon HaLevi). The Meiri proves that in certain cases, when halakhic problems arise with regard to the betrothal itself, the Sages used this procedure to invalidate it.

The early and later commentaries discussed at length the precise mechanism through which the Sages invalidate the betrothal retroactively. Some explain that just as a man can betroth a woman and stipulate that it will take effect contingent on the approval of his father, so too, in every act of betrothal there is an implicit stipulation: This betrothal will take effect contingent upon the approval of the Sages, or on the condition that the Sages do not object to it (Ritva).

Rashi goes a step further and asserts that the betrothal takes effect only when the Sages actively ratify it. Apparently, that is the opinion of *Tosafot*, who explain that this is the reason that the groom adds, when reciting the formula of the betrothal: In accordance with the law of Moses and Israel, which acknowledges that the betrothal takes effect in accordance with the provisions of both Torah and rabbinic law.

The explanation in *Sefer Hafla'a* is that there are two complementary mechanisms mentioned in the Gemara that together resolve potential difficulties. On the one hand, it is difficult to explain how the Sages can invalidate the betrothal by rendering the money with which the man betrothed the woman, which is no longer in existence, ownerless retroactively. On the other hand, there is the concern that certain people will not make their betrothal contingent on rabbinic approval. The combination of both mechanisms facilitates invalidation of the betrothal in all cases.

אֲמַר לֵיהּ רָבִינָא לְרַב אַשִׁי: תֵּינַח קָדֵישׁ בְּכַסְפָּא, קָדֵישׁ בְּבִיאָה מַאי אִיכָּא לְמֵימַר? שַׁוְיוּהָ רַבָּנַן לִבְעִילָתוֹ בְּעִילַת זְנוּת.

Ravina said to Rav Ashi: That **works out well if he betrothed** her **with money,**[N] as in that case, the courts could declare the money ownerless, and one cannot betroth a woman with money that is not his. However, if **he betrothed** her **with intercourse, what can be said?** Rav Ashi answered: **The Sages rendered his intercourse licentious intercourse.**

אִיכָּא דְּאָמְרִי, אֲמַר רָבָא: וְכֵן לְעִנְיַן גִּיטִּין. אַלְמָא קָסָבַר רָבָא: יֵשׁ אוֹנֶס בְּגִיטִּין,

Some say, to the contrary, that **Rava said:** Just as with regard to postponement of a wedding due to circumstances beyond his control, the groom is not obligated to provide sustenance for his betrothed, **the same is true with regard to the matter of bills of divorce.** The Gemara concludes that **apparently Rava maintains: Unavoidable circumstances** have legal standing **with regard to bills of divorce.**[N]

מֵיתִיבֵי: ״הֲרֵי זֶה גִּיטֵּיךְ אִם לֹא בָּאתִי מִכָּאן וְעַד שְׁנֵים עָשָׂר חֹדֶשׁ וּמֵת בְּתוֹךְ שְׁנֵים עָשָׂר חֹדֶשׁ – אֵינוֹ גֵּט״. מֵת – הוּא דְּאֵינוֹ גֵּט, הָא חָלָה – הֲרֵי זֶה גֵּט!

The Gemara raises an objection from a mishna (*Gittin* 76b): With regard to one who said to his wife: **This is your bill of divorce if I do not return from now until** the conclusion of **twelve months, and he died within** those **twelve months,** the document **is not a bill of divorce.** The Gemara infers: If **he died,** that **is when it is not a bill of divorce,** since a divorce cannot take effect posthumously. However, in cases involving other circumstances beyond his control, e.g., if **he fell ill** and therefore did not return, **it is a bill of divorce** and it does take effect.

לְעוֹלָם אֵימָא לָךְ חָלָה נַמִי אֵינוֹ גֵּט, וְהִיא גּוּפָהּ קָא מַשְׁמַע לָן, דְּאֵין גֵּט לְאַחַר מִיתָה.

The Gemara answers: **Actually, I will say to you** that in the case where **one falls ill it is also not a bill of divorce,** and death is merely an example of circumstances beyond one's control. **And** the fact that the mishna cited **that** example **itself teaches us that there is no bill of divorce posthumously.**

אֵין גֵּט לְאַחַר מִיתָה – הָא תָּנָא לֵיהּ רֵישָׁא! דִּלְמָא לְאַפּוּקֵי מִדְּרַבּוֹתֵינוּ.

The Gemara asks: Does it come to teach that **there is no bill of divorce posthumously? Wasn't it already taught in the first clause** of that mishna? The Gemara answers: **Perhaps** it was necessary for the first clause to mention specifically the case of death, **to exclude** the opinion **of our Rabbis.**

תָּא שְׁמַע: ״מֵעַכְשָׁיו אִם לֹא בָּאתִי מִכָּאן וְעַד שְׁנֵים עָשָׂר חֹדֶשׁ״ וּמֵת בְּתוֹךְ שְׁנֵים עָשָׂר חֹדֶשׁ – הֲרֵי זֶה גֵּט. מַאי לָאו – הוּא הַדִּין לְחָלָה? לָא, מֵת דַּוְקָא, דְּלָא נִיחָא לֵיהּ דְּתִפּוֹל קַמֵּי יָבָם.

Come and hear an additional proof from the latter clause of that mishna: If one said: This is your bill of divorce **from now if I have not returned from now until** the conclusion of **twelve months, and he died within** those **twelve months,** then **this** document **is a bill of divorce. What, is it not that the same is true** if his failure to return is due to the fact that **he fell ill?** The Gemara rejects that proof. The divorce takes effect **specifically** in the case where **he died,** and he wrote the bill of divorce because **he was not amenable** to have his wife **happen before** her ***yavam,*** his brother, for levirate marriage if he had no children. However, in cases where that is not a consideration, if other circumstances beyond his control caused the condition to be fulfilled, his intention is that the bill of divorce will not take effect.

תָּא שְׁמַע: מֵהַהוּא דַּאֲמַר לְהוּ: ״אִי לָא אָתֵינָא מִכָּאן וְעַד שְׁלֹשִׁים יוֹם לֶיהֱוֵי גִּיטָּא״, אֲתָא בְּסוֹף תְּלָתִין יוֹמִין וּפְסַקֵיהּ מַבְרָא, וַאֲמַר לְהוּ: ״חֲזוּ דַּאֲתַאי, חֲזוּ דַּאֲתַאי!״ וַאֲמַר שְׁמוּאֵל: לָא שְׁמֵיהּ מָתְיָא.

Come and hear an additional proof **from** the case of **a certain** man **who said to** the agents with whom he entrusted the bill of divorce: **If I do not return from now until thirty days** have passed, **let this be a bill of divorce. He came at the end of thirty days,** before the deadline passed, **but was prevented** from crossing the river **by the ferry** that was located on the other side of the river, so he did not come within the designated time. **He said to the** people across the river: **See that I have come, see that I have come. Shmuel said:** It **is not considered** to be **a return.** Apparently, even if the condition was fulfilled due to circumstances beyond his control, the condition is considered fulfilled.

אוּנְסָא דִּשְׁכִיחַ שָׁאנֵי, דְּכֵיוָן דְּאִיבָּעֵי לֵיהּ לְאַתְנוּיֵי וְלָא אַתְנֵי – אִיהוּ הוּא דְּאַפְסֵיד אַנַּפְשֵׁיהּ.

The Gemara rejects that proof: **Perhaps unavoidable circumstances that are common** and could be anticipated, e.g., the ferry being located at the other side of the river, **are different, since he should have stipulated** that exception when giving his wife the bill of divorce. **And** since he did not **stipulate it, he brought the failure upon himself.**

NOTES

That works out well if he betrothed her with money – תֵּינַח קָדֵישׁ בְּכַסְפָּא: Rashi rejects the explanation raised by several commentaries, that betrothal effected with money can be invalidated because this means of betrothal is not effective by Torah law. According to the Rambam, only betrothal effected by means of sexual intercourse or with a betrothal document is by Torah law. Rather, the simple explanation is that the courts have the power to declare the money ownerless, thereby retroactively invalidating the betrothal.

With regard to betrothal through sexual intercourse, many explain the difficulty raised by the Gemara as: How can the Sages retroactively transform an action performed as a mitzva into a transgression? (see *Tosafot*). With regard to invalidation of betrothal with a betrothal document, some explain that the Sages retroactively disqualify the witnesses who signed the document (*Tashbetz*).

Unavoidable circumstances have legal standing with regard to bills of divorce – יֵשׁ אוֹנֶס בְּגִיטִּין: A related dilemma is raised in the Jerusalem Talmud with regard to betrothal: If a man stipulated that his betrothal is contingent on fulfillment of a certain condition, and the condition was not fulfilled due to circumstances beyond his control, is the betrothal nevertheless valid? The dilemma remains unresolved.

אָמַר רַב שְׁמוּאֵל בַּר יִצְחָק: לֹא שָׁנוּ אֶלָּא מִתַּקָּנַת עֶזְרָא וְאֵילָךְ, שֶׁאֵין בָּתֵּי דִינִין קְבוּעִין אֶלָּא בַּשֵּׁנִי וּבַחֲמִישִׁי. אֲבָל קוֹדֶם תַּקָּנַת עֶזְרָא, שֶׁבָּתֵּי דִינִין קְבוּעִין בְּכׇל יוֹם – אִשָּׁה נִשֵּׂאת בְּכׇל יוֹם.

§ **Rav Shmuel bar Yitzḥak said:** The Sages **teach** that this *halakha* that a virgin is married on Wednesday is in effect **only from** the institution of **the ordinance of Ezra**[NB] **that courts are in regular session only on Monday and Thursday. However,** prior to the institution of **the ordinance of Ezra, when courts** were in **regular** session **every day,**[NH] **a woman was married on any day** of the week.

קוֹדֶם תַּקָּנַת עֶזְרָא? מַאי דַּהֲוָה הֲוָה! הָכִי קָאָמַר: אִי אִיכָּא בָּתֵּי דִינִין דִּקְבוּעִין הָאִידָּנָא כְּקוֹדֶם תַּקָּנַת עֶזְרָא – אִשָּׁה נִשֵּׂאת בְּכׇל יוֹם.

The Gemara asks: **Prior to** the institution of **the ordinance of Ezra? What was** in the past **was** in the past. There are no halakhic ramifications to that statement. The Gemara answers: **This is what** Rav Shmuel bar Yitzḥak **is saying: If there are courts** in **regular** daily session **today, as** they were **prior to** the institution of **the ordinance of Ezra, a woman is married on any day** of the week.[N]

הָא בָּעֵינַן שֶׁקָּדוּ! דְּטָרַח לֵיהּ.

The Gemara asks: **Don't we require** the additional reason that a virgin is married on Wednesday because the Sages **were assiduous** in seeing to the well-being of Jewish women and made certain that the groom would have several days to prepare for the wedding feast prior to the wedding? The Gemara answers: This is referring to a case **where he** already **exerted himself**[N] and prepared everything before Shabbat, so the feast will be prepared even if the wedding is Sunday or Monday.

NOTES

The ordinance of Ezra – תַּקָּנַת עֶזְרָא: The early commentaries ask: What was the objective of the ordinance? Did Ezra seek to limit the activity of the courts? They answer that prior to the ordinance, the court convened each day in a different city, or there were no fixed hours when the court was in session. Ezra instituted an ordinance to ensure that in each city, the courts would regularly convene in session at fixed hours (Ritva; *Shita Mekubbetzet*).

When courts are in regular session every day – שֶׁבָּתֵּי דִינִין קְבוּעִין בְּכׇל יוֹם: The early commentaries ask: Based on the principle that one court can abrogate ordinances instituted by another court only if the court is greater in wisdom and number, even if the reason for the ordinance is obsolete, how could a court abrogate the ordinance of the court of Ezra that determined Wednesday as the day for the marriage of a virgin, since no court was greater than the court of Ezra? Some suggest that in the original ordinance there was a provision that if the court schedule changed, the marriage day would change accordingly (Ritva). On a similar note, others explain that the essence of the original ordinance was that a wedding should take place on the day before the court is in session. If the court convenes daily, every day is suitable for a wedding (*Ḥatam Sofer*).

A woman is married on any day of the week – אִשָּׁה נִשֵּׂאת בְּכׇל יוֹם: Some hold that the phrase every day is not to be taken literally, as the courts do not convene on Friday or Shabbat, and there are other reasons precluding getting married on those days. They explain that although the courts do not convene on Friday on a regular basis, when the need arose, they would convene on that day as well. In addition, since today betrothal, marriage, and consummation of the marriage take place consecutively on the same day, the primary reason for limiting weddings to the day before the courts convene is no longer in effect, and weddings may be held any day of the week.

Where he already exerted himself – דְּטָרַח לֵיהּ: Rav Aḥai writes that even today, when the reasons relating to the court convening on Thursday are no longer relevant, a distinction remains between Wednesday and other days. When the wedding is on Wednesday, the groom's claim that he exerted himself in preparing the wedding feast is accorded credibility. When the wedding is on other days, he must provide proof to support his claim. Some prove from here that although the Sages remain insistent with regard to ensuring that the groom exert himself in preparing the feast, even when the wedding takes place on a day other than Wednesday, there is no such insistence with regard to ensuring that the wedding take place on a day when the blessing for procreation was stated (Ritva).

BACKGROUND

The ordinance of Ezra – תַּקָּנַת עֶזְרָא: The Gemara (*Bava Kamma* 82a) cites a tradition that Ezra the Scribe instituted ten ordinances whose purpose was to promote fulfillment of Torah law and observance of ancient customs. The focus of these ordinances was to imbue the daily existence of the people with sanctity. For example, by Torah law, one who experiences a seminal emission is ritually impure, and it is prohibited for him to partake of consecrated foods. In his ordinance, Ezra instituted that the individual must immerse himself for purification before praying or engaging in Torah study. Although this ordinance was repealed several generations later, it remained the custom in many communities, as well as a custom of the pious throughout the generations.

HALAKHA

When courts are in regular session every day – שֶׁבָּתֵּי דִינִין קְבוּעִין בְּכׇל יוֹם: In places where the courts convene only on Monday and Thursday, a virgin is married on Wednesday. In places where the courts convene every day, or where they do not regularly convene on any particular day, she may marry on any day of the week, provided that the groom exerted himself in preparing the feast three days prior to the wedding.

Some early commentaries (Ran; Meiri) rule that since today betrothal, marriage, and consummation of the marriage take place consecutively on the same day, the primary reason for limiting weddings to the day before the courts convene, i.e., so that the groom can make a claim concerning virginity, is no longer in effect, and therefore weddings may be held on any day of the week (Rambam *Sefer Nashim*, *Hilkhot Ishut* 10:14–15; *Shulḥan Arukh*, *Even HaEzer* 64:3).

מַאי שָׁקְדוּ? דְּתַנְיָא: מִפְּנֵי מָה אָמְרוּ בְּתוּלָה נִשֵּׂאת לְיוֹם הָרְבִיעִי – שֶׁאִם הָיָה לוֹ טַעֲנַת בְּתוּלִים הָיָה מַשְׁכִּים לְבֵית דִּין. וְתִנָּשֵׂא בְּאֶחָד בְּשַׁבָּת, וְאִם הָיָה לוֹ טַעֲנַת בְּתוּלִים – הָיָה מַשְׁכִּים לְבֵית דִּין! שָׁקְדוּ חֲכָמִים עַל תַּקָּנַת בְּנוֹת יִשְׂרָאֵל, שֶׁיְּהֵא אָדָם טוֹרֵחַ בִּסְעוּדָה שְׁלֹשָׁה יָמִים: אֶחָד בְּשַׁבָּת, וְשֵׁנִי בְּשַׁבָּת, וּשְׁלִישִׁי בְּשַׁבָּת, וּבִרְבִיעִי כּוֹנְסָהּ.

The Gemara asks: **What is the meaning of:** The Sages **were assiduous?**[N] It is **as it is taught in a** *baraita*: **Due to what** reason **did** the Sages in the mishna **say** that **a virgin is married on Wednesday?** It is so **that if** the husband **had a claim concerning** the bride's **virginity, he would go early** the next day **to court** and make his claim. The *baraita* continues: **But** if that is the reason, **let her marry on Sunday,** as then too, **if** the husband **had a claim concerning** the bride's **virginity, he would go early** the next day **to court** and make his claim. The Gemara answers: The Sages **were assiduous in seeing to the well-being of Jewish women** and preferred Wednesday, **so that** the husband **would exert** himself **in** arranging **the wedding feast for three days, Sunday, Monday and Tuesday, and on Wednesday, he marries her.**

וּמִסַּכָּנָה וְאֵילָךְ נָהֲגוּ הָעָם לִכְנוֹס בִּשְׁלִישִׁי, וְלֹא מִיחוּ בְּיָדָם חֲכָמִים. וּבְשֵׁנִי לֹא יִכְנוֹס, וְאִם מֵחֲמַת הָאוֹנֶס – מוּתָּר. וּמַפְרִישִׁין אֶת הֶחָתָן מִן הַכַּלָּה לֵילֵי שַׁבָּת תְּחִלָּה, מִפְּנֵי שֶׁהוּא עוֹשֶׂה חַבּוּרָה.

The *baraita* continues: **And from** the time of **danger and onward, the people adopted the custom to marry on Tuesday** as well, **and the Sages did not reprimand them. And on Monday one may not marry** even in time of danger. **However, if it is due to the coercion,** it is **permitted.**[N] The *baraita* concludes: **One isolates the groom from the** virgin **bride,** so that he will not engage in intercourse with her for the **first** time **on Shabbat evening, because** by rupturing the hymen **he inflicts a wound,** which is a labor prohibited on Shabbat.

מַאי סַכָּנָה? אִילֵימָא דְּאָמְרִי: בְּתוּלָה הַנִּשֵּׂאת לְיוֹם הָרְבִיעִי תֵּיהָרֵג, נָהֲגוּ?! לִגְמְרֵי נִיעַקְרֵיהּ!

The Gemara elaborates: **What is the danger** mentioned in the *baraita*? **If we say** it is referring to a situation where the government **said that a virgin who is married on Wednesday will be executed,** would the response be merely **that they adopted the custom** to marry on Tuesday? **Let them** totally **abolish** the ordinance[N] to marry on Wednesday in the face of life-threatening danger.

אָמַר רַבָּה, דְּאָמְרִי: בְּתוּלָה הַנִּשֵּׂאת בְּיוֹם הָרְבִיעִי – תִּיבָּעֵל לְהֶגְמוֹן תְּחִלָּה. הָאי סַכָּנָה?! אוֹנֶס הוּא! מִשּׁוּם דְּאִיכָּא צְנוּעוֹת דְּמָסְרָן נַפְשַׁיְיהוּ לִקְטָלָא, וְאָתְיָין לִידֵי סַכָּנָה.

Rabba said: The *baraita* is referring to a period where the government **said that a virgin who is married on Wednesday will** submit to **intercourse with the prefect** [*hegmon*][L] **first.**[B] The Gemara questions the formulation of the *baraita*: **Is that** characterized as **danger? It is coercion.** The Gemara answers: There is also danger involved, **as there are virtuous women who give their lives** rather than allow themselves to be violated, **and they will come to** mortal **danger.**

LANGUAGE

Prefect [*hegmon*] – הֶגְמוֹן: From the Greek ἡγεμών, *heguemon*, meaning leader, in particular a military leader. In a later period, this served as the title for local Roman governors. In the Talmud it is a term meaning general or high government official.

BACKGROUND

Will submit to intercourse with the prefect first – תִּיבָּעֵל לְהֶגְמוֹן תְּחִלָּה: These decrees, which underscore the total domination by a ruler of his subjects, were in effect in several countries in the ancient world. Even in the Middle Ages, *jus primae noctis*, the right of the first night, was one of the rights the feudal lords held over their serfs and vassals. There are several sources of uncertain credibility indicating that a decree of this kind was in effect in the period prior to the Hasmonean revolt.

NOTES

What is the meaning of the Sages were assiduous – מַאי שָׁקְדוּ: Why is this question raised here when the assiduousness of the Sages was mentioned earlier? Rashi explains that the Gemara is not seeking to ascertain the meaning of their assiduousness but is attempting to determine its tannaitic source. An explanation more in keeping with the language of the Gemara is cited in the *Shita Mekubbetzet*: One of the reasons for the ordinance to marry on Wednesday is to ensure that the groom prepare the wedding feast. This was discussed extensively. However, the other reason cited, that the wedding take place on the day that the blessing of procreation was given, was not discussed at length. What was the significance of the former reason that led the Sages to devote so much discussion to it? The Gemara cites the *baraita* that indicates that the Sages were so insistent about preparations for the wedding feast that they enforced its observance even in the face of danger.

Others explain that the question is: Where in the mishna is there an allusion to the assiduousness of the Sages on this matter (*Sefer Hafla'a*)? Their answer, based on the Rosh, is that the Sages were particularly assiduous in ensuring that the groom exert himself for three days in preparing the wedding to prevent any possibility of making false allegations against his bride. That also answers the difficulty raised by the Ran: Why must the three days be consecutive? The answer is that the Sages wanted the groom to be busy preparing the wedding feast during the three days immediately prior to the wedding to prevent discord between the bride and the groom.

Adopted the custom…permitted – נָהֲגוּ...מוּתָּר: Rashi explains: They adopted the custom, means that most people accepted it as the norm. It is permitted, means that if one did so, it is acceptable after the fact.

Tosafot explain to the contrary: They adopted the custom, means that it is permitted after the fact, and: It is permitted, means that it is permitted even *ab initio*. Support for the opinion of Rashi appears in the Jerusalem Talmud, where it is stated that only in exigent circumstances may one marry on Monday. The reason for that statement is that the longer the break between consummating the marriage and convening the court, the greater the chance that the groom's resolve will cool.

They adopted the custom, let them totally abolish the ordinance – נָהֲגוּ, לִגְמְרֵי נִיעַקְרֵיהּ: Some explain this as an answer to the question: If it was a decree of religious persecution, why weren't they required to sacrifice their lives as martyrs rather than violate Jewish customs, and all the more so rabbinic ordinances? They answer that since the decree was directed at the women, the Sages, who were not directly affected by the decree, would have been free to repeal their ordinance, thereby negating the prohibition altogether (Rivash). A slight variation of that explanation is that although in that situation it is prohibited to violate a rabbinic ordinance, the court should initiate a repeal of the ordinance and create a situation where martyrdom would not be required (*Shita Mekubbetzet*).

LANGUAGE

Decree of religious persecution [*shemada*] – שמדא: The term: Decree of religious persecution was changed by the Christian censor to decree or royal decree. The term *shemada* is a pejorative term describing the act of a Jew adopting another religion in general, Christianity in particular. The *ge'onim* explain that the term is from the Aramaic term *amad*, meaning wash or immerse. However, there is also a secondary meaning, something disgusting, e.g., a container filled with urine. The term *meshumad*, apostate, literally means immersed. However, *shemada* is commonly used in reference to any law or punitive action designed to convert Jews to other religions. In addition, it is associated with the related Hebrew term *hashmada*, destruction.

ולידרוש להו דאונס שרי! איכא פרוצות, ואיכא נמי כהנות.

The Gemara asks: **And** if so, **let** the Sages **instruct** these women **that** in cases of **coercion** it is **permitted**[N] to submit to violation rather than sacrifice their lives, and they will not be forbidden to their husbands. The Gemara answers: The Sages cannot issue an instruction of that sort, because **there are licentious women**[N] who would exploit the situation to engage in intercourse willingly, rendering them forbidden to their husbands. **And** furthermore, **there are also** women married to **priests,**[N] who are rendered forbidden to their husbands even if they are raped.

וליעקריה! שמדא עבידא דבטלא, ותקנתא דרבנן מקמי שמדא לא עקרינן. אי הכי בשלישי נמי אתי ובעיל! מספיקא לא עקר נפשיה.

The Gemara asks: **And let** the Sages completely **abolish** the ordinance to marry on Wednesday and establish marriage on a different day. The Gemara answers: **A decree of religious persecution [*shemada*]**[L] **is likely to be abrogated, and we do not abolish a rabbinic ordinance in the face of a decree of religious persecution.**[N] Rather, a lenient ruling is issued instructing them not to follow the ordinance, as long as the decree of persecution is in effect. The Gemara asks: **If so,** what is accomplished by moving the marriage to Tuesday? The prefect **will come on Tuesday too,** to violate them. The Gemara answers: The date of the marriage is not fixed, and **for** a situation of **uncertainty** the prefect will not **uproot himself** to violate the bride.

ובשני לא יכנוס, ואם מחמת האונס – מותר. מאי אונס? אילימא הא דאמרן – התם קרי ליה סכנה והכא קא קרי ליה אונס? ותו, התם נהגו, הכא – מותר!

The *baraita* continues: **And on Monday one may not marry** even in time of danger. **However, if it is due to the coercion, it is permitted.** The Gemara asks: **What is the coercion**[N] mentioned in the *baraita*? **If we say it is referring to that which we mentioned** with regard to the decree of *prima nocta* it is difficult, as **there** the *tanna* **calls it danger, and here he calls it coercion. Furthermore, there** it says that they **adopted the custom** to marry on Tuesday; **here** it states that it is **permitted.**

NOTES

That in cases of coercion it is permitted – דאונס שרי: Although one forced to perform a forbidden action under duress is not considered a transgressor, in this case, two difficulties arise. First, this is a case involving forbidden sexual relations, which is one of the three transgressions for which one is required to sacrifice his life rather than violate them. Second, this was a decree of religious persecution, for which one must be killed even if it involves a minor transgression.

Several solutions are suggested. *Tosafot* explain that one must give his life rather than perform a forbidden action. However, since the woman plays a passive role in intercourse, she need not submit to being killed.

Tosafot cite a second explanation in the name of Rabbeinu Tam: Intercourse with a gentile does not fall into the category of forbidden sexual relations that require martyrdom. The Ramban explains that there is a distinction between a decree intended to cause apostasy among the Jews, in which case one must be killed rather than violate the prohibition, and a decree motivated by self-gratification, for which martyrdom is not required. The Ra'avad disagrees.

There are licentious women – איכא פרוצות: The commentaries raise the question: Must virtuous women give their lives due to the concern that licentious women will engage in illicit relations? They answer that the existence of licentious women is not the reason that the Sages did not issue a ruling that a raped woman is permitted to her husband. Rather, it is the reason that the Sages allowed the ordinance to be changed. Because there are licentious women who are likely to be forbidden to their husbands by willingly engaging in intercourse, it is preferable to change the day designated for marriage and avoid that pitfall (*Shita Mekubbetzet*). The *Ḥatam Sofer* writes that there is an additional concern that once licentious women are aware that intercourse with the prefect is permitted, they will allow themselves to engage in forbidden intercourse with others, as once the woman is no longer a virgin, it is impossible to ascertain with whom they engaged in intercourse.

And there are also women married to priests – ואיכא נמי כהנות: Since women married to priests know they will be rendered forbidden to their husbands if raped, they will give their lives rather than submit to the rape. Therefore, there is mortal danger involved (Ritva).

And we do not abolish a rabbinic ordinance in the face of a decree of religious persecution – ותקנתא דרבנן מקמי שמדא לא עקרינן: With regard to the decree that anyone who marries on Wednesday will be killed, the Sages explicitly abolished the ordinance to marry on Wednesday. However, in this case, where the decree would not necessarily lead to death, as it is permitted for women to submit to rape, the Sages did not want to abolish the ordinance, due to licentious women and the wives of priests who opted to give their lives rather than submit to rape (Ritva).

What is the coercion – מאי אונס: In the Jerusalem Talmud, the phrase: Due to the coercion, is explained to mean due to sorcery. Some explain that the concern is that the gentiles will attribute the fact that Jews insist on marrying on the same day as due to sorcery (*Penei Moshe*). Others explain that the concern is that if the sorcerers knew when the wedding was taking place, they would cast a spell on the bride and the groom (*Korban HaEda*).

אֲמַר רָבָא: דְּאָמְרִי שַׂר צָבָא בָּא לָעִיר. הֵיכִי דָּמֵי? אִי דְּאָתֵי וְחָלֵיף – לִיעַכַּב! לָא צְרִיכָא, דְּאָתֵי וְקָבַע. בִּשְׁלִישִׁי מִיהָא לִכְנוֹס! אַסְפַּרְוָוא דִּידֵיהּ בִּשְׁלִישִׁי קָאָתוּ.

Rava said: Coercion refers to a case **where they said: A general** and his army **are coming to the city** on Wednesday, and the concern is that the troops will appropriate the supplies for the feast. **What are the circumstances? If** it is a situation **where** the general **comes and passes** through, **let** them **postpone** the wedding until the following week. **Rather, it is necessary** to teach the *halakha* with regard to the general only in a case **where he comes and establishes** himself there. The Gemara asks: **In any case, let one marry on Tuesday.** Why does the *baraita* permit marrying on Monday? The Gemara answers: It was necessary to move the wedding to Monday because **his entourage [*asperava*]**[L] **arrives on Tuesday.**

וְאִיבָּעֵית אֵימָא: מַאי מֵחֲמַת הָאוֹנֶס – כִּדְתַנְיָא: הֲרֵי שֶׁהָיָה פִּתּוֹ אָפוּי, וְטִבְחוֹ טָבוּחַ, וְיֵינוֹ מָזוּג, וּמֵת אָבִיו שֶׁל חָתָן אוֹ אִמָּהּ שֶׁל כַּלָּה – מַכְנִיסִין אֶת הַמֵּת לְחֶדֶר, וְאֶת הֶחָתָן וְאֶת הַכַּלָּה לַחוּפָּה,

And if you wish, say instead: **What is** the meaning of: **Due to the coercion?** It is **as it is taught** in a *baraita*: **If one's bread was baked, and his animal slaughtered, and his wine diluted,** and all preparations for the wedding feast were complete, **and the father of the groom or the mother of the bride died**[H] before the wedding, then before burying the deceased, which would trigger the onset of mourning, **one moves the corpse into a room, and the bride and groom** are ushered **to the wedding canopy** and they are married.

LANGUAGE

Entourage [*asperava*] – **אַסְפַּרְוָוא:** The source of this word and its precise meaning are unknown. Some claim that it is the Persian form of the Greek σπεῖρα, *speira*, meaning the garrison of a military unit, a group of people stationed around a temple, or an organization.

HALAKHA

If one's bread was baked…and the father of the groom or the mother of the bride died – הֲרֵי שֶׁהָיָה פִּתּוֹ אָפוּי...וּמֵת אָבִיו שֶׁל חָתָן אוֹ אִמָּהּ שֶׁל כַּלָּה: If the groom's father dies after the wedding preparations were completed, and it is a place where the prepared items cannot be sold and will be lost if the wedding is postponed, or similarly, if the bride's mother dies and it will be impossible to reproduce the preparation invested in the hair, clothing, and jewelry of the bride, the corpse is placed in a separate room, and the wedding proceeds as planned. The groom engages in intercourse with the bride to fulfill the mitzva, and this is followed by the seven-day period of rejoicing. During this period, mourning is observed in private. Therefore, the couple may not engage in conjugal relations, nor may they sleep in the same room. Afterward, the seven-day period of mourning is observed.

If, however, the bride and groom are in a place where the prepared items can be sold, and no loss will be incurred if the wedding is postponed, or if it was the groom's mother or the bride's father who died and the groom's father and the bride's mother will be able to assist in preparations for the postponed wedding (see 4a), then the deceased is buried immediately and the seven day mourning period ensues. Afterward, the wedding takes place, followed by seven days of rejoicing (Rambam *Sefer Shofetim, Hilkhot Evel* 11:8; *Shulḥan Arukh, Yoreh De'a* 342:1).

Perek **I**
Daf **4** Amud **a**

וּבוֹעֵל בְּעִילַת מִצְוָה וּפוֹרֵשׁ, וְנוֹהֵג שִׁבְעַת יְמֵי הַמִּשְׁתֶּה, וְאַחַר כָּךְ נוֹהֵג שִׁבְעַת יְמֵי אֲבֵילוּת. וְכׇל אוֹתָן הַיָּמִים הוּא יָשֵׁן בֵּין הָאֲנָשִׁים וְהִיא יְשֵׁנָה בֵּין הַנָּשִׁים. וְאֵין מוֹנְעִין תַּכְשִׁיטִין מִן הַכַּלָּה כׇּל שְׁלֹשִׁים יוֹם.

And the groom then **engages in intercourse** with the bride to fulfill the **mitzva,**[N] and then he **withdraws**[N] from his wife, and the corpse is buried. **And** the groom then **observes the seven days of** the wedding **feast,** which are a personal festival for him, when the obligation of mourning rites does not take effect, **and thereafter he observes the seven days of mourning. And throughout those days** of rejoicing and mourning, the groom **sleeps among the men, and the bride sleeps among the women,** and they are not permitted to enter into seclusion. **And** in the event of mourning, **one does not withhold jewels from the bride**[HN] for the **entire thirty-day** period after the wedding, so that she not be undesirable to her husband.

HALAKHA

And one does not withhold jewels from the bride – וְאֵין מוֹנְעִין תַּכְשִׁיטִין מִן הַכַּלָּה: A bride whose close relative dies within thirty days after the marriage ceremony need not refrain from adorning herself, even during the seven-day mourning period (see Rashi; Rambam *Sefer Shofetim, Hilkhot Evel* 11:8; *Shulḥan Arukh Yoreh De'a* 342, 381:6).

NOTES

And the groom then engages in intercourse to fulfill the mitzva – וּבוֹעֵל בְּעִילַת מִצְוָה: Until the deceased is buried, the *halakhot* of mourning are not in effect. However, between the death and the burial, there is a period of acute mourning. During that period, various leniencies are in effect to allow the mourner to tend to the burial. Some maintain that, fundamentally, none of those matters forbidden to a mourner are forbidden to an acute mourner, and therefore the Rambam writes that he may bathe, smear himself with oil, eat meat, drink wine, and engage in sexual relations. Only eating consecrated foods and performing the Temple service are prohibited. According to that opinion, it is clear why the groom would be permitted to engage in the initial intercourse to fulfill the mitzva. According to the Ramban and others, it is prohibited by rabbinic law for an acute mourner to engage in sexual relations; however, the Sages permitted the groom to do so in order to fulfill a mitzva (Meiri).

With regard to the concept that the wedding celebration overrides mourning, some explain that even on the day of death and burial, there is no explicit mitzva of mourning by Torah law. The Sages derived this from the verse "And I will make it as the mourning for an only son, and the end thereof as a bitter day" (Amos 8:10). Similarly, the mitzva of the wedding celebration is not by Torah law, but according to Rabbi Meir HaLevi there is an allusion from the verse "On the day of his marriage and the day of the gladness of his heart" (Song of Songs 3:11). According to the Meiri, it is derived from the verse "The voice of mirth and the voice of gladness, the voice of the bridegroom and the voice of the bride" (Jeremiah 16:9). Since failure to perform the wedding would lead to financial loss, and there is concern that postponement would undermine the wedding celebration, the week of rejoicing is not postponed. The Radbaz adds that since the mourning is not completely annulled, but merely postponed, no Torah law or rabbinic law is actually being abrogated.

And engages in intercourse…and withdraws – וּבוֹעֵל...וּפוֹרֵשׁ: Rashi explains that after intercourse the husband withdraws and the deceased is immediately buried (see *Tosafot*). Others say that were they to bury the deceased immediately, that day would be the day of death and burial on which, according to many opinions, the mourning would be by Torah law. If so, it would be prohibited to engage in intercourse that day. Therefore, they maintain that the deceased is buried only the next day, at which point the mourning period begins. In this case, one is allowed to postpone the burial. Although postponing a burial is generally prohibited so as not to compromise the dignity of the deceased, doing so here is permitted, as it enhances the dignity of the deceased by preventing the humiliation his son would suffer by postponing his wedding (Meiri). The Ramban, however, prohibits postponing the burial, as doing so violates a Torah prohibition. Rather, once the groom consummates the marriage, the deceased is buried that same day.

And one does not withhold jewels from the bride – וְאֵין מוֹנְעִין תַּכְשִׁיטִין מִן הַכַּלָּה: Rashi explains that this refers to a bride whose mourning period was postponed due to the wedding. Most commentaries interpret it as referring to any bride in mourning.

וְדַוְקָא אָבִיו שֶׁל חָתָן אוֹ אִמָּהּ שֶׁל כַּלָּה, דְּלֵיכָּא אִינִישׁ דְּטָרַח לְהוּ, אֲבָל אִיפְּכָא – לָא.

And the wedding takes place and is followed by seven days of feasting and seven days of mourning, **specifically** if it is **the father of the groom or the mother of** the **bride**[N] who died, **as** in that case **there is no** other **person who** would **exert** themselves **for them.** They are the ones responsible for the wedding preparations, and therefore the preparations that were completed must be utilized. **However,** if **the opposite** takes place, i.e., the mother of the groom or the father of the bride dies, **no,** the practice is different. The corpse is buried immediately, the seven-day mourning period is observed, and only afterward is the couple married.

אָמַר רַפְרַם בַּר פַּפָּא אָמַר רַב חִסְדָּא: לֹא שָׁנוּ אֶלָּא שֶׁנָּתַן מַיִם עַל גַּבֵּי בָשָׂר. אֲבָל לֹא נָתַן מַיִם עַל גַּבֵּי בָשָׂר – מִזְדַּבַּן.

Rafram bar Pappa said that **Rav Ḥisda said:** The Sages **taught** that they are married immediately **only if one** already **placed water on the meat.** In that case, it will be impossible to sell it to others, and if it is not cooked immediately it will spoil and a significant loss will be incurred, potentially resulting in cancellation of the wedding feast. **However, if he did not place water on the meat, it can be sold.** No significant loss will be incurred, so the mourning period need not be postponed.

אָמַר רָבָא: וּבִכְרָךְ, אַף עַל פִּי שֶׁנָּתַן מַיִם עַל גַּבֵּי בָשָׂר – מִזְדַּבַּן. אָמַר רַב פַּפָּא: וּבִכְפָר, אַף עַל פִּי שֶׁלֹּא נָתַן מַיִם עַל גַּבֵּי בָשָׂר – לָא מִזְדַּבַּן. וְאֶלָּא, דְּרַב חִסְדָּא הֵיכִי מַשְׁכַּחַתְּ לָהּ? אֲמַר רַב אַשִׁי: כְּגוֹן מָתָא מְחַסְיָא, דְּמַפְּקָא מִכְּרָךְ וּמַפְּקָא מִכְּפָר,

Rava said: And in a city, where there are typically many buyers, **even if he placed water on the meat it** can be **sold,** and the mourning period need not be postponed. **Rav Pappa said: And in a village, even if he did not place water on the meat, it cannot** be **sold,** because no buyers can be found to purchase a quantity of meat that great. Based on the statements of Rava and Rav Pappa, whether or not water was placed on the meat is irrelevant both in a large city and in a village. The Gemara asks: **Where do you find** a case where the statement **of Rav Ḥisda** applies? **Rav Ashi says:** It can be found in a place **like** his city of **Mata Meḥasya,**[NB] **which is removed from** the category of **a city,** as it is too small, **and removed from** the category of **a village,** as it is too large.

תַּנְיָא כְּוָותֵיהּ דְּרַב חִסְדָּא: הֲרֵי שֶׁהָיְתָה פִּתּוֹ אֲפוּיָה וְטִבְחוֹ טָבוּחַ וְיֵינוֹ מָזוּג, וְנָתַן מַיִם עַל גַּבֵּי בָשָׂר, וּמֵת אָבִיו שֶׁל חָתָן אוֹ אִמָּהּ שֶׁל כַּלָּה – מַכְנִיסִין אֶת הַמֵּת לְחֶדֶר וְאֶת הֶחָתָן וְאֶת הַכַּלָּה לַחוּפָּה, וּבוֹעֵל בְּעִילַת מִצְוָה וּפוֹרֵשׁ, וְנוֹהֵג שִׁבְעַת יְמֵי הַמִּשְׁתֶּה, וְאַחַר כָּךְ נוֹהֵג שִׁבְעַת יְמֵי אֲבֵילוּת. וְכָל אוֹתָן הַיָּמִים הוּא יָשֵׁן בֵּין הָאֲנָשִׁים וְאִשְׁתּוֹ יְשֵׁנָה בֵּין הַנָּשִׁים.

The following *baraita* was **taught in accordance** with the opinion **of Rav Ḥisda: If one's bread was baked, and his animal slaughtered, and his wine diluted, and he placed water on the meat, and the father of the groom or the mother of the bride died,**[N] **one moves the corpse into a room, and the bride and groom** are ushered **to the wedding canopy,** and they are married. The groom then **engages in intercourse** with the bride to fulfill the **mitzva,**[N] and he then **withdraws** from his wife, and the corpse is buried. **And** the groom then **observes the seven days of** the wedding **feast, and thereafter observes the seven days of mourning. And throughout those days** of feast and mourning, the groom **sleeps among the men, and his wife sleeps among the women,** and they are not permitted to be alone together.

וְכֵן מִי שֶׁפֵּירְסָה אִשְׁתּוֹ נִדָּה – הוּא יָשֵׁן בֵּין הָאֲנָשִׁים וְהִיא יְשֵׁנָה בֵּין הַנָּשִׁים. וְאֵין מוֹנְעִין תַּכְשִׁיטִין מִן הַכַּלָּה כָּל שְׁלֹשִׁים יוֹם. בֵּין כָּךְ וּבֵין כָּךְ לֹא יִבְעוֹל לֹא בְּעֶרֶב שַׁבָּת וְלֹא בְּמוֹצָאֵי שַׁבָּת.

And likewise, a groom **whose wife began to menstruate**[H] at the time of the wedding, **he sleeps among the men and she sleeps among the women,** until she becomes ritually pure. **However,** the Sages **do not withhold jewels from the bride** while she is in mourning for the **entire thirty-day** period after the wedding. **In any event, the** groom **may not engage in intercourse** with his virgin bride, **neither on Shabbat evening,**[N] as he will thereby inflict a wound, **nor at the conclusion of Shabbat.**

NOTES

The mother of the bride – אִמָּהּ שֶׁל כַּלָּה: Some explain that the reason the wedding is not postponed is that the mother of the bride is the one who undertakes the wedding preparations in general (Rambam; see *Kesef Mishne* and *Talmidei Rabbeinu Yona*). Most early commentaries, beginning with Rav Hai Gaon, explain that the mother of the bride is involved with preparing the bride's jewelry. The Ramban asks why that is considered a major loss, as most jewelry will not be ruined in the course of an additional week. He explains that the concern is with regard to items that lose value over time. Furthermore, the term used in the Gemara, *takhshit*, refers not only to jewelry but also to makeup and body treatments. In the mother of the bride's absence, there will be no one to see to those details.

Like Mata Meḥasya – כְּגוֹן מָתָא מְחַסְיָא: *Tosafot* ask why Rav Ḥisda establishes this in so limited a case. They explain that this is prototypical of most places that are neither small villages nor large cities. Some explain that Rav Ḥisda himself does not accept the distinction of Rava and Rav Pappa but holds that even in a large city there would be financial loss, since it would not be possible to sell this meat in the market, but only in private homes. Therefore, the ruling is applicable everywhere (*Shita Mekubbetzet*). This explains the proof cited from the *baraita*, which establishes a general ruling without distinguishing between different places.

The father of the groom…died, etc. – מֵת אָבִיו שֶׁל חָתָן וכו׳: The early commentaries discuss the ruling in the case of the death of a relative of the bride or the groom not mentioned in the Gemara, e.g., a brother or sister.

Some authorities rule that in those cases, too, the couple engages in initial intercourse to fulfill the mitzva, after which the groom withdraws from his wife; however, the seven days of mourning precede the seven days of rejoicing (*Ba'al Halakhot Gedolot*). Others hold that the wedding is postponed until after the mourning period (Rosh). There are those who also make a distinction between the groom's mother and the bride's father and other relatives (see Meiri).

Intercourse to fulfill the mitzva – בְּעִילַת מִצְוָה: See *Tosafot* for an explanation why this is referred to as intercourse to fulfill the mitzva. Some early commentaries write that since conjugal relations are an essential component of marriage, the seven days of rejoicing begin only after the marriage is consummated.

In any event, the groom may not engage in intercourse, neither on Shabbat evening – בֵּין כָּךְ וּבֵין כָּךְ לֹא יִבְעוֹל לֹא בְּעֶרֶב שַׁבָּת: Some explain that this *halakha* is cited here because if one marries a virgin on Wednesday and waits until the thirty-day mourning period ends before consummating the marriage, the thirtieth day is Friday evening.

HALAKHA

And likewise, a groom whose wife began to menstruate – וְכֵן מִי שֶׁפֵּירְסָה אִשְׁתּוֹ נִדָּה: If the bride begins to menstruate before the couple engaged in conjugal relations for the first time, the couple may not enter into seclusion together. The groom sleeps among the men and the bride sleeps among the women (Rambam *Sefer Kedusha, Hilkhot Issurei Bia* 22:1; *Shulḥan Arukh, Even HaEzer* 22:1).

BACKGROUND

Mata Meḥasya – מָתָא מְחַסְיָא: Mata Meḥasya was a city adjacent to Sura in Babylonia. In its day, Sura was a large city and even served as the capital of the Parthian Empire. Mata Meḥasya was relatively small. Apparently, most of its inhabitants were Jews, and it is said to date back to the beginning of Jewish settlement in Babylonia. In the time of Rav Ashi, the yeshiva in Sura moved to Mata Meḥasya. Due to the proximity of the two cities, during the geonic period, the academy was sometimes called the Sura Yeshiva and sometimes called the Meḥasya Yeshiva. Throughout all these periods, the city of Meḥasya remained the same, larger than a village but never reaching the size of a large city.

אָמַר מָר: הוּא יָשֵׁן בֵּין הָאֲנָשִׁים וְהִיא יְשֵׁנָה בֵּין הַנָּשִׁים. מְסַיֵּיעַ לֵיהּ לְרַבִּי יוֹחָנָן. דְּאָמַר רַבִּי יוֹחָנָן: אַף עַל פִּי שֶׁאָמְרוּ אֵין אֲבֵילוּת בַּמּוֹעֵד – אֲבָל דְּבָרִים שֶׁל צִינְעָא נוֹהֵג.

The Gemara proceeds to analyze the *baraita*. **The Master said: He sleeps among the men and she sleeps among the women.** This **supports** the opinion **of Rabbi Yoḥanan, as Rabbi Yoḥanan said: Although they stated that there is no mourning** observed **on a Festival, yet one observes matters of privacy,**[NH] i.e., mourning practices not apparent to onlookers. Therefore, the groom and the bride may not engage in relations during the seven days of rejoicing, as the legal status of those days is like that of a Festival for them.

דָּרַשׁ רַב יוֹסֵף בְּרֵיהּ דְּרָבָא מִשְּׁמֵיהּ דְּרָבָא: לֹא שָׁנוּ אֶלָּא שֶׁלֹּא בָּעַל, אֲבָל בָּעַל – אִשְׁתּוֹ יְשֵׁנָה עִמּוֹ.

Rav Yosef, son of Rava, taught in the name of Rava: They taught the *halakha* that if the bride began menstruating, the bride and groom may not be alone together, **only if he did not engage in intercourse** with her. **However, if he engaged in intercourse** with her, and afterward she begins menstruating, **his wife sleeps with him,** and there is no concern that this will lead to their engaging in forbidden relations.

וְהָא הָכָא, דִּבְבָעַל עָסְקִינַן, וְקָתָנֵי: הוּא יָשֵׁן בֵּין הָאֲנָשִׁים וְהִיא יְשֵׁנָה בֵּין הַנָּשִׁים! כִּי קָאָמַר – אַפֵּירְסָה אִשְׁתּוֹ נִדָּה.

The Gemara asks: **But here,** with regard to mourning, **we are dealing** with a case **where he** already **engaged in intercourse** that was permitted prior to the funeral, **and** yet the *tanna* **teaches: He sleeps among the men and she sleeps among the women.** The Gemara answers: **When he states** the ruling that if they already engaged in intercourse she sleeps with him, it was **concerning** only a case where **his wife began menstruating,** and it is not a case of mourning.

הָא ״וְכֵן״ קָתָנֵי!

The Gemara asks: But **doesn't it state: And likewise,** indicating that the legal status of the mourner and the legal status of the groom whose wife is menstruating are the same?

NOTES

One observes matters of privacy – דְּבָרִים שֶׁל צִינְעָא נוֹהֵג: There is a difference of opinion among the early commentaries with regard to the meaning of: One observes. Some explain that it means that he must observe those matters. Others maintain that he may do so. However, that dispute is with regard to the intermediate days of the Festival. During the seven days of rejoicing after a wedding, whose legal status is like that of a Festival by rabbinic law, everyone agrees that it means one must observe these mourning practices.

HALAKHA

One observes matters of privacy – דְּבָרִים שֶׁל צִינְעָא נוֹהֵג: If the close relative of an individual dies during a Festival, although the seven-day period of mourning does not begin until the conclusion of the Festival, private mourning practices are still observed, and sexual relations are forbidden, in accordance with the opinion of Rabbi Yoḥanan. That is the ruling of most authorities, following the ruling of *Ba'al Halakhot Gedolot* and contrary to the ruling of the Rambam (Rambam *Sefer Shofetim*, *Hilkhot Evel* 10:3; *Shulḥan Arukh*, *Yoreh De'a* 399:2).

Perek **I**
Daf **4** Amud **b**

הָכִי קָאָמַר: וְכֵן מִי שֶׁפֵּירְסָה אִשְׁתּוֹ נִדָּה וְלֹא בָּעַל – הוּא יָשֵׁן בֵּין הָאֲנָשִׁים, וְאִשְׁתּוֹ יְשֵׁנָה בֵּין הַנָּשִׁים.

This is what the *tanna* **is saying: And likewise,** with regard to a groom **whose wife began to menstruate, and he had not** yet **engaged in intercourse** with her, **he sleeps among the men, and his wife sleeps among the women.** However, in the case of a mourner, even if they already engaged in sexual relations, he sleeps among the men and she sleeps among the women.

לְמֵימְרָא דַּאֲבֵילוּת קִילָּא לֵיהּ מִנִּדָּה?

The Gemara asks: **Is that to say that** the prohibition against relations during **mourning is more lenient in his opinion than** the prohibition against relations with **a menstruating woman?**[N] That is apparently the case, as after engaging in the initial intercourse, he may enter into seclusion with his menstruating wife but not with his wife when either of them is in mourning.

NOTES

Is that to say that mourning is more lenient in his opinion than a menstruating woman – לְמֵימְרָא דַּאֲבֵילוּת קִילָּא לֵיהּ מִנִּדָּה: The Meiri notes that the discussion here is clearly not with regard to their relative halakhic stringency, as intercourse with a menstruating woman is forbidden by Torah law and punishable by *karet*, while intercourse during the mourning period is forbidden by rabbinic law. However, since the discussion in the Gemara relates to the measures instituted by the Sages to distance one from transgression, this depends more on the way one subjectively relates to these matters. There are major prohibitions that one takes lightly and minor prohibitions with regard to which one is especially observant (see *Shita Mekubbetzet*).

וְהָאָמַר רַבִּי יִצְחָק בַּר חֲנִינָא אָמַר רַב הוּנָא: כָּל מְלָאכוֹת שֶׁאִשָּׁה עוֹשָׂה לְבַעְלָהּ, נִדָּה עוֹשָׂה לְבַעְלָהּ, חוּץ מִמְּזִיגַת הַכּוֹס וְהַצָּעַת הַמִּטָּה וְהַרְחָצַת פָּנָיו יָדָיו וְרַגְלָיו. וְאִלּוּ גַּבֵּי אֲבֵילוּת תַּנְיָא: אַף עַל פִּי שֶׁאָמְרוּ: אֵין אָדָם רַשַּׁאי לָכוֹף אֶת אִשְׁתּוֹ לִהְיוֹת כּוֹחֶלֶת וְלִהְיוֹת פּוֹקֶסֶת, בֶּאֱמֶת אָמְרוּ: מוֹזֶגֶת לוֹ הַכּוֹס, וּמַצַּעַת לוֹ הַמִּטָּה, וּמַרְחֶצֶת לוֹ פָּנָיו יָדָיו וְרַגְלָיו!

The Gemara continues: **But didn't Rav Yitzḥak bar Ḥanina** say that **Rav Huna said: All tasks that a woman** typically **performs for her husband, a menstruating woman performs for her husband,**[H] **except for pouring** his drink into the **cup;**[N] **arranging** his **bed; and washing his face, hands, and feet,** as these actions are particularly intimate. **Whereas with regard to mourning, it is taught** in a *baraita*: **Although they said that a man may not compel** his mourning **wife, to paint** her eyes blue **or to rouge** [*pokeset*][L] her face, **in truth they said that she may pour**[H] his drink into **the cup; arrange his bed; and wash his face, hands, and feet.** Apparently, the concern lest they come to engage in relations while in mourning is less pressing than the concern while she is menstruating.

לָא קַשְׁיָא, כָּאן – בַּאֲבֵילוּת דִּידֵיהּ, כָּאן – בַּאֲבֵילוּת דִּידָהּ.

The Gemara answers: This is **not difficult. Here,** where the Sages required them to sleep apart, it is **in** a case of the husband's **mourning; there,** where the Sages allowed her to pour his drink and perform other intimate activities, it is **in** a case of the wife's **mourning.**[N] The prohibition against relations when one is mourning is not perceived to be as severe as the prohibition against relations with a menstruating woman. However, when his wife is mourning, even were he unable to restrain himself, his wife would not be complicit. Therefore, the Sages did not restrict their interaction.

וְהָא אָבִיו שֶׁל חָתָן אוֹ אִמָּהּ שֶׁל כַּלָּה קָתָנֵי! כִּי קָתָנֵי – אַשְּׁאָרָא.

The Gemara asks: **But isn't it taught** in that *baraita*: **The father of the groom and the mother of the bride?** This indicates that it makes no difference which of them was in mourning. **When** the *tanna* **teaches** that there is no distinction between which of them was in mourning, it was **concerning the rest** of the mourning practices cited there, not with regard to prohibiting their seclusion.

HALAKHA

A menstruating woman performs for her husband – נִדָּה עוֹשָׂה לְבַעְלָהּ: A menstruating woman may perform all the tasks that a wife normally performs for her husband, except for washing his face, hands, or feet; serving him his drink; and arranging his bed (Rambam *Sefer Kedusha, Hilkhot Issurei Bia* 11:19; *Shulḥan Arukh, Yoreh De'a* 195:10–12).

In truth they said that she may pour – בֶּאֱמֶת אָמְרוּ מוֹזֶגֶת: It is prohibited for a mourner to engage in conjugal relations. However, if either the husband or the wife is in mourning, acts of intimacy are permitted. Therefore, the wife is permitted to serve a drink to her husband; wash his face, hands, or feet; and arrange his bed, whether it is he or she that is in mourning. This ruling is in accordance with the opinion of Rav Ashi, a later *amora*. In his opinion he does not distinguish whether it is the husband or the wife who is the mourner (Ran; *Shulḥan Arukh, Yoreh De'a* 383:1).

LANGUAGE

Rouge [*pokeset*] – פּוֹקֶסֶת: From the Greek φῦκος, *fukos*, meaning a red dye made of a kind of seaweed. Some claim that the origin of the Greek word is the Hebrew *pukh*, meaning eye shadow.

NOTES

Except for pouring his drink into the cup – חוּץ מִמְּזִיגַת הַכּוֹס: Following Rashi, the Ritva explains that the reference here is not to the actual pouring, but to serving the drink to her husband. Similarly, he explains that arranging the bed is prohibited only when she does so in his presence. He also cites the opinion of *Tosafot*, who explain that it is referring specifically to placing the sheets on the bed and not arranging the mattress or similar tasks. With regard to washing his face, the reference is not to actual washing, as contact is forbidden. Rather, the reference is to preparing water for him to wash himself. Common to all of these cases is a degree of intimacy unique to a man and his wife, and these actions could lead to conjugal relations.

His mourning…her mourning – בַּאֲבֵילוּת דִּידֵיהּ...בַּאֲבֵילוּת דִּידָהּ: Some cite a variant reading with the opposite meaning: His mourning is a greater deterrent to intimacy than hers. When he is in mourning, there is no concern that he will come to commit a transgression. However, her mourning does not have the same effect upon him, and he is more likely to be tempted and to commit a transgression. There is a variant reading in the continuation of the Gemara as well. However, most commentaries subscribe to Rashi's reading and explanation of the Gemara, that stringency is necessary when he is in mourning. Although he is in mourning, there is still concern that he will not be able to control his urges. In fact, the Sages say that even during the period of acute mourning, one's temptations are powerful. However, when a woman is in mourning, she would refuse her husband even if he were to approach her, as her urges are less powerful. The Rashash adds that women are more sensitive than men and therefore mourning affects them more than it does men.

וּמִי שָׁאנֵי בֵּין אֲבֵילוּת דִּידֵיהּ לַאֲבֵילוּת דִּידַהּ? וְהָתַנְיָא: מִי שֶׁמֵּת חָמִיו אוֹ חֲמוֹתוֹ אֵינוֹ יָכוֹל לָכוֹף אֶת אִשְׁתּוֹ לִהְיוֹת כּוֹחֶלֶת וְלִהְיוֹת פּוֹקֶסֶת, אֶלָּא כּוֹפֶה מִטָּתוֹ וְנוֹהֵג עִמָּהּ אֲבֵילוּת. וְכֵן הִיא שֶׁמֵּת חָמִיהָ אוֹ חֲמוֹתָהּ אֵינָהּ רַשָּׁאָה לִהְיוֹת כּוֹחֶלֶת וְלִהְיוֹת פּוֹקֶסֶת, אֶלָּא כּוֹפָה מִטָּתָהּ וְנוֹהֶגֶת עִמּוֹ אֲבֵילוּת!

The Gemara asks: **And do** the Sages **distinguish between his mourning and her mourning? But isn't it taught** in a *baraita*: With regard to **one whose father-in-law or mother-in-law died, he may not compel his wife to paint** her eyes **blue**[B] **or to rouge** her face.[H] **Rather, he overturns his bed,** as was the practice among mourners, **and observes** the **mourning** period **with her.**[N] **And likewise, if** a wife's **father-in-law or mother-in-law dies, she is not allowed to paint** her eyes **blue or to rouge** her face. **Rather, she overturns her bed and observes** the **mourning** period **with him.** There is no mention in the context of his mourning that he must not be alone with his wife.

תְּנֵי בַּאֲבֵילוּת דִּידֵיהּ: הוּא יָשֵׁן בֵּין הָאֲנָשִׁים וְאִשְׁתּוֹ יְשֵׁנָה בֵּין הַנָּשִׁים. הָא "וְכֵן" קָתָנֵי! כִּי קָתָנֵי – אַכִּיחוּל וְאַפִּירְכּוּס. וְהָא "עִמּוֹ" קָתָנֵי, מַאי לָאו עִמּוֹ בְּמִטָּה? לָא, עִמּוֹ בְּבַיִת. וּכְדַאֲמַר לֵיהּ רַב לְחִיָּיא בְּרֵיהּ: בְּאַפַּהּ – נְהוֹג אֲבֵילוּתָא, דְּלָא בְּאַפַּהּ – לָא תִּנְהוֹג אֲבֵילוּתָא.

The Gemara emends the *baraita*. **Teach with regard to his mourning: He sleeps among the men and his wife sleeps among the women.** The Gemara asks: But **doesn't** the *tanna* **teach: And likewise?** This indicates that there is no difference between the two cases. The Gemara answers: **When** the *tanna* **teaches** that there is no distinction between which of them is mourning, it is with regard to **painting and rouge.** The Gemara asks: But **doesn't** the *tanna* **teach: With him? What,** does it **not** mean **with him** together **in bed,** and there is no concern that it will lead to sexual relations? **No,** it means **with him at home, and** it is **as that which Rav said to Ḥiyya, his son,** when his wife's father died: **Before her, observe mourning** practices;[H] **not before her, do not observe mourning** practices. Understood in this context, the term, With him, means in his presence.

רַב אַשִׁי אֲמַר: מִי קָמְדַמֵּית אֲבֵילוּתָא דְּהָכָא לַאֲבֵילוּתָא דְּעָלְמָא? אֲבֵילוּתָא דְּעָלְמָא – חֲמִיר, וְלָא אָתֵי לְזַלְזוּלֵי בֵּיהּ. אֲבֵילוּת דְּהָכָא, כֵּיוָן דְּאַקִּילוּ רַבָּנַן – אָתֵי לְזַלְזוּלֵי בֵּיהּ.

Rav Ashi said that the question was based on a mistaken premise: **Can you compare the mourning here with mourning in general? Mourning in general is stringent, and one will not come to take it lightly.** However, with regard to **mourning here,** immediately following the wedding, **since the Sages were lenient, one will come to take it lightly.**[N]

HALAKHA

He may not compel his wife to paint her eyes blue or to rouge her face – אֵינוֹ יָכוֹל לָכוֹף אֶת אִשְׁתּוֹ לִהְיוֹת כּוֹחֶלֶת וְלִהְיוֹת פּוֹקֶסֶת: If a man's wife is in mourning for her father or mother, he may not compel her to apply makeup during her mourning period (Rambam *Sefer Shofetim, Hilkhot Evel* 2:5; *Shulḥan Arukh, Yoreh De'a* 381:6).

Before her, observe mourning practices – בְּאַפַּהּ, נְהוֹג אֲבֵילוּתָא: If a man's father-in-law or mother-in-law dies, he is not obligated to observe mourning practices together with his wife, but he should observe them when he is in his wife's presence. So too, a wife is obligated to observe mourning practices in her husband's presence when he is in mourning for his father or mother, in accordance with the opinion of Rav (Rambam *Sefer Shofetim, Hilkhot Evel* 2:5; *Shulḥan Arukh, Yoreh De'a* 374:6, 381:6).

NOTES

And observes the mourning period with her – וְנוֹהֵג עִמָּהּ אֲבֵילוּת: The Ritva cites two explanations. The first is a literal explanation: If he is actually in her presence, i.e., at home with her, he observes the mourning practices with her. The second explanation, which seems more reasonable in this context, says that he observes mourning practices in any place where she will be informed of his conduct, even if he is not actually in her presence. The Ramban rules that these mourning practices for the relative of a spouse are no longer observed. The reason for these practices is to show deference to one's spouse, not due to any obligation of mourning. The custom today is to forgo that deference.

Mourning here…one will come to take it lightly – אֲבֵילוּת דְּהָכָא...אָתֵי לְזַלְזוּלֵי בֵּיהּ: Some commentaries ask why this explanation wasn't already suggested earlier, seeing as it is the least complicated of those suggested (*Shita Mekubbetzet*). They explain that the case of death before a wedding was likened to death during a Festival, where the mourning is delayed until after the Festival and there is no concern that one will take it lightly.

Based on the Gemara here, the Rosh raises the possibility that even on a Festival the bride and groom must separate for similar reasons. However, he draws a distinction between the cases. Since the Festival predated the mourning, the mourning never takes effect and there is no active postponement of the mourning, the husband and wife engaging in conjugal relations will not lead them to take mourning lightly. However, in the case of a wedding there is concern that they will take mourning lightly, as even though they did not yet marry, the period of mourning is postponed, and they are allowed to engage in conjugal relations on the first night.

BACKGROUND

To paint her eyes blue – לִהְיוֹת כּוֹחֶלֶת: The eye shadow described here is kohl, apparently a black-blue color that was derived from the mineral stibnite, Sb_2S_3. The stibnite crystals were ground into powder and women would color the area around their eyes to draw attention to them and create the impression that they were larger. It was apparently also utilized for medicinal purposes.

Stibnite

Ancient kohl tube

Ancient kohl applicator

NOTES

That mourning has not yet taken effect upon him – דְּלָא חָל עָלָיו אֲבֵילוּתָא: The question is raised: Although mourning does not take effect before the burial, isn't he an acute mourner? The Rashba and the Ritva answer that there is a difference between the status of a mourner before his relative's burial and his status thereafter. Although both statuses are effected by the death of a relative, clearly the mourning that takes places before burial is more lenient.

BACKGROUND

Covering of the grave – גּוֹלֵל: This covering is a large stone that was rolled to seal the opening of a grave. In the burial caves of significant families, this stone is in the shape of a large wheel, which is not susceptible to ritual impurity and could be moved in order to gain access to the cave.

Stone covering of the grave of the royal house of Herod, from the end of the Second Temple period

מַאי קוּלָּא? אִילֵימָא דְּקָתָנֵי בּוֹעֵל בְּעִילַת מִצְוָה וּפוֹרֵשׁ – הָתָם מִשּׁוּם דְּלָא חָל עָלָיו אֲבֵילוּתָא; אִי לְרַבִּי אֱלִיעֶזֶר – עַד שֶׁיֵּצֵא מִפֶּתַח הַבַּיִת, אִי לְרַבִּי יְהוֹשֻׁעַ – עַד שֶׁיִּסָּתֵם הַגּוֹלֵל!

What leniency did the Sages enact in this case? If we say it is that which the *tanna* teaches: The groom engages in the initial intercourse with the bride to fulfill the mitzva and then he withdraws from his wife, then there, where the corpse is placed into a room in the house, it is due to the fact that mourning has not yet taken effect upon him.[N] Consequently, there is no leniency with regard to mourning practices. If it is according to the opinion of Rabbi Eliezer, mourning does not take effect until the corpse emerges from the entrance of the house for burial. If it is according to the opinion of Rabbi Yehoshua, mourning does not take effect until the covering of the grave[B] is sealed.

אֶלָּא דְּקָתָנֵי: נוֹהֵג שִׁבְעַת יְמֵי הַמִּשְׁתֶּה, וְאַחַר כָּךְ נוֹהֵג שִׁבְעַת יְמֵי אֲבֵילוּת.

Rather, the leniency is that which the *tanna* teaches: And the groom then observes the seven days of feast following the wedding, and thereafter he observes the seven days of mourning. Since the Sages were lenient and allowed him to observe the wedding feast, despite the fact that he is a mourner, they prohibited his being alone with his wife so he would be less likely to practice additional leniencies in his mourning.

אֲמַר מָר: בֵּין כָּךְ וּבֵין כָּךְ לֹא יִבְעוֹל לֹא בְּעֶרֶב שַׁבָּת וְלֹא בְּמוֹצָאֵי שַׁבָּת. בִּשְׁלָמָא בְּעֶרֶב שַׁבָּת – מִשּׁוּם חַבּוּרָה, אֶלָּא בְּמוֹצָאֵי שַׁבָּת אַמַּאי לֹא?

§ The Master said in the *baraita*: In any event, the groom may not engage in intercourse with his virgin bride, neither on Shabbat evening, nor at the conclusion of Shabbat.[H] Granted, on Shabbat evening he may not engage in intercourse due to the prohibition against inflicting a wound on Shabbat. However, at the conclusion of Shabbat, why may he not engage in intercourse with his virgin bride?

אֲמַר רַבִּי זֵירָא:

Rabbi Zeira said:

HALAKHA

In any event, the groom may not engage in intercourse with his virgin bride, neither on Shabbat evening nor at the conclusion of Shabbat – בֵּין כָּךְ וּבֵין כָּךְ לֹא יִבְעוֹל לֹא בְּעֶרֶב שַׁבָּת וְלֹא בְּמוֹצָאֵי שַׁבָּת: According to the Rambam, a wedding may not take place on Friday or at the conclusion of Shabbat, lest one desecrate Shabbat in the course of preparing the wedding feast. This ruling is in accordance with the conclusion of the Gemara, based on the *baraita* (Ramban). Other authorities maintain that this restriction was said only in places where courts convene on Monday and Thursday (Rosh; *Tur*). Furthermore, they rule based on the Gemara's conclusion that the initial intercourse with one's virgin wife is permitted on Shabbat evening, and there is no concern lest it lead to desecration of Shabbat. In fact, there were periods when the custom was to schedule weddings on Friday to benefit the poor, so that the wedding feast and the Shabbat meal would coincide (Mordekhai). However, there was no widespread custom to marry on Sunday, because that is the day when gentiles marry, and it is prohibited to follow the statutes of the gentiles (Rema in a responsum; Rambam *Sefer Nashim, Hilkhot Ishut* 10:14; *Shulḥan Arukh, Even HaEzer* 63:4).

Perek **I**
Daf **5** Amud **a**

NOTES

Calculations for a mitzva – חֶשְׁבּוֹנוֹת שֶׁל מִצְוָה: The source of the prohibition against speaking about mundane matters on Shabbat is the verse "And call Shabbat a delight…and you shall honor it…neither pursuing your business, nor speaking thereof" (Isaiah 58:13). However, the Gemara infers (*Shabbat* 140b): Your business is forbidden, but matters of Heaven are permitted. The question is raised: If matters of Heaven are permitted, why on Shabbat is it prohibited to consecrate an item? That is a matter of Heaven par excellence. Some early commentaries answer: Since consecration typically involves transfer of a clearly defined object into the treasury of God, so to speak, it resembles a transaction, which is prohibited on Shabbat.

מִשּׁוּם חֶשְׁבּוֹנוֹת.

It is due to calculations performed on Shabbat to prepare for the wedding. He would thereby engage in weekday matters on Shabbat.

אֲמַר לֵיהּ אַבַּיֵי: וְחֶשְׁבּוֹנוֹת שֶׁל מִצְוָה מִי אֲסִירִי? וְהָא רַב חִסְדָּא וְרַב הַמְנוּנָא דְּאָמְרִי תַּרְוַיְיהוּ: חֶשְׁבּוֹנוֹת שֶׁל מִצְוָה מוּתָּר לְחַשְּׁבָן בְּשַׁבָּת! וְאָמַר רַבִּי אֶלְעָזָר: פּוֹסְקִין צְדָקָה לַעֲנִיִּים בְּשַׁבָּת! וְאָמַר רַבִּי יַעֲקֹב אָמַר רַבִּי יוֹחָנָן: הוֹלְכִין לְבָתֵּי כְנֵסִיּוֹת וּלְבָתֵּי מִדְרָשׁוֹת לְפַקֵּחַ עַל עִסְקֵי רַבִּים בְּשַׁבָּת. וְאָמַר רַבִּי יַעֲקֹב בַּר אִידִי אָמַר רַבִּי יוֹחָנָן: מְפַקְּחִין פִּיקּוּחַ נֶפֶשׁ בְּשַׁבָּת.

Abaye said to him: And are calculations for a mitzva prohibited on Shabbat? But wasn't it Rav Ḥisda and Rav Hamnuna who both said: With regard to calculations for a mitzva,[NH] it is permitted to reckon them on Shabbat? And Rabbi Elazar said: One may allocate charity[H] to the poor on Shabbat. And Rabbi Ya'akov said that Rabbi Yoḥanan said: One goes to synagogues and study halls to supervise matters affecting the multitudes on Shabbat. And Rabbi Ya'akov bar Idi said that Rabbi Yoḥanan said: One supervises matters of saving a life on Shabbat.[H]

HALAKHA

Calculations for a mitzva – חֶשְׁבּוֹנוֹת שֶׁל מִצְוָה: One may engage in calculations with regard to a mitzva on Shabbat (Rambam *Sefer Zemanim, Hilkhot Shabbat* 24:5; *Shulḥan Arukh, Oraḥ Ḥayyim* 306:6).

One may allocate charity – פּוֹסְקִין צְדָקָה: One may allocate charity to the poor and pledge to donate money for the purpose of a mitzva on Shabbat (Rambam *Sefer Zemanim, Hilkhot Shabbat* 24:5; *Shulḥan Arukh, Oraḥ Ḥayyim* 306:6).

One supervises matters of saving a life on Shabbat – מְפַקְּחִין פִּיקּוּחַ נֶפֶשׁ בְּשַׁבָּת: One may violate all Shabbat prohibitions in order to save a life, and he need not seek permission from the courts before doing so. On the contrary, anyone who takes the initiative is praiseworthy (Rambam *Sefer Zemanim, Hilkhot Shabbat* 2:16; *Shulḥan Arukh, Oraḥ Ḥayyim* 328:13).

וְאָמַר רַב שְׁמוּאֵל בַּר נַחְמָנִי אָמַר רַבִּי יוֹנָתָן: הוֹלְכִין לְטַרְטִיָּיאוֹת וּלְקַרְקִיָּיאוֹת לְפַקֵּחַ עַל עִסְקֵי רַבִּים בְּשַׁבָּת. וְתָנָא דְּבֵי מְנַשְּׁיָא: מְשַׁדְּכִין עַל הַתִּינוֹקֶת לֵיאָרֵס בְּשַׁבָּת, וְעַל הַתִּינוֹק לְלַמְּדוֹ סֵפֶר וּלְלַמְּדוֹ אוּמָּנוּת!

And Rabbi Shmuel bar Naḥmani said that Rabbi Yoḥanan said: One goes to theaters [*tartiyyaot*][BL] **and circuses** [*karkiyyaot*][L] **to supervise matters** affecting the **multitudes on Shabbat,**[H] because the fate of the Jewish people or of individual Jews is often decided there and one's presence could prevent calamity. **And the Sage of the school of Menashya taught: One makes matches** [*meshadkhin*][L] among the families concerned **for a young girl to be betrothed on Shabbat,**[H] **and** similarly one may make arrangements **for a young boy to teach him Torah and to teach him a craft.** Apparently, calculations for a mitzva may be reckoned on Shabbat, including calculations for a wedding. Therefore, this cannot be the reason for the prohibition against marrying at the conclusion of Shabbat.

אֶלָּא אָמַר רַבִּי זֵירָא: גְּזֵירָה שֶׁמָּא יִשְׁחוֹט בֶּן עוֹף. אֲמַר לֵיהּ אַבַּיֵי: אֶלָּא מֵעַתָּה, יוֹם הַכִּפּוּרִים שֶׁחָל לִהְיוֹת בְּשֵׁנִי בְּשַׁבָּת יִדָּחֶה, גְּזֵירָה שֶׁמָּא יִשְׁחוֹט בֶּן עוֹף! הָתָם, דִּלְנַפְשֵׁיהּ, לָא טָרִיד, הָכָא דִּלַאֲחֵרִים – טָרִיד. אִי נַמִי: הָתָם – אִית לֵיהּ רַוְחָא, הָכָא – לֵית לֵיהּ רַוְחָא.

Rather, Rabbi Zeira said: It is a decree lest one slaughter a young fowl[N] **on Shabbat,** due to his preoccupation with the preparations for that night's wedding feast. **Abaye said to him: If that is so, Yom Kippur that occurs on Monday should be postponed**[N] when fixing the calendar, due to **a decree lest one slaughter a young fowl** on Shabbat for the meal on Yom Kippur eve, which is a mitzva. The Gemara distinguishes between the cases. **There,** with regard to Yom Kippur eve, when one is preparing a meal **for himself, he is not preoccupied,** and he will not overlook the fact that it is Shabbat. **Here,** in the case of a wedding, one is preparing a meal **for others** and is **preoccupied. Alternatively, there,** on Yom Kippur eve, **he has an interval** of time during which he can slaughter the bird, as the mitzva is to eat the meal on Yom Kippur eve the next day. **Here, he does not have an interval** of time, because the wedding and the feast take place at night at the conclusion of Shabbat.

הַשְׁתָּא דְּאָתֵית לְהָכִי – עֶרֶב שַׁבָּת נַמִי, גְּזֵירָה שֶׁמָּא יִשְׁחוֹט בֶּן עוֹף.

The Gemara says: **Now that we have come to this** understanding of the prohibition against marrying at the conclusion of Shabbat, the prohibition not to engage in sexual intercourse on **Shabbat evening, too,**[N] is not due to the intercourse. Rather, it is **a decree lest one slaughter a young fowl** for the wedding feast.

אִיבַּעְיָא לְהוּ: בְּתוּלָה נִשֵּׂאת בִּרְבִיעִי וְנִבְעֶלֶת בִּרְבִיעִי, וְלָא חָיְישִׁינַן לְאִיקְּרוּרֵי דַּעְתָּא, אוֹ דִּלְמָא: בְּתוּלָה נִשֵּׂאת בִּרְבִיעִי וְנִבְעֶלֶת בַּחֲמִישִׁי, דְּחָיְישִׁינַן לְאִיקְּרוּרֵי דַּעְתָּא?

§ The Gemara **raises a dilemma: Is a virgin married on Wednesday and** does she **engage in intercourse on** that **Wednesday, and we are not concerned** lest **his resolve** to take his bride to court upon discovering that she was not a virgin **cool** overnight? Rather, he will certainly go to court the next morning. **Or perhaps, a virgin is married on Wednesday but engages in intercourse on Thursday,**[H] **as we are concerned that his resolve will cool.** [N]

NOTES

Lest one slaughter a young fowl – שֶׁמָּא יִשְׁחוֹט בֶּן עוֹף: The commentaries provide several explanations for use of the term young fowl, as opposed to another source of meat that requires slaughter. Some explain that since young fowl are typically available in the proximity of the house, the concern is that one will forget that it is Shabbat and slaughter one (*ge'onim*). Others explain that, contrary to slaughtering an animal, slaughtering a young fowl requires little effort. Due to that relative ease, one will slaughter the fowl without realizing that it is Shabbat (Ritva). The Meiri explains that it was customary to specifically slaughter young chickens for the wedding feast as a portent that the couple will procreate like chickens. This custom remains in effect in several places.

Yom Kippur…should be postponed – יוֹם הַכִּפּוּרִים...יִדָּחֶה: The *ge'onim* explain that the concern with regard to young fowl is due to the fact that it is customary to slaughter roosters and chickens for the meal preceding Yom Kippur. The early commentaries question the notion of postponing Yom Kippur for so insignificant a concern. They answer that the calendar is fixed to prevent Yom Kippur from occurring on Sunday or Friday for similar reasons.

An additional question is raised. If Yom Kippur is postponed until Tuesday, the seventh day of *Sukkot* will coincide with Shabbat. The very reason that the calendar is fixed to prevent Rosh HaShana from occurring on Sunday is to preclude that coincidence. The commentaries answer that the Gemara is not suggesting that Yom Kippur be postponed specifically until Tuesday. Rather, in a case where, based on calculations, Yom Kippur was going to occur on Sunday, it would be preferable to postpone it until Tuesday rather than Monday.

Shabbat evening too – עֶרֶב שַׁבָּת נַמִי: This answer is difficult, as a *baraita* cited later in the Gemara prohibits intercourse on Friday night because it causes a wound. The Rashba explains that Rabbi Zeira sought to interpret the *baraita* in accordance with the *halakha*, that there is no concern lest one cause a wound during intercourse. In the *Shita Mekubbetzet* an explanation is cited that Rabbi Zeira preferred to explain the entire *baraita* according to the same reason. With regard to the actual concern that one will slaughter a young fowl, some explain that if one engages in relations on Shabbat, the groomsmen will need to remain with him, and in seeking to feed them, he will come to slaughter a young fowl (*Talmidei Rabbeinu Yona*). Others suggest that the wedding feast will not take place on Friday night in any case. Rather, the intention is that one will prepare the feast for the conclusion of Shabbat, and the concern is that he will slaughter the fowl on Shabbat for the purpose of this meal (Rabbi Meir HaLevi).

As we are concerned that his resolve will cool – דְּחָיְישִׁינַן לְאִיקְּרוּרֵי דַּעְתָּא: The Ramban and many other early commentaries following discuss the relationship between this problem and the adjacent *halakha*, that one may engage in intercourse with his virgin wife on Shabbat. Ostensibly, if the wedding was on Friday, the concern that his resolve will cool is even greater, as the court reconvenes only the following Monday. The Ramban explains that the Gemara is not discussing a wedding that took place on Friday. Rather, the Gemara is discussing a wedding that took place on Wednesday but was not consummated until Shabbat.

BACKGROUND

One goes to theaters – הוֹלְכִין לְטַרְטִיָּיאוֹת: Theaters, circuses, and arenas occasionally served as venues for public gatherings. Furthermore, riots would erupt, often over the outcome of sporting events, and would escalate into large-scale riots that went beyond the walls of those structures. More often than not, this led to pogroms directed against the Jews. Some of the performances in the theaters, at least in Eretz Yisrael, were of a distinctly anti-Jewish nature and often incited riots. The presence of Jews at those events could be effective either in preventing the riots or in warning the Jews that a riot was developing. In addition, Jews were sometimes among the participants in the battles in the circuses as gladiators, and the presence of Jewish spectators would enable them to outshout the supporters of the gentile combatant and prevent the Jew from being thrown to the beasts.

LANGUAGE

Theaters [*tartiyyaot*] **– טַרְטִיָּיאוֹת:** One form of the Greek θέατρον, *theatron,* meaning theater, or place for seeing.

Circuses [*karkiyyaot*] **– קַרְקִיָּיאוֹת:** One form of the Latin word circus. Some claim that it derives from the Latin carcer, meaning an enclosed place.

Makes matches [*meshadkhin*] **– מְשַׁדְּכִין:** Apparently from Aramaic, the term's primary meaning is to quiet or to calm. Its additional related meaning in Hebrew is to appease both sides and reach an agreement, in particular, a marriage agreement.

HALAKHA

One goes…to supervise matters affecting the multitudes on Shabbat – הוֹלְכִין...לְפַקֵּחַ עַל עִסְקֵי רַבִּים בְּשַׁבָּת: One may go to the synagogues and study halls, and even to the theaters and palaces of gentiles, in order to supervise matters affecting the multitudes on Shabbat (Rambam *Sefer Zemanim, Hilkhot Shabbat* 24:5 *Shulḥan Arukh, Oraḥ Ḥayyim* 306:6).

One makes matches among the families concerned for a young girl to be betrothed on Shabbat – מְשַׁדְּכִין עַל הַתִּינוֹקֶת לֵיאָרֵס בְּשַׁבָּת: It is permitted to engage in matchmaking on Shabbat to arrange one's daughter's betrothal. Similarly, one may undertake arrangements necessary for his son's Torah education or vocational training on Shabbat (Rambam *Sefer Zemanim, Hilkhot Shabbat* 24:5; *Shulḥan Arukh, Oraḥ Ḥayyim* 306:6).

A virgin is married on Wednesday but engages in intercourse on Thursday – בְּתוּלָה נִשֵּׂאת בִּרְבִיעִי וְנִבְעֶלֶת בַּחֲמִישִׁי: The Rabbis instituted that a virgin is married on Wednesday during the day, and the marriage is consummated on Wednesday night, so that if the groom has a claim concerning the bride's virginity he can go to court on Thursday when the courts convene. In places where the courts are in session every day, the couple may marry any day of the week, provided that the groom completed the preparations for the wedding feast, because the blessing to the fish on the fifth day of Creation is not sufficient reason to fix a specific day for the wedding (*Tur, Even HaEzer* 64; *Beit Yosef*, citing Rosh).

תָּא שְׁמַע, דְּתָנֵי בַּר קַפָּרָא: בְּתוּלָה נִשֵּׂאת בְּרְבִיעִי וְנִבְעֶלֶת בַּחֲמִישִׁי, הוֹאִיל וְנֶאֶמְרָה בּוֹ בְּרָכָה לַדָּגִים. אַלְמָנָה נִשֵּׂאת בַּחֲמִישִׁי וְנִבְעֶלֶת בְּשִׁשִּׁי, הוֹאִיל וְנֶאֶמְרָה בּוֹ בְּרָכָה לָאָדָם. טַעֲמָא – מִשּׁוּם בְּרָכָה, אֲבָל מִשּׁוּם אִיקְרוּרֵי דַּעְתָּא – לָא חָיְישִׁינַן.

Come and hear proof, as bar Kappara taught: A virgin is married on Wednesday and engages in intercourse on Thursday, since the blessing to the fish:[N] Be fruitful and multiply, was **stated** on the fifth day of Creation. **A widow is married on Thursday and engages in intercourse on Friday,**[H] **since the blessing** of procreation **was stated to man** on the sixth day of Creation. It may be inferred that **the reason is due to the blessing, but with regard to** the possibility lest **his resolve cool, we are not concerned.**

אִי הָכִי, אַלְמָנָה נַמִי תִּיבָּעֵל בַּחֲמִישִׁי, הוֹאִיל וְנֶאֶמְרָה בּוֹ בְּרָכָה לַדָּגִים! בְּרָכָה דְּאָדָם עֲדִיפָא לֵיהּ.

The Gemara asks: **If so, a widow should also engage in intercourse on Thursday, since the blessing to the fish was stated then.**[N] The Gemara answers: Since there is the option to postpone engaging in relations to the day on which **the blessing of man** was stated, doing so **is preferable for him.**

וְאִי נַמִי – מִשּׁוּם שָׁקְדוּ. דְּתַנְיָא: מִפְּנֵי מָה אָמְרוּ אַלְמָנָה נִשֵּׂאת בַּחֲמִישִׁי וְנִבְעֶלֶת בְּשִׁשִּׁי? שֶׁאִם אַתָּה אוֹמֵר תִּיבָּעֵל בַּחֲמִישִׁי – לְמָחָר מַשְׁכִּים לְאוּמָּנְתּוֹ וְהוֹלֵךְ לוֹ, שָׁקְדוּ חֲכָמִים עַל תַּקָּנַת בְּנוֹת יִשְׂרָאֵל, שֶׁיְּהֵא שָׂמֵחַ עִמָּהּ שְׁלֹשָׁה יָמִים: חֲמִישִׁי בְּשַׁבָּת, וְעֶרֶב שַׁבָּת, וְשַׁבָּת.

Alternatively, that day was established as the day for a widow to engage in sexual relations **due to** the fact that the Sages **were assiduous**[N] in seeing to the well-being of Jewish women, **as it is taught** in a *baraita*: **Why did** the Sages **say that a widow is married on Thursday and engages in intercourse on Friday?** It is **because if you say that she should engage in intercourse on Thursday, on the next day** the groom will **go to ply his craft early**[N] and leave his wife alone. When a man marries a widow, there is no observance of the seven days of rejoicing, whose legal status is like that of a Festival, during which he does not go to work. Therefore, **the Sages were assiduous in seeing to the well-being of Jewish women** and ensured **that** the groom **rejoice with her** for **three days:**[H] **Thursday,** the day of the wedding; **and Shabbat eve,** the day when they engage in sexual relations; **and Shabbat.**

מַאי אִיכָּא בֵּין ״בְּרָכָה״ לְ״שָׁקְדוּ״? אִיכָּא בֵּינַיְיהוּ אָדָם בָּטֵל, אִי נַמִי יוֹם טוֹב שֶׁחָל לִהְיוֹת בְּעֶרֶב שַׁבָּת.

What practical difference **is there between** the two reasons given to engage in relations on Friday, i.e., the **blessing** of procreation for man **and** the fact that the Sages **were assiduous?**[N] The Gemara answers: **There is** a practical difference **between them** in the case of **an idle person,** who has no job, in which case the reason of blessing applies and the reason that the Sages were assiduous does not, as no matter what he will not go to work early. **Alternatively,** there is a practical difference in the case of **a Festival that occurs on Shabbat eve.** There too, the reason of blessing applies but the Sages' assiduousness does not apply, as one does not work on a Festival.

HALAKHA

A widow is married on Thursday and engages in intercourse on Friday – אַלְמָנָה נִשֵּׂאת בַּחֲמִישִׁי וְנִבְעֶלֶת בְּשִׁשִּׁי: The Sages instituted that a widow is married on Thursday during the day, and the couple consummates the marriage on Thursday night, so that the husband will celebrate with his wife for three days and not go to work the morning after the wedding. One who is unemployed may marry a widow any day of the week (*Tur, Even HaEzer* 64; *Beit Yosef*).

That he rejoice with her for three days – שֶׁיְּהֵא שָׂמֵחַ עִמָּהּ שְׁלֹשָׁה יָמִים: The Sages instituted that a man who marries a woman who is not a virgin is obligated to rejoice with her for three days. The Rema notes that since this ordinance was instituted for the bride's benefit, she may waive that benefit (Rambam *Sefer Nashim, Hilkhot Ishut* 10:12; *Shulḥan Arukh, Even HaEzer* 64:2).

NOTES

The blessing to the fish – בְּרָכָה לַדָּגִים: Although there was a blessing of procreation for the birds as well, the Gemara mentions the fish because their blessing preceded the blessing of the birds: "Be fruitful, and multiply, and fill the waters in the seas, and let fowl multiply in the earth" (Genesis 1:22). Furthermore, the language of the blessing to the birds is similar to the blessing of procreation given to man (see Genesis 1:28; *Shita Mekubbetzet*). In certain respects, the blessing to the fish is superior to the blessing to man, as the fish are more numerous, and the evil eye has no dominion over them (Ritva; *HaBoneh*). Alternatively, with regard to man, the blessing could be interpreted as a mitzva more than a blessing. For the fish, it is clearly a blessing (*Penei Yehoshua*).

Since the blessing to the fish was stated then – הוֹאִיל וְנֶאֶמְרָה בּוֹ בְּרָכָה לַדָּגִים: The Ritva explains that the question is: If the blessing to the fish is a reason to hold the wedding on Wednesday, why is the wedding of a widow on Thursday? The Gemara then answers that if the content of the blessing is considered, the blessing to man is preferable.

Blessing, the Sages were assiduous – בְּרָכָה, שָׁקְדוּ: Some explain that even bar Kappara himself held that there are two reasons for the ordinance of the Sages: One, the Sages were assiduous or the claim concerning virginity; two, the blessing of procreation. Others say that bar Kappara considered the latter reason to be an auxiliary reason for the ordinance, not one that stands on its own (Ramban; Rabbi Aharon HaLevi). However, the Meiri says that bar Kappara considered the blessing of procreation as an independent and significant reason for the ordinance. That appears to be the conclusion of the Jerusalem Talmud, contrary to the conclusion of the Gemara here.

The groom will go to ply his craft early – מַשְׁכִּים לְאוּמָּנְתּוֹ וְהוֹלֵךְ לוֹ: Based on the Gemara here, it is fundamentally permitted for the groom to work, but the Sages prevented him from doing so by instituting ordinances seeing to the well-being of Jewish women. This line of reasoning is difficult, because several sources indicate that it is prohibited for a groom to work for seven days after marrying a virgin and for three days after marrying a widow. The Ritva suggests two solutions. Although it is prohibited for him to work, there is still concern that he might ignore the prohibition. Therefore, for the benefit of the bride, the Sages fixed the wedding on a day when the groom would be unable to go to work. Alternatively, the prohibition mentioned in the other sources ensued from the ordinance of the Sages that the widow marries on Thursday, so that the groom will remain with his wife and not work for three days.

What practical difference is there between the blessing and the Sages were assiduous – מַאי אִיכָּא בֵּין בְּרָכָה לְשָׁקְדוּ: This Gemara is asking: What element is added by the reason of the blessing of procreation? Clearly, the reason that the Sages were assiduous introduces the element of the authority of the Sages. Although one could assert that the groom can be indifferent with regard to the blessing, he cannot be indifferent to an ordinance instituted by the Sages.

דרש בר קפרא: גדולים מעשה צדיקים יותר ממעשה שמים וארץ, דאילו במעשה שמים וארץ כתיב: "אף ידי יסדה ארץ וימיני טפחה שמים" ואלו במעשה ידיהם של צדיקים כתיב "מכון לשבתך פעלת ה׳ מקדש אדני כוננו ידיך".

§ The Gemara cites additional aggadic statements of bar Kappara. **Bar Kappara taught: The handiwork of the righteous is greater**[N] **than the creation of heaven and earth, as with regard to the creation of heaven and earth it is written: "My hand also has laid the foundation of the earth, and My right hand has spanned the heavens"** (Isaiah 48:13). There, hand is written in the singular. **Whereas with regard to the handiwork of the righteous it is written: "The place which You have made for Yourself to dwell in, Lord, the Sanctuary, Lord, which your hands**[N] **have established" (Exodus 15:17).** The reference is to the Temple, which is the handiwork of man, and hand is written in the plural.

השיב בבלי אחד, ורבי חייא שמו: "וִיבשת ידיו יצרו"! "ידו" כתיב. והכתיב "יצרו"! אמר רב נחמן בר יצחק: יצרו אצבעותיו, כדכתיב "כי אראה שמיך מעשה אצבעותיך ירח וכוכבים אשר כוננתה".

A certain Babylonian, and his name is Rabbi Ḥiyya, responded[N] with a challenge. It is written with regard to creation of the earth: **"And His hands formed the dry land"** (Psalms 95:5). The Gemara answers: **"His hand"** is the way it **is written.** Although the word is vocalized in the plural, it is written in the singular, without the letter *yod*. **But isn't it written: "Formed,"** in the plural? **Rav Naḥman bar Yitzḥak said:** The plural is referring to **His fingers, as it is written: "When I see Your heavens, the work of Your fingers, the moon and stars, which You have established"** (Psalms 8:4).

מיתיבי: "השמים מספרים כבוד אל ומעשה ידיו מגיד הרקיע"! הכי קאמר: מעשה ידיהם של צדיקים מי מגיד – הרקיע, ומאי ניהו – מטר.

The Gemara raises an objection: "The heavens declare the glory of God, and the firmament proclaims the work of His hands" (Psalms 19:2). The heavens were created by His hands. The Gemara answers that **this** is what the verse **is saying: Who attests to the handiwork of the righteous,** that they are performing the will of God? It is **the heavens. And what is** the avenue through which the heavens do so? It is by means of **rain** that falls due to the prayers of the righteous.

דרש בר קפרא: מאי דכתיב "ויתד תהיה לך על אזנך" – אל תקרי "אזנך" אלא "על אזנך", שאם ישמע אדם דבר שאינו הגון,

Bar Kappara taught: What is the meaning of that which is **written: And you shall have a peg among your weapons** [*azenekha*]" (Deuteronomy 23:14)? **Do not read** it as: **Your weapons** [*azenekha*].[N] **Rather,** read it: **On your ear** [*oznekha*], meaning **that if a person hears an inappropriate matter,**

Perek **I**
Daf **5** Amud **b**

יניח אצבעו באזניו. והיינו דאמר רבי אלעזר: מפני מה אצבעותיו של אדם דומות ליתידות? מאי טעמא? אילימא משום דמחלקן – כל חדא וחדא למילתיה עבידא, דאמר מר: זו זרת, זו קמיצה, זו אמה, זו אצבע, זה גודל!

he should place his finger, which is shaped like a peg, **into his ears. And that is what Rabbi Elazar said: Why are the fingers of a person similar to pegs?** The Gemara asks: **What is the reason** that Rabbi Elazar said that fingers are like pegs? **If we say** that it is **due to** the fact **that they are discrete**[N] from each other, **each and every** finger **was designated for its** own discrete, sacred **matter, as the Master said: This** small finger is for measuring **a span,** the distance between the little finger to the tip of the thumb used in measuring the breastplate of the High Priest; **this** next finger is used for taking **a fistful** of the meal-offering; **this** middle finger is used for measuring **a cubit,** the distance from the elbow to the tip of the middle finger; **this** one next to the thumb is the **finger** used to sprinkle the blood of offerings on the altar; **this is the thumb,** on which the blood and oil is placed in the purification ritual of a leper.

NOTES

The handiwork of the righteous is greater – גדולים מעשה צדיקים: The obvious connection between this passage and those that precede it is that they are taught by the same Sage. Some add that this statement of bar Kappara comes to explain his preference for the blessing to man over the blessing to the fish. The actions of man are greater than God's Creation of the world (see *Shita Mekubbetzet* and *Ḥatam Sofer*).

One hand or two hands – יד אחת שתי ידים: In the *Otzar HaKavod*, it is explained that there is a dichotomy between heaven and earth, between the spiritual and the corporeal, and symbolically each was created with a different hand. However, the handiwork of the righteous, i.e., the Temple, unites the heavenly and the earthly. This is represented by both hands.

Others explain that the world of creation is static and unchanging, whereas the actions of man are constantly developing. The question in the Gemara notes that even in the heavens there is change. The Gemara explains that those changes are minor changes within a fixed framework. They are characterized as: The work of Your fingers (*Leḥem Shlomo*).

A certain Babylonian…responded – השיב בבלי אחד: In the *Shita Mekubbetzet*, there is an explanation why the Gemara mentioned that he was a Babylonian. The reason, as stated in tractate *Kiddushin*, is that the Babylonians were not expert enough in the spelling in the Bible to know whether a word is written with a *yod* or a *vav*. The answer to the question in the Gemara is based on that distinction.

Do not read it as. Your weapons – אל תקרי אזנך. The Maharal in *Be'er HaGola* explains this statement at great length according to the plain meaning of the verses. He writes that the verse says that there are certain matters that are best concealed. The term: Your weapons [*azenekha*], is redundant. It would have been sufficient to write that one should use the peg to obscure those matters. Where one suspends that peg is irrelevant (Rav Yoshiya Pinto; Maharal). Furthermore, the term for your weapons should have been [*zayinkha*]. The additional *alef* at the beginning of the word alludes to an additional meaning (*Shita Mekubbetzet*; Maharsha).

NOTES

Due to the fact that they are discrete – משום דמחלקן: See *Tosafot*, who explain the need for the thumb as also being related to the fistful of flour in a meal-offering. With regard to the question of *Tosafot*, that the thumb could have served its role even if it were not discrete, see *Shita Mekubbetzet*, where it is explained that the same question could have been asked with regard to the middle finger and fourth finger as well. However, since each has its own role, they must be discrete, and it is clear why they were separated.

אֶלָּא: מַה טַּעַם מְשׁוּפּוֹת כִּיתֵידוֹת? שֶׁאִם יִשְׁמַע אָדָם דָּבָר שֶׁאֵינוֹ הָגוּן יַנִּיחַ אֶצְבְּעוֹתָיו בְּאׇזְנָיו. תָּנָא דְּבֵי רַבִּי יִשְׁמָעֵאל: מִפְּנֵי מָה אוֹזֶן כּוּלָּהּ קָשָׁה וְהָאַלְיָה רַכָּה? שֶׁאִם יִשְׁמַע אָדָם דָּבָר שֶׁאֵינוֹ הָגוּן – יָכוֹף אַלְיָה לְתוֹכָהּ. תָּנוּ רַבָּנַן: אַל יַשְׁמִיעַ אָדָם לְאׇזְנָיו דְּבָרִים בְּטֵלִים מִפְּנֵי שֶׁהֵן נִכְווֹת תְּחִלָּה לָאֵיבָרִים.

Rather, the question is: **What is the reason that they are pointed like pegs?** It is so **that if a person hears an inappropriate matter, he will place his fingers in his ears.** Similarly, a Sage **of the school of Rabbi Yishmael taught: Why is the entire ear hard and the earlobe soft?** It is so **that if a person hears an inappropriate matter, he will bend his earlobe into** his ear to seal it. **The Sages taught: A person should not allow his ears to hear idle matters.**[N] **Because** of the fact **that** ears are very sensitive and **are the first of the limbs burned,**[B] one should make certain not to expose them to anything problematic.

אִיבַּעְיָא לְהוּ: מַהוּ לִבְעוֹל בְּתְחִלָּה בְּשַׁבָּת, דָּם מִיפְקַד פְּקִיד אוֹ חַבּוּרֵי מִיחַבַּר?

§ **A dilemma was raised** before the Sages: **What is** the *halakha* with regard **to engaging in intercourse** with one's virgin bride **for the first time on Shabbat?**[N] The dilemma is with regard to the nature of the blood that emerges as a result of the piercing of the hymen. Is it that the **blood is pooled,** and it is released once the hymen is pierced, so that no prohibition is violated? **Or,** is the blood flowing through vessels **attached**[B] to the body, and it emerges as a result of a wound, so that he does violate a prohibition?

וְאִם תִּימְצֵי לוֹמַר דָּם מִיפְקַד פְּקִיד, לְדָם הוּא צָרִיךְ – וְשָׁרֵי, אוֹ דִּלְמָא לְפֶתַח הוּא צָרִיךְ – וַאֲסִיר?

And if you say that **it is pooled** and the intercourse does not cause a wound, there is an additional dilemma: Does the husband **require the blood**[N] to flow, and that is his objective in performing the act, in which case it is **permitted?**[N] **Or, perhaps he requires the opening**[N] caused by the rupture of the hymen, **and** creating that opening is **prohibited** on Shabbat.

וְאִם תִּימְצֵי לוֹמַר לְדָם הוּא צָרִיךְ, וּפֶתַח מִמֵּילָא קָאָתֵי, הֲלָכָה כְּרַבִּי שִׁמְעוֹן דְּאָמַר: דָּבָר שֶׁאֵין מִתְכַּוֵּין מוּתָּר, אוֹ הֲלָכָה כְּרַבִּי יְהוּדָה דְּאָמַר: דָּבָר שֶׁאֵין מִתְכַּוֵּין אָסוּר?

And if you say that **he requires the blood, and the opening comes** about **incidentally**[N] as an unintended consequence, **is the *halakha* in accordance with** the opinion of **Rabbi Shimon, who said: An unintentional act,**[N] i.e., a permitted action from which a forbidden labor inadvertently ensued, **is permitted? Or, is the *halakha* in accordance with** the opinion of **Rabbi Yehuda, who said: An unintentional act is forbidden?**

BACKGROUND

They are the first of the limbs burned – הֵן נִכְווֹת תְּחִלָּה לָאֵיבָרִים: The surface area of the auricle of the ear is large relative to its volume, due to its thin, soft tissue and lack of bone. It is therefore more sensitive to changes in temperature than other parts of the body. That is why the ears are the first of the body parts burned.

The blood is pooled or flowing through vessels attached – דָּם מִיפְקַד פְּקִיד אוֹ חַבּוּרֵי מִיחַבַּר: The medical explanation for the blood that flows after the rupture of the hymen is that it occurs due to the bleeding from the blood vessels in the hymen. In that way, it is similar to bleeding from any other part of the body. However, there are cases, albeit uncommon ones, where the hymen creates an impermeable seal, and menstrual blood pools behind the hymen. In that case, the blood that results from intercourse with a virgin is halakhically characterized as pooled blood.

NOTES

Idle matters – דְּבָרִים בְּטֵלִים: After prohibiting listening to inappropriate matters and suggesting the actions that one should take to avoid doing so, the Gemara adds that one should avoid idle matters as well. Although they are not inappropriate, one should refrain from hearing them, as one is influenced by what he hears. The characterization that one's ears are the first body parts that burn alludes to this idea (Maharal).

What is the *halakha* with regard to engaging in intercourse with one's virgin bride for the first time on Shabbat – מַהוּ לִבְעוֹל בְּתְחִלָּה בְּשַׁבָּת: Rashi, *Tosafot*, and other early commentaries discuss the connection between this passage in the Gemara and the *baraitot* in which it is explicitly taught, that one may not engage in intercourse with his virgin bride for the first time on Shabbat. Rashi suggests two solutions: First, the Sages of the Gemara were unaware of the *baraitot* (see *Tosafot* and Rabbi Aharon HaLevi). Second, they were aware of the *baraitot* and were either debating whether they were in accordance with the *halakha* or assumed that they were not in accordance with the *halakha* (see *Derush VeḤiddush*).

Those who consider this passage a continuation of the previous one discuss why the concern lest one slaughter a young fowl was not raised. The Ramban explains that the case here is one where the wedding took place the previous day, but it has not yet been consummated. The Ritva and others explain that it is referring to a case where the groom already completed the wedding preparations.

Does the husband require the blood – לְדָם הוּא צָרִיךְ: Two reasons were suggested as to why the husband would require the blood. First, he wants as much blood as possible to flow the first time, so that when they engage in relations on subsequent occasions there will be less blood. Second, he wants to see the blood flow to verify that she is a virgin (see *Tosafot* and Ritva). The phrase: The husband requires the blood, is more appropriate according to the latter explanation.

Does the husband require the blood and it is permitted – לְדָם הוּא צָרִיךְ וְשָׁרֵי: The term permitted is problematic, as even if he requires the blood, the question whether or not it is permitted hinges on the tannaitic dispute cited in the Gemara. The Rashba has a variant reading in which the words: And it is permitted, are omitted. According to that version, the legal status of the act in a case where one needs the blood is clarified in the subsequent discussion.

Others, based on Rashi, include the term: And it is permitted, and explain that it is not a decisive ruling but a conditional statement: Even if you say that it is permitted according to one tannaitic opinion, the question of its status remains according to the other opinion (Ritva).

He requires the opening – לְפֶתַח הוּא צָרִיךְ: With regard to the prohibition against creating an opening on Shabbat, Rashi explains that it is categorized under the rubric of the forbidden labor of building.

Others explain that it falls under the category of one who strikes a blow with a hammer, which includes all activities that complete production of a vessel. In this case, consummating the marriage completes the forging of the bond between the husband and wife.

The Rashba writes that if the husband requires the opening and that is his intention, although it is a fundamentally destructive action, it is not a full-fledged destructive action because it contains a constructive element.

And the opening comes about incidentally – וּפֶתַח מִמֵּילָא קָאָתֵי: Even Rabbi Shimon, who holds that it is permitted to perform an unintentional act, agrees that it is prohibited to do so when the forbidden result is inevitable.

Rashi discusses the question: Since rupturing the hymen during intercourse with a virgin is inevitable, why is intercourse permitted according to Rabbi Shimon? Rashi explains that the ruling in the Gemara is limited to one who is adept at engaging in intercourse without rupturing the hymen. Others explain that even if the groom in question is not capable of doing so, since there are those who are, that suffices to generally characterize this case as one where the consequences are not inevitable (Ritva; Meiri).

An unintentional act – דָּבָר שֶׁאֵין מִתְכַּוֵּין: The dispute between Rabbi Yehuda and Rabbi Shimon with regard to unintentional actions with forbidden results is discussed extensively in tractate *Shabbat*. Although this is an issue pertinent to other areas of *halakha* as well, in the context of the *halakhot* of Shabbat there is a unique aspect.

Labor is forbidden only if it is planned, thoughtful, constructive labor. Unintentional actions, with regard to which there is a dispute between Rabbi Yehuda and Rabbi Shimon, are not actions performed accidentally or unwittingly. Rather, they are permitted actions that one intends to perform, from which a forbidden action unintentionally ensues. Rabbi Shimon permits performing these actions and Rabbi Yehuda prohibits doing so.

וְאִם תִּימְצֵי לוֹמַר הֲלָכָה כְּרַבִּי יְהוּדָה – מְקַלְקֵל הוּא אֵצֶל הַפֶּתַח אוֹ מְתַקֵּן הוּא אֵצֶל הַפֶּתַח?

And even if you say that the *halakha* is in accordance with the opinion of **Rabbi Yehuda** in this regard, is this **a destructive** action **vis-à-vis the opening,** and is it consequently permitted on Shabbat because only constructive actions are forbidden? **Or,** perhaps it is **a constructive** action **vis-à-vis the opening.**

אִיכָּא דְּאָמְרִי: וְאִם תִּימְצֵי לוֹמַר דָּם חַבּוּרֵי מִיחַבַּר – לְדָם הוּא צָרִיךְ וְאָסוּר, אוֹ דִּלְמָא לַהֲנָאַת עַצְמוֹ הוּא צָרִיךְ וְשָׁרֵי?

Some say that the series of dilemmas is as follows: **And if you say that the blood is** flowing through vessels **attached** to the body and emerges as a result of a wound, **does** the husband **require the blood,** and engaging in intercourse is consequently **prohibited,** as his intent is to cause the wound? **Or, perhaps he requires** the act of intercourse solely **for his own pleasure, and** it is **permitted.**

וְאִם תִּימְצֵי לוֹמַר לַהֲנָאַת עַצְמוֹ הוּא צָרִיךְ, וְדָם מִמֵּילָא קָאָתֵי – הֲלָכָה כְּרַבִּי יְהוּדָה אוֹ הֲלָכָה כְּרַבִּי שִׁמְעוֹן?

And if you say that he requires the act of intercourse solely **for his own pleasure, and the blood comes incidentally,** as it was not his intent to draw blood, **is the *halakha* in accordance with** the opinion of **Rabbi Yehuda** with regard to an unintentional act, **or** is it **in accordance with** the opinion of **Rabbi Shimon?**

וְאִם תִּימְצֵי לוֹמַר הֲלָכָה כְּרַבִּי יְהוּדָה – מְקַלְקֵל בְּחַבּוּרָה אוֹ מְתַקֵּן בְּחַבּוּרָה הוּא?

And if you say that the ***halakha* is in accordance with** the opinion of **Rabbi Yehuda** and unintentional acts are forbidden, is one **destructive in** causing **the wound** or **constructive in** causing the **wound?**

וְאִם תִּימְצֵי לוֹמַר מְקַלְקֵל בְּחַבּוּרָה הוּא – בִּמְקַלְקֵל הֲלָכָה כְּרַבִּי יְהוּדָה

And if you say that he is **destructive in** causing **the wound,**[N] in cases involving **destructive** acts **is the *halakha* in accordance with** the opinion of **Rabbi Yehuda,**[N] who rules that one who performs any destructive act on Shabbat is exempt, even if he did so intentionally?

NOTES

Destructive in causing the wound – מְקַלְקֵל בְּחַבּוּרָה: The Ramban cites an explanation that he himself rejects, that the reference here is to the wound caused by slaughtering young fowl. In the *Shita Mekubbetzet*, a defense of that explanation is cited.

The Gemara seems to be saying that if the intercourse is considered destructive, it is permitted *ab initio* according to Rabbi Yehuda. The commentaries ask: Isn't performance of a destructive action prohibited by rabbinic law (see *Tosafot*)? They respond that there are two factors here dictating leniency: The action is destructive action and unintentional. Others add a third factor: It is in the course of performing a mitzva. The Rashba contends that the Sages issue decrees prohibiting certain actions, only due to the concern that otherwise one might come to perform a similar action prohibited by Torah law. Here, although creating the opening falls into the category of building, people do not consider it building and will not come to perform the forbidden labor of building as a result of the intercourse. Others explain that since the intercourse is a destructive action as far as the woman is concerned, it is in no way comparable to the forbidden labor of building, and no decree was issued (*Ha'amek She'ala*).

In cases involving destructive acts is the *halakha* in accordance with the opinion of Rabbi Yehuda – בִּמְקַלְקֵל הֲלָכָה כְּרַבִּי יְהוּדָה: Some ask why the ruling with regard to intercourse with his virgin bride, which is a mitzva, is not the same as the ruling with regard to circumcision, which is considered a constructive act due to the mitzva involved (*Sefer Hafla'a*). Some distinguish between circumcision, where creating the wound is the essence of the mitzva, and intercourse with a virgin, where the wound is ancillary to the mitzva.

Perek **I**
Daf **6** Amud **a**

אוֹ הֲלָכָה כְּרַבִּי שִׁמְעוֹן?

Or, is the *halakha* in accordance with the opinion of **Rabbi Shimon,** who ruled that one who is destructive in causing a wound on Shabbat is liable if he did so intentionally?

(אִיתְּמַר), בְּבֵי רַב אָמְרִי: רַב שָׁרֵי וּשְׁמוּאֵל אָסַר. בִּנְהַרְדְּעָא אָמְרִי: רַב אָסַר וּשְׁמוּאֵל שָׁרֵי. אָמַר רַב נַחְמָן בַּר יִצְחָק, וְסִימָנֵיךְ: אֵלּוּ מְקִילִין לְעַצְמָן וְאֵלּוּ מְקִילִין לְעַצְמָן.

With regard to the *halakha* of engaging in intercourse with one's virgin bride on Shabbat, **it was stated** that **in the school of Rav they say: Rav permitted** doing so **and Shmuel prohibited** doing so. **In Neharde'a,**[B] where Shmuel lived, **they say: Rav prohibited** doing so **and Shmuel permitted** doing so. **Rav Naḥman bar Yitzḥak said: And your mnemonic is: These are lenient** with regard **to themselves, and those are lenient** with regard **to themselves.** Each attributes the lenient ruling to the local halakhic authority, whose ruling is binding in that locale.

BACKGROUND

Neharde'a – נְהַרְדְּעָא: This city, located on the Euphrates near the Malka River, was one of the oldest Jewish communities in Babylonia. According to tradition, Jews lived in Neharde'a as early as the First Temple period, in the sixth century BCE, beginning with the exile of King Jehoiachin of Judea. Neharde'a was one of the most important Jewish communities in Babylonia. It was a center of Torah study from an early period, and its yeshiva was the oldest in Babylonia. Many of the greatest *tanna'im* visited Neharde'a, among them Rabbi Akiva, who intercalated the calendar there (*Yevamot* 122b). In Rav's time, the first half of the third century CE, the Neharde'a Yeshiva was headed by Rav Sheila and then by Shmuel. Since the city was located near the border between the Roman and Persian empires, it frequently suffered from wars between the two, and Pappa ben Nazer Odonathus, king of Tadmor, destroyed it completely in 259 CE. Later, however, Jews resettled there, and many Torah scholars remained in Neharde'a even after its yeshiva relocated to Meḥoza and Pumbedita.

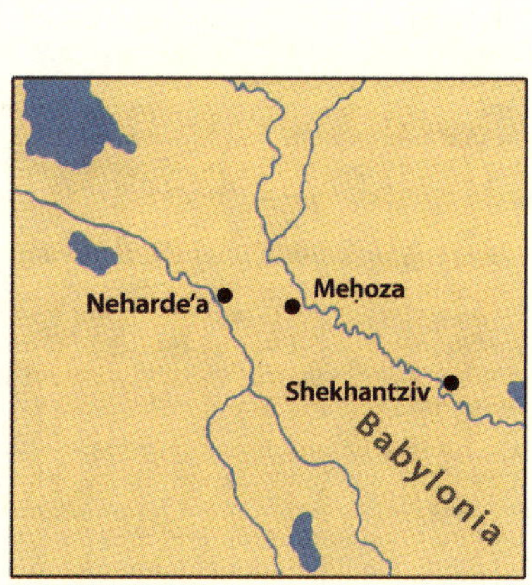

Location of Neharde'a

וְרַב שָׁרֵי?! וְהָאָמַר רַב שִׁימִי בַּר חִזְקִיָּה מִשְּׁמֵיהּ דְּרַב: הַאי מְסוֹכְרִיָּא דְּנַזְיָיתָא אָסוּר לַהֲדוּקָהּ בְּיוֹמָא טָבָא!

The Gemara asks: **And did Rav permit** engaging in intercourse in those circumstances? **But didn't Rav Shimi bar Ḥizkiyya say in the name of Rav:** In the case of **this** cloth **stopper of a barrel** [*nazyata*],[LHN] it **is prohibited to insert it tightly**[N] in the spout of the barrel **on a Festival,** because in the process liquid will be squeezed from the cloth, and squeezing liquids is prohibited on Shabbat and Festivals. Apparently, Rav prohibits even unintentional actions.

בְּהַהוּא אֲפִילּוּ רַבִּי שִׁמְעוֹן מוֹדֶה. דְּאַבַּיֵי וְרָבָא דְּאָמְרִי תַּרְוַיְיהוּ: מוֹדֶה רַבִּי שִׁמְעוֹן בִּפְסִיק רֵישֵׁיהּ וְלָא יָמוּת.

The Gemara answers: **In the case** of the barrel, **even Rabbi Shimon concedes, as it is Abaye and Rava who both say: Rabbi Shimon concedes in** the case of: **Cut off its head**[N] **and will it not die,** i.e., a case that involves inevitable consequences like the decapitation of an animal, that the action is forbidden. Here, the liquid will inevitably be squeezed from the cloth.

וְהָא אָמַר רַב חִיָּיא בַּר אַשִׁי אָמַר רַב: הֲלָכָה כְּרַבִּי יְהוּדָה, וְרַב חָנָן בַּר אַמִי אָמַר שְׁמוּאֵל: הֲלָכָה כְּרַבִּי שִׁמְעוֹן. וְרַב חִיָּיא בַּר אָבִין מַתְנֵי לָהּ בְּלָא גַּבְרֵי, רַב אָמַר: הֲלָכָה כְּרַבִּי יְהוּדָה, וּשְׁמוּאֵל אָמַר: הֲלָכָה כְּרַבִּי שִׁמְעוֹן!

The Gemara asks: **But didn't Rav Ḥiyya bar Ashi say** that **Rav said** with regard to unintentional acts: **The *halakha* is in accordance with** the opinion of **Rabbi Yehuda, and Rav Ḥanan bar Ami said** that **Shmuel said: The *halakha* is in accordance with** the opinion of **Rabbi Shimon. And Rav Ḥiyya bar Avin taught** these rulings directly, **without** citing additional **men** who transmitted them. **Rav said: The *halakha* is in accordance with** the opinion of **Rabbi Yehuda, and Shmuel said: The *halakha* is in accordance with** the opinion of **Rabbi Shimon.** How then did Rav permit intercourse with one's virgin bride on Shabbat?

לְעוֹלָם רַב כְּרַבִּי יְהוּדָה סְבִירָא לֵיהּ לְהָךְ לִישָּׁנָא דְּאָמַר דָּם מִיפְקַד פְּקִיד – מְקַלְקֵל הוּא אֵצֶל הַפֶּתַח. לְהָךְ לִישָּׁנָא דְּאָמַר דָּם חַבּוּרֵי מִיחַבַּר – מְקַלְקֵל בְּחַבּוּרָה הוּא.

The Gemara answers: **Actually, Rav holds in accordance with** the opinion of **Rabbi Yehuda.** According **to that version that said** that **the blood is pooled, he is destructive vis-à-vis the opening.** According **to that version that said** that blood is flowing through blood vessels **attached** to the body, **he is destructive in** causing the **wound,** and Rabbi Yehuda concedes that it is permitted.

מְתִיב רַב חִסְדָּא: תִּינוֹקֶת שֶׁלֹּא הִגִּיעַ זְמַנָּהּ לִרְאוֹת וְנִשֵּׂאת, בֵּית שַׁמַּאי אוֹמְרִים: נוֹתְנִין לָהּ אַרְבָּעָה לֵילוֹת, וּבֵית הִלֵּל אוֹמְרִים: עַד שֶׁתֶּחְיֶה הַמַּכָּה.

Rav Ḥisda raised an objection from a mishna (*Nidda* 64b). With regard to **a young girl whose time to see** the flow of menstrual blood **has not arrived,**[N] as she has not yet reached puberty, **and she married,**[H] **Beit Shammai say: One gives her four nights** during which she may engage in intercourse, as any blood is attributed to the ruptured hymen. **Beit Hillel say:** There is no limit. Rather, any blood she sees is attributed to the ruptured hymen **until the wound heals.**[BN]

BACKGROUND

Until the wound heals – עַד שֶׁתֶּחְיֶה הַמַּכָּה: The period of time in which a wound forms a scab and the bleeding ceases is determined by different variables and differs from person to person. Clearly, additional wounds irritating the affected area, e.g., by means of additional acts of intercourse, would extend that period of time. Therefore, no time limit is set, and the duration of the healing process varies based on the circumstances in each case.

LANGUAGE

Barrel [*nazyata*] – נַזְיָיתָא: From the ancient Syriac-Aramaic *nazanta* or *nazita*, meaning large barrel. Its source is the Akkadian namzitu, meaning vessel for fermenting alcoholic beverages.

HALAKHA

Stopper of a barrel – מְסוֹכְרִיָּא דְּנַזְיָיתָא: According to some authorities, it is permitted to remove and return the cloth stopper that is inserted into the opening in the side of the barrel, although it is inevitable that liquid will be squeezed out of the cloth, since that is an undesirable inevitable consequence (*Tur*, based on *Arukh*). Others prohibit performing a permitted action with an inevitable forbidden consequence in all circumstances (Ri). It is customary to adopt the lenient ruling, but one must be certain to avoid placing a vessel under the stopper to receive the dripping wine, as doing so renders the action permitted with an inevitable forbidden consequence that is desirable (*Shulḥan Arukh, Oraḥ Ḥayyim* 320:18).

A young girl whose time to see has not arrived and she married – תִּינוֹקֶת שֶׁלֹּא הִגִּיעַ זְמַנָּהּ לִרְאוֹת וְנִשֵּׂאת: If a man marries a young girl whose time to see the flow of menstrual blood has not yet arrived, she is permitted to her husband until the wound heals, as any blood that flows is from the ruptured hymen (Rambam; see Rif). Nevertheless, the accepted custom is that even in the case of a minor girl, they engage in intercourse to fulfill the mitzva, then the groom withdraws, and they refrain from further relations until the wound heals. This is the opinion of the Rambam and the Ra'avad, and most authorities, based on the conclusion of the Gemara (*Nidda* 65b; Rambam *Sefer Kedusha, Hilkhot Issurei Bia* 5:19, 11:8; *Shulḥan Arukh, Yoreh De'a* 193:1).

NOTES

Stopper of a barrel – מְסוֹכְרִיָּא דְּנַזְיָיתָא: There are various opinions with regard to the nature of this item, as well as with regard to the halakhic issue involved. According to Rashi and several of the *ge'onim*, the reference is to a cloth stopper or one covered in cloth that plugs a hole in the side of the barrel, and the halakhic problem relates to squeezing the liquid from the cloth. A similar explanation is that the reference is to a garment used to cover the top of the barrel, and there too the concern is with regard to squeezing the liquid from the garment (*Tosefot Rid*; Meiri). In both of those cases, one does not intend to squeeze the liquid, but that consequence is inevitable.

The *Arukh* cites a different opinion, based on a geonic tradition, that the reference is to a wooden covering used to seal the side of the barrel, and the concern is with regard to the prohibited labor of building. Although one's intention is merely to prevent the wine from leaking, by fixing the covering in place, he is essentially building the side of the barrel.

It it is prohibited to insert it tightly – אָסוּר לַהֲדוּקָהּ: According to most opinions, the halakhic issue under discussion is the prohibited labor of squeezing a liquid. The question arises: Under the rubric of which of the thirty-nine primary categories of prohibited labor does this action fall? The question is not merely academic, as each of the categories of labor is unique with regard to its objective, its typical method of performance, and the manner in which one incurs complete liability.

The Ritva summarizes the various opinions, enumerating three primary categories under whose rubric squeezing could fall: (1) Threshing, i.e., extracting a substance suitable for use from an outer covering unfit for use. This is prohibited by Torah law only with regard to substances that grow from the ground. (2) Whitening, i.e., laundering, cleaning, etc., as immersing the cloth in water is a form of laundering. (3) Dyeing, as the wine changes the color of the cloth (see *Tosafot*). An interesting proof that it cannot fall under extracting, a subcategory of threshing, is cited in *Shoel UMeshiv*. The Gemara states that this activity is forbidden on a Festival. Extracting, which is necessary for preparation of food, is permitted on a Festival.

Cut off its head – פְּסִיק רֵישֵׁיהּ: The opinion of Rava and Abaye is that in cases where the forbidden consequence is inevitable, even Rabbi Shimon concedes that there is no exemption based on lack of intent. However, there is an additional consideration, cited in the *Arukh*, which is whether the inevitable consequence is desirable to the one performing the permitted action, whether he is indifferent to it, or whether it is undesirable to him. Some authorities rule that in the latter cases, Rabbi Shimon holds that the action is permitted.

A young girl whose time to see has not arrived – תִּינוֹקֶת שֶׁלֹּא הִגִּיעַ זְמַנָּהּ לִרְאוֹת: These discussions are based on two fundamental principles. By Torah law, the blood from a ruptured hymen is not a source of ritual impurity, and its halakhic status is like that of blood from any other wound. In many cases, however, the concern is that during intercourse, or immediately thereafter, the bride began to menstruate, and there is no clear way to distinguish between menstrual blood and the blood from the hymen.

Furthermore, at one point, Jewish women adopted the stringency that any blood that emerges from the womb is treated as the blood of a *zava*, who is eligible for purification only after counting seven clean days without blood. The combination of these two factors forms the basis for the disputes of the *tanna'im* and later halakhic authorities on this matter.

Until the wound heals – עַד שֶׁתֶּחְיֶה הַמַּכָּה: In other words, even if the wound takes a long time to heal, they may engage in intercourse. Beit Hillel also permits relations for four nights even after the wound heals. There is no alternative to understanding the dispute in this manner, as otherwise, this would be a case where the opinion of Beit Shammai is more lenient than the opinion of Beit Hillel, and it is not enumerated among the leniencies of Beit Shammai in tractate *Eduyyot*.

הִגִּיעַ זְמַנָּהּ לִרְאוֹת וְנִשֵּׂאת. בֵּית שַׁמַּאי אוֹמְרִים: נוֹתְנִין לָהּ לַיְלָה הָרִאשׁוֹן. וּבֵית הִלֵּל אוֹמְרִים: עַד מוֹצָאֵי שַׁבָּת, אַרְבָּעָה לֵילוֹת.

If, however, **her time to see** the flow of menstrual blood **has arrived,**[H] as she has reached the age of puberty, even if she has not yet menstruated, **and she married, Beit Shammai say: One gives her the first night,** during which the blood is attributed to the wound. Thereafter, the blood is presumed to be menstrual blood, and she is forbidden to her husband. **Beit Hillel say: One gives her** from Wednesday, the day designated for marriage of a virgin, **until the conclusion of Shabbat, four nights.** During that period, any blood is attributed to the wound, and she is permitted to her husband.

HALAKHA

Her time to see has arrived – הִגִּיעַ זְמַנָּהּ לִרְאוֹת: A girl who reached the age of menstruation but has not yet menstruated is permitted to her husband for four days following the first act of intercourse, even if there is some bleeding, provided the wound has not healed. According to the Rosh, she is permitted even if the wound has healed. Today, however, Jewish women adopted the stringency that any blood that emerges from the womb is treated as the blood of a *zava*. Therefore, the accepted custom is to engage in intercourse and withdraw until the wound is completely healed and there is no bleeding (Rambam *Sefer Kedusha, Hilkhot Issurei Bia* 5:19, 11:8; *Shulḥan Arukh, Yoreh De'a* 193:1, *Even HaEzer* 63:1).

Perek **I**
Daf **6** Amud **b**

מַאי לָאו דְּאִי לָא בָּעַל מָצֵי בָּעֵיל אֲפִילּוּ בְּשַׁבָּת! אָמַר רָבָא: לָא, לְבַר מִשַּׁבָּת. אָמַר לֵיהּ אַבָּיֵי: וְהָא עַד מוֹצָאֵי שַׁבָּת אַרְבָּעָה לֵילוֹת קָתָנֵי! אֶלָּא אָמַר רָבָא: כְּשֶׁבָּעַל.

What, is it not referring to a case **where if he did not** yet **engage in** full-fledged **intercourse,** i.e., rupturing the hymen, with his bride, **he may engage in** full-fledged **intercourse** with her **even on Shabbat?** Apparently, it is permitted to engage in intercourse with a virgin on Shabbat. **Rava said: No,** it is referring to any other day **except for Shabbat. Abaye said to him: But isn't it taught: Until the conclusion of Shabbat, four nights?** Four nights from Wednesday until the conclusion of Shabbat includes Shabbat. **Rather, Rava said:** It is referring to a case **where he engaged in** full-fledged **intercourse** with his bride before Shabbat. Therefore, there is no concern lest he cause a wound on Shabbat.

אִי כְּשֶׁבָּעַל – מַאי קָא מַשְׁמַע לַן? קָא מַשְׁמַע לַן דְּשָׁרֵי לְמִיבְעַל בְּשַׁבָּת, כִּדְשְׁמוּאֵל. דְּאָמַר שְׁמוּאֵל: פִּירְצָה דְּחוּקָה מוּתָּר לִיכָּנֵס בָּהּ בְּשַׁבָּת, וְאַף עַל פִּי שֶׁמַּשִּׁיר צְרוֹרוֹת.

However, **if** it is referring to a case where **he** already **engaged in intercourse, what is** the *tanna* **teaching us** when he says that it is permitted to have intercourse with her even on Shabbat? **He teaches us that** although it might cause bleeding, **it is permitted to engage in intercourse on Shabbat, in accordance with** the statement of **Shmuel, as Shmuel said:** It is **permitted to enter into a narrow opening** in a wall **on Shabbat, although** doing so **causes pebbles to fall** from the wall. Here too, although it might cause a wound and bleeding, intercourse is permitted on Shabbat.

מֵתִיב רַב יוֹסֵף: חָתָן פָּטוּר מִקְּרִיַּת שְׁמַע לַיְלָה הָרִאשׁוֹן עַד מוֹצָאֵי שַׁבָּת אִם לֹא עָשָׂה מַעֲשֶׂה. מַאי לָאו – דִּטְרִיד, דְּבָעֵי לְמִיבְעַל? אָמַר לֵיהּ אַבָּיֵי: לָא, דִּטְרִיד דְּלָא בְּעֵיל.

Rav Yosef raised an objection from a mishna (*Berakhot* 16a): **A groom is exempt from the mitzva of reciting *Shema* on the first night**[H] of his marriage to a virgin on Wednesday night, **until Saturday night, if he has not taken action** and consummated the marriage. **What, is it not** that he is exempt due to the fact **that he is preoccupied because he wishes to engage in intercourse** with her and is concerned that he will fail to do so properly? Apparently, if he did not yet consummate the marriage, he is exempt from reciting *Shema* even on Shabbat, indicating that it is permitted to engage in intercourse on Shabbat. **Abaye said to him: No.** It can be explained **that he** is exempt from reciting *Shema* because he **is preoccupied** due to the fact **that** he did **not** yet **engage in intercourse** with her. No proof may be cited with regard to engaging in intercourse on Shabbat.

אָמַר לֵיהּ רָבָא: וּמִשּׁוּם טִירְדָּא פָּטוּר?! אֶלָּא מֵעַתָּה טָבְעָה סְפִינָתוֹ בַּיָּם הָכִי נַמִי דְּפָטוּר?! וְכִי תֵּימָא הָכִי נַמִי – וְהָאָמַר רַבִּי אַבָּא בַּר זַבְדָּא אָמַר רַב: אָבֵל חַיָּיב בְּכָל הַמִּצְוֹת הָאֲמוּרוֹת בַּתּוֹרָה חוּץ מִן הַתְּפִילִּין, שֶׁנֶּאֱמַר בָּהֶן "פְּאֵר"!

Rava said to Abaye: **And is one exempt due to preoccupation?**[N] **If that is so, would one whose ship sunk at sea also** be exempt? The Gemara reinforces its question: **And if you would say:** In fact, **that is so, didn't Rabbi Abba bar Zavda say that Rav said: A mourner is obligated in all the mitzvot**[N] **in the Torah except for** the mitzva to don **phylacteries,**[H] as the term **splendor is stated with regard to** phylacteries:[N] "Make no mourning for the dead; bind your splendor upon yourself" (Ezekiel 24:17). Splendor is antithetical to mourning. If a mourner, who is clearly pained and preoccupied, is obligated to recite *Shema,* then certainly all others who are preoccupied due to events that transpired in the past should be obligated. If the groom is exempt, it must be due to his preoccupation with a mitzva that remains incumbent upon him to perform in the future.

HALAKHA

A groom is exempt from the mitzva of reciting *Shema* on the first night – חָתָן פָּטוּר מִקְּרִיַּת שְׁמַע לַיְלָה הָרִאשׁוֹן: A groom who marries a virgin is exempt from reciting *Shema* until he consummates the marriage because he is preoccupied that he will discover that she is not a virgin. Since he is preoccupied with the performance of a mitzva, he is exempt from performing another. If he has not engaged in sexual relations three nights after the wedding, he is obligated to recite *Shema*, since he is more comfortable with his bride and no longer preoccupied. That exemption applied in earlier generations. However, today most people typically recite *Shema* without the proper intent, so a groom who marries a virgin recites *Shema* as well (Rambam *Sefer Ahava, Hilkhot Keriat Shema* 4:1; *Shulḥan Arukh, Oraḥ Ḥayyim* 70:3).

A mourner is obligated in all the mitzvot in the Torah except for the mitzva to don phylacteries – אָבֵל חַיָּיב בְּכָל הַמִּצְוֹת הָאֲמוּרוֹת בַּתּוֹרָה חוּץ מִן הַתְּפִילִּין: It is prohibited for a mourner to don phylacteries on the day of the burial (Rambam *Sefer Shofetim, Hilkhot Evel* 4:9; *Shulḥan Arukh, Oraḥ Ḥayyim* 38:5).

NOTES

Preoccupation – טִירְדָּא: Several explanations are provided for the preoccupation of one who marries a virgin. They must be taken together in order to understand the course of the Gemara's discussion here. In the Rambam's Commentary on the Mishna it is explained that he is anxious that he will discover that his bride is not a virgin. In the *Shita Mekubbetzet*, an opinion is cited that his concern is that he might falsely suspect his wife of not being a virgin. Apparently, he is also worried that he will be unable to engage properly in full-fledged intercourse.

Is obligated in all the mitzvot – חַיָּיב בְּכָל הַמִּצְוֹת: The Ritva notes that a mourner is also prohibited from studying Torah, which means that the statement here is not completely accurate. The Sages, in various formulations, stated that practical *halakha* cannot be learned from principles stated in the mishna, as there are no principles without exceptions.

As the term splendor is stated with regard to phylacteries – שֶׁנֶּאֱמַר בָּהֶן פְּאֵר: Rashi adds that since a mourner is downhearted and despondent, it is inappropriate for him to place splendor on his head. The Ritva explains that Rashi did not suffice with merely citing the verse from Ezekiel, from which it is derived that the mourner is exempt from the mitzva of phylacteries, because he wanted to explain, in passing, why all mitzvot are not derived from the mitzva of phylacteries by means of an analogy.

אֶלָּא אֲמַר רָבָא: תַּנָּאֵי הִיא. דְּתָנָא חֲדָא: אִם לֹא עָשָׂה מַעֲשֶׂה בָּרִאשׁוֹן – פָּטוּר אַף בַּשֵּׁנִי, בַּשֵּׁנִי – פָּטוּר אַף בַּשְּׁלִישִׁי.

Rather, Rava said: This matter of intercourse with a virgin on Shabbat **is subject to a dispute between** ***tanna'im*****, as one** ***tanna*** **taught: If he did not take action on the first** night **he is exempt** from reciting *Shema* **even on the second.** If he failed to consummate the marriage on the **second** night **he is exempt even on the third** night, which is Shabbat evening.

וְתַנְיָא אִידָּךְ: רִאשׁוֹן וְשֵׁנִי – פָּטוּר, שְׁלִישִׁי – חַיָּיב.

And another *baraita* **is taught:** On the **first and second** nights **he is exempt;** on the **third he is obligated** to recite *Shema*. He is obligated on the third night, even if he did not yet consummate the marriage, because the third night is Shabbat, when intercourse with his virgin wife is forbidden. The different rulings in the two *baraitot* indicate that there is a tannaitic dispute with regard to intercourse with a virgin on Shabbat.

וְאַבָּיֵי: הָתָם נַמִּי בְּטִירְדָּא פְּלִיגִי.

And how does **Abaye** respond to this proof? He says that **there too,** it can be explained that it **is with regard to preoccupation** that the *tanna'im* **disagree.** Everyone agrees that it is prohibited to engage in intercourse with a virgin on Shabbat. The dispute is whether or not one's preoccupation with the fact that he has not yet performed the mitzva of consummating the marriage in the past is considered preoccupation with a mitzva, which would exempt him from reciting *Shema*?

וְהָנֵי תַּנָּאֵי כִּי הָנֵי תַּנָּאֵי; דְּתַנְיָא: הַכּוֹנֵס אֶת הַבְּתוּלָה לֹא יִבְעוֹל בַּתְּחִלָּה בְּשַׁבָּת, וַחֲכָמִים מַתִּירִין.

And the dispute between **these** ***tanna'im*** in the *baraitot* cited is **parallel** to the dispute between **these** ***tanna'im*****, as it is taught** in another *baraita*: With regard to **one who marries a virgin, he may not engage in intercourse** with her for the **first** time **on Shabbat, and the Rabbis permit** doing so.

מַאן חֲכָמִים? אֲמַר רַבָּה: רַבִּי שִׁמְעוֹן הִיא, דְּאָמַר: דָּבָר שֶׁאֵין מִתְכַּוֵּין מוּתָּר.

The Gemara asks: **Who are the Rabbis** that permit doing so? **Rabba said: It is** the opinion of **Rabbi Shimon, who said: An unintentional act is permitted** on Shabbat. Since one's intention is to perform a permitted action, i.e., the consummation of the marriage, and there is no intent to perform a forbidden action, any forbidden action that may ensue is not a source of concern.

אֲמַר לֵיהּ אַבָּיֵי: וְהָא מוֹדֶה רַבִּי שִׁמְעוֹן בִּפְסִיק רֵישֵׁיהּ וְלָא יָמוּת! אֲמַר לֵיהּ: לֹא כְּהַלָּלוּ בַּבְלִיִּים שֶׁאֵין בְּקִיאִין בְּהַטָּיָה, אֶלָּא יֵשׁ בְּקִיאִין בְּהַטָּיָה.

Abaye said to Rabba: **But doesn't Rabbi Shimon concede** that **in** the case of: **Cut off its head and will it not die,** i.e., inevitable consequences, one is not exempted by lack of intent. Since rupture of the hymen and the subsequent bleeding is inevitable, Rabbi Shimon would concede that intercourse with a virgin is forbidden. Rabba **said to him: Unlike these Babylonians, who are not experts in diverting**[B] during intercourse and are unable to engage in intercourse without rupturing the hymen, **there are** those who are **experts in diverting.** Therefore, rupture of the hymen is not an inevitable consequence.

אִם כֵּן טוֹרֶד לָמָּה? לְשֶׁאֵינוֹ בָּקִי. יֹאמְרוּ בָּקִי – מוּתָּר, שֶׁאֵינוֹ בָּקִי – אָסוּר! רוֹב בְּקִיאִין הֵן.

The Gemara asks: **If so,** and the groom is expert in diverting, **why** is there **preoccupation** that renders him exempt from reciting *Shema*? The Gemara answers: The exemption due to preoccupation is limited to **one who is not expert.** The Gemara asks: If so, the Sages **should say** explicitly: One who is **expert is permitted** to have intercourse with a virgin on Shabbat, and one **who is not expert**[N] **is prohibited** from doing so. The Gemara answers: The **majority** of men **are experts** in this matter. Therefore, rupture of the hymen is not an inevitable consequence, and intercourse is permitted on Shabbat.

BACKGROUND

Diverting – הַטָּיָה: Diverting can be accomplished in several manners. It can be a form of intercourse without penetrating the vagina, which is one of the possibilities raised by the Gemara with regard to the preliminary stage of intercourse. Here, it seems more likely that we are dealing with a case of complete penetration that avoids rupturing the hymen. This is possible when the hymen is naturally perforated sufficiently to allow entry. In the case of most mature grown women, the hymen is no longer intact and there is often an opening large enough to enable penetration at a certain angle without causing rupture.

NOTES

One who is expert…one who is not expert – בָּקִי...שֶׁאֵינוֹ בָּקִי: The early commentaries analyzed this brief passage very closely, since the different reasons cited are apparently contradictory (see *Tosafot*). They conclude that even those who are not expert at diverting are at times successful in doing so. However, due to their lack of expertise, they will not know in advance whether or not they will be successful. On the other hand, those who are expert may decide to engage in full-fledged intercourse. On that basis, the various statements can be reconciled.

אָמַר לֵיהּ רָבָא בַּר רַב חָנָן לְאַבָּיֵי: אֶלָּא מֵעַתָּה שׁוֹשְׁבִינִין לָמָּה? מַפָּה לָמָּה? אָמַר לֵיהּ: הָתָם שֶׁמָּא יִרְאֶה וִיאַבֵּד.

Rava bar Rav Ḥanan said to Abaye: If that is so, and most people are able to engage in intercourse with a virgin without rupturing the hymen, **why are groomsmen** stationed to ensure that no deceit is employed by the groom with regard to the bride's virginity? And **why is a sheet** necessary to determine whether there was blood? The absence of blood proves nothing if intercourse is possible without blood. Abaye **said to him: There,** the groomsmen and the sheet are necessary **lest** the groom **see** blood **and** seek to **destroy** it intentionally. Certainly, if he seeks to engage in intercourse and keep the hymen intact he can do so. However, if he engages in full-fledged intercourse and the hymen is ruptured, the Sages sought to ensure that the facts are clear.

מְתִיב רַבִּי אַמֵּי: הַמֵּפִיס מוּרְסָא בְּשַׁבָּת, אִם לַעֲשׂוֹת לָהּ פֶּה – חַיָּיב. וְאִם לְהוֹצִיא מִמֶּנָּה לֵיחָה,

Rav Ami raised an objection from a mishna (*Eduyyot* 2:5): With regard to **one who drains an abscess**[NHB] **on Shabbat, if** his intent is **to create** a permanent **opening** so that the abscess will dry, **he is liable** to receive punishment for performing an action similar to the prohibited labor of building on Shabbat. **However, if** he created the opening **to remove pus,**

NOTES

One who drains an abscess – הַמֵּפִיס מוּרְסָא: Rashi explains that creating a permanent opening in the abscess falls under the rubric of the prohibited labor of building, which is applicable to human bodies as well. The Rambam explains that creating this opening is included in the category of striking with a hammer, i.e., completing production of a vessel. The purpose of this opening is to facilitate the exit of the pus and the entry of air (*Tosafot*). Others, citing *Tosafot*, explain that the opening facilitates exit of the pus and the introduction of medicine.

HALAKHA

One who drains an abscess – הַמֵּפִיס מוּרְסָא: One who lances a pus-filled abscess on Shabbat in order to create a permanent opening to facilitate healing is liable to receive punishment for performing the prohibited labor of striking with a hammer, i.e., completing production of a vessel. However, it is permitted for one to lance the abscess if his intention is to drain the pus (Rambam *Sefer Zemanim, Hilkhot Shabbat* 10:17; *Shulḥan Arukh, Oraḥ Ḥayyim* 328:28).

BACKGROUND

Drains an abscess – מֵפִיס מוּרְסָא: An abscess is a wound filled with pus that is drained by means of squeezing. The continued drainage of the pus is a necessary step in healing the abscess. The accumulation of pus in a closed abscess causes significant pain, and lancing the abscess and draining the pus temporarily relieves that pain.

Perek **I**
Daf **7** Amud **a**

פָּטוּר! הָתָם פָּקִיד וַעֲקִיר, הָכָא – פָּקִיד וְלָא עֲקִיר.

he is exempt. In this case, exempt means permitted *ab initio*. Ostensibly, intercourse with a virgin is comparable to creating an opening in an abscess. Why then, would intercourse with a virgin be forbidden on Shabbat? The Gemara rejects the proof: **There,** the pus in the abscess **is pooled** in one place **and** completely **removed** from the vessels in the flesh. In creating the opening, he creates nothing enduring. **Here,** however, in the case of the ruptured hymen, even according to the opinion that the blood **is pooled, it is not** completely **removed** from the blood vessels in the flesh. Through intercourse, the blood is removed from its place, which constitutes an aspect of a prohibited labor.

רַבִּי אַמֵּי שְׁרָא לְמִיבְעַל בְּתְחִלָּה בְּשַׁבָּת. אָמְרִי לֵיהּ רַבָּנַן: וְהָא לָא כְּתִיבָא כְּתוּבָּתָהּ! אָמַר לְהוּ: אַתְפְּסוּהָ מְטַלְטְלִין.

The Gemara relates: **Rav Ami permitted** one **to engage in intercourse** with his virgin wife for the **first** time **on Shabbat. The Sages said to him: But her marriage contract is not** yet **written.** Engaging in conjugal relations with one's wife without a marriage contract is considered an act of promiscuity. **He said to them: Have her seize** a portion of her husband's **movable property**[H] equivalent to the value of her marriage contract, and that will serve as a deposit until he writes the marriage contract. He may then engage in sexual relations with her.

רַב זְבִיד שְׁרָא לְמִיבְעַל בְּתְחִלָּה בְּשַׁבָּת. אִיכָּא דְּאָמְרִי: רַב זְבִיד גּוּפֵיהּ בָּעַל בְּתְחִלָּה בְּשַׁבָּת.

The Gemara relates: **Rav Zevid permitted** one **to engage in intercourse** with his virgin wife for the **first** time **on Shabbat. There are those who say: Rav Zevid himself engaged in intercourse** with his virgin wife for the **first** time **on Shabbat.**

רַב יְהוּדָה שְׁרָא לְמִיבְעַל בְּתְחִלָּה בְּיוֹם טוֹב. אָמַר רַב פַּפִּי מִשְּׁמֵיהּ דְּרָבָא: לָא תֵּימָא בְּיוֹם טוֹב דִּשְׁרֵי, הָא בְּשַׁבָּת אָסוּר – דְּהוּא הַדִּין דַּאֲפִילּוּ בְּשַׁבָּת נַמִי שְׁרֵי, וּמַעֲשֶׂה שֶׁהָיָה כָּךְ הָיָה.

It was further related: **Rav Yehuda permitted** one **to engage in intercourse** with his virgin wife for the **first** time **on a Festival. Rav Pappi said in the name of Rava: Do not** infer and say: It is **on a Festival that** it is **permitted,** but **on Shabbat** it is **prohibited,** similar to actions involving food preparation, which are permitted on Festivals and prohibited on Shabbat, **as the same is true that even on Shabbat it is permitted. And** the reason Rav Yehuda issued his ruling with regard to a Festival is due to the fact that **the incident that took place, took place in this way.**

HALAKHA

Have her seize her husband's movable property – אַתְפְּסוּהָ מְטַלְטְלִין: If a man neglected to or is unable to write a marriage contract for his wife, e.g., on Shabbat, he may give her movable property corresponding to the value of the marriage contract accompanied by a guarantee that he will compensate her for any loss of value. He may then engage in intercourse with his wife until he has the opportunity to draft a marriage contract, at which point he is obligated to do so (Rambam *Sefer Nashim, Hilkhot Ishut* 10:9; *Shulḥan Arukh, Even HaEzer* 66:2).

NOTES

Since…was permitted – מִתּוֹךְ שֶׁהוּתְּרָה: There is a dispute between Beit Shammai and Beit Hillel in tractate *Beitza* with regard to the principle: Since it was permitted for the purpose of food preparation, it was also permitted when not performed for the purpose of food preparation. According to Beit Hillel, since certain actions were permitted for the purpose of food preparation, they are permitted for other purposes as well. *Tosafot* and the Rashba note that this is not blanket permission to perform these activities for any purpose. These activities are permitted only when performed for the purpose of that day, even if it is not for food preparation.

And is there a ruling issued to prohibit – וּמִי אִיכָּא הוֹרָאָה לְאִיסּוּר: Apparently, the question arises from the use of the term: Issued a ruling, which typically connotes a novel element. A Sage may rule that a matter is prohibited merely to avoid entering a situation of uncertainty, not due to any novel understanding. However, in order to rule that a matter is permitted, it must be based on a clear-cut, often novel understanding (see Rashi). In the *Shita Mekubbetzet*, an explanation is cited that the question of the Gemara is: Perhaps Rabbi Ya'akov bar Idi was mistaken, and based on the fact that he heard that Rabbi Yoḥanan issued a ruling, he assumed that he had ruled that it is permitted.

LANGUAGE

Incense [*mugmar*] – **מוּגְמָר:** From the Aramaic *gomra* or *gomarta*, meaning coal. Incense consisted of various spices placed on hot coals that would fill the home with a pleasant fragrance.

רַב פַּפָּא מִשְּׁמֵיהּ דְּרָבָא אָמַר: בְּיוֹם טוֹב – שָׁרֵי, בְּשַׁבָּת – אָסוּר. אֲמַר לֵיהּ רַב פַּפִּי לְרַב פַּפָּא: מַאי דַּעְתָּיךְ, מִתּוֹךְ שֶׁהוּתְּרָה חַבּוּרָה לְצוֹרֶךְ הוּתְּרָה נַמִּי שֶׁלֹּא לְצוֹרֶךְ? אֶלָּא מֵעַתָּה מוּתָּר לַעֲשׂוֹת מוּגְמָר בְּיוֹם טוֹב, דְּמִתּוֹךְ שֶׁהוּתְּרָה הַבְעָרָה לְצוֹרֶךְ – הוּתְּרָה נַמִּי שֶׁלֹּא לְצוֹרֶךְ!

Rav Pappa said in the name of Rava: According to Rav Yehuda, **on a Festival** it is **permitted, on Shabbat** it is **prohibited. Rav Pappi said to Rav Pappa: What is your thinking?** Is it: **Since** causing **a wound was permitted**[N] on a Festival when performed **for the purpose** of food preparation, it **was also permitted** when **not** performed **for the purpose** of food preparation? **If that is so,** it would be **permitted to prepare incense** [*mugmar*][LB] **on a Festival** due to the following reason: **Since kindling** a fire **was permitted** on a Festival when performed **for the purpose** of food preparation, it **was also permitted** when **not** performed **for the purpose** of food preparation.

אֲמַר לֵיהּ: עָלֶיךָ אָמַר קְרָא "אַךְ אֲשֶׁר יֵאָכֵל לְכָל נֶפֶשׁ" דָּבָר הַשָּׁוֶה לְכָל נֶפֶשׁ.

Rav Pappa **said to him:** It is **about your** assertion that **the verse states** with regard to a Festival: **"Save that which every person must eat,** that alone may be done by you" (Exodus 12:16), indicating a **matter that is equal for every person.** Incense is burned only by those who are particularly delicate. It is not equally utilized by everyone, and therefore it is not permitted. Intercourse, on the other hand, is universally practiced.

אֲמַר לֵיהּ רַב אַחָא בְּרֵיהּ דְּרָבָא לְרַב אַשִׁי: אֶלָּא מֵעַתָּה, נִזְדַּמֵּן לוֹ צְבִי בְּיוֹם טוֹב, הוֹאִיל וְאֵינוֹ שָׁוֶה לְכָל נֶפֶשׁ – הָכִי נַמִּי דְּאָסוּר לְמִשְׁחָטֵיהּ?! אֲמַר לֵיהּ: אֲנָא דָּבָר הַצּוֹרֵךְ לְכָל נֶפֶשׁ קָאָמִינָא, צְבִי צָרִיךְ לְכָל נֶפֶשׁ הוּא.

Rav Aḥa, son of Rava, said to Rav Ashi: If that is so, if a deer happened to come into **his** possession **on a Festival, since** it is **not** a food that is **equal for every person,** would the ruling **also** be **that** it is **prohibited to slaughter it?** Rav Ashi **said to him: I said a matter** that is **a need for every person,** and **deer** meat **is a matter** that although difficult to acquire, is **a need for every person.** Incense, even when available, is not universally utilized.

אָמַר רַבִּי יַעֲקֹב בַּר אִידִי: הוֹרָה רַבִּי יוֹחָנָן בְּצַיְידָן: אָסוּר לִבְעוֹל בַּתְּחִלָּה בְּשַׁבָּת. וּמִי אִיכָּא הוֹרָאָה לְאִיסּוּר?

Rabbi Ya'akov bar Idi said: Rabbi Yoḥanan issued a ruling in the city of **Tzaidan:**[B] **It is prohibited to engage in intercourse** with one's virgin wife for the **first** time **on Shabbat.** The Gemara asks: **And is there a ruling issued to prohibit**[N] an action? Typically, that language is utilized in reference to a firmly established ruling. A stringent ruling can be issued even based on uncertainty. In contrast, a lenient ruling can be issued only if the matter is clearly established by means of tradition or the reasoning of the Sage issuing the ruling.

BACKGROUND

Incense – מוּגְמָר: Incense vessels, also called censers, were at times fashioned with a perforated cover in order to allow the fragrance to diffuse. Others were sealed, and the cover was removed only when one wanted the fragrance to diffuse throughout the house or to perfume one's garments. The use of various types of incense was customary among well-to-do families.

Censer from Eretz Yisrael dating back to the period of the *ge'onim*

Ruins of Tzaidan

Tzaidan – צַיְידָן: Tzaidan was a town on the northern bank of the Sea of Galilee, adjacent to the place where the Jordan River flows into the Sea of Galilee. It is also called Beit Tzaida in other sources, and Josephus used its Roman name, Julias. The Sages of Tiberias frequently visited there and issued various rulings.

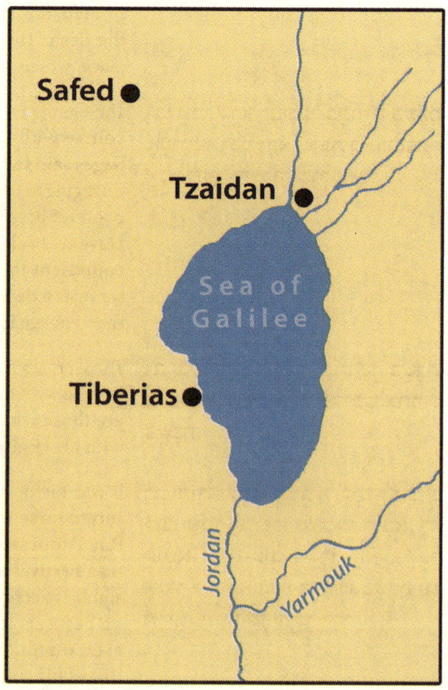

Location of Tzaidan

אִין. וְהָתְנַן: הוֹרוּהָ בֵּית הִלֵּל שֶׁתְּהֵא נְזִירָה עוֹד שֶׁבַע שָׁנִים אֲחֵרוֹת,

The Gemara answers: **Yes,** that language is used with regard to a stringent ruling, as **didn't we learn** the following in a mishna (*Nazir* 19b): When Queen Helene's son went to war, she took a vow to be a nazirite for seven years, and she fulfilled that vow for the duration of her stay in the Diaspora? When she immigrated to Eretz Yisrael, **Beit Hillel issued a ruling that she shall be a nazirite for seven additional years.**[HN] Apparently, rulings are issued to prohibit an action as well.

וְאִי נַמִי כִּי הָא, דְּתַנְיָא: חוּט הַשִּׁדְרָה שֶׁנִּפְסַק – בְּרוּבּוֹ, דִּבְרֵי רַבִּי. רַבִּי יַעֲקֹב אוֹמֵר: אֲפִילּוּ נִיקַּב. הוֹרָה רַבִּי כְּרַבִּי יַעֲקֹב. אָמַר רַב הוּנָא: אֵין הֲלָכָה כְּרַבִּי יַעֲקֹב.

And alternatively, this is **similar** to **that which is taught** in a *baraita*: **If a majority of the spinal cord** of an animal **is severed,**[H] the animal is a *tereifa*; **this is the statement of Rabbi** Yehuda HaNasi. **Rabbi Ya'akov says: Even** if the spinal cord is **perforated** but otherwise intact, the animal is a *tereifa*. The *baraita* continues: **Rabbi** Yehuda HaNasi **issued a ruling in accordance with** the opinion of **Rabbi Ya'akov.** Here too, the term: Issue a ruling, is employed with regard to a stringent ruling. **Rav Huna said:** Despite the fact that Rabbi Yehuda HaNasi ruled in accordance with his opinion, **the *halakha* is not in accordance with** the opinion of **Rabbi Ya'akov,** but rather it is in accordance with the opinion of Rabbi Yehuda HaNasi. This is one version of this discussion.

רַב נַחְמָן בַּר יִצְחָק מַתְנֵי הָכִי: אָמַר רַבִּי אַבָּהוּ שָׁאַל רַבִּי יִשְׁמָעֵאל בֶּן יַעֲקֹב דְּמִן צוֹר אֶת רַבִּי יוֹחָנָן בְּצַיְידָן, וַאֲנָא שְׁמָעִי: מַהוּ לִבְעוֹל בַּתְּחִלָּה בְּשַׁבָּת? וַאֲמַר לֵיהּ: אָסוּר. וְהִלְכְתָא: מוּתָּר לִבְעוֹל בַּתְּחִלָּה בְּשַׁבָּת.

Rav Naḥman bar Yitzḥak taught this alternative version of the ruling of Rabbi Yoḥanan. **Rav Abbahu said: Rabbi Yishmael ben Ya'akov, who is from Tyre, asked Rabbi Yoḥanan in Tzaidan, and I heard** the exchange: **What is** the *halakha* with regard **to engaging in intercourse** with one's virgin wife for the **first** time **on Shabbat? And he said to** him: It is **prohibited.** The Gemara concludes: **And the *halakha*** is that it is **permitted to engage in intercourse** with one's virgin wife for the **first** time **on Shabbat,**[H] and one need not be concerned lest he cause a wound, create an opening, or initiate bleeding.

אָמַר רַבִּי חֶלְבּוֹ אָמַר רַב הוּנָא אָמַר רַבִּי אַבָּא בַּר זַבְדָּא אָמַר רַב: אַחַת בְּתוּלָה וְאַחַת אַלְמָנָה טְעוּנָה בְּרָכָה. וּמִי אֲמַר רַב הוּנָא הָכִי? וְהָאָמַר רַב הוּנָא: אַלְמָנָה אֵינָהּ טְעוּנָה בְּרָכָה! לָא קַשְׁיָא; כָּאן – בְּבָחוּר שֶׁנָּשָׂא אַלְמָנָה, כָּאן – בְּאַלְמוֹן שֶׁנָּשָׂא אַלְמָנָה.

§ **Rabbi Ḥelbo said** that **Rav Huna said** that **Rabbi Abba bar Rav Zavda said** that **Rav said: Both a virgin and a widow** who marry **require** that the **benediction**[N] of the grooms be recited. The Gemara asks: **Did Rav Huna say that? But didn't Rav Huna say: A widow does not require** that **a benediction** be recited? The Gemara answers: This is **not difficult. Here,** where Rav Huna said that a widow requires a benediction, it is **with regard to a bachelor who married a widow. There,** where Rav Huna said she does not require a benediction, it is **with regard to a widower who married a widow.**[H]

וְאַלְמוֹן שֶׁנָּשָׂא אַלְמָנָה לָא? וְהָאֲמַר רַב נַחְמָן, אֲמַר לִי הוּנָא בַּר נָתָן, תָּנָא: מִנַּיִן לְבִרְכַּת חֲתָנִים בַּעֲשָׂרָה? שֶׁנֶּאֱמַר "וַיִּקַּח עֲשָׂרָה אֲנָשִׁים מִזִּקְנֵי הָעִיר וַיֹּאמֶר שְׁבוּ פֹה וַיֵּשֵׁבוּ", וּבוֹעַז אַלְמוֹן שֶׁנָּשָׂא אַלְמָנָה הֲוָה!

The Gemara asks: **And does a widower who married a widow not** require a benediction to be recited? **But didn't Rav Naḥman say: Huna bar Natan said to me** that it was **taught: From where** is it derived **that the benediction of the grooms** is recited **in a** quorum of **ten men?**[H] **It is as it is stated** with regard to Boaz, who married Ruth: **"And he took ten men of the Elders of the city and said: Sit you here, and they sat"** (Ruth 4:2). **And** when **Boaz** married Ruth, **he was a widower marrying a widow.**[N] As that is the primary source for the obligation to recite the benediction, apparently the benediction is recited even in that case.

HALAKHA

Beit Hillel issued a ruling that she shall be a nazirite for seven additional years – הוֹרוּהָ בֵּית הִלֵּל שֶׁתְּהֵא נְזִירָה עוֹד שֶׁבַע שָׁנִים אֲחֵרוֹת: The vows of a nazirite can be fulfilled only in Eretz Yisrael. If one takes a nazirite vow outside of Eretz Israel, he is obligated to go to Eretz Yisrael and observe the entire period of the vow, and the period that he observed outside of Eretz Yisrael is discounted. According to the Rambam, even today he is obligated to go to Eretz Yisrael and observe the vow there until he dies or until the Temple is rebuilt, at which point he can sacrifice the requisite offerings and conclude his tenure as a nazirite. The Ra'avad disagrees, contending that today there is no point in the nazirite going to Eretz Yisrael, as there is no way for him to purify himself from impurity imparted by a corpse (Rambam *Sefer Hafla'a, Hilkhot Nezirut* 2:21; see Radbaz).

If a majority of the spinal cord of an animal is severed – חוּט הַשִּׁדְרָה שֶׁנִּפְסַק בְּרוּבּוֹ: If more than half the sheath enveloping an animal's spinal cord is severed, it is a *tereifa* and may not be eaten, in accordance with the ruling of Rabbi Yehuda HaNasi (Rambam *Sefer Kedusha, Hilkhot Sheḥita* 9:1; *Shulḥan Arukh, Yoreh De'a* 32:1).

It is permitted to engage in intercourse with one's virgin wife for the first time on Shabbat – מוּתָּר לִבְעוֹל בַּתְּחִלָּה בְּשַׁבָּת: It is permitted to engage in intercourse with one's virgin wife for the first time on Shabbat, and there is no concern that causing a wound or pain entail desecration of Shabbat. Some (Rosh) rule that in places where the custom is to rule stringently and to refrain from engaging in intercourse with a virgin for the first time on Shabbat, one may not rule leniently unless there are compelling circumstances (*Pitḥei Teshuva*; Rambam *Sefer Zemanim, Hilkhot Shabbat* 30:14; *Shulḥan Arukh, Even HaEzer* 63:1).

A widower who married a widow – אַלְמוֹן שֶׁנָּשָׂא אַלְמָנָה: If a widower marries a widow, the benediction of the grooms is recited only on the day of the wedding. However, whenever a virgin is married, whether the groom is marrying for the first time or has been married before, the benediction of the grooms is recited on all seven days of the wedding celebration (Rambam *Sefer Ahava, Hilkhot Berakhot* 2:9; *Shulḥan Arukh, Even HaEzer* 62:6).

The benediction of the grooms is recited in a quorum of ten men – בִּרְכַּת חֲתָנִים בַּעֲשָׂרָה: The benediction of the grooms is recited only if there is a quorum of ten adult, free males present. Therefore, the wedding should not be held without a quorum. However, if there is no alternative, the wedding may be held without the benediction, and the benediction is recited later (Rashba; *Ḥelkat Meḥokek*). Others maintain that the presence of ten men is not critical after the fact, and so in cases where assembling the quorum would require a major effort, one need not insist on the presence of the quorum (*Darkhei Moshe*; *Beit Shmuel*; *Be'er Heitev*; Rambam *Sefer Ahava, Hilkhot Berakhot* 2:10; *Shulḥan Arukh, Even HaEzer* 62:4).

NOTES

That she shall be a nazirite for seven additional years – שֶׁתְּהֵא נְזִירָה עוֹד שֶׁבַע שָׁנִים: The essential reason was that a decree of ritual impurity was issued with regard to the land of the gentiles, and since it is prohibited for a nazirite to become impure with impurity imparted by a corpse, the naziriteship observed outside of Eretz Yisrael is disregarded.

A bride requires the benediction – טְעוּנָה בְּרָכָה כַּלָּה: In tractate *Kalla*, it states more forcefully that a bride without a blessing is forbidden to her husband like a menstruating woman. See *Tosafot* and Rav Yoshiya Pinto, who note that an additional source for the wedding benediction is cited there, from the verse "And they blessed Rebecca, and said to her: Our sister, may you be the mother of thousands of ten thousands" (Genesis 24:60).

He was a widower marrying a widow – אַלְמוֹן שֶׁנָּשָׂא אַלְמָנָה הֲוָה: Some derive that Boaz was a widower from the fact that he is identified with Ibzan, one of the judges from Bethlehem, about whom it is written that he had many children. In the Jerusalem Talmud, a midrash is cited with regard to the verse that describes Naomi and Ruth's arrival: "All the city was astir" (Ruth 1:22). It wasn't astir due to their arrival; rather, it was astir due to the funeral of Boaz's wife.

NOTES

However that which is taught in a *baraita* that the Sages were assiduous – אֶלָּא הָא דְּתַנְיָא שָׁקְדוּ: The connection between rejoicing at a wedding and the blessing is underscored by the *halakha* cited later in the Gemara, that the wedding benediction is recited at occasions celebrating the wedding and not specifically on the days of the wedding feast itself.

HALAKHA

The marriage celebration – שִׂמְחַת נִשּׂוּאִין: If a man marries a virgin, he must rejoice with her for a period of seven days. However, if he marries a woman who was previously married, he must rejoice with her for a period of three days. According to most authorities, who consider the two versions of the Gemara not mutually exclusive, this applies whether or not the groom was married before. However, the Rashba and others maintain that in the case of a widow marrying a man who was never married, he must also rejoice with her for seven days. In their opinion, the two versions are mutually exclusive, and the *halakha* is in accordance with the latter version, and that is the custom (*Be'er HaGola*; Rambam *Sefer Nashim, Hilkhot Ishut* 10:12; *Shulḥan Arukh, Even HaEzer* 64:2).

מַאי אֵינָהּ טְעוּנָה בְּרָכָה דַּאֲמַר רַב הוּנָא – אֵינָהּ טְעוּנָה בְּרָכָה כָּל שִׁבְעָה – אֲבָל יוֹם אֶחָד טְעוּנָה בְּרָכָה.

The Gemara answers: **What is** the meaning of: **Does not require a benediction, that Rav Huna stated?** It means that **she does not require a benediction all seven** days of the wedding celebration, **but** everyone agrees that for **one day, she requires** that a **benediction** be recited.

אֶלָּא הָא דְּתַנְיָא: שָׁקְדוּ חֲכָמִים עַל תַּקָּנַת בְּנוֹת יִשְׂרָאֵל שֶׁיְּהֵא שָׂמֵחַ עִמָּהּ שְׁלֹשָׁה יָמִים, בְּמַאי? אִי בְּבָחוּר – הָאָמַרְתְּ שִׁבְעָה, אִי בְּאַלְמוֹן – הָאָמַרְתְּ יוֹם אֶחָד!

The Gemara asks: **However, that which is taught** in a *baraita*, that **the Sages were assiduous**[N] **in seeing to the well-being of Jewish women,** ensuring **that** the groom **will rejoice with her three days,** and that is why they established that a widow is married on Thursday, **with regard to what** circumstance is the *baraita* speaking? **If** it is **with regard to a bachelor** who marries a widow, **didn't you say** he celebrates **seven** days; why then did the Sages see to a mere three-day celebration? **If** it is **with regard to a widower** who marries a widow, **didn't you say** he celebrates for **one** day? Why then did the Sages see to a three-day celebration?

אִיבָּעֵית אֵימָא: בְּאַלְמוֹן – יוֹם אֶחָד לִבְרָכָה וּשְׁלֹשָׁה לְשִׂמְחָה, וְאִיבָּעֵית אֵימָא: בְּבָחוּר – שִׁבְעָה לִבְרָכָה וּשְׁלֹשָׁה לְשִׂמְחָה.

The Gemara answers that this can be resolved in several manners. **If you wish, say:** In the case of **a widower** marrying a widow, there is **one day for benediction and three days for celebration.** The wedding is scheduled on Thursday to facilitate a three-day celebration. **And if you wish, say** instead: **In the case of a bachelor** marrying a widow, there are **seven days for benediction and** there are **three days for celebration,** during which he must refrain from going to work.[H]

Perek **I**
Daf **7** Amud **b**

מֵיתִיבֵי: מְבָרְכִין לִבְתוּלָה שִׁבְעָה וּלְאַלְמָנָה יוֹם אֶחָד. מַאי לָאו – אֲפִילּוּ אַלְמָנָה שֶׁנִּשֵּׂאת לְבָחוּר! לָא, לְאַלְמוֹן. אֲבָל לְבָחוּר מַאי – שִׁבְעָה, אִי הָכִי לִיתְנֵי: מְבָרְכִין לִבְתוּלָה שִׁבְעָה, וּלְאַלְמָנָה שֶׁנִּשֵּׂאת לְבָחוּר שִׁבְעָה, וּלְאַלְמָנָה יוֹם אֶחָד!

The Gemara raises an objection from a *baraita*: **One recites a benediction for a virgin** who marries for **seven** days **and for a widow** who marries for **one** day. **What, is it not even** in the case of **a widow who is married to a bachelor,** that one recites the benediction for one day? The Gemara answers: **No,** it is only in the case of a widow who is married **to a widower** that the benediction is recited for one day. The Gemara asks: **However,** one may then infer that in the case of a widow who is married **to a bachelor, what** is the *halakha*? The blessing is recited **seven** days? **If so,** let the *tanna* **teach** the *baraita*: **One recites a benediction for a virgin** who marries for **seven** days, **and for a widow** who marries **a bachelor seven** days, **and for a widow** marrying a widower for **one day.** Why was the middle case omitted?

מִילְּתָא פְּסִיקְתָּא קָתָנֵי, דְּלֵיכָּא בְּתוּלָה דְּבָצְרָה מִשִּׁבְעָה, וְלֵיכָּא אַלְמָנָה דְּבָצְרָה מִיּוֹם אֶחָד.

Although the *tanna* could have included that case in the *baraita*, **he taught categorical matters.** He preferred to avoid entering into detail, **as there is no virgin** for **whom** the benediction is recited **fewer than seven** days, **and there is no widow** for **whom** the benediction is recited for **less than one day.** However, there are circumstances where even for a widow the benediction is recited for more than one day.

גּוּפָא, אֲמַר רַב נַחְמָן: אֲמַר לִי הוּנָא בַּר נָתָן, תָּנָא: מִנַּיִן לְבִרְכַּת חֲתָנִים בַּעֲשָׂרָה – שֶׁנֶּאֱמַר "וַיִּקַּח עֲשָׂרָה אֲנָשִׁים מִזִּקְנֵי הָעִיר וַיֹּאמֶר שְׁבוּ פֹה". וְרַבִּי אַבָּהוּ אֲמַר מֵהָכָא: "בְּמַקְהֵלוֹת בָּרְכוּ אֱלֹהִים ה׳ מִמְּקוֹר יִשְׂרָאֵל".

§ Apropos the source for the benediction of the grooms, the Gemara discusses **the matter itself. Rav Naḥman said: Huna bar Natan said to me** that it was **taught: From where** is it derived **that the benediction of the grooms** is recited **in** a quorum of **ten** men? It is **as it is stated: "And he took ten men of the Elders of the city and said: Sit you here,** and they sat" (Ruth 4:2). **And Rabbi Abbahu said** that the source is **from here: "In assemblies [*mak'helot*], bless God, the Lord, from the source of Israel"** (Psalms 68:27). This verse indicates that a congregation [*kahal*], which contains at least ten men, blesses God when reciting a benediction related to the source of Israel, i.e., conjugal relations, which will lead to the birth of Jewish children.

וְרַב נַחְמָן בְּהַאי קְרָא דְּרַבִּי אַבָּהוּ מַאי דָּרֵישׁ בֵּיהּ? מִיבְּעֵי לֵיהּ לְכִדְתַנְיָא: הָיָה רַבִּי מֵאִיר אוֹמֵר: מִנַּיִן שֶׁאֲפִילּוּ עוּבָּרִים שֶׁבִּמְעֵי אִמָּן אָמְרוּ שִׁירָה עַל הַיָּם? שֶׁנֶּאֱמַר ״בְּמַקְהֵלוֹת בָּרְכוּ אֱלֹהִים ה׳ מִמְּקוֹר יִשְׂרָאֵל״. וְאִידָךְ – אִם כֵּן לֵימָא קְרָא ״מִבֶּטֶן״, מַאי ״מִמְּקוֹר״ עַל עִסְקֵי מָקוֹר.

And what does Rav Naḥman derive from this verse from which **Rabbi Abbahu** derived that *halakha*? **He requires** the verse **to** derive **that which is taught** in a *baraita*: **Rabbi Meir would say: From where** is it derived **that even fetuses in their mother's womb recited** the **song at the** Red **Sea?** It is **as it is stated** in the chapter of Psalms that describes the exodus from Egypt: **"In assemblies, bless God, the Lord, from the source of Israel."** Even those fetuses that were still in the source, i.e., the womb, joined the assemblies in blessing God. **And the other** Sage, Rabbi Abbahu says: **If that is** the meaning, **let the verse say: From the belly of Israel. What is** the meaning of the term **"source"?** Clearly, it is referring **to matters** related to **the source**[N] of Israel, i.e., the benediction of the grooms, which must be recited in a congregation, a quorum of ten.

וְרַבִּי אַבָּהוּ בְּהַאי קְרָא דְּרַב נַחְמָן מַאי דָּרֵישׁ בֵּיהּ? הַהוּא מִיבְּעֵי לֵיהּ לְמִידְרַשׁ: ״עַמּוֹנִי וְלֹא עַמּוֹנִית, מוֹאָבִי וְלֹא מוֹאָבִית״. דְּאִי סָלְקָא דַּעְתָּךְ לִבְרָכָה – לָא סַגְיָא דְּלָאו זְקֵנִים?

And what does Rabbi Abbahu derive from this verse from which **Rav Naḥman** derived his *halakha*? **He requires** the verse stating that Boaz assembled ten men in order **to teach** that the Torah prohibition with regard to marrying members of the nations of Ammon and Moab is limited to a male **Ammonite and not a female Ammonite,**[H] and to a male **Moabite and not a female Moabite, as, if it would enter your mind** that Boaz gathered the men only **to** recite **a benediction,** would it **not** have been **sufficient** if they **were not Elders?**[N] From the fact that he convened a quorum of Elders, apparently it was to engage in halakhic discourse and to issue a halakhic ruling.

וְאִידָךְ: אִי סָלְקָא דַּעְתָּךְ לְמִידְרַשׁ – לָא סַגְיָא דְּלָאו עֲשָׂרָה? אִין, לְפַרְסוּמֵי מִילְּתָא. וּכְדַאֲמַר לֵיהּ שְׁמוּאֵל לְרַב חָנָא בַּגְדָּתָאָה: פּוּק וְאַיְיתִי לִי בֵּי עַשְׂרָה, וְאֵימָא לָךְ בְּאַנְפַּיְיהוּ: הַמְזַכֶּה לְעוּבָּר – קָנָה. וְהִלְכְתָא: הַמְזַכֶּה לְעוּבָּר – לֹא קָנָה.

And the other Sage, Rav Naḥman, would reject that proof. **If it would enter your mind** that he gathered the men **in order to teach** a *halakha*, would it **not** have been **sufficient** if they **were not ten?** The Gemara answers: **Yes,** in fact a quorum of ten is not necessary to issue a halakhic ruling. Nevertheless, Boaz convened ten Elders **to publicize the matter, as Shmuel said to Rav Ḥana of Baghdad: Go and bring me an assembly of ten** men **and I will say to you before them** a *halakha* that I seek to disseminate: With regard to **one who transfers ownership** of an object **to a fetus,** the fetus **acquires** it, although it has not yet entered the world. Boaz too assembled ten Elders to publicize the matter. Apropos the *halakha* that Shmuel publicized, the Gemara rules: **And the *halakha*** is: With regard to **one who transfers ownership** of an object **to a fetus,** the fetus **does not acquire it.**[NH]

תָּנוּ רַבָּנַן: מְבָרְכִין בִּרְכַּת חֲתָנִים בְּבֵית חֲתָנִים. רַבִּי יְהוּדָה אוֹמֵר: אַף בְּבֵית הָאֵרוּסִין מְבָרְכִין אוֹתָהּ.

The Sages taught in a *baraita*: **One recites the benediction of the grooms in the house of the grooms,** when the bride enters into the wedding canopy. **Rabbi Yehuda said: One recites it even in the house of the betrothal,** at the time of the betrothal.

אָמַר אַבָּיֵי: וּבִיהוּדָה שָׁנוּ, מִפְּנֵי שֶׁמִּתְיַיחֵד עִמָּהּ.

Abaye said: And the Sages **taught** the statement of Rabbi Yehuda **in Judea because** there the custom was **that** the groom **be secluded with** his betrothed,[H] leading to the concern lest he engage in conjugal relations with her. Therefore, the blessing is recited already at that stage.

NOTES

To matters related to the source – עַל עִסְקֵי מָקוֹר: The early commentaries disagree whether a quorum of ten is required not only for the wedding blessing but for the betrothal blessing as well (see Rabbi Shmuel HaNagid and Rosh). Support for those who maintain that it is required can be cited from this Gemara, as betrothal is also a matter relating to the source of Israel.

Would it not have been sufficient if they were not Elders – לָא סַגְיָא דְּלָאו זְקֵנִים: The Ritva writes that although it is not derived from here that the quorum must be Elders, it is derived that the ten must have reached the age of majority, as the verse employs the term men.

And the *halakha* is: With regard to one who transfers ownership of an object to a fetus, the fetus does not acquire it – וְהִלְכְתָא, הַמְזַכֶּה לְעוּבָּר לֹא קָנָה: This ruling was stated explicitly to ensure that one does not rule in accordance with Shmuel, who issued his ruling publicly.

HALAKHA

A male Ammonite and not a female Ammonite – עַמּוֹנִי וְלֹא עַמּוֹנִית: An Ammonite or Moabite who converted to Judaism may not marry a Jewish woman, nor may male descendants of those converts marry Jewish women, regardless of the number of generations that have passed since the conversion of their ancestor. However, a female Ammonite or Moabite who converted to Judaism may marry a Jewish man, like any other convert (Rambam *Sefer Kedusha, Hilkhot Issurei Bia* 12:18; *Shulḥan Arukh, Even HaEzer* 4:2).

One who transfers ownership of an object to a fetus, the fetus does not acquire it – הַמְזַכֶּה לְעוּבָּר לֹא קָנָה: If one consigns a gift to a fetus, the latter does not acquire it. However, if one consigns a gift to a fetus that he fathered, the fetus does acquire it (*Bava Batra* 142b). Some maintain that the fetus acquires a gift from its father only if it is a gift bequeathed on his deathbed (*Sefer HaIttur*, citing Rav Hai Gaon), but most authorities disagree (see *Shakh*; Rambam *Sefer Kinyan, Hilkhot Mekhira* 22:10, *Hilkhot Zekhiya* 8:5; *Shulḥan Arukh, Ḥoshen Mishpat* 210:1).

Because the custom was that the groom be secluded with his betrothed – מִפְּנֵי שֶׁמִּתְיַיחֵד עִמָּהּ: In places where it is customary for a betrothed couple to be secluded together, the wedding benediction is recited at the betrothal, as in that case everyone agrees that it is permitted for the bride to engage in relations with the groom, in accordance with the statements of Rabbi Yehuda and Abaye. Even those authorities who do not rule in accordance with the statement of Rabbi Yehuda infer from this statement that if the groom does not enter into seclusion with his betrothed, the wedding benediction is not recited then (Rambam *Sefer Nashim, Hilkhot Ishut* 10:6; *Shulḥan Arukh, Even HaEzer* 55:1–2).

תַּנְיָא אִידָךְ: מְבָרְכִין בִּרְכַּת חֲתָנִים בְּבֵית חֲתָנִים, וּבִרְכַּת אֵרוּסִין בְּבֵית הָאֵרוּסִין. בִּרְכַּת הָאֵרוּסִין מַאי מְבָרֵךְ? רָבִין בַּר רַב אַדָּא וְרַבָּה בַּר רַב אַדָּא, תַּרְוַיְיהוּ מִשְּׁמֵיהּ דְּרַב יְהוּדָה אָמְרִי: בָּרוּךְ אַתָּה ה׳ אֱלֹהֵינוּ מֶלֶךְ הָעוֹלָם אֲשֶׁר קִדְּשָׁנוּ בְּמִצְוֹתָיו וְצִוָּנוּ עַל הָעֲרָיוֹת וְאָסַר לָנוּ אֶת הָאֲרוּסוֹת וְהִתִּיר לָנוּ אֶת הַנְּשׂוּאוֹת עַל יְדֵי חוּפָּה וְקִדּוּשִׁין. רַב אַחָא בְּרֵיהּ דְּרָבָא מְסַיֵּים בָּהּ מִשְּׁמֵיהּ דְּרַב יְהוּדָה: בָּרוּךְ אַתָּה ה׳ מְקַדֵּשׁ יִשְׂרָאֵל עַל יְדֵי חוּפָּה וְקִדּוּשִׁין.

It is taught in **another** ***baraita*****: One recites the benediction of the grooms**[H] **in the house of the grooms, and the benediction of the betrothal in the house of the betrothal.** With regard to **the benediction of the betrothal,**[N] **what** formula **does one recite?**[H] **Ravin bar Rav Adda and Rabba bar Rav Adda both said in the name of Rav Yehuda: Blessed are You, Lord our God, King of the universe, Who sanctified us through His mitzvot, and commanded us concerning the forbidden relatives,**[N] **and prohibited to us those women who are betrothed,**[N] **and permitted to us** those women **who are married**[N] **by means of the wedding canopy and betrothal. Rav Aḥa, son of Rava, concludes** the blessing **in the name of Rav Yehuda: Blessed are You, Lord, Who sanctifies Israel by means of the wedding canopy and betrothal.**[HN]

מַאן דְּלָא חָתֵים – מִידֵי דַּהֲוָה אַבִּרְכַּת פֵּרוֹת וְאַבִּרְכַּת מִצְוֹת, וּמַאן דְּחָתֵים – מִידֵי דַּהֲוָה אַקִּידּוּשָׁא.

One who does not conclude the benediction of the betrothal in accordance with the opinion of Rav Aḥa, but instead recites it without a concluding blessing, deems the formula of this blessing **just as** the formula **is in the blessing** recited over **fruits and the blessing** recited over **mitzvot,** in which the words: Blessed are You, Lord, appear only at the beginning of the blessing. **And one who concludes** the benediction of the betrothal in accordance with the opinion of Rav Aḥa, deems the formula of this blessing **just as** the formula **is** in the blessing **of** ***kiddush*****,** in which the words: Blessed are You, Lord, appears both at the beginning and the conclusion of the blessing.

HALAKHA

The time for reciting the benediction of the grooms – זְמַן בִּרְכַּת חֲתָנִים: The wedding benediction is recited for the first time when the bride enters the wedding canopy. It is subsequently recited at each of the wedding meals in the groom's house (Rambam *Sefer Ahava, Hilkhot Berakhot* 2:9 and *Sefer Nashim, Hilkhot Ishut* 10:3; *Shulḥan Arukh, Even HaEzer* 62:1).

The formula for the benediction of the betrothal – נוּסַח בִּרְכַּת הָאֵרוּסִין: Today the formula for the benediction of the betrothal is consistent with the formula that appears in the Gemara, with minor variations, based on variant readings and divergent halakhic rulings. The formula of the benediction according to the Ashkenazic custom is: Blessed are You, Lord our God, King of the universe, Who sanctified us through His mitzvot, and commanded us concerning the forbidden relations, and has prohibited to us those women who are betrothed, and has permitted to us those women who are married to us by the rite of the wedding canopy and betrothal. The added phrase: Married to us, is an emendation by Rabbeinu Tam. According to the Sephardic custom, the benediction concludes: By the rite of the wedding canopy with betrothal (*Beit Yosef*, based on *Sefer HaIttur*). The Yemenite custom, based on the Rambam, is: Who has sanctified us through His mitzvot, and distanced us from the forbidden relations, and prohibited to us those women who are betrothed, and permitted to us those women who are married by the rite of the wedding canopy and betrothal (see *Maggid Mishne*; Rambam *Sefer Nashim, Hilkhot Ishut* 3:24; *Shulḥan Arukh, Even HaEzer* 34:1).

The conclusion of the benediction of the grooms – חֲתִימַת בִּרְכַּת חֲתָנִים: The prevalent custom is to end the betrothal benediction with a concluding blessing, in accordance with the statement of Rav Aḥa. According to both the Ashkenazic and the Sephardic customs, based on the text in the Gemara and the prayer book of Rav Amram Gaon and the Maḥzor Vitri, the benediction concludes: Blessed are You, Lord, Who sanctifies Israel by means of the wedding canopy and betrothal. Alternatively, it concludes as follows: With betrothal, according to the Sephardic custom. The Yemenite custom concludes with: Who sanctifies Israel (Rav Hai Gaon; Rif; Rambam; Rambam *Sefer Nashim, Hilkhot Ishut* 3:24; *Shulḥan Arukh, Even HaEzer* 34:1).

NOTES

The benediction of the betrothal – בִּרְכַּת הָאֵרוּסִין: The early commentaries (Ramban) note that this blessing is anomalous, as there are no blessings on prohibitions, and the formula of this blessing refers to the prohibitions governing sexual relations between a man and woman. They explain that the blessing is not recited over observance of those prohibitions. Rather, it is a blessing of thanksgiving to God for sanctifying the Jewish people by commanding them to fulfill mitzvot. Analysis of Rashi's commentary reveals that he alluded to this as well. In the *Roke'aḥ*, it is explained that because these prohibitions are unique to the Jewish people, there is room to recite a blessing over them. The Meiri writes that the blessing is recited not over the prohibitions. Rather, it is recited over the mitzva of betrothal.

And commanded us concerning the forbidden relations – וְצִוָּנוּ עַל הָעֲרָיוֹת: The use of the term: And commanded us, is difficult in this context, as it does not indicate what the command is. The Rambam has a variant reading: And distanced us from the forbidden relatives (see *Maggid Mishne*). The term: Commanded us, is more easily understood in light of the explanation of the Ramban cited above, that this is not a blessing over performance of a mitzva, but a blessing of thanksgiving. Others write that in this context the term: Forbidden relatives, is referring not only to illicit sexual intercourse, but to sexual relations in the broader sense. Therefore, the blessing means: Who commanded us, both with regard to the prohibition against relations with those who are forbidden and with regard to the positive mitzva to betroth those who are permitted (*Ḥatam Sofer*).

And prohibited to us those women who are betrothed – וְאָסַר לָנוּ אֶת הָאֲרוּסוֹת: Rashi explains that although the prohibition against engaging in relations with one's betrothed is by rabbinic law, the expression: Who commanded us, is appropriate even for rabbinic mitzvot, e.g., kindling Hanukkah lights. Others write that since the Gemara proves that the obligation to enter into the wedding canopy is by Torah law, then the bride is forbidden to him by Torah law (see Rosh). With regard to the reason for the blessing, the Ramban explains that since it was customary for the betrothal to take place up to a year before the wedding, it was necessary to remind the groom that the betrothed woman was forbidden to him until marriage.

And permitted to us those women who are married – וְהִתִּיר לָנוּ אֶת הַנְּשׂוּאוֹת: The prevalent custom is in accordance with the opinion of Rabbeinu Tam, who says that although the intention is clear, the formula of a blessing must nevertheless be unambiguous. Therefore, he emended the blessing and added: Those women who are married to us. In the opinion of Rav Hai Gaon, the phrase: And permitted to us those who are married, is omitted. Rather, the formula is: And permitted them to us, referring to the aforementioned betrothed women. This was the custom in the Babylonian academies. The early commentaries approve of that formula. However, that custom never became prevalent elsewhere.

Who sanctifies Israel by means of the wedding canopy and betrothal – מְקַדֵּשׁ יִשְׂרָאֵל עַל יְדֵי חוּפָּה וְקִדּוּשִׁין: According to Rav Hai Gaon, the blessing concludes merely: Who sanctifies Israel, as it is inappropriate to attribute the sanctity of Israel to the wedding canopy and betrothal. However, according to the understanding that this is a blessing of thanksgiving, it can be explained as thanksgiving for this additional element of sanctity, similar to the Sages' interpretation of the verse "You shall be sacred" (Leviticus 19:2) as: You shall be separate.

תָּנוּ רַבָּנַן: מְבָרְכִין בִּרְכַּת חֲתָנִים בַּעֲשָׂרָה כׇּל שִׁבְעָה. אָמַר רַב יְהוּדָה: וְהוּא שֶׁבָּאוּ פָּנִים חֲדָשׁוֹת.

§ **The Sages taught: One recites the benediction of the grooms in** a quorum of **ten** men **all seven** days of the wedding celebration. **Rav Yehuda said: And that is** the case only **when new faces**[HN] who did not previously participate in the festivities **came** to join the celebration.

מַאי מְבָרֵךְ? אָמַר רַב יְהוּדָה: בָּרוּךְ אַתָּה ה׳ אֱלֹהֵינוּ מֶלֶךְ הָעוֹלָם

The Gemara asks: **What** blessings does one recite?[N] **Rav Yehuda said** that these are the seven blessings: **Blessed are You, Lord our God, King of the universe,**

NOTES

New faces – פָּנִים חֲדָשׁוֹת: Some learn from the fact that this term is in the plural that at least two new people are required. In the *Shita Mekubbetzet*, that conclusion is rejected, as the plural refers to all the guests who will participate in the festivities throughout the seven days.

The order of the wedding blessings – סֵדֶר בִּרְכוֹת נִשּׂוּאִין: Rashi explains the order of the wedding blessings as follows: The first was instituted in deference to the congregation attending the wedding, followed by a blessing over the creation of man and his union with his spouse in the Garden of Eden. Before proceeding to blessing the couple upon their entry beneath the wedding canopy, there is a blessing over the solace of Jerusalem, to fulfill the verse "If I set not Jerusalem above my greatest joy" (Psalms 137:6). That is followed by the blessing wishing the couple happiness together for the rest of their lives, followed by the final blessing wishing them joy at the wedding. That is the approach adopted by most early commentaries (see Ritva).

The Maharsha explains the order as follows: First comes God, then the creation of man, followed by the creation of woman, and subsequently God's providence in the world, including celebration of the wedding.

HALAKHA

New faces – פָּנִים חֲדָשׁוֹת: For the seven days of the celebration following the wedding, the wedding benedictions are recited at each meal where new faces are present. There are various opinions as to who qualifies as a new face. Some maintain that people who did not hear the wedding benedictions at the wedding are considered new faces (Rambam). Others maintain that even people who attended the wedding may be considered new faces if they did not yet participate in one of the wedding meals. The *Shulḥan Arukh* notes that this is the prevalent custom. The Rema writes that even if the new guests do not actually partake of the meal that they attend, the wedding benedictions may be recited on that night and the following day. According to *Tosafot*, only new guests whose presence enhances the festive nature of the occasion qualify as new faces. Some maintain that Shabbat and Festivals are also considered new faces, so that the benedictions are recited on Friday and Festival nights and the following day. The Rema adds that the Ashkenazic custom is to recite the benediction even at the third Shabbat meal (Rambam *Sefer Ahava, Hilkhot Berakhot* 2:10; *Shulḥan Arukh, Even HaEzer* 62:7–8).

שֶׁהַכֹּל בָּרָא לִכְבוֹדוֹ,

Who has created all for His glory.

וְ״יוֹצֵר הָאָדָם״,

And the second blessing is: Blessed are You… **Creator of mankind.**

וַ״אֲשֶׁר יָצַר אֶת הָאָדָם בְּצַלְמוֹ בְּצֶלֶם דְּמוּת תַּבְנִיתוֹ וְהִתְקִין לוֹ מִמֶּנּוּ בִּנְיַן עֲדֵי עַד. בָּרוּךְ אַתָּה ה׳ יוֹצֵר הָאָדָם״,

And the third blessing is: Blessed are You… **Who made humanity**[N] **in His image, in the image of the likeness of His form, and out of His very self formed a building** (see Genesis 2:22) **for eternity. Blessed are You, Lord, Creator of mankind.**

״שׂוֹשׂ תָּשִׂישׂ וְתָגֵל הָעֲקָרָה בְּקִבּוּץ בָּנֶיהָ לְתוֹכָהּ בְּשִׂמְחָה. בָּרוּךְ אַתָּה ה׳ מְשַׂמֵּחַ צִיּוֹן בְּבָנֶיהָ״,

The fourth blessing is: **May the barren** city of Jerusalem **greatly rejoice and delight**[N] **with the ingathering of her children within her in joy. Blessed are You, Lord, Who gladdens Zion through her children.**

״שַׂמֵּחַ תְּשַׂמַּח רֵעִים הָאֲהוּבִים כְּשַׂמֵּחֲךָ יְצִירְךָ בְּגַן עֵדֶן מִקֶּדֶם. בָּרוּךְ אַתָּה ה׳ מְשַׂמֵּחַ חָתָן וְכַלָּה״,

The fifth blessing is: **Bring great joy to these loving friends, as You gave joy to Your creations**[N] **in Eden in ancient times. Blessed are You, Lord, Who brings joy to the groom and bride.**

״בָּרוּךְ אַתָּה ה׳ אֱלֹהֵינוּ מֶלֶךְ הָעוֹלָם אֲשֶׁר בָּרָא שָׂשׂוֹן וְשִׂמְחָה חָתָן וְכַלָּה גִּילָה רִינָּה דִּיצָה חֶדְוָה אַהֲבָה וְאַחֲוָה וְשָׁלוֹם וְרֵיעוּת, מְהֵרָה ה׳ אֱלֹהֵינוּ יִשָּׁמַע בְּעָרֵי יְהוּדָה וּבְחוּצוֹת יְרוּשָׁלַיִם קוֹל שָׂשׂוֹן וְקוֹל שִׂמְחָה קוֹל חָתָן וְקוֹל כַּלָּה קוֹל מִצְהֲלוֹת חֲתָנִים מֵחוּפָּתָם וּנְעָרִים מִמִּשְׁתֵּה נְגִינָתָם. בָּרוּךְ אַתָּה ה׳ מְשַׂמֵּחַ חָתָן עִם הַכַּלָּה״.

The sixth blessing is: **Blessed are You, Lord our God, King of the universe, Who has created joy and gladness, groom and bride, delight, exultation, happiness, jubilation, love and brotherhood, and peace and friendship. Soon, Lord our God, may there be heard in the cities of Judea and in the streets of Jerusalem the sound of joy and the sound of gladness, the sound of the groom and the sound of the bride, the joyous sound of grooms from their wedding canopy and of young people from their feast of song** (see Jeremiah 33:11). **Blessed are You, Lord, Who makes the groom rejoice with the bride.** Together with the blessing over the wine, these are the seven wedding blessings.

NOTES

Who made humanity – אֲשֶׁר יָצַר אֶת הָאָדָם: Many commentaries are of the opinion that the first blessing: Creator of mankind, refers to the creation of Adam, and the second refers to the creation of Eve. Despite the fact that the formula of the second blessing also employs the term *adam*, in the Bible that term refers to women as well (see Numbers 31:35 and Isaiah 44:13).

May the barren city of Jerusalem greatly rejoice and delight – שׂוֹשׂ תָּשִׂישׂ וְתָגֵל הָעֲקָרָה: In addition to the primary reason for this blessing, i.e., to fulfill the verse "If I set not Jerusalem above my greatest joy" (Psalms 137:6), the Meiri cites an additional reason: In many places in the Bible, the relationship between God and the Jewish people is likened to the relationship between a man and woman, or a bride and groom, e.g., "And as the bridegroom rejoices over the bride, so shall your God rejoice over you" (Isaiah 62:5). Therefore, while reciting blessings over the marriage of a man and a woman, it is appropriate to mention the relationship of God and His people.

As You gave joy to Your creations – כְּשַׂמֵּחֲךָ יְצִירְךָ: In the midrash there is a description of how God prepared the wedding celebration for Adam and Eve, and the angels were the wedding guests (see *Eiruvin* 18a).

לוי איקלע לבי רבי בהלוליה דרבי שמעון בריה, בריך חמש. רב אסי איקלע לבי רב אשי בהלוליה דמר בריה, בריך שית.

The Gemara relates: **Levi happened** to come **to the house of** Rabbi Yehuda HaNasi **during the wedding celebration of** Rabbi **Shimon,**[P] **his son, and recited five** of these **blessings. Rav Asi happened** to come **to the house of Rav Ashi during the wedding celebration of Mar, his son, and recited six**[N] of these **blessings.**[H]

לימא בהא קמיפלגי, דמר סבר חדא יצירה הואי, ומר סבר: שתי יצירות הואי?

The Gemara suggests: **Let us say that they disagree about this:** One **Sage holds: It was one** act of **creation** with which man was created. **And** one **Sage holds: It was two** acts of **creation** with which man was created.[N] The first opinion, that there was one act of creation, is based on the concept that man was created with two sides, one male and one female. There was no additional act of creation. Man and woman were subsequently separated into two independent beings. Therefore, there is no need for the two blessings: Who created mankind, and: Who created mankind in His image. The second opinion is that there were in fact two separate acts of creation. Therefore, it is appropriate to recite two blessings with regard to the creation of mankind.

לא, דכולי עלמא חדא יצירה הואי, מר סבר: בתר מחשבה אזלינן, ומר סבר: בתר מעשה אזלינן. כי הא דרב יהודה רמי: כתיב ״ויברא אלהים את האדם בצלמו״, וכתיב ״זכר ונקבה בראם״, הא כיצד? בתחלה עלה במחשבה לבראות שנים, ולבסוף נברא אחד.

The Gemara rejects that suggestion: **No, everyone agrees that** it was only **one** act of **creation.** However, one **Sage holds:** It is **according to** the initial **thought** that **we proceed. And** one **Sage holds:** It is **according to the action** that **we proceed.** God's initial thought was to create man and woman as separate entities. Ultimately, they were created as one entity. That explanation is **like the following. Rav Yehuda raises a contradiction.** In one verse **it is written: "And God created man in His own image"** (Genesis 1:27), indicating one act of creation, **and** in another verse **it is written: "Male and female He created them"** (Genesis 5:2), indicating two acts. **How** can **this** apparent contradiction be resolved? **Initially, the thought entered** God's mind **to create two, but ultimately only one was** actually **created.**[N]

רב אשי איקלע לבי רב כהנא, יומא קמא בריך כולהו, מכאן ואילך, אי איכא פנים חדשות – בריך כולהו, ואי לא – אפושי שמחה בעלמא הוא, מברך ״שהשמחה במעונו״ ו״אשר ברא״.

The Gemara relates: **Rav Ashi happened** to come **to the house of Rav Kahana** to attend a wedding. **The first day he recited all** seven **blessings.**[H] **From that point forward, if there were new faces** present,[H] **he recited all the blessings, and if not,**[H] he would say: **It is merely an extension of the** original **celebration, and he would recite the blessing: In Whose dwelling is joy,** in the *zimmun* prior to Grace after Meals, **and** the sixth blessing after Grace after Meals: **Who has created.**

PERSONALITIES

Rabbi Shimon – רבי שמעון: Rabbi Shimon was the youngest son of Rabbi Yehuda HaNasi and his foremost student. He was a member of the group of prominent students of Rabbi Yehuda HaNasi and discussed halakhic issues with them. He was especially close to Rabbi Ḥiyya, who was also his close friend and his partner in the silk business. In many sources, it is evident that Rabbi Shimon was very scrupulous with regard to his honor, which he considered to be related to the honor of the office of the *Nasi*. He was especially careful to ensure that nothing he did or said would reflect poorly on the reverence due his prominent father.

At least one of his statements is cited in the Mishna, although he a member of the transitional generation between *tanna'im* and *amora'im*. His statements are often introduced with the term: It was stated, characteristic of statements of *amora'im*.

Rabbi Yehuda HaNasi considered Rabbi Shimon a Torah luminary and before his death appointed him *Ḥakham*, the third-highest position in the Sanhedrin after the *Nasi* and the deputy *Nasi*. He appointed Rabbi Shimon's older brother, Rabban Gamliel, to succeed him as *Nasi*.

NOTES

Recited six blessings – בריך שית: There is a dispute with regard to which blessing is the one omitted by Levi and Rav Asi. According to Rashi, it is the second blessing. According to the Ri Migash, it is the third blessing.

The Gemara is referring to either five or six blessings that are recited. However, the custom of referring to the wedding blessings as the seven blessings is an early one. The practice, originating with the *ge'onim*, is to recite the blessing over wine prior to the six wedding blessings. In other places, a blessing was recited over a myrtle branch (*Seder Rav Amram Gaon*), or even over wine and incense. Rabbeinu Tam adopted a different approach. Because today betrothal and marriage are held consecutively, the blessing of betrothal that precedes the six wedding blessings brings the total to seven.

One act of creation or two acts of creation – יצירה אחת או שתים: Most commentaries understand this question like the question raised in tractate *Eiruvin*: Were man and woman created separately, or was Adam created with two faces and subsequently separated into man and woman? Rabbeinu Ḥananel, however, explains it differently. The opinion that says that there were two separate creations holds that man and woman were created separately. However, the first woman fled and a second woman was created from man.

Initially, the thought entered God's mind to create two, but ultimately only one was actually created – בתחלה עלה במחשבה לבראות שנים, ולבסוף נברא אחד: The Maharsha explains that initially God thought to create man and woman separately, as He had all the other species. However, anticipating potential discord, He ultimately created them together and then separated them, to enhance the potential of peaceful coexistence.

HALAKHA

Recited six blessings – בריך שית: The six blessings recited at the wedding are (1) Blessed…Who has created all for His glory, (2) Blessed…Creator of man, (3) Blessed…Who created man…Creator of man, (4) May the barren city greatly rejoice…Blessed…Who gladdens Zion through her children, (5) Bring great joy to these loving friends…Blessed…Who makes groom and bride rejoice, (6) Blessed…Who has created…Blessed…Who makes the groom rejoice with the bride (Rambam *Sefer Ahava, Hilkhot Berakhot* 2:11, *Sefer Nashim, Hilkhot Ishut* 10:3; *Shulḥan Arukh, Even HaEzer* 62:7).

The first day he recited all seven blessings – יומא קמא בריך כולהו: Most authorities rule that all seven blessings, the six mentioned in the Gemara and the benediction over wine, are recited at the first wedding meal, even if there are no new faces who did not attend the wedding ceremony partaking of the meal (Rosh; *Tur*), and even in the marriage of a widower to a widow. According to the Rif, the Rambam, and *Tosafot*, when there are no new guests the six blessings are not recited, even at the first meal. However, if there are new faces, one recites the blessings at the conclusion of all meals throughout the day (see *Beit Shmuel*; *Arukh HaShulḥan*; Rambam *Sefer Ahava, Hilkhot Berakhot* 2:9–10; *Tur, Even HaEzer* 62, *Shulḥan Arukh, Even HaEzer* 62:1).

From this point forward if there were new faces present – מכאן ואילך, אי איכא פנים חדשות: The seven blessings are recited at each of the meals during the seven days of the wedding feast, when new faces are in attendance (Rambam *Sefer Ahava, Hilkhot Berakhot* 2:9–10; *Shulḥan Arukh, Even HaEzer* 62:7).

And if not – ואי לא: When there are no new faces at the meal during the seven days of the wedding feast, only the final marriage blessing: Who has created joy and gladness, is recited. The Rema writes that the prevalent custom is in accordance with those who maintain that this blessing is recited only when there are guests in attendance due to the wedding (Ramban; Ran). However, if they are dining with their family, even that blessing is not recited (Rambam *Sefer Ahava, Hilkhot Berakhot* 2:9–10; *Shulḥan Arukh, Even HaEzer* 62:7).

מִשִּׁבְעָה וְעַד שְׁלֹשִׁים, בֵּין אֲמַר לְהוּ מֵחֲמַת הִלּוּלָא וּבֵין לָא אֲמַר לְהוּ מֵחֲמַת הִלּוּלָא – מְבָרֵךְ ״שֶׁהַשִּׂמְחָה בִּמְעוֹנוֹ״. מִכָּאן וְאֵילָךְ, אִי אֲמַר לְהוּ מֵחֲמַת הִלּוּלָא – מְבָרֵךְ ״שֶׁהַשִּׂמְחָה בִּמְעוֹנוֹ״, וְאִי לָא – לָא.

§ Apropos the wedding blessings, the Gemara continues: **From seven** days after the wedding **until** the **thirtieth** day, **whether** the groom **said** to the guests that he is inviting them **due to the wedding celebration or whether he did not say to them** that he is inviting them **due to the wedding celebration, he recites the blessing: In Whose dwelling is joy.**[H] **From this** point, thirty days after the wedding, **forward, if he said to them** that he is inviting them **due to the wedding celebration** [*hillula*],[L] **he recites the blessing: In Whose dwelling is joy, and if not, he doesn't.**

וְכִי אֲמַר לְהוּ מֵחֲמַת הִלּוּלָא עַד אֵימַת? אֲמַר רַב פַּפִּי מִשְּׁמֵיהּ דְּרָבָא: עַד תְּרֵיסַר יַרְחֵי שַׁתָּא. וּמֵעִיקָּרָא מֵאֵימַת? אֲמַר רַב פַּפָּא: מִכִּי רָמוּ שַׂעֲרֵי בְּאָסִינְתָּא. אִינִי? וְהָא רַב פַּפָּא אִיעֲסַק לְאַבָּא מָר בְּרֵיהּ, וּבְרֵיךְ מִשְּׁעַת אֵירוּסִין! שָׁאנֵי רַב פַּפָּא דַּהֲוָה טְרִיחַ לֵיהּ.

The Gemara asks: **And when** the groom **said to them** that he is inviting them **due to the wedding celebration, until when** is this blessing recited? **Rav Pappi said in the name of Rava: Until twelve months of the year**[N] have passed since the wedding. Since his legal status remains that of a groom, the blessing: In Whose dwelling is joy, may be recited. The Gemara asks: **And initially,** prior to the wedding, **from when** is that blessing recited? **Rav Pappa**[P] **said: From when they cast barley into the mortar**[NB] to prepare beer for the wedding. The Gemara asks: **Is that so? But didn't Rav Pappa, involve** himself in preparations **for the** wedding of **his son, Abba Mar, and** begin **reciting the blessing from the time of betrothal? Rav Pappa is different, because** the wedding preparations had already been **prepared for him,** and it was merely a matter of waiting for the designated time to arrive. Therefore, the wedding celebration began for him from the time of betrothal.

רָבִינָא אִיעֲסַק לֵיהּ לִבְרֵיהּ בֵּי רַב חֲבִיבָא, וּבְרֵיךְ מִשְּׁעַת אֵירוּסִין. אֲמַר: קִים לִי בְּגַוַּייהוּ דְּלָא הָדְרִי בְּהוּ. לָא אִסְתַּיַּיע מִילְּתָא, וְהָדְרִי בְּהוּ. רַב תַּחְלִיפָא בַּר מַעַרְבָא אִיקְּלַע לְבָבֶל, בְּרֵיךְ שִׁית אֲרִיכָתָא. וְלֵית הִלְכְתָא כְּוָותֵיהּ.

The Gemara relates: **Ravina arranged for his son** to marry a woman from **the house of Rav Ḥaviva and recited the blessing from the time of betrothal. He said: I am certain with regard to them, that they will not retract** their commitment and terminate the betrothal, and the wedding will take place on time. Nevertheless, **the matter was not to be, and** ultimately **they retracted** their commitment, and the wedding was canceled. The Gemara relates: **Rav Taḥlifa, from the West,** i.e., Eretz Yisrael, **happened** to come **to Babylonia,** and he elaborated on the themes of the wedding blessings **and recited six long blessings.**[N] The Gemara concludes: **And the *halakha* is not in accordance with his** opinion. Rather, one must adhere to the formula coined by the Sages.

רַב חֲבִיבָא אִיקְּלַע לְבֵי מְהוּלָא, בְּרֵיךְ ״שֶׁהַשִּׂמְחָה בִּמְעוֹנוֹ״, וְלֵית הִלְכְתָא כְּוָותֵיהּ, מִשּׁוּם דִּטְרִידִי, דְּאִית לֵיהּ צַעֲרָא לְיָנוֹקָא.

It is further related: **Rav Ḥaviva happened** to come **to the house** where **a circumcision** was taking place. **He recited the blessing: In Whose dwelling is joy.**[N] The Gemara concludes: **And the *halakha* is not in accordance with his** opinion. **Since the** parents of the baby **are anxious, as the baby is** experiencing **pain,** it is not appropriate to recite the blessing under those circumstances.

HALAKHA

In Whose dwelling is joy – שֶׁהַשִּׂמְחָה בִּמְעוֹנוֹ: If one dines in the wedding house, he recites in the *zimmun* prior to the Grace after Meals: In Whose dwelling there is joy. According to Rav Pappa, this applies once the preparations for the wedding feast have begun. According to Rav Pappi, this applies within the thirty days after the wedding or at a meal celebrating the marriage throughout the first year of the marriage. If there is a quorum of ten men present, one recites: Our God, in Whose dwelling there is joy. That is the *halakha* as cited in the Gemara. In later times, in the wake of the numerous tragedies that befell the Jewish people, the prevalent custom is to recite: In Whose dwelling there is joy, only during the seven days of the wedding feast. In the case of a widower who married a widow, it is recited only during the first three days of marriage (Rambam *Sefer Ahava, Hilkhot Berakhot* 5:5; *Shulḥan Arukh, Even HaEzer* 62:13, citing *Tur*).

LANGUAGE

Wedding celebration [*hillula*] – הִלּוּלָא: From the Hebrew *hallel*, meaning praise. The Aramaic form, *hillula*, is used specifically for a wedding or a wedding celebration.

NOTES

Until twelve months of the year – עַד תְּרֵיסַר יַרְחֵי שַׁתָּא: The Ritva finds an allusion in the Torah to the fact that the marriage celebration lasts a year: "When a man takes a new wife…he shall be free for his house one year, and shall cheer his wife whom he has taken" (Deuteronomy 24:5).

From when they cast barley into the mortar – מִכִּי רָמוּ שַׂעֲרֵי בְּאָסִינְתָּא: Another explanation is that they would crush the shell of the barley to prepare from it sweet toasted grain, which they would eat at the wedding meal (*Shita Mekubbetzet*).

Recited six long blessings – בְּרֵיךְ שִׁית אֲרִיכָתָא: Rav Hai Gaon explains that the problem was not that Rav Taḥlifa emended or added to the formula of the blessing. Rather, he deviated from the formula coined by the Sages in blessings. He changed short blessings, which do not both begin and conclude with: Blessed, into long blessings, which both begin and conclude with: Blessed.

In Whose dwelling is joy – שֶׁהַשִּׂמְחָה בִּמְעוֹנוֹ: Rav Ḥaviva's reasoning for reciting this blessing was that circumcision is a joyous occasion for the parents of the baby. There are several *halakhot* that reflect that celebratory aspect, e.g., the *taḥanun* prayer is not recited that day. Some proposed reciting this formula at the redemption of the firstborn, where the baby does not experience pain. That was rejected, as it is only with regard to circumcision that there is an allusion in the Bible to special rejoicing (see *Megilla* 16b).

PERSONALITIES

Rav Pappa – רַב פַּפָּא: Rav Pappa was a fifth-generation Babylonian *amora*. He was a student of both Abaye and Rava in Pumbedita. Rav Pappa established an academy in Neresh, where he was joined by his close friend Rav Huna, son of Rav Yehoshua, who delivered the principal lecture. After Rava's death, many of his students came to study with Rav Pappa, and more than two hundred students attended his lectures.

Rav Pappa's father was a wealthy merchant who supported him throughout his many years of study. Rav Pappa became a wealthy businessman in his own right, successful as a brewer of date beer as well as in his other business ventures. The Talmud records that he engaged in trade with both Jews and gentiles and had a reputation for fairness and generosity in his business dealings. Rav Huna, son of Rav Yehoshua, was his partner in many of those and also became wealthy.

Rav Pappa was blessed with ten sons, all of whom were Torah scholars. Traditionally, the names of the ten sons of Rav Pappa are enumerated as part of the formula recited upon completion of the study of a tractate. While the source of this tradition is unclear and the identities of the sons are uncertain, the Rema suggests that it commemorates the celebrations of Rav Pappa and his sons upon completion of a tractate.

BACKGROUND

From when they cast barley into the mortar [*asinta*] – מִכִּי רָמוּ שַׂעֲרֵי בְּאָסִינְתָּא: *Asinta* is a synonym, or perhaps a diminutive, for *asita*, meaning mortar, which is a bowl used in crushing. Rashi cites two possible explanations that appear in geonic literature. One explanation is that the reference is to placing barley seeds into a vessel to soak them in preparation for brewing beer. There is a variant reading: Once the barley is soaked. *Tosafot* on *Avoda Zara* 8b question that explanation because in the talmudic period, beer was brewed from dates, not barley. Furthermore, *Tosafot* note that mortars are not used for soaking.

The second explanation in Rashi, which is also cited in the *Arukh*, is that there was a custom to sow barley seeds before the wedding and to bring the barley sprouts before the bride and groom as an auspicious sign for fertility. The *Arukh* cites an additional explanation: The reference is to crushing barley in the mortar to prepare sweet toasted grain.

אָמַר רַב נַחְמָן אָמַר רַב: חֲתָנִים מִן הַמִּנְיָן, וְאֵין אֲבֵלִים מִן הַמִּנְיָן. מֵיתִיבֵי: חֲתָנִים וַאֲבֵלִים מִן הַמִּנְיָן! מַתְנִיתָא קָא רָמֵית עֲלֵיהּ דְּרַב – רַב תַּנָּא הוּא, וּפָלֵיג. אִיתְּמַר, אָמַר רַבִּי יִצְחָק אָמַר רַבִּי יוֹחָנָן: חֲתָנִים מִן הַמִּנְיָן, וְאֵין אֲבֵלִים מִן הַמִּנְיָן. מֵיתִיבֵי: חֲתָנִים וַאֲבֵלִים מִן הַמִּנְיָן!

§ **Rav Naḥman said** that **Rav said:** With regard to the quorum of ten required to recite the wedding blessings, **grooms are included in the tally.**[NH] **And mourners are not included in the tally** for the blessing of the mourners. The Gemara **raises an objection** from a *baraita*: **Grooms and mourners are included in the tally.** The Gemara responds: **Are you raising a contradiction from a *baraita* against** the opinion of **Rav? Rav** himself had ***tanna*** status **and** therefore, unlike later *amora'im*, could **disagree**[N] with opinions of *tanna'im*. **It was stated: Rabbi Yitzḥak said** that **Rabbi Yoḥanan said: Grooms are included in the tally, but mourners are not included in the tally. The Gemara raises an objection** from the *baraita* cited above: **Grooms and mourners are included in the tally.**

NOTES

Grooms are included in the tally – חֲתָנִים מִן הַמִּנְיָן: The simple reason for this *halakha* is that at the wedding the groom participates in the celebration, and therefore he is included in the tally, as it is written: "And shall cheer his wife whom he has taken" (Deuteronomy 24:5). A mourner does not participate in the comforting of mourners, and therefore he is not included in the tally (*Talmidei Rabbeinu Yona*). An alternative explanation is that a mourner, who is in a state of despondency and sadness, cannot be included in the quorum of ten, where the Divine Presence rests, as the Divine Presence does not rest in an atmosphere of sadness (*Penei Yehoshua*).

Rav himself had *tanna* status and could disagree – רַב תַּנָּא הוּא וּפָלֵיג: Rav Hai Gaon writes that in at least three places in the Talmud (see, e.g., *Ketubot* 81a), a *tanna* by the name of Rav Abba is mentioned and the reference is to Rav, indicating that Rav was one of the last *tanna'im* cited in *baraitot*.

HALAKHA

Grooms are included in the tally – חֲתָנִים מִן הַמִּנְיָן: The benediction of the grooms is recited only in the presence of a quorum of ten adult males, and the groom himself is included in the tally (Rambam *Sefer Nashim, Hilkhot Ishut* 10:5; *Shulḥan Arukh, Even HaEzer* 62:4).

Perek **I**
Daf **8** Amud **b**

כִּי תַּנְיָא הַהִיא – בְּבִרְכַּת הַמָּזוֹן, כִּי קָאָמַר רַבִּי יוֹחָנָן – בְּשׁוּרָה.

The Gemara answers: **When that *baraita* is taught,** it is **with regard to** combining with others to form a quorum of three to recite **Grace after Meals,**[H] as a mourner is obligated to recite Grace after Meals. However, **when Rabbi Yoḥanan says** that mourners are not included in the tally, it is **with regard to** the quorum of ten men required to form **a line**[HN] to comfort the mourners following the burial.

וְאֶלָּא הָא דְּאָמַר רַבִּי יִצְחָק אָמַר רַבִּי יוֹחָנָן: מְבָרְכִים בִּרְכַּת חֲתָנִים בַּעֲשָׂרָה – וַחֲתָנִים מִן הַמִּנְיָן, וּבִרְכַּת אֲבֵלִים בַּעֲשָׂרָה – וְאֵין אֲבֵלִים מִן הַמִּנְיָן. בְּרָכָה בְּשׁוּרָה מִי אִיכָּא? אֶלָּא, כִּי קָאָמַר רַבִּי יוֹחָנָן – בִּרְחָבָה.

And the Gemara raises an objection: **However, that which Rabbi Yitzḥak said** that **Rabbi Yoḥanan said: One recites the blessing of the grooms in** a quorum **of ten, and the grooms are included in the tally, and one recites the blessing of the mourners in** a quorum **of ten, and the mourners are not included in the tally. Is there a blessing** recited **in the line** formed to comfort the mourners? Clearly, this statement of Rabbi Yoḥanan cannot be explained as referring to the line. **Rather, when Rabbi Yoḥanan said** that mourners are not included in the tally, it was **with regard to** the blessing recited **in the square**[N] adjacent to the cemetery, where the meal of comfort takes place and various blessings are recited to comfort the mourners. Mourners are not included in the requisite quorum of ten.

וְאֶלָּא הָא דְּאָמַר רַבִּי יִצְחָק אָמַר רַבִּי יוֹחָנָן: מְבָרְכִין בִּרְכַּת חֲתָנִים בַּעֲשָׂרָה כׇּל שִׁבְעָה – וַחֲתָנִים מִן הַמִּנְיָן, וּבִרְכַּת אֲבֵלִים בַּעֲשָׂרָה כׇּל שִׁבְעָה – וְאֵין אֲבֵלִים מִן הַמִּנְיָן, בִּרְכַּת רְחָבָה כׇּל שִׁבְעָה מִי אִיכָּא? מַשְׁכַּחַתְּ לַהּ בְּפָנִים חֲדָשׁוֹת.

The Gemara asks: **However,** with regard to **that which Rabbi Yitzḥak said** that **Rabbi Yoḥanan said: One recites the blessing of the grooms in** a quorum of **ten all seven** days of celebration, **and the grooms are included in the tally; and one recites the blessing of the mourners all seven** days of mourning **in** a quorum of **ten, and the mourners are not included in the tally, is there a blessing** recited **in the square all seven** days? The meal of comfort and the associated blessings take place directly after the burial, not throughout the seven days of mourning. The Gemara answers: **You find** blessings recited throughout the seven-day mourning period **in** a case where **new faces** who did not attend the burial are present.[N] In that case, eulogies and words of comfort are repeated, and the blessing of the mourners is recited again.

HALAKHA

When that *baraita* is taught, it is with regard to Grace after Meals – כִּי תַּנְיָא הַהִיא בְּבִרְכַּת הַמָּזוֹן: A mourner is included in the tally of people required in order to recite the *zimmun*, the invitation to Grace After Meals, both for the quorum of three and for the quorum of ten, in accordance with the explanation of Rashi. Some authorities question whether this ruling applies even at the meal of comfort, the first meal eaten by the mourners upon returning from the cemetery after a funeral (see Mordekhai; *Shakh*; *Dagul MeRevava*; Rambam *Sefer Shofetim, Hilkhot Evel* 4:6; *Shulḥan Arukh, Yoreh De'a* 379:5).

With regard to a line – בְּשׁוּרָה: After the burial, only if there is a quorum of ten, not including the mourners, do those assembled stand in a line and offer the mourners words of consolation (Rambam *Sefer Shofetim, Hilkhot Evel* 13:1; *Tur, Yoreh De'a* 376).

NOTES

With regard to a line – בְּשׁוּרָה: Rav Hai Gaon writes that the custom was that after the burial, those comforting the mourners would stand in rows. In the first row, those with the closest ties to the mourner would stand; in the second row, those with ties that were not as close, etc. Each row would consist of at least ten of those providing comfort.

The blessing recited in the square – בִּרְחָבָה: During talmudic times, the practice was to perform the rite of standing and sitting in the square next to the cemetery. They would sit and then stand, and sit, and stand again. While they were sitting, and each time they sat, statements of comfort like those cited in the Gemara were said (*ge'onim*).

In a case where new faces are present – בְּפָנִים חֲדָשׁוֹת: During festive times, the joy is enhanced when people who did not yet participate in the celebration arrive, and it is therefore appropriate to recite the wedding blessing. So too, when new people come to comfort the mourner, the feelings of mourning are again aroused and statements of comfort are appropriate.

כִּי הָא דְּרַב חִיָּיא בַּר אַבָּא מַקְרֵי בְּנֵיהּ דְּרֵישׁ לָקִישׁ הֲוָה, וְאָמְרִי לָהּ מַתְנֵי בְּרֵיהּ דְּרֵישׁ לָקִישׁ הֲוָה. שְׁכֵיב לֵיהּ יָנוּקָא. יוֹמָא קַמָּא לָא אֲזַל לְגַבֵּיהּ, לְמָחָר דַּבְרֵיהּ לִיהוּדָה בַּר נַחְמָנִי מְתוּרְגְּמָנֵיהּ, אֲמַר לֵיהּ: קוּם אֵימָא מִלְּתָא כָּל קְבֵיל יָנוּקָא. פְּתַח וַאֲמַר: ״וַיַּרְא ה׳ וַיִּנְאָץ מִכַּעַס בָּנָיו וּבְנוֹתָיו״, דּוֹר שֶׁאָבוֹת מְנָאֲצִים לְהַקָּדוֹשׁ בָּרוּךְ הוּא – כּוֹעֵס עַל בְּנֵיהֶם וְעַל בְּנוֹתֵיהֶם, וּמֵתִים כְּשֶׁהֵם קְטַנִּים.

§ This is similar to that incident involving Rav Ḥiyya bar Abba, who was the Bible teacher of the sons of Reish Lakish, and some say that he was the Mishna teacher of the son of Reish Lakish. His child died. On the first day, Reish Lakish did not go to comfort him. The next day, he took Yehuda bar Naḥmani,[P] his disseminator, with him to comfort Rav Ḥiyya bar Abba. Reish Lakish said to his disseminator: Stand and say a matter of comfort with regard to the death of the child.[N] He began and said: "And the Lord saw it and He abhorred them,[N] due to the provocation of His sons and His daughters" (Deuteronomy 32:19). A generation in which the fathers abhor the Holy One, Blessed be He, He is angered at their sons and their daughters, and they die when they are small.

וְאִיכָּא דְּאָמְרִי: בָּחוּר הֲוָה, וְהָכִי קָאָמַר לֵיהּ: ״עַל כֵּן עַל בַּחוּרָיו לֹא יִשְׂמַח ה׳ וְאֶת יְתוֹמָיו וְאֶת אַלְמְנוֹתָיו לֹא יְרַחֵם כִּי כֻלּוֹ חָנֵף וּמֵרַע וְכָל פֶּה דֹּבֵר נְבָלָה בְּכָל זֹאת לֹא שָׁב אַפּוֹ וְעוֹד יָדוֹ נְטוּיָה״, מַאי ״וְעוֹד יָדוֹ נְטוּיָה״? אָמַר רַב חָנָן בַּר רַב: הַכֹּל יוֹדְעִין כַּלָּה לָמָּה נִכְנְסָה לַחוּפָּה, אֶלָּא כָּל הַמְנַבֵּל פִּיו וּמוֹצִיא דְּבַר נְבָלָה מִפִּיו, אֲפִילּוּ נֶחְתַּם לוֹ גְּזַר דִּינוֹ שֶׁל שִׁבְעִים שָׁנָה לְטוֹבָה – נֶהְפָּךְ עָלָיו לְרָעָה.

And there are those who say that the child who died was not a small child, but a youth, and this is what the disseminator said to him: "Therefore the Lord shall have no joy in their young men, nor shall He have compassion on their orphans and widows, for everyone is a flatterer and an evildoer, and every mouth speaks obscenity. For all this His anger is not turned away, and His hand is still outstretched" (Isaiah 9:16). What is the meaning of the phrase "And His hand is still outstretched"? Rav Ḥanan bar Rav said: Everyone knows why a bride enters the wedding canopy.[N] It is the step before consummation of the marriage. However, one should not speak about it unnecessarily, as anyone who profanes his mouth and issues a matter of profanity from his mouth, even if a positive decree of seventy years was sealed for him, nevertheless, it is transformed for him into an evil decree.

אֲתָא לְנַחוּמֵי, צַעוּרֵי קָמְצַעֵר לֵיהּ?! הָכִי קָאָמַר לֵיהּ: חָשֵׁיב אַתְּ לְאִתְפּוּסֵי אַדָּרָא.

The Gemara asks about this incident: He came at the behest of Reish Lakish to comfort Rav Ḥiyya bar Abba and instead he upset him by attributing the death of his son to his transgressions. The Gemara answers: It was not his intention to upset Rav Ḥiyya bar Abba and to attribute the death of his son to his actions. Rather, this is what he is saying to him: You are sufficiently significant to be seized, i.e., to die or suffer, for the sins of the generation, as it is specifically the righteous few who are punished for the transgressions of a sinful generation.

אֲמַר לֵיהּ: קוּם אֵימָא מִלְּתָא כְּנֶגֶד שִׁבְחוֹ שֶׁל הַקָּדוֹשׁ בָּרוּךְ הוּא. פְּתַח וַאֲמַר: הָאֵל הַגָּדוֹל בְּרוֹב גָּדְלוֹ, אַדִּיר וְחָזָק בְּרוֹב נוֹרָאוֹת, מְחַיֶּה מֵתִים בְּמַאֲמָרוֹ, עוֹשֶׂה גְּדוֹלוֹת עַד אֵין חֵקֶר וְנִפְלָאוֹת עַד אֵין מִסְפָּר, בָּרוּךְ אַתָּה ה׳ מְחַיֶּה הַמֵּתִים.

Reish Lakish said to his disseminator: Stand and say a statement with regard to the praiseworthiness of the Holy One, Blessed be He. He began and said: God, Who is great in the abundance of His greatness, mighty and strong in the abundance of His awesome deeds, Who revives the dead in fulfillment of His statement, Who does great deeds beyond comprehension, wondrous deeds without number. Blessed are You, Lord, Who revives the dead.

אֲמַר לֵיהּ: קוּם אֵימָא מִלְּתָא כְּנֶגֶד אֲבֵלִים. פְּתַח וַאֲמַר: אַחֵינוּ הַמְיוּגָּעִים הַמְדוּכָּאִין בָּאֵבֶל הַזֶּה, תְּנוּ לְבַבְכֶם לַחֲקוֹר אֶת זֹאת. זֹאת הִיא עוֹמֶדֶת לָעַד, נָתִיב הוּא מִשֵּׁשֶׁת יְמֵי בְרֵאשִׁית, רַבִּים שָׁתוּ רַבִּים יִשְׁתּוּ, כְּמִשְׁתֵּה רִאשׁוֹנִים כָּךְ מִשְׁתֵּה אַחֲרוֹנִים. אַחֵינוּ, בַּעַל נֶחָמוֹת יְנַחֵם אֶתְכֶם, בָּרוּךְ מְנַחֵם אֲבֵלִים.

Reish Lakish said to him: Stand and say a statement with regard to the mourners. He began and said: Our brothers, who are exhausted, who are overwhelmed by this mourning, set your heart to examine this: This is what stands forever. It is a path from the six days of Creation, i.e., death exists since Creation, and it is well known that this is the fate of man. Many have drunk from the poisonous cup of death, and many will drink. As was the consequence of the drink of the first who have drunk, so too will be the consequence of the drink of the last who will drink. Our brothers, may the Master of solace comfort you. Blessed are You, Lord, Who comforts the mourners.

NOTES

With regard to the death of the child – כָּל קְבֵיל יָנוּקָא: The Maharsha explains that this is mentioned here because ostensibly, young children are not subject to punishment at all, and those younger than twenty years old are not punished at the hand of Heaven. Therefore, when children suffer, one might have a grievance against God. Consequently, Reish Lakish asked his disseminator to explain that their deaths are attributable to the sins of others.

And the Lord saw it and He abhorred them – וַיַּרְא ה׳ וַיִּנְאָץ: Fundamentally, a minor is not considered an independent individual with personal responsibility who is subject to reward and punishment for his actions. Rather, minors are without sin. Their deaths are merely to torment their relatives.

Everyone knows why a bride enters the wedding canopy – הַכֹּל יוֹדְעִין כַּלָּה לָמָּה נִכְנְסָה לַחוּפָּה: The Maharsha writes that the punishment fits the crime in this case. Anyone who profanes his mouth with regard to the bride entering the wedding canopy will die young before entering the wedding canopy.

PERSONALITIES

Rabbi Yehuda bar Naḥmani – רַבִּי יְהוּדָה בַּר נַחְמָנִי: Rabbi Yehuda bar Naḥmani was also known as Rabbi Yudan, and his father was identified at times as bar Naḥman or bar Neḥemya. He was one of the great homiletic experts of his generation. In addition to his role as disseminator of the Torah of Reish Lakish, both he and his colleague Rabbi Levi would lecture on *aggada* before the congregation, as a prelude to the central lecture of Rabbi Yoḥanan. The Talmud and Midrash cite several homiletic interpretations attributed to him, and he often cited the statements of Reish Lakish.

אָמַר אַבָּיֵי: "רַבִּים שָׁתוּ" – לֵימָא: "רַבִּים יִשְׁתּוּ" – לָא לֵימָא. "מִשְׁתֵּה רִאשׁוֹנִים" – לֵימָא: "מִשְׁתֵּה אַחֲרוֹנִים" – לָא לֵימָא. דְּאָמַר רַבִּי שִׁמְעוֹן בֶּן לָקִישׁ, וְכֵן תָּנָא מִשְּׁמֵיהּ דְּרַבִּי יוֹסֵי: לְעוֹלָם אַל יִפְתַּח אָדָם פִּיו לַשָּׂטָן. אָמַר רַב יוֹסֵף: מַאי קְרָא – "כִּסְדוֹם הָיִינוּ לַעֲמוֹרָה דָּמִינוּ" מַאי אַהְדַר לֵיהּ – "שִׁמְעוּ דְבַר ה' קְצִינֵי סְדוֹם" וגו'.

Abaye said with regard to the statement concerning the mourners: **Let him say: Many have drunk;**[N] **let him not say: Many will drink. Let him say: The drink of the first; let him not say: The drink of the last.** This is as **Rabbi Shimon ben Lakish said, and likewise it was taught in the name of Rabbi Yosei: A person should never open his mouth to Satan**[N] and speculate about potential disasters. **Rav Yosef said: What is the verse** from which it is derived? **"We should have almost been as Sodom, we should have been like unto Gomorrah"** (Isaiah 1:9), after which, **what did** the prophet **reply to them? "Hear the word of the Lord, rulers of Sodom;** give ear unto the law of our God, people of Gomorrah" (Isaiah 1:10). Isaiah drew the analogy and immediately it was realized.

אָמַר לֵיהּ: קוּם אֵימָא מִלְּתָא כְּנֶגֶד מְנַחֲמֵי אֲבֵלִים. פְּתַח וַאֲמַר: אַחֵינוּ גּוֹמְלֵי חֲסָדִים בְּנֵי גּוֹמְלֵי חֲסָדִים, הַמַּחֲזִיקִים בִּבְרִיתוֹ שֶׁל אַבְרָהָם אָבִינוּ, (שֶׁנֶּאֱמַר "כִּי יְדַעְתִּיו לְמַעַן אֲשֶׁר יְצַוֶּה אֶת בָּנָיו" וגו'). אַחֵינוּ, בַּעַל הַגְּמוּל יְשַׁלֵּם לָכֶם גְּמוּלְכֶם, בָּרוּךְ אַתָּה מְשַׁלֵּם הַגְּמוּל.

Reish Lakish **said to** the disseminator: **Stand and say a statement with regard to those who comfort the mourners. He began and said: Our brothers, bestowers of loving-kindness, sons of bestowers of loving-kindness, who embrace the covenant of Abraham our Patriarch, as it is stated: "For I know him, that he will command his children…** to do righteousness and justice" (Genesis 18:19). **Our brothers, may the Master of reward pay you your just deserts. Blessed are You,** Lord, **Who pays the just deserts.**

אָמַר לֵיהּ: קוּם אֵימָא מִלְּתָא כְּנֶגֶד כָּל יִשְׂרָאֵל. פְּתַח וַאֲמַר: רִבּוֹן הָעוֹלָמִים, פְּדֵה וְהַצֵּל מַלֵּט הוֹשַׁע עַמְּךָ יִשְׂרָאֵל מִן הַדֶּבֶר, וּמִן הַחֶרֶב, וּמִן הַבִּיזָּה, וּמִן הַשִּׁדָּפוֹן, וּמִן הַיֵּרָקוֹן, וּמִכָּל מִינֵי פּוּרְעָנִיּוֹת הַמִּתְרַגְּשׁוֹת וּבָאוֹת לָעוֹלָם. טֶרֶם נִקְרָא וְאַתָּה תַּעֲנֶה, בָּרוּךְ אַתָּה עוֹצֵר הַמַּגֵּפָה.

Reish Lakish **said to** the disseminator: **Stand and say a statement with regard to the entire Jewish people. He began and said: Master of the worlds, redeem and save, rescue and deliver Your people, Israel, from the pestilence and from the sword, and from spoil, and from the blight, and from the mildew, and from all types of afflictions that suddenly erupt and come to the world. Before we call and You will respond. Blessed are You,** Lord, **Who halts the plague.** Apparently, several blessings are recited on the days following the burial.

אָמַר עוּלָּא, וְאָמְרִי לַהּ בְּמַתְנִיתָא תָּנָא: עֲשָׂרָה כּוֹסוֹת תִּקְּנוּ חֲכָמִים בְּבֵית הָאָבֵל; שְׁלֹשָׁה קוֹדֶם אֲכִילָה – כְּדֵי לִפְתּוֹחַ אֶת בְּנֵי מֵעָיו, שְׁלֹשָׁה בְּתוֹךְ אֲכִילָה – כְּדֵי לִשְׁרוֹת אֲכִילָה שֶׁבְּמֵעָיו, וְאַרְבָּעָה לְאַחַר אֲכִילָה – אֶחָד כְּנֶגֶד "הַזָּן", וְאֶחָד כְּנֶגֶד בִּרְכַּת הָאָרֶץ, וְאֶחָד כְּנֶגֶד "בּוֹנֵה יְרוּשָׁלַיִם", וְאֶחָד כְּנֶגֶד "הַטּוֹב וְהַמֵּטִיב".

§ In connection with comforting mourners, **Ulla said, and some say that it was taught in a** ***baraita*****: The Sages instituted ten cups of wine**[N] to be drunk **in the house of the mourner:**[H] **Three** cups **prior to the meal, in order to open his intestines,**[B] i.e., whet his appetite; **three during the meal, to soak the food in his intestines** in order to facilitate digestion; **and four** cups **after the meal,** each corresponding to a blessing in the Grace after Meals. **One corresponds to** the first blessing: **Who feeds all;**[N] **one corresponds to the** second blessing, the **blessing of the land; one corresponding to the third** blessing: **Who builds Jerusalem; and one corresponding to** the fourth blessing: **Who is good and does good.**

הוֹסִיפוּ עֲלֵיהֶם אַרְבָּעָה: אֶחָד כְּנֶגֶד חַזָּנֵי הָעִיר, וְאֶחָד כְּנֶגֶד פַּרְנָסֵי הָעִיר, וְאֶחָד כְּנֶגֶד בֵּית הַמִּקְדָּשׁ, וְאֶחָד כְּנֶגֶד רַבָּן גַּמְלִיאֵל. הִתְחִילוּ, הָיוּ שׁוֹתִין וּמִשְׁתַּכְּרִין. הֶחֱזִירוּ הַדָּבָר לְיוֹשְׁנָהּ.

Later, the Sages **added to those four** additional blessings: **One,** noting the actions **of the attendants of the city** [***ḥazzanei ha'ir***],[L] who tend to burials and other communal needs; **one,** noting the actions **of the leaders of the city,** who would provide funding for the burial of the poor; **one, noting the Temple,** commemorating its destruction; **and one, noting** the actions of **Rabban Gamliel.** The people **began** observing this ordinance instituted by the Sages, **and they would drink and become intoxicated.** Therefore, the Sages **restored the matter to its previous status**[N] and established that they drink no more than ten cups.

NOTES

Many have drunk – רַבִּים שָׁתוּ: Some explain that this dispute is dependent on the question of whether, at the end of days, when people will live much longer, death will still exist. Abaye was of the opinion that at that time death will no longer exist. Therefore, the expression that death is ubiquitous is inappropriate (*Iyyun Ya'akov*).

A person should never open his mouth to Satan – לְעוֹלָם אַל יִפְתַּח אָדָם פִּיו לַשָּׂטָן: When a person explicitly makes a statement about some event, he thereby prepares himself psychologically for its occurrence. He thereby renders it a genuine possibility, enhancing its potential for realization. Therefore, one should avoid speaking badly about himself (Maharsha).

Ten cups of wine – עֲשָׂרָה כּוֹסוֹת: It appears from the commentary of Rashi and the Meiri that the ten cups mentioned here are considered obligatory, to ease the pain of the mourner. However, from the comments of the Rambam and others, it appears that it was not required, although the custom was to drink one cup of wine.

One corresponding to the first blessing: Who feeds all – אֶחָד כְּנֶגֶד הַזָּן וכו': The Ritva writes that there is an inherent connection between each of the blessings and mourning. The first blessing: Who feeds all, states that God provides sustenance to all His creations. The request for sustenance is therefore a request for life. The second blessing, the blessing of the land, reflects the verse: "So that your days will be lengthened…upon the land which the Lord swore unto your fathers to give them" (Deuteronomy 11:21). The third blessing: Who builds Jerusalem, is connected to mourning because it written that with the restoration of Zion: "He will swallow up death forever" (Isaiah 25:8). The fourth blessing: Who is good and does good, was instituted in praise of God for the fact that those massacred in Beitar were ultimately buried. According to the variant reading of the Vilna Gaon, this passage is omitted. He explains that perhaps the four cups were instituted parallel to the four blessings of consolation spoken by the disseminator.

The Sages restored the matter to its previous status – הֶחֱזִירוּ הַדָּבָר לְיוֹשְׁנָהּ: According to Rashi and the Rambam, the explanation is that they restored the custom of drinking ten cups and no more. The Ramban, the Rashba, the Ritva, and Rabbi Aharon HaLevi explain that they restored the custom that the mourner drinks wine only during the meal, and they do not drink ten cups, and this is the prevalent custom.

HALAKHA

The Sages instituted ten cups of wine in the house of the mourner – עֲשָׂרָה כּוֹסוֹת תִּקְּנוּ חֲכָמִים בְּבֵית הָאָבֵל: According to the Rambam, mourners may not drink more than ten cups of wine each: Three prior to the meal, three during the meal, and four after the meal. They may drink no more than that lest they get drunk. The *Beit Yosef* notes that according to the Rambam there is no obligation to drink ten cups of wine. There is merely a prohibition against drinking more than that quantity. The *Shulḥan Arukh*, based on the Rambam (*Sefer Shofetim*, *Hilkhot Evel* 4:6), rules that after the burial, the mourner is permitted to drink a small amount of wine in order to facilitate digestion, but not enough to become drunk (Rambam *Sefer Shofetim*, *Hilkhot Evel* 13:8; *Shulḥan Arukh*, *Yoreh De'a* 378:8).

BACKGROUND

To open his intestines – לִפְתּוֹחַ אֶת בְּנֵי מֵעָיו: A small amount of wine stimulates secretion of stomach enzymes and thereby whets the appetite. That quality, along with its ability to ease inhibitions, makes wine an ideal drink for a mourner. Mourning often suppresses one's appetite, and eating and drinking help the mourner deal with the emotional strain of his mourning.

LANGUAGE

Attendants of the city [*ḥazzanei ha'ir*] – חַזָּנֵי הָעִיר: In the Talmud and the Mishna, the word *ḥazzan* means a caretaker, one responsible for upkeep and seeing to the needs of a particular place. In this vein, there is a *ḥazzan* in a synagogue, in the court, and in the city.

There are several opinions with regard to the source of the word. According to early authorities, it comes from the word *ḥaza*, meaning one who sees or oversees the particular needs of a certain place (*Dunash*). Others associate the word with the Akkadian ahazan, meaning officer, because the *ḥazzan* would fill the role of the local police and low-level government officials. Here too, the reference is to attendants, among whose tasks was dealing with the burial of the dead.

The use of the term *ḥazzan* in the exclusive sense of prayer leader in the synagogue is a later phenomenon, although it appears in medieval Jewish literature. Perhaps one of the duties of the *ḥazzan* in ancient times was that of prayer leader.

מַאי רַבָּן גַּמְלִיאֵל? דְּתַנְיָא: בָּרִאשׁוֹנָה הָיְתָה הוֹצָאַת הַמֵּת קָשָׁה לִקְרוֹבָיו יוֹתֵר מִמִּיתָתוֹ, עַד שֶׁהָיוּ מַנִּיחִים אוֹתוֹ וּבוֹרְחִין. עַד שֶׁבָּא רַבָּן גַּמְלִיאֵל וְנָהַג קַלּוּת בְּעַצְמוֹ, וְהוֹצִיאוּהוּ בִּכְלֵי פִשְׁתָּן. וְנָהֲגוּ כׇּל הָעָם אַחֲרָיו לְהוֹצִיא בִּכְלֵי פִשְׁתָּן, אֲמַר רַב פַּפָּא: וְהָאִידָּנָא נְהוּג עָלְמָא אֲפִילּוּ בִּצְרָדָא בַּר זוּזָא.

What is the connection between **Rabban Gamliel** and a house of mourning? It is **as it is taught** in a *baraita*: **Initially, the funeral** expenditures **for the deceased were more taxing for his relatives than his death,** as the burials were opulent, **until** it reached a point where people **would abandon the deceased and flee.** This continued **until Rabbi Gamliel came and conducted himself in a self-deprecatory** manner, instructing the people that they were **to take him** for burial **in** plain **linen garments. And all the people conducted themselves following his** example, and instructed their families **to take** them for burial **in** plain **linen garments.**[H] **Rav Pappa said: And today, everyone is accustomed** to bury the dead in plain garments, **even in rough cloth** [*tzerada*][L] **worth one** *zuz*.

אָמַר רַבִּי אֶלְעָזָר:

Rabbi Elazar said:

HALAKHA

And all the people conducted themselves following his example and instructed to take them for burial in linen garments – וְנָהֲגוּ כׇּל הָעָם אַחֲרָיו לְהוֹצִיא בִּכְלֵי פִשְׁתָּן: The prevalent custom is to bury the deceased in white linen shrouds, as per the allusion in the Gemara. The Rambam writes that according to the custom of the Sages, the shrouds should be worth no more than a dinar. However, if one wants to add to that sum, he is not reprimanded (Radbaz; Rambam *Sefer Shofetim, Hilkhot Evel* 4:1; *Shulḥan Arukh, Yoreh De'a* 352:2).

LANGUAGE

Rough cloth [*tzerada*] – צְרָדָא: In the *Arukh*, this word is written *tzedara*. It is apparently related to the Middle Persian čādur, meaning a veil.

Perek **I**
Daf **9** Amud **a**

הָאוֹמֵר ״פֶּתַח פָּתוּחַ מָצָאתִי״ – נֶאֱמָן לְאוֹסְרָהּ עָלָיו.

A groom **who says: I encountered an unobstructed orifice,**[HN] claiming that when he consummated the marriage he discovered that his bride was not a virgin, **is credible**[N] **to render her forbidden to himself.** Although it is not always possible to corroborate his claim with testimony that his wife committed adultery after betrothal, he is credible to render her forbidden to him as though she had in fact committed adultery.

וְאַמַּאי? סָפֵק סְפֵיקָא הוּא: סָפֵק תַּחְתָּיו סָפֵק אֵין תַּחְתָּיו, וְאִם תִּמְצָא לוֹמַר תַּחְתָּיו – סָפֵק בְּאוֹנֶס סָפֵק בְּרָצוֹן!

The Gemara asks: **But why** is she forbidden to him? It **is** a case of **compound uncertainty.**[N] It is **uncertain** whether she engaged in intercourse while **under his** jurisdiction, after betrothal, in which case she would be forbidden to him, and it is **uncertain** whether she engaged in intercourse while **not under his** jurisdiction, in which case she would not be forbidden to him. **And if you say** that she engaged in intercourse while **under his** jurisdiction, it is **uncertain** whether she engaged in intercourse **by coercion,** in which case she would not be forbidden to him, and it is **uncertain** whether she engaged in intercourse **willingly,** in which case she would be forbidden to him. In cases of compound uncertainty, the ruling is lenient. Why, then, is his claim deemed credible?

HALAKHA

A groom who says: I encountered an unobstructed orifice – הָאוֹמֵר פֶּתַח פָּתוּחַ מָצָאתִי: If a priest betroths a woman, marries her after a period of time, and claims that he discovered that his wife was not a virgin when consummating the marriage, then the woman is forbidden to him, as there is only one uncertainty, whether she lost her virginity before or after she was betrothed to her husband. However, if the man is not a priest, the woman is permitted to her husband, as there is compound uncertainty: Did she lose her virginity before or after betrothal? And even if she lost her virginity after betrothal, it may have been by means of rape, in which case she is not forbidden to her non-priest husband (Rambam *Sefer Kedusha, Hilkhot Issurei Bia* 18:10; *Shulḥan Arukh, Even HaEzer* 68:7).

NOTES

I encountered an unobstructed orifice – פֶּתַח פָּתוּחַ מָצָאתִי: A fundamental question addressed by all the early commentaries is: What of the bleeding that accompanies rupture of the hymen? The presence or absence of blood clearly indicates whether or not a woman is a virgin. Rashi explains that perhaps the Gemara is referring to a woman from a family where the women do not bleed from a ruptured hymen, or perhaps the sheet was lost and it cannot be ascertained whether or not there was bleeding. Rabbeinu Ḥananel explains that the Gemara is dealing with a grown woman who does not bleed, although her hymen is intact (see *Tosafot*). The Ramban explains that even if there was bleeding, the groom could claim that it was the result of a wound or deceit. The Meiri adds that he could claim that it was menstrual blood.

With regard to the case itself, the groom is making a claim that cannot be corroborated by witnesses. Therefore, the matter is entirely dependent on the credibility of the husband and whether he is sufficiently knowledgeable to ascertain the matter.

Credible – נֶאֱמָן: The early commentaries write that the groom is accorded credibility specifically when the bride denies the matter, claiming that she is a virgin and the husband is falsely accusing her, or when she remains silent. However, if she can explain the lack of a hymen by claiming that she was raped or that she engaged in intercourse before betrothal, or that her hymen was ruptured by a foreign object, she is accorded credibility not only with regard to monetary claims, i.e., that she does not lose the right to payment of the marriage contract, but also with regard to the prohibition, i.e., she is not forbidden to her husband as an adulteress. This is because the husband's claim is not a certain one, as even if it is true that the orifice was unobstructed, he can only speculate how that came to be, while hers is a certain claim.

The early commentaries also question why the court doesn't make one of those effective claims on her behalf if she remains silent. They answer that the court does not do so because those occurrences are rare.

It is a case of compound uncertainty – סָפֵק סְפֵיקָא הוּא: This principle that the ruling is lenient in cases where there are multiple elements of uncertainty is unique to the Babylonian Talmud. According to the Jerusalem Talmud, she remains forbidden to him, just as she is in the case of *sota*, where he suspects that she committed adultery, although he is not accorded credibility to prohibit her to others or to void her marriage contract.

Various explanations were proposed with regard to the reason that the ruling is lenient in cases of compound uncertainty. The Rambam is of the opinion that in any case of uncertainty with regard to a Torah prohibition, the ruling is lenient by Torah law. The stringent ruling in those cases is by rabbinic law. Therefore, the second uncertainty is uncertainty with regard to a rabbinic prohibition, in which case the ruling is lenient.

According to *Tosafot*, who maintain that in any case of uncertainty with regard to a Torah prohibition the ruling is stringent by Torah law, the reason for leniency in the case of compound uncertainty is, according to the Rashba, based on the principle of majority. Since any uncertainty is essentially an equally balanced uncertainty, with each possibility carrying a probability of 50 percent, the second uncertainty, which is based on one of those possibilities, carries with it only a 25 percent probability of prohibition. The *Shakh*, in his summary of the principles of compound uncertainty (*Yoreh De'a* 110), writes that not every case of multiple uncertainties has the legal status of a compound uncertainty. In addition, based on the modern discipline of statistics and probability, there are cases where the elements of uncertainty are factored together and others where they are not. Later authorities greatly elaborate on this topic, conceptually and practically.

לָא צְרִיכָא בְּאֵשֶׁת כֹּהֵן. וְאִיבָּעֵית אֵימָא בְּאֵשֶׁת יִשְׂרָאֵל, וּכְגוֹן דְּקַבֵּיל בָּהּ אֲבוּהּ קִידּוּשִׁין פְּחוּתָה מִבַּת שָׁלֹשׁ שָׁנִים וְיוֹם אֶחָד.

No, it is necessary to teach this ruling only **in the case of the wife of a priest,**[N] who is rendered forbidden to her husband even if she engaged in intercourse by coercion. In that case, there is a single uncertainty. **And if you wish, say** instead that this ruling is relevant **even to the wife of an Israelite, and** it is in a case **where her father accepted** her **betrothal** when she was **less than three years and one day old.**[H] Intercourse with a girl less than three years old does not permanently rupture the hymen, and therefore there is no uncertainty whether she engaged in intercourse before or after betrothal. Clearly, it took place after betrothal, and there is only one uncertainty: Did she engage in intercourse by coercion or willingly?

מַאי קָא מַשְׁמַע לָן? תְּנֵינָא. הָאוֹמֵר לְאִשָּׁה ״קִדַּשְׁתִּיךְ״. וְהִיא אוֹמֶרֶת ״לֹא קִדַּשְׁתַּנִי״ – הִיא מוּתֶּרֶת בִּקְרוֹבָיו, וְהוּא אָסוּר בִּקְרוֹבוֹתֶיהָ!

The Gemara asks: If this is a case where there is only one uncertainty, **what is it teaching us? We** already **learned** this explicitly: With regard to **a man who says to a woman: I betrothed you,**[H] **and she says: You did not betroth me,** and there are no witnesses to corroborate either claim, **she is permitted to** marry any of **his relatives,** e.g., his brother, because based on her claim they are not related. **And** it is **prohibited** for **him to** marry **her relatives,** as based on his claim she is his betrothed. Apparently, one is capable of creating a prohibition for himself without corroborating witnesses.

מַהוּ דְּתֵימָא: הָתָם וַדַּאי קִים לֵיהּ, אֲבָל הָכָא – מֵיקָם הוּא דְּלָא קִים לֵיהּ, קָא מַשְׁמַע לָן.

The Gemara says that it was necessary to teach the case of the claim of virginity, **lest you say: There, where certainly** it is **clear to him** that he betrothed her, it is prohibited for him to marry her relatives. **However, here,** perhaps it is **not clear to him** that she was not a virgin, as he is not experienced in these matters and is mistaken. Therefore, Rabbi Elazar **teaches us** that his claim is nevertheless credible and she is forbidden to him.

וּמִי אֲמַר רַבִּי אֶלְעָזָר הָכִי? וְהָאָמַר רַבִּי אֶלְעָזָר: אֵין הָאִשָּׁה נֶאֱסֶרֶת עַל בַּעְלָהּ: אֶלָּא עַל עִסְקֵי קִינּוּי וּסְתִירָה, וּכְמַעֲשֶׂה שֶׁהָיָה!

And did Rabbi Elazar say that? But didn't Rabbi Elazar say: A woman is forbidden to her husband due to adultery, **only over matters of jealous warning and seclusion,**[N] **and as** it was in **the incident that transpired**[N] involving David and Bathsheba? A wife is forbidden to her husband only in a case where he warns her not to seclude herself with a certain man and witnesses testify that she subsequently entered into seclusion with him.

וְתִסְבְּרָא, מַעֲשֶׂה שֶׁהָיָה בְּקִינּוּי וּסְתִירָה הֲוָה?! וְעוֹד: מִי אֲסָרוּהָ?

And how can **you understand** it in that manner? **Was the incident that transpired with jealous warning and seclusion? Furthermore, did** the Sages **render** Bathsheba **forbidden** to her husband? Had she been forbidden to her husband, she would have also been forbidden to David, based on the following principle: Just as an adulteress is forbidden to her husband, she is also forbidden to her paramour.

הָא לָא קַשְׁיָא; הָכִי קָאָמַר: אֵין הָאִשָּׁה נֶאֱסֶרֶת עַל בַּעְלָהּ אֶלָּא עַל עִסְקֵי קִינּוּי וּסְתִירָה, מִמַּעֲשֶׂה שֶׁהָיָה דְּלָא הֲוָה קִינּוּי וּסְתִירָה, וְלָא אִיתַּסְרָא. מִכׇּל מָקוֹם קַשְׁיָא: קִינּוּי וּסְתִירָה – אִין, פֶּתַח פָּתוּחַ – לָא!

That is not difficult, as **this is** what Rabbi Elazar **is saying:** The fact that **a woman is forbidden to her husband** due to adultery **only over matters of jealous warning and seclusion** is derived **from the incident that transpired** involving David and Bathsheba, **as there was no jealous warning and seclusion,** and therefore **she was not forbidden** to her husband. **In any case,** it is **difficult,** as the statements of Rabbi Elazar are contradictory. It may be inferred: By means of **jealous warning and seclusion, yes,** a man renders his wife forbidden to him; by means of the claim that he encountered **an unobstructed orifice, no,** he does not render her forbidden.

וּלְטַעְמִיךְ, קִינּוּי וּסְתִירָה – אִין, עֵדִים – לָא?!

The Gemara rejects that inference: **And** according **to your reasoning,** that the statement of Rabbi Elazar restricts to jealous warning and seclusion the manner in which a husband can render his wife forbidden, infer: By means of **jealous warning and seclusion, yes,** a man renders his wife forbidden to him; by means of the testimony of two **witnesses** that she engaged in adulterous relations, **no,** he does not render her forbidden. That cannot be so, as clearly two witnesses establish her as one who committed adultery and render her forbidden to her husband.

NOTES

In the case of the wife of a priest – בְּאֵשֶׁת כֹּהֵן: The Ramban asks: Why is there not a compound uncertainty in this case as well, as, even if the women's hymens were ruptured after betrothal, perhaps it was ruptured by a foreign object and she is permitted to her husband? He answers that there is an additional reason to rule stringently, as, even if the hymen were ruptured before betrothal, a woman who had relations with one disqualified from entering the congregation of Israel renders her forbidden to a priest. Others answer that, as cited previously, the possibility that her hymen was ruptured by a foreign object is uncommon and therefore cannot be classified as an uncertainty. The early commentaries discuss at length whether or not that circumstance is uncommon.

Only over matters of jealous warning and seclusion – אֶלָּא עַל עִסְקֵי קִינּוּי וּסְתִירָה: The Ritva proves at length that this statement is not to be taken literally. If it were to be taken literally, even if a man actually witnessed his wife committing adultery she would not be forbidden to him. He therefore explains that the Gemara means that in a case of uncertainty, where there is no full-fledged testimony that she committed adultery, a woman is rendered forbidden to her husband only through warning followed by seclusion. Others reject his proof and explain that perhaps Rabbi Elazar maintains that by Torah law a woman is rendered forbidden to her husband only by means of the testimony of witnesses, and the Gemara can be explained that in bringing his wife to court, the matter will be publicized and witnesses will come to testify against her (Rabbi Akiva Eiger).

And as it was in the incident that transpired – וּכְמַעֲשֶׂה שֶׁהָיָה: Rabbeinu Ḥananel explains that there is a tradition that the incident in question is the incident involving David and Bathsheba, and the reference is obscure in deference to David. He adds that the correct understanding of the Gemara is: Either over matters of jealous warning and seclusion or as it was in the incident that transpired.

HALAKHA

In a case where her father accepted her betrothal when she was less than three years and one day old – וּכְגוֹן דְּקַבֵּיל בָּהּ אֲבוּהּ קִידּוּשִׁין פְּחוּתָה מִבַּת שָׁלֹשׁ שָׁנִים וְיוֹם אֶחָד: If a man accepts betrothal on behalf of his daughter when she is less than three years and one day old, and if her husband claims that when consummating the marriage he discovered that his wife is not a virgin, she is forbidden to her husband. In that case, there is only one uncertainty: Whether or not she was raped. She could not have lost her virginity before betrothal, as the hymen of a girl younger than three years old does not rupture (Rambam *Sefer Kedusha, Hilkhot Issurei Bia* 18:11; *Shulḥan Arukh, Even HaEzer* 68:7).

A man who says to a woman: I betrothed you – הָאוֹמֵר לְאִשָּׁה קִדַּשְׁתִּיךְ: If a man says to a woman that he betrothed her in the presence of two witnesses who are currently unavailable to testify, e.g., they died or moved, and she claims that she had never been betrothed to him, it is prohibited for him to marry any of her relatives, e.g., her mother or sister, but it is permitted for her to marry any of his relatives (Rambam *Sefer Nashim, Hilkhot Ishut* 9:15–16; *Shulḥan Arukh, Even HaEzer* 48:5).

אֶלָּא הָכִי קָאָמַר: אֵין הָאִשָּׁה נֶאֱסֶרֶת עַל בַּעְלָהּ בְּעֵד אֶחָד אֶלָּא בִּשְׁנֵי עֵדִים, וְקִינּוּי וּסְתִירָה – אֲפִילּוּ בְּעֵד אֶחָד נַמִּי, וּפֶתַח פָּתוּחַ – כִּשְׁנֵי עֵדִים דָּמֵי.

The Gemara explains: **Rather, this is** what Rabbi Elazar **is saying: A woman is not rendered forbidden to her husband through** the testimony of **one witness. Rather,** she is rendered forbidden **only by means of** the testimony of **two witnesses**[H] who testify that she engaged in adulterous relations. **And** if there was **jealous warning and seclusion,** she is rendered forbidden **even by means of** the testimony of **one witness as well,**[H] if he comes after the husband warned his wife and testifies that she engaged in adulterous relations. **And** the legal status of the claim: I encountered **an unobstructed orifice,** is **like** that of **two witnesses,** and it renders her forbidden even without jealous warning and seclusion.

וְכִי תֵּימָא: מַעֲשֶׂה שֶׁהָיָה מִפְּנֵי מָה לֹא אֲסָרוּהָ – הָתָם אוֹנֶס הֲוָה. וְאִיבָּעֵית אֵימָא, כִּי הָא דְּאָמַר רַבִּי שְׁמוּאֵל בַּר נַחְמָנִי אָמַר רַבִּי יוֹנָתָן:

And if you would say with regard to **the incident that transpired** involving David and Bathsheba: **For what** reason did the Sages **not deem her forbidden,** when clearly David committed adultery with a married woman? The Gemara answers: **There it was rape,** and she did not engage in intercourse willingly. **And if you wish, say** instead[N] that the Sages did not deem her forbidden, **as that which Rabbi Shmuel bar Naḥmani said that Rabbi Yonatan said:**

NOTES

And if you wish, say instead – וְאִיבָּעֵית אֵימָא: There is a practical halakhic difference between these two answers. According to the first, since a woman who is raped is not forbidden to her husband, after her husband dies she would be permitted to the rapist. Although the rapist raped her intentionally, the reason that a woman who commits adultery is forbidden to her paramour is based only on her being forbidden to her husband (*Beit Shmuel*). Others add that this is dependent on a tannaitic dispute (*Sota* 28a) with regard to the source of her prohibition to her paramour. If it is derived from an amplification in the verse that prohibits her to the husband, then she is not forbidden to the rapist since she is not forbidden to her husband. However, if there is an independent source for her prohibition to the paramour, it is entirely possible that she is forbidden to the rapist even in the absence of a prohibition to her husband, if he has died (*Ḥatam Sofer*).

HALAKHA

A woman is not rendered forbidden to her husband… Rather, only by means of the testimony of two witnesses – אֵין הָאִשָּׁה נֶאֱסֶרֶת עַל בַּעְלָהּ...אֶלָּא בִּשְׁנֵי עֵדִים: Although the Sages said that one who notices improper conduct in his wife, leading him to the conclusion that his wife committed adultery, is obligated to divorce her, the court compels him to divorce her only when there are two witnesses who testify that they saw the woman committing adultery of her own volition (Rambam *Sefer Nashim, Hilkhot Ishut* 24:18; *Tur, Even HaEzer* 115; *Shulḥan Arukh, Even HaEzer* 11:1).

And if there was jealous warning and seclusion, even by means of the testimony of one witness as well – וְקִינּוּי וּסְתִירָה אֲפִילּוּ בְּעֵד אֶחָד נַמִּי: If a man grows suspicious of his wife and warns her not to enter into seclusion with a specific man, then even if only a single witness testifies that she engaged in relations with that man, she does not drink the ritual water of a *sota*, but rather he divorces her immediately and she does not receive payment of her marriage contract. This is the case even if the witness is one who is ordinarily disqualified from giving testimony, e.g., a relative (Rambam *Sefer Nashim, Hilkhot Sota* 1:14–15; *Shulḥan Arukh, Even HaEzer* 178:14).

Perek **I**
Daf **9** Amud **b**

כָּל הַיּוֹצֵא לְמִלְחֶמֶת בֵּית דָּוִד גֵּט כְּרִיתוּת כּוֹתֵב לְאִשְׁתּוֹ, דִּכְתִיב "וְאֶת אַחֶיךָ תִּפְקֹד לְשָׁלוֹם וְאֶת עֲרֻבָּתָם תִּקָּח". מַאי "וְאֶת עֲרֻבָּתָם תִּקָּח" – תָּנֵי רַב יוֹסֵף: דְּבָרִים הַמְעוֹרָבִין בֵּינוֹ לְבֵינָהּ.

Anyone who goes to a war waged by the royal **house of David writes** a conditional **bill of divorce to his wife.**[N] This was done to prevent a situation in which the wife of the soldier would be unable to remarry because her husband did not return from battle and there were no witnesses with regard to his fate. The conditional bill of divorce accorded the wife the status of a divorcée and freed her to remarry, **as it is written: "And to your brothers bring greetings and take their pledge [*arubatam*]"** (I Samuel 17:18).[N] **What is the** meaning of: **And take *arubatam*? Rav Yosef taught:** It is referring **to matters that are shared [*hame'oravin*] between** the husband **and** his wife, i.e., marriage. Since apparently it was customary for men at war to send their wives a conditional divorce, and since Uriah later died, Bathsheba assumed divorced status retroactively from the time that he set out to war. Therefore, she was not forbidden to David.

NOTES

Writes a conditional bill of divorce to his wife – גֵּט כְּרִיתוּת כּוֹתֵב לְאִשְׁתּוֹ: From Rashi's explanation, it appears that this was a bill of divorce that was given conditionally, to take effect if the husband dies at war, to spare his wife the obligation to enter into levirate marriage with her brother-in-law. The question is raised: If that is its purpose, it affects only a small segment of the population, i.e., men with a brother and no children. Rather, to prevent their wives from assuming the status of a deserted wife, all those going out to war would write a conditional bill of divorce that would take effect retroactively from the time the bill of divorce was written (*Tosafot*; Ramban).

Another problem discussed is with regard to the legal status of the wife between receipt of the bill of divorce and the husband's failure to return. *Tosafot* note that there is a tannaitic dispute whether during that interim period the woman is considered married or divorced. Apparently, according to the opinion in the Gemara that Uriah gave his wife a conditional bill of divorce, it is determined retroactively that she was not married in the interim. However, many authorities question that from the statement in *Bava Metzia* (59a), where Bathsheba is characterized, even according to that opinion, as a woman whose marital status is uncertain, not a woman who is considered divorced and permitted.

Tosafot explain simply that at the time that David had relations with Bathsheba, there was uncertainty with regard to whether or not Uriah would return. The Ramban explains that although the matter was ultimately resolved, David did not know what the resolution would be when he engaged in relations with Bathsheba. Therefore, ostensibly he engaged in relations with a woman whose marital status is uncertain.

Rabbeinu Tam (see *Tosafot*) explains the Gemara in its plain sense, as follows: Those going to war, who were uncertain about their fate, would write an unconditional bill of divorce and divorce their wives; upon their return, they betrothed and married them a second time. Therefore, David did not commit even an uncertain transgression; nevertheless, taking Uriah's wife before it became clear that Uriah died in battle was despicable.

As it is written…and take their pledge – דִּכְתִיב...וְאֶת עֲרֻבָּתָם תִּקָּח: Although this verse is written with regard to the wars of King Saul, apparently it was the custom of Yishai, David's father. When David assumed the throne, he taught this practice to all his troops (Ritva; see Rashi).

אֲמַר אַבַּיֵי: אַף אֲנַן נַמִּי תָּנֵינָא, בְּתוּלָה נִשֵּׂאת לְיוֹם הָרְבִיעִי. לְיוֹם רְבִיעִי – אִין, לְיוֹם חֲמִישִׁי – לָא, מַאי טַעֲמָא – מִשּׁוּם אִיקְּרוּרֵי דַּעְתָּא.

§ Apropos the credibility of the claim: I encountered an unobstructed orifice, **Abaye said: We, too, learn** in the mishna proof for the opinion of Rabbi Elazar: **A virgin is married on Wednesday.** Abaye infers: **On Wednesday, yes,** a virgin is married; **on Thursday, no,**[N] she is not married. **What is the reason** for this ruling? It is **due to** the fact **that** if the marriage were to be held on Thursday, several days would elapse before the court would next convene, and in the interim **his resolve will cool**[N] and his anger subside. The concern is that consequently he will fail to claim before the court that his bride was not a virgin.

וּלְמַאי? אִי לְמֵיתַב לָהּ כְּתוּבָּה – נֵיתִיב לָהּ, אֶלָּא לְאוֹסְרָהּ עָלָיו, וּדְקָא טָעֵין טַעֲנָה.

The Gemara asks: **And for what** matter is that a source of concern? **If** the concern is with regard **to giving her** payment for her **marriage contract,** i.e., if he fails to go to court, her legal status at the time of marriage will remain that of a virgin, and when the time comes she will receive payment for her marriage contract to which she is not entitled; then **let him give it to her** if he wishes. Why is that a concern? **Rather, it is** with regard **to rendering her forbidden to him, and** that would result in a case **where he makes a claim.**

מַאי לָאו דְּקָטָעֵין טַעֲנַת ״פֶּתַח פָּתוּחַ״! לָא, דְּקָטָעֵין טַעֲנַת דָּמִים.

What, is it not referring to a case **where he makes the claim:** I encountered **an unobstructed orifice,** after engaging in intercourse with his bride, and his claim is accorded credibility to render her forbidden to him in accordance with the opinion of Rabbi Elazar? The Gemara rejects that proof: **No,** it can be explained that it is a case **where he makes the claim** that there was no **blood,**[NHB] which would have resulted from rupture of the hymen had she been a virgin. That is a claim based on objective, verifiable evidence and not merely dependent on his subjective sensation.

אָמַר רַב יְהוּדָה אָמַר שְׁמוּאֵל: הָאוֹמֵר ״פֶּתַח פָּתוּחַ מָצָאתִי״ נֶאֱמָן לְהַפְסִידָהּ כְּתוּבָּתָהּ. אֲמַר רַב יוֹסֵף: מַאי קָא מַשְׁמַע לַן? תָּנֵינָא: הָאוֹכֵל אֵצֶל חָמִיו בִּיהוּדָה שֶׁלֹּא בְּעֵדִים – אֵינוֹ יָכוֹל לִטְעוֹן טַעֲנַת בְּתוּלִים, מִפְּנֵי שֶׁמִּתְיַיחֵד עִמָּהּ. בִּיהוּדָה הוּא דְּלָא מָצֵי טָעֵין, הָא בַּגָּלִיל – מָצֵי טָעֵין.

§ **Rav Yehuda said** that **Shmuel said** that a groom **who says: I encountered an unobstructed orifice, is deemed credible** with regard **to causing her to lose her marriage contract.**[N] **Rav Yosef said: What is he teaching us? We already learned** explicitly in a mishna (12a): A man **who eats at** the house of **his father-in-law in Judea** after betrothal, **without witnesses** to attest to the fact that he was not alone with her, **cannot make a claim about** his bride's **virginity** after marriage, **because** in accordance with the custom in Judea, the assumption is **that he secluded himself with her** and it was he who engaged in intercourse with her. The Gemara infers: It is **in Judea that he cannot claim** that she is not a virgin, **but in the Galilee, he can claim** that this is the case.

NOTES

On Thursday, no – לְיוֹם חֲמִישִׁי לָא: Some ask: Why is this inference necessary, when the reason for this ordinance, i.e., to enable him to go to court the next day and make the claim concerning virginity, is articulated explicitly in the mishna? Rashi explains that if the groom marries on Thursday, he would need to wait several days until Monday.

The *Shita Mekubbetzet* cites an explanation why Thursday is emphasized rather than simply another day: The blessing to procreate, "Be fruitful, and multiply" (Genesis 1:22), was first stated on Thursday, and therefore one might think that marriage can be held on Thursday. Even so, the Sages insisted that a virgin should marry specifically on Wednesday. The inference was necessary to prove that the Sages were concerned that the groom's resolve will cool, and therefore it is clear that they were concerned due to the prohibition.

His resolve will cool – אִיקְּרוּרֵי דַּעְתָּא: The distinction between the claim of an unobstructed orifice and a claim that there was no blood from the rupture of the hymen is that in the former case the groom lacks confidence in his claim and is concerned that perhaps he is mistaken, either due to his lack of sexual experience or due to his lack of familiarity with a woman's body. Therefore, with the passage of time, if he grows fond of his bride, or as it is phrased in the Jerusalem Talmud, his acquisition is pleasant in his eyes, the feeling he had when he consummated the marriage and discovered an unobstructed orifice is forgotten. However, with regard to a claim of the lack of blood, there is no uncertainty or lack of confidence and the passage of time will not compromise that fact (see *Tosafot*; Ritva).

Where he makes the claim that there was no blood – דְּקָטָעֵין טַעֲנַת דָּמִים: The commentaries discuss the difference between these two claims at length, and there are different opinions with regard to both the explanation and the halakhic implications of that difference. Some say that in the claim of an unobstructed orifice, there is concern that he is lying, and there is no way to disprove his claim. In the claim that there was no blood, she could bring proof to refute that claim (Rabbeinu Ḥananel). Rashi explains that in a claim of an unobstructed orifice, there is uncertainty with regard to the degree of the husband's expertise in those matters. Accordingly, there would be a distinction between a bachelor and one who was previously married. The claim that there was no blood requires no expertise. Others explain on a similar note that the claim of an unobstructed orifice is based on feeling and the claim of blood is based on empirical evidence and can be verified (see Ramban; Rashba).

He is deemed credible with regard to causing her to lose her marriage contract – נֶאֱמָן לְהַפְסִידָהּ כְּתוּבָּתָהּ: There are numerous opinions among the early commentaries with regard to the relationship between the statements of Rav Yehuda in the name of Shmuel and the earlier statement of Rabbi Elazar that the groom is deemed credible with regard to rendering her forbidden to him. Some suggest that Shmuel agrees with Rabbi Elazar, i.e., that she is forbidden to the husband; he is merely adding that she loses her marriage contract. Others are of the opinion that Shmuel holds that the groom is accorded credibility only with regard to losing the marriage contract but not to rendering her forbidden to him (see *Tosafot*; Ramban).

Yet others claim that the Sages agree with each other, but that each formulates the ruling in a far-reaching and novel manner. Rabbi Elazar holds that the fact that she is forbidden is a more novel element, as despite her presumptive status of being permitted, she is rendered forbidden by his claim. In contrast, the fact that his claim is credible in monetary matters is clear, as the burden of proof is incumbent upon the claimant. On the other hand, Shmuel holds that he is accorded credibility with regard to the monetary issue, where there is room for leniency, as stringency for one party is leniency for the other. Once his claim is deemed credible with regard to the marriage contract, the result is that she is forbidden, as with regard to the prohibition there is certainly greater concern (Ritva).

HALAKHA

The claim of an unobstructed orifice and the claim that there was no blood – טַעֲנַת פֶּתַח פָּתוּחַ וְטַעֲנַת דָּמִים: If the groom claims after engaging in intercourse with his virgin bride for the first time that she is not a virgin, based on the absence of blood from the ruptured hymen, and that absence cannot be attributed to illness, malnutrition, or a genetic anomaly, his claim is accepted, whether the woman in question is an adult or a minor. If, however, his claim that she is not a virgin is based on encountering an unobstructed orifice and she is a grown woman, i.e., more than twelve and a half years old, his claim is not accepted and it is attributed to the fact that he did not sense that the hymen was intact. If she is a young woman, i.e., less than twelve and a half years old, his claim is accepted even if there is evidence of bleeding (Rambam). Others maintain that if there is blood, the claim of an unobstructed orifice is not accepted, even if the bride is less than twelve and half years old years old (Ri; Ramban; Rashba; Rambam *Sefer Nashim*, *Hilkhot Ishut* 11:12–13; *Shulḥan Arukh*, *Even HaEzer* 68:3, 6).

BACKGROUND

An unobstructed orifice and blood – פֶּתַח פָּתוּחַ וְדָמִים: Most women have some opening in the hymen, the size of which varies from woman to woman and is influenced by age. If the opening is relatively large it is conceivable that one could engage in intercourse with a virgin without encountering that membrane at all. Nevertheless, if the hymen is at all ruptured it bleeds. However, unlike bleeding, where there is a clear, objective criterion to determine the matter, his sensing that he encountered an unobstructed orifice is subjective. It is entirely possible that the hymen was intact, but it simply had a relatively large opening (see 36a).

וְלְמַאי? אִי לְאוֹסְרָהּ עָלָיו – בִּיהוּדָה אַמַּאי לָא? אֶלָּא לָאו – לְהַפְסִידָהּ כְּתוּבָּתָהּ, וּדְקָא טָעֵין טַעֲנָה, מַאי לָאו דְּקָא טָעֵין טַעֲנַת ״פֶּתַח פָּתוּחַ״! לָא, דְּקָא טָעֵין טַעֲנַת דָּמִים.

The Gemara asks: **And for what** matter is this claim directed? **If it is to render her forbidden to him,** then **in Judea why** is the claim **not** credible? If he is certain that he did not engage in intercourse with her, and finds that she is not a virgin, apparently she committed adultery and that claim should render her forbidden. **Rather, is it not** that he is seeking **to cause her to lose her marriage contract**[N] in a case **where he makes a claim? And what, is it not** referring to a case **where he makes the claim:** I encountered **an unobstructed orifice,** and apparently he is accorded credibility? The Gemara rejects that proof: **No,** it can be explained that it is a case **where he makes the claim** that there was no **blood.**[N]

NOTES

To cause her to lose her marriage contract – לְהַפְסִידָהּ כְּתוּבָּתָהּ: The Gemara later (13a) cites a dispute among the *amora'im* whether this means that she loses the marriage contract of two hundred dinars to which a virgin is entitled, and instead receives one hundred as a non-virgin, or whether she loses her entire marriage contract, since the entire marriage was based on false pretenses and is therefore a mistaken transaction. The early halakhic authorities (Rif, citing Rav Hai Gaon) write that the dispute is only with regard to the standard payment of the marriage contract. However, the groom is required to pay any sum that he committed to add to the marriage contract.

In Judea…where he makes the claim that there was no blood – בִּיהוּדָה...דְּקָא טָעֵין טַעֲנַת דָּמִים: Some explain that with regard to the claim of an unobstructed orifice, it is conceivable that they engaged in intercourse while betrothed and were both under the impression that it was not full-fledged intercourse. However, with regard to bleeding, had they engaged in intercourse in Judea, and she saw blood, she would have told both him and her parents, to avoid suspicion later. However, if she said nothing at the time, it is likely that she had engaged in intercourse with another man (*Tosefot Yeshanim*).

Perek **I**
Daf **10** Amud **a**

אִיתְּמַר, אָמַר רַב נַחְמָן אָמַר שְׁמוּאֵל מִשּׁוּם רַבִּי שִׁמְעוֹן בֶּן אֶלְעָזָר: חֲכָמִים תִּקְּנוּ לָהֶם לִבְנוֹת יִשְׂרָאֵל, לִבְתוּלָה מָאתַיִם, וּלְאַלְמָנָה מָנֶה. וְהֵם הֶאֱמִינוּהוּ, שֶׁאִם אָמַר ״פֶּתַח פָּתוּחַ מָצָאתִי״ נֶאֱמָן. אִם כֵּן מָה הוֹעִילוּ חֲכָמִים בְּתַקָּנָתָם?

§ **It was stated: Rav Naḥman said** that **Shmuel said in the name of Rabbi Shimon ben Elazar: The Sages instituted** the marriage contract **for Jewish women:**[N] **For a virgin two hundred** dinars[N] **and for a widow one hundred dinars.**[H] And they **deemed** the groom **credible in that if he says** with regard to his virgin bride: **I encountered an unobstructed orifice** and she is not a virgin, **he is deemed credible,** causing her to lose her marriage contract. The Gemara asks: **If so,** and the Sages deemed him credible, **what did the Sages accomplish in their ordinance** that the marriage contract of a virgin is two hundred dinars, if his claim that she is not a virgin is effective?

אָמַר רָבָא: חֲזָקָה, אֵין אָדָם טוֹרֵחַ בִּסְעוּדָה וּמַפְסִידָהּ.

Rava said: The ordinance is effective due to the **presumption** that **a person does not**[N] **exert** himself to prepare a wedding **feast and** then **cause it to be lost.**[N] Investing in the wedding preparations clearly indicates that the groom's intention is to marry the bride and rejoice with her. If, nevertheless, he claims that she is not a virgin, apparently he is telling the truth.

HALAKHA

For a virgin two hundred dinars and for a widow one hundred dinars – לִבְתוּלָה מָאתַיִם וּלְאַלְמָנָה מָנֶה: If a man marries a virgin, even if she was widowed or divorced after betrothal to another man, she is entitled to a marriage contract of two hundred dinars. However, if a man marries a woman who was widowed or divorced after marriage to another man, or who engaged in sexual relations while single, she is entitled to a marriage contract of only one hundred dinars (Rambam *Sefer Nashim*, *Hilkhot Ishut* 11:1; *Shulḥan Arukh*, *Even HaEzer* 66:6, 67:1–2).

NOTES

The Sages instituted the marriage contract for Jewish women – חֲכָמִים תִּקְּנוּ לָהֶם לִבְנוֹת יִשְׂרָאֵל: Rashi states that the Gemara explained the fact that the Sages accorded credibility to the claim of the groom to void the marriage contract, by stating that the marriage contract is an obligation by rabbinic law. The commentaries discuss why his claim would not be accepted if it was an obligation by Torah law.

For a virgin two hundred dinars – לִבְתוּלָה מָאתַיִם: According to Rabban Shimon ben Gamliel, who holds that the marriage contract is an obligation by Torah law, the source of two hundred dinars for a virgin is clear, as that is the sum of the dowry of a virgin in the Torah. According to the Rabbis, who hold that it is an obligation by rabbinic law, the reason that the Sages instituted two hundred dinars is that they concluded that one with that sum, which was approximately the basic annual wage, is not considered poor, and they sought to ensure that the divorcée or widow would not be dependent on the aid of society. For a widow, who already received a certain sum from the marriage contract of her first husband, one hundred dinars was sufficient (*Ramat Shmuel*).

The presumption that a person does not, etc. – חֲזָקָה אֵין אָדָם וכו׳: The early commentaries discuss the fundamental legal situation with regard to the woman's claim that she is entitled to payment of the marriage contract. On the one hand, since the husband is currently in possession of the disputed funds, the burden of proof is incumbent upon the woman, who is the claimant in this case. On the other hand, the woman's claim is supported by the presumptive status of her body, as most women marry as virgins. As a rule, the presumptive status of her body takes precedence over the possession of disputed property. Therefore, it was necessary to buttress the husband's claim with an additional presumption: A person does not exert himself to prepare a wedding feast and then cause it to be lost.

A person does not exert himself to prepare a wedding feast and then cause it to be lost – אֵין אָדָם טוֹרֵחַ בִּסְעוּדָה וּמַפְסִידָהּ: *Tosafot* infer that this presumption is relevant only in a case where he stands to lose his entire investment in the feast because the wedding is voided, e.g., where the groom is a priest and therefore there is only one uncertainty, or where he claims that the betrothal was a mistaken transaction. However, if his claim is merely to reduce the marriage contract payment to the one hundred dinars of a non-virgin, his claim is not accorded credibility. Similarly, the Rosh explains that in any case where his intention is for her to remain his wife, then since he doesn't actually lose the value of the entire feast, his claim is not credible. The Ramban writes that the primary reason is not that he will lose the money invested in the feast, but rather, in a broader sense, that a person does not get married in order to immediately cast aspersions upon the woman he just married. Or, as he phrased it: A person does not spit in the cup from which he is drinking. According to all of these explanations, the groom's credibility is based on the assumption that he will behave rationally.

תָּנָא: הוֹאִיל וּקְנַס חֲכָמִים הוּא – לֹא תִּגְבֶּה אֶלָּא מִן הַזִּיבּוּרִית. קְנָסָא?! מַאי קְנָסָא? אֶלָּא אֵימָא: הוֹאִיל וְתַקָּנַת חֲכָמִים הוּא – לֹא תִּגְבֶּה אֶלָּא מִן הַזִּיבּוּרִית. רַבָּן שִׁמְעוֹן בֶּן גַּמְלִיאֵל אוֹמֵר: כְּתוּבַּת אִשָּׁה מִן הַתּוֹרָה.

§ A Sage **taught** in a *baraita*: **Since** payment of the marriage contract **is a penalty** instituted by the **Sages,**[N] **she may collect only from the** husband's **land of the most inferior quality.**[H] The Gemara asks: **A penalty? What penalty** is there in a marriage contract? **Rather,** emend the *baraita* and **say: Since it is a rabbinic ordinance**[H] and not a Torah obligation, **she may collect only from the** husband's **land of the most inferior quality. Rabban Shimon ben Gamliel says: The marriage contract of a woman is** an obligation **by Torah** law.

וּמִי אֲמַר רַבָּן שִׁמְעוֹן בֶּן גַּמְלִיאֵל הָכִי? וְהָתַנְיָא: ״כֶּסֶף יִשְׁקֹל כְּמֹהַר הַבְּתוּלֹת״ שֶׁיְּהֵא זֶה כְּמוֹהַר הַבְּתוּלוֹת, וּמוֹהַר הַבְּתוּלוֹת כָּזֶה. מִכָּאן סָמְכוּ חֲכָמִים לִכְתוּבַּת אִשָּׁה מִן הַתּוֹרָה. רַבָּן שִׁמְעוֹן בֶּן גַּמְלִיאֵל אוֹמֵר: כְּתוּבַּת אִשָּׁה אֵינָהּ מִדִּבְרֵי תוֹרָה אֶלָּא מִדִּבְרֵי סוֹפְרִים!

The Gemara asks: **And did Rabban Shimon ben Gamliel say that? But isn't it taught** in a *baraita* that it is written with regard to a seducer: **"He shall pay money according to the dowry of virgins"** (Exodus 22:16)? The Torah establishes that **this** fine **will be like the dowry of a virgin,** and that **the dowry of a virgin** will be **like this** fine, i.e., fifty silver *sela*, or two hundred dinars. **From here the Sages based**[N] their determination **that a woman's marriage contract** is an obligation **by Torah** law. **Rabban Shimon ben Gamliel says: The marriage contract of a woman is not** an obligation **by Torah law, but is by rabbinic law.**[N]

אֵיפּוֹךְ. וּמַאי חָזֵית דְּאַפְּכַתְּ בַּתְרַיְיתָא? אֵיפּוֹךְ קַמַּיְיתָא!

The Gemara resolves the contradiction between the statements of Rabban Shimon ben Gamliel: **Reverse** the attribution of opinions in this *baraita*. The Gemara asks: **And what did you see that** led **you to reverse** the attribution of opinions **in the latter** *baraita*? **Reverse** the attribution of opinions in **the former,** in the *baraita*, and say that Rabban Shimon ben Gamliel is the one who holds that the marriage contract is a rabbinic ordinance.

הָא שְׁמַעִינָא לֵיהּ לְרַבָּן שִׁמְעוֹן בֶּן גַּמְלִיאֵל דַּאֲמַר כְּתוּבַּת אִשָּׁה מִדְּאוֹרַיְיתָא, דִּתְנַן: רַבָּן שִׁמְעוֹן בֶּן גַּמְלִיאֵל אוֹמֵר: נוֹתֵן לָהּ מִמְּעוֹת קַפּוֹטְקִיָא.

The Gemara answers: The reason is **that we learned that** it is **Rabban Shimon ben Gamliel who said** elsewhere **that the marriage contract of a woman is** an obligation **by Torah** law, **as we learned** in a mishna (110b) that **Rabban Shimon ben Gamliel says** that if a man marries a woman in Cappadocia, where the currency is more valuable, and he divorces her in Eretz Yisrael, **he gives her** payment for the marriage contract **from the money of Cappadocia.**[N] From the fact that he is obligated to pay the marriage contract in the currency of the place where he undertook the obligation, apparently the marriage contract of a woman is an obligation by Torah law.

וְאִי בָּעֵית אֵימָא: כּוּלָּהּ רַבָּן שִׁמְעוֹן בֶּן גַּמְלִיאֵל הִיא, וְחַסּוּרֵי מִיחַסְּרָא וְהָכִי קָתָנֵי: מִכָּאן סָמְכוּ חֲכָמִים לִכְתוּבַּת אִשָּׁה מִן הַתּוֹרָה. כְּתוּבַּת אַלְמָנָה אֵינָהּ מִדִּבְרֵי תוֹרָה אֶלָּא מִדִּבְרֵי סוֹפְרִים, שֶׁרַבָּן שִׁמְעוֹן בֶּן גַּמְלִיאֵל אוֹמֵר כְּתוּבַּת אַלְמָנָה אֵינָהּ מִדִּבְרֵי תוֹרָה אֶלָּא מִדִּבְרֵי סוֹפְרִים.

And if you wish, say instead that the **entire** latter *baraita* **is** in accordance with the opinion of **Rabban Shimon ben Gamliel,** but the *baraita* **is incomplete and it is teaching the following:**[B] **From here, the Sages based** their determination **that a woman's marriage contract** in the case of a virgin is an obligation **by Torah** law. However, the **marriage contract of a widow is not** an obligation **by Torah law but** is an ordinance **by rabbinic law, as Rabban Shimon ben Gamliel says: The marriage contract of a widow is not** an obligation **by Torah law but** is an ordinance **by rabbinic law.**

NOTES

Since it is a penalty instituted by the Sages – הוֹאִיל וּקְנַס חֲכָמִים הוּא: The use of the term penalty in this context is questionable, even though it is ultimately abandoned. The Ya'avetz writes that fundamentally the marriage contract was instituted as a type of penalty to deter the husband from coveting another woman and divorcing his wife for no good reason. Even though the marriage contract applies in all cases, even where there is justification for the divorce, this was the initial motive for the ordinance.

From here the Sages based – מִכָּאן סָמְכוּ חֲכָמִים: From a precise analysis of the language, the early commentaries conclude that even according to Rabban Shimon ben Gamliel, the sum written in the marriage contract is a rabbinic ordinance and not fixed by Torah law. However, the fundamental obligation to write a marriage contract is derived from the verse in the Torah: "He shall pay money according to the dowry of virgins" (Ritva).

The marriage contract of a woman…is an ordinance by rabbinic law – כְּתוּבַּת אִשָּׁה...מִדִּבְרֵי סוֹפְרִים: There are various opinions as to whether the marriage contract is by Torah law or by rabbinic ordinance (see HALAKHA). The dispute dates back at least to the geonic period and may have been the subject of a dispute between the Sages in Babylonia, where the ruling is in accordance with the opinion of Shmuel and Rav Naḥman, and those in Eretz Yisrael, where the ruling is in accordance with the opinion of Rabban Shimon ben Gamliel. That could also explain some of the differences between the formulas of the marriage contract employed in those places.

With regard to the standard formula of the marriage contract, which includes the expression: Two hundred dinars to which you are entitled by Torah law, many authorities reprimanded those who included that phrase, and some ruled the marriage contract invalid. However, the Ritva and the Meiri explain that the wording is merely to enhance the authority of the marriage contract enabling the woman to collect payment as if it were a commitment by Torah law (see *Tosafot*).

He gives her payment from the money of Cappadocia – נוֹתֵן לָהּ מִמְּעוֹת קַפּוֹטְקִיָא: The early commentaries discuss the significance of the coins used to pay the marriage contract if ultimately the amount of the payment is the same (see *Tosafot*). The Meiri writes that if the groom did not specify the coinage, his intention is to use the legal tender in the place where the contract was signed. Others explain that although the values are the same, currency that is universally accepted is preferable.

BACKGROUND

The *baraita* is incomplete and it is teaching the following – חַסּוּרֵי מִיחַסְּרָא וְהָכִי קָתָנֵי: This method of explanation appears throughout the Talmud. Generally speaking, it does not suggest an actual emendation of the text of the *baraita*. The addition introduced by the Gemara is a necessary elaboration upon that which is written in the *baraita*, which is insufficiently clear in its current form. The addition provides the necessary clarification.

HALAKHA

She may collect only from the land of the most inferior quality – לֹא תִּגְבֶּה אֶלָּא מִן הַזִּיבּוּרִית: A wife collects payment of her entire marriage contract, both the standard payment and any additional commitment assumed by the husband, from the land of the lowest quality belonging to the husband, in accordance with the *baraita*. The early commentaries disagree with regard to the ruling in a case where the husband expressly stipulates that his wife will collect payment of the marriage contract from his highest quality land. The *Shulḥan Arukh* (*Ḥoshen Mishpat* 108:18) rules that a condition of that kind takes effect. In the *Beit Shmuel* it is written that since today the prevalent custom is to include in the marriage contract the phrase: The choicest of properties, the wife collects payment of the marriage contract from land of the highest quality (Rambam *Sefer Nashim, Hilkhot Ishut* 16:3; *Shulḥan Arukh, Even HaEzer* 100:2).

Since it is a rabbinic ordinance – הוֹאִיל וְתַקָּנַת חֲכָמִים הוּא: Some authorities (Rabbeinu Tam) rule in accordance with the statement of Rabban Shimon Ben Gamliel, whose statements in the mishna are generally the basis for the halakhic ruling that the marriage contract is an obligation by Torah law. However, most authorities rule that the marriage contract is an ordinance by rabbinic law. This in accordance with the statement cited by Rav Naḥman in the name of Shmuel, as the halakhic ruling is generally in accordance with both Shmuel and Rav Naḥman in civil matters (Rambam *Sefer Nashim, Hilkhot Ishut* 10:7; *Shulḥan Arukh, Even HaEzer* 66:6).

הַהוּא דַּאֲתָא לְקַמֵּיהּ דְּרַב נַחְמָן, אֲמַר לֵיהּ: פֶּתַח פָּתוּחַ מָצָאתִי. אֲמַר לֵיהּ רַב נַחְמָן: אַסְבְּוּהוּ כּוּפְרֵי, מְבָרַכְתָּא חֲבִיטָא לֵיהּ.

§ The Gemara relates: **A certain** man **who** had never been married **came before Rav Naḥman and said to him: I encountered an unobstructed orifice** when I consummated the marriage. **Rav Naḥman said** in his regard: **Flog him with palm branches** [***kufrei***];[L] **prostitutes** [***mevarakhta***][LN] **are common** around **him.**[N] As he was never previously married, how was he able to determine whether or not the orifice was unobstructed, if he did not gain experience with prostitutes?

וְהָא רַב נַחְמָן הוּא דַּאֲמַר מְהֵימָן! מְהֵימָן, וּמַסְבִּינַן לֵיהּ כּוּפְרִי. רַב אַחַאי מְשַׁנֵּי: כָּאן – בְּבָחוּר, כָּאן – בְּנָשׂוּי.

The Gemara asks: **But isn't Rav Naḥman he who said that he is deemed credible** when he claims that he encountered an unobstructed orifice? The Gemara answers: Yes, **he is deemed credible,** and nevertheless, **we flog him with palm branches. Rav Aḥai answered: Here,** in the case where he is flogged, it is **with regard to a bachelor,** who is not accorded credibility, because he lacks experience. **There,** in the case where he is accorded credibility, it is **with regard to** one who has been **married.**[H]

הַהוּא דַּאֲתָא לְקַמֵּיהּ דְּרַבָּן גַּמְלִיאֵל, אֲמַר לֵיהּ: פֶּתַח פָּתוּחַ מָצָאתִי. אֲמַר לֵיהּ: שֶׁמָּא הִטִּיתָהּ? אֶמְשׁוֹל לְךָ מָשָׁל, לְמָה הַדָּבָר דּוֹמֶה – לְאָדָם שֶׁהָיָה מְהַלֵּךְ בְּאִישׁוֹן לַיְלָה וַאֲפֵילָה, הִיטָּה – מְצָאוֹ פָּתוּחַ, לֹא הִיטָּה – מְצָאוֹ נָעוּל.

The Gemara relates a similar incident from an earlier era: **A certain** man **who came before Rabban Gamliel said to him: I encountered an unobstructed orifice.** Rabban Gamliel **said to him: Perhaps you diverted** your approach[NH] and therefore, you encountered no obstruction? **I will tell you a parable to which this is similar.** It is similar **to a man who was walking in the blackness of night and darkness** and he arrived at the entrance to the house; if **he diverts** the object preventing the door from opening, **he finds it open;** if **he does not divert it, he finds it locked.** Perhaps you too diverted your approach and entered from a different angle and that is why you did not encounter an obstruction.

אִיכָּא דְּאָמְרִי, הָכִי אֲמַר לֵיהּ: שֶׁמָּא בְּמֵזִיד הִטִּיתָהּ וְעָקַרְתָּ לְדַשָּׁא וְעַבְרָא? אֶמְשׁוֹל לְךָ מָשָׁל לְמָה הַדָּבָר דּוֹמֶה – לְאָדָם שֶׁהוּא מְהַלֵּךְ בְּאִישׁוֹן לַיְלָה וַאֲפֵילָה; הִיטָּה בְּמֵזִיד – מְצָאוֹ פָּתוּחַ. לֹא הִיטָּה בְּמֵזִיד – מְצָאוֹ נָעוּל.

Some say this is what Rabban Gamliel **said to him: Maybe you diverted** your approach **intentionally and you displaced the door**[N] **and the bolt. I will tell you a parable to which this is similar.** It is similar **to a man who is walking in the blackness of night and darkness** and he arrives at his entrance. **If he diverts intentionally, he finds it open; if he does not divert intentionally, he finds it locked.**

הַהוּא דַּאֲתָא לְקַמֵּיהּ דְּרַבָּן גַּמְלִיאֵל בַּר רַבִּי, אֲמַר לֵיהּ: רַבִּי, בָּעַלְתִּי וְלֹא מָצָאתִי דָּם. אָמְרָה לוֹ: רַבִּי, בְּתוּלָה הָיִיתִי. אָמַר לָהֶם: הָבִיאוּ לִי אוֹתוֹ סוּדָר. הֵבִיאוּ לוֹ הַסּוּדָר וּשְׁרָאוֹ בַּמַּיִם, וְכִבְּסוֹ, וּמָצָא עָלָיו כַּמָּה טִיפֵּי דָמִים. אָמַר לוֹ: לֵךְ זְכֵה בְּמִקָּחֲךָ.

The Gemara relates: **A certain man who came before Rabban Gamliel bar Rabbi** Yehuda HaNasi **said to him: My teacher, I engaged in intercourse and did not find blood.** The bride **said to him: My teacher, I was a virgin.** Rabban Gamliel bar Rabbi Yehuda HaNasi **said to them: Bring me that cloth** [***sudar***][L] on which you consummated the marriage. **They brought him the cloth, and he soaked it in water and laundered it and found upon it several drops of blood** from the rupture of the hymen. Rabban Gamliel bar Rabbi Yehuda HaNasi **said to** the groom: **Go take possession of your acquisition,** as she was a virgin and there is no need for concern.

אֲמַר לֵיהּ הוּנָא מָר בְּרֵיהּ דְּרָבָא מִפַּרְזַקְיָא לְרַב אַשִׁי: אֲנַן נַמִי נַעֲבֵיד הָכִי – אֲמַר לֵיהּ

Huna Mar, son of Rava, from Parzakya, said to Rav Ashi: Let us do so as well in similar cases and examine whether there is blood that is obscured by semen or another substance. Rav Ashi **said to him:**

LANGUAGE

Palm branches [*kufrei*] – **כּוּפְרֵי:** An Aramaic word, similar to the Arabic كفري, *kafarrā*, meaning palm fronds and palm branches.

Prostitutes [*mevarakhta*] – **מְבָרַכְתָּא:** According to Rashi, this is the name of a village or town near Meḥoza whose name means caravan or convoy of camels. Therefore, it may have been a market town frequented by prostitutes. Some say that the word means convoy, and in this context, a group of prostitutes.

In Syriac, the term *mevarekh* is employed as a euphemism for debased or shameful. Therefore, it is possible that *mevarakhta* means prostitutes.

Cloth [*sudar*] – **סוּדָר:** From the Greek σουδάριον, *sudarion*, or the Latin sudarium, meaning towel or napkin. In the language of the Sages a *sudar* is apparently a cloth with a variety of functions, e.g., a scarf, a head covering, or a tablecloth.

NOTES

Prostitutes – **מְבָרַכְתָּא:** Rashi writes, and it is also cited in the *Arukh*, that this is the name of a place frequented by prostitutes. Rabbeinu Ḥananel explains, and it is also cited in the *Arukh* and elsewhere in the name of the *ge'onim*, that it means a small pool. In this context, it is a euphemism for the female genitalia. Others explain that because the word contains the Hebrew root for bless, it is a euphemism for prostitutes, substituting blessed for cursed.

Flog him with palm branches, prostitutes are common around him – **אַסְבְּוּהוּ כּוּפְרֵי מְבָרַכְתָּא חֲבִיטָא לֵיהּ:** Rashi understands the expression: Prostitutes are common around him, as a statement. The Gemara is saying that he is accorded credibility and flogged because he is suspect of gaining experience through licentious relations. *Tosafot* understand the expression as a rhetorical question. The Gemara is saying that the bachelor is not accorded credibility because he is not expert in the matter.

Some explain that there are three distinct cases. If a bachelor makes the claim it is considered impertinent and slanderous; his claim is not accorded credibility and he is flogged for slander. If he is insistent and states that he is certain, his claim is accepted but he is flogged for licentiousness. If he was previously married, his claim is credible and there are no sanctions (see Meiri).

The Ritva asks: If a bachelor claiming that his bride is not a virgin is flogged, he will refrain from coming to court at all, and that undermines the whole purpose of the ordinance of marrying a virgin on Wednesday. He answers that there remains the claim that no bleeding resulted from the rupture of the hymen. Furthermore, once his claim is a certain one and he is angry, he will certainly not be deterred from making his claim in court even if as a result he will be flogged.

Perhaps you diverted your approach, etc. – **שֶׁמָּא הִטִּיתָהּ וכו׳:** The Ritva notes that there were no grounds to prohibit the woman here, e.g., she was the wife of a non-priest and therefore there was compound uncertainty. Rabban Gamliel simply sought to appease the husband, so that he would not be resentful toward his wife for no reason. Indeed, based on the questions that Rabban Gamliel asked and the groom's silence in response, it appears that he was appeased.

And you displaced the door – **וְעָקַרְתָּ לְדַשָּׁא:** The explanation is that in his passion, he engaged in intercourse so forcefully that he did not sense her hymen (Ritva; see Rambam and *Shulḥan Arukh*).

HALAKHA

Here it is with regard to a bachelor, there it is with regard to one who has been married – **כָּאן בְּבָחוּר, כָּאן בְּנָשׂוּי:** According to the Rambam, if a groom claims that he encountered an unobstructed orifice when consummating his marriage with his bride, whom he presumed was a virgin, his claim is accorded credibility, whether or not he was previously married, in accordance with the first answer cited in the Gemara and the second explanation of *Tosafot* (see Gra). However, if he is a bachelor, he is deserving of lashes because he is suspected of gaining experience through licentious relations (*Ḥelkat Meḥokek*). The Rema cites authorities (Rif; *Tur*) who rule that the groom's claim is credible only if he was previously married. If not, his claim is rejected and he is flogged for slandering his wife (Rambam *Sefer Nashim*, *Hilkhot Ishut* 11:12; *Shulḥan Arukh*, *Even HaEzer* 68:6).

Perhaps you diverted your approach – **שֶׁמָּא הִטִּיתָהּ:** If a groom claims that he encountered an unobstructed orifice when consummating his marriage with his bride, whom he presumed was a virgin, the court asks him whether he diverted his approach during intercourse or if perhaps he employed force and therefore did not sense when the hymen was ruptured. This is in accordance with the opinion of Rambam Gamliel (Rambam *Sefer Nashim*, *Hilkhot Ishut* 11:12; *Shulḥan Arukh*, *Even HaEzer* 68:6).

גִּיהוּץ שֶׁלָּנוּ כְּכִבּוּס שֶׁלָּהֶם. וְאִי אָמְרַתְּ נִיעֲבַד גִּיהוּץ – מַעַבְּרָא לֵיהּ חוּמְרְתָא.

Our calendering in Babylonia, which includes passing an abrasive stone over the garments to scrape off dirt, **is like their laundering** in Eretz Israel, and only in that manner do the garments in Babylonia reach that level of cleanliness. **And if you say: Let us perform** the process of **calendering** on cloths brought as proof that she was not a virgin, **the stone removes** any trace of blood. Therefore, the process would be ineffective.

הַהוּא דַּאֲתָא לְקַמֵּיהּ דְּרַבָּן גַּמְלִיאֵל בַּר רַבִּי, אֲמַר לֵיהּ: רַבִּי, בָּעַלְתִּי וְלֹא מָצָאתִי דָּם. אָמְרָה לֵיהּ: רַבִּי, עֲדַיִין בְּתוּלָה אֲנִי. אָמַר לָהֶן: הָבִיאוּ לִי שְׁתֵּי שְׁפָחוֹת, אַחַת בְּתוּלָה וְאַחַת בְּעוּלָה. הֵבִיאוּ לוֹ, וְהוֹשִׁיבָן עַל פִּי חָבִית שֶׁל יַיִן. בְּעוּלָה – רֵיחָהּ נוֹדֵף, בְּתוּלָה – אֵין רֵיחָהּ נוֹדֵף, אַף זוֹ הוֹשִׁיבָהּ, וְלֹא הָיָה רֵיחָהּ נוֹדֵף, אָמַר לוֹ: לֵךְ זְכֵה בְּמִקָּחֲךָ.

The Gemara relates: **A certain** man **who came before Rabban Gamliel bar Rabbi** Yehuda HaNasi **said to him: My teacher, I engaged in intercourse and did not find blood.** The bride **said to him: My teacher, I am still a virgin.** Rabban Gamliel bar Rabbi Yehuda HaNasi **said to them: Bring me two maidservants,**[H] **one a virgin and one a non-virgin,** to conduct a trial. **They brought him** the two maidservants, **and he seated them on the opening of a barrel of wine.** From **the non-virgin,** he discovered that the **scent** of the wine in the barrel **diffuses** from her mouth; from **the virgin** he discovered that the **scent does not diffuse** from her mouth.[B] Then, **he also seated that** bride on the barrel, **and** the scent of the wine **did not diffuse** from her mouth. Rabban Gamliel bar Rabbi Yehuda HaNasi **said to** the groom: **Go take possession of your acquisition,** as she is a virgin.

וְנִבְדּוֹק מֵעִיקָּרָא בְּגַוָּהּ? גְּמָרָא הֲוָה שְׁמִיעַ לֵיהּ, מַעֲשֶׂה לָא הֲוָה חָזֵי, וְסָבַר דִּלְמָא לָא קִים לֵיהּ בְּגַוָּהּ דְּמִלְּתָא שַׁפִּיר, וְלָאו אוֹרַח אַרְעָא לְזַלְזוּלֵי בִּבְנוֹת יִשְׂרָאֵל.

The Gemara asks: Since Rabban Gamliel was familiar with this method of examination, **let him** use it to **examine her initially.** Why was the trial with the maidservants necessary? The Gemara answers: **He learned** that it was effective through **tradition;**[N] however, **he had never seen it in action, and he thought perhaps he was not sufficiently expert in** that **manner** of examination, **and it is improper conduct to demean Jewish women** by subjecting them to that indignity for naught. Once he established the effectiveness of that method, he proceeded to examine the bride to resolve the matter.

הַהוּא דַּאֲתָא לְקַמֵּיהּ דְּרַבָּן גַּמְלִיאֵל הַזָּקֵן, אָמַר לוֹ: רַבִּי, בָּעַלְתִּי וְלֹא מָצָאתִי דָּם. אָמְרָה לוֹ: רַבִּי, מִמִּשְׁפַּחַת דּוֹרְקְטִי אֲנִי, שֶׁאֵין לָהֶן לֹא דַּם נִדָּה וְלֹא דַּם בְּתוּלִים. בָּדַק רַבָּן גַּמְלִיאֵל בִּקְרוֹבוֹתֶיהָ וּמָצָא כִּדְבָרֶיהָ. אָמַר לוֹ: לֵךְ זְכֵה בְּמִקָּחֲךָ, אַשְׁרֶיךָ שֶׁזָּכִיתָ לְמִשְׁפַּחַת דּוֹרְקְטִי.

The Gemara relates: **A certain** man **who came before Rabban Gamliel the Elder said to him: My teacher, I engaged in intercourse and did not find blood.** The bride **said to him: My teacher, I am from the family of Dorketi,**[HLB] **who have neither menstrual blood nor blood** from the rupture of **the hymen. Rabban Gamliel investigated among her relatives** to determine whether the claim with regard to her family was true, **and discovered** that the truth was **in accordance with her statement. He said to him: Go take possession of your acquisition. Happy are you that you were privileged** to marry a member of **the Dorketi family,** as those forms of blood will never pose a problem for you.

HALAKHA

Bring me two maidservants – הָבִיאוּ לִי שְׁתֵּי שְׁפָחוֹת: If the groom claims he discovered that his bride was not a virgin, and she claims in response that she is still a virgin, she is examined. The *Maggid Mishne* explains that the Rambam did not specifically mention examination by means of a barrel of wine because any examination that is effective is appropriate (see *Taz*; Rambam *Sefer Nashim, Hilkhot Ishut* 11:12; *Shulḥan Arukh, Even HaEzer* 68:4).

I am from the family of Dorketi – מִמִּשְׁפַּחַת דּוֹרְקְטִי אֲנִי: In a case where the groom claims that he found no traces of blood upon consummating the marriage and the bride claims that the women in her family do not bleed, if the court determined the latter to be true, her presumptive status is that she was a virgin before the marriage was consummated (Rambam *Sefer Nashim, Hilkhot Ishut* 11:12; *Shulḥan Arukh, Even HaEzer* 68:5).

NOTES

He learned that it was effective through tradition, etc. – גְּמָרָא הֲוָה שְׁמִיעַ לֵיהּ וכו׳: The commentaries ask: If there was a tradition that this examination is effective, why didn't Rabban Gamliel examine the bride herself? They explain, based on the responsa of the *ge'onim*, that this examination requires extreme attention to detail, both in terms of the manner in which the woman is seated on the barrel and in terms of ascertaining the aroma of wine in her breath. His lack of expertise was with regard to those details, as he knew based on tradition that it was effective (*Tur*; *Maggid Mishne*).

LANGUAGE

Dorketi – דּוֹרְקְטִי: The source of this word is unclear. Some suggest, especially according to the variant reading *trokati*, that it is from the Greek τρυγᾶν, *trugan*, meaning to harvest or to rob.

BACKGROUND

The scent of the virgin does not diffuse – בְּתוּלָה אֵין רֵיחָהּ נוֹדֵף: Although there is no direct connection between the reproductive system and the lungs, different systems in the body are connected by means of the diffusion of volatile substances. An example of this is that although there is no direct connection between the digestive and respiratory systems, the fact is that alcohol that one drinks diffuses through the membranes of the lungs.

Apparently, the examination discussed in the Gemara is based on the phenomenon of diffusion through the vagina. Based on the assumption that there is a palpable difference between the diffusion of alcohol vapors between a virgin and a non-virgin, this difference would eventually be discernible in the air exhaled from the lungs.

The reliability of this examination is clearly dependent on the manner in which the woman is seated on the barrel, the percentage of alcohol in the wine, and the speed at which the alcohol fumes diffuse. Therefore, Rabban Gamliel performed a preliminary examination because he thought perhaps he was not sufficiently expert in that manner of examination.

The family of Dorketi – מִשְׁפַּחַת דּוֹרְקְטִי: Apparently, there is a genetic factor that influences the prevalence or lack of blood. As a rule, the assumption is that a woman with no menstrual blood is infertile and incapable of bearing children. In the case of the Dorketi family mentioned here, there was presumably a hereditary factor in the women that caused the absolute lack of menstrual blood. The women in the family who did not menstruate were barren, and the family was perpetuated by the women who menstruated at least somewhat. However, as even they were carriers of that same genetic factor, the result was that as many as half the women in the family were barren. For this reason they were called a truncated generation.

מַאי דּוֹרְקְטִי – דּוֹר קָטוּעַ. אָמַר רַבִּי חֲנִינָא: תַּנְחוּמִים שֶׁל הֶבֶל נִיחֲמוֹ רַבָּן גַּמְלִיאֵל לְאוֹתוֹ הָאִישׁ. דְּתָנֵי רַבִּי חִיָּיא: כְּשֵׁם שֶׁהַשְּׂאוֹר יָפֶה לָעִיסָּה כָּךְ דָּמִים יָפִים לָאִשָּׁה. וְתָנָא מִשּׁוּם רַבִּי מֵאִיר: כׇּל אִשָּׁה שֶׁדָּמֶיהָ מְרוּבִּין – בָּנֶיהָ מְרוּבִּים.

The Gemara elaborates: **What is the meaning of Dorketi?** It means **truncated generation** [***dor katua***].[N] **Rabbi Ḥanina said: Rabban Gamliel consoled that man with vain** words of **consolation,** because the absence of blood in this woman is a drawback. **As Rabbi Ḥiyya taught: Just as leaven is fortuitous for dough, so too, blood is fortuitous for a woman. And it was taught in the name of Rabbi Meir: Any woman whose blood is plentiful, her children are plentiful.**[B] This bride, who lacks blood, will not produce many children.

אִתְּמַר, רַבִּי יִרְמְיָה בַּר אַבָּא אָמַר: ״זְכֵה בְּמִקָּחֲךָ״ אָמַר לֵיהּ. וְרַבִּי יוֹסֵי בַּר אָבִין אָמַר: ״נִתְחַיֵּיב בְּמִקָּחֲךָ״ אָמַר לֵיהּ. בִּשְׁלָמָא לְמַאן דְּאָמַר ״נִתְחַיֵּיב״ – הַיְינוּ דְּרַבִּי חֲנִינָא, אֶלָּא לְמַאן דְּאָמַר ״זְכֵה״ – מַאי זְכוּתָא? דְּלָא אָתֵי לִידֵי סְפֵק נִדָּה.

It was stated that there is a dispute with regard to Rabban Gamliel's reply. **Rabbi Yirmeya bar Abba said** that Rabban Gamliel **said to** the groom: **Exercise your privilege** and take possession **of your acquisition.**[N] **And Rabbi Yosei bar Avin said** that Rabban Gamliel **said to him:** It is your **misfortune** to take possession **of your acquisition. Granted, according to the one who says:** It is your **misfortune, that is** in accordance with the opinion **of Rabbi Ḥanina,** who said the consolation was vain. **However, according to the one who says: Exercise your privilege, what is the privilege** to which he is referring? The Gemara answers: The privilege is **that** thanks to the condition of the women of this family, **he will not come to a situation of uncertainty** whether she has the halakhic status of a **menstruating woman.**

הַהוּא דַּאֲתָא לְקַמֵּיהּ דְּרַבִּי, אֲמַר לֵיהּ: רַבִּי, בָּעַלְתִּי וְלֹא מָצָאתִי דָּם. אָמְרָה לוֹ: רַבִּי, עֲדַיִין בְּתוּלָה הָיִיתִי, וּשְׁנֵי בַּצּוֹרֶת הֲוָה. רָאָה רַבִּי שֶׁפְּנֵיהֶם שְׁחוֹרִים, צִוָּה עֲלֵיהֶן וְהִכְנִיסוּם לַמֶּרְחָץ, וְהֶאֱכִילוּם וְהִשְׁקוּם, וְהִכְנִיסוּם לַחֶדֶר, בָּעַל וּמָצָא דָּם. אָמַר לוֹ: לֵךְ זְכֵה בְּמִקָּחֲךָ. קָרֵי רַבִּי עֲלֵיהֶם: ״צָפַד עוֹרָם עַל עַצְמָם יָבֵשׁ הָיָה כָעֵץ״.

The Gemara relates: **A certain man who came before Rabbi** Yehuda HaNasi **said to him: My teacher, I engaged in intercourse and did not find blood.** The bride **said to him: My teacher, I was still a virgin. And** the Gemara comments that this incident **was during years of drought.**[H] **Rabbi** Yehuda HaNasi **saw that their faces were black**[BN] due to hunger. **He instructed** his attendants to tend **to them and they took them into the bathhouse** and bathed them **and they fed them and gave them drink.** Then **they took them into a room,** and the groom **engaged in intercourse** with her **and found blood,** as it was due to the famine that there was no blood. Rabbi Yehuda HaNasi **said to him: Go take possession of your acquisition. Rabbi** Yehuda HaNasi **read** this verse **in their regard: "Their skin is shriveled upon their bones, it is withered, it has become like a stick"** (Lamentations 4:8), in the sense that no blood flows from them.

מתני׳ בְּתוּלָה כְּתוּבָּתָהּ מָאתַיִם וְאַלְמָנָה מָנֶה. בְּתוּלָה, אַלְמָנָה, גְּרוּשָׁה, וַחֲלוּצָה מִן הָאֵירוּסִין – כְּתוּבָּתָן מָאתַיִם, וְיֵשׁ לָהֶן טַעֲנַת בְּתוּלִים.

MISHNA With regard to **a virgin, her marriage contract is two hundred dinars,**[H] **and** with regard to **a widow,** her marriage contract **is one hundred** dinars. With regard to **a virgin** who is **a widow, a divorcée, or a *ḥalutza***[N] who achieved that status **from** a state of **betrothal,** before marriage and before consummation of the marriage, for all of these **their marriage contract is two hundred** dinars, **and they are subject to a claim concerning** their **virginity,** as their presumptive status of virginity is intact.

BACKGROUND

Her blood and her children – דָּמֶיהָ וּבָנֶיהָ: There is a connection between a woman's menstrual blood and the degree of her fertility. A woman who does not experience a monthly period but rather menstruates once every few months or even less frequently will tend to be less fertile, as the menstrual blood is an indicator of the ovulation that preceded it. Similarly, when the amount of menstrual blood is less than is typical, it can indicate a hormonal, nutritional, or physiological problem, which could also prevent conception.

He saw that their faces were black – רָאָה...שֶׁפְּנֵיהֶם שְׁחוֹרִים: Severe malnutrition could cause a simple wound, e.g., the rupture of the hymen, not to bleed. Similarly, starvation and exhaustion could have affected the husband, rendering him unable to engage in the full act of intercourse. Treatment that addresses this condition could alleviate the problem.

HALAKHA

Years of drought – שְׁנֵי בַּצּוֹרֶת: If the groom claims that upon consummating the marriage he found no traces of blood, and it is a period of famine or the woman appears to be suffering from malnutrition, she is brought to the bathhouse and treated and given food and drink. Then the next time she engages in intercourse she is examined for bleeding (Rambam *Sefer Nashim, Hilkhot Ishut* 11:12; *Shulḥan Arukh, Even HaEzer* 68:5).

With regard to a virgin, her marriage contract is two hundred dinars – בְּתוּלָה כְּתוּבָּתָהּ מָאתַיִם: The marriage contract of a virgin is at least two hundred dinars, and that of a widow is at least one hundred dinars (Rambam *Sefer Nashim, Hilkhot Ishut* 11:12; *Shulḥan Arukh, Even HaEzer* 66:6).

NOTES

Truncated generation [*dor katua*] – דּוֹר קָטוּעַ: According to Rashi, the menstrual cycles of the female members of the family were truncated. Alternatively, the *Arukh* posits that the generations of that family were truncated, as their women were incapable of giving birth.

Exercise your privilege [*zekhe*] and take possession of your acquisition, etc. – זְכֵה בְּמִקָּחֲךָ וכו׳: The *Shita Mekubbetzet* explains that the dispute was not with regard to the language employed by Rabban Gamliel. Rather, the dispute is whether he employed the term *zekhe* in the positive sense of privilege, or whether it was in the neutral sense of taking possession. There is a similar dispute in the Jerusalem Talmud with regard to that which Rabbi Yishmael, son of Rabbi Yosei, said to a woman with the same condition: May there be many like you among the Jewish people. Some say he was implying that it was a positive phenomenon, as the potential for rendering ritually pure items impure was non-existent in those women. Others say that he was speaking euphemistically, and actually considered it a negative phenomenon.

That their faces were black – שֶׁפְּנֵיהֶם שְׁחוֹרִים: There is a variant reading: That her face grew pale. This would indicate that that the ruling was dependent on the physical condition of the woman, who due to hunger and weakness did not bleed (*Piskei Rid*; *Yam shel Shlomo*). This appears to be the position of the Rambam as well. According to that understanding, they fed the husband merely as an act of loving-kindness, not because his condition influenced hers. The halakhic authorities write that even if the woman does not claim that the failure to bleed was due to her weakness, nevertheless when it can be attributed to that condition, the matter is examined.

A widow, a divorcée, or a *ḥalutza* – אַלְמָנָה גְּרוּשָׁה וַחֲלוּצָה: See *Tosafot* for an explanation of the novel element with regard to a *ḥalutza*. *Shita Mekubbetzet* explains that the novelty for each of the women listed is greater than for the previous one. Not only does a widow from betrothal receive the marriage contract of a virgin, but even a divorcée receives two hundred dinars, although one might contend that divorce carries with it a stigma rendering her less desirable. Had only the widow and the divorcée been listed, one might have contended that the *ḥalutza*, who is not only a widow but has suffered the indignity of performing the *ḥalitza* ceremony in court and at times even in public, would not receive a marriage contract of two hundred dinars due to the stigma involved.

גמ׳ מַאי אַלְמָנָה? אָמַר רַב חָנָא בַּגְדָּתָאָה: אַלְמָנָה – עַל שֵׁם מָנֶה. אַלְמָנָה מִן הָאֵירוּסִין מַאי אִיכָּא לְמֵימַר? אַיְּידֵי דְּהָא קָרֵי לָהּ אַלְמָנָה – הָא נַמִי קָרֵי לָהּ אַלְמָנָה.

GEMARA What is the relationship between the term *almana*[L] and its meaning, widow? **Rav Ḥana of Baghdad said:** A widow is called **an *almana* after** the *maneh*,[N] one hundred dinars, which is the sum of her marriage contract. The Gemara asks: With regard to **a widow from betrothal,** whose marriage contract is two hundred dinars and not a *maneh*, **what is there to say?** The Gemara answers: **Since they called this** widow from marriage ***almana*, this** widow from betrothal **they also called *almana*.**

אַלְמָנָה דִּכְתִיבָא בְּאוֹרַיְיתָא מַאי אִיכָּא לְמֵימַר? דַּעֲתִידִין רַבָּנַן דְּמִתַקְּנִי לָהּ מָנֶה. וּמִי כָּתַב קְרָא לֶעָתִיד? אִין, דִּכְתִיב ״וְשֵׁם הַנָּהָר הַשְּׁלִישִׁי חִדֶּקֶל הוּא הַהוֹלֵךְ קִדְמַת אַשּׁוּר״, וְתָנָא רַב יוֹסֵף: אַשּׁוּר זוֹ סֵלֵיקָא. וּמִי הֲוַאי? אֶלָּא דַּעֲתִידָה, הָכָא נַמִי – דַּעֲתִידָה.

The Gemara asks: That explains the use of *almana* in the terminology of the Sages. However, with regard to the term ***almana* that is written in the Torah, what is there to say?** The rabbinic ordinance that the marriage contract of a widow is a *maneh* was not yet instituted. The Gemara answers: The Torah employs the term *almana* **because the Sages are destined to institute** the sum of a ***maneh* for her** in her marriage contract. The Gemara asks: **And is a verse written for the future?** The Gemara answers: **Yes,** indeed it is, **as it is written: "And the name of the third river is Tigris; that is it which goes toward the east of Asshur"** (Genesis 2:14). **And Rav Yosef taught: Asshur, that is Seleucia.**[B] **And did** that city **exist** when the Torah was written? **Rather,** the Torah is referring to that city **because** it was **destined** to exist in the future. **Here too,** the Torah employs the term *almana* **because** a widow was **destined** to have a marriage contract of a *maneh* instituted for her.

וְאָמַר רַב חָנָא בַּגְדָּתָאָה: מָטָר מַשְׁקֶה, מַרְוֶה, וּמְזַבֵּל, וּמְעַדֵּן, וּמַמְשִׁיךְ. אֲמַר רָבָא בַּר רַבִּי יִשְׁמָעֵאל וְאִיתֵּימָא רַב יֵימַר בַּר שֶׁלֶמְיָא: מַאי קְרָא – ״תְּלָמֶיהָ רַוֵּה נַחֵת גְּדוּדֶיהָ בִּרְבִיבִים תְּמֹגְגֶנָּה צִמְחָהּ תְּבָרֵךְ״.

Apropos the statement of Rav Ḥana of Baghdad, the Gemara cites additional statements of his. **And Rav Ḥana of Baghdad said: Rain irrigates, saturates, and fertilizes** the land, **and refines** the fruit **and** causes it to **proliferate. Rava bar Rabbi Yishmael, and some say** it was **Rav Yeimar bar Shelamya who said: What is the verse** that alludes to this? **"Watering its ridges abundantly, settling its furrows, You make it soft with showers, You bless its growth"** (Psalms 65:11). "Watering its ridges abundantly" indicates that the rain irrigates and saturates the land, "You make it soft with showers" indicates that it fertilizes the land, and "You bless its growth" indicates that it refines the fruit and causes it to proliferate.

אָמַר רַבִּי אֶלְעָזָר: מִזְבֵּחַ – מֵזִיחַ, וּמֵזִין, מְחַבֵּב, מְכַפֵּר. הַיְינוּ מְכַפֵּר הַיְינוּ מֵזִיחַ! מֵזִיחַ גְּזֵירוֹת וּמְכַפֵּר עֲוֹנוֹת.

Rabbi Elazar said: The term ***mizbe'aḥ***, altar, is a rough acrostic representing its qualities. **It moves [*meziaḥ*]** sins **and sustains [*mezin*]**, because as a result of the offerings sacrificed on the altar, sustenance is provided to all. **It endears [*meḥabev*]**, and **atones [*mekhapper*]**. *Mizbe'aḥ* evokes the letters *mem* and *zayin* from the first two qualities, *bet* from *meḥabev* and the *kaf* from *mekhapper*. The Gemara asks: **This** quality, that the altar **atones, is** the same as **that** quality, that it **moves** sins. Why are they listed separately? The Gemara answers: The altar **moves** evil **decrees, and atones** for **sins.**

וַאֲמַר רַב חָנָא בַּגְדָּתָאָה: תַּמְרֵי מְשַׁחֲנָן, מַשְׂבְּעָן, מְשַׁלְשְׁלָן, מְאַשְּׁרָן וְלָא מְפַנְּקָן. אָמַר רַב: אָכַל תְּמָרִים אַל יוֹרֶה. מֵיתִיבֵי: תְּמָרִים, שַׁחֲרִית וְעַרְבִית – יָפוֹת, בְּמִנְחָה – רָעוֹת, בַּצָּהֳרַיִם – אֵין כְּמוֹתָן. וּמְבַטְּלוֹת שְׁלֹשָׁה דְּבָרִים: מַחֲשָׁבָה רָעָה, וְחוֹלִי מֵעַיִם, וְתַחְתּוֹנִיּוֹת!

And Rav Ḥana of Baghdad said: Dates warm and satiate, loosen the bowels, strengthen, but do not pamper. Rav said: If one ate dates[B] **he should not issue** halakhic **rulings,**[NH] as dates are intoxicating. The Gemara **raises an objection:** With regard to **dates,** in the **morning and evening** they have a **positive** effect on one who eats them; **in the afternoon,** they have a **negative** effect on one who eats them. **At noon, their** positive effect is **unparalleled, and they negate three matters: A troubling thought, intestinal illness, and hemorrhoids.** Apparently, the effect of dates is primarily a positive one.

LANGUAGE

Widow [*almana*] – אַלְמָנָה: The derivation of this word is not at all simple. The early grammarians claimed that it is from the Hebrew word for mute, *illem*, and the letter *nun* is a suffix. This is also the case in the Hebrew words for complacent [*sha'anan*] and fresh [*ra'anan*].

In similar Semitic languages there are various forms of the word *almana*, e.g., the Aramaic *armalta*, which is similar to the Hebrew. This would indicate that the word *almana* is an independent term and not an extension of a different Hebrew root. The word *armalta* underwent a not uncommon transposition of the letters *lamed* and *reish* and *nun* and *lamed*, respectively, creating the word *almana*. Due to this apparent difficulty in ascertaining the source of the term, the Gemara thought it appropriate to add a homiletic interpretation.

NOTES

A widow is called an *almana* after the *maneh* – אַלְמָנָה עַל שֵׁם מָנֶה: The Ritva writes that the source of the term *almana* stems from the Hebrew word for mute, *illem*, as she is alone and there is no one to fight her battles. This consigns her to silence, unable to defend herself. The interpretation in the Gemara is based on the suffix *na*. Rashi explains that the word *almana* is an abbreviation meaning: Merely a *maneh* [*ela maneh*], while the *ge'onim* interpret it as an abbreviation for: Not a *maneh* [*al maneh*], because she receives one hundred dinars less than her virgin counterpart.

If one ate dates he should not issue halakhic rulings – אָכַל תְּמָרִים אַל יוֹרֶה: The source of the *halakha* that it is prohibited for one who is intoxicated to issue halakhic rulings is the prohibition, punishable by death at the hand of Heaven, against priests performing the Temple service under the influence of alcohol or any other food or drink capable of causing intoxication or confusion (Leviticus 10:9). The next two verses state: "And that you may distinguish between the holy and the profane, and between the impure and the pure; and that you may teach the children of Israel all the statutes which the Lord has spoken unto them by the hand of Moses" (Leviticus 10:10–11), indicating that the prohibition goes beyond Temple service and applies to teaching the Jewish people as well.

BACKGROUND

Seleucia – סְלֵיקָא: This seems to be referring to the large city of Σελεύκεια, *Silukia*, on the Tigris River. The city was established by King Seleucus I in the beginning of the third century BCE on the ruins of an ancient city, and became the capital of the Seleucid Empire and one of the largest cities in the East. It had a large population as well, and was an important commercial center. It remained an important city during the Parthian Empire. Seleucia was destroyed in the year 153 CE, and the city of Ardashir was built on its ruins.

Eating dates – אֲכִילַת תְּמָרִים: Dates are high in calories, which are mostly delivered in the form of simple carbohydrates that are digested rapidly. Therefore, eating dates satiates, raises the body temperature, and due to their high level of fiber acts as a laxative. Satiation that is not accompanied by a sense of overeating creates a general sense of calm and thereby negates troubling thoughts.

Because dates satiate, it is recommended not to eat them before a meal. However, after a meal they are beneficial; first, because they satiate, and secondly, because their laxative property is beneficial for digestion. This latter property helps ease the pain of those suffering from hemorrhoids, and there could be an element in dates that aids in healing that ailment.

Eating a large quantity of a concentrated, sweet substance could create an excess of sugar in the blood, which could cause dizziness and drowsiness, similar to the effects of drinking alcohol. Therefore, the Sages said that one may not issue a halakhic ruling after eating dates.

HALAKHA

If one ate dates he should not issue halakhic rulings – אָכַל תְּמָרִים אַל יוֹרֶה: A rabbinic scholar may not render a halakhic decision while intoxicated. Even if he ate dates or drank milk, leading to slight lightheadedness, he may not issue a halakhic ruling, in accordance with the opinion of Rav (Rambam *Sefer Avoda, Hilkhot Biat HaMikdash* 1:3; *Shulḥan Arukh, Yoreh De'a* 242:13 and in the comment of Rema).

מִי אָמְרִינַן דְּלָא מַעֲלוּ? עִלּוּיֵי מַעֲלוּ, וּלְפִי שַׁעְתָּא טָרְדָא. מִידֵּי דַּהֲוָה אַחַמְרָא, דְּאָמַר מָר הַשּׁוֹתֶה רְבִיעִית יַיִן אַל יוֹרֶה. וְאִיבָּעֵית אֵימָא: לָא קַשְׁיָא; הָא – מִקַּמֵּי נַהֲמָא, הָא – לְבָתַר נַהֲמָא. דְּאָמַר אַבָּיֵי, אָמְרָה לִי אֵם: תַּמְרֵי מִקַּמֵּי נַהֲמָא – כִּי נַרְגָּא לְדִיקוּלָא, בָּתַר נַהֲמָא – כִּי עַבְרָא לְדַשָּׁא.

The Gemara answers that there is no contradiction. **Did we say that they are not exemplary? They are exemplary, and** at the same time **cause temporary distraction** and **intoxication, just as it is** in the case **of wine, as the Master said: One who drinks a quarter-*log* of wine should not issue** halakhic **rulings. And if you wish, say** instead: This apparent contradiction is **not difficult. This** statement, which prohibits issuing a ruling under the influence of dates, is referring to one eating dates **before** he eats **bread,** when eating them can lead to intoxication. **That** statement, which enumerates the salutary effects of dates, is referring **to** one eating dates **after** he eats **bread. As Abaye said: My mother told me** that **dates** eaten **before** eating **bread** are destructive **like an ax to a palm tree;** dates eaten **after** eating **bread** they are beneficial **like a bolt to a door,** which provides support.

דַּשָּׁא, אָמַר רָבָא: דֶּרֶךְ שָׁם. דַּרְגָּא, אָמַר רָבָא: דֶּרֶךְ גַּג. פּוּרְיָא, אָמַר רַב פַּפָּא: שֶׁפָּרִין וְרָבִין עָלֶיהָ. אָמַר רַב נַחְמָן בַּר יִצְחָק:

Apropos the term door [*dasha*], the Gemara cites statements referring to its etymology as well as that of several other Aramaic terms. With regard to the word ***dasha*,** door, **Rava said:** It is an acrostic for ***derekh sham*,** meaning through there. With regard to the word ***darga*,** ladder or stair, **Rava said:** It is an acrostic for ***derekh gag*,** meaning way to the roof. With regard to the word ***purya*,** bed, **Rav Pappa said:** It is an acrostic for ***parin veravin aleha*,** meaning one procreates upon it. **Rav Naḥman bar Yitzḥak said:**

Perek **I**
Daf **11** Amud **a**

אַף אָנוּ נֹאמַר: אַיְילוֹנִית – דּוּכְרָנִית דְּלָא יָלְדָה.

We too will say: *Ailonit*, a sexually underdeveloped woman,[B] is a term meaning: Like a **ram** [***dukhranit***],[L] **because** like a male sheep [*ayyil*] **she does not bear children.**

מתני׳ הַגִּיּוֹרֶת וְהַשְּׁבוּיָה וְהַשִּׁפְחָה, שֶׁנִּפְדּוּ וְשֶׁנִּתְגַּיְּירוּ וְשֶׁנִּשְׁתַּחְרְרוּ פְּחוּתוֹת מִבְּנוֹת שָׁלֹשׁ שָׁנִים וְיוֹם אֶחָד – כְּתוּבָּתָן מָאתַיִם, וְיֵשׁ לָהֶן טַעֲנַת בְּתוּלִין.

MISHNA With regard to **a female convert, or a captive woman,**[N] **or a maidservant,**[B] **who were ransomed** with regard to the captive, or **who converted** with regard to the convert, **or who were freed** with regard to the maidservant, when they were **less than three years and one day old,**[H] **their marriage contract is two hundred** dinars, as their presumptive status is that of a virgin. Even if they were subject to intercourse when they were younger than that age, the hymen remains intact. **And they are** subject to **a claim** concerning their **virginity.**

BACKGROUND

Sexually underdeveloped woman [*ailonit*] – אַיְילוֹנִית: From the detailed discussions in the Talmud, primarily in tractate *Yevamot*, an *ailonit* is apparently a woman suffering from a genetic condition that renders her unable to have children. This is not to be confused with sterility, which is a condition caused by certain secondary defects; the physical and sexual development of a sterile woman is standard. The *ailonit* is also characterized by different physical development in secondary sexual characteristics, e.g., growth of pubic hair. There are different theories as to the causes of this condition, ranging from those who attribute it to overproduction of male hormones to those who identify it as Turner's syndrome.

There are detailed halakhic discussions with regard to the legal status of an *ailonit*, primarily due to the total lack or delayed development of secondary sexual characteristics. As a result, various questions are raised with regard to determining when the *ailonit* assumes the status of a young woman and a grown woman.

Maidservant – שִׁפְחָה: This refers to a Canaanite maidservant, a female gentile purchased by a Jew as a slave. Like a male Canaanite slave, after she is purchased she must be immersed in a ritual bath and subsequently her personal status changes: She henceforth must observe all of the Torah's prohibitions and is obligated to observe positive mitzvot that apply to a Jewish woman. Nevertheless, she is not fully Jewish and may not marry a Jewish man, except under special circumstances, where her master arranges a marriage for her with a Hebrew slave for the purpose of producing children whose status is like her own. As with a male Canaanite slave, it is permitted to sell a maidservant to other Jews but not to non-Jews. Although the *halakha* is that her master is ordinarily prohibited from freeing her, if she receives a bill of manumission, it takes effect, and her status as a freed maidservant is similar to that of a convert.

LANGUAGE

Like a ram [*dukhranit*] – דּוּכְרָנִית: In Aramaic a ram [*ayyil*] is called *dikhra*, meaning male. Consequently, the term *ailonit* is derived from the Hebrew word for ram, whose Aramaic equivalent means male or masculine. An *ailonit*, therefore, is a woman incapable of having children, often masculine in appearance.

NOTES

A female convert, or a captive woman, etc. – הַגִּיּוֹרֶת וְהַשְּׁבוּיָה וכו׳: The Ritva points out that the order of the verbs: Ransomed, converted, and freed, does not correspond to the order of the subjects: Convert, captive, and maidservant. He explains that both the subjects and the verbs are listed in their respective order of importance. Converts, as people who consciously chose to join the Jewish people, are listed before victims of captivity and maidservants. Likewise, ransoming, i.e., fulfilling the mitzva of freeing captives, is the highest form of lovingkindness and takes precedence over conversion. Conversion, in turn, takes precedence over the freeing of slaves, as the latter is generally prohibited.

HALAKHA

A female convert…less than three years and one day old, etc. – הַגִּיּוֹרֶת...פְּחוּתוֹת מִבְּנוֹת שָׁלֹשׁ שָׁנִים וְיוֹם אֶחָד וכו׳: A female convert, redeemed captive, or freed slave who converted or was redeemed or freed when she was less than three years and one day old retains the presumptive status of a virgin. Therefore, she is entitled to a marriage contract of two hundred dinars and her husband may make a claim concerning her virginity (Rambam *Sefer Nashim*, *Hilkhot Ishut* 11:1; *Shulḥan Arukh*, *Even HaEzer* 67:3).

HALAKHA

With regard to a convert who is a minor, one immerses him with the consent of the court – גֵּר קָטָן מַטְבִּילִין אוֹתוֹ עַל דַּעַת בֵּית דִּין: A gentile minor may be immersed in a ritual bath for the purpose of conversion with the consent of the court, because the conversion is considered to be to his benefit, in accordance with the opinion of Rav Huna (Rambam *Sefer Kedusha, Hilkhot Issurei Bia* 13:7; *Shulḥan Arukh, Yoreh De'a* 268:7).

One may act in a person's interests in his absence – זָכִין לְאָדָם שֶׁלֹּא בְּפָנָיו: One may accept a gift on another's behalf or perform actions that benefit him without his knowledge; however, one may not act on his behalf to his detriment without his agreement (Rambam *Sefer Kinyan, Hilkhot Zekhiya* 4:2; *Shulḥan Arukh, Ḥoshen Mishpat* 243:1).

גמ׳ אָמַר רַב הוּנָא: גֵּר קָטָן מַטְבִּילִין אוֹתוֹ עַל דַּעַת בֵּית דִּין.

GEMARA Rav Huna said: With regard to a convert who is a minor,[N] one immerses him[N] in a ritual bath with the consent of the court.[H] As a minor lacks the capacity to make halakhic decisions, the court is authorized to make those decisions in his stead.

מַאי קָא מַשְׁמַע לַן – דִּזְכוּת הוּא לוֹ, וְזָכִין לְאָדָם שֶׁלֹּא בְּפָנָיו – תְּנֵינָא: זָכִין לְאָדָם שֶׁלֹּא בְּפָנָיו, וְאֵין חָבִין לְאָדָם שֶׁלֹּא בְּפָנָיו!

What is Rav Huna **coming to teach us?** Is he teaching **that it is a privilege for** the minor to convert,[N] **and one may act in a person's interests** even **in his absence?**[HN] **We** already **learned** that explicitly in a mishna (*Eiruvin* 81b): One **may act in a person's interests in his absence, but one may not act against a person's interests in his absence.**

מַהוּ דְּתֵימָא: גּוֹי בְּהֶפְקֵירָא נִיחָא לֵיהּ, דְּהָא קַיְימָא לַן דְּעֶבֶד וַדַּאי בְּהֶפְקֵירָא נִיחָא לֵיהּ,

Rav Huna's statement was necessary **lest you say:** With regard to **a gentile, licentiousness is preferable for him,** so conversion is contrary to his interests, just **as we maintain that** with regard to **a slave, licentiousness is certainly preferable.**[N] Just as a slave has no interest in assuming the restrictions that come with freedom, in that a freed Canaanite slave is a convert to Judaism, a gentile would have the same attitude toward conversion.

קָא מַשְׁמַע לַן: דְּהָנֵי מִילֵּי – גָּדוֹל, דְּטָעַם טַעַם דְּאִיסּוּרָא. אֲבָל קָטָן – זְכוּת הוּא לוֹ.

Therefore, Rav Huna **teaches us: That applies** only with regard to **an adult, who has experienced a taste of prohibition.** Therefore, presumably he prefers to remain a slave and indulge in licentiousness. **However,** with regard to a **minor,** who did not yet engage in those activities, **it is a privilege for him**[N] to convert.

לֵימָא מְסַיַּיע לֵיהּ: הַגִּיּוֹרֶת וְהַשְּׁבוּיָה וְהַשִּׁפְחָה שֶׁנִּפְדּוּ וְשֶׁנִּתְגַּיְּירוּ וְשֶׁנִּשְׁתַּחְרְרוּ פְּחוּתוֹת מִבְּנוֹת שָׁלֹשׁ שָׁנִים וְיוֹם אֶחָד. מַאי לָאו – דְּאַטְבְּלִינְהוּ עַל דַּעַת בֵּית דִּין?

The Gemara suggests: **Let us say** that the mishna **supports** Rav Huna's statement: With regard to **a female convert, or a captive woman, or a maidservant, who were ransomed** with regard to the captive, or **who converted** with regard to the convert, **or who were freed** with regard to the maidservant, when they were **less than three years and one day old; what, is it not** referring to a case where **they immersed** the minor converts and the maidservants **with the consent of the court?** Apparently, a conversion of that sort is valid.

NOTES

A convert who is a minor – גֵּר קָטָן: Rashi explains that this case is one of a fatherless, gentile child, whose mother is bringing him to be converted. The early commentaries seek to clarify: If the reference is to a case where the mother is converting with the child, then that is identical to the case cited later of a father converting his children; there is no distinction between the father and the mother in this matter (see Rashba). Some explain that this is a case where both the father and the mother want the child to convert, although they themselves are not converting (Ritva, citing Rashi). Others say that the child comes on his own initiative, as although he has not reached majority, he has the capacity, albeit limited, to make advised decisions.

Later commentaries explain, based on various sources, that the determination of majority as the age when one is halakhically capable of independent decision is a Torah law that applies uniquely to Jews. With regard to gentiles, that capacity is determined based on the ability of each individual, unrelated to age. According to all these opinions, the initiative for this conversion must originate either with the convert or with his parents; the court does not proselytize (see Mordekhai, citing Ra'avya). The Ran holds that if the court initiates conversion, the conversion is valid after the fact.

One immerses him – מַטְבִּילִין אוֹתוֹ: The early commentaries ask why Rav Huna did not mention the requirement of circumcision. They explain that he sought to address conversion that applies to all, not only to males (Ritva). The Meiri concurs, adding that the conversion process culminates with immersion even for males. The Rashba adds that there is a novel element with regard to immersion. Circumcision performed when one is a minor obviously remains into his adulthood. However, with regard to immersion, which leaves no lasting imprint, one might have thought that when he reaches majority he would require an additional immersion.

The *Shita Mekubbetzet* cites an opinion that since immersion is wholly beneficial, one may therefore act in the minor's interests and immerse him. However, circumcision is accompanied by pain, and therefore it is not an unadulterated privilege and cannot be performed for a minor convert. According to this explanation, Rav Huna is referring to a convert who is already circumcised.

It is a privilege for the minor to convert – זְכוּת הוּא לוֹ: *Tosafot* ask how the principle that one can act in another's interests even in his absence can be applied in this case. That principle is based on agency, and both a child and a gentile are halakhically incapable of appointing an agent. The *Shakh* explains in the book *Nekuddot HaKesef* that the conversion is not effected for the gentile child based on agency, but rather on the authority of the court to act on his behalf.

One may act in a person's interests in his absence – זָכִין לְאָדָם שֶׁלֹּא בְּפָנָיו: The *Shita Mekubbetzet* cites an opinion that provided an action is not completely to the detriment of another, it can be considered to be in his interests. That is why although converting to Judaism carries with it certain difficulties, e.g., the onus of the mitzvot, it is considered to be in his interests.

We maintain that with regard to a slave licentiousness is certainly preferable – הָא קַיְימָא לַן דְּעֶבֶד וַדַּאי בְּהֶפְקֵירָא נִיחָא לֵיהּ: *Tosafot* note that only according to Rabbi Meir is freeing a slave considered contrary to his interests, as he prefers his unrestricted lifestyle. According to the Rabbis, that is not the case. *Tosafot* ask why the Gemara cites that opinion as the consensus. For this reason, some early commentaries prefer a variant reading of the Gemara: With regard to a gentile, licentiousness is certainly preferable. The Ritva explains that even the Rabbis concede that the slave prefers his unrestricted lifestyle; however, they hold that the prospect of freedom outweighs that preference.

With regard to a minor, it is a privilege for him – קָטָן, זְכוּת הוּא לוֹ: Some maintain that until he reaches majority he is a convert by rabbinic law. Only upon reaching majority and accepting the mitzvot does he become a full-fledged convert by Torah law. The Ritva and others prove that he is considered a full-fledged convert by Torah law immediately, although he may renounce his conversion when reaching majority.

לא, הכא במאי עסקינן, בגר שנתגיירו בניו ובנותיו עמו, דניחא להו במאי דעביד אבוהון.

The Gemara rejects that proof: **No, with what are we dealing here?** It is **with a convert whose** minor **sons and daughters converted with him, as they are content with whatever their father does**[HN] in their regard. However, that does not apply to a child who is converting on his own.

אמר רב יוסף: הגדילו יכולין למחות. איתיביה אביי: הגיורת והשבויה והשפחה שנפדו ושנתגיירו ושנשתחררו פחותות מבנות שלש שנים ויום אחד – כתובתן מאתים. ואי סלקא דעתך הגדילו יכולין למחות – יהבינן לה כתובה דאזלה ואכלה בגיותה?!

Rav Yosef said: In any case where minors convert, when **they reach majority**[N] **they can protest**[HN] and annul their conversion.[N] **Abaye raised an objection to his** opinion from the mishna: With regard to **a female convert, or a captive woman, or a maidservant who were ransomed, or who converted, or who were freed** when they were **less than three years and one day old, their marriage contract is two hundred** dinars. **And if it enters your mind** to say that when **they reach majority they can protest** and annul their conversion, **do we give her** the payment of the **marriage contract that she will go and consume in her gentile** state?

לכי גדלה. לכי גדלה נמי, ממחייא ונפקא! כיון שהגדילה שעה אחת ולא מיחתה – שוב אינה יכולה למחות.

The Gemara answers: She receives payment of her marriage contract **once she has reached majority**[H] and does not protest, but not while still a minor. The Gemara asks: **When she reaches majority too,** is there not the same concern that **she will protest and abandon** Judaism? The Gemara answers: **Once she reached majority** for even **one moment**[H] **and did not protest, she may no longer protest.** This mishna poses no difficulty to the opinion of Rav Yosef.

מתיב רבא: אלו נערות שיש להן קנס: הבא על הממזרת, ועל הנתינה, ועל הכותית, ועל הגיורת, ועל השבויה, ועל השפחה שנפדו ושנתגיירו ושנשתחררו פחותות מבנות שלש שנים ויום אחד – יש להן קנס. ואי אמרת הגדילו יכולין למחות – יהבינן לה קנס דאזלה ואכלה בגיותה?!

Rava raised an objection from a mishna (29a): **These are the** cases of **young women for whom there is a fine** paid to their fathers by one who rapes them: **One who engages in intercourse with a** ***mamzeret*****; or with a Gibeonite woman [*****netina*****],** who are given [*netunim*] to the service of the people and the altar (see Joshua 9:27); **or with a Samaritan**[B] **woman [*****kutit*****].** In addition, the same applies to one who engages in intercourse **with a female convert, or with a captive woman, or with a maidservant,** provided **that** the captives **were ransomed or that** the converts **converted, or that** the maidservants **were freed** when they were **less than three years and one day old,** as only in that case do they maintain the presumptive status of a virgin. In all of these cases, **there is a fine** paid **to their** fathers if they are raped. **And if you say** that **when they reach majority they can protest** and annul their conversion, **do we give her** payment **of the fine that she will go and consume in her gentile** state?

לכי גדלה. לכי גדלה נמי, ממחייא ונפקא! כיון שהגדילה שעה אחת ולא מיחתה – שוב אינה יכולה למחות.

The Gemara answers: Her father receives payment of the fine **once she has reached majority** and does not protest, but not while she is still a minor. The Gemara asks: **When she reaches majority too,** is there not the same concern that **she will protest and abandon** Judaism? The Gemara answers: **Once she reached majority** for even **one moment and did not protest, she may no longer protest.**

HALAKHA

They are content with whatever their father does – ניחא להו במאי דעביד אבוהון: A gentile child may be converted to Judaism by his father (*Shulḥan Arukh, Yoreh De'a* 268:7).

When they reach majority they can protest – הגדילו יכולין למחות: A child who converted to Judaism, whether he converted alone with the consent of the court, or whether he converted with his father or mother, may protest and renounce the conversion once he reaches majority. According to some authorities, if the child converted together with his parents, he may not renounce his conversion when he comes of age (*Ba'al Halakhot Gedolot*; see Rambam; *Ḥatam Sofer*; *Pitḥei Teshuva*; Rambam *Sefer Shofetim*, *Hilkhot Melakhim* 10:3; *Shulḥan Arukh, Yoreh De'a* 268:7).

Once she has reached majority – לכי גדלה: If a female child who converted marries and is then widowed or divorced, her marriage contract remains in the hands of the court until she reaches majority. This is in order to prevent a situation where she will protest her conversion and renounce her Judaism upon reaching adulthood, and benefit from payment of the marriage contract as a gentile (Rambam *Sefer Shofetim*, *Hilkhot Melakhim* 10:3).

Once she reached majority for even one moment – כיון שהגדילה שעה אחת: If a child who converted reaches majority and continues to practice Jewish customs he is considered a full-fledged convert. He can no longer protest his conversion and abandon Judaism. This is in accordance with the opinion of Rav Yosef, as explained by *Tosafot* (Rambam *Sefer Shofetim*, *Hilkhot Melakhim* 10:3; *Shulḥan Arukh, Yoreh De'a* 268:8).

BACKGROUND

Samaritan – כותי: The Samaritans are the descendants of the nations displaced by Sennacherib, King of Assyria, and relocated to Eretz Yisrael. Eventually, they accepted upon themselves several mitzvot (II Kings 17). At the beginning of the Second Temple period, during the times of Ezra and Nehemiah, relations between the Samaritans and the Jews deteriorated. Later, the Samaritans established a center of worship on Mount Gerizim, as they claimed that the sanctity of that mountain was established by one of the Ten Commandments.

Some generations of Sages recognized Samaritans as half Jewish. They went so far as to say: In the mitzvot that the Samaritans adopted, they are extremely exacting in their fulfillment, even more than the Jews are. Ultimately, as the Samaritans continued to distance themselves from the Jewish people in virtually every regard, they were accorded the legal status of gentiles.

NOTES

As they are content with whatever their father does – דניחא להו במאי דעביד אבוהון: According to the Rashba, there is no difference between a father and a mother in this regard. In fact, it is reasonable to assume that the child would tend more to follow his mother. The Meiri, however, suggests that the Sages stated this *halakha* only with regard to the father.

When they reach majority – הגדילו: *Talmidei Rabbeinu Yona* ask: As majority is reached at a given moment, just prior to that moment he is a minor and just after that moment he is an adult. How, then, is it possible to determine the precise moment when she may protest and renounce the conversion? *Tosafot* explain that reaching majority and conducting oneself as a Jew indicates that he is not protesting. The Rosh elaborates: If after reaching majority one performs an action unmistakably characteristic of Judaism, this would indicate he is not protesting. Others explain that the protest need not coincide precisely with reaching majority. Rather, when the convert comes of age he is informed of the onus of mitzvot. If he accepts, he is a full-fledged Jew (Ritva).

The Ra'avad and the Rashba require that the process of acceptance or rejection of Judaism must begin during the latter stages of a child's minority and continue into the beginning of majority. According to *Tosefot Rid*, the process must be completed during the final days of minority, when the minor has the intellectual capacity to make decisions but has not yet reached the age of legal capacity to accept the mitzvot as a Jew.

When they reach majority they can protest – הגדילו יכולין למחות: The halakhic authorities disagree whether this applies only to a case where the child is converted with the consent of the court, or even in a case where he converted with his father. The Rashba and others cite the fact that Rav Yosef formulated his statement in the plural, indicating that it applies in the case of all child converts.

They can protest and annul their conversion – יכולין למחות: The question is asked: Once the convert renounces Judaism, is he retroactively considered a gentile who never converted? There is a practical ramification to this question with regard to wine with which he came into contact prior to his protest. If he is retroactively considered a gentile, the wine is forbidden. The Ḥatam Sofer maintains that this is the ruling, although he was unaware of that which the Meiri cited in the name of the *ge'onim*, that the wine is not forbidden after the fact. Fundamentally, the prohibition of wine with which a gentile child came into contact is by rabbinic decree. As it is uncommon for converts to renounce their Judaism, the Sages do not issue decrees in uncommon cases.

אַבַּיֵי לָא אֲמַר כְּרָבָא – הָתָם קְנָסָא, הַיְינוּ טַעֲמָא שֶׁלֹּא יְהֵא חוֹטֵא נִשְׂכָּר.

Abaye did not state his objection from the same source **as** did Rava, because **there,** in the mishna cited by Rava, it is referring to **a fine,** and in that case **this is the reason: So that the sinner will not profit.** The Sages did not absolve the rapist from payment of the fine merely due to the concern that the woman he raped may ultimately negate the conversion.

רָבָא לָא אֲמַר כְּאַבַּיֵי – כְּתוּבָּה הַיְינוּ טַעֲמָא – שֶׁלֹּא תְּהֵא קַלָּה בְּעֵינָיו לְהוֹצִיאָהּ.

Rava did not state his objection from the same source **as** did **Abaye,** as with regard to **a marriage contract, this is the reason**[NH] that the Sages instituted it: **So that** his wife **will not be inconsequential in his eyes,** enabling him **to** easily **divorce her.** As long as this woman does not negate her conversion, she is a Jewish woman and the Sages saw to her interests.

מתני׳ הַגָּדוֹל שֶׁבָּא עַל הַקְּטַנָּה, וְקָטָן שֶׁבָּא עַל הַגְּדוֹלָה, וּמוּכַּת עֵץ – כְּתוּבָּתָן מָאתַיִם, דִּבְרֵי רַבִּי מֵאִיר. וַחֲכָמִים אוֹמְרִים: מוּכַּת עֵץ – כְּתוּבָּתָהּ מָנֶה.

MISHNA With regard to **an adult man who engaged in intercourse with a minor girl** less than three years old; **or a minor boy** less than nine years old **who engaged in intercourse with an adult woman;**[H] **or a** woman who had her hymen **ruptured by wood** or any other foreign object, for all these women **their marriage contract is two hundred** dinars, as their legal status is that of a virgin. This is **the statement of Rabbi Meir. And the Rabbis say: The marriage contract** of a woman whose hymen was **ruptured by wood is one hundred dinars,**[H] as physically, since her hymen is not intact, she is no longer a virgin.

בְּתוּלָה, אַלְמָנָה, גְּרוּשָׁה וַחֲלוּצָה מִן הַנִּישּׂוּאִין – כְּתוּבָּתָן מָנֶה,

With regard to **a virgin** who is either **a widow,** a **divorcée, or** a ***ḥalutza*** who achieved that status **from** a state of **marriage,**[NH] for all these women **their marriage contract is one hundred dinars,**

NOTES

With regard to a marriage contract this is the reason, etc. – **כְּתוּבָּה הַיְינוּ טַעֲמָא וכו׳**: The Ritva explains this in a unique manner: If he doesn't give her a marriage contract at all the concern is that she will consider the lack of a marriage contract demeaning, as the lack will ease the way for her husband to divorce her. That itself may lead to her renunciation of Judaism.

A virgin…from a state of marriage – **בְּתוּלָה...מִן הַנִּישּׂוּאִין**: In explaining why a virgin who was married receives a marriage contract of only one hundred dinars, Rashi writes that upon entering the wedding canopy, she assumes the presumptive status of a non-virgin. The early commentaries add that this is the ruling even if she claims that she is still a virgin and brings proof to that effect. Nevertheless, the concern is that she is seeking to be valued more highly by her groom, and the witnesses share that objective.

Although there are certainly cases where it is clear that she did not engage in intercourse, the Sages did not distinguish between the cases. The Rashba explains the reason for this *halakha* based on the Jerusalem Talmud: A virgin receives a marriage contract of two hundred dinars from the groom because she finds favor in his eyes. The fact that she previously entered the wedding canopy with another man mitigates that favor. That is also the reason that according to one opinion, a woman whose hymen was ruptured by a foreign object receives a marriage contract of one hundred dinars.

HALAKHA

With regard to a marriage contract this is the reason – **כְּתוּבָּה הַיְינוּ טַעֲמָא**: The Sages instituted payment of the marriage contract to the wife so that she will not be inconsequential in her husband's eyes, enabling him to easily divorce her (Rambam *Sefer Nashim, Hilkhot Ishut* 10:7; *Tur, Even HaEzer* 66).

With regard to an adult man who engaged in intercourse with a minor girl, or a minor boy who engaged in intercourse with an adult woman – **הַגָּדוֹל שֶׁבָּא עַל הַקְּטַנָּה וְקָטָן שֶׁבָּא עַל הַגְּדוֹלָה**: A girl who engaged in intercourse when she was less than three years and one day old, even if it was with an adult man, is entitled, when she marries, to a marriage contract of two hundred dinars. Similarly, an adult woman who engaged in intercourse with a boy less than nine years and one day old is entitled, when she marries, to a marriage contract of two hundred dinars (Rambam *Sefer Nashim, Hilkhot Ishut* 11:3; *Shulḥan Arukh, Even HaEzer* 67:4).

The marriage contract of a woman whose hymen was ruptured by wood is one hundred dinars – **מוּכַּת עֵץ כְּתוּבָּתָהּ מָנֶה**: A woman whose hymen was ruptured by means of a foreign object, not through intercourse, is entitled to a marriage contract of one hundred dinars, in accordance with the opinion of the Rabbis (Rambam *Sefer Nashim, Hilkhot Ishut* 11:3; *Shulḥan Arukh, Even HaEzer* 67:5).

A virgin…from a state of marriage – **בְּתוּלָה...מִן הַנִּישּׂוּאִין**: A woman who was widowed or divorced or who underwent *ḥalitza* after marriage, even if the marriage was not consummated, no longer has the legal status of a virgin, and is entitled to a marriage contract of one hundred dinars. In addition, her husband cannot later make a claim concerning her virginity (Rambam *Sefer Nashim, Hilkhot Ishut* 11:1; *Shulḥan Arukh, Even HaEzer* 67:2).

וְאֵין לָהֶן טַעֲנַת בְּתוּלִים.

and they are not subject to **a claim** concerning their **virginity.** Since they were married, even if they did not engage in intercourse with their husband, their presumptive status is that of non-virgins, and the second husband cannot claim that he was misled with regard to their status as virgins.

הַגִּיּוֹרֶת וְהַשְּׁבוּיָה וְהַשִּׁפְחָה שֶׁנִּפְדּוּ וְשֶׁנִּתְגַּיְּירוּ וְשֶׁנִּשְׁתַּחְרְרוּ יְתֵירוֹת עַל בְּנוֹת שָׁלֹשׁ שָׁנִים וְיוֹם אֶחָד – כְּתוּבָּתָן מָנֶה, וְאֵין לָהֶן טַעֲנַת בְּתוּלִין.

And similarly, with regard to **a female convert, or a captive woman, or a maidservant, who were ransomed** with regard to the captive, or **who converted** with regard to the convert, **or who were freed** with regard to the maidservant, when they were **more than three years and one day old,**[NH] **their marriage contract is one hundred dinars and they are not** subject to **a claim** concerning their **virginity.** When they married, their presumptive status was that of a non-virgin.

גמ׳ אָמַר רַב יְהוּדָה אָמַר רַב: קָטָן הַבָּא עַל הַגְּדוֹלָה עֲשָׂאָהּ מוּכַּת עֵץ. כִּי אָמְרִיתָהּ קַמֵּיהּ דִּשְׁמוּאֵל, אֲמַר: אֵין מוּכַּת עֵץ בְּבָשָׂר.

GEMARA Rav Yehuda said that **Rav said: A minor boy who engaged in intercourse with an adult woman**[N] **renders her** as one whose hymen was **ruptured by wood,** as the act is not considered full-fledged intercourse. Rav Yehuda continues: **When I said** this statement **before Shmuel,** he **said** to me: A woman does **not** achieve the status of one whose hymen was **ruptured by wood** by means of **flesh,**[H] i.e., intercourse.

אִיכָּא דְּמַתְנֵי לַהּ לְהָא שְׁמַעְתָּא בְּאַפֵּי נַפְשַׁהּ: קָטָן הַבָּא עַל הַגְּדוֹלָה, רַב אָמַר: עֲשָׂאָהּ מוּכַּת עֵץ, וּשְׁמוּאֵל אָמַר: אֵין מוּכַּת עֵץ בְּבָשָׂר.

Some teach this *halakha* independent of Rav Yehuda: With regard to **a minor boy who engaged in intercourse with an adult woman, Rav said: He renders her** as one whose hymen was **ruptured by wood. And Shmuel said:** A woman does **not** achieve the status of one whose hymen was **ruptured by wood** by means of **flesh.**

מֵתִיב רַב אוֹשַׁעְיָא: גָּדוֹל שֶׁבָּא עַל הַקְּטַנָּה, וְקָטָן הַבָּא עַל הַגְּדוֹלָה, וּמוּכַּת עֵץ – כְּתוּבָּתָן מָאתַיִם, דִּבְרֵי רַבִּי מֵאִיר. וַחֲכָמִים אוֹמְרִים: מוּכַּת עֵץ כְּתוּבָּתָהּ מָנֶה!

Rav Oshaya raised an objection to the opinion of Rav from the mishna: With regard to **an adult man who engaged in intercourse with a minor girl** less than three years old, **or a minor boy** less than nine years old **who engaged in intercourse with an adult woman, or a** woman who had her hymen **ruptured by wood**[B] or any other foreign object, **the marriage contract** for each of these women **is two hundred** dinars. This is **the statement of Rabbi Meir. And the Rabbis say: The marriage contract** of a woman whose hymen was **ruptured by wood is one hundred dinars.** Contrary to Rav's opinion, the Rabbis distinguish between the *halakha* in the case of the intercourse of a minor boy and the *halakha* in the case of a woman whose hymen was ruptured by wood.

אָמַר רָבָא: הָכִי קָאָמַר גָּדוֹל הַבָּא עַל הַקְּטַנָּה – וְלֹא כְלוּם, דְּפָחוֹת מִכָּאן כְּנוֹתֵן אֶצְבַּע בָּעַיִן דָּמֵי. וְקָטָן הַבָּא עַל הַגְּדוֹלָה – עֲשָׂאָהּ מוּכַּת עֵץ, וּמוּכַּת עֵץ גּוּפָא – פְּלוּגְתָּא דְּרַבִּי מֵאִיר וְרַבָּנַן.

Rava said that **this is what** the mishna **is saying: An adult man who engaged in intercourse with a minor girl** less than three years old has done **nothing,** as intercourse with a girl **less than** three years old **is tantamount to poking a finger into the eye.** In the case of an eye, after a tear falls from it another tear forms to replace it. Similarly, the ruptured hymen of the girl younger than three is restored. **And a young boy who engaged in intercourse with an adult woman renders her** as one whose hymen **was ruptured by wood. And** with regard to the case of a woman whose hymen was **ruptured by wood itself,** there is a **dispute between Rabbi Meir and the Rabbis.** Rabbi Meir maintains that her marriage contract is two hundred dinars, and the Rabbis maintain that it is one hundred dinars.

NOTES

More than three years and one day old – יְתֵירוֹת עַל בְּנוֹת שָׁלֹשׁ שָׁנִים וְיוֹם אֶחָד: In all these cases, these women no longer have the presumptive status of a virgin either due to the fact that they are subject to the control of others or because chastity is not their concern. This is not age dependent; however, for a girl younger than three, intercourse is not considered intercourse at all.

A minor boy who engaged in intercourse with an adult woman – קָטָן הַבָּא עַל הַגְּדוֹלָה: With regard to the dispute between Rav and Shmuel, there are two primary approaches. According to *Tosafot*, they disagree with regard to a case where her hymen remained intact. The dispute is whether a woman who engaged in intercourse with a boy younger than nine is comparable to a woman whose hymen was ruptured by a foreign object according to the opinion of the Rabbis that her marriage contract is one hundred dinars, or whether that does not apply in this case as the intercourse of a boy less than nine is inconsequential.

Tosefot Rid, however, maintains that they disagree even in a case where the hymen was ruptured. Based on the understanding that the amount in the marriage contract is determined based on the degree that the woman finds favor in the eyes of the groom, the definition of virgin is not necessarily dependent on whether or not the hymen is intact. Rather, it is dependent on whether or not she engaged in intercourse. The Rid explicitly writes that if she herself ruptured her hymen, she is still considered a virgin. According to Rav, intercourse with a boy less than nine years old is considered intercourse in the sense that it mitigates the favor that she finds in the eyes of the groom. The same is true of a woman whose hymen was ruptured by a foreign object according to the Rabbis. According to Shmuel, intercourse with a minor is not considered intercourse at all, and it carries with it less of a stigma than a woman whose hymen was ruptured by a foreign object according to the Rabbis.

HALAKHA

A female convert…more than three years and one day old – הַגִּיּוֹרֶת...יְתֵירוֹת עַל בְּנוֹת שָׁלֹשׁ שָׁנִים וְיוֹם אֶחָד: A female gentile, captive, or slave who was converted, redeemed, or freed respectively when she was more than three years and one day old has lost her presumptive status of a virgin and is entitled to a marriage contract of only one hundred dinars. On the other hand, her husband cannot make a claim concerning her virginity (Rambam *Sefer Nashim, Hilkhot Ishut* 11:1; *Shulḥan Arukh, Even HaEzer* 67:3).

A woman does not achieve the status of one whose hymen was ruptured by wood by means of flesh – אֵין מוּכַּת עֵץ בְּבָשָׂר: If a grown woman engages in intercourse with a boy younger than nine years old, she is still entitled to a marriage contract of two hundred dinars in accordance with the opinion of Shmuel, as the *halakha* is ruled in accordance with his opinion in civil matters. This ruling applies only if the woman's hymen was not ruptured as a result of that intercourse; however, if the hymen was ruptured, she is entitled to a marriage contract of one hundred dinars, like a woman whose hymen was ruptured by a foreign object (*Tosafot*; Rambam *Sefer Nashim, Hilkhot Ishut* 11:3; *Shulḥan Arukh, Even HaEzer* 67:4).

BACKGROUND

A woman who had her hymen ruptured by wood – מוּכַּת עֵץ: Penetration of the vagina with a hard, foreign object can rupture the hymen, e.g., if a girl falls and a hard, protruding object comes into contact with the vagina (see 36b). This is an unlikely occurrence, as a typical fall would not lead to such a result (see *Tosafot* 9b).

אֲמַר רָמִי בַּר חָמָא: מַחֲלוֹקֶת כְּשֶׁהִכִּיר בָּהּ; דְּרַבִּי מֵאִיר מְדַמֵּי לָהּ לְבוֹגֶרֶת, וְרַבָּנַן מְדַמּוּ לָהּ לִבְעוּלָה. אֲבָל לֹא הִכִּיר בָּהּ – דִּבְרֵי הַכֹּל וְלֹא כְּלוּם.

Rami bar Ḥama said: This dispute is specifically in a case **where** the husband **was aware that her** hymen was ruptured by wood, **as** in that case **Rabbi Meir likens her to a grown woman,**[N] whose hymen does not completely obstruct the orifice as a result of the maturation process. Nevertheless, her marriage contract is that of a virgin, two hundred dinars. **And the Rabbis liken her to a non-virgin** who engaged in intercourse in the past. Her marriage contract is one hundred dinars. **However, if he was not aware that her** hymen was ruptured by wood and was under the impression that she was a full-fledged virgin, **everyone agrees** that she receives **no** marriage contract **at all** when he becomes aware of her condition, as the marriage was a mistaken transaction.

וְרַבִּי מֵאִיר אַמַּאי מְדַמֵּי לָהּ לְבוֹגֶרֶת? נְדַמְּיָהּ לִבְעוּלָה! בְּעוּלָה אִיתְעֲבֵיד בָּהּ מַעֲשֶׂה בִּידֵי אָדָם. הָא – לָא אִיתְעֲבֵיד בָּהּ מַעֲשֶׂה בִּידֵי אָדָם. וְרַבָּנַן, אַדִּמְדַמּוּ לָהּ לִבְעוּלָה נְדַמְּיָהּ לְבוֹגֶרֶת! בּוֹגֶרֶת לָא אִיתְעֲבֵיד בָּהּ מַעֲשֶׂה כְּלָל, הָא – אִיתְעֲבֵיד בָּהּ מַעֲשֶׂה,

The Gemara asks: **And why does Rabbi Meir liken her to a grown woman? Let him liken her to a non-virgin,** who engaged in intercourse in the past. The Gemara answers: In the case of **a non-virgin, an action was performed on her by a person;** but with regard to **this** woman, whose hymen was ruptured by wood, **an action was not performed on her by a person.** The Gemara asks: **And** with regard to **the Rabbis, rather than likening her to a non-virgin, let them liken her to a grown woman.** The Gemara answers: In the case of **a grown woman, no action was performed on her;** but with regard to **this** woman, whose hymen was ruptured by wood, **an action was performed on her.**

אֲבָל לֹא הִכִּיר בָּהּ – לְדִבְרֵי הַכֹּל וְלֹא כְּלוּם. מְתִיב רַב נַחְמָן: הִיא אוֹמֶרֶת "מוּכַּת עֵץ אֲנִי" וְהוּא אוֹמֵר "לֹא כִּי, אֶלָּא דְּרוּסַת אִישׁ אַתְּ". רַבָּן גַּמְלִיאֵל וְרַבִּי אֱלִיעֶזֶר אוֹמְרִים: נֶאֱמֶנֶת!

Rami bar Ḥama concluded his statement: **However, if he was not aware that her** hymen was ruptured by wood, **everyone agrees** that she receives **no** marriage contract **at all. Rav Naḥman raised an objection** from a mishna (13a): In a case where **she says: I am** one whose hymen was **ruptured by wood,**[N] i.e., she admits that her hymen is not intact but claims that it was not ruptured through intercourse, **and the** groom **says: No; rather, you are** one who **was violated by a man** and you are no longer a virgin, **Rabban Gamliel and Rabbi Eliezer say: She is deemed credible** and her claim is accepted. In that case, she is claiming that she is entitled to a marriage contract. Despite the fact that the groom had no prior awareness of her condition, Rabban Gamliel and Rabbi Eliezer maintain that she is deemed credible and receives a marriage contract of at least one hundred dinars. Apparently, not everyone agrees that in that case she receives nothing at all.

אֶלָּא אָמַר רָבָא: בֵּין הִכִּיר בָּהּ וּבֵין לֹא הִכִּיר בָּהּ, לְרַבִּי מֵאִיר – מָאתַיִם, לְרַבָּנַן; הִכִּיר בָּהּ – מָנֶה, לֹא הִכִּיר בָּהּ – וְלֹא כְּלוּם.

Rather, Rava said: This is what the mishna is saying: **Whether** the husband **was aware that her** hymen was ruptured by wood **and whether he was not aware of her** condition, according **to Rabbi Meir** she receives a marriage contract of **two hundred** dinars and it is not a mistaken transaction. According **to the Rabbis, if he was aware of her** condition she receives a marriage contract of **one hundred dinars** like a non-virgin; if **he was not aware of her** condition she receives **no** marriage contract **at all,** since it is a mistaken transaction, as when he married her he believed that her hymen was intact. According to this explanation, the mishna cited by Rav Naḥman is in accordance with the opinion of Rabbi Meir.

וַהֲדַר בֵּיהּ רָבָא, דְּתַנְיָא: כֵּיצַד הוֹצָאַת שֵׁם רַע? בָּא לְבֵית דִּין וְאָמַר: פְּלוֹנִי, לֹא מָצָאתִי לְבִתְּךָ בְּתוּלִים. אִם יֵשׁ עֵדִים שֶׁזִּינְּתָה תַּחְתָּיו – יֵשׁ לָהּ כְּתוּבָּה מָנֶה. אִם יֵשׁ עֵדִים שֶׁזִּינְּתָה תַּחְתָּיו?! בַּת סְקִילָה הִיא! הָכִי קָאָמַר: אִם יֵשׁ עֵדִים שֶׁזִּינְּתָה תַּחְתָּיו – בִּסְקִילָה, זִינְּתָה מֵעִיקָּרָא – יֵשׁ לָהּ כְּתוּבָּה מָנֶה.

And Rava retracted his opinion, **as it is taught** in a *baraita*: **How** does the **slander**[N] described in the Torah come about? If the groom **comes to court and says: So-and-so,** father of the bride, **I did not find in your daughter** an intact **hymen. If there are witnesses that she committed adultery** while **under** the husband's jurisdiction after betrothal, **she** receives **a marriage contract of one hundred dinars.** The Gemara asks: **If there are witnesses that she committed adultery** while **under his** jurisdiction after betrothal, **she is subject to** execution by **stoning.**[N] Obviously, she is in no position to receive a marriage contract. The Gemara answers that **this is what** the mishna **is saying: If there are witnesses that she committed adultery** while **under his** jurisdiction after betrothal, she is subject **to** execution by **stoning.** However, **if she engaged in intercourse initially,** prior to betrothal, **she receives a marriage contract of one hundred dinars,** like any non-virgin.

NOTES

Likens her to a grown woman – מְדַמֵּי לָהּ לְבוֹגֶרֶת: The commentaries agree that the comparison is not perfect, as in the case of a grown woman, whose hymen, as a result of the maturation process, does not completely obstruct the orifice, whether or not her husband was aware of that phenomenon her marriage contract is two hundred dinars (Rashba). In the Jerusalem Talmud this discussion is tied to the matter of a woman whose hymen was ruptured by a foreign object, in terms of the degree in which the woman finds favor in the eyes of the groom. Does a woman whose hymen was ruptured by a foreign object receive a marriage contract of two hundred dinars like a grown woman, who receives two hundred dinars, even though her hymen does not completely obstruct the orifice due to maturation?

She says I am one whose hymen was ruptured by wood – הִיא אוֹמֶרֶת מוּכַּת עֵץ אֲנִי: The early commentaries ask: Why doesn't the Gemara explain that the woman claims that her husband was aware of the fact that her hymen was ruptured; and he claims that he was unaware, and that he married her assuming that she was a virgin but she in fact engaged in intercourse with a man (Rashba; Ritva)? They add that this is the explanation in the Jerusalem Talmud. According to the Gemara here, apparently, in that case where there is a dispute between the groom and the bride with regard to the nature of the agreement between them, there is no reason why Rabban Gamliel would accord credibility specifically to the woman.

Slander – הוֹצָאַת שֵׁם רַע: This source of the *halakha* of a man who accuses his wife of adultery and claims that she was not a virgin is from the Torah (Deuteronomy 22:13–21), and is explained at length by the Gemara (44b–46b). The conclusion drawn from the verses is that it is not merely the claim of a suspicious groom but is a claim corroborated by witnesses. The difference between the various cases depends on the essence of the witnesses' testimony and an examination of their credibility.

She is subject to execution by stoning – בַּת סְקִילָה הִיא: The Rashba writes that it does not mean that she will actually be executed, as stoning is administered only after forewarning. It means that if there are witnesses that she committed adultery she does not receive payment of her marriage contract at all, as a *sota*, a woman suspected of adultery, also does not receive payment.

וְאָמַר רַב חִיָּיא בַּר אָבִין אָמַר רַב שֵׁשֶׁת: זֹאת אוֹמֶרֶת כְּנָסָהּ בְּחֶזְקַת בְּתוּלָה וְנִמְצֵאת בְּעוּלָה – יֵשׁ לָהּ כְּתוּבָּה מָנֶה. וּמוֹתֵיב רַב נַחְמָן: הַנּוֹשֵׂא אֶת הָאִשָּׁה וְלֹא מָצָא לָהּ בְּתוּלִים, הִיא אוֹמֶרֶת ״מִשֶּׁאֵרַסְתַּנִי נֶאֱנַסְתִּי וְנִסְתַּחְפָה שָׂדֵהוּ״ וְהוּא אוֹמֵר ״לֹא כִּי, אֶלָּא עַד שֶׁלֹּא אֵירַסְתִּיךְ, וְהָיָה מִקָּחִי מִקַּח טָעוּת״, וְלֵית לָהּ כְּלָל?

And Rav Ḥiyya bar Avin said that **Rav Sheshet said: That is to say,** if the groom **married** a woman **with the presumptive status of a virgin and she is found to be a non-virgin,** she receives **a marriage contract of one hundred dinars. And Rav Naḥman raised an objection** to the statement of Rav Sheshet from a mishna (12b): There is a case of one **who marries a woman and did not find her hymen** intact, and **she says: After you betrothed me I was raped, and his,** i.e., her husband's, **field was inundated,** meaning that it is his misfortune that she is not a virgin, as she was raped after betrothal. **And he says: No;** rather, you were raped **before I betrothed you, and my transaction was a mistaken transaction.** The betrothal was predicated on your presumptive status as a virgin and in fact, you were not a virgin then. In that case, **she does not** receive **any** marriage contract **at all.**

וְאָמַר לְהוּ רַב חִיָּיא בַּר אָבִין: אֶפְשָׁר רַב עַמְרָם וְכָל גְּדוֹלֵי הַדּוֹר יָתְבִי כִּי אֲמַר רַב שֵׁשֶׁת לְהָא שְׁמַעְתָּא, וְקַשְׁיָא לְהוּ, וְשַׁנִּי: מַאי מִקַּח טָעוּת – נַמִי מִמָּאתַיִם, אֲבָל מָנֶה – אִית לָהּ. וְאַתְּ אָמְרַתְּ לֵית לָהּ כְּלָל?!

And Rav Ḥiyya bar Avin said to those present: Is it **possible** that **Rav Amram and all the prominent** Sages **of the generation were sitting when Rav Sheshet said this *halakha*, and** Rav Naḥman's question **was difficult for them, and they answered: What is** the meaning of **mistaken transaction** in this context? It **too** means that he is absolved **from** his commitment to pay the marriage contract of a virgin, **two hundred** dinars, because she is not entitled to that sum. **However, she** is entitled to **one hundred dinars. And,** contrary to that consensus, **you say that she does not** receive any marriage contract **at all?**

וְאָמַר רָבָא: מַאן דְּקָא מוֹתֵיב – שַׁפִּיר קָא מוֹתֵיב, מִקַּח טָעוּת – לְגַמְרֵי מַשְׁמַע. וְאֶלָּא קַשְׁיָא הָךְ! תָּרֵיץ וְאֵימָא הָכִי: אִם יֵשׁ עֵדִים שֶׁזִּינְּתָה תַּחְתָּיו – בִּסְקִילָה, זִינְּתָה מֵעִיקָּרָא – וְלֹא כְּלוּם, נִמְצֵאת מוּכַּת עֵץ – יֵשׁ לָהּ כְּתוּבָּה מָנֶה.

And Rava said: The one who raised the objection, Rav Naḥman, **raises the objection well,** as the term: **Mistaken transaction, indicates** that the betrothal is dissolved **totally.**[H] The Gemara asks: **But that** *baraita* with regard to slander remains **difficult,** as in that case, if he discovered that she was not a virgin, she receives a marriage contract of one hundred dinars. The Gemara answers: **Resolve** the apparent contradiction **and say this** in the text of the *baraita*: **If there are witnesses that she committed adultery** while **under his** jurisdiction after betrothal, she is subject **to** execution by **stoning. If she engaged in intercourse initially,** prior to betrothal, she receives **nothing at all. If she was discovered** to be one whose hymen was **ruptured by wood,**[H] **she is entitled to a marriage contract of one hundred dinars.**

וְהָא רָבָא הוּא דַּאֲמַר לְרַבָּנַן לֹא הִכִּיר בָּהּ וְלֹא כְּלוּם! אֶלָּא שְׁמַע מִינָּהּ: הֲדַר בֵּיהּ רָבָא מֵהַהִיא.

But isn't it Rava himself who said that according **to the Rabbis,** in the case of a woman whose hymen was ruptured by wood, if **he was not aware of her** condition she receives **no** marriage contract **at all? Rather, conclude from it** that **Rava retracted that** statement, and he holds that even according to the Rabbis, even if he was unaware of her condition she receives a marriage contract of one hundred dinars.

תָּנוּ רַבָּנַן: כְּנָסָהּ רִאשׁוֹן לְשׁוּם נִישּׂוּאִין, וְיֵשׁ לָהּ עֵדִים שֶׁלֹּא נִסְתְּרָה. אִי נַמִי, נִסְתְּרָה וְלֹא שָׁהֲתָה כְּדֵי בִּיאָה – אֵין הַשֵּׁנִי יָכוֹל לִטְעוֹן טַעֲנַת בְּתוּלִים, שֶׁהֲרֵי כְּנָסָהּ רִאשׁוֹן.

§ **The Sages taught:** If her **first** husband **brought her into** his home **for the purpose of marriage,**[N] **and she has witnesses** who testified **that she did not seclude herself** with him,[N] or **alternatively,** they testified that **she secluded herself** with him **and did not stay** in seclusion with him for a period **equivalent** to the time required to engage in **intercourse,** if the first husband dies or divorces her and she remarries, despite the testimony of the witnesses, **the second** husband **cannot make a claim concerning virginity,**[H] and say the betrothal was predicated on the assumption that she was a virgin and she should lose her marriage contract. Since the **first husband brought her into** his home, the second husband should have considered that a woman who entered her husband's home is no longer a virgin.

HALAKHA

Mistaken transaction indicates that the betrothal is dissolved totally – מִקַּח טָעוּת לְגַמְרֵי מַשְׁמַע: If a man marries a woman under the assumption that she is a virgin and he discovers that she was not a virgin, even if it was due to rape, the marriage contract is voided and she receives no payment, in accordance with the ruling of Rav Sheshet (Rambam *Sefer Nashim, Hilkhot Ishut* 11:3; *Shulḥan Arukh, Even HaEzer* 67:5).

If she was discovered to be one whose hymen was ruptured by wood – נִמְצֵאת מוּכַּת עֵץ: A woman whose hymen was ruptured by a foreign object is entitled to a marriage contract of one hundred dinars. Even if the groom married her under the assumption that she was a virgin and he discovers that her hymen was ruptured by a foreign object, she is still entitled to a marriage contract of one hundred dinars, in accordance with the opinion of Rami bar Ḥama, as Rava eventually conceded to his opinion (Rambam *Sefer Nashim, Hilkhot Ishut* 11:3; *Shulḥan Arukh, Even HaEzer* 67:5).

The second husband cannot make a claim concerning virginity – אֵין הַשֵּׁנִי יָכוֹל לִטְעוֹן טַעֲנַת בְּתוּלִים: If a woman was widowed or divorced or underwent *ḥalitza*, she is entitled to a marriage contract of only one hundred dinars when she remarries. The second husband cannot make a claim with regard to her virginity, even if there are witnesses who testify that she never entered into seclusion with her first husband (*Shulḥan Arukh, Even HaEzer* 67:2).

NOTES

If her first husband brought her into his home for the purpose of marriage – כְּנָסָהּ רִאשׁוֹן לְשׁוּם נִישּׂוּאִין: Some conclude based on the mishna and other sources that once the woman enters the wedding canopy, which is a prelude to consummation of the marriage, she loses her presumptive status of virginity even though intercourse did not actually take place yet.

Witnesses that she did not seclude herself with him – עֵדִים שֶׁלֹּא נִסְתְּרָה: In the *Shita Mekubbetzet* an explanation appears why these two examples were cited. In the case where the witnesses testified that she did not seclude herself with him there is room for concern that she was indeed secluded, as perhaps they are attempting to have the husband value her more highly. However, in the case where the witnesses testify that she entered into seclusion but did not remain there long, since they testified that she entered the wedding canopy, they are clearly not seeking to praise her; therefore, one might have thought that their testimony is reliable. Furthermore, when they testify that she did not enter into seclusion, perhaps their testimony is not accurate, as their intention was not to observe in order to testify; however, when they testify that she entered into seclusion and they indicate that they had calculated its duration, one might have thought that their testimony is reliable.

NOTES

Because the first husband brought her into his house – **שֶׁהֲרֵי כְּנָסָהּ רִאשׁוֹן**: The commentaries ask: Ostensibly, the distinction suggested by the Gemara is obvious, as the reason for the *halakha* is written explicitly. Why did Rabba think otherwise? The Rivam, cited in *Tosafot*, explains that Rabba understood the phrase to mean that since the first husband brought her into his house and caused her to receive a marriage contract of one hundred dinars, the second husband can no longer make a claim with regard to the other hundred dinars, as a claim of virginity can affect only the hundred dinars to which a virgin is entitled. The Ramban explains that Rabba understood that the phrase adds a novel element, as although he could claim that he relied on the witnesses and did not pay the additional amount of the marriage contract, he would not have married her if he did not believe that she was a virgin. Therefore, even though he could say that he relied on the witnesses, and even though he did not add anything to the one hundred dinars of the marriage contract, he would not have married her had he not thought she was a virgin. Therefore, it states that since she entered the wedding canopy, he can no longer be said to be certain that she is a virgin.

Because she entered the wedding canopy – **שֶׁהֲרֵי נִכְנְסָה לַחוּפָּה**: Rabbeinu Ḥananel writes that since the groom should have determined whether or not the bride previously engaged in intercourse, as there were indications that this was the case, and he failed to investigate, he appears to have assumed that she was not a virgin. The Ramban and others explain that since she had entered the wedding canopy, she no longer finds favor in the eyes of the groom in the manner that a full-fledged virgin does.

אָמַר רַבָּה: זֹאת אוֹמֶרֶת; כְּנָסָהּ בְּחֶזְקַת בְּתוּלָה וְנִמְצֵאת בְּעוּלָה יֵשׁ לָהּ כְּתוּבָּה מָנֶה. רַב אַשִׁי אֲמַר: בְּעָלְמָא לְעוֹלָם אֵימָא לָךְ – לֵית לָהּ כְּלָל, וְשָׁאנֵי הָכָא – שֶׁהֲרֵי כְּנָסָהּ רִאשׁוֹן.

Rabba said: That is to say, if **one married** a woman **with the presumptive status of a virgin,** as there were witnesses that she did not engage in intercourse, **and she was found** to be **a non-virgin, she is** entitled to **a marriage contract of one hundred dinars.** The Gemara rejects the proof. **Rav Ashi said: In general, actually, I** would **say to you** that in that case **she does not** receive a marriage contract **at all,** as it is a mistaken transaction. **But here it is different,** and she does not totally lose her marriage contract, **because the first** husband **brought her into** his house.[N] Therefore, the second husband should have considered that a woman who entered her husband's home is no longer a virgin.

וְנֵיחוּשׁ שֶׁמָּא תַּחְתָּיו זִינְּתָה! אָמַר רַב שֵׁרֵבְיָא: כְּגוֹן שֶׁקִּידֵּשׁ וּבָעַל לְאַלְתַּר.

The Gemara asks: **And** since there are witnesses that she did not engage in intercourse with the first husband, **let us be concerned that perhaps she committed adultery** after betrothal, **while under** the jurisdiction of the second husband, and rule that she is forbidden to him due to suspicion of adultery and is not entitled to a marriage contract at all. **Rav Sherevya said:** The *baraita* is referring to a case **where he betrothed** her **and engaged in intercourse immediately.** Therefore, there was no opportunity to engage in adultery between her betrothal and her marriage to the second husband.

וְאִיכָּא דְּמַתְנֵי לָהּ אַמַּתְנִיתִין: בְּתוּלָה אַלְמָנָה, גְּרוּשָׁה, חֲלוּצָה, מִן הַנִּישּׂוּאִין – כְּתוּבָּתָן מָנֶה, וְאֵין לָהֶן טַעֲנַת בְּתוּלִין. בְּתוּלָה מִן הַנִּישּׂוּאִין הֵיכִי מַשְׁכַּחַתְּ לָהּ? כְּגוֹן שֶׁנִּכְנְסָה לַחוּפָּה וְלֹא נִבְעֲלָה.

Others taught this statement of Rabba **with regard to the mishna:** Concerning **a virgin** who is **a widow, a divorcée,** or a *ḥalutza* who achieved that status **from** a state of **marriage,** for all these women **their marriage contract is one hundred dinars, and they are not subject** to **a claim** concerning their **virginity.** The Gemara asks: **How can you find a virgin from** a state of **marriage?** It is in a case **where she entered the wedding canopy and did not engage in intercourse.**

אָמַר רַבָּה: זֹאת אוֹמֶרֶת; כְּנָסָהּ בְּחֶזְקַת בְּתוּלָה וְנִמְצֵאת בְּעוּלָה – כְּתוּבָּתָהּ מָנֶה. רַב אַשִׁי אֲמַר: בְּעָלְמָא לְעוֹלָם אֵימָא לָךְ – לֵית לָהּ כְּלָל, וְשָׁאנֵי הָכָא – שֶׁהֲרֵי נִכְנְסָה לַחוּפָּה.

Rabba said: That is to say, if **one married** a woman **with the presumptive status of a virgin and she was found** to be **a non-virgin, her marriage contract is one hundred dinars.** The Gemara rejects the proof. **Rav Ashi said: In general, actually, I** would **say to you** that **in general, she does not** receive a marriage contract **at all,** as it is a mistaken transaction. **But here it is different,** and she does not totally lose her marriage contract, **because she entered the wedding canopy.**[N] Therefore, the second husband should have considered that a woman who entered her husband's home is no longer a virgin.

וְנֵיחוּשׁ שֶׁמָּא תַּחְתָּיו זִינְּתָה! אָמַר רַב שֵׁרֵבְיָא: כְּגוֹן שֶׁקִּידֵּשׁ וּבָעַל לְאַלְתַּר.

The Gemara asks: **And let us be concerned that perhaps she committed adultery** after betrothal, **while under** the jurisdiction of the second husband. **Rav Sherevya said:** The *baraita* is referring to a case **where he betrothed** her **and engaged in intercourse immediately.** Therefore, there was no opportunity to engage in adultery between her betrothal and her marriage to the second husband.

מַאן דְּמַתְנֵי לָהּ אַבָּרַיְיתָא – כׇּל שֶׁכֵּן אַמַּתְנִיתִין, וּמַאן דְּמַתְנֵי לָהּ אַמַּתְנִיתִין – אֲבָל אַבָּרַיְיתָא לָא, מִשּׁוּם דְּמָצֵי אָמַר לַהּ: אֲנָא אַעֵדִים סָמְכִי.

The Gemara notes: **The one who taught** the exchange between Rabba and Rav Ashi **with regard to the *baraita*,** where there is explicit testimony that she did not engage in intercourse with the first husband and nevertheless no proof can be brought that if he discovers that she is not a virgin she receives a marriage contract of one hundred dinars, **all the more so** would he say that the same is true **with regard to the mishna.** And **the one who taught** the exchange **with regard to the mishna, however,** would **not** say the same **with regard to the *baraita*, due to** the fact **that** the husband could **say to her: I relied on witnesses.** Therefore, proof can be brought from the *baraita* that if he discovered that she is not a virgin, she receives a marriage contract of one hundred dinars.

מתני׳ הָאוֹכֵל אֵצֶל חָמִיו בִּיהוּדָה שֶׁלֹּא בְּעֵדִים – אֵינוֹ יָכוֹל לִטְעוֹן טַעֲנַת בְּתוּלִים, מִפְּנֵי שֶׁמִּתְיַיחֵד עִמָּהּ.

MISHNA A man **who eats at** the house of **his father-in-law**[HN] **in Judea** after betrothal and **without witnesses** to attest to the fact that he was not alone with his betrothed **is unable to make a claim concerning virginity** after marriage **because** in accordance with the custom in Judea, the assumption is **that he secluded himself with her,** and the concern is that it was he who engaged in intercourse with her.

גמ׳ מִדְּקָתָנֵי ״הָאוֹכֵל״ מִכְּלָל דְּאִיכָּא דּוּכְתָּא בִּיהוּדָה נַמִי דְּלָא אָכֵיל! אֲמַר אַבַּיֵי: שְׁמַע מִינָּהּ בִּיהוּדָה נַמִי מְקוֹמוֹת מְקוֹמוֹת יֵשׁ. כִּדְתַנְיָא, אָמַר רַבִּי יְהוּדָה: בִּיהוּדָה, בָּרִאשׁוֹנָה הָיוּ מְיַיחֲדִין אֶת הֶחָתָן וְאֶת הַכַּלָּה שָׁעָה אַחַת קוֹדֶם כְּנִיסָתָן לַחוּפָּה, כְּדֵי שֶׁיְּהֵא לִבּוֹ גַּס בָּהּ. וּבַגָּלִיל לֹא הָיוּ עוֹשִׂין כֵּן.

GEMARA The Gemara infers: **From the fact that the** mishna **teaches the** *halakha* employing the phrase: A man **who eats, by inference** one may conclude **that there is also a place in Judea where** the groom **does not eat** at the house of his father-in-law, and does not enter into seclusion with his betrothed. **Abaye said: Conclude from it that in Judea too there are** different **places** with different customs, **as it is taught** in a *baraita* that **Rabbi Yehuda said: In Judea, at first they would seclude the groom and bride** together **for a brief period before their entry into the wedding canopy, so that he would** grow **accustomed to her** companionship in order to ease the awkwardness when they would consummate the marriage. **And in the Galilee they did not do so.**

בִּיהוּדָה, בָּרִאשׁוֹנָה הָיוּ מַעֲמִידִין לָהֶם שְׁנֵי שׁוֹשְׁבִינִין, אֶחָד לוֹ וְאֶחָד לָהּ, כְּדֵי לְמַשְׁמֵשׁ אֶת הֶחָתָן וְאֶת הַכַּלָּה בִּשְׁעַת כְּנִיסָתָן לַחוּפָּה, וּבַגָּלִיל לֹא הָיוּ עוֹשִׂין כֵּן.

The *baraita* continues. **In Judea, at first they would appoint for them two groomsmen** [*shushvinin*],[LN] **one for him and one for her, in order to examine**[N] **the groom and the bride at the time of their entry into the wedding canopy** and thereafter, to ensure that neither would engage in deception with regard to the presence or absence of blood from the rupture of the hymen. **And in the Galilee**[B] **they would not do so.**[N] As the custom of appointing groomsmen would be relevant only in a case where the groom and the bride had not been together in seclusion prior to marriage, this is apparently a custom in Judea different from the first custom cited in the mishna, where they would enter into seclusion prior to marriage.

בִּיהוּדָה, בָּרִאשׁוֹנָה הָיוּ שׁוֹשְׁבִינִין יְשֵׁנִים בַּבַּיִת שֶׁחָתָן וְכַלָּה יְשֵׁנִים בָּהּ. וּבַגָּלִיל לֹא הָיוּ עוֹשִׂין כֵּן.

The *baraita* continues. **In Judea, at first the groomsmen would sleep in the house in which the groom and bride sleep,** in order to examine the sheet on which the marriage was consummated immediately following intercourse. This was in order to ensure that the groom would not attempt to obscure the blood of the rupture of the hymen and claim that the bride was not a virgin. **And in the Galilee they would not do so.**

NOTES

A man who eats at the house of his father-in-law – הָאוֹכֵל אֵצֶל חָמִיו: The reason for this custom in Judea is cited by several commentaries in the Jerusalem Talmud. It was related to the Roman decree that virgin brides submit to intercourse with the prefect first. To ensure that the woman would not submit to the prefect willingly, they sought in Judea to bolster the relationship between the bride and groom by cultivating a more intimate relationship between them. Rabbeinu Yehonatan adds that once the prefect discovered that the woman was not a virgin, he would not be insistent in exercising his right. From most commentaries it appears that this seclusion included physical intimacy and at times involved intercourse. The Meiri writes that when they entered into seclusion they would make a festive meal, and this is why it is referred to as: A man who eats in the house of his father-in-law. In the Jerusalem Talmud it is noted that the custom remained in effect in Judea even after the decree was revoked.

In Judea at first they would appoint for them two groomsmen – בִּיהוּדָה בָּרִאשׁוֹנָה הָיוּ מַעֲמִידִין לָהֶם שְׁנֵי שׁוֹשְׁבִינִין: The Rashba and the Ritva explain that this custom was prevalent specifically in Judea because the people of Judea were deceitful and required supervision. It appears from several sources that Judeans were educated and quick witted, in contrast to those in the Galilee who were simpler people.

The Meiri explains that there is a connection between this custom and the custom to enter into seclusion. Since it was common in Judea for the bride to enter the wedding canopy when no longer a virgin, there was naturally more suspicion as well as additional opportunity for deception by both the groom and the bride. Others explain that the examination by the groomsmen was effective only with regard to the claim of blood from the rupture of the hymen, but not with regard to the claim of an unobstructed orifice. The Meiri writes that in places where there was suspicion with regard to these matters, women would be enlisted to examine the bride and ensure that she was not seeking to deceive the groom with regard to her virginity.

Examination – מִשְׁמוּשׁ: The meaning of this term here and elsewhere (see Genesis 31:37), is examination. This examination was to ensure that the bride did not bring a bloodstained sheet and replace the sheet of the marriage bed with it, and also that the groom did not bring a clean sheet and replace the bloodstained sheet of the marriage bed with it in order to make a false claim against the bride. See the Meiri and other sources, who point out that there were other forms of deception employed by the bride on the wedding night in order to create an impression that she was indeed a virgin. The examination was designed to prevent all forms of deception.

And in the Galilee they would not do so – וּבַגָּלִיל לֹא הָיוּ עוֹשִׂין כֵּן: The Rashba writes that even though there were groomsmen in the Galilee, these would examine the bride to ensure that she did not bring a cloth already stained with blood, but they would not examine the groom.

HALAKHA

A man who eats at the house of his father-in-law – הָאוֹכֵל אֵצֶל חָמִיו: If the groom enters into seclusion with the bride before the wedding, he cannot then make a claim concerning her virginity. See, however, *Beit Shmuel*, which points out that according to *Tosafot*, this applies only in places where the seclusion is sanctioned according to local custom, not where it happened unsanctioned (Rambam *Sefer Nashim*, *Hilkhot Ishut* 11:8; *Shulḥan Arukh*, *Even HaEzer* 68:1).

LANGUAGE

Groomsmen [*shushvinin*] – שׁוֹשְׁבִינִין: This word, which appears in both Aramaic and Hebrew, apparently derives from Syriac. Some assert that it is from the root *yod, shin, beit*, meaning sit, indicating the one who seats the groom at the wedding. In Aramaic, *shushvinim* are the friends and those who accompany the groom. Apparently, during the mishnaic and talmudic eras the *shushvinim* did not merely fill the symbolic function of escorting the groom to the wedding; rather, they gave him gifts and assisted him at the wedding.

The role of *shushvin* was firmly established to the extent that it was considered a legal obligation for the groom, or his family, to reciprocate and serve as groomsman at the wedding of his groomsman or members of his family. This Gemara notes that the groomsman filled the additional role of ensuring that there was no deception on the part of the groom or the bride with regard to claims concerning virginity.

BACKGROUND

Judea and Galilee – יְהוּדָה וְגָלִיל:

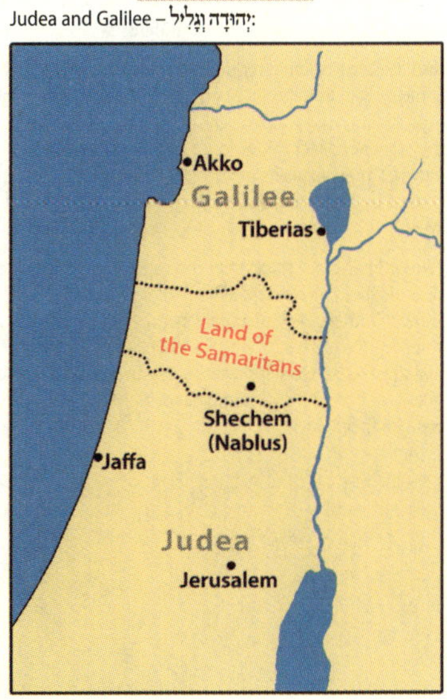

Location of Judea and Galilee

וְכָל שֶׁלֹּא נָהַג כַּמִּנְהָג הַזֶּה אֵינוֹ יָכוֹל לִטְעוֹן טַעֲנַת בְּתוּלִים. אַהֵייָא? אִילֵימָא אַרֵישָׁא – ״כָּל שֶׁנָּהַג״ מִיבְּעֵי לֵיהּ!

The *baraita* concludes: **And anyone who did not conduct** himself **in accordance with this custom cannot make a claim concerning virginity** against the bride. The Gemara asks: **Concerning which** case in the *baraita* was this principle stated? **If we say** it is **concerning the first clause** of the *baraita*, regarding the custom to seclude the couple prior to marriage, in that case, the phrase: **Anyone who conducted** himself in accordance with this custom cannot make a claim concerning virginity, is what **it needed to say,** due to the concern that perhaps they had sexual relations before the marriage.

אֶלָּא אַסֵּיפָא – ״כָּל שֶׁלֹּא מוּשְׁמָשׁ״ מִיבְּעֵי לֵיהּ!

Rather, it is **concerning the latter clause** of the *baraita*: They would appoint for them two groomsmen to examine them, that the principle was stated. In that case, the phrase: **Anyone who was not examined**[H] by the groomsmen, is what **it needed** to say, as it is dependent on the family of the bride, and not the phrase: Anyone who did not conduct himself in accordance with this custom, which indicates that it depends on him.

אָמַר אַבַּיֵי: לְעוֹלָם אַרֵישָׁא, וּתְנֵי: ״כָּל שֶׁנָּהַג״. אֲמַר לֵיהּ רָבָא: וְהָא ״כָּל שֶׁלֹּא נָהַג״ קָתָנֵי! אֶלָּא אָמַר רָבָא, הָכִי קָאָמַר: כָּל שֶׁלֹּא נָהַג מִנְהַג גָּלִיל בַּגָּלִיל אֶלָּא מִנְהַג יְהוּדָה בַּגָּלִיל אֵינוֹ יָכוֹל לִטְעוֹן טַעֲנַת בְּתוּלִים. רַב אַשִׁי אָמַר: לְעוֹלָם אַסֵּיפָא, וּתְנֵי: ״כָּל שֶׁלֹּא מוּשְׁמָשׁ״.

Abaye said: Actually, the principle is stated **concerning the first clause; and** emend the *baraita* **and teach: Anyone who conducted** himself in accordance with this custom. **Rava said to him: But isn't it teaching** explicitly: **Anyone who did not conduct** himself in accordance with this custom? One should not corrupt a *baraita* due to a difficulty that arose in understanding it. **Rather, Rava said** that **this is what** the *baraita* **is saying: Anyone who did not practice the custom of the Galilee in the Galilee, but** instead observed **the custom of Judea in the Galilee, cannot make a claim concerning virginity** against the bride. **Rav Ashi said: Actually,** this principle could be applied **concerning the latter clause, and teach: Anyone who was not examined.**[N] When it said in the *baraita*: Anyone who did not conduct himself in accordance with this custom, it is referring to the custom of being examined.

מתני׳ אַחַת אַלְמְנַת יִשְׂרָאֵל וְאַחַת אַלְמְנַת כֹּהֲנִים כְּתוּבָּתָהּ מָנֶה. בֵּית דִּין שֶׁל כֹּהֲנִים הָיוּ גּוֹבִין לִבְתוּלָה אַרְבַּע מֵאוֹת זוּז, וְלֹא מִיחוּ בְּיָדָם חֲכָמִים.

MISHNA For **both a widow** who is **an Israelite woman**[N] **and a widow** who is the daughter **of priests, her marriage contract is one hundred dinars. A court of priests**[NB] **would collect** a marriage contract of **four hundred dinars for a virgin** daughter of a priest, twice the sum of the standard marriage contract for a virgin, **and the Sages did not reprimand them.**[N]

גמ׳ תָּנָא: וְאַלְמְנַת כֹּהֲנִים כְּתוּבָּתָהּ מָאתַיִם. וְהָאֲנַן תְּנַן: אַחַת אַלְמְנַת יִשְׂרָאֵל וְאַחַת אַלְמְנַת כֹּהֲנִים כְּתוּבָּתָן מָנֶה!

GEMARA A Sage **taught** in a *baraita*: **And** for a widow who is the daughter **of priests, her marriage contract is two hundred** dinars. The Gemara asks: **But didn't we learn** in the mishna: For **both a widow** who is **an Israelite woman and a widow** who is the daughter **of priests, their marriage contract is one hundred dinars?**

אָמַר רַב אַשִׁי: שְׁתֵּי תַקָּנוֹת הָווּ; מֵעִיקָּרָא תַּקִּינוּ לִבְתוּלָה אַרְבַּע מֵאוֹת זוּז, וּלְאַלְמָנָה מָנֶה.

Rav Ashi said: There were two ordinances[N] instituted: **Initially,** the court of priests **instituted for a virgin** daughter of a priest a marriage contract of **four hundred dinars, and for a widow,** a marriage contract of **one hundred dinars.**

HALAKHA

Anyone who was not examined – כָּל שֶׁלֹּא מוּשְׁמָשׁ: If it is the local custom to appoint witnesses to examine the bride and groom to prevent deception with regard to the groom's claim concerning virginity, and none were appointed, the husband cannot make a claim. However, in places where this is not the custom, the husband's claim is accepted based on the presumption that a person does not exert himself to prepare a wedding feast and then cause it to be lost (*Ḥelkat Meḥokek*; *Shulḥan Arukh, Even HaEzer* 68:2).

NOTES

And teach: Anyone who was not examined – וּתְנֵי כָּל שֶׁלֹּא מוּשְׁמָשׁ: The Rivam explains that Rav Ashi disagrees with the presumption: A person does not exert himself to prepare a wedding feast and then cause it to be lost (10a), because in his opinion whether the groom can make a claim concerning virginity is dependent upon the examination. Rabbeinu Tam says that Rav Ashi does not disagree with the presumption, but that he adds that since in Judea the custom was to be examined and the groom failed to observe it, there is suspicion that the failure was not due to forgetfulness but rather it was intentional, in order to cast aspersions on the bride. Therefore, his claim is groundless (*Tosefot Yeshanim*; Rosh).

Both a widow who is an Israelite woman – אַחַת אַלְמְנַת יִשְׂרָאֵל: Rabbeinu Yehonatan writes that the basis for specifying this is that since this mishna is discussing even a woman marrying a priest, one might say that since she is improving her social status she would be satisfied with any amount, even less than one hundred dinars.

A court of priests – בֵּית דִּין שֶׁל כֹּהֲנִים: It is explained in the name of the *ge'onim* that these were courts that were in cities in which the majority of the population consisted of priests. Such cities existed during the second Temple period and thereafter.

And the Sages did not reprimand them – וְלֹא מִיחוּ בְּיָדָם חֲכָמִים: Some explain that the Sages approved of this practice, and that even if the sum was not explicitly written in the marriage contract they would collect this amount based on general agreement (Ritva). Others explains that despite the potential for jealousy caused by the inequality, the Sages did not reprimand them (Meiri).

Two ordinances – שְׁתֵּי תַקָּנוֹת: The early commentaries discuss: How did they arrive at a total of two ordinances, and how do they know that there were two ordinances? According to Rav Ashi it was only one ordinance, which was later revoked. Rashi explains that there were two steps taken for the benefit of the widows of priests, as both the original ordinance and its subsequent repeal were for their benefit.

BACKGROUND

A court of priests – בֵּית דִּין שֶׁל כֹּהֲנִים: Based on descriptions in various talmudic sources, there were apparently several courts under the jurisdiction of the Great Sanhedrin that convened in the Temple and that addressed different problems. One of those courts was the court of priests. This court addressed problems relating to the Temple and its service, e.g., examining the lineage of the priests who came to serve, as well as additional matters, and there are sources indicating that it was the responsibility of this court to establish the New Moon. The court, and the priests in general, had special traditions and customs. See later in the Gemara (14a), where it says that the priests would not always accept the rulings of other courts with regard to the lineage of the priests. Based on the Gemara here, this tribunal also served as the official court of the priests, establishing matters applicable to all priests.

כֵּיוָן דְּחָזוּ דִּמְזַלְזְלִי בְּהוּ – תַּקִּינוּ לְהוּ מָאתָן. כֵּיוָן דְּחָזוּ דְּקָא פָּרְשִׁין מִינַּיְיהוּ, דְּאָמְרִי: עַד דְּנָסְבִינַן אַלְמָנַת כֹּהֲנִים – נֵיזִיל נִיסִיב בְּתוּלָה בַּת יִשְׂרָאֵל, אַהֲדְרִינְהוּ לְמִלְּתַיְיהוּ.

Once the members of the court **saw that** the priests **were demeaning** the widows, **they instituted for them** a marriage contract of **two hundred** dinars, so that they would treat them with greater esteem. **Once they saw that** the grooms **were distancing** themselves **from them, as they said: Instead of marrying a widow** who is the daughter of **priests** and paying a marriage contract of two hundred, **let us go marry a virgin Israelite woman** for the same price. Since men would no longer marry widows from priestly families, **they restored** matters **to their** original **status.** This indicates that the mishna and the *baraita* are addressing different time periods and different ordinances.

״בֵּית דִּין שֶׁל כֹּהֲנִים״ כו׳. אָמַר רַב יְהוּדָה אָמַר שְׁמוּאֵל: לֹא בֵּית דִּין שֶׁל כֹּהֲנִים בִּלְבַד אָמְרוּ, אֶלָּא אֲפִילּוּ מִשְׁפָּחוֹת הַמְיוּחָסוֹת בְּיִשְׂרָאֵל, אִם רָצוּ לַעֲשׂוֹת כְּדֶרֶךְ שֶׁהַכֹּהֲנִים עוֹשִׂין – עוֹשִׂין.

§ It is stated in the mishna that **a court of priests** would collect a marriage contract of four hundred dinars for a virgin daughter of a priest. **Rav Yehuda said** that **Shmuel said: Not only with regard to a court of priests did** the Sages **say that**[H] they could collect a greater sum for the marriage contract of their daughters, **but even families of distinguished lineage**[N] **in Israel. If they wanted to act as the priests do, they may act** in that manner.

מֵיתִיבֵי: הָרוֹצֶה לַעֲשׂוֹת כְּדֶרֶךְ שֶׁהַכֹּהֲנִים עוֹשִׂין, כְּגוֹן בַּת יִשְׂרָאֵל לְכֹהֵן וּבַת כֹּהֵן לְיִשְׂרָאֵל – עוֹשִׂין. בַּת יִשְׂרָאֵל לְכֹהֵן, וּבַת כֹּהֵן לְיִשְׂרָאֵל הוּא דְּאִיכָּא צַד כְּהוּנָּה, אֲבָל בַּת יִשְׂרָאֵל לְיִשְׂרָאֵל – לָא!

The Gemara **raises an objection** from a *baraita*: **One who sought to act as the priests do,** as in cases **where an Israelite woman** is married **to a priest, or the daughter of a priest** is married **to an Israelite, may act** in that manner. The Gemara infers: This allowance is specifically in cases where **an Israelite woman** is married **to a priest, or the daughter of a priest** is married **to an Israelite, where there is an aspect of priesthood**[N] involved. **However,** apparently, in a case where **the daughter of an Israelite** is married **to an Israelite, no,** it is not allowed.

לָא מִבַּעְיָא קָאָמַר; לָא מִבַּעְיָא בַּת יִשְׂרָאֵל לְיִשְׂרָאֵל, דְּלָא מָצֵי אָמַר לָהּ עַלּוּיֵי קָא מַעֲלֵינַן לֵיךְ, אֲבָל בַּת יִשְׂרָאֵל לְכֹהֵן, דְּמָצֵי אָמַר לָהּ עַלּוּיֵי קָא מַעֲלֵינַן לֵיךְ, אֵימָא לָא – קָא מַשְׁמַע לָן.

The Gemara rejects that inference. The *baraita* **is stated** employing the style of: **It is not necessary. It is not necessary** to state a case where **the daughter of an Israelite** is married **to an Israelite, as** in that case the groom **cannot say to her:** By marrying you, **I am raising your** social status, and it is clear that women from distinguished families would demand a marriage contract with a greater sum. **However,** in a case where **an Israelite woman** is married **to a priest,**[N] **where he can say to her: I am raising your** social status, as you are marrying into the priesthood, you might think to **say no,** the woman cannot demand a marriage contract with a greater sum. Therefore, the *baraita* **teaches us** that even in the case of a woman from a distinguished family of Israelites marrying a priest, she may demand a marriage contract with a greater sum.

HALAKHA

Not only with regard to a court of priests did the Sages say that – לֹא בֵּית דִּין שֶׁל כֹּהֲנִים בִּלְבַד אָמְרוּ: If a family has a custom to write in their marriage contract a sum greater than the standard sum established by the Sages, they are not reprimanded. Furthermore, if a member of that family did not write a marriage contract for his wife, the court collects payment for her in the amount corresponding to the family custom (*Ḥelkat Meḥokek*; *Shulḥan Arukh, Even HaEzer* 66:7).

NOTES

But even families of distinguished lineage – אֶלָּא אֲפִילּוּ מִשְׁפָּחוֹת הַמְיוּחָסוֹת: The courts would support this practice and collect the greater sum for the women according to the family custom. It was necessary to state this in order to emphasize that this practice does not constitute violation of the rabbinic ordinance of two hundred dinars for a virgin and one hundred for a non-virgin (*Tosefot Rid*). The *ge'onim* note that despite the approval expressed in the Gemara, this practice was not adopted in Babylonia. The Meiri writes that this *halakha* applies only to families of distinguished lineage.

Where there is an aspect of priesthood – דְּאִיכָּא צַד כְּהוּנָּה: This explanation appears strange, since the reason for the greater sum is relevant only to the daughter of a priest but not to the daughter of a non-priest. Ritva explains that the priests did not want to flaunt their prominence conspicuously, so they instituted a marriage contract with a greater sum in any case involving a priestly family, even if the groom was the priest and the bride the daughter of a non-priest. Rashba explains the matter in terms of interpersonal relationships. Were the daughter of a non-priest marrying a priest to receive a standard marriage contract, lower than the one received by her mother-in-law and sister-in-law, she would be jealous and resentful of them.

An Israelite woman married to a priest – בַּת יִשְׂרָאֵל לְכֹהֵן: In the Jerusalem Talmud, explanations are cited supporting the payment of a greater sum in each of the cases. On the one hand, the daughter of a priest marrying a non-priest should receive a greater sum in her marriage contract, as in general priests receive gifts from non-priests, and in contrast, the daughter of a non-priest marrying a priest should suffice with her newly acquired elevated social status and no additional sum should be necessary.

On the other hand, the daughter of a non-priest marrying a priest should receive a greater sum in her marriage contract because she is now being elevated into the priesthood, i.e., she may now partake of *teruma*. Her marriage contract should reflect that elevated status. And in contrast, the daughter of a priest marrying a non-priest should receive a standard marriage contract since she thereby forfeits all rights of the priesthood.

The conclusion is that in both cases there is a marriage contract with a greater sum. In addition, in order to encourage people to marry within their own tribe, the Sages levied a fine penalizing the non-priest groom who marries the daughter of a priest.

HALAKHA

She says: After you betrothed me I was raped – הִיא אוֹמֶרֶת מִשֶּׁאֵרַסְתַּנִי נֶאֱנַסְתִּי: A woman who married with the presumptive status of a virgin, whose husband discovered that she was not, and she admits that she is not a virgin but claims that she was raped after the betrothal, is accorded credibility and is entitled to a marriage contract of two hundred dinars in accordance with the opinions of Rabban Gamliel and Rabbi Eliezer. However, in an effort to ensure that the woman is telling the truth, the *ge'onim* instituted that the husband may request that the court excommunicate her if it is discovered that she made a false claim in order to obligate him to pay money (Rambam *Sefer Nashim, Hilkhot Ishut* 11:11; *Shulḥan Arukh, Even HaEzer* 68:9).

One says I have one hundred dinars in your possession and the other says I don't know – מָנֶה לִי בְּיָדְךָ וְהַלָּה אוֹמֵר אֵינִי יוֹדֵעַ: If one claims that another owes him money that he loaned him or deposited with him, and the other person asserts that he is uncertain whether he borrowed money or received the deposit from the claimant, the respondent is exempt from payment in accordance with the opinions of Rav Naḥman and Rabbi Yoḥanan. However, he is required by rabbinic law to take an oath of inducement, instituted to induce him to tell the truth, that he does not know. Furthermore, one may request the court to excommunicate anyone making false claims to collect money from him (Rambam *Sefer Mishpatim, Hilkhot To'en VeNitan* 1:9; *Shulḥan Arukh, Ḥoshen Mishpat* 75:9).

מתני׳ הַנּוֹשֵׂא אֶת הָאִשָּׁה וְלֹא מָצָא לָהּ בְּתוּלִים, הִיא אוֹמֶרֶת: מִשֶּׁאֵרַסְתַּנִי נֶאֱנַסְתִּי, וְנִסְתַּחֲפָה שָׂדֵהוּ. וְהוּא אוֹמֵר: לֹא כִּי, אֶלָּא עַד שֶׁלֹּא אֵרַסְתִּיךְ, וְהָיָה מִקָּחִי מִקַּח טָעוּת. רַבָּן גַּמְלִיאֵל וְרַבִּי אֱלִיעֶזֶר אוֹמְרִים: נֶאֱמֶנֶת. רַבִּי יְהוֹשֻׁעַ אוֹמֵר: לֹא מִפִּיהָ אָנוּ חַיִּין, אֶלָּא הֲרֵי זוֹ בְּחֶזְקַת בְּעוּלָה עַד שֶׁלֹּא תִּתְאָרֵס וְהִטְעַתּוּ, עַד שֶׁתָּבִיא רְאָיָה לִדְבָרֶיהָ.

MISHNA There is a case of one **who marries a woman and did not find her hymen** intact, and **she says: After you betrothed me I was raped,**[H] and **his,** i.e., her husband's, **field was inundated,** meaning that it is his misfortune that she is not a virgin, as she was raped after betrothal. **And he says: No; rather,** you were raped **before I betrothed you, and my transaction was a mistaken transaction. Rabban Gamliel and Rabbi Eliezer say: She is deemed credible.**[N] **Rabbi Yehoshua says:** It is **not** based on the statement emerging **from her mouth** that **we conduct our lives;**[N] **rather, this** woman assumes **the presumptive status of one who engaged in intercourse when she was not yet betrothed and she misled him, until she brings proof** supporting **her statement.**

גמ׳ אִתְּמַר: ״מָנֶה לִי בְּיָדְךָ״ וְהַלָּה אוֹמֵר ״אֵינִי יוֹדֵעַ״. רַב יְהוּדָה וְרַב הוּנָא אָמְרִי: חַיָּיב, וְרַב נַחְמָן וְרַבִּי יוֹחָנָן אָמְרִי: פָּטוּר. רַב הוּנָא וְרַב יְהוּדָה אָמְרִי: חַיָּיב, בָּרִי וְשֶׁמָּא – בָּרִי עָדִיף. רַב נַחְמָן וְרַבִּי יוֹחָנָן אָמְרִי: פָּטוּר, אוֹקֵי מָמוֹנָא בְּחֶזְקַת מָרֵיהּ.

GEMARA **It was stated:** With regard to one who approaches another and says: **I have one hundred dinars in your possession, and the other says: I don't know,**[H] **Rav Yehuda and Rav Huna say:** The respondent is **obligated** to pay, because he did not deny the claim, **and Rav Naḥman and Rabbi Yoḥanan**[N] **say:** He is **exempt** from payment. The Gemara elaborates. **Rav Huna and Rav Yehuda say** that the respondent is **obligated** to pay based on the principle: When there is a **certain** claim, e.g., that of the claimant, **and an uncertain** claim,[N] e.g., that of the respondent, the **certain** claim **prevails.**[N] **Rav Naḥman and Rabbi Yoḥanan say:** The respondent is **exempt** based on the principle: **Establish the money in the possession of its owner,** and the burden of proof rests upon the claimant. Since the claimant does not support his claim with proof, the money remains in the possession of the respondent.

אָמַר לֵיהּ אַבַּיֵי לְרַב יוֹסֵף: הָא דְּרַב הוּנָא וְרַב יְהוּדָה – דִּשְׁמוּאֵל הִיא. דִּתְנַן: הָיְתָה מְעוּבֶּרֶת, וְאָמְרוּ לָהּ: מַה טִּיבוֹ שֶׁל עוּבָּר זֶה? מֵאִישׁ פְּלוֹנִי, וְכֹהֵן הוּא. רַבָּן גַּמְלִיאֵל וְרַבִּי אֱלִיעֶזֶר אוֹמְרִים: נֶאֱמֶנֶת. וְאָמַר רַב יְהוּדָה אָמַר שְׁמוּאֵל: הֲלָכָה כְּרַבָּן גַּמְלִיאֵל.

Abaye said to Rav Yosef: This ruling **of Rav Huna and Rav Yehuda** is essentially the statement **of Shmuel, as we learned** in a mishna (13a): In the case of an unmarried woman **who was pregnant,** and the Sages **said to her: What is the nature of this fetus,** i.e., who is the father. And she says: It is **from a man** called **so-and-so and he is a priest** and is certainly of valid lineage. **Rabban Gamliel and Rabbi Eliezer say: She is deemed credible,** and the fetus is deemed to be of valid lineage. **Rav Yehuda said** that **Shmuel said: The *halakha* is in accordance with** the opinion **of Rabban Gamliel.**

NOTES

She is deemed credible – נֶאֱמֶנֶת: In the Jerusalem Talmud the question is raised: If she is accorded credibility then there is no case where the groom's claim concerning virginity would be accepted. It would be far-fetched to explain that all the discussions concerning that claim up to this point were exclusively according to the opinion of Rabbi Yehoshua. The explanation there is that there is a distinction between a case where the bride denies the groom's claim and asserts that she was a virgin, in which case the groom's certain claim that she was not is accorded credibility; and a case where she admits that she was not a virgin but provides an alternative explanation for the situation (see *Tosefot Rid*).

It is not based on the statement emerging from her mouth that we conduct our lives – לֹא מִפִּיהָ אָנוּ חַיִּין: This unique formulation contains an allusion to a mishna in tractate *Avot* (1:18), which states: On three matters does the world stand, on truth, on justice, and on peace. Since Rabbi Yehoshua maintains that she is not deemed credible and that she is not telling the truth, then based on that mishna he says: It is not based on her statement that we conduct our lives; it is based on truth (Ritva; Radbaz; *Melekhet Shlomo*, citing the Ari).

Rav Naḥman and Rabbi Yoḥanan – רַב נַחְמָן וְרַבִּי יוֹחָנָן: It is unusual that Rav Naḥman is cited before Rabbi Yoḥanan, as not only was Rabbi Yoḥanan greater than Rav Naḥman, he preceded him chronologically as well. The Rosh explains that this *halakha* was formulated in Babylonia, where Rav Naḥman's opinion was the only one known. Later, when the Sages discovered that Rabbi Yoḥanan shared his opinion, they appended his name to the statement.

A certain claim and an uncertain claim – בָּרִי וְשֶׁמָּא: *Tosafot* and many early commentaries analyze at length the various issues concerning the subject of certain and uncertain claims as it relates to different areas of *halakha*, and in terms of how the various opinions can be reconciled with the sources. They explain that although in general a certain claim prevails over an uncertain claim, there are distinctions drawn between different types of claims. Some claims have lesser certainty, due to additional factors and considerations that oppose them, e.g., presumptions, majorities, or logic. Similarly, there are uncertain claims that are enhanced in a situation where there is no way for the claimant to ascertain the facts, and all the more so where there are elements supporting his contention. When one claims: I don't know, in the case of a loan, this would be an inferior uncertain claim, because he should know whether or not there was a loan. However, the uncertain claim of the husband is enhanced by the fact that the rape never became public, even though rape is usually publicized.

The certain claim prevails – בָּרִי עָדִיף: In the *Penei Yehoshua* the question is raised: Why is this principle not applied to lost articles? The finder can make only an uncertain claim, as he does not know whether he is the owner, and the owner can claim with certainty that it belongs to him. Why must the owner provide identifying indicators that the item belongs to him? He answers that since the article could have belonged to anyone and the majority of the world is not the one claiming ownership, the claim of the finder is supported by that majority. Others explain that even one making an uncertain claim can request time to clarify the matter, and in this case the finder could say that he prefers waiting before returning the article, as someone else may claim it and provide indicators or witnesses (*Ḥatam Sofer*).

Rav Ḥayyim Soloveitchik explains that with regard to returning lost articles there is another consideration, since the verse states: "And it shall be with you until your brother demands it" (Deuteronomy 22:2), meaning that it is incumbent upon the finder to investigate whether the claimant is indeed the one who lost it. Therefore, even a certain claim does not suffice.

וְאָמַר לֵיהּ רַב שְׁמוּאֵל בַּר יְהוּדָה לְרַב יְהוּדָה: שִׁינָּנָא, אָמְרַתְּ לָן מִשְּׁמֵיהּ דִּשְׁמוּאֵל הֲלָכָה כְּרַבָּן גַּמְלִיאֵל אַף בָּרִאשׁוֹנָה. מַאי ״אַף בָּרִאשׁוֹנָה״? אַף עַל גַּב דְּאִיכָּא לְמֵימַר אוּקֵי מָמוֹנָא בְּחֶזְקַת מָרֵיהּ – אָמַר רַבָּן גַּמְלִיאֵל בָּרִי עָדִיף.

And Rav Shmuel bar Yehuda said to Rav Yehuda: Big-toothed one [*shinnana*],[L] **you said to us in the name of Shmuel that the** ***halakha*** **is in accordance with** the opinion of **Rabban Gamliel even in the first** dispute, the dispute cited in the mishna, which is the first in a series of disputes with regard to conflicting claims. The Gemara asks: **What** is the meaning of **even the first?** What is unique about that dispute relative to the others? The Gemara answers: The novel element in the first dispute is that the claim of the bride is accepted **despite the fact that** although **there is** room **to say: Establish the money in the possession of its owner,** and since the money is in the possession of the husband and the woman is the claimant, **Rabban Gamliel said** that the **certain** claim of the bride **prevails** over the uncertain claim of the groom, who can only speculate about when she was raped.

לֵימָא רַב יְהוּדָה וְרַב הוּנָא דְּאָמְרִי כְּרַבָּן גַּמְלִיאֵל, וְרַב נַחְמָן וְרַבִּי יוֹחָנָן דְּאָמְרִי כְּרַבִּי יְהוֹשֻׁעַ?

The Gemara suggests: **Let us say** that it is **Rav Yehuda and Rav Huna who say** their ruling **in accordance with** the opinion of **Rabban Gamliel,** who says that a certain claim prevails over an uncertain one even to collect money from the possession of the respondent. **And** it is **Rav Naḥman and Rabbi Yoḥanan who say** their ruling **in accordance with** the opinion of **Rabbi Yehoshua,** that one does not collect money based merely on a claim.

אָמַר לָךְ רַב נַחְמָן: אֲנָא דַּאֲמַרִי אֲפִילּוּ כְּרַבָּן גַּמְלִיאֵל; עַד כָּאן לֹא קָאָמַר רַבָּן גַּמְלִיאֵל הָתָם אֶלָּא דְּאִיכָּא מִגּוֹ, אֲבָל הָכָא – מַאי מִגּוֹ אִיכָּא?

The Gemara rejects that suggestion. **Rav Naḥman** could have **said to you:** That **which I said, is even in accordance with** the opinion of **Rabban Gamliel. Rabban Gamliel says his ruling only there,** with regard to claims of a groom and a bride, **where there is a** ***miggo*****,**[N] a halakhic argument that the ability to make a more advantageous claim grants credibility to the claim one actually makes, that bolsters the bride's claim. She could have claimed that she wasn't raped at all, but rather that her hymen was ruptured by wood. That is a more advantageous claim because she is not disgraced in the eyes of the groom. Therefore, her claim that she was raped is accorded credibility. **However here,** where one claims that another owes him money, **what** ***miggo*** **is there** bolstering his claim and according it credibility?

אִי נַמִּי, עַד כָּאן לֹא קָאָמַר רַבָּן גַּמְלִיאֵל הָתָם אֶלָּא דְּאָמְרִינַן אוֹקְמַהּ אַחֲזָקָה, אֲבָל הָכָא – מַאי חֲזָקָה אִית לֵיהּ לְהַאי?

Alternatively, Rav Naḥman could have said to you: **Rabban Gamliel says his ruling only there, where we say: Establish her** legal status according to her **presumptive status**[N] as a virgin, and the husband's claim seeks to undermine that presumptive status. **However here, what presumptive status does this** claimant **have** supporting the claim that another owes him money? Therefore, even Rabban Gamliel would concede that his certain claim does not prevail.

הָכִי נַמִּי מִסְתַּבְּרָא כִּדְקָא מְשַׁנֵּינַן, דְּרַב נַחְמָן הוּא דַּאֲמַר כְּרַבָּן גַּמְלִיאֵל.

The Gemara notes: **Indeed,** it is **also reasonable** to explain **as we are teaching, that it is Rav Naḥman who said** his ruling **in accordance** with the opinion of **Rabban Gamliel.**

LANGUAGE

Big-toothed one [*shinnana*] **– שִׁינָּנָא:** A nickname for Rabbi Yehuda, appearing in several places in the Talmud, that was explained by several commentaries to mean sharp or brilliant. However, the *ge'onim* assert that they are certain that this is an expression describing one with large teeth, noting that the expression was still employed in their time.

NOTES

Where there is a ***miggo*** **– דְּאִיכָּא מִגּוֹ:** The *miggo* in this case is that the bride could have claimed that her hymen was ruptured by a foreign object. This is a more advantageous claim, as it does not disqualify her from marrying a priest. Moreover, an additional advantage of that claim is that the stigma associated with a claim of rape does not exist (Meiri).

Many reservations were raised with regard to the applicability of the principle of *miggo* in this context. In fact, there are variant readings in which the reason of *miggo* does not appear and only the second reason of presumptive status is cited (see Ritva and Rabbi Aharon HaLevi). The primary difficulty is that, according to most authorities, *miggo* is effective only to exempt from payment, not to collect payment from the possession of its owner, and in this case the bride is receiving payment of her marriage contract from the husband.

Several early commentaries conclude based on this discussion that the principle of *miggo* is effective to collect payment as well (Maharshak; *Haggahot Mordekhai*). Others explain that in this case it is not the *miggo* that is effective in collecting the money. Rather, it is that the certain claim prevails over the uncertain claim (see Ritva and Meiri).

Establish her legal status according to her presumptive status – אוֹקְמַהּ אַחֲזָקָה: This is referring to the presumptive status of the bride's body; since she was born as a virgin, she maintains that status until proven otherwise. The Rid and the Rosh add that although the bride does not receive payment of her marriage contract before she enters the wedding canopy, fundamentally, she is entitled to it even after betrothal. They did not want to rely solely on her presumptive status of virginity; that presumption itself was undermined, as she is no longer a virgin when the claim is made. Later commentaries discuss this subject extensively, from various perspectives (see Maharam Schiff and *Shev Shemateta*).

דְּאִם כֵּן קַשְׁיָא הִלְכְתָא אַהִלְכְתָא, דְּקַיְימָא לָן הִלְכְתָא כְּרַב נַחְמָן בְּדִינֵי, וּבְהָא אָמַר רַב יְהוּדָה אָמַר שְׁמוּאֵל הֲלָכָה כְּרַבָּן גַּמְלִיאֵל. אֶלָּא לָאו שְׁמַע מִינָּהּ כִּדְמְשַׁנֵּינַן, שְׁמַע מִינָּהּ.

Because if that were not **so, it is difficult,** as there would be a contradiction between one ***halakha*** and another ***halakha.* Since,** on the one hand, **we maintain** a principle in halakhic ruling that **the *halakha* is in accordance with** the opinion of **Rav Naḥman in civil law; and,** on the other hand, **in that** case involving the claims of the bride and the groom **Rav Yehuda said** that **Shmuel said: The *halakha* is in accordance with** the opinion of **Rabban Gamliel. Rather,** can we **not conclude from** this apparent contradiction that the matter must be understood **as we are teaching,** that the opinion of Rav Naḥman can be reconciled with the opinion of Rabban Gamliel? The Gemara affirms: Indeed, **conclude from it** that this is the case.

מתני׳ הִיא אוֹמֶרֶת: ״מוּכַּת עֵץ אֲנִי״, וְהוּא אוֹמֵר: ״לֹא כִּי, אֶלָּא דְּרוּסַת אִישׁ אַתְּ״. רַבָּן גַּמְלִיאֵל וְרַבִּי אֱלִיעֶזֶר אוֹמְרִים: נֶאֱמֶנֶת, וְרַבִּי יְהוֹשֻׁעַ אוֹמֵר: לֹא מִפִּיהָ אָנוּ חַיִּין, אֶלָּא הֲרֵי זוֹ בְּחֶזְקַת דְּרוּסַת אִישׁ עַד שֶׁתָּבִיא רְאָיָה לִדְבָרֶיהָ.

MISHNA In a case where **she says:** I am one whose hymen was **ruptured by wood,** i.e., she admits that her hymen is not intact but claims that it was not ruptured through intercourse, **and the groom says: No; rather, you are** one who was **trampled by a man,**[NH] and your hymen was ruptured through intercourse, **Rabban Gamliel and Rabbi Eliezer say: She is deemed credible** and her claim is accepted because she certainly knows what actually happened. **Rabbi Yehoshua says:** It is **not** based on the statement emerging **from her mouth** that **we conduct our lives; rather, she** retains **the presumptive status of** one who **was trampled by a man, until she brings proof** supporting **her statement** that her hymen was ruptured by wood.

גמ׳ טַעֲנָתַיְיהוּ בְּמַאי? רַבִּי יוֹחָנָן אָמַר: בְּמָאתַיִם וּמָנֶה, רַבִּי אֶלְעָזָר אָמַר: בְּמָנֶה וְלֹא כְלוּם.

GEMARA The Gemara asks: **What are their** respective financial **claims?**[N] **Rabbi Yoḥanan said:** The bride claims that since her hymen was ruptured by wood, her legal status is that of a virgin and she is entitled to a marriage contract of **two hundred** dinars; **and** the groom claims that she engaged in intercourse and is entitled to a marriage contract of **one hundred dinars.**[N] **Rabbi Elazar said:** The bride claims that although her hymen is not intact she did not completely deceive him, as she never engaged in intercourse, and therefore she is entitled to a marriage contract of **one hundred dinars; and** the groom claims that she engaged in intercourse, rendering the betrothal a mistaken transaction, and therefore she is entitled to **nothing at all.**

רַבִּי יוֹחָנָן אָמַר: בְּמָאתַיִם וּמָנֶה, סָבַר לָהּ כְּרַבִּי מֵאִיר, דְּאָמַר: בֵּין הִכִּיר בָּהּ וּבֵין לֹא הִכִּיר בָּהּ – מָאתַיִם. וְרַבִּי אֶלְעָזָר אוֹמֵר: בְּמָנֶה וְלֹא כְלוּם, סָבַר לָהּ כְּרַבָּנַן דְּאָמְרִי: בֵּין הִכִּיר בָּהּ בֵּין לֹא הִכִּיר בָּהּ – מָנֶה.

The Gemara elaborates. **Rabbi Yoḥanan said:** The dispute between the bride and groom is whether the marriage contract **is two hundred** dinars **or one hundred dinars,** because the *tanna* of the mishna **holds in accordance with** the opinion of **Rabbi Meir, who said: Whether** the husband **was aware that her** hymen was ruptured by wood **or whether he was not aware of her** condition, she receives payment of her marriage contract of **two hundred** dinars and it is not a mistaken transaction. **And Rabbi Elazar says: The dispute** between the bride and groom is whether the marriage contract **is one hundred dinars or** whether she is entitled to **nothing at all,** because the *tanna* of the mishna **holds in accordance with** the opinion of **the Rabbis, who said: Whether** the husband **was aware that her** hymen was ruptured by wood or **whether he was not aware of her** condition, she receives payment of her marriage contract of **one hundred dinars.**

NOTES

No, rather you are one who was trampled by a man – לֹא כִּי אֶלָּא דְּרוּסַת אִישׁ אַתְּ: In the Jerusalem Talmud the question is raised: How is this exchange possible? The husband has no way of knowing that she her hymen was ruptured through intercourse and not by means of a foreign object. Therefore, the case is explained there that the bride claims she informed the groom before betrothal that her hymen was ruptured by a foreign object, and that he agreed to marry her. The groom claims that he married her based on her presumptive status as a virgin, and he concludes from the fact that she did not tell him that her hymen was ruptured by a foreign object that in fact she lost her virginity through intercourse.

What are their respective financial claims – טַעֲנָתַיְיהוּ בְּמַאי: In the *Shita Mekubbetzet* both the question and the basis of the dispute are explained. In the previous mishna (12b), the objective of the claim of each of the parties is articulated. The bride claims that she is entitled to two hundred dinars and the groom claims that she is entitled to nothing, as it is a mistaken transaction. Here, however, the objectives are unarticulated. Therefore, Rabbi Yoḥanan prefers establishing this mishna parallel to the previous mishna, with the bride claiming two hundred dinars despite the fact that this explanation is possible only according to the opinion of Rabbi Meir (11a). Rabbi Elazar prefers establishing this mishna in accordance with the opinion of the Rabbis, although that means that the bride's claim in this mishna is not parallel to the claim in the previous mishna.

Two hundred dinars and one hundred dinars – בְּמָאתַיִם וּמָנֶה: Many early commentaries note that ostensibly this is a classic case of partial admission in response to a claim, as the bride claims two hundred dinars and the groom admits that he owes one hundred. In such a case, the Torah imposed an oath upon the respondent. In this case the groom is unable to take the oath, as he does not know what happened, and the principle is that one unable to take an oath is required to pay. Some explain that this principle applies only in a case where there is a reasonable expectation that he knows what happened, but refuses to take an oath. In this case, where there is no such expectation, he is not obligated to pay (Ri, cited in *Tosafot, Bava Kamma* 46a). Many commentaries dispute that explanation. Others explain that the hundred dinars that he acknowledges owing her are not in dispute. They certainly belong to the bride. It is not an admission on his part; rather, the dispute is solely with regard to the additional one hundred dinars, which he completely denies owing (Ritva).

HALAKHA

Ruptured by wood or trampled by a man – מוּכַּת עֵץ אוֹ דְּרוּסַת אִישׁ: If a man marries a woman with the presumptive status of a virgin and claims that he discovered that she is not a virgin, and she admits that her hymen was not intact when they consummated the marriage but claims that her hymen was ruptured by a foreign object, her claim is accepted and she is entitled to receive payment of a marriage contract of one hundred dinars. This is in accordance with the opinion of Rabbi Elazar. Even if the husband claims that his wife may have lost her virginity by engaging in intercourse with another man and that the betrothal was a mistaken transaction, his claim is ignored. However, the husband may request that the court excommunicate her if she is lying (Rambam *Sefer Nashim, Hilkhot Ishut* 11:10; *Shulḥan Arukh, Even HaEzer* 68:9).

בִּשְׁלָמָא רַבִּי אֶלְעָזָר לָא קָאָמַר כְּרַבִּי יוֹחָנָן – דְּקָא מוֹקֵי לָהּ כְּרַבָּנַן, אֶלָּא רַבִּי יוֹחָנָן מַאי טַעֲמָא לָא אֲמַר כְּרַבִּי אֶלְעָזָר?

The Gemara asks: **Granted, Rabbi Elazar did not state** his explanation of the mishna **in accordance with** the explanation of **Rabbi Yoḥanan because he** preferred to **establish** the mishna **in accordance with** the opinion of **the Rabbis,** according to which the *halakha* is ruled, and not the opinion of Rabbi Meir. **However, what is the reason that Rabbi Yoḥanan did not state** his explanation of the mishna **in accordance with** the explanation of **Rabbi Elazar?**

קָסָבַר: כְּנָסָהּ בְּחֶזְקַת בְּתוּלָה וְנִמְצֵאת בְּעוּלָה – יֵשׁ לָהּ כְּתוּבָּה מָנֶה. הָכָא, הוּא קָאָמַר מָנֶה וְהִיא קָאָמְרָה מָנֶה, מַאי אִיכָּא בֵּין טַעֲנָה דִּידֵיהּ לְטַעֲנָה דִּידָהּ?

The Gemara answers: The reason that Rabbi Yoḥanan explained the mishna in that manner is that **he holds:** If the groom **married** a woman **with the presumptive status of a virgin, and she is found to be a non-virgin, she** receives payment of her **marriage contract of one hundred** dinars. Therefore, **here,** according to the explanation of Rabbi Elazar, who explains the mishna according to the opinion of the Rabbis, **he is saying** that she engaged in intercourse and is entitled to a marriage contract of **one hundred dinars; and she is saying** that her hymen was ruptured by wood and she is entitled to a marriage contract of **one hundred dinars. What** difference **is there between his claim and her claim?** Therefore, Rabbi Yoḥanan explains the mishna in accordance with the opinion of Rabbi Meir, who holds that the dispute between the bride and the groom is whether she is entitled to a marriage contract of two hundred dinars or a marriage contract of one hundred dinars.

בִּשְׁלָמָא לְרַבִּי אֶלְעָזָר – הַיְינוּ דְּקָתָנֵי תַּרְתֵּי: חֲדָא – לְאַפּוּקֵי מִדְּרָמִי בַּר חָמָא,

Again we question: **Granted, according to Rabbi Elazar,** who explains that the dispute between the bride and the groom is with regard to whether she is entitled to a marriage contract of one hundred dinars because her hymen was ruptured by wood, or whether she is entitled to nothing because she engaged in intercourse, **that is** why the *tanna* **teaches two** similar disputes, in this mishna and in the previous one. **One** dispute, in this mishna, comes **to exclude** the opinion **of Rami bar Ḥama,** who said: If he was not aware that her hymen was ruptured by wood, everyone agrees that she receives no marriage contract at all, as the marriage was a mistaken transaction. From this mishna it is clear that according to her claim that her hymen was ruptured by wood, she is entitled to one hundred dinars.

וַחֲדָא – לְאַפּוּקֵי מִדְּרַב חִיָּיא בַּר אָבִין אָמַר רַב שֵׁשֶׁת. אֶלָּא לְרַבִּי יוֹחָנָן, תַּרְתֵּי לָמָּה לִי?

And one dispute, in the previous mishna, is brought in order **to exclude** that **which Rav Ḥiyya bar Avin** said that **Rav Sheshet said:** If the groom married a woman with the presumptive status of a virgin and she is found to be a non-virgin, she receives payment of her marriage contract of one hundred dinars. In the previous mishna he claims: Before I betrothed you, you were raped and my transaction was a mistaken transaction, indicating that she is entitled to nothing. **However,** according **to Rabbi Yoḥanan, why do I** need the *tanna* to teach **two** similar disputes? In his opinion, the previous mishna could not have been taught to exclude that which Rav Ḥiyya bar Avin said that Rav Sheshet said. It has already been established that Rabbi Yoḥanan agrees with the opinion that if she is found to be a non-virgin, she receives payment of her marriage contract of one hundred dinars.

חֲדָא לְהוֹדִיעֲךָ כֹּחוֹ דְּרַבָּן גַּמְלִיאֵל, וַחֲדָא לְהוֹדִיעֲךָ כֹּחוֹ דְּרַבִּי יְהוֹשֻׁעַ. קַמַּיְיתָא לְהוֹדִיעֲךָ כֹּחוֹ דְּרַבִּי יְהוֹשֻׁעַ, דְּאַף עַל גַּב דְּאִיכָּא לְמֵימַר מִיגּוֹ – לָא מְהֵימְנָא, בַּתְרַיְיתָא לְהוֹדִיעֲךָ כֹּחוֹ דְּרַבָּן גַּמְלִיאֵל, דְּאַף עַל גַּב דְּלֵיכָּא לְמֵימַר מִיגּוֹ – מְהֵימְנָא.

The Gemara answers: The two similar disputes were necessary. **One** is **to convey to you the far-reaching nature** of the opinion **of Rabban Gamliel** and the extent of the credibility that he accords to her claim; **and one** is **to convey to you the far-reaching nature** of the opinion **of Rabbi Yehoshua** and the extent to which he does not accord credibility to her claim. The Gemara elaborates: **The first** mishna, where she admits she was raped but claims that it was after betrothal, **conveys to you the far-reaching nature** of the opinion **of Rabbi Yehoshua: That even though there is** room **to say** that her claim is bolstered by a *miggo*, **she is not deemed credible. The second** mishna, where she claims that her hymen was ruptured by wood and he claims that she engaged in intercourse, **conveys to you the far-reaching nature** of the opinion **of Rabban Gamliel: That even though there is no** room **to say** that her claim is bolstered by a *miggo*, in his opinion **she is deemed credible.**

LANGUAGE

Nature [*tivo*] – טִיבוֹ: The meaning of the word *tivo* was discussed by the early commentaries. According to the Rambam it means reason. Others explain that in general it means matter or concern. According to Rabbi Binyamin Musafya it most closely approximates the Hebrew word *teva*, meaning nature. The question then is: What is the nature of this man (see *Melekhet Shlomo*)?

BACKGROUND

***Mamzer* – מַמְזֵר:** A *mamzer* is a child born from an incestuous or adulterous relationship, i.e., a child born from relations between a married woman and a man other than her husband, or between relatives for whom relations are proscribed by a prohibition punishable by *karet*. An offspring conceived with a menstruating woman is an exception to this principle, because although the prohibition in that case is punishable by *karet*, the offspring is not a *mamzer*. The offspring born of an unmarried couple is not a *mamzer*. A *mamzer* inherits from his biological father and is considered his son in every respect. A *mamzer* may marry only a female *mamzer* or a convert to Judaism, and the offspring of that union is a *mamzer*. Likewise, a female *mamzer* may marry only a *mamzer* or a convert. The offspring of that union is a *mamzer* as well.

HALAKHA

What is the meaning of speaking – מַאי מְדַבֶּרֶת: If an unmarried woman was seen engaging in sexual relations with an unidentified man, and she claims that he is of unflawed lineage, her claim is accepted and she is permitted to marry into the priesthood. Although Rav Asi's opinion is not consistent with the mishna, Ze'eiri does not disagree with his halakhic conclusion (Vilna Gaon; Rambam *Sefer Kedusha, Hilkhot Issurei Bia* 15:11, 18:13; *Shulḥan Arukh, Even HaEzer* 6:17).

מתני׳ רָאוּהָ מְדַבֶּרֶת עִם אֶחָד, וְאָמְרוּ לָהּ: ״מַה טִיבוֹ שֶׁל אִישׁ זֶה״? ״אִישׁ פְּלוֹנִי, וְכֹהֵן הוּא״. רַבָּן גַּמְלִיאֵל וְרַבִּי אֱלִיעֶזֶר אוֹמְרִים: נֶאֱמֶנֶת, וְרַבִּי יְהוֹשֻׁעַ אוֹמֵר: לֹא מִפִּיהָ אָנוּ חַיִּין, אֶלָּא הֲרֵי זוֹ בְּחֶזְקַת בְּעוּלָה לְנָתִין וּלְמַמְזֵר, עַד שֶׁתָּבִיא רְאָיָה לִדְבָרֶיהָ.

MISHNA If people saw a woman **speaking to one** man, but they did not recognize him, **and they said to her: What is the nature** [***tivo***][L] **of this man?** And she said to them: **He is a man** called so-and-so **and he is a priest;**[N] **Rabban Gamliel and Rabbi Eliezer say: She is deemed credible, and Rabbi Yehoshua says:** It is **not** based on the statement emerging **from her mouth** that **we conduct our lives. Rather,** she assumes **the presumptive status of** one who **engaged in intercourse with a Gibeonite or with a *mamzer*,**[BN] men of flawed lineage who disqualify her from marrying a priest, **until she brings proof** supporting **her statement.**[N]

הָיְתָה מְעוּבֶּרֶת, וְאָמְרוּ לָהּ: ״מַה טִיבוֹ שֶׁל עוּבָּר זֶה״? ״מֵאִישׁ פְּלוֹנִי, וְכֹהֵן הוּא״. רַבָּן גַּמְלִיאֵל וְרַבִּי אֱלִיעֶזֶר אוֹמְרִים: נֶאֱמֶנֶת, וְרַבִּי יְהוֹשֻׁעַ אוֹמֵר: לֹא מִפִּיהָ אָנוּ חַיִּין, אֶלָּא הֲרֵי זוֹ בְּחֶזְקַת מְעוּבֶּרֶת לְנָתִין וּלְמַמְזֵר, עַד שֶׁתָּבִיא רְאָיָה לִדְבָרֶיהָ.

Similarly, **if** a single woman **was pregnant, and** people **said to her: What is the nature of this fetus?** And she says to them: **It is from** a man called so-and-so **and he is a priest; Rabban Gamliel and Rabbi Eliezer say: She is deemed credible, and Rabbi Yehoshua says:** It is **not** based on the statement emerging **from her mouth** that **we conduct our lives. Rather, she** assumes **the presumptive status of** one who **conceived from a Gibeonite or a *mamzer*, until she brings proof** supporting **her statement.**

גמ׳ מַאי ״מְדַבֶּרֶת״? זְעֵירִי אָמַר: נִסְתְּרָה, רַב אַסִי אָמַר, נִבְעֲלָה. בִּשְׁלָמָא לִזְעֵירִי – הַיְינוּ דְּקָתָנֵי ״מְדַבֶּרֶת״, אֶלָּא לְרַב אַסִי מַאי ״מְדַבֶּרֶת״? לִישָּׁנָא מַעַלְיָא, כְּדִכְתִיב ״אָכְלָה וּמָחֲתָה פִּיהָ וְאָמְרָה לֹא פָעַלְתִּי אָוֶן״.

GEMARA The Gemara asks: **What is** the meaning **of speaking**[HN] mentioned in the mishna? **Ze'eiri said:** It means that **she secluded herself** with a man and it is unknown whether she engaged in intercourse. **Rav Asi said:** It means that **she engaged in intercourse. Granted, according to Ze'eiri, that is** why the mishna **teaches** the case employing the term **speaking,** as it is certain only that they were in seclusion. Perhaps all they did was speak. **However, according to Rav Asi, what is** the reason the mishna employed the term **speaking** if the reference is to intercourse? The Gemara answers: The mishna employed **a euphemism, as it is written** with regard to licentious women: **"She eats and wipes her mouth and says: I have done no wickedness"** (Proverbs 30:20). The verse euphemistically ascribes the act of intercourse to the mouth instead of to the appropriate body part.

NOTES

He is a man called so-and-so and he is a priest – אִישׁ פְּלוֹנִי וְכֹהֵן הוּא: Even according to Rabban Gamliel, who says that her claim is accepted, this does not mean that her identification of a man as the one who engaged in intercourse with her or as the father of the child, is similarly accepted. The early commentaries write, and it is likewise cited in the name of the *ge'onim*, that her claim is neither accepted with regard to feeding her child *teruma* if the man she identified as the father was a priest, nor with regard to inheritance, and certainly not with regard to service in the Temple. Others contend that her claim is partially accepted, e.g., to enable her to feed her son produce that is *teruma* by rabbinic law (Meiri). On a similar note, some commentaries maintain that her claim is partially accepted in the sense that if she is the daughter of a priest, she does not forfeit the right to eat *teruma* due to her son. Were he deemed an Israelite and not a priest, she would lose that right.

Engaged in intercourse with a Gibeonite or with a *mamzer* – בְּעוּלָה לְנָתִין וּלְמַמְזֵר: In the Jerusalem Talmud the dispute is explained in the following manner: Rabbi Yehoshua holds that licentiousness is more common among people of flawed lineage. As the case in question involves licentiousness, there is reason for concern that a man of flawed lineage was involved. The Rabbis, based on the principle: There is no steward for restraining sexual immorality, hold that all men are equally suspect with regard to licentiousness. Later commentaries note that the fact that Rabbi Yehoshua is concerned that perhaps she engaged in intercourse with a *mamzer* or a Gibeonite, and not that she engaged in intercourse with a gentile, although they are more common, proves that the majority is not a factor. Therefore, even in a place where the majority of men are of unflawed lineage, Rabbi Yehoshua does not accept her claim. Furthermore, Rabbi Yehoshua does not accept her claim even in a city where the majority are Jews, where there would be only minor concern that she engaged in intercourse with a *mamzer* (*Ahavat Tziyyon*).

Until she brings proof supporting her statement – עַד שֶׁתָּבִיא רְאָיָה לִדְבָרֶיהָ: Rabbi Akiva Eiger asks: Even if she brings proof that the man was of unflawed lineage, since she was immodest with one man there is concern that she was immodest with another, and there is no proof with regard to the anonymous second man. He answers: Once she brings proof for her claim, she restores her presumptive status of unflawed lineage. Even though the possibility exists that she engaged in intercourse with another man, it is a concern by rabbinic law, and everyone agrees that her claim is accepted.

What is the meaning of speaking – מַאי מְדַבֶּרֶת: The commentaries explain that since the term speaking is clearly not to be taken literally, as no woman is disqualified from marrying a priest by speaking to a man, the question arises: Is it a euphemism for entering into seclusion or a euphemism for intercourse?

בִּשְׁלָמָא לִזְעֵירִי – הַיְינוּ דְּקָתָנֵי תַּרְתֵּי: "מְדַבֶּרֶת" "וּמְעוּבֶּרֶת". אֶלָּא לְרַב אַסִי, תַּרְתֵּי לָמָּה לִי?

The Gemara asks: **Granted, according to Ze'eiri,** who said that speaking means that she secluded herself with him, **that is** the reason **that** the *tanna* **teaches two** cases in the mishna: A woman **speaking** to a man **and** a woman who is **pregnant. However, according to Rav Asi,** if speaking means that she engaged in intercourse, **why do I need two** cases addressing the same issue?

חֲדָא לְהַכְשִׁיר בָּהּ, וַחֲדָא לְהַכְשִׁיר בְּבִתָּהּ.

The Gemara answers: The *tanna* teaches **one** case, the case of speaking to a man, **to deem her fit** to marry a priest, because although she engaged in intercourse, Rabbi Eliezer and Rabban Gamliel rule that she is deemed credible and is not considered to have engaged in intercourse with a man of flawed lineage. **And** the *tanna* teaches **one** case, the case of the single woman who is pregnant, in order **to deem her daughter** born from that pregnancy **fit** to marry a priest, as Rabbi Eliezer and Rabban Gamliel rule the mother is deemed credible.

הָנִיחָא לְמַאן דְּאָמַר: לְדִבְרֵי הַמַּכְשִׁיר בָּהּ מַכְשִׁיר בְּבִתָּהּ, אֶלָּא לְמַאן דְּאָמַר: לְדִבְרֵי הַמַּכְשִׁיר בָּהּ פּוֹסֵל בְּבִתָּהּ, מַאי אִיכָּא לְמֵימַר? רַב אַסִי סָבַר כְּמַאן דְּאָמַר לְדִבְרֵי הַמַּכְשִׁיר בָּהּ מַכְשִׁיר בְּבִתָּהּ.

The Gemara asks: **This works out well according to the one who says:** With regard **to the statement of the one who deems her fit** to marry a priest, **he deems her daughter fit**[N] to do so as well. **However, according to the one who says:** With regard **to the statement of the one who deems her fit** to marry a priest, **he** nevertheless **deems her daughter unfit, what is there to say?** Why did the mishna cite two cases addressing the same issue? The Gemara answers: **Rav Asi holds in accordance with** the opinion of **the one who said:** With regard **to the statement of the one who deems her fit** to marry a priest, **he deems her daughter fit** to do so as well.

אֲמַר לֵיהּ רַב פָּפָּא לְאַבָּיֵי: לִזְעֵירִי, דְּאָמַר מַאי "מְדַבֶּרֶת" נִסְתְּרָה, וְאָמַר רַבִּי יְהוֹשֻׁעַ לָא מְהֵימְנָא – הָאָמַר רַב: מַלְקִין עַל הַיִּחוּד וְאֵין אוֹסְרִין עַל הַיִּחוּד,

Rav Pappa said to Abaye: According **to Ze'eiri, who said: What is** the meaning of the term **speaking?** It means that **she secluded herself, and Rabbi Yehoshua said** that she is **not deemed credible** to say that she engaged in intercourse with a man of proper lineage, but the assumption is that she engaged in intercourse with a man of flawed lineage. **Didn't Rav say: One flogs** a man and a woman **for** entering into **seclusion,**[H] for violating rabbinic law, **but one does not render** a woman **forbidden** to her husband **for** entering into **seclusion?**[N] Only if it is established as a certainty that she engaged in intercourse with a man other than her husband, is she forbidden to her husband.

לֵימָא דְּלָא כְּרַבִּי יְהוֹשֻׁעַ! אֲפִילּוּ תֵּימָא רַבִּי יְהוֹשֻׁעַ, מַעֲלָה עָשׂוּ בְּיוּחֲסִין.

Let us say that this statement of Rav is **not in accordance with** the opinion of **Rabbi Yehoshua,** as Rabbi Yehoshua rules that she assumes the presumptive status of one who engaged in intercourse with a Gibeonite or with a *mamzer*, and she is forbidden to marry a priest even for entering into seclusion. The Gemara rejects that conclusion. **Even** if you **say** that Rav's statement is **in accordance with** the opinion of **Rabbi Yehoshua,** the Sages **established a higher standard with regard to** matters of **lineage.** Although she is not forbidden to her husband for entering into seclusion, she is deemed unfit to marry a priest.

מֵיתִיבִי: רָאוּהָ שֶׁנִּכְנְסָה עִם אֶחָד לְסֵתֶר,

The Gemara **raises an objection: If** people **saw that** a woman **entered with one** man **into seclusion,**

HALAKHA

One flogs a man and a woman for entering into seclusion – מַלְקִין עַל הַיִּחוּד: King David's court decreed that a man may not enter into seclusion with an unmarried woman, and if he does so, both he and the woman are flogged with lashes of rebelliousness. However, a married woman is not forbidden to her husband by entering into seclusion with another man, nor is an unmarried woman forbidden to a priest by entering into seclusion with a man of flawed lineage (Rambam *Sefer Kedusha, Hilkhot Issurei Bia* 22:3; *Shulḥan Arukh, Even HaEzer* 22:2).

NOTES

Deems her daughter fit – מַכְשִׁיר בְּבִתָּהּ: The question is not only relevant to a female child but to a male child as well. The Gemara discusses a female child here because she is disqualified by her mother's intercourse with a man of flawed lineage in more ways than male offspring. For example, she may not marry a priest. By contrast, with regard to a male child, the only relevant concerns are whether she engaged in intercourse with a *mamzer* or a Gibeonite, or one with whom relations are forbidden.

One flogs a man and a woman for entering into seclusion but one does not render a woman forbidden to her husband for entering into seclusion – מַלְקִין עַל הַיִּחוּד וְאֵין אוֹסְרִין עַל הַיִּחוּד: The early commentaries discuss whether these two statements refer to the same case or to two different cases, and whether the reference is to a married or an unmarried woman. Most hold that since it is stated in tractate *Kiddushin* that one does not flog a married woman for entering into seclusion with a man, to avoid slandering her children, the Gemara here must be referring to an unmarried woman. *Tosefot Rid*, as well, holds that an unmarried woman is flogged. Others explain that the phrase: One does not render a woman forbidden to her husband for entering into seclusion, is referring specifically to an unmarried woman and her future husband. The Ritva, however, explains that it is referring to a married woman. The Meiri writes that it is referring to both cases, as even an unmarried woman is not rendered forbidden for entering into seclusion with one with whom relations are forbidden, and all the more so a married woman is not rendered forbidden.

אוֹ לְחוּרְבָּה, וְאָמְרוּ לָהּ: ״מַה טִּיבוֹ שֶׁל אִישׁ זֶה״? ״כֹּהֵן הוּא, וּבֶן אֲחִי אַבָּא הוּא״. רַבָּן גַּמְלִיאֵל וְרַבִּי אֱלִיעֶזֶר אוֹמְרִים: נֶאֱמֶנֶת. רַבִּי יְהוֹשֻׁעַ אוֹמֵר: לֹא מִפִּיהָ אָנוּ חַיִּין, אֶלָּא הֲרֵי זוֹ בְּחֶזְקַת בְּעוּלָה לְנָתִין וּלְמַמְזֵר, עַד שֶׁתָּבִיא רְאָיָה לִדְבָרֶיהָ.

or into a ruin, which is typically located outside the city, and if a man and woman meet there it is presumably in order to engage in sexual relations, and people **said to her: What is the nature of this man** with whom you secluded? She said to them: **He is a priest, and he is the son of my father's brother,**[N] a respectable person of impeccable lineage. **Rabban Gamliel and Rabbi Eliezer say: She is deemed credible.**[N] **Rabbi Yehoshua says:** It is not based on the statement emerging **from her mouth** that **we conduct our lives; rather, she** assumes **the presumptive status of** one who **engaged in intercourse with a Gibeonite or with a** ***mamzer***, men of flawed lineage who disqualify her from marrying a priest, **until she brings proof** supporting **her statement.**

בִּשְׁלָמָא לִזְעֵירִי – הַיְינוּ דְּקָתָנֵי תַּרְתֵּי: ״לְסֵתֶר אוֹ לְחוּרְבָּה״. אֶלָּא לְרַב אַסִּי, דְּאָמַר נִבְעֲלָה – תַּרְתֵּי לָמָּה לִי? חֲדָא קָתָנֵי, לְסֵתֶר דְּחוּרְבָּה.

Granted, according to Ze'eiri, who said that speaking means that she secluded herself, **that is** the reason **that the** ***tanna*** **teaches two** cases where there is merely concern: The case of: **Into seclusion,** where there is lesser concern that she engaged in intercourse, **and** the case of: **Into a ruin,** where there is greater concern. **However, according to Rav Asi, who said** that speaking means that **she had intercourse,** and only in that case is she not deemed credible according to Rabbi Yehoshua, **why do I need two** cases? The Gemara answers: According to Rav Asi, the *tanna* **is teaching one** case: If people saw a woman enter with one man **into the seclusion of a ruin,** where the likelihood is that that they entered to engage in relations.

וְהָא ״לְסֵתֶר אוֹ לְחוּרְבָּה״ קָתָנֵי! חֲדָא לְחוּרְבָּה דְּמָתָא, וַחֲדָא לְחוּרְבָּה דְּדַבְרָא. וּצְרִיכִי, דְּאִי אַשְׁמְעִינַן חוּרְבָּה דְּמָתָא – בְּהָא קָמַכְשַׁר רַבָּן גַּמְלִיאֵל, מִשּׁוּם דְּרוֹב כְּשֵׁרִים אֶצְלָהּ. אֲבָל לְחוּרְבָּה דְּדַבְרָא, דְּרוֹב פְּסוּלִין אֶצְלָהּ – אֵימָא מוֹדֶה לֵיהּ לְרַבִּי יְהוֹשֻׁעַ.

The Gemara asks: **But isn't** the mishna **teaching** two different cases: **Into seclusion or into a ruin?** The Gemara suggests a different explanation. According to Rav Asi, two cases are necessary, **one** with regard **to a ruin in the city and one** with regard **to a ruin in the field,** distant from the city. **And** both cases **are necessary, because if** the *tanna* **taught us** only the case of **a ruin in the city,** one might have concluded that **in that** case **Rabban Gamliel deems her fit** to marry a priest **due to** the fact **that the majority** of the people **in its proximity are honorable** and of impeccable lineage. **However,** with regard **to a ruin in the field, where the majority** of the people **in its proximity are unfit** and of flawed lineage, as people from all over the world pass the ruin in the field and the majority of the people in the world are of flawed lineage, **say** that Rabban Gamliel **concedes to Rabbi Yehoshua** and deems her unfit to marry a priest.

וְאִי אַשְׁמְעִינַן בְּהַהִיא – בְּהַהִיא קָאָמַר רַבִּי יְהוֹשֻׁעַ, אֲבָל בְּהָא – אֵימָא מוֹדֶה לְרַבָּן גַּמְלִיאֵל, צְרִיכָא.

And if the *tanna* **taught us** only **that** case of a ruin in the field, one might have concluded that **in that** case **Rabbi Yehoshua said** she is not deemed credible, because the majority of the people there are of flawed lineage. **However here,** in the case of a ruin in the city, where the majority of the people are of impeccable lineage, **say** that Rabbi Yehoshua **concedes to Rabban Gamliel** that she is deemed credible. Therefore, both cases were **necessary.**

מֵיתִיבִי: זוֹ עֵדוּת שֶׁהָאִשָּׁה כְּשֵׁרָה לָהּ, וְרַבִּי יְהוֹשֻׁעַ אוֹמֵר: אֵינָהּ נֶאֱמֶנֶת. אָמַר לָהֶם רַבִּי יְהוֹשֻׁעַ: אִי אַתֶּם מוֹדִים בִּשְׁבוּיָה שֶׁנִּשְׁבֵּית וְיֵשׁ לָהּ עֵדִים שֶׁנִּשְׁבֵּית וְהִיא אוֹמֶרֶת ״טְהוֹרָה אֲנִי״, שֶׁאֵינָהּ נֶאֱמֶנֶת?

The Gemara **raises an objection** from the *Tosefta*: **This,** i.e., that she engaged in intercourse with a man of impeccable lineage, **is testimony that a woman is fit** to testify.[N] **And Rabbi Yehoshua says: She is not deemed credible. Rabbi Yehoshua said to the** Sages: **Do you not agree in the case of a woman who was taken captive,**[N] **and she has witnesses** testifying **that she was taken captive,**[H] **and she says: I am pure,** i.e., I was not violated by my captors, **that she is not deemed credible?** The assumption in that case is that most captive women are violated by their captors.

NOTES

And he is the son of my father's brother – וּבֶן אֲחִי אַבָּא הוּא: In the *Shita Mekubbetzet* an explanation is cited asserting that this formulation supports the opinion of Ze'eiri, as it is reasonable to assume that when one asks the woman why she entered into seclusion she would answer that the man was a relative with whom she was speaking. It is also explained there why the Gemara did not cite proof for Ze'eiri's opinion from here.

She is deemed credible – נֶאֱמֶנֶת: The Ramban cites two opinions. The first is that she is deemed credible in a case where the man with whom she engaged in intercourse cannot be located and therefore cannot be questioned. The second, in the name of Ri Migash, is that this is referring to a case where the man confirms that he engaged in intercourse with her but states that he does not know whether she did so with others as well. Later commentaries discuss whether in a case where the man denies having engaged in intercourse with her, Rabban Gamliel would say that her claim is accepted.

This is testimony that a woman is fit to testify – זוֹ עֵדוּת שֶׁהָאִשָּׁה כְּשֵׁרָה לָהּ: The term "this" in the phrase is not to the exclusion of all other testimony, as there are other areas of *halakha* in which a woman is fit to testify. The unique element here is that the woman's testimony is accepted with regard to herself, from which it is inferred that the testimony is accepted with regard to herself and not with regard to her daughter (*Shita Mekubbetzet*).

A woman who was taken captive – שְׁבוּיָה שֶׁנִּשְׁבֵּית: The Ritva explains that in the case of a captive woman there are two factors leading to stringency. First, most men who were in her proximity and potentially violated her while she was in captivity are gentiles, who are sexually immoral and who disqualify her from marrying a priest. Furthermore, she is subject to rape by her captors. Consequently, were she taken captive by Jews, or by gentiles who were unable to rape her, she would not have the legal status of a captive.

HALAKHA

A woman who was taken captive, and she has witnesses that she was taken captive – שְׁבוּיָה שֶׁנִּשְׁבֵּית וְיֵשׁ לָהּ עֵדִים שֶׁנִּשְׁבֵּית: If there are witnesses that the woman was taken into captivity, her claim that she was not violated by her captors is not accepted; rather, she assumes the presumptive status of one who was raped by a gentile and unfit to marry into the priesthood (Rambam *Sefer Kedusha, Hilkhot Issurei Bia* 18:21; *Shulḥan Arukh, Even HaEzer* 7:4).

אָמְרוּ לוֹ: אֲבָל – וּמָה הֶפְרֵשׁ יֵשׁ בֵּין זוֹ לָזוֹ? לָזוֹ – יֵשׁ עֵדִים, וְלָזוֹ – אֵין לָהּ עֵדִים.

The Sages **said to him: But** there is a difference between the cases. **And what difference is there between this** case of a captive, where the woman is not accorded credibility, **and that** case of a woman who secluded herself with a man? **For this** captive, **there are witnesses** that she was taken captive, and due to the prevalent immorality in that situation, she loses the presumptive status of virtue and is considered to have certainly engaged in intercourse. **But for this** woman who secluded herself with a man, **she does not have witnesses** that she engaged in intercourse. Since she could have claimed that she did not engage in intercourse and instead admitted that she engaged in intercourse and claimed that it was with a man of impeccable lineage, she should be accorded credibility.

אָמַר לָהֶם: אַף לָזוֹ יֵשׁ עֵדִים, שֶׁהֲרֵי כְּרֵיסָהּ בֵּין שִׁינֶּיהָ! אָמְרוּ לוֹ: רוֹב גּוֹיִם פְּרוּצִים בַּעֲרָיוֹת הֵם. אָמַר לָהֶן: אֵין אַפּוֹטְרוֹפּוֹס לַעֲרָיוֹת.

Rabbi Yehoshua **said to them: Even for that** woman, the one who secluded herself, **there are witnesses, because her belly is between her teeth,** i.e., her pregnancy is conspicuous and therefore she does not have the option of claiming that she did not engage in intercourse. The Sages **said to him:** There remains a difference between the cases, as **most gentiles are steeped in sexual immorality.** Therefore, presumably, they engaged in intercourse with the captive woman. However, in the case of the woman in seclusion there is no presumption that she engaged in intercourse specifically with a man with flawed lineage. Rabbi Yehoshua **said to them: There is no steward for** restraining **sexual immorality,**[N] and therefore, everyone is suspect in that regard. Therefore, this woman, since she engaged in intercourse, lost her presumptive status of virtue, and there is no basis to trust her that it was with a person of impeccable lineage.

בַּמֶּה דְּבָרִים אֲמוּרִים – בְּעֵדוּת אִשָּׁה בְּגוּפָהּ, אֲבָל עֵדוּת אִשָּׁה בְּבִתָּהּ – דִּבְרֵי הַכֹּל הַוָּלָד שְׁתוּקִי.

The *baraita* continues: **In what** case **are these** divergent **statements** of Rabban Gamliel and Rabbi Yehoshua **said?** It is **in the case of the testimony of a woman with regard to herself,** to render her fit to marry a priest. **However,** in the case of **testimony of a woman with regard to** the fact that the father of **her daughter** is a man of unflawed lineage, **everyone agrees** that her testimony is not deemed credible, and the legal status of **the child** is that of **a** ***shetuki,***[B] the identity of whose father is unknown and to whom all the stringencies that apply to a *mamzer* apply, due the uncertainty of his lineage.

מַאי קָאָמַר לְהוּ וּמַאי קָמְהַדְּרִי לֵיהּ? הָכִי קָאָמְרִי לֵיהּ: הֲשַׁבְתָּנוּ עַל הַמְעוּבֶּרֶת, מַה תְּשִׁיבֵנוּ עַל הַמְדַבֶּרֶת? אָמַר לָהֶם: מְדַבֶּרֶת הַיְינוּ שְׁבוּיָה. אָמְרוּ לוֹ: שָׁאנֵי שְׁבוּיָה דְּרוֹב גּוֹיִם פְּרוּצִים בַּעֲרָיוֹת הֵם. אָמַר לָהֶם: הָא נַמִּי, כֵּיוָן דְּאִיסְתַּתַּר – אֵין אַפּוֹטְרוֹפּוֹס לַעֲרָיוֹת.

The Gemara seeks to understand the exchange between Rabbi Yehoshua and the Sages. **What did he say to them and what did they reply to him?** It appears that they were not discussing the same case. **This is what** the Sages **are saying to him: You answered us concerning the pregnant woman,** asserting that there is testimony in the case of the pregnant woman comparable to the testimony in the case of the captive. However, **what will you answer us concerning the** woman who was seen **speaking** to a man? In that case, there is no testimony that she had intercourse. Rabbi Yehoshua **said to them:** The case of **speaking is the same as** the case of the **captive,** as there is reason to believe that she engaged in intercourse. The Sages **said to him:** The case of **a captive is different, as most gentiles are steeped in sexual immorality,** and presumably they engaged in intercourse with the captive woman. Rabbi Yehoshua **said to them:** In **this** case **too, since she secluded herself** with a man, based on the principle: **There is no steward for** restraining **sexual immorality,** presumably she engaged in intercourse with him.

קָתָנֵי מִיהַת תַּרְתֵּי, מְדַבֶּרֶת וּמְעוּבֶּרֶת, תְּיוּבְתָּא דְּרַב אַסִי! תְּיוּבְתָּא.

With regard to the dispute over the meaning of the term: Speaking, the Gemara says: **In any event,** from this discussion it is clear that the *tanna* **is teaching two** different cases, one case of **speaking,** where there is uncertainty whether she engaged in intercourse, **and** one case where she is **pregnant,** and there is no uncertainty in that regard. The Gemara suggests: This is **a conclusive refutation** of the opinion **of Rav Asi,** who explained that speaking in the mishna means that she engaged in intercourse. The Gemara concludes: Indeed, this is a **conclusive refutation** of his opinion.

NOTES

There is no steward for restraining sexual immorality – אֵין אַפּוֹטְרוֹפּוֹס לַעֲרָיוֹת: Rashi explains this to mean that once she entered into seclusion, the Sages cannot guarantee that she did not engage in intercourse. Rabbeinu Ḥananel explains the principle in the way in which it is typically applied: Even the most righteous individual cannot be appointed as a steward for restraining sexual immorality. Therefore, there is no distinction between moral and immoral people in this regard.

BACKGROUND

***Shetuki* – שְׁתוּקִי:** A child whose father's identity is not known is referred to as a *shetuki*, from the Hebrew root *shin, tav, kuf*, meaning silence. The Gemara (*Kiddushin* 70a) explains that he is called *shetuki* because when he calls his father, his mother silences him. His legal status is that of an uncertain *mamzer*.

וְתֵיפּוֹק לֵיהּ דְּהָתָם רוֹב פְּסוּלִין אֶצְלָהּ, וְהָכָא רוֹב כְּשֵׁרִין אֶצְלָהּ! מְסַיַּיע לֵיהּ לְרַבִּי יְהוֹשֻׁעַ בֶּן לֵוִי, דְּאָמַר רַבִּי יְהוֹשֻׁעַ בֶּן לֵוִי: לְדִבְרֵי הַמַּכְשִׁיר – מַכְשִׁיר אֲפִילּוּ בְּרוֹב פְּסוּלִין, לְדִבְרֵי הַפּוֹסֵל – פּוֹסֵל אֲפִילּוּ בְּרוֹב כְּשֵׁרִים.

The Gemara asks with regard to the *baraita*: **And let** the *tanna* **derive** this distinction between a captive woman and a woman who secluded herself with a man from the fact **that there,** in the case of the captive, **the majority** of the men **in her proximity are unfit**[N] and of flawed lineage, **but here,** where she was secluded, **the majority of the men in her proximity are honorable** and of impeccable lineage. Since she is unmarried, most men are not unfit for her. The Gemara notes: The fact that the *tanna* did not derive the distinction from that source **supports** the opinion **of Rabbi Yehoshua ben Levi, as Rabbi Yehoshua ben Levi said:** According **to the statement of** Rabban Gamliel, **the one who deems her fit** to marry a priest, **he deems her fit even in** a case **where the majority of the men** in her proximity **are unfit.**[N] According **to the statement of** Rabbi Yehoshua, **the one who deems her unfit** to marry a priest, **he deems her unfit even in** a case where **the majority** of the men in her proximity **are fit.**

אָמַר רַבִּי יוֹחָנָן: לְדִבְרֵי הַמַּכְשִׁיר בָּהּ – מַכְשִׁיר בְּבִתָּהּ, לְדִבְרֵי הַפּוֹסֵל בָּהּ – פּוֹסֵל בְּבִתָּהּ. וְרַבִּי אֶלְעָזָר אוֹמֵר: לְדִבְרֵי הַמַּכְשִׁיר בָּהּ – פּוֹסֵל בְּבִתָּהּ.

Rabbi Yoḥanan said: According **to the statement of the one who deems her fit** to marry a priest and accepts her claim that she engaged in intercourse with a man of unflawed lineage, **he deems her daughter fit**[HN] as well. According **to the statement of the one who deems her unfit, he deems her daughter unfit** as well. **But Rabbi Elazar says:** According **to the statement of the one who deems her fit, he deems her daughter unfit.**

אֲמַר רַבָּה: מַאי טַעְמָא דְּרַבִּי אֶלְעָזָר? בִּשְׁלָמָא אִיהִי – אִית לָהּ חֲזָקָה דְּכַשְׁרוּת, בִּתָּהּ – לֵית לָהּ חֲזָקָה דְּכַשְׁרוּת.

Rabba said: What is the reason for the opinion **of Rabbi Elazar,** who distinguishes between the effectiveness of the woman's claim in determining her own status and its effectiveness in determining the status of her daughter? The reason is that **granted,** her claim is effective with regard to her status because **she has the presumptive status of fitness.** Therefore, until proven otherwise, she retains that status. **Her daughter,** the identity of whose father is unknown, **does not have the presumptive status of fitness.** Therefore, a full-fledged proof is required to establish her fitness.

אֵיתִיבֵיהּ רַבִּי אֶלְעָזָר לְרַבִּי יוֹחָנָן: בַּמֶּה דְּבָרִים אֲמוּרִים – בְּעֵדוּת אִשָּׁה בְּגוּפָהּ. אֲבָל עֵדוּת אִשָּׁה בְּבִתָּהּ – דִּבְרֵי הַכֹּל הַוָּלָד שְׁתוּקִי. מַאי לָאו – שְׁתוּקִי וּפָסוּל? לָא, שְׁתוּקִי וְכָשֵׁר.

Rabbi Elazar raised an objection to the opinion of **Rabbi Yoḥanan** from the *baraita*: **In what** case **are these** disputing **statements** of Rabban Gamliel and Rabbi Yehoshua **said?** It is **in the case of a woman's testimony with regard to herself. However,** in the case of **testimony of a woman with regard to her daughter, everyone agrees** that her testimony is not credible, and the legal status of **the child is** that of **a *shetuki*. What, is it not** that contrary to the opinion of Rabbi Yoḥanan, the *baraita* means that the child is **a *shetuki* and unfit** until proof can be brought that the lineage of the father is unflawed? The Gemara rejects that objection: **No,** the *baraita* means that the child is **a *shetuki*,** as her lineage is unclear, but she is nevertheless **fit.**[N]

HALAKHA

The one who deems her fit…deems her daughter fit – הַמַּכְשִׁיר בָּהּ מַכְשִׁיר בְּבִתָּהּ: If an unmarried woman is pregnant and the identity of the father is unknown, and she claims that the father is a man of unflawed lineage, her claim is accepted, and both she and her daughter born from that pregnancy are fit to marry into the priesthood, in accordance with the opinion of Rabbi Yoḥanan. The ruling is in accordance with his opinion because he was Rabbi Elazar's teacher, and because he holds in accordance with the opinion of Abba Shaul in tractate *Kiddushin*, according to whose opinion the *halakha* was ruled as authoritative (Rosh; Rambam *Sefer Kedusha, Hilkhot Issurei Bia* 15:11; *Shulḥan Arukh, Even HaEzer* 6:17).

NOTES

And let the *tanna* derive from the fact that there the majority of the men in her proximity are unfit – וְתֵיפּוֹק לֵיהּ דְּהָתָם רוֹב פְּסוּלִין אֶצְלָהּ: According to Rashi, this passage is a question on the opinion of Rabbi Yehoshua. According to the Rosh and the Ritva, the difficulty is with regard to the opinion of Rabban Gamliel. In their opinion, the question is: Why did he cite the reason that most gentiles are steeped in sexual immorality? He could have cited a different reason: The majority of the men in her proximity are unfit.

Deems her fit even where the majority of the men in her proximity are unfit – מַכְשִׁיר אֲפִילּוּ בְּרוֹב פְּסוּלִין: Rabbeinu Tam, cited in *Tosafot*, asks: Isn't there a distinction between the case of a captive woman and the case of a woman entering into seclusion? With regard to a captive woman, all the men in her proximity are unfit, not just the majority, as she is subject to coercion and rape by her captors and all intercourse with them renders her unfit. Rabbeinu Tam answers that in this regard there is no halakhic distinction between most and all. Even according to the opinion that the combination of the minority of men who are fit and her presumptive status of fitness neutralizes the majority of unfit men, this situation remains an equally balanced uncertainty in which the ruling is stringent.

Others explain that when Rabbi Yehoshua ben Levi deems her fit even when the majority of men are unfit, he does not distinguish between most and all. Even if all of the men in her proximity are of flawed lineage, perhaps a man of unflawed lineage happened to be there. This is based on the principle: A woman does not engage in intercourse with a man before ascertaining that he is of unflawed lineage.

One who deems her fit…deems her daughter fit – הַמַּכְשִׁיר בָּהּ מַכְשִׁיר בְּבִתָּהּ: The commentaries explain the reason for Rabbi Yoḥanan's opinion in different ways. According to the Rosh, the certain claim of the mother is effective in rendering the daughter fit, as according to the Rabbis when a certain claim clashes with an uncertain claim, one relies on the certain claim unequivocally. According to the *Maggid Mishna*, by Torah law the daughter should be fit, as the Sages said that it is prohibited for a *mamzer* to marry into the congregation of Israel only if he is a definite *mamzer* but not if there is uncertainty with regard to his status.

In cases of uncertainty, the prohibition is by rabbinic law, and in those cases the mother's claim is sufficient to render her daughter fit. Others explain that the mother's presumptive status of fitness, by virtue of which the Rabbis determine that she engaged in intercourse with a man of unflawed lineage, is effective to render the daughter fit as well (*Nimmukei Yosef*; see Ritva; *Shev Shemateta*).

The child is a *shetuki* but she is fit – שְׁתוּקִי וְכָשֵׁר: The *ge'onim* write that based on the conclusion of the Gemara there are two types of *shetuki*. One is a child born to an unmarried woman who does not know the child's father. In that case, due to the possibility that the child is a *mamzer*, he may not marry into the congregation of Israel. The second type of *shetuki* is one born to an unmarried woman who claims that she knows the child's father and he is a man of unflawed lineage. Although, based on her claim, he is neither that man's heir nor fit to perform the Temple service if the man is a priest, he may marry into the congregation of Israel.

ומִי אִיכָּא שְׁתוּקִי כָּשֵׁר? אִין, כְּדִשְׁמוּאֵל, דַּאֲמַר שְׁמוּאֵל: עֲשָׂרָה כֹּהֲנִים עוֹמְדִים, וּפֵירַשׁ אֶחָד מֵהֶם וּבָעַל – הַוָּלָד שְׁתוּקִי.

The Gemara asks: **And is there** a case of **a *shetuki*** who is nevertheless **fit?** The Gemara answers: **Yes, as in the statement of Shmuel. As Shmuel said:** If **ten priests were standing and one of them left and engaged in intercourse, the child is a *shetuki*,** literally one who is silenced, because the identity of the father is unclear. In that case it is clear that the child is fit, because it is known that the father is a priest of flawless lineage.

מַאי שְׁתוּקִי? אִילֵימָא שֶׁמַּשְׁתִּיקִין אוֹתוֹ מִנִּכְסֵי אָבִיו – פְּשִׁיטָא, וּמִי יָדְעִינַן אֲבוּהּ מַנּוּ? אֶלָּא שֶׁמַּשְׁתִּיקִין אוֹתוֹ מִדִּין כְּהוּנָּה, דִּכְתִיב ״וְהָיְתָה לוֹ וּלְזַרְעוֹ אַחֲרָיו בְּרִית כְּהֻנַּת עוֹלָם״ – מִי שֶׁזַּרְעוֹ מְיוּחָס אַחֲרָיו, יָצָא זֶה שֶׁאֵין זַרְעוֹ מְיוּחָס אַחֲרָיו.

The Gemara asks: In **what** sense **is** this child **a *shetuki*? If we say** that it means **that one silences him from** a claim to **his father's assets** and he does not inherit his estate, that is **obvious. Do we know who his father is?** It could be any one of the ten. **Rather,** it means **that one silences him from** a claim to **the status of priesthood.**[NH] Although there is no doubt that his father is a priest, the son is not a priest, **as it is written: "And it shall be for him and for his offspring after him an everlasting covenant of priesthood"** (Numbers 25:13). From this it is derived: In the case of a priest **whose offspring are attributed to him,** his offspring are priests; to the **exclusion of this** priest, **whose offspring are not attributed to him,** and whose offspring are not priests. This child, therefore, is a *shetuki* only in the sense that he may not perform the Temple service as a priest. However, he is permitted to marry a Jewish woman.

הַהוּא אָרוּס וַאֲרוּסָתוֹ דַּאֲתוֹ לְקַמֵּיהּ דְּרַב יוֹסֵף, הִיא אָמְרָה: מִינֵּיהּ, וְהוּא אֲמַר:

Apropos paternity, the Gemara relates: There was **a certain betrothed man and his betrothed,** who was pregnant, **who came before Rav Yosef. She said** that she conceived **from** relations with **him, and he said:**

NOTES

One silences him from a claim to the status of priesthood – מַשְׁתִּיקִין אוֹתוֹ מִדִּין כְּהוּנָּה: The Gemara here holds that there is a special *halakha* with regard to the priesthood: Mere knowledge that a child is the son of a priest is not sufficient. Rather, a specific priest must be identified as his father. Early and later commentaries discuss whether his entire lineage must be known or whether it is sufficient if his grandfather can be identified. See *Tosafot*, who explain that this demand is by rabbinic law and the verse cited is merely an allusion. There are early commentaries who disagree and hold that it is a demand by Torah law, although they dispute whether it applies only to Temple service or even to partaking of *teruma* and reciting the Priestly Blessing as well.

HALAKHA

One silences him from a claim to the status of priesthood – מַשְׁתִּיקִין אוֹתוֹ מִדִּין כְּהוּנָּה: If the identity of a child born to an unmarried woman is unknown, he may not function as a priest. For example, if one of a group of ten priests had relations with a woman, but his identity is unknown, the child born of that union is definitely of priestly lineage. If he marries a divorcée or subjects himself to impurity imparted by a corpse, he is flogged, but he may neither perform the Temple service nor partake of *teruma* (Rambam *Sefer Kedusha, Hilkhot Issurei Bia* 20:20; *Shulḥan Arukh, Even HaEzer* 3:9).

Perek **I**
Daf **14** Amud **a**

אִין, מִינַּאי. אֲמַר רַב יוֹסֵף: לְמַאי נֵיחוּשׁ לָהּ? חֲדָא – דְּהָא קָא מוֹדֶה, וְעוֹד: הָא אָמַר רַב יְהוּדָה אָמַר שְׁמוּאֵל: הֲלָכָה כְּרַבָּן גַּמְלִיאֵל.

Yes, she conceived **from** relations with **me.**[NH] **Rav Yosef said:** The ruling here is clear, as **with regard to what** suspicion need **we be concerned? First, he concedes** that he is the father. **And furthermore, didn't Rav Yehuda say**[N] that **Shmuel said: The *halakha* is in accordance with** the opinion of **Rabban Gamliel,**[H] and even if he didn't admit that the child was his, the woman's claim is accorded credibility?

NOTES

Yes, she conceived from relations with me – אִין, מִינַּאי: This entire passage in the Gemara is tied to a passage in tractate *Yevamot* (69b), where a dispute between Rav and Shmuel is cited with regard to the legal status of a child born to a betrothed woman. There, the concern is raised that perhaps she conceived the child of another man. With regard to that concern, two possibilities are raised. Is it a concern only when she has a reputation of promiscuity? Or perhaps it is even a concern when she has no reputation of that sort, and it was apparently her betrothed who impregnated her. Some commentaries explain that the discussion in the Gemara here is based on the first opinion there. Therefore, provided that she does not have a reputation of promiscuity and the man to whom she is betrothed admits that he is the father, the offspring is attributed to him, she may marry into the priesthood, and the lineage of the offspring is unflawed (Ramban; Rashba).

Tosafot hold that the Gemara here is not referring to a case where they engaged in relations once. Rather, it is referring to a case where the betrothed couple lived together as husband and wife. Therefore, the presumptive status of the offspring is that he is the child of her betrothed. This is based on the principle: Most acts of intercourse are attributed to the husband. Others insist that the Gemara here is referring only to a case where the betrothed woman never left the side of her betrothed until she discovered that she was pregnant. Only then can her betrothed state with certainty that the child is his (Rabbi Yosef Migash; Ritva).

And furthermore didn't Rav Yehuda say – וְעוֹד הָא אָמַר רַב יְהוּדָה: The early commentaries disagree with regard to the meaning of the phrase: And furthermore, etc. What was Rav Yosef's opinion? According to *Tosafot*, it means that if her betrothed is not present one relies on the claim of the woman. However, if her betrothed is present, her claim is not accepted at all (Ramban; Rosh; Ran). The Rambam holds that if her claim is contradicted by her betrothed, his statement is not effective to disqualify the woman from marrying into the priesthood, but the offspring is a *mamzer*. Others explain that the claim of the woman is accepted even if it is contradicted by her betrothed, but his statement renders her forbidden to him (*Tosefot Rid; Shiltei HaGibborim*). Although the conclusion of the Gemara is that if there is a majority of people of flawed lineage in her proximity she is disqualified from marrying into the priesthood, the offspring is fit to marry into the priesthood because that is a situation after the fact.

HALAKHA

A betrothed woman who becomes pregnant – אֲרוּסָה שֶׁנִּתְעַבְּרָה: If a betrothed woman becomes pregnant before the wedding and claims that the man to whom she is betrothed is the father of her unborn child, and he admits that he is the father or is not present to confirm or deny her claim, the lineage of the child is unflawed and he is considered the groom's child in every sense, even with regard to inheritance (Rema, based on Ran). If the groom denies his paternity the woman remains fit to marry into the priesthood, although his claim renders her forbidden to him. There are additional distinctions with regard to the *halakha* in a case where she has a reputation of promiscuity with others. These are discussed in tractate *Yevamot* (Rambam *Sefer Kedusha, Hilkhot Issurei Bia* 15:17; *Shulḥan Arukh, Even HaEzer* 4:27).

The *halakha* is in accordance with the opinion of Rabban Gamliel – הֲלָכָה כְּרַבָּן גַּמְלִיאֵל: With regard to an unmarried woman who became pregnant and claims that she had relations with a man of unflawed lineage, her claim is accepted and she may marry a priest, even if the majority of men in her proximity are of flawed lineage. The Sages, however, established a higher standard for priestly lineage, and accepted her claim only if there are two majorities of men of unflawed lineage. Otherwise, she is disqualified from marrying a priest (Rambam). Some authorities (*Tur*, citing Ramban and Rashba) maintain that one majority is sufficient (Rambam *Sefer Kedusha, Hilkhot Issurei Bia* 18:13–14; *Shulḥan Arukh, Even HaEzer* 6:17).

אמר ליה אביי: ובהא, כי לא מודה מכשר רבן גמליאל? והאמר ליה שמואל לרב יהודה: שיננא! הלכה כרבן גמליאל, ואת לא תעביד עובדא עד דאיכא רוב כשרין אצלה. והכא – רוב פסולין אצלה!

Abaye said to him: And in this case, based on the fact that you cited two reasons to deem the child fit, is that to say **when he does not admit** that he is the father **Rabban Gamliel deems** the child **fit?**[N] **But didn't Shmuel say to Rav Yehuda: Big-toothed** one, **the *halakha* is in accordance with** the opinion of **Rabban Gamliel,** i.e., that she is accorded credibility, **but you should not perform an action** based on this ruling **unless the majority of the men in her proximity are honorable** and of impeccable lineage, corroborating her claim. **And here,** since she is betrothed, **the majority of the men in her proximity are unfit,** as a child fathered by any man other than her betrothed is a *mamzer*. Shmuel should not have ruled that the *halakha* was in accordance with the opinion of Rabban Gamliel.

וליטעמיך, תקשי לך היא גופא: הלכה – ואת לא תעביד עובדא?! אלא מאי אית לך למימר: הא – לכתחלה, הא – דיעבד, והא נמי, כדיעבד דמי.

Rav Yosef said to Abaye: **And according to your reasoning,** the ***halakha* itself should pose a difficulty for you,** as on the one hand Shmuel rules that it is the ***halakha*** **and** on the other hand he adds: **But you should not perform an action** based on this ruling. **Rather, what have you to say** to explain this contradiction? **This** statement that one relies on the woman's claim only if a majority of men in her proximity are of unflawed lineage is ***ab initio*****. That** statement that one may rely on the woman's claim regardless of the status on the men in her proximity is **after the fact. And this** case of the betrothed woman, **too, is like** a case **after the fact,**[N] as failure to rely on her claim will render her child a *mamzer*. Therefore, in this case, Shmuel would rule that the *halakha* is in accordance with the opinion of Rabban Gamliel.

רמי ליה אביי לרבא: ומי אמר רבי יהושע אינה נאמנת? ורמינהו: העיד רבי יהושע ורבי יהודה בן בתירא על אלמנת עיסה שהיא כשרה לכהונה!

§ **Abaye raised a contradiction before Rava** from a mishna (*Eduyyot* 10:3): **Did Rabbi Yehoshua say that** the woman **is not deemed credible** and her claim is not accepted? **And** the Gemara **raises a contradiction: Rabbi Yehoshua and Rabbi Yehuda ben Beteira testified concerning the widow** whose late husband was a member **of a** priestly **family of questionable lineage** [*issa*],[HLN] **that she is fit to** marry into the **priesthood.** Since the matter is uncertain, the woman retains her presumptive status of fitness and her late husband is presumed to be of unflawed lineage.

אמר ליה: הכי השתא! התם – אשה נישאת – בודקת ונישאת, הכא – אשה מזנה – בודקת ומזנה?!

Rava **said to him: How can** these cases **be compared? There,** in the case of the widow, one could say: **A woman** who **marries investigates** the lineage of her prospective husband before the wedding **and** only then **marries.**[N] Therefore, one may rely on her presumptive status of fitness and deem her fit to marry a priest. **Here,** can it be said that **a woman** who **engages in licentious intercourse investigates** the lineage of her partner and only then **engages in licentious intercourse?**

HALAKHA

The widow whose late husband was a member of a priestly family of questionable lineage – אלמנת עיסה: If a woman married a man from a family in which one of the members is an uncertain *ḥalal*, and was then widowed, it is prohibited for her to marry a priest; this is in accordance with the opinion of Rabban Gamliel. However, if she married a priest she may remain married to him, as Rabban Gamliel did not say that it is prohibited for a priest to marry her. Rather, he said that the priests did not accept the leniency (Rambam *Sefer Kedusha, Hilkhot Issurei Bia* 19:23; *Shulḥan Arukh, Even HaEzer* 2:5).

LANGUAGE

A family of questionable lineage [*issa*] – עיסה: Rav Hai Gaon explains that this expression evokes kneaded dough, in which it is difficult to determine exactly what is mixed into the dough. By contrast, the metaphor used to describe a family of impeccable lineage is pure, fine flour. The *Arukh* explains that the reference is to dough from which *ḥalla* was separated, which remains non-sacred. Rashi in tractate *Kiddushin* explains that the reference is to a doughy paste made of grapes from which the juice was squeezed.

NOTES

Rabban Gamliel deems the child fit – מכשר רבן גמליאל: The Ramban cites a variant reading that omits the words: Rabban Gamliel. According to that version, the Gemara is analyzing the opinion of Shmuel and not the opinion of Rabban Gamliel.

And this too is like a case after the fact – והא נמי כדיעבד דמי: The Ra'avad explains that even though with regard to the woman there is an element of after the fact, as she is rendered forbidden to her betrothed, with regard to the offspring the matter is apparently *ab initio*. Nevertheless, he explains that there is an element of a situation after the fact with regard to the offspring. If the question is whether or not her daughter is fit to marry into the priesthood, this would be an *ab initio* situation. However, if the question pertains to classifying the offspring as a *mamzer*, or even worse as an uncertain *mamzer*, who may not marry even another *mamzer*, that is considered after the fact (*Tosafot*; *Tosefot Rid*; Ramban). The Ritva notes that this is the meaning of the phrase: Like a case after the fact, as even though it is not actually after the fact, it is treated as if it were.

The Ra'avad further explains that the use of the term: Like, is due to the fact that they are not yet married and therefore the situation is not actually after the fact. The Ran explains that it is permitted even for the offspring to marry into the priesthood. The reason is that the case is treated as if it were after the fact, because the fate of the woman is tied to the fate of the child. If her betrothed is told that her child is unfit, it is likely that he will divorce the woman.

The widow whose late husband was a member of a priestly family of questionable lineage – אלמנת עיסה: There are several opinions with regard to the meaning of this concept. Although everyone agrees that there is uncertainty with regard to the *ḥalal* status of the family, there is disagreement with regard to the essence of this uncertainty. Rashi explains that the reference is to a widow whose husband was the son of a priest who married a woman with regard to whom there is uncertainty whether she was a divorcée or whether she was a widow. An example of this would be if her first husband threw a bill of divorce to her and it is unclear whether it landed closer to her or closer to him; and then he died.

Rabbeinu Ḥananel cites two explanations. In one, he agrees with Rashi. In the other, he explains that she is the widow of a man whose status as a priest is uncertain, e.g., if two babies were intermingled. See Rashi, who cites an additional explanation in the name of Rabbi Yosef Tuv-Elem.

The *ge'onim*, the Rambam, and *Tosafot* all explain that the reference is to an uncertain *ḥalal* who joined a family or moved to a city, but it is not known who he is. There is a compound uncertainty with regard to the widow of a man from that family. The first uncertainty is whether her late husband is the member of that family with regard to whom the uncertainty exists. Even if it is established that her late husband is indeed the one with regard to whom the uncertainty exists, there remains an uncertainty whether he is in fact a *ḥalal*. The term *issa*, meaning dough, is especially appropriate according to that explanation, as the family is like dough whose ingredients are unknown.

With regard to the legal status of a child born from this union, although the widow enjoys presumptive status of fitness, her offspring does not. Furthermore, as with regard to lineage, the status of the child is determined by the status of the father; since the father is an uncertain *ḥalal*, the same is true of the offspring (*Ayyelet Ahavim*; *Beit Ya'akov*).

A woman who marries, investigates and marries – אשה נישאת, בודקת ונישאת: The Rashash explains that since a woman who is getting married plans on spending her entire life with this man, she will investigate his lineage so she does not live her life in sin. However, when it is a one-time, licentious liaison, she is not as careful. Furthermore, before marriage the woman has the time and opportunity to investigate her potential husband. In a licentious liaison, perhaps it is the result of a moment of passion and there is no opportunity to investigate.

אֲמַר רָבָא: דְּרַבִּי יְהוֹשֻׁעַ אַדְּרַבִּי יְהוֹשֻׁעַ קַשְׁיָא, דְּרַבָּן גַּמְלִיאֵל אַדְּרַבָּן גַּמְלִיאֵל לָא קַשְׁיָא? וְהָא קָתָנֵי סֵיפָא, אָמַר לָהֶן רַבָּן גַּמְלִיאֵל: קִבַּלְנוּ עֵדוּתְכֶם, אֲבָל מַה נַּעֲשֶׂה שֶׁהֲרֵי גָּזַר רַבָּן יוֹחָנָן בֶּן זַכַּאי שֶׁלֹּא לְהוֹשִׁיב בֵּית דִּין עַל כָּךְ, שֶׁהַכֹּהֲנִים שׁוֹמְעִין לָכֶם לְרַחֵק אֲבָל לֹא לְקָרֵב!

Rava said with regard to the contradiction that was raised: Is the contradiction between one statement **of Rabbi Yehoshua and** another statement **of Rabbi Yehoshua difficult,** and the contradiction between one statement **of Rabban Gamliel and** another statement **of Rabban Gamliel not difficult? But isn't it taught in the latter clause** of that mishna with regard to the widow whose late husband was from a priestly family of questionable lineage that **Rabban Gamliel said to them: We accept your testimony** that this is the *halakha*, **but what can we do, as Rabban Yoḥanan ben Zakkai decreed not to convene a court for this** purpose of ruling the woman fit, **because the priests obey you** when your ruling calls **to distance** a woman of questionable lineage from marrying them, **but not** when your ruling calls **to bring her near** and deem her fit to marry them. Apparently, Rabban Gamliel did not accept the lenient ruling in the case of the widow, contrary to his statement here that she is accorded credibility.

אֶלָּא אֲמַר רָבָא: דְּרַבָּן גַּמְלִיאֵל אַדְּרַבָּן גַּמְלִיאֵל לָא קַשְׁיָא; הָתָם – בָּרִי, הָכָא – שֶׁמָּא.

Rather, Rava said: The contradiction between one statement **of Rabban Gamliel and** another statement **of Rabban Gamliel is not difficult. There,** in the case of the woman who engaged in intercourse with an unidentified man, her claim that the lineage of the man is unflawed is **a certain** claim. **Here,** in the case of the widow, her claim that his lineage is unflawed is **an uncertain** claim, because there is objective uncertainty with regard to his lineage.

דְּרַבִּי יְהוֹשֻׁעַ אַדְּרַבִּי יְהוֹשֻׁעַ נַמִּי לָא קַשְׁיָא; הָתָם – חַד סְפֵיקָא, הָכָא – תְּרֵי סְפֵיקֵי.

The contradiction between one statement **of Rabbi Yehoshua and** another statement **of Rabbi Yehoshua is** similarly **not difficult. There,** in the case of the woman who engaged in intercourse with an unidentified man, there is only **one uncertainty:**[N] Is the lineage of the man with whom she engaged in intercourse flawed or unflawed? In the case of one uncertainty, the ruling is stringent. **Here,** in the case of the widow, there are **two uncertainties**[N] with regard to the objective situation. It is established that there is uncertainty with regard to one of the members of the family whether or not he is a *ḥalal*. The first uncertainty is whether her late husband is the member of that family with regard to whom the uncertainty exists. Even if it is established that her late husband is indeed the one with regard to whom the uncertainty exists, there remains an uncertainty whether he is in fact a *ḥalal*.

הִלְכָּךְ, לְרַבָּן גַּמְלִיאֵל – אַלִּים לֵיהּ בָּרִי, דַּאֲפִילּוּ בְּחַד סְפֵיקָא נַמִּי מַכְשִׁיר. וְקִיל לֵיהּ שֶׁמָּא, דַּאֲפִילּוּ בִּסְפֵק סְפֵיקָא – נַמִּי פָּסֵיל. לְרַבִּי יְהוֹשֻׁעַ אַלִּים לֵיהּ חַד סְפֵיקָא, דַּאֲפִילּוּ בְּבָרִי נַמִּי פָּסֵיל וְקִיל לֵיהּ סְפֵק סְפֵיקָא, דַּאֲפִילּוּ בְּשֶׁמָּא – נַמִּי מַכְשִׁיר.

Therefore, according **to Rabban Gamliel, a certain** claim is so **powerful for him**[N] **that even in** a case where there is **one uncertainty, he also deems her fit** to marry a priest. **And an uncertain** claim is so **insignificant for him that even in** a case where there is **a compound uncertainty, he also deems her unfit** to marry a priest. According **to Rabbi Yehoshua,** a case where there is **one uncertainty** is so **powerful for him that even in** a case where she makes **a certain** claim, **he also deems her unfit. And** the case of **a compound uncertainty** is so **insignificant for him that even if she makes an uncertain** claim, **he also deems her fit.**

NOTES

There, there is one uncertainty – **הָתָם חַד סְפֵיקָא**: Some ask: Isn't there a compound uncertainty in the case of a woman who entered into seclusion as well, the uncertainty whether or not she engaged in intercourse, and even if she did engage in intercourse, perhaps her paramour was of unflawed lineage? The Ramban explains that according to Rabbi Yehoshua, once she enters into seclusion there is no longer uncertainty whether or not she engaged in intercourse, as there is no steward for restraining sexual immorality, i.e., presumably she engaged in intercourse with him.

Here, there are two uncertainties – **הָכָא תְּרֵי סְפֵיקֵי**: According to the opinion of the Rambam and the *ge'onim* with regard to the widow whose late husband was from a priestly family of questionable lineage, the compound uncertainty is clear: There is uncertainty whether there was a *ḥalal* at all, and even if there was a *ḥalal*, whether her husband was that *ḥalal*. In the *Shita Mekubbetzet* another explanation is cited: Since there is uncertainty with regard to the status of the husband, the resultant uncertainty with regard to his widow is considered a second uncertainty. Since she has the presumptive status of fitness, the flaw in lineage is not dependent on her but originates elsewhere and perhaps there was no flaw at all (see *Beit Shmuel*; *Ayyelet Ahavim*).

A certain claim is so powerful for him – **אַלִּים לֵיהּ בָּרִי**: The Ritva explains that there is not merely a claim of certainty here. It is bolstered by the presumptive status of her body.

תָּנוּ רַבָּנַן: אֵיזוֹהִי אַלְמְנַת עִיסָּה – כׇּל שֶׁאֵין בָּהּ לֹא מִשּׁוּם מַמְזֵרוּת, וְלֹא מִשּׁוּם נְתִינוּת, וְלֹא מִשּׁוּם עַבְדֵי מְלָכִים. אָמַר רַבִּי מֵאִיר:

§ Apropos the widow, **the Rabbis taught: Who is the widow** whose late husband was a member **of a** priestly **family of questionable lineage** and is fit to marry a priest? It is one who married into **any** family **that does not have** the status of being unfit, **neither due to** uncertain ***mamzer*** **status, nor due to** uncertain **Gibeonite status, nor due to** uncertain status as **slaves of kings,**[N] who would force Jewish women, even daughters of priests, to marry them. **Rabbi Meir said:**

NOTES

Slaves of kings – **עַבְדֵי מְלָכִים**: Most commentaries explain that the concern is due to the prohibition against marrying slaves. The Meiri, however, explains that the reference here is to gentiles, who exercised their power and took Jewish women. Although the *halakha* is that a child born to a Jewish woman and a gentile or slave is permitted to marry into the congregation of Israel, a female child is disqualified from marrying into the priesthood.

Perek **I**
Daf **14** Amud **b**

שָׁמַעְתִּי כׇּל שֶׁאֵין בָּהּ אֶחָד מִכׇּל אֵלּוּ – מַשִּׂיאִין לִכְהוּנָּה.

I heard that with regard to the widow of **any family that has none of these** uncertainties associated with it, **one** allows **her to marry** members of **the priesthood.** The only uncertainty where this ruling applies is in the case of uncertain *ḥalal* status.

רַבִּי שִׁמְעוֹן בֶּן אֶלְעָזָר אוֹמֵר מִשּׁוּם רַבִּי מֵאִיר, וְכֵן הָיָה רַבִּי שִׁמְעוֹן בֶּן מְנַסְיָא אוֹמֵר כִּדְבָרָיו: אֵיזוֹהִי אַלְמְנַת עִיסָּה – כׇּל שֶׁנִּטְמַע בָּהּ סְפֵק חָלָל.

Rabbi Shimon ben Elazar says in the name of Rabbi Meir, and likewise Rabbi Shimon ben Menasya would say in accordance with his statement: Who is the widow whose late husband was a member **of a** priestly **family of questionable lineage?** It is a widow who marries into **any** family in **which** a person with regard to whom there is **uncertainty** whether or not he is a ***ḥalal*** **was assimilated** among its members. Therefore, she is referred to as a widow of dough [*issa*]. Just as dough is the result of a mixture of several ingredients, this family too has a person with regard to whom there is uncertainty whether he is a *ḥalal* mixed within it.

מַכִּירִין יִשְׂרָאֵל מַמְזֵרִים שֶׁבֵּינֵיהֶם, וְאֵין מַכִּירִין חֲלָלִין שֶׁבֵּינֵיהֶם.

The reason for the distinction between uncertain *ḥalal* status and uncertain *mamzer* status is that **Jews identify the** ***mamzerim*** **that are among them,**[N] and there is no concern lest they assimilate into families of unflawed lineage. **But they do not identify the** ***ḥalalin*** **among them.** Therefore, there is concern lest a *ḥalal* assimilate into the family.

אָמַר מָר: אֵיזוֹהִי אַלְמְנַת עִיסָּה – כׇּל שֶׁאֵין בָּהּ לֹא מִשּׁוּם מַמְזֵרוּת, וְלֹא מִשּׁוּם נְתִינוּת, וְלֹא מִשּׁוּם עַבְדֵי מְלָכִים. הָא חָלָל – כָּשֵׁר.

The Gemara analyzes the *baraita*. **The Master said** in the *baraita*: **Who is the widow** whose late husband was a member **of a** priestly **family of questionable lineage?** It is one who married into **any** family **that does not have** the status of being unfit, **neither due to** uncertain ***mamzer*** **status,**[N] **nor due to** uncertain **Gibeonite status, nor due to** uncertain status as **slaves of kings.** The Gemara infers: **However,** if it is due to uncertain ***ḥalal*** status, her marriage to a priest is deemed **fit.**

מַאי שְׁנָא הָנָךְ – דְּאוֹרָיְיתָא, חָלָל נָמֵי דְּאוֹרָיְיתָא! וְתוּ, אָמַר רַבִּי מֵאִיר: שָׁמַעְתִּי כׇּל שֶׁאֵין בָּהּ אֶחָד מִכׇּל אֵלּוּ מַשִּׂיאִין לִכְהוּנָּה, הַיְינוּ תַּנָּא קַמָּא!

The Gemara asks: **What is different** about **these** flaws in lineage, uncertain *mamzer* status and Gibeonite status, which render her unfit to marry a priest **by Torah** law?[N] **A** ***ḥalal*** also renders her unfit **by Torah** law. **And furthermore,** the *baraita* continues: **Rabbi Meir said: I heard** that with regard to the widow of **any family that has none of these** uncertainties associated with it, **one marries her to** members of **the priesthood. That is** identical to the opinion of the **first** ***tanna.***[N] If there is uncertainty with regard to one in the late husband's family that he is a *mamzer* or a Gibeonite, she is unfit to marry a priest; if the uncertainty is with regard to *ḥalal* status, she is fit to marry a priest. What novel element does Rabbi Meir introduce?

NOTES

Jews identify the *mamzerim* that are among them – **מַכִּירִין יִשְׂרָאֵל מַמְזֵרִים שֶׁבֵּינֵיהֶם**: The same is true of the other men of flawed lineage enumerated there, because people identify all those prohibited from entering the congregation of Israel. However, since the *ḥalal* is prohibited only with regard to the priesthood and the prohibition is irrelevant to all other people, they are likely to forget the prohibition.

That does not have the status of being unfit…due to uncertain *mamzer* status – **שֶׁאֵין בָּהּ לֹא מִשּׁוּם מַמְזֵרוּת**: Most commentaries explain that other examples of flawed lineage by Torah law, e.g., Ammonites, Moabites, Egyptians, and Edomites, were not cited here for various reasons: Ammonites and Moabites because there is a difference between males, who may never enter into the congregation, and females, who may do so immediately; Egyptians and Edomites because they may enter into the congregation three generations after conversion. Rather, only those people of flawed lineage for whom the prohibition is universal and permanent were enumerated here.

These flaws which render her unfit by Torah law – **הָנָךְ דְּאוֹרָיְיתָא**: Rashi explains that all these are derived from the verse: "And if a priest's daughter be married to a common man" (Leviticus 22:12). However, the lack of fitness of a *ḥalal* does not fall into that category because he is a priest, not a common man. The status of a *ḥalal* is derived from a different verse.

That is identical to the opinion of the first *tanna* – **הַיְינוּ תַּנָּא קַמָּא**: Some early commentaries ask: Why didn't the Gemara explain that Rabbi Meir disagrees and holds that the dispute between Rabban Gamliel and Rabbi Yehoshua is limited to a case where there is uncertainty with regard to the fitness of other categories of flawed lineage, but where there is uncertainty with regard to *ḥalal* status Rabban Gamliel would concede? They answer that since all of these categories of flawed lineage are derived from the Torah, there is no reason to distinguish between them (Ramban; Rabbi Aharon HaLevi; Ritva).

וְתוּ, רַבִּי שִׁמְעוֹן בֶּן אֶלְעָזָר אוֹמֵר מִשּׁוּם רַבִּי מֵאִיר, וְכֵן הָיָה רַבִּי שִׁמְעוֹן בֶּן מְנַסְיָא אוֹמֵר כִּדְבָרָיו: אֵיזוֹהִי אַלְמָנַת עִיסָּה – כׇּל שֶׁנִּטְמַע בָּהּ סְפֵק חָלָל, מַכִּירִין יִשְׂרָאֵל מַמְזֵרִים שֶׁבֵּינֵיהֶן וְאֵין מַכִּירִין חֲלָלִין שֶׁבֵּינֵיהֶן, וְהָא אָמְרַתְּ רֵישָׁא חָלָל כָּשֵׁר!

The *baraita* continues: **And furthermore, Rabbi Shimon ben Elazar says in the name of Rabbi Meir, and likewise, Rabbi Shimon ben Menasya would say in accordance with his statement: Who is the widow** whose late husband was a member **of a** priestly **family of questionable lineage?** It is a widow who marries into **any** family in **which** a person with regard to whom there is **uncertainty** whether or not he is a ***ḥalal* was assimilated.** Because **Jews identify the *mamzerim* that are among them** there is no concern that they will assimilate into families of unflawed lineage, **but** Jews **do not identify the *ḥalalin* among them.** Due to the concern that a *ḥalal* assimilated into the family, the widow is unfit to marry a priest. The Gemara asks: **But didn't you say** in **the first clause** of the *baraita* that if there is uncertainty whether or not a ***ḥalal*** was assimilated among its members, her marriage to a priest is deemed **fit?**

אָמַר רַבִּי יוֹחָנָן: "מַמְזֵר" – צוֹוֵחַ, וְ"חָלָל" – שׁוֹתֵק, אִיכָּא בֵּינַיְיהוּ. תַּנָּא קַמָּא סָבַר: כׇּל פְּסוּל דְּקָרוּ לֵיהּ וְשָׁתֵיק – פָּסוּל. וְהָכִי קָאָמַר תַּנָּא קַמָּא: אֵיזוֹהִי אַלְמָנַת עִיסָּה – כׇּל שֶׁאֵין בָּהּ לֹא שְׁתוּק מַמְזֵרוּת, וְלֹא שְׁתוּק נְתִינוּת, וְלֹא שְׁתוּק עַבְדֵי מְלָכִים, וְלֹא שְׁתוּק חָלָל.

Rabbi Yoḥanan said: The case of one who when called *mamzer* **screams** and protests that he is being slandered, **and** when called ***ḥalal* is silent,**[N] is the subject of the dispute **between** the *tanna'im* in the *baraita*. **The first *tanna* holds: Anyone who** when others **call him unfit and he is silent, is unfit,**[H] as his silence confirms the allegation. **And this is what the first *tanna* is saying: Who is the widow** whose late husband was a member **of a** priestly **family of questionable lineage,** who is fit to marry a priest? It is one who married into **any** family **that has neither** unfitness due to **silence** in response to allegations of ***mamzer* status, nor silence** in response to allegations of **Gibeonite status, nor silence** in response to allegations that they are **slaves of kings, nor silence** in response to allegations of ***ḥalal*** status.[N] Only a woman who was married into a family that protested in response to all these allegations is fit to marry a priest.

וְקָאָמַר לֵיהּ רַבִּי מֵאִיר: הָנָךְ הוּא – דְּקָא פָּסֵיל לֵיהּ בְּקָהָל, אֲבָל שְׁתוּק חָלָל – כָּשֵׁר, וְהָא דְּשָׁתֵיק – מִשּׁוּם דְּלָא אִיכְפַּת לֵיהּ.

And Rabbi Meir is saying to him: Specifically, each of **those** silent in response to allegations of *mamzer* or Gibeonite status or allegations that they are slaves of kings are rendered unfit **because these** allegations **render him unfit** to marry **into the congregation** of Israel. **However,** despite **silence** in response to allegations of ***ḥalal*** status, her marriage to a priest is deemed **fit. And** the fact **that he is silent is due to his indifference,** as even were he deemed a *ḥalal* the only restriction would be with regard to marriage to priests.

וְקָאָמַר לֵיהּ רַבִּי שִׁמְעוֹן בֶּן אֶלְעָזָר לְתַנָּא קַמָּא דְּרַבִּי מֵאִיר: אִי שְׁמִיעַ לָךְ דְּמַכְשַׁר רַבִּי מֵאִיר בִּשְׁתִיקָה – לָא דְּקָרוּ לֵיהּ חָלָל וְשָׁתֵיק, אֶלָּא דְּקָרוּ לֵיהּ מַמְזֵר וְשָׁתֵיק, וְהַאי דְּשָׁתֵיק – סָבַר: מַמְזֵר קָלָא אִית לֵיהּ. אֲבָל "מַמְזֵר" וְצוֹוֵחַ: "חָלָל" וְשׁוֹתֵק, פָּסוּל, וְהַאי דְּאִשְׁתִּיק – סָבַר: מִיסְתַּיֵּיהּ דְּלָא מַפְּקֵי לֵיהּ מִקָּהָל.

And Rabbi Shimon ben Elazar is saying to the first *tanna* who quoted **Rabbi Meir** as saying: I heard, etc. **If you heard that Rabbi Meir deems** her marriage to a priest **fit,** in a case of **silence** in response to allegations, it is **not** in a case **where they called him *ḥalal* and he is silent; rather,** it is in a case **where they call him *mamzer* and he is silent.** In that case, the reason **he is silent** is **that he holds:** The fact that one is a ***mamzer*** generates **publicity,** and since he is not reputed to be a *mamzer*, he is indifferent to the allegation. **However,** in a case where he is called ***mamzer* and he screams** in protest, or where he is called ***ḥalal* and he is silent, he is unfit. And** the fact **that he is silent** and does not protest is because **he holds:** It is **sufficient for him that they do not expel him from the congregation** of Israel.

NOTES

One who when called *mamzer* screams and protests that he is being slandered, and when called *ḥalal* is silent – **מַמְזֵר צוֹוֵחַ וְחָלָל שׁוֹתֵק**: The early commentaries discuss the matter of unfitness resulting from the silence of the accused, and there are different explanations with halakhic ramifications. Some explain that according to the first *tanna*, his silence is tantamount to an admission that the allegation of unfitness is accurate (Rambam; Meiri). Some explain that silence is incriminating only if there were rumors of flawed lineage surrounding the accused and his family; otherwise, his silence proves nothing (Ramban; Rashba). The Ra'avad explains that the distinction between screaming and silence was in effect only in those generations when the courts would punish one who slanders another in this manner.

Today, however, the opposite is true. Silence in reaction to an allegation during a quarrel indicates unflawed lineage; it is considered admission of flawed lineage only if the allegation is leveled not in the context of a quarrel. According to these opinions, the matter of one who screams in response to allegations of a *mamzer* is irrelevant. The Ramban cites in the name of Rav Hai Gaon that there is a variant reading that omits the phrase: One who when called *mamzer* screams. However, others hold that confirmation of the allegation is specifically with regard to one who when called *mamzer* screams and protests, and when called *ḥalal* is silent. If one is consistently silent in the face of allegations, perhaps he is one of those people who never scream, even when quarreling with others.

In tractate *Kiddushin*, silence is an indication of impeccable lineage. However, one who screams when called *mamzer* indicates that he reacts to and protests false allegations. If he is then silent when called *ḥalal*, that confirms the allegation (Ritva; Ran).

Silence in response to allegations of *ḥalal* status – **שְׁתוּק חָלָל**: The significance of silence in the face of allegations of *ḥalal* is understood according to those who explain that the *ḥalal* is certain that he is a *ḥalal* and it is everyone else who is uncertain. However, according to those opinions who explain that there is an objective uncertainty, how can the silence be considered an admission if the *ḥalal* himself is uncertain of his status? The Ritva explains that his silence is an admission that he is a member of the family with regard to which there is uncertainty.

HALAKHA

Anyone who hears an allegation of unfitness that others call him and is silent, is unfit – **כׇּל פְּסוּל דְּקָרוּ לֵיהּ וְשָׁתֵיק פָּסוּל**: If one is silent in the face of allegations that he is of flawed lineage, e.g., he is called a *mamzer*, a *ḥalal*, or a Gibeonite, the suspicion is that his silence confirms those allegations, and one may marry him or members of his family only after those allegations are investigated and refuted, in accordance with the opinion of the first *tanna*. Some maintain that this is the case only if it is known that a person of flawed lineage married into the family; otherwise, his silence proves nothing (*Tur*, citing Rabbeinu Yitzḥak; *Beit Yosef*, citing Ramban and Rashba). The Ra'avad explains that the distinction between silence and screaming was in effect only in those generations when the courts would punish one who slanders another in this manner.

Today, however, the opposite is true. Silence in reaction to an allegation during a quarrel indicates unflawed lineage. Yet others hold that his silence confirms the allegations only if he is not silent in response to other allegations (Ran; Rambam *Sefer Kedusha*, *Hilkhot Issurei Bia* 19:22; *Shulḥan Arukh*, *Even HaEzer* 2:4).

תָּנֵי חֲדָא: רַבִּי יוֹסֵי אוֹמֵר שְׁתוּק מַמְזֵר – כָּשֵׁר, שְׁתוּק חָלָל – פָּסוּל. וְתַנְיָא אִידָךְ: שְׁתוּק חָלָל – כָּשֵׁר, שְׁתוּק מַמְזֵר – פָּסוּל!

The Gemara notes: **It is taught in one** *baraita* that **Rabbi Yosei says:** Despite the fact that with **silence** in response to allegations of ***mamzer*** one is **fit; silence** in response to allegations of ***ḥalal*** renders one **unfit. It is taught in another** *baraita*: Despite the fact that with **silence** in response to allegations of ***ḥalal*** one is **fit; silence** in response to allegations of ***mamzer*** renders one **unfit.**

לָא קַשְׁיָא; הָא – תַּנָּא קַמָּא אַלִּיבָּא דְּרַבִּי מֵאִיר, הָא – דְּרַבִּי שִׁמְעוֹן בֶּן אֶלְעָזָר אַלִּיבָּא דְּרַבִּי מֵאִיר.

The Gemara explains: The contradiction between the *baraitot* is **not difficult. This** second *baraita* is the opinion of **the first** ***tanna*** **in accordance with** the opinion of **Rabbi Meir,** who holds that silence in response to allegations of *ḥalal* does not render one unfit. And **this** first *baraita* is the opinion **of Rabbi Shimon ben Elazar in accordance with** the opinion of **Rabbi Meir,** who holds that silence in response to allegations of *mamzer* is motivated by indifference and does not render him unfit; however, silence in response to allegations of *ḥalal* is an indication that the allegations are true and he is unfit.

מתני׳ אָמַר רַבִּי יוֹסֵי: מַעֲשֶׂה בְּתִינוֹקֶת שֶׁיָּרְדָה לְמַלְּאוֹת מַיִם מִן הָעַיִן וְנֶאֶנְסָה, אָמַר רַבִּי יוֹחָנָן בֶּן נוּרִי: אִם רוֹב אַנְשֵׁי הָעִיר מַשִּׂיאִין לִכְהוּנָּה – הֲרֵי זוֹ תִּינָּשֵׂא לִכְהוּנָּה.

MISHNA **Rabbi Yosei said:** There was **an incident involving a young girl who descended**[N] **to fill** her jug with **water from the spring, and she was raped,** and the identity of the rapist was unknown. **Rabbi Yoḥanan ben Nuri said: If the majority of the people of the city marry** their daughters to members of the **priesthood,**[N] **this young girl may be married to** a member of the priesthood.

גמ׳ אֲמַר לֵיהּ רָבָא לְרַב נַחְמָן: רַבִּי יוֹחָנָן בֶּן נוּרִי דַּאֲמַר כְּמַאן? אִי כְּרַבָּן גַּמְלִיאֵל, אֲפִילּוּ בְּרוֹב פְּסוּלִין נַמִי מַכְשַׁר! אִי כְּרַבִּי יְהוֹשֻׁעַ, אֲפִילּוּ בְּרוֹב כְּשֵׁרִים נַמִי פָּסֵיל! אֲמַר לֵיהּ, הָכִי אֲמַר רַב יְהוּדָה אֲמַר רַב:

GEMARA **Rava said to Rav Naḥman: In accordance with whose** opinion **is it that Rabbi Yoḥanan ben Nuri stated** his opinion?[N] **If** it is **in accordance with** the opinion of **Rabban Gamliel, even in** a case where **the majority** of the people **are of flawed lineage as well, he deems** her **fit** to marry into the priesthood. **If** it is **in accordance with** the opinion of **Rabbi Yehoshua,**[N] **even in** a case where **the majority** of the people **are of unflawed lineage, he deems** her **unfit** to marry into the priesthood. Rav Naḥman **said to** Rava that **this** is what **Rav Yehuda said** that **Rav said:**

NOTES

A young girl who descended – תִּינוֹקֶת שֶׁיָּרְדָה: One of the questions raised by the early commentaries is whether the girl who was raped claims that she is certain that the man who raped her is of unflawed lineage. The fact is that according to Rabban Gamliel, her certain claim is part of the reason that she is not disqualified. Many prove from the formulation of the mishna, where no claim is mentioned, that the girl made no claim with regard to the identity of the rapist. This is underscored by the fact that the mishna is referring to a young girl and by the fact that the incident transpired among the wagons (see 15a) where there are many strangers whose lineage is unknown (Ramban; Ritva).

If the majority of the people of the city marry their daughters to members of the priesthood – אִם רוֹב אַנְשֵׁי הָעִיר מַשִּׂיאִין לִכְהוּנָּה: Rashi writes that this means simply that most of the people in the city are of unflawed lineage and could marry their daughters to priests. Others explain that it means that most of the residents in fact marry their daughters to priests (*ge'onim*).

In accordance with whose opinion is it that Rabbi Yoḥanan ben Nuri stated his opinion – רַבִּי יוֹחָנָן בֶּן נוּרִי דַּאֲמַר כְּמַאן: The early commentaries ask: Since Rabbi Yoḥanan ben Nuri is a *tanna*, why was it necessary to align his opinion with the opinion of one of the *tanna'im*? Why not say that his is a third opinion? They answer that his opinion was introduced by means of an incident, and the mishna typically cites incidents in support of what was stated previously. Furthermore, were this a third opinion, Rabbi Yosei should have cited it earlier and stated that there is an opinion that the entire matter is dependent on the question whether the majority of the people are of flawed or unflawed lineage (Rabbi Yosef MiGash; Ritva).

If it is in accordance with the opinion of Rabbi Yehoshua – אִי כְּרַבִּי יְהוֹשֻׁעַ: The conclusion of the Jerusalem Talmud differs from the Gemara here. There it is stated that the statement of Rabbi Yoḥanan ben Nuri is in accordance with the opinion of Rabbi Yehoshua. The reason that Rabbi Yoḥanan ben Nuri rules that she is fit to marry into the priesthood is that she was raped. Rabbi Yehoshua deems her unfit because her presumptive status of fitness is compromised by her volitional promiscuity. However, one who is raped does not lose her presumptive status of fitness. That status together with the majority of people of unflawed lineage in her proximity is sufficient to render her fit to marry into the priesthood.

בִּקְרוֹנוֹת שֶׁל צִיפּוֹרִי הָיָה מַעֲשֶׂה, וְכִדְרַבִּי אַמִי, דְּאָמַר רַבִּי אַמִי: וְהוּא שֶׁהָיְתָה סִיעָה שֶׁל בְּנֵי אָדָם כְּשֵׁרִין עוֹבֶרֶת לְשָׁם, וְכִדְרַבִּי יַנַּאי. דְּאָמַר רַבִּי יַנַּאי: נִבְעֶלֶת בִּקְרוֹנוֹת – כְּשֵׁרָה לִכְהוּנָּה.

The **incident** transpired **among the wagons** [*keronot*][LN] in the marketplace **of Tzippori**[B] on the market day, and this *halakha* is **in accordance with** the statement **of Rabbi Ami, as Rabbi Ami said: And this is** the ruling only in a case **where there was a contingent of men of unflawed lineage passing there.**[N] Due to the fact that both the lineage of the majority of the people of the city where the girl was raped and the lineage of the majority of the passersby is unflawed, the rape is attributed to a man of unflawed lineage. **And** this ruling is **in accordance with** the statement of **Rabbi Yannai, as Rabbi Yannai said: If she engaged in intercourse in the wagons, she is fit to** marry a member of the **priesthood.**

בִּקְרוֹנוֹת סָלְקָא דַּעְתָּךְ?! אֶלָּא: נִבְעֶלֶת בִּשְׁעַת קְרוֹנוֹת – כְּשֵׁרָה לִכְהוּנָּה. אֲבָל פֵּירַשׁ אֶחָד מִצִּיפּוֹרִי וּבָעַל – הַוָּלָד שְׁתוּקִי.

The Gemara asks: Does it **enter your mind** to say that the woman was raped **in the wagons,** in the crowded area of the marketplace where business is conducted? **Rather,** Rabbi Yannai is saying that if **she** was forced to **engage in intercourse at the time of the wagons,** i.e., when the convoys pass, **she is fit to** marry a member of the **priesthood. However,** if **one** individual, whose lineage is unknown, **left Tzippori**[N] **and engaged in intercourse** with a woman, **the child is a *shetuki*** and deemed unfit to marry into the priesthood even though the majority of the inhabitants of city are of unflawed lineage.

כִּי הָא דְּכִי אֲתָא רַב דִּימִי אָמַר זְעֵירִי אָמַר רַבִּי חֲנִינָא, וְאָמְרִי לָהּ אָמַר זְעֵירִי אָמַר רַבִּי חֲנִינָא: הוֹלְכִין אַחַר רוֹב הָעִיר, וְאֵין הוֹלְכִין אַחַר רוֹב סִיעָה.

The Gemara notes: That is **similar** to **this** statement **that when Rav Dimi came** from Eretz Yisrael to Babylonia, **Ze'eiri said** that **Rabbi Ḥanina said, and some say** directly that **Ze'eiri said** that **Rabbi Ḥanina said: One follows the** flawed lineage of the **majority of** the people in **the city and one does not follow** the unflawed lineage of **the majority of the** traveling **contingent,** and the woman who engaged in intercourse with a member of the itinerant contingent is deemed unfit to marry into the priesthood.

כְּלַפֵּי לַיָּיא?! הָנֵי נָיְידֵי וְהָנֵי קְבִיעִי וְקַיְימִי!

The Gemara asks: **On the contrary** [*kelapei layya*],[L] the opposite is logical. **These** members of the contingent **are moving,** and in that case the principle is that one follows the majority. **And these** people of the city **are fixed and standing** in one place, and in that case the principle is that even if the lineage of the majority is unflawed, the uncertainty is treated as if it were equally balanced.

NOTES

Among the wagons – בִּקְרוֹנוֹת: Most commentaries explain that the reference here is to wagons that travel from place to place. Others explain that the reference is to the place where the wagons stop and sell their merchandise, i.e., the marketplace (*Talmidei Rabbeinu Yona*).

And this is where there was a contingent of men of unflawed lineage passing there – וְהוּא שֶׁהָיְתָה סִיעָה שֶׁל בְּנֵי אָדָם כְּשֵׁרִין עוֹבֶרֶת לְשָׁם: There are different opinions regarding the connection of this matter to the dispute between Rabban Gamliel and Rabbi Yehoshua, leading to different halakhic conclusions. According to Rashi, this is in accordance with the opinion of Rabbi Yehoshua; however, he does not explain what Rabban Gamliel would hold in this case. The Ritva explains that according to Rashi, Rabban Gamliel holds that two majorities are no more effective than one, just as he holds that a compound uncertainty is insignificant when the woman's claim is certain. According to most commentaries, there is no dispute between Rabban Gamliel and Rabbi Yehoshua in this case.

Rabbeinu Zeraḥya HaLevi understands Rashi's opinion differently. He explains that this entire discussion is conducted according to the opinion of Rabbi Yehoshua; however, Rabban Gamliel does not require two majorities at all. See the Ramban in *Milḥamot Hashem* with the Ra'avad, both of whom reject that opinion.

However if one left Tzippori – אֲבָל פֵּירַשׁ אֶחָד מִצִּיפּוֹרִי: Most of the early commentaries hold that this ordinance requiring two majorities is universally applied. Therefore, even if it is known that the man with whom she engaged in intercourse was from the city, in the absence of a second majority the child is of flawed lineage. The Meiri disagrees and holds that in this case one majority is sufficient.

LANGUAGE

Wagons [*keronot*] – קְרוֹנוֹת: From the Latin carrum, and perhaps the Greek κάρρον, *karron*, meaning carriage or wagon. In the Jerusalem Talmud, the phrase *kerona shel Tzippori* appears, which based on context is from the Greek κρήνη, *krēnē*, meaning spring or well. According to that understanding, the reference would be to the spring in Tzippori, corresponding to the mishna that is referring to a young girl who descended to the spring.

On the contrary [*kelapei layya*] – כְּלַפֵּי לַיָּיא: This expression is employed in response to a statement that seems contrary to reason. Some say it is a variation of the phrase *kelapei le'an*, meaning: Toward where are you going? Shouldn't you be going in the opposite direction? Some explain it as a contraction of *kelapei alya*, meaning toward the tail, evoking the image of riding a horse facing the tail. That too is contrary to reason.

BACKGROUND

Tzippori – צִיפּוֹרִי: Tzippori was a large town in the Upper Galilee and the perennial rival of Tiberias for recognition as the religious capital of Galilee. During the Second Temple period it enjoyed special status among the towns of the Galilee because of its large and learned Jewish community. Among the *tanna'im* who lived there were Rabbi Yoḥanan ben Nuri, Rabbi Ḥalafta, and his renowned son Rabbi Yosei.

Rabbi Yehuda HaNasi moved to Tzippori toward the end of his life, and it was the seat of the Sanhedrin for approximately one generation. Rabbi Yehuda HaNasi's leading disciples lived in Tzippori: Rabbi Yishmael, son of Rabbi Yosei; Rabban Gamliel, son of Rabbi Yehuda HaNasi, who later succeeded his father as *Nasi*; his brother Rabbi Shimon; Rabbi Ḥanina bar Ḥama, who later headed the Tzippori yeshiva; and Rabbi Yannai. Even after the Sanhedrin moved to Tiberias, Torah scholars continued to live in Tzippori, among them the prominent *amora'im* of Eretz Yisrael, Rabbi Ḥanina of Tzippori and Rabbi Mana.

Ruins at Tzippori

אֶלָּא: הוֹלְכִין אַחַר רוֹב הָעִיר וְהוּא דְּאִיכָּא רוֹב סִיעָה בַּהֲדָהּ. וְאֵין הוֹלְכִין אַחַר רוֹב הָעִיר גְּרֵידְתָּא וְלֹא אַחַר רוֹב סִיעָה גְּרֵידְתָּא. מַאי טַעְמָא – גְּזֵרָה רוֹב סִיעָה אַטּוּ רוֹב הָעִיר.

Rather, this is what Rabbi Yannai is saying: **One follows the** lineage of the **majority of the city,**[N] **and that is** specifically in a case **where there is a majority** of men of unflawed lineage in the passing **contingent**[H] together **with** the city's unflawed majority. In that case, from both perspectives the intercourse can be attributed to a man of unflawed lineage. **However, neither does one follow the** unflawed lineage of the **majority of the city alone, nor** does he **follow the** unflawed lineage of the **majority of the contingent alone. What is the reason** that one does not follow the lineage of the majority of the moving contingent? It is because the Sages issued **a decree** not to follow **the majority of the contingent**[N] **due to the majority of the city,** where one does not follow the majority.

וְרוֹב הָעִיר נַמִי, אִי דְּקָא אָזְלֵי אִינְהוּ לְגַבָּהּ – כָּל דְּפָרֵישׁ מֵרוּבָּא פָּרֵישׁ! לָא צְרִיכָא, דְּקָא אָזְלָא אִיהִי לְגַבַּיְיהוּ, דַּהֲוָה לֵיהּ קָבוּעַ, וְאָמַר רַבִּי זֵירָא: כָּל קָבוּעַ כְּמֶחֱצָה עַל מֶחֱצָה דָּמֵי.

The Gemara asks: **But** aren't there cases where one follows **the majority of the city as well,** as, **if** one of the residents of the city **goes** out of the city **to her** and rapes her, the principle is: The legal status of **any** item **that is separated** from the group is that of one **separated from the majority?**[N] Therefore, there is no reason to issue a decree. The Gemara answers: The decree is **necessary only** due to a case **where she went**[N] into the city **to them,** in which case the rapist **is** an indistinguishable member of a **fixed** set, **and Rabbi Zeira said:** The legal status of uncertainty with regard to **any** item **fixed** in its place is that of an uncertainty that is **equally balanced,** and one does not follow the majority.

וּמִי בָּעֵינַן תְּרֵי רוּבֵּי? וְהָתַנְיָא: תֵּשַׁע חֲנוּיוֹת, כּוּלָּן מוֹכְרוֹת בְּשַׂר שְׁחוּטָה, וְאַחַת מוֹכֶרֶת בְּשַׂר נְבֵלָה, וְלָקַח מֵאַחַת מֵהֶן וְאֵינוֹ יוֹדֵעַ מֵאֵי זֶה מֵהֶן לָקַח – סְפֵיקוֹ אָסוּר. וּבַנִּמְצָא – הַלֵּךְ אַחַר הָרוֹב!

The Gemara questions the statement of Rabbi Ami: **And do we require two majorities** to overcome the minority? **Isn't it taught** in a *baraita*: With regard to **nine stores**[N] in a city, **all of which sell** kosher **meat** from **a slaughtered** animal,[H] **and one** other store that **sells meat** from unslaughtered **animal carcasses, and** a person **bought** meat **from one of** the stores **and he does not know from which** store **he bought** the meat, in this case of **uncertainty,** the meat **is prohibited.** The legal status of uncertainty with regard to any item fixed in its place is that of an uncertainty that is equally balanced, and one does not follow the majority. This *baraita* continues: **And in** the case of meat **found** in the street, outside the stores, **follow the majority**[H] of stores that sell kosher meat. In other words, the meat is kosher.

NOTES

Rather, one follows the lineage of the majority of the city – **אֶלָּא הוֹלְכִין אַחַר רוֹב הָעִיר**: The Rashba notes that the language used here appears to indicate that the majority of the city is the primary consideration. However, it is clear from the context that this is not the case, as the majority of the city is a fixed majority. Therefore, in order to reconcile the sources, he explains that although the majority of the city is not as significant as the majority of the contingent, it is required in support of the majority of the contingent.

A decree not to follow the majority of the contingent – **גְּזֵרָה רוֹב סִיעָה**: The Ritva explains that although the fundamental *halakha* in this case is a decree, the second decree is not issued to prevent violation of the first, as both were issued as one decree. In terms of the halakhic ruling, in the *Penei Yehoshua* it is explained based on the *Beit Shmuel* that ultimately, the final conclusion of the Gemara is that this is not a decree. Rather, there is a special ordinance instituted by the Sages to require two majorities in cases relating to lineage. The practical halakhic difference would be in a case where all the people in the city are of unflawed lineage. In that case the decree would not be relevant, even if it is a case where the residents of the city are fixed (see Rashash).

Any item that is separated is separated from the majority – **כָּל דְּפָרֵישׁ מֵרוּבָּא פָּרֵישׁ**: The early commentaries explain, and thereby resolve a related contradiction in tractate *Kinnim*, that even though those separated from the majority ultimately returned to their original fixed state, as the man with whom she engaged in intercourse ultimately went home, the determining moment is when the incident took place (Rosh).

The decree is necessary only due to a case where she went – **לָא צְרִיכָא דְּקָא אָזְלָא אִיהִי**: There is a variant reading: There are cases where she went. There is a significant difference between the two versions. According to the version in the Gemara, two majorities are required only in a case where it is clear that she went to them. According to the variant reading (Rashi; *Yam shel Shlomo*), the very concern that perhaps she went to them is sufficient for the decree to be issued, and the decree is in effect even in cases where it is unclear whether or not she went to them (see *Beit Yosef*).

Nine stores – **תֵּשַׁע חֲנוּיוֹת**: The distinction here is between fixed items and items that are not fixed. Rabbeinu Ḥananel explains that one does not follow the majority of kosher stores because the price of non-kosher meat is lower and therefore the likelihood that he bought meat in the non-kosher store is greater. Some ask: Even in the case of meat that was found, presumably the meat fell from someone who had purchased it in one of the stores. Why, then, isn't the ruling that it is an equally balanced uncertainty? They answer that the determining moment is the moment that the uncertainty developed. When the question with regard to its status was raised, the item was not fixed (*Shita Mekubbetzet*).

HALAKHA

A majority of the city and a majority of the contingent – **רוֹב הָעִיר וְרוֹב סִיעָה**: With regard to an unmarried woman who engaged in intercourse, even if she became pregnant, and she claims that the man is of unflawed lineage, her claim is accepted and she and her daughter are both fit to marry into the priesthood. That is the *halakha*, provided the majority of the passersby are of unflawed lineage and the majority of the residents of the city from which the passersby came are of unflawed lineage. The Sages established a higher standard with regard to lineage, requiring two majorities.

If there was only one majority, either of the city or of the passersby, she may not marry a priest. However, if she went ahead and married a priest, even if there was a majority of people of flawed lineage, they may remain married (Rambam). If she does not claim that the man was of unflawed lineage, e.g., she did not know his identity, some say that according to the Rambam, unless there are two majorities, she may not marry a priest *ab initio*, and if she does, they may not remain married (*Maggid Mishne*; see Ramban; Rashba; Ran).

Others hold that according to the Rambam, even if there are two majorities, she may not marry a priest *ab initio* (*Beit Yosef*). Others hold that if she claims that she is certain that the man was of unflawed lineage she may marry a priest *ab initio* even if there is only one majority. Furthermore, even if there is a majority of people of unflawed lineage, she may remain married after the fact (Rambam *Sefer Kedusha, Hilkhot Issurei Bia* 18:13–14; *Shulḥan Arukh, Even HaEzer* 6:17).

Nine stores all of which sell meat from a slaughtered animal – **תֵּשַׁע חֲנוּיוֹת כּוּלָּן מוֹכְרוֹת בְּשַׂר שְׁחוּטָה**: If the majority of stores in the city sell kosher meat and a minority of stores sell non-kosher meat, and a person entered one of the stores and purchased meat and does not know which store he entered, since it is a fixed majority, its legal status is that of a balanced uncertainty and the meat is forbidden (Rambam *Sefer Kedusha, Hilkhot Ma'akhalot Assurot* 8:11; *Shulḥan Arukh, Yoreh De'a* 110:3).

And in the case of meat found outside follow the majority – **וּבַנִּמְצָא הַלֵּךְ אַחַר הָרוֹב**: With regard to one who finds meat in the marketplace or in the possession of a gentile, one follows the majority; if the majority of stores sell kosher meat, the meat is permitted by Torah law. However, the Sages prohibited all meat that is found and all meat that was out of the sight of Jews even if all those who slaughter and sell meat are Jewish, unless it is clear that it is kosher (Rambam *Sefer Kedusha, Hilkhot Ma'akhalot Assurot* 8:11; *Shulḥan Arukh, Yoreh De'a* 63:1, 110:3).

וְכִי תֵּימָא בְּשֶׁאֵין דַּלְתוֹת מְדִינָה נְעוּלוֹת, דְּקָא אָתֵי לָהּ רוּבָּא מֵעָלְמָא – וְהָא אָמַר רַבִּי זֵירָא: אַף עַל פִּי שֶׁדַּלְתוֹת מְדִינָה נְעוּלוֹת! מַעֲלָה עָשׂוּ בְּיוּחֲסִין.

And if you would say that one follows the majority only in a case **where the gates of the city are unlocked, where** the meat could have **come** to the city **from the majority** of kosher meat **outside** the city and only by combining that majority with the majority of kosher meat stores inside the city, creating two majorities, is the meat ruled kosher; **but didn't Rabbi Zeira say: Even if the city gates are locked,** one follows the majority and the meat is kosher even without a double majority? The Gemara answers: The Sages require two majorities only in cases such as establishing the identity of the child's father, because they **established a higher standard with regard to** matters of **lineage.** However, in other cases, e.g., concerning kosher meat, a single majority is sufficient.

גּוּפָא, אָמַר רַבִּי זֵירָא: כָּל קָבוּעַ כְּמֶחֱצָה עַל מֶחֱצָה דָּמֵי, בֵּין לְקוּלָּא בֵּין לְחוּמְרָא.

§ In terms of the matter **itself, Rabbi Zeira said:** The legal status of uncertainty with regard to **any** item **fixed** in its place is that of an uncertainty that is **equally balanced, both** when it leads to **leniency,** e.g., in a case where, were one to follow the majority, the ruling would be stringent, and when it leads to **stringency,** e.g., in a case where, were one to follow the majority, the ruling would be lenient.

מְנָא לֵיהּ לְרַבִּי זֵירָא הָא? אִילֵימָא מִתֵּשַׁע חֲנוּיוֹת כּוּלָּן מוֹכְרוֹת בְּשַׂר שְׁחוּטָה וְאַחַת בְּשַׂר נְבֵלָה, וְלָקַח מֵאַחַת מֵהֶן, וְאֵינוֹ יוֹדֵעַ מֵאֵיזֶה מֵהֶן לָקַח – סְפֵיקוֹ אָסוּר, וּבַנִּמְצָא – הַלֵּךְ אַחַר הָרוֹב, הָתָם לְחוּמְרָא!

The Gemara asks: **From where does Rabbi Zeira** learn that the legal status of uncertainty with regard to any item fixed in its place is that of an uncertainty that is equally balanced, both when it leads to leniency and when it leads to stringency? **If we say** that it is derived **from** the case of **nine stores** in a city, **all of which sell** kosher **meat** from **a slaughtered** animal, **and one** other store that sells **meat from unslaughtered animal carcasses, and** a person **bought** meat **from one of** the stores **and he does not know from which** store **he bought** the meat, in this case of **uncertainty** the meat **is prohibited. And in the** case of meat **found** in the street, outside the stores, **follow the majority** of stores that sell kosher meat, and therefore the meat would be kosher. **There,** in the first case, ruling it an equally balanced uncertainty is **a stringency,** as there is a majority of kosher stores.

אֶלָּא, מִתִּשְׁעָה צְפַרְדְּעִים וְשֶׁרֶץ אֶחָד בֵּינֵיהֶם, וְנָגַע בְּאֶחָד מֵהֶן וְאֵינוֹ יוֹדֵעַ בְּאֵיזֶה מֵהֶן נָגַע, סְפֵיקוֹ טָמֵא. הָתָם נַמִי לְחוּמְרָא!

Rather, Rabbi Zeira learns that *halakha* **from** a different *baraita*. If there were **nine frogs,** which is a creeping animal that does not impart ritual impurity while alive or when dead, **and one** ritually impure **creeping animal,**[HB] whose carcass imparts ritual impurity, **among them, and** a person **touched one of the** ten creatures, **and he does not know which of them he touched,** in this case of **uncertainty** the person is **ritually impure. There too,** ruling it an equally balanced uncertainty is **a stringency,** as the majority of the creeping animals do not impart impurity.

אֶלָּא מִתִּשְׁעָה שְׁרָצִים וּצְפַרְדֵּעַ אֶחָד בֵּינֵיהֶם, וְנָגַע בְּאֶחָד מֵהֶן, וְאֵינוֹ יוֹדֵעַ בְּאֵיזֶה מֵהֶן נָגַע, בִּרְשׁוּת הַיָּחִיד סְפֵיקוֹ טָמֵא, בִּרְשׁוּת הָרַבִּים סְפֵיקוֹ טָהוֹר.

Rather, Rabbi Zeira learns that *halakha* **from** the continuation of that *baraita*. If there are **nine creeping animals,** whose carcasses impart ritual impurity, **and one frog**[H] **among them, and** a person **touched one of them, and he does not know which of them he touched,** if it was **in the private domain,** in this case of **uncertainty** the person is **ritually impure,** as all cases of uncertainty with regard to ritual impurity are ruled impure in the private domain. This is derived from the case of *sota*. However, **in the public domain,** in that case of **uncertainty** the person is **ritually pure.**[N] Although contact with a creeping animal from the majority would render him ritually impure, since the uncertainty is with regard to a fixed group, its legal status is that of an equally balanced uncertainty, and in the public domain he is ritually pure. Rabbi Zeira learns that *halakha* from this case of leniency.

HALAKHA

Nine frogs and one creeping animal – תִּשְׁעָה צְפַרְדְּעִים וְשֶׁרֶץ אֶחָד: If there were nine frogs and one ritually impure creeping animal among them in the private domain, and a person touched one of them but he does not know which, he is ritually impure, as uncertain ritual impurity in the private domain is ritually impure (Rambam *Sefer Tahara, Hilkhot Avot HaTumot* 18:2).

Nine creeping animals and one frog – תִּשְׁעָה שְׁרָצִים וּצְפַרְדֵּעַ אֶחָד: If there were nine creeping animals and one frog among them in the private domain, and a person touched one of them and he does not know which, he is ritually impure, as uncertain ritual impurity in the private domain is ritually impure. However, in the public domain he is ritually pure, because the legal status of a fixed majority is that of an equally balanced uncertainty, and uncertain ritual impurity in the public domain is ritually pure (Rambam *Sefer Tahara, Hilkhot Avot HaTumot* 18:2).

BACKGROUND

Creeping animal – שֶׁרֶץ: Generally, this term includes rodents, lizards, insects, and any other small creature that crawls. Ritual impurity is imparted by the carcasses of the eight creeping animals enumerated in Leviticus (11:29–37), and the Talmud often refers to these eight creatures with the unmodified term creeping animal. The Sages stated that since the smallest of these eight animals was at least the size of a lentil-bulk at birth, one contracts ritual impurity only through contact with a portion of the carcass of a creeping animal no smaller than a lentil-bulk. Moreover, one is liable to receive lashes for eating a lentil-bulk of a creeping animal.

NOTES

In the public domain, in that case of uncertainty the person is ritually pure – בִּרְשׁוּת הָרַבִּים סְפֵיקוֹ טָהוֹר: The distinction between the private and public domains with regard to uncertain ritual impurity is derived from the case of *sota*, as the *halakha* is that she is forbidden to her husband in a case of uncertainty and her status is expressed in the Torah in terms of ritual impurity. Just as in the case of *sota* the uncertainty developed when the woman entered into seclusion with the man with whom her husband warned her not to seclude herself, which was clearly in the private and not the public domain, so too in a case of uncertain ritual impurity, the person is deemed impure only in the private domain.

Additional details are also derived from *sota*, e.g., the distinction between an item that does not have knowledge to be asked, which is deemed ritually pure in a case of uncertainty, and an item that has knowledge to be asked, which is deemed ritually impure in that case.

וּמִדְּאוֹרַיְיתָא מְנָא לַן? אָמַר קְרָא ״וְאָרַב לוֹ וְקָם עָלָיו״ – עַד שֶׁיִּתְכַּוֵּין לוֹ. וְרַבָּנַן? אָמְרִי דְּבֵי רַבִּי יַנַּאי: פְּרָט לְזוֹרֵק אֶבֶן לְגוֹ.

After citing a tannaitic source for Rabbi Zeira's opinion, the Gemara asks: **And from where in the Torah do we** derive that the legal status of any item fixed in its place is like that of an uncertainty that is equally balanced, both when it leads to leniency and when it leads to stringency? It is derived from **the verse** that **states** with regard to a murderer: **"And lie in wait for him, and rise up against him"** (Deuteronomy 19:11), indicating that one is liable **only** in a case **where he intends to** kill **him.**[HN] One who intended to kill one person and inadvertently killed another is exempt from punishment. **And** how do **the Rabbis,** who hold that one is liable in that case, interpret that verse? The Sages **of the school of Rabbi Yannai say:** It **excludes** the case **of** one who **throws a stone into a crowd** and did not intend to kill a specific person.

הֵיכִי דָּמֵי? אִילֵימָא דְּאִיכָּא תִּשְׁעָה גּוֹיִם וְאֶחָד יִשְׂרָאֵל בֵּינֵיהֶם – וְתֵיפּוֹק לֵיהּ דְּרוּבָּא גּוֹיִם נִינְהוּ! אִי נַמִי פַּלְגָא וּפַלְגָא – סְפֵק נְפָשׁוֹת לְהָקֵל!

The Gemara asks: **What are the circumstances** of the case where he threw the stone and is exempt? **If we say that there are nine gentiles** in the crowd **and one Jew among them,** even without the verse, **let him derive** the exemption from the fact **that they are a majority of gentiles. Alternatively,** even if we say that **half** of the ten people are considered gentiles **and half** are considered Jews, let him derive the exemption from the principle: In a case of **uncertainty** concerning a **life-threatening** situation, the *halakha* **is lenient.**

לָא צְרִיכָא, דְּאִיכָּא תִּשְׁעָה יִשְׂרְאֵלִים וְגוֹי אֶחָד בֵּינֵיהֶם, דַּהֲוָה לֵיהּ גּוֹי קָבוּעַ, וְכָל קָבוּעַ כְּמֶחֱצָה עַל מֶחֱצָה דָּמֵי.

The Gemara answers: **No,** the verse is **necessary** only in a case where **there are nine Jews and one gentile among them.** Were the ruling to follow the majority the one who threw the stone would be liable. But in that case, **because the gentile is fixed** among them, **and** the legal status of **any** item **fixed** in its place is **like** that of an uncertainty that is **equally balanced,** he is exempt, based on the principle: In a case of uncertainty concerning a life-threatening situation, the *halakha* is lenient. Apparently, even in cases of Torah law in which the result would be a leniency, i.e., exemption from the death penalty for murder, the legal status of any item fixed in its place is like that of an uncertainty that is equally balanced.

אִיתְּמַר רַב חִיָּיא בַּר אַשִׁי אָמַר רַב: הֲלָכָה כְּרַבִּי יוֹסֵי, וְרַב חָנָן בַּר רָבָא אָמַר רַב: הוֹרָאַת שָׁעָה הָיְתָה.

§ With regard to the matter of following the majority in cases of lineage, it **was stated** that there is an amoraic dispute: **Rav Ḥiyya bar Ashi** said that **Rav said: The** ***halakha*** **is in accordance with** the opinion of **Rabbi Yosei** in the mishna, and it is permitted for the young girl who was raped to marry a priest. **And Rav Ḥanan bar Rava** said that **Rav said:** That **was a provisional edict**[N] issued in exigent circumstances. However, typically, with regard to matters of lineage two majorities are required.

מְתִיב רַבִּי יִרְמְיָה: וּלְיוּחֲסִין לָא בָּעֵינַן תְּרֵי רוּבֵּי? וְהָתְנַן:

Rav Yirmeya raised an objection to the ruling of Rav Ḥiyya bar Ashi, who apparently ruled that even in cases where there is one majority the *halakha* is in accordance with the opinion of Rabbi Yosei: **And in matters of lineage, do we not require two majorities,** a majority of the city's inhabitants and a majority of the passing contingent? **But didn't we learn** in a mishna (*Makhshirin* 2:7):

HALAKHA

Only in a case where he intends to kill him – עַד שֶׁיִּתְכַּוֵּין לוֹ: One who intended to kill one person but killed another is exempt from court-imposed execution, from payment, and from exile. Therefore, one who throws a stone into a crowd and kills one of those present is exempt, even if the crowd consisted only of Jews.

The Ra'avad wonders why the Rambam ruled in accordance with the opinion of Rabbi Shimon, which is an individual opinion. Some explain that the ruling of the Rambam is not in accordance with the opinion of Rabbi Shimon. Rather, it is in accordance with the opinion of the Sages of the school of Ḥizkiyya (38a), as the discourse in the Gemara is according to his opinion (*Migdal Oz*; *Kesef Mishne*). The second explanation in the *Kesef Mishne* says that the Rambam holds in accordance with the opinion of the Rabbis, and the reason the murderer is exempt is due to the lack of forewarning (Rambam *Sefer Nezikin, Hilkhot Rotze'aḥ UShmirat HaNefesh* 4:1).

NOTES

Only in a case where he intends to kill him – עַד שֶׁיִּתְכַּוֵּין לוֹ: According to Rabbi Shimon, one is liable to be executed for murder only if he intended to murder a specific individual. This is consistent with Rabbi Shimon's opinion in many areas of *halakha*; an action is significant only if the result reflects the perpetrator's specific intent. Even according to the opinion of the Rabbis, who hold that one can be liable even if the action does not reflect his specific intent, the question is raised: How can the murderer be executed? Even if he was forewarned, wasn't the forewarning an uncertain forewarning, which is ineffective? The commentaries answer: Since it is possible to forewarn the murderer with regard to both individuals present, it is no longer considered an uncertain forewarning (*Shita Mekubbetzet*).

That was a provisional edict – הוֹרָאַת שָׁעָה הָיְתָה: The simple understanding is that the provisional edict was to be lenient; the Sages issued the edict due to reasons for leniency that existed at that time (see Rashi). However, early commentaries commented that the term provisional edict could be understood in various ways. Some explained that the edict was to be stringent and require two majorities (see *Shita Mekubbetzet*).

מָצָא בָּהּ תִּינוֹק מוּשְׁלָךְ, אִם רוֹב גּוֹיִם – גּוֹי, אִם רוֹב יִשְׂרָאֵל – יִשְׂרָאֵל, מֶחֱצָה עַל מֶחֱצָה – יִשְׂרָאֵל.

If there is a city in which both Jews and gentiles reside, and **one found** an unidentified, **abandoned baby in** the city,[N] **if** there is a **majority of gentiles** in the city the baby is deemed **a gentile;** **if** there is a **majority of Jews** in the city the baby is deemed **a Jew. If half** the population is gentile and **half** Jewish, the baby is deemed **a Jew.**

וְאָמַר רַב: לֹא שָׁנוּ אֶלָּא לְהַחֲיוֹתוֹ, אֲבָל לְיוֹחֲסִין – לֹא, וּשְׁמוּאֵל אָמַר: לְפַקֵּחַ עָלָיו אֶת הַגַּל!

And Rav said with regard to this mishna: The Sages **taught** that if there is a majority of Jews in the city the baby is deemed a Jew **only** with regard **to sustaining him;**[NH] **however,** with regard **to lineage,** e.g., marrying him to a Jewish woman, **no,** he is not deemed a Jew based on the majority and would require conversion. **And Shmuel said:** It was taught that he is deemed a Jew in order **to create an opening** in **a heap** of debris **on his** behalf on Shabbat, i.e., desecrating Shabbat in order to save his life. Apparently, contrary to the ruling of Rav Ḥiyya bar Ashi, Rav holds that a single majority is insufficient to deem him Jewish in matters of lineage.

אִשְׁתַּמִּיטְתֵּיהּ הָא דַּאֲמַר רַב יְהוּדָה אָמַר רַב: בִּקְרוֹנוֹת שֶׁל צִפּוֹרִי הֲוָה מַעֲשֶׂה.

The Gemara answers: Rav Yirmeya **overlooked that which Rav Yehuda said** that **Rav said** with regard to the mishna: The **incident** of the rape of the young girl transpired **among the wagons** in the marketplace **of Tzippori,** and there were two majorities; the majority of the inhabitants of the city and the majority of the passing contingent. Therefore, when Rav Ḥiyya bar Ashi ruled that the *halakha* is in accordance with the opinion of Rabbi Yosei, i.e., that the young girl may marry a priest, it was in a case of two majorities.

וּלְרַב חָנָן בַּר רָבָא דַּאֲמַר: הוֹרָאַת שָׁעָה הָיְתָה, קַשְׁיָא. הָא! מַאן דְּמַתְנֵי הָא לָא מַתְנֵי הָא.

The Gemara asks: **And** if the case in the mishna is one of two majorities, according **to Rav Ḥanan bar Rava who said** in the name of Rav: **That was a provisional edict** issued in exigent circumstances, meaning that two majorities were required in that case but typically one majority is sufficient, it is **difficult.** Didn't Rav say that in matters of lineage one majority is insufficient? The Gemara answers: **That** is not difficult. **The one who teaches this,** that the ruling in our mishna was a provisional edict, **does not teach that**[N] statement that Rav Yehuda said that Rav said that the incident took place among the wagons in the marketplace of Tzippori. Rather, he holds that there was a single majority and nevertheless, due to exigent circumstances, the girl was permitted to marry into the priesthood, although generally two majorities are required in cases of lineage.

גּוּפָא, מָצָא בָּהּ תִּינוֹק מוּשְׁלָךְ, אִם רוֹב גּוֹיִם – גּוֹי, אִם רוֹב יִשְׂרָאֵל – יִשְׂרָאֵל, מֶחֱצָה עַל מֶחֱצָה – יִשְׂרָאֵל, אָמַר רַב: לֹא שָׁנוּ אֶלָּא לְהַחֲיוֹתוֹ, אֲבָל לְיוֹחֲסִין – לֹא, וּשְׁמוּאֵל אָמַר: לְפַקֵּחַ עָלָיו אֶת הַגַּל.

§ Apropos the case of the abandoned baby, the Gemara analyzes the matter **itself:** If there is a city in which both Jews and gentiles reside, and **one found** an unidentified, **abandoned baby in** the city, **if** there is a **majority of gentiles** in the city the baby is deemed **a gentile. If** there is a **majority of Jews** in the city the baby is deemed **a Jew.** If **half** the population is gentile and **half** Jewish, the baby is deemed **a Jew. Rav said:** The Sages **taught** that the baby is deemed a Jew **only** with regard **to sustaining him; however,** with regard **to lineage, no.**[H] **And Shmuel said:** It was taught that he is deemed a Jew in order **to create an opening** in **a heap** of debris **on his** behalf on Shabbat.

NOTES

One found an unidentified abandoned baby in the city – מָצָא בָּהּ תִּינוֹק מוּשְׁלָךְ: The commentaries ask: Why not resolve the problem by immersing the child for the purpose of conversion? In that way he will grow among the Jews and his legal status will be that of a full-fledged Jew. Several explanations were suggested. According to the opinion that the court converts only a minor who initiates the conversion or who is brought by his parents, in this case conversion is impossible. According to the opinion that the court can initiate conversion, since upon reaching majority the convert can reconsider his conversion, the conversion does not solve the problem (*Shita Mekubbetzet*).

To sustaining him – לְהַחֲיוֹתוֹ: Although it is possible to explain that the term: To sustaining him [*lehaḥayoto*], means saving his life according to Rav, who agrees with Shmuel, the language and context indicate that this was not his intention. Based on this understanding, there is a novel element in Rav's opinion that a Jew is required not merely to save his life but even to tend to his daily needs. There is a novel element in the opinion of Shmuel as well: One may save his life even if it involves desecrating Shabbat.

The one who teaches this does not teach that – מַאן דְּמַתְנֵי הָא לָא מַתְנֵי הָא: Rabbeinu Ḥananel and Rabbi Zeraḥya HaLevi explain: That which Rav Ḥanan does not teach is the segment of Rav's statement: However, with regard to lineage, no. Most of the early commentaries reject that explanation (*Tosafot*; Ramban; Rashba). Most commentaries agree with Rashi, who explains that Rav Ḥanan does not teach the statement cited in the name of Rav that the incident transpired among the wagons of Tzippori. Although that explanation is somewhat problematic as well, as it is difficult to say that their dispute is with regard to the details of an incident that transpired, most early commentaries accept it.

The Ramban in *Milḥamot Hashem* cites a third approach: This *halakha* was not taught in reference to the case of an abandoned baby that was found. Rather, a question was raised from the statement of Rav Yehuda in the name of Rav, who requires two majorities, on the statement of Rav Ḥanan. The Gemara answers that there are two traditions cited in the name of Rav. Early commentaries noted that the expression: The one who teaches this does not teach that, is not typically employed to describe a dispute between two opinions. Rather, it is employed to describe two statements that are redundant or inconsistent in their formulation.

HALAKHA

To sustaining him – לְהַחֲיוֹתוֹ: The legal status of an abandoned baby found in a city with a Jewish majority is that of a Jew in terms of sustaining him. Likewise, if half the population is Jewish and half is gentile, there is a mitzva to sustain the baby (Rambam). The Rema writes that there are those who say that there is a mitzva to sustain him only if there is a Jewish majority (Rashi; *Tosafot*). The dispute is whether Rav's statement in the Gemara addresses the first *halakha* cited in the mishna or the second one (Vilna Gaon; Rambam *Sefer Kedusha, Hilkhot Issurei Bia* 15:26; *Shulḥan Arukh, Even HaEzer* 4:34).

However, with regard to lineage, no – אֲבָל לְיוֹחֲסִין לֹא: The legal status of an abandoned baby found in a city with a population of Jews and gentiles, even if there is a Jewish majority, is that of a gentile whose status is uncertain with regard to his lineage. If, after reaching majority, he betrothed a Jewish woman, if he seeks to divorce her he may do so only by giving her a bill of divorce due to that uncertainty, in accordance with the statement of Rav. If he was immersed and converted by the court, or if he himself converted, when he reaches majority his legal status is that of a foundling, and his conversion is effective only in the sense that he is no longer considered a gentile (Rambam *Sefer Kedusha, Hilkhot Issurei Bia* 15:25–26; *Shulḥan Arukh, Even HaEzer* 4:33).

ומִי אֲמַר שְׁמוּאֵל הָכִי? וְהָאָמַר רַב יוֹסֵף אָמַר רַב יְהוּדָה אָמַר שְׁמוּאֵל: אֵין הוֹלְכִין בְּפִיקּוּחַ נֶפֶשׁ אַחַר הָרוֹב! אֶלָּא, כִּי אִיתְּמַר דִּשְׁמוּאֵל – אַרֵישָׁא אִתְּמַר: אִם רוֹב גּוֹיִם – גּוֹי, אָמַר שְׁמוּאֵל: וּלְפַקֵּחַ עָלָיו אֶת הַגַּל – אֵינוֹ כֵּן.

The Gemara asks: **And did Shmuel say that? But didn't Rav Yosef say that Rav Yehuda said that Shmuel said: One does not follow the majority in matters** involving **saving a life?**[N] Even if there is the slightest concern that the life of a Jew may be in danger, one takes all steps necessary to save him, even on Shabbat. **Rather, when the statement of Shmuel was stated** with regard to saving a life **it was stated concerning the first clause** of the mishna: **If** there is a **majority of gentiles**[N] in the city the baby is deemed **a gentile. Shmuel said: And** with regard **to creating an opening in a heap** of debris **on his** behalf [*lefake'aḥ alav et hagal*][HN] on Shabbat, **that is not so.** Even if there is a gentile majority in the city, one does not follow the majority in cases involving the saving of a life.

"אִם רוֹב גּוֹיִם – גּוֹי". לְמַאי הִלְכְתָא? אָמַר רַב פַּפָּא: לְהַאֲכִילוֹ נְבֵילוֹת.

The mishna continues: **If** there is a **majority of gentiles** the baby is deemed **a gentile.** The Gemara asks: With regard **to what *halakha*** was this stated? **Rav Pappa said:** It was stated in order **to feed** the baby **animal carcasses,**[H] i.e., non-kosher food.

"אִם רוֹב יִשְׂרָאֵל – יִשְׂרָאֵל, לְמַאי הִלְכְתָא? אָמַר רַב פַּפָּא: לְהַחֲזִיר לוֹ אֲבֵידָה.

And it is taught in the mishna: **If** there is a **majority of Jews** the baby is deemed **a Jew.** The Gemara asks: With regard **to what *halakha*** was this stated?[N] **Rav Pappa said:** It was stated in order **to return lost property to him,**[HN] as one is required to return lost property to a Jew.

HALAKHA

To create an opening in a heap of debris on his behalf – לְפַקֵּחַ עָלָיו אֶת הַגַּל: One may create an opening in a heap of debris on Shabbat on behalf of an abandoned baby found in a city in which half the population is Jewish and half is gentile. However, if there is a gentile majority in the city one may not desecrate Shabbat on his behalf. This is the ruling of the Rambam, who holds that Rav and Shmuel disagree about this matter, and the ruling in disputes between Rav and Shmuel is in accordance with the opinion of Rav in ritual matters.

The Rambam, in his responsa to the Sages of Lunel, cites proof from the related discourse in tractate *Yoma* (84b–85a). The Rema cites the opinion of the *Tur* based on the Ramban and the Rashba, which agrees with the opinions of Rashi and *Tosafot*, that even in a city with a gentile majority one may create an opening in a heap of debris on Shabbat on behalf of an abandoned baby that was found. This is because they hold that Rav and Shmuel did not disagree about this matter (Vilna Gaon; Rambam *Sefer Kedusha, Hilkhot Issurei Bia* 15:26 and *Sefer Zemanim, Hilkhot Shabbat* 2:21; *Shulḥan Arukh, Even HaEzer* 4:34).

To feed the baby animal carcasses – לְהַאֲכִילוֹ נְבֵילוֹת: The legal status of an abandoned baby found in a city with a gentile majority is that of a gentile, and one may feed him foods forbidden to Jews, in accordance with the opinion of Rav Pappa (Rambam *Sefer Kedusha, Hilkhot Issurei Bia* 15:26; *Shulḥan Arukh, Even HaEzer* 4:34).

To return lost property to him – לְהַחֲזִיר לוֹ אֲבֵידָה: The legal status of an abandoned baby found in a city with a Jewish majority is that of a Jew, and one who found lost objects belonging to him returns them to him, in accordance with the opinion of Rav Pappa (Rambam *Sefer Kedusha, Hilkhot Issurei Bia* 15:26; *Shulḥan Arukh, Even HaEzer* 4:34).

NOTES

One does not follow the majority in matters involving saving a life – אֵין הוֹלְכִין בְּפִיקּוּחַ נֶפֶשׁ אַחַר הָרוֹב: The reason that one does not follow a majority in that case is that once the Gemara interpreted the verse: "And he shall live by them" (Leviticus 18:5) and not that he shall die by them, it means that under no circumstances may he be allowed to die. Therefore, in every case of uncertainty with regard to saving a life, whether due to the situation or due to the identity of the person in danger, one must take the minority into consideration and may not act on the basis of the majority (*Tosafot Yeshanim*; Rosh).

If there is a majority of gentiles – אִם רוֹב גּוֹיִם: Some explain that this question is posed specifically according to the opinion of Shmuel, as it is possible to say that Rav disagrees with Shmuel and holds that in a case where there is a gentile majority one does not rescue the person from beneath the debris (Ramban). Others disagree, as they maintain that Rav and Shmuel do not disagree with regard to that matter.

To create an opening in a heap of debris on his behalf [*lefake'aḥ alav et hagal*] – לְפַקֵּחַ עָלָיו אֶת הַגַּל: The root *peh, kuf, ḥet* in this context is employed in the manner that it is employed throughout the Talmud, in the sense of observation or examination. It refers to opening one's eyes in order to ascertain whether the person under the debris remains alive and to extract him from beneath it. Some explain that it refers not to opening one's eyes but to creating an opening in the heap to release the person who is trapped.

If there is a majority of Jews…with regard to what *halakha* was this stated – אִם רוֹב יִשְׂרָאֵל...לְמַאי הִלְכְתָא: Here too, some explain that this question is posed specifically according to the opinion of Shmuel, who holds that even if there is a gentile majority one rescues the person from beneath the debris (*Shita Mekubbetzet*). Others explain that this question is based on the previous question: If you say that the *halakha* is not in accordance with the opinion of Rav, what is the difference between a situation where the population is half Jewish and half gentile, and a Jewish majority?

To return lost property to him – לְהַחֲזִיר לוֹ אֲבֵידָה: The commentaries ask: Why is the case of lost property different from the case of damages? The person who found the lost object should say to a person with regard to whom there is uncertainty whether or not he is a Jew who is seeking to recover the lost object: Prove that you are a Jew and take your object. Although there is a Jewish majority, it is not effective in removing property from the hands of the person possessing it.

They answer that there is a distinction between damages and a lost object. In the case of damages, the victim is seeking to receive damages from money that is clearly in the possession of the one who caused the damage. In that case the principle is: The burden of proof is incumbent upon the claimant. However, concerning a lost object, it is not considered completely in the possession of the one who found it, and therefore the majority is effective in facilitating recovery of the object (Ramban; Rashba).

Some later commentaries explain that although in a standard case of one seeking to exact payment from another, possession of the property is the determining factor, in the case of recovery of a lost object, since there is a mitzva to return it, the fact that the object is in one's possession does not supersede the mitzva to return it. See *Tosafot*, where this matter is discussed from a different perspective.

"מֶחֱצָה עַל מֶחֱצָה – יִשְׂרָאֵל" לְמַאי הִלְכְתָא? אָמַר רֵישׁ לָקִישׁ: לִנְזָקִין. הֵיכִי דָמֵי? אִי נֵימָא דִּנְגַחֵיהּ תּוֹרָא דִידַן לְתוֹרָא דִידֵיהּ – לֵימָא לֵיהּ: אַיְיתִי רְאָיָה דְּיִשְׂרָאֵל אַתְּ וּשְׁקוֹל!

And it is taught in the mishna: If **half** the population is gentile and **half** Jewish, the baby is deemed **a Jew.** The Gemara asks: With regard **to what *halakha*** was this stated? **Reish Lakish said:** It was stated with regard **to damages.**[H] In terms of payment of damages, the courts judge him as a Jew. The Gemara asks: **What are the circumstances? If we say that our ox,** one belonging to a Jew, **gored his ox,** one belonging to a person of uncertain status, and he claims that he should be compensated for the damages as a Jew, **let the** owner of the ox that gored **say to him: Bring proof that you are a Jew, and take** payment. Due to the uncertainty surrounding his status, he is unable to produce any proof.

לָא צְרִיכָא, דִּנְגַחֵיהּ תּוֹרָא דִידֵיהּ לְתוֹרָא דִידַן. פַּלְגָא – מְשַׁלֵּם, וְאִידָךְ פַּלְגָא – אָמַר לְהוּ: אַיְיתוּ רְאָיָה דְּלָאו יִשְׂרָאֵל אֲנָא, וְאֶתֵּן לְכוֹן.

Rather, this *halakha* is **necessary only** in a case **where his ox gored our ox,** one belonging to a Jew. In that case, there is no question that **he pays half** the damage, which is the payment when an innocuous ox belonging to a Jew gores an ox belonging to a Jew. **And** with regard to **the other half,** which the owner of the gored ox is claiming, asserting that this person of uncertain status is a gentile and therefore liable to pay full damages, the owner of the ox that gored can **say to** the claimants:[N] **Bring proof that I am not a Jew and I will give you** payment of the other half of the damages. It is with regard to that case that Reish Lakish ruled that in a case of uncertainty, the baby has the presumptive status of a Jew, and it is incumbent upon the claimant to prove otherwise.

הדרן עלך בתולה נשאת

HALAKHA

With regard to damages – לִנְזָקִין: In a case where one caused damage to a person who was an abandoned baby found in a city in which half the population is Jewish and half is gentile, or even in a city with a Jewish majority, it is a standard case of uncertainty with regard to monetary matters and the burden of proof is incumbent upon the claimant. If his innocuous ox gored the ox of a full-fledged Jew, he pays half the damage. If the Jew wishes to collect the other half he must bring proof that the owner of the ox is a gentile. If the innocuous ox of a Jew gores his ox, the Jew need not pay him damages, because the owner of the gored ox cannot prove that he is a Jew (Rambam *Sefer Kedusha, Hilkhot Issurei Bia* 15:26; *Tur, Even HaEzer* 4:34).

NOTES

And with regard to the other half, he can say to the claimants – וְאִידָךְ פַּלְגָא אָמַר לְהוּ: The question is raised: Isn't this a case of partial admission in response to a claim, where one is obligated to take an oath on the portion of the claim that he denies? Based on the principle: One who is obligated to take an oath and is unable to take that oath is required to pay, since he is unable to take the oath because there is uncertainty whether he is Jewish, he should be obligated to pay. However, this is not a problem according to the opinion that this principle applies only in a case where there is a reasonable expectation that he could have known what happened but refuses to take an oath; here, therefore, since there is no way to ascertain whether he is a Jew or a gentile he is not required to pay. Even according to those who say that one is required to pay even if he did not take the oath because there is no way for him to know what happened, here he is not required to take an oath at all, as both the claim of the claimant and the claim of the respondent are uncertain (Ritva; *Shita Mekubbetzet*).

Summary of **Perek I**

The Sages designated certain days for marriage because they were assiduous in seeing to the well-being of Jewish women and ensuring that the wedding feast be appropriately elaborate. They also valued the integrity of marriage by scheduling the wedding on a day that would not delay a husband from bringing to court a claim, if he suspected his bride was forbidden to him. Throughout later generations as well, when a wedding could take place any day of the week, including Friday, one must take those two ordinances into account. It is possible to have a wedding on Friday due to the halakhic ruling that it is permitted to engage in intercourse with a virgin on Shabbat. Since there is sanctity and blessing in the wedding celebration, the Sages instituted six special blessings recited whenever and wherever there is a wedding celebration.

With regard to the definition of a virgin in the context of a marriage contract, the Sages determined that a woman who never married and whose hymen is intact is a virgin. The legal status of a woman who married but did not engage in intercourse, or that of a woman whose hymen was ruptured by wood, even though she never engaged in intercourse, is that of a non-virgin. The presumptive status of an unmarried woman with regard to whom there is no information to the contrary is that of a virgin, unless she converted, was liberated from slavery, or was redeemed from captivity after reaching the age of three.

The Gemara concluded that a husband who claims that his bride was not a virgin is deemed credible unless the bride is in possession of proof that his claim is false. However, when there are conflicting claims with regard to the manner in which the bride lost her virginity, with the husband claiming that she engaged in licentious intercourse or that she deceived him and the bride claiming that the circumstances were different, the bride is deemed credible as long as the husband can bring no proof to support his claim.

Just as one relies on the credibility of the bride in this case, so too one relies on her credibility with regard to lineage when she claims that she engaged in intercourse with a man who does not disqualify her from marrying into the priesthood. Likewise, one relies on her credibility to establish the unflawed lineage of an offspring that she conceived while single. The Sages imposed strictures with regard to the *halakhot* of lineage, especially when the woman is unable to identify the father of her unborn child. In order to establish the unflawed lineage of both mother and child, a double majority is required, i.e., a majority of people with unflawed lineage in the place where she engaged in intercourse and a majority of people with unflawed lineage in the place where she originated.

Image **Credits**

p21 1st image © Magnus Manske; **p21** 2nd image © acquired by Henry Walters, 1914; **p22** © Galyn Wiemers; **p32** top left image © andrewgabrielrose; **p32** bottom left image © Chmee2; **p79** © Ori~.

My Notes

My Notes

My Notes

My Notes

My Notes

My Notes

תלמוד בבלי

— מהדורת נאה —

כתובות חלק א

Steinsaltz Center

KOREN

Please note that the number ranges that appear at the bottom of each daf of the Vilna pages indicate the corresponding pages of the Koren Talmud Bavli translation and commentary.

תלמוד בבלי

הוצאת קורן ירושלים

מהדורת נאה

מסכת כתובות

דף ב. עד דף טו:

COMMENTARY BY

Rabbi Adin Even-Israel Steinsaltz

EDITOR-IN-CHIEF

Rabbi Dr Tzvi Hersh Weinreb

EXECUTIVE EDITOR

Rabbi Joshua Schreier

•

STEINSALTZ CENTER
KOREN PUBLISHERS JERUSALEM

בתולה

מתני׳ *[א]נשאת ליום הרביעי, ואלמנה ליום החמישי. שפעמים בשבת בתי דינין יושבין בעיירות: ביום השני וביום החמישי, שאם היה לו טענת בתולים היה משכים לבית דין.§ **גמ׳** אמר רב יוסף אמר רב יהודה אמר שמואל: מפני מה אמרו בתולה נשאת ליום הרביעי — לפי ששנינו: *הגיע זמן ולא נישאו — אוכלות משלו, ואוכלות בתרומה. יכול הגיע זמן באחד בשבת יהא מעלה לה מזונות — לכך שנינו: בתולה נשאת ליום הרביעי. אמר רב יוסף: *מריה דאברהם! תלי תניא בדלא תניא. הי תניא והי לא תניא? הא תניא והא תניא! אלא: תלי תניא דמפרש טעמא, בדתניא דלא מפרש טעמא! אלא, אי איתמר הכי איתמר, אמר רב יהודה אמר שמואל: מפני מה אמרו בתולה נשאת ליום הרביעי — שאם היה לו טענת בתולים היה משכים לב"ד. ותינשא באחד בשבת, שאם היה לו טענת בתולים היה משכים לבית דין? *[ב]שקדו חכמים על תקנת בנות ישראל, שיהא טורח בסעודה שלשה ימים: אחד בשבת ושני בשבת ושלישי בשבת, וברביעי כונסה. ועכשו ששנינו "שקדו", אותה ששנינו הגיע זמן ולא נישאו אוכלות משלו ואוכלות בתרומה, [ג]הגיע זמן באחד בשבת, מתוך שאינו יכול לכנוס — אינו מעלה לה מזונות. לפיכך, [ד]חלה הוא, או שחלתה היא, או שפירסה נדה — אינו מעלה לה מזונות. ואיכא דבעי לה מיבעיא: חלה הוא מהו? התם טעמא מאי — משום דאנים, והכא נמי — הא אנים. או דלמא: התם אנים בתקנתא דתקינו ליה רבנן, הכא — לא. ואם תמצי לומר חלה הוא מעלה לה מזונות, חלתה היא מהו? מצי אמר לה: אנא הא קאימנא, או דלמא, מציא אמרה ליה "נסתחפה שדהו"? ואם תמצי לומר אמרה ליה "נסתחפה שדהו", פירסה נדה מהו? בשעת ווסתה — לא תיבעי לך, דלא

רש"י

בתולה נשאת ליום הרביעי. תקנת חכמים היא שתנשא ברביעי בשבת, כדמפרש טעמא. שפעמים בשבת. אבתולה קאי. בשני ובחמישי. אחת מעשר תקנות שתקן עזרא. בבבא קמא בפרק "מרובה" (דף פב.) מפרש לכולהו. ולכך תקנו שתנשא ברביעי, שאם היה לו טענת בתולים — ישכים לב"ד בעוד כעסו עליו. [ואם יש שהות בינתים — יש לחוש] שמא יתפייס ותתקרר דעתו, ויקיימנה. ושמא היא זינתה תחתיו, ונאסרה עליו, כדילפינן (סוטה דף כח.) מ"ונסתרה והיא נטמאה", ומתוך שילך לבית דין — יתברר הדבר כשיצא הקול, שמא יבואו עדים. ובגמרא פריך: ותינשא באחד בשבת! **גמ׳** לפי ששנינו כו׳. לקמן מקשי עלה. הגיע זמן ולא נישאו. לקמן בפרק "אף על פי" תנן: נותנין לבתולה שנים עשר חדש משתבעה הבעל והזהיר על הנישואין, לפרנס עצמה בתכשיטין. לפרנס = קנדיר"ר בלע"ז. ולאלמנה שלשים יום. הגיע זמן. זה ולא נישאו לחופה, לקמן מפרש שעכב הבעל. **אוכלות משלו.** שהבעל חייב במזונות אשתו מתקנת ב"ד, כדלקמן בפרק "נערה" (דף מו:). **ואוכלות בתרומה.** אם כהן הוא והיא בת ישראל. שהכהן מאכיל את אשתו תרומה, כדיליף (לקמן דף נז:) מ"וכהן כי יקנה נפש". לכך שנינו בתולה נשאת כו׳. להודיע שתקנת חכמים מעכבתו מלכנוס, ואין עכבה זו שלו. מריה דאברהם כו׳. תמה על דברי רבו, ואמר: מריה דאברהם! מה זה היה לשמואל לומר כן? ועוד, שחלה רב יוסף ושכח תלמודו, ותוהה על דבריו הראשונים. תלי תניא בדלא תניא. תולה טעם משנה שנויה במשנה שאינה שנויה: ומקשינן לרב יוסף. הי תניא והי לא תניא? הא תניא והא תניא. זו שנויה וזו שנויה. **אלא** תלי תניא דמפרש טעמא בדתניא דלא מפרש טעמא. משנתינו טעמא מפורש בתוכה — כדי שישכים לבית דין. והגיע זמן אין שום טעם מפורש בה, לומר מפני מה אם הגיע זמן באחד בשבת אינו מעלה לה מזונות. **ותינשא** באחד בשבת. כולה רב יוסף קאמר לה. ועכשיו ששנינו שקדו. ובשביל תקנה זו הוא מעוכב מלכנוס באחד בשבת, מעתה אותה ששנינו כו׳. לפיכך. רב יוסף מסיים לה משמיה דנפשיה ומסבריה, ואמר: לפיכך, הואיל ולמדנו שהמעוכב מחמת אונס אינו חייב לזונה — חלה הוא כו׳. **הא קאימנא.** הנני מזומן. נסתחפה שדהו. לשון "מטר סוחף" (משלי כח) נשטפה שדך, כלומר: מזלך גרם, כי מהיום אני מוטלת עליך לזון. פשיט

תוספות

בתולה · הא דלא קתני "הבתולה" כדתני "האשה נקנית", "היבמה ניקנית" (קדושין דף ב.) — משום דהתם אקרא קאי "כי יקח איש אשה" (דברים כב) — האשה הכתובה, וכן היבמה, אבל הכא — לא קאי אקרא. והא דלא תנן בפ"ק דקידושין (דף יד:) "העבד עברי" אף על פי דכתיב בקרא (שמות כא) "כי תקנה עבד עברי" — משום דא"כ ה"ל למתני "העבד העברי", שאינו דבוק, ואין דרך התלמוד לדבר כן. ומיהו, גבי איש ואשה רגילים בכל מקום לשנות בה׳ אע"ג דלא קאי אקרא כמו "האשה שהלכה" (יבמות דף קיד:) "האשה שנתארמלה" (לקמן דף טו:) "האיש מדיר את בנו בנזיר" (נזיר ד׳ כח:). **נשאת** · הא דלא קתני "נושאין את הבתולה" כמו "האיש מקדש" (קדושין דף מא.) — לפי שעתה מקצר יותר. ועוד: דאי תנא הכי ה"א אפי׳ בעל כרחה, כדמשני (שם דף ב:) גבי הא דפריך וליתני "האיש קונה". ועוד, דהתם אקרא קאי כי יקח איש אשה". **ליום** הרביעי. ולא בליל חמישי, כדאמר בפרק בתרא דנדה (דף סה:) *דליכא כתובה דלא רמו בה תיגרא. כ"ש אם יעשה נשואין בליל ה׳, דאיכא למיחש שיטרד בנשואין וכתובה ולא יבעול. **שאם** היה לו טענת וכו׳. ואם תאמר: הא תינח אשת כהן או פחותה מבת שלש דליכא אלא חד ספיקא, כדאמרינן בגמרא (לקמן ט.) אבל בשאר נשים, דאיכא ספק ספיקא — אמאי תנשא ליום ד׳? ואומר ר"ת: דלא פלוג רבנן בתקנתא, ומשום אשת כהן ופחותה מג׳ תקנו בכל הנשים שינשאו ביום ד׳. ובקונטרס פי׳: שמתוך כך יתברר הדבר ויבואו עדים שזינתה ברצון. וקשה לפירושו, דאמרינן בגמרא (שם:) אמר אביי אף אנן נמי תנינא, דהאומר פתח פתוח מצאתי נאמן לאוסרה עליו: בתולה נשאת כו׳, מאי לאו דקטעין פתח פתוח? והשתא היכי מייתי ראיה לפ"ה? הא אע"ג דאינו נאמן — מכל מקום ישכים לבית דין, שמתוך כך יצא הקול ויבואו עדים ויתברר הדבר? וי"ל: דלא מייתי אביי ראיה לרבי אלעזר אלא שהוא בקי ומכיר אם הוא פתח פתוח, דאם אינו בקי — לא יצא הקול, ולא יבא לידי בירור, כי יאמרו שהוא טעה וסבור שמצא פתח פתוח ואינו כן, ולא יחושו לדבריו. ועי"ל: דגם לפ"ה לא היו מתקנים שתהא ניסת ליום ד׳ משום שמא יתברר על ידי עדים, אבל כיון דבאשת כהן ובפחותה מבת שלש, דנאמן לאוסרה עליו, תקנו שתהא ניסת ברביעי — גם בשאר נשים תקנו, משום שמתוך כך יצא הקול ויתברר הדבר על ידי עדים. והשתא מייתי אביי שפיר ממתניתין דבאשת כהן ובפחותה מבת שלש נאמן לאוסרה עליו. ותימה: דהכא משמע דמשום חששא דזנות תקנו שתהא ניסת ברביעי, ובפ"ב דגטין (דף יז. ושם) איכא מ"ד דתקנו זמן בגטין משום פירי, אבל משום שמא יחפה על בת אחותו לא חיישינן, משום דזנות לא שכיח? וי"ל: דהתם קאמר זנות דאתי לידי מיתה, דהיינו בהתראה ובעדים, לא שכיח. אי נמי: הכא שלא תשב עמו באיסור כל ימיו — חשו אפילו לזנות, אע"ג דלא שכיח. **מפני** מה אמרו בתולה נשאת ליום הרביעי לפי ששנינו כו׳. אין שואל הטעם למה נשאת ברביעי, דאם כן לא הוה משני מידי. אלא הכי פירושו: "מפני מה אמרו" כלומר, מאי נפקא מינה שתיקנו שנשאת ברביעי? ומשני: נפקא מינה לענין מזונות ותרומה. ורב יוסף קא מתמה "מריה דאברהם", דהא נפקותא מפרשה בהדיא "שאם היה לו טענת בתולים", והוא מניח נפקותא זו המפורשת ותופס נפקותא אחרינא. **אלא** אי אתמר הכי אתמר א"ר יהודה אמר שמואל. ולא גרסינן רב יוסף, דהא רב יוסף גופיה קאמר: אלא אי איתמר. **מפני** מה אמרו כו׳. בניחותא גרסינן לה, ולא בא להקשות אלא "ותנשא באחד בשבת". **ותנשא** באחד בשבת. לא בעי לשנויי דנשאת ברביעי כדי שתבעל בחמישי משום ברכה שנאמרה בו לדגים, כדאמרינן לקמן (דף ה.)! ועוד: למה לי טעם דשקדו? תיפוק ליה משום ברכה! ואומר ר"י: דטעם דברכה אינה אלא עצה טובה, ולא מקרי עבריינא. אבל משום שקדו — מקרי עבריינא. וכן משמע לקמן דאמר טעמא משום ברכה. אבל משום איקרורי דעתא — לא חיישינן, ומאי נפקא מינה? אלא ודאי דמשום ברכה לא מקרי עבריינא.

מליא [?]

עין משפט נר מצוה

א א ב מיי׳ פ"י מהל׳ אישות הל׳ טו סמג עשין מח טוש"ע אה"ע סימן סד סעי׳ ג:

ב ג ד מיי׳ שם הלכה יט וסמג שם טוש"ע שם סי׳ נו סעי׳ ג:

[הך דליכא כתובה וכו׳ ליתא בנדה אך בשבת קל. ונראה כוונת התוס׳ במ"ש כדאמר בפ׳ בתרא דנדה סה: ר"ל שאמרו שם שאני כתובה דמגהי בה טפי ע׳ רש"י וערוך שם והא דכתבו דליכא כתובה הוא טעס בפ"ע]

תוספות רי"ד

בתולה נשאת ביום ד׳ ואלמנה ביום ה׳ שפעמים בשבת ב"ד יושבין בעיירות ביום ב׳ וביום ה׳ ואם היה לו טענת בתולים היה משכים לב"ד. פי׳ חכמים תקנו שתנשא הבתולה בד׳ כדי שיבעול בליל ה׳ ואם לא ימצא לה בתולים ילך בבוקר לב"ד טרם שיתקרר דעתו שיפיים עמה ויחקרו ב"ד מתי זינתה שמא תחתיו זינתה והיא אסורה לו. שפעמים בשבת וכו׳. פי׳ אבתולה יהיב טעמא וטעמא דאלמנה מפרש לקמן. ותקנות עזרא הוא שישבו ב"ד בעיירות בב׳ ובה׳. כדאמרינן בפ׳ מרובה מי׳ תקנות שתיקן עזרא. ואע"פ שבכל עיר ועיר היתה סנהדרין קבוע. בכל ימות השבוע היו עוסקים בתורה ובב׳ ובה׳ עוסקים בדינים. ולקמן פריך ותנשא באחד בשבת: אמר ר"י מפני מה אמרו בתולה נשאת בד׳ שאם היה לו טענת בתולים היה משכים לב"ד. ותנשא בא׳ בשבת ואם היה לו טענת בתולים היה משכים לב"ד שקדו חכמים על תקנות בנות ישראל שיהא טורח ג׳ ימים בסעודה א׳ בשבת שני ושלישי וברביעי כונסה. ועכשיו ששנינו שקדו. אותה ששנינו לקמן בפ׳ אע"פ נותנים לבתולה י"ב חודש משתבעה הבעל לפרנס א"ע. כשם שנותנים לאשה כך נותנים לאיש לפרנס א"ע ולאלמנה ל׳ יום הגיע זמן ולא נשאו אוכלות משלו. פי׳ וכגון שהבעל מעכב הגיע זמן בא׳ בשבת מתוך שאינו יכול לכונסה אינו מעלה לה מזונות לפיכך חלה הוא או שחלתה היא או שפירסה נדה אינו מעלה לה מזונות. א"ר שמואל בר רב יצחק ל"ש אלא מתקנות עזרא ואילך שאין ב"ד יושבין אלא בב׳ ובה׳. אבל אי איכא ב"ד קבועים בכל יום כקודם תקנות עזרא אשה נשאת בכל יום והא בעינן שקדו דטריח לה. והכי אסיק רב אחא דכל אונסא לא אכלה בין חלתה היא ובין חלה הוא. והכי הילכתא:

נ"י כ"י

לקמן ט:

לקמן מח. נז. ע: [נדרים עג:]

ב"ב קלו: שבת כג. [עירובין עה:]

לקמן ג. ה.

דְּלָא מָצְיָא אָמְרָה לֵיהּ "נִסְתַּחֲפָה שָׂדֵהוּ". כִּי תִּיבָּעֵי לָךְ — שֶׁלֹּא בִּשְׁעַת וְוסְתָּהּ מַאי? כֵּיוָן דְּלָא בִּשְׁעַת וְוסְתָּהּ הֲוַיָא — מָצְיָא אָמְרָה לֵיהּ "נִסְתַּחֲפָה שָׂדֵהוּ", אוֹ דִּלְמָא, כֵּיוָן דְּאִיכָּא נָשֵׁי דְּקָא מְשַׁנְּיָא וְוסְתַּיְיהוּ, כִּשְׁעַת וְוסְתָּהּ דָּמֵי? פָּשֵׁיט רַב אַחַאי: הִגִּיעַ זְמַן וְלֹא נִישְּׂאוּ אוֹכְלוֹת מִשֶּׁלּוֹ וְאוֹכְלוֹת בִּתְרוּמָה. "לֹא נָשְׂאוּ" לָא קָתָנֵי, אֶלָּא "לֹא נִישְּׂאוּ", הֵיכִי דָּמֵי, אִי דְּקָא מְעַכְּבָן אִינְהִי — אַמַּאי אוֹכְלוֹת מִשֶּׁלּוֹ וְאוֹכְלוֹת בִּתְרוּמָה? אֶלָּא לָאו דְּאִיתְנִיס כִּי הַאי גַּוְונָא, וְקָתָנֵי: אוֹכְלוֹת מִשֶּׁלּוֹ וְאוֹכְלוֹת בִּתְרוּמָה! אָמַר רַב אַשִׁי: לְעוֹלָם אֵימָא לָךְ: כָּל אוֹנְסָא לָא אָכְלָה, וְדְקָא מְעַכְּבֵי אִינְהוּ, וּבְדִין הוּא דְּאִיבָּעֵי לֵיהּ לְמִיתְנֵי "לֹא נָשְׂאוּ", וְאַיְּידֵי דִּתְנָא רֵישָׁא בְּדִידְהִי תְּנָא נַמִי סֵיפָא בְּדִידְהִי.§ אָמַר רָבָא: וּלְעִנְיַן גִּיטִּין אֵינוֹ כֵּן. [א]אַלְמָא קָסָבַר רָבָא: *אֵין אוֹנֶס בְּגִיטִּין. מְנָא לֵיהּ לְרָבָא הָא? אִילֵימָא מֵהָא דִּתְנַן: *[ב]"הֲרֵי זֶה גִּיטֵּיךְ אִם לֹא בָּאתִי מִכָּאן וְעַד שְׁנֵים עָשָׂר חֹדֶשׁ", וּמֵת בְּתוֹךְ שְׁנֵים עָשָׂר חֹדֶשׁ, אֵינוֹ גֵּט. מֵת — הוּא דְּאֵינוֹ גֵּט, הָא חָלָה — הֲרֵי זֶה גֵּט. וְדִלְמָא לְעוֹלָם אֵימָא לָךְ: חָלָה נַמִי אֵינוֹ גֵּט, וְהִיא גּוּפָא קמ"ל: דְּאֵין גֵּט לְאַחַר מִיתָה? אֵין גֵּט לְאַחַר מִיתָה — הָא תְּנָא לֵיהּ רֵישָׁא: [ג]"הֲרֵי זֶה גִּיטֵּיךְ אִם *מַתִּי" "הֲרֵי זֶה גִּיטֵּיךְ מֵחוֹלִי זֶה" "הֲרֵי זֶה גִּיטֵּיךְ לְאַחַר מִיתָה" — לֹא אָמַר כְּלוּם. דִּלְמָא לְאַפּוּקֵי מִדְּרַבּוֹתֵינוּ? דְּתַנְיָא: וְרַבּוֹתֵינוּ הִתִּירוּהָ לְהִנָּשֵׂא, וְאָמְרִינַן: מַאן רַבּוֹתֵינוּ? אָמַר רַב יְהוּדָה אָמַר שְׁמוּאֵל: בֵּי דִינָא דְּשָׁרוּ מִשְׁחָא. סְבִירִי לָהּ כְּרַבִּי יוֹסֵי, דְּאָמַר: זְמַנּוֹ שֶׁל שְׁטָר מוֹכִיחַ עָלָיו. וְאֶלָּא מִסֵּיפָא: *[ד]"מֵעַכְשָׁיו אִם לֹא בָּאתִי מִכָּאן וְעַד י"ב חֹדֶשׁ" וּמֵת בְּתוֹךְ שְׁנֵים עָשָׂר חֹדֶשׁ — הֲרֵי זֶה גֵּט. מֵת — וְהוּא הַדִּין לְחָלָה. דִּלְמָא מֵת דַּוְקָא, דְּלָא נִיחָא לֵיהּ דְּתִפּוֹל קַמֵּי יָבָם! אֶלָּא מֵהָא: *דְּהַהוּא דַּאֲמַר לְהוּ "אִי לָא אָתֵינָא מִיכָּן וְעַד תְּלָתִין יוֹמִין לֶיהֱוֵי גִּיטָּא", אֲתָא בְּסוֹף תְּלָתִין יוֹמִין [ה]וּפְסַקֵיהּ מַבְרָא, אֲמַר לְהוּ: "חֲזוּ דַּאֲתַאי, חֲזוּ דַּאֲתַאי!" אֲמַר שְׁמוּאֵל: לָאו שְׁמֵיהּ מָתְיָא. וְדִלְמָא אוֹנְסָא דִּשְׁכִיחַ שָׁאנֵי, דְּכֵיוָן דְּאִיבָּעֵי לֵיהּ לְאַתְנוּיֵי וְלָא אַתְנֵי — אִיהוּ דְּאַפְסֵיד אַנַּפְשֵׁיהּ! אֶלָּא רָבָא סְבָרָא דְּנַפְשֵׁיהּ קָאָמַר, מִשּׁוּם צְנוּעוֹת וּמִשּׁוּם פְּרוּצוֹת; מִשּׁוּם צְנוּעוֹת, דְּאִי אָמְרַתְּ לָא לֶהֱוֵי גֵּט — זִימְנִין

רש"י

פשיט רב אחאי. הך בעיא ממתניתין, דקתני: לא נישאו, ולא קתני לא נשאו, דלישתמע שהבעלים מעכבים. אלא לא נישאו. הן לבעלים, תלה העכבה בנשים. ואיידי דתנא רישא בדידהי. נותנין לבתולה שנים עשר חדש, ולאלמנה שלשים יום. ולענין גיטין אינו כן. אלפיכך קאי, דאשמעינן שעכבת האונס פוטרתו מן המזונות — לענין גיטין אין טענת אונס מועלת; אם נתן גט לאשתו ע"מ אם לא אבא עד זמן פלוני יהא גט, [ונאנס] ולא בא — הרי זה גט, ואינו יכול לומר אנוס הייתי. אלמא קסבר אין אונס בגטין. אין טענת אונס בגיטין. ולקמיה מפרש טעמא. אינו גט. ואם אין לה בנים זקוקה ליבם. מת הוא דאינו גט. דהא לא שויא גיטא עד י"ב חדש, והוא מת בתוך הזמן, ומאן קא מגרש לה מהשתא? אין המתים מגרשים. מת הוא דאינו גט. משום דאין גט לאחר מיתה. אבל משום אונס אחרינא — לא מפקע גיטא. אלמא: אין אונס בגטין. דאי סלקא דעתך חלה נמי אינו גט — ניתני חלה וכל שכן מת, שאין אונס גדול מזה. היא גופא קמ"ל. כלומר: האי דתנא מת לאו לדיוקא דילה תנייה, למידק: הא חלה — הרי זה גט; אלא לאשמועינן היא גופא, דאין גט לאחר מיתה, ואסי' בלא תנאי. כגון, האומר לאשתו: הרי זה גיטיך לאחר מותי — אינו גט לפוטרה מן היבם. זה גיטך אם מתי. שכיב מרע שכתב גט לאשתו באחד מן הלשונות הללו: זה גיטך אם מתי, או זה גיטך מחולי זה — משיפסוק חולי זה (מעלי) משמע, והוא מת מאותו חולי — לא אמר כלום, שהרי משפסק אינו בחיים ואינו יכול לגרש. דלמא. הא דאיצטריך סיפא אם לא באתי וכו' — לאפוקי מדרבותינו איצטריך, דפליגי עלה, ואמרי דאין גט לאחר מיתה הוא, דכיון דכתוב בגט זמן כתיבתו — הוא מוכיח שכך אמר לה: אם לא באתי לאותו זמן — יהא גט למפרע מהיום. דאי לא משוה גיטא עד שנים עשר חדש, למה כתב יום כתיבת הגט בתוכו? לכתוב: אם לא באתי לר"ח פלוני יהא גט. התירוה לינשא. בלא חליצה, להיא ד"אם לא באתי". זמנו של שטר מוכיח עליו. לא לחנם נכתב זמנו לתוכו, אם לא להודיע שמיום הכתיבה והמסירה הוא מגרשה אם לא יבא לאותו זמן. הלכך, אע"ג דלא כתב: זה גיטך מהיום אם לא באתי כו' — כמאן דכתב "מהיום" דמי. ובבבא בתרא (דף קלו.) אמרה רבי יוסי, דתנן: הכותב נכסיו לבנו צריך שיכתוב "מהיום ולאחר מיתה", ואם לא כתב "מהיום" — אינה מתנה. רבי יוסי אומר: אינו צריך. ואלא מסיפא. גמר רבא דאין אונס בגיטין. הרי זה גט. ואע"ג דאין אונס גדול ממיתה. אלמא: אין אונס בגיטין, והוא הדין לחלה. דלמא מת דוקא. דכל עצמו שכתב לה גט מחמת כן כתב לה, שאם ימות יהיה גט למפרע, שלא תיזקק ליבם. ובהאי אונסא לא ניחא ליה למיבטל גיטא. אבל באונסא אחרינא, דניחא ליה לבטולי גיטא ביה — אימא לך: יש אונס בגיטין. ופסקיה מברא. הנהר הפסיקו. שהיתה המעבורת מצד העיר, ולא יכול לעבור. חזו דאתאי. שבאתי. לא שמיה מתיא. והוי גיטא. ואם רצתה — תינשא לאחר, וגם לכהונה נפסלת מהיום.

תוספות

מציא אמרה ליה נסתחפה שדהו. ואינו יכול לטעון: דאדרבה מזלה גרם. דכיון דלא מיפקדא אפריה ורביה לא מיענשא, כדאמרינן ב"הבא על יבמתו" (יבמות דף סד:) ועוד: דהאשה היא שדה של הבעל, ואין הבעל שדה שלה. לפיכך חלה הוא אינו מעלה לה מזונות. קשה לר"י: דאמר ב"החולץ" (שם דף מא: ושם) עמד בדין וברח — זונות משל יבם, ומפרש בירושלמי: ברח — ה"ה חלה, והכא אמרי' דחלה אין מעלה לה מזונות! ואור"י: דהתם חלה או ברח לאחר שעמד בדין, שכבר נתחייב לה במזונות. אבל הכא בחלה קודם הגעת הזמן. ובקונט' פי' שם: דוקא ברח, אבל חלה — לא, ואין נראה, כדמשמע בירושלמי. ולפירושו אין להקשות מאיכא דבעו לה מיבעיא, אמאי לא פשיט לה מהתם? דיש לומר: דארוסתו אגידא ביה טפי מיבמתו, כדאמרינן ביבמות בכמה דוכתי. פשיט רב אחאי. לא כמו שפירש רשב"ם דהיינו רב אחאי גאון שעשה שאלתות, והיה בסוף כל האמוראים, ולכך משנה לשונו בכל התלמוד: פריך רב אחאי: פשיט רב אחאי. שהרי כאן רב אשי *עונה על דבריו. אלא אומר רבינו תם שהוא אמורא, וכל אמורא היה תופס לשונו, כמו: מגדף בה ר' אבהו (סנהדרין ג:) תהי בה ר' יוחנן (ב"ק קיב:), לייט עלה אביי (ברכות כט.). לא נשאו לא קתני אלא לא נישאו. *מקובלין היו כך לקרות "לא נישאו". ועוד: דאי "לא נשאו" אאנשים קאי — ה"ל למימר נמי בלשון רבים: ואוכלות משלהם. אלא לא נישאו. פירוש: דמשמע נמי דמעכבי אינהי. אבל אין לומר דמשמע דוקא דמעכבי אינהי אבל לא אינהו, מדקאמר: לעולם דמעכבי אינהו, ואיידי דתנא רישא בדידהי כו', דמשום איידי אין לשנות טעות בסיפא. מת הוא דאינו גט. דאין גט לאחר מיתה, הא חלה — הרי זה גט. דאי חלה נמי אינו גט, וטעמא דהכא דאינו גט משום אונס — אם כן לישמעינן חלה, דהוי אונס מועט, וכ"ש מת! דהשתא אכתי לא אסיק אדעתיה דבמת איכא למימר ניחא ליה דלא תפול קמי יבם. ודלמא לעולם אימא לך חלה נמי אינו גט. ויש טענת אונס. ודקאמר ליתני חלה וכ"ש מת, הא דקתני מת — הא קמ"ל דאין גט לאחר מיתה. ואתא לאשמועינן תרוייהו: דיש אונס, ואין גט לאחר מיתה. דאי יש אונס גרידא אתא לאשמועינן, אבל יש גט לאחר מיתה — הוה ליה למינקט חלה, ואי אין גט לאחר מיתה גרידא הוה בעי לאשמועינן — לא הוה ליה למינקט הרי זה גיטך אם לא באתי, שעושה תנאי, אלא הרי זה גיטך לאחר מיתה. הרי זה גיטך אם מתי מחולי זה לאחר מיתה. לאחר מיתה הוי טעמא דכולהו כמו "אתם" — ולא אפוטרופסין ולא שותפין ולא אריסין. ולא כל התורם את שאינו שלו (גיטין דף נב.) דכולהו הוו משום תורם את שאינו שלו. וא"ת: ההיא משנה גופה אמאי איצטריך? הא תנן בהדיא בפ"ק דגיטין (דף יג. שם): דאין גט לאחר מיתה, דתנן: האומר תנו גט זה לאשתי — לא יתנו לאחר מיתה. ובפרק קמא דגיטין (שם ד"ה "לא") פירשנו. דלמא לאפוקי מדרבותינו. אבל מההיא דרישא לא שמעינן לאפוקי מדרבותינו, דאיכא לאוקמה בשאין כתוב זמן בשטר. והא דאמרינן (בגיטין דף פו.) שלשה גיטין פסולין וחד מינייהו שאין בו זמן — הא אמרינן אם נשאת הולד כשר, ומשום דאין גט לאחר מיתה קתני הכא לא אמר כלום, אפילו נשאת. אי נמי בשכתוב בו *שבוע או שנה או חדש, דאמר בפרק שני דגיטין (דף יז:) דכשר ואין זמנו מוכיח עליו. אי נמי במאוחר. דלמא מת דוקא דלא ניחא ליה דתפול קמי יבם. וא"ת: בפרק "מי שאחזו" (גיטין דף עג. ושם) דאמרי': אכלו אחרי אין לנו. פירוש: אין לנו שיהא גט. ואמאי לא הוי גט? הא לא ניחא ליה דתפול קמי יבם? וי"ל: דבאונס דלא שכיח כלל לא אסיק אדעתיה שירצה שיהא גט. וסברה

עין משפט נר מצוה

ג א מיי' פ"ט מהל' גירושין הל' ח סמג עשין נ טוש"ע אה"ע סי' קמד סעי' א:
ד ב מיי' שם הל' ב (טוש"ע שם סעי' ב):
ה ג מיי' שם הל' יב סמג שם טוש"ע שם סי' קמה סעי' א:
ו ד מיי' שם הל' יא וסמג שם טוש"ע שם סי' קמד סעי' ג:
ז ה מיי' שם הל' ח טוש"ע שם סעי' א:

מסורת הש"ס

[גיטין ל. לד.]
גיטין עו: ע"ז לז.
גיטין עב. ב"ב קלו.
גיטין עו:
שם ל. לד. נדרים כז.
[ועי' תוס' זבחים קב: ד"ה פריך]
[שבוע שנה חודש כצ"ל]

תוספות רי"ד

אמר רבא ולענין גיטין אינו כן. פי' לענין גיטין אין טענת אונס מועלת שאם נתן גט לאשתו שאם לא אבוא עד זמן פלוני יהא גט. ונאנס ולא בא ה"ז גט ואין יכול לומר אנוס הייתי. אלמא קסבר אין אונס בגיטין. א"ד אמר רבא וכן לענין גיטין. אלמא קסבר יש אונס בגיטין. ואע"ג דקי"ל הלכה כלישנא בתרא. הכא הלכה כלישנא קמא דהכי אמרי' בגיטין בשמעתא קמייתא בפ' השולח. ההוא דא"ל אי לא נסיבנא מכאן ועד תלתין יומין להוי גיטא כי מטא יום תלתין א"ל הא טרחנא למאי נחוש לה. אי משום אונסא אין אונס בגיטין. אלמא קסבר לה לתלמודא דאין אונס בגיטין:

גליון הש"ס

תום' ד"ה לא נשאו וכו' מקובלין היו כך. וכן בנדרים דף לה ע"א בר"ן ד"ה דיקא נמי:

זימנין דלא אניס, וסברה דאניס, ומיעגנא ויתבה. ומשום פרוצות, דאי אמרת לא ליהוי גיטא, זימנין דאניס ואמרה לא אניס, ואזלא ומינסבא, ונמצא גט בטל ובניה ממזרים. ומי איכא מידי דמדאורייתא לא להוי גט ומשום צנועות ומשום פרוצות שרינן אשת איש לעלמא?! אין, *כל דמקדש – אדעתא דרבנן מקדש, °ואפקעינהו רבנן לקידושי מיניה. אמר ליה רבינא לרב אשי: תינח קדיש בכספא, קדיש בביאה מאי איכא למימר? שויוה רבנן לבעילתו בעילת זנות. איכא דאמרי, אמר רבא: וכן לענין גיטין. אלמא קסבר רבא: יש אונס בגיטין, מיתיבי: "הרי זה גיטיך אם לא באתי מכאן ועד שנים עשר חדש" ומת בתוך שנים עשר חדש – אינו גט. מת – הוא דאינו גט, הא חלה – הרי זה גט! לעולם אימא לך חלה נמי אינו גט, והיא גופה קמ"ל, דאין גט לאחר מיתה. אין גט לאחר מיתה – הא תנא ליה רישא! דלמא לאפוקי מדרבותינו. ת"ש: "מעכשיו אם לא באתי מכאן ועד שנים עשר חדש" ומת בתוך שנים עשר חדש – הרי זה גט. מאי לאו – הוא הדין לחלה? לא, מת דוקא, דלא ניחא ליה דתפול קמי יבם. ת"ש: מההוא דאמר להו: "אי לא אתינא מכאן ועד שלשים יום ליהוי גיטא", אתא בסוף תלתין יומין ופסקיה מברא, ואמר להו: "חזו דאתאי, חזו דאתאי!" ואמר שמואל: לא שמיה מתיא. אונסא דשכיח שאני, דכיון דאיבעי ליה לאתנויי ולא אתני – איהו הוא דאפסיד אנפשיה. אמר רב שמואל בר יצחק: לא שנו אלא מתקנת עזרא ואילך, שאין בתי דינין קבועין אלא בשני ובחמישי. אבל קודם תקנת עזרא, שבתי דינין קבועין בכל יום – אשה נשאת בכל יום. קודם תקנת עזרא? מאי דהוה הוה! הכי קאמר: אאי איכא בתי דינין דקבועין האידנא כקודם תקנת עזרא – אשה נשאת בכל יום. הא בעינן *שקדו! דטריח ליה. מאי

רש"י

זימנין דלא אניס. והוי גיטא. וסברה. דלמא אניס, ואינו גט, ותדאג להינשא. ומינסבא. וכשיבא ויאמר "נאנסתי" – נמצא גט בטל, ובניה מן האחרון ממזרים. לפיכך אמרו יהא גט. דמדאורייתא לא הוי גיטא. שמצינו טענת אונס מן התורה, שנאמר (דברים כב) "ולנערה לא תעשה דבר". כל המקדש.

כל המקדש אשה – על דעת שהנהיגו חכמי ישראל בישראל הוא מקדשה, שיהיו קיימין קידושין לפי דברי חכמים, ויהיו בטילים לפי דברי חכמים, על ידי גיטין שהכשירו חכמים. ואפקעוה רבנן לקידושין. כשיצא גט כזה אחריהם. תינח. למימר אפקעתא כדקדיש בכספא, דנימא: גט זה עוקר הקידושין, ועושה מעות מתנה מעיקרן. קדיש בביאה מאי. אפקעתא מעיקרא היכא? בשלמא על ידי גט כשר, אע"פ שהקידושין קיימים עד עכשיו – גזירת הכתוב היא שהגט כורתו ומתיר איסורו מכאן ולהבא. אבל זה, שאינו גט מן התורה, ואתה מכשירו מפני דעתו של זה שקידשה על דעת חכמים, ושביטלו על פי חכמים – צריך אתה לומר שמעיקרן לא יהו קידושין, ואי קדיש בביאה, ואתה עוקר קידושין למפרע, מה תהא על ביאתו? שויוה רבנן לבעילתו. למפרע, על ידי גט שהוא מדבריהם, בעילת זנות. ויש בהן כח לעשות כן, שהרי הוא תלה בהן. שמעתי כל רבותי מפרשים "דקדיש בכספא" – דקידושי דרבנן נינהו. ואי אפשר לומר כן. חדא: דגזירה שוה היא "קיחה" "קיחה" משדה עפרון (קידושין דף ב.), וכל הלמד מגזירה שוה כמו שכתוב מפורש הוא לכל דבר. ועוד: אי דרבנן נינהו – היאך סוקלין על ידו, ומביאין חולין לעזרה על שגגתן? וסוף סוף כי קא משנינן שויוה רבנן לבעילתו בעילת זנות – על כרחך צריך אתה לפרש כמו שפירשתי, שהקידושין נעקרין מעיקרן ולא מכאן ולהבא. והמפרש לומר שויוה רבנן לכל מקדשי ביאה בעילת זנות – טעות גמור הוא, ובא להתיר אשת איש המתקדשת בביאה בלא גט מן הטעם הזה, ולא מצינו זאת בהתלמוד. וכן לענין גיטין. אלפיכך קאי, דטענינן טענת אונס בתנאי הגט להפקיעו. שבתי דינין קבועין בכל יום. כלומר, שקביעות כל הימים שוה. והא בעינן שקדו. שיהא טורח בסעודה שלשה ימים. דטריח ליה. אם טרח לפני השבת ותיקן צרכי סעודה – כונסה באחד בשבת או בשני בשבת. מאי

תוספות

וסברה דאנים. ומן הדין לית לן למיחש דלמא אניס הוא, דרובן לא אניסי. ולהכי קרי להו צנועות, שמחמירים על עצמן אע"ג דמצי לאינסובי. א] וגבי פרוצות לא גרסינן וסברה דלא אניס, אלא: ואמרה דלא אניס. פי': אפילו כשיצא הקול דאניס, אמרה דלא אניס. או אפילו כשתדע היא עצמה דאניס, ואחרים לא ידעו. ואם תאמר: מת תוך י"ב חודש נמי יהא גט מהאי טעמא? דזימנין דלא מת וסברה דמת, ומיעגנא ויתבה! ויש לומר: דמיתה קלא אית לה.

אדעתא דרבנן מקדש. לכן אומרים בשעת קידושין "כדת משה וישראל".

ואפקעינהו רבנן לקידושין מינה. בריש "השולח" (גיטין לג.) פירשתי.

תינח דקדיש בכספא. דהפקר ב"ד היה הפקר, והוו מעות מתנה, וממילא יהו כל בעילותיו זנות. קדיש בביאה מאי איכא למימר, איך יפקיעו ביאה של קידושין? ואפי' למ"ד ב"האשה רבה" (יבמות פט: ושם) דיש כח לחכמים לעקור דבר מן התורה – היינו כגון דליכא עבירה, כההיא ד"האשה רבה" דהדר לטיבלא. אבל היכא דאיכא עבירה, דמקודשת היא בביאה – מאי איכא למימר? ומשני: שויוה רבנן בעילותיו בעילת זנות, ואין כאן קדושין*.

איכא דאמרי אמר רבא וכן לענין גיטין. פסק ר"ת כלישנא קמא, דאין אונס בגיטין. והביא ראיה מדקאמר סתמא התלמוד בריש "השולח" (גיטין לד. ושם) גבי ההוא דאמר אי לא נסיבנא עד תלתין יומין ליהוי גיטא כו', ואי משום אונס – אין אונס בגיטין. וכן נראה, דאליבא דאיכא דאמרי הוו פירכי מכל הני דמייתי סייעתא ללישנא קמא, ולא סמכינן אשינויי דחיקי. וקשה לר"י: דמסיק בפרק "מי שאחזו" (שם עג. ושם) דבין דאמר הרי זה גיטיך אם מתי מחולי זה, בין אם אמר אם לא אעמוד מחולי זה, ונפל עליו הבית או נשכו נחש או אכלו ארי – דלא הוי גט. אלמא דיש אונס בגיטין! וליכא למימר דהתם לא מטעם דיש אונס קאמר דלא הוי גט, אלא משום דבין אם מתי מחולי זה בין אם לא אעמוד – משמע שימות מחמת זה החולי, וכשנפל עליו הבית או נשכו נחש – אינו גט דאין זה מחולי זה. דהא מוכח בהדיא התם דמטעם דיש אונס הוא, גבי ההוא גברא דזבין ארעא לחבריה וקביל עליה כל אונסא דאיתיליד בה כו', אמר רבא: אונס דלא שכיח הוא. ומייתי רבא סייעתא מהא דאכלו ארי אינו גט, אלמא אונס דלא שכיח יש טענת אונס לרבא, והכא קאמר רבא גופיה בלישנא קמא, שהוא עיקר, דאין אונס אפילו באונס דלא שכיח, כדמוכח הסוגיא! ואור"י: דג' ענייני אונס הן; דאונס דלא שכיח כלל כההיא ד"מי שאחזו", אפי' ללישנא קמא דרבא דהכא – יש אונס, דלא שייך התם לתקן משום צנועות ומשום פרוצות, דלעולם לא סברי צנועות דנפל עליו הבית או שהכישו נחש, כיון דלא שכיח כלל. ומשום פרוצות נמי ליכא למיחש, כיון דלא שכיח שיעשה כן. ואונס דשכיח, כגון ההיא דפסקיה מברא – אפילו לאיכא דאמרי אין אונס, דאיבעי ליה לאתנויי. אבל אונס דשכיח ולא שכיח – בהא פליגי תרי לישני דרבא. והלכתא כלישנא קמא דרבא כדפירשנו.

שבתי דינין קבועים בכל יום. וא"ת: וכי תיקן עזרא שלא יהו בתי דינין קבועים בכל יום אלא בב' וה' בלבד? ועוד קשה: דאמרינן בשבת (ד' קכט: ושם) מי שיש לו זכות אבות יקיז בב' וה'. וכי קודם תקנת עזרא לא היו מקיזין כל עיקר? ואומר ר"ת: דקודם תקנת עזרא לא היו קבועים בכל יום, אלא כשהיו צריכין לשום דין היו יושבין בכל יום ויום, ועזרא תיקן שיהיו קבועין בב' וה', וכל הרוצה לדון יבא וידון. והיו יכולין להקיז בכל יום קודם תקנת עזרא, כיון שלא היו קבועים. ור"י תירץ: שלא היו קבועים תחלה אלא בעיר אחת, ועזרא תיקן בכל עיר ועיר בב' וה'.

אשה נשאת בכל יום. קשה לרשב"א: אמאי נשאת בכל יום? תהא כאלמנה ותינשא בה' ותיבעל בששי, לפי שנאמר בו ברכה לאדם! וי"ל: דמשום ברכה לא היו קובעים יום, כדפרישית לעיל. ובאלמנה נמי לא קבעו שתיבעל בששי משום ברכה גרידא, אלא משום שקדו, שיהא שמח עמה ג' ימים, כדאמר לקמן (דף ה.). ובתולה דלא שייך ההוא טעמא, דליכא למימר משכים לאומנתו והולך לו, לפי שיש בה שבעת ימי המשתה – הלכך משום ברכה גרידא לא היו קובעים יום.

אי איכא בתי דינין כו'. נראה לר"י: דמכל מקום אין נשאת בשבת, דהא אין דנין בשבת, ועתה נוהגין לישא אף בששי, משום דאין ב"ד קבועין. ואם יש לו טענת בתולין – יכול לקבול בשבת בפני שלשה כמו בשאר ימות השבוע. ועוד: לפירוש הקונטרס, דוקא בימיהם קבעו יום הנישואין משום שעל ידי כך יתברר הדבר ויבואו עדים, מתוך שמתאספים העם לב"ד, ואין שייך לומר עכשיו כך.

ובשני

עין משפט נר מצוה

ח א מיי' פ"י מהל' אישות הל' טו סמג עשין מח טוש"ע אה"ע סי' סד סעי' ג:

מסורת הש"ס

יבמות ל: קי. גיטין לג. עג. בבא בתרא מח:

[ועי' תוס' ב"ב מח:]

[לעיל ב. לקמן ה.]

גליון הש"ס

גמ' ואפקעינהו רבנן. עי' תשובת רשב"א סי' אלף קסב:

הגהות מהר"ב רנשבורג

א] תד"ה וסברה דאנים וכו' וגבי פרוצות ל"ג וכו'. עי' נדה יב ע"א תד"ה לנוע וכו':

מַאי שָׁקְדוּ? דְּתַנְיָא: מִפְּנֵי מָה אָמְרוּ בְּתוּלָה נִשֵּׂאת לְיוֹם הָרְבִיעִי – שֶׁאִם הָיָה לוֹ טַעֲנַת בְּתוּלִים הָיָה מַשְׁכִּים לְב"ד. וְתִנָּשֵׂא בְּאֶחָד בְּשַׁבָּת, וְאִם הָיָה לוֹ טַעֲנַת בְּתוּלִים – הָיָה מַשְׁכִּים לְב"ד! שֶׁקָּדוּ חֲכָמִים עַל תַּקָּנַת בְּנוֹת יִשְׂרָאֵל, שֶׁיְּהֵא אָדָם טוֹרֵחַ בִּסְעוּדָה שְׁלֹשָׁה יָמִים: אֶחָד בְּשַׁבָּת, וְשֵׁנִי בְּשַׁבָּת, וּשְׁלִישִׁי בְּשַׁבָּת, וּבָרְבִיעִי כּוֹנְסָהּ. וּמִסַּכָּנָה וְאֵילָךְ נָהֲגוּ הָעָם לִכְנוֹס בִּשְׁלִישִׁי, וְלֹא מִיחוּ בְּיָדָם חֲכָמִים. וּבְשֵׁנִי לֹא יִכְנוֹס, וְאִם מֵחֲמַת הָאוֹנֶס – מוּתָּר. וּמַפְרִישִׁין אֶת הֶחָתָן מִן הַכַּלָּה לֵילֵי שַׁבָּת תְּחִלָּה, מִפְּנֵי שֶׁהוּא עוֹשֶׂה חַבּוּרָה. מַאי סַכָּנָה? אִילֵימָא דְּאָמְרִי: בְּתוּלָה הַנִּשֵּׂאת לְיוֹם הָרְבִיעִי תֵּיהָרֵג – נָהֲגוּ?! לְגַמְרֵי נִיעַקְרֵיהּ! אָמַר רַבָּה, דְּאָמְרִי: בְּתוּלָה הַנִּשֵּׂאת בְּיוֹם הָרְבִיעִי – תִּיבָּעֵל לַהֶגְמוֹן תְּחִלָּה. הַאי סַכָּנָה?! אוֹנֶס הוּא! מִשּׁוּם דְּאִיכָּא צְנוּעוֹת דְּמָסְרָן נַפְשַׁיְיהוּ לִקְטָלָא, וְאָתְיָין לִידֵי סַכָּנָה. וְלִידְרוֹשׁ לְהוּ דְּאוֹנֶס שָׁרֵי! אִיכָּא פְּרוּצוֹת, וְאִיכָּא נַמִי כֹּהֲנוֹת. וְלִיעַקְרֵיהּ! גְּזֵירָה עֲבִידָא דְּבָטְלָא, וְתַקַּנְתָּא דְּרַבָּנַן מִקַּמֵּי גְּזֵירָה לָא עָקְרִינַן. אִי הָכִי בִּשְׁלִישִׁי נַמִי אָתֵי וּבָעֵיל! מִסְּפֵיקָא לָא עָקַר נַפְשֵׁיהּ. וּבְשֵׁנִי לֹא יִכְנוֹס, וְאִם מֵחֲמַת הָאוֹנֶס – מוּתָּר. מַאי אוֹנֶס? אִילֵימָא הָא דַּאֲמַרַן – הָתָם קָרֵי לֵיהּ סַכָּנָה וְהָכָא קָא קָרֵי לֵיהּ אוֹנֶס? וְתוּ, הָתָם נָהֲגוּ, הָכָא – מוּתָּר! אָמַר רָבָא: דְּאָמְרִי שַׂר צָבָא בָּא לָעִיר. ה"ד? אִי דְּאָתֵי וְחָלֵיף – לִיעַכַּב! לָא צְרִיכָא, דְּאָתֵי וְקָבַע. בְּג' מִיהָא לִכְנוֹס! אַסְפַּרְוָוא דִּידֵיהּ בְּג' קָאָתוּ. וְאִיבָּעֵית אֵימָא: מַאי מֵחֲמַת הָאוֹנֶס – כִּדְתַנְיָא: הֲרֵי שֶׁהָיָה פִּתּוֹ אָפוּי, וְטִבְחוֹ טָבוּחַ, וְיֵינוֹ מָזוּג, וּמֵת אָבִיו שֶׁל חָתָן אוֹ אִמָּהּ שֶׁל כַּלָּה – מַכְנִיסִין אֶת הַמֵּת לְחֶדֶר, וְאֶת הֶחָתָן וְאֶת הַכַּלָּה לַחוּפָּה וּבוֹעֵל

מאי שקדו. היכן שנינו שקדו דמקשינן לה הכא? אי משום דאמר שמואל לעיל – לית לן לאותביה מינה לאמוראה אחרינא. **ומן הסכנה ואילך.** לקמן מפרש לה. **ובשני לא יכנום.** בשביל אותה סכנה, ואין צריך לעקור בשבילה תקנת חכמים אלא יום אחד, ויהיה טורח מיהת שני ימים בצורכי סעודה. **ואם מחמת האונס.** לקמן מפרש. **תחלה.** אם ביאה ראשונה היא, מפרישין אותה ממנו לילי שבת. **נהגו.** בתמיה. סכנת נפשות היא, ואת אמרת נהגו לכנוס ביום שלישי, אבל מיעקר רביעי לגמרי לא עקרו? **ניעקריה.** ויתקנו להם ימים אחרים. **ולדרוש להו דאונס שרי.** דנבעלת באונס אינה נאסרת על בעלה, דילפינן לקמן בפרק ד' (דף נא:) מ"והיא לא נתפשה", ולא לימסרו נפשייהו למיתה. **איכא פרוצות.** דאי מקילינן להו עבדי ברצון, ונאסרות על בעליהן. **ואיכא נמי כהנות.** שנאסרות על בעליהן אף באונס. ואינהו מסרן נפשייהו למיתה, דאשת כהן שנאנסה אסורה לבעלה, ולקמן בפרק ד' (שם) ילפינן לה. **וליעקריה.** הואיל וזמנין דאיכא סכנה. **בשלישי נמי אתי ובעיל.** כיון דידע שהתחילו לנהוג בשלישי. **מספיקא לא עקר נפשיה.** כיון דלאו קביעות גמור הוא על ידי תקנת ב"ד, ספיקא היא לו אם יש נישואין היום בעיר, ולא עקר נפשיה לבא בעיר. **התם נהגו.** משמע רובם נהגו. **הכא מותר.** לא גרסינן לכתחילה. והכי קא מתמה: הכא מותר קתני, דמשמע: אם ימלך איש יחידי בבית דין – יתירו לו, אבל נהגו – לא קתני. **שר צבא בא לעיר.** ויחטפו צורכי סעודה מאשר ימלאו. **וחליף.** לאחר רביעי. **לעכב.** עד יום רביעי של שבת הבא. **בשלישי לכנום.** למה נתיר לו לקדום כל כך, שלא יטריח בסעודה אלא יום אחד, ומיעקרא תקנתא דשקדו? **איספרווא דידיה.** חיל משרתיו המכינים לו צורכי סעודה, בלשון לעז הירניי"ש. **כדתניא.** חתן שמת אביו בשני ואין יכול להמתין עד למחר, שצריך להשהות את המת עד שיכנסו לחופה. **ויינו מזוג.** במים, שיהא ראוי לשתיה, ושוב אינו מתקיים. **אביו של חתן או אמה של כלה.** דווקא נקט אביו של חתן, שהוא הטורח בצורכי סעודה, ואמה של כלה היא המכינה לה תכשיטין. לפיכך, אם יעבור המועד שוב אין מכין להם, והתירו להם להכניס את המת לחדר שלא יקברוהו, דאם כן חלה אבילות על החתן בסתימת הגולל, כדלקמן, ושוב לא יוכל לכנוס עד שיעבור האבילות. **ופורש**

ובשני לא יכנום. פ"ה: אפילו בשעת הסכנה, דאין לעקור בשבילה תקנת חכמים אלא יום אחד. וקשה לר"י, דאמר לקמן: מאי אונס? אילימא הא דאמרן התם קרי ליה כו', הוה ליה למיפרך טפי רישא לסיפא, דקתני רישא ובשני לא יכנום אפי' בשעת הסכנה! ואומר ריצב"א: דמשום הכי לא פריך ליה משום דאיכא לפרושי ואם מחמת האונס, פירוש: שיש סכנה אף ביום שלישי – מותר לכנום בשני. ונראה לר"י: דמילתא באנפי נפשה היא, ולא איירי בסכנה. ובשני לא יכנום – הוא הדין בג', אלא נקט בב' משום דבעי למיתני: ואם מחמת האונס מותר. **ולדרוש** להו דאונס שרי. וא"ת: והא אמרינן בפ' "בן סורר ומורה" (סנהדרין עד. ושם) על כל עבירות יעבור ואל יהרג, חוץ מעבודה זרה וג"ע וש"ד! ותירץ ר"ת: דאין חייבין מיתה על בעילת נכרי, דרחמנא אפקריה לזרעיה דנכרי, דכתיב (יחזקאל כג) "וזרמת סוסים זרמתם". ומייתי ראיה, דפריך בפ' "בן סורר ומורה" (שם:): הא אסתר פרהסיא הואי! ולא פריך והא אסתר גילוי עריות הויא, משמע דמשום עריות לא הוה מיחייבא. ומתוך כך התיר ר"ת לבת ישראל שהמירה ובא עליה גוי לקיימה לאותו גוי כשנתגייר, דלא שייך למימר אחד לבעל ואחד לבועל בביאת נכרי דהויא כביאת בהמה. ואין נראה לריב"ם, דהא ע"י ביאת גוי נאסרה לבעלה, כדאמר הכא דאיכא פרוצות. ובפ' "האשה שנתארמלה" (לקמן כו: ושם) גבי האשה שנחבשה בין הגוים אמרי' דברצון אסורה לבעלה. ואמר נמי במגילה (דף טו.): "כאשר אבדתי אבדתי" כאשר אבדתי מבית אבא אבדתי ממך, אלמא לגבי בעלה לא חשיבא בעילת נכרי כביאת בהמה, והוא הדין לבועל. אע"ג דאין זנות לבהמה ואין ביאת בהמה פוסלת ואוסרת, כדאמרי' בפ' "הבא על יבמתו" (יבמות נט:), ביאת נכרי הויא ביאה, וכי אפקריה רחמנא לזרעיה – הני מילי לענין דאין לו חיים, וזרעו חשוב כזרע בהמה! ויש לומר, דהכי פריך: ולדרוש להו דאונס שרי, לפי שהאשה היא קרקע עולם ולא עבדה מעשה, כדמשני בפרק "בן סורר ומורה": אסתר קרקע עולם היתה. והא דלא פריך התם גילוי עריות הויא – דפשיטא ליה דאיכא לשנויי קרקע עולם היא ואין לה למסור עצמה, אבל לענין חילול השם לא היה נראה לו שיועיל טעם דקרקע עולם, ומשני: קרקע עולם היתה, ואפילו חילול השם ליכא. ובפרק "מצות חליצה" (שם קג. ושם) דפריך גבי יעל: והא קמתהניא מעבירה! ומשני: טובתן של רשעים רעה היא אצל צדיקים, שהטיל בה זוהמא. ולא משני קרקע עולם היתה – משום דהתם לא פריך אמאי מסרה עצמה, דהא לא היה רוצה להמיתה, דאדרבה היה צריך שתשמרהו, אלא הכי פירושו: והא מתהניא מעבירה, למה משבחה הכתוב "מנשים באהל תבורך" ודרשינן בנזיר (דף כג: שם): גדולה עבירה לשמה ממצוה שלא לשמה, ופריך דיעל נמי הוה עבירה שלא לשמה, דהא מתהניא מעבירה! ומשני: דלא מתהניא, ועשתה עבירה לשמה כדי להציל את ישראל. **בתולה** הנשאת ברביעי תיבעל. לאו דוקא ברביעי, מדפריך לקמן: בשלישי נמי אתי ובעיל, שאינו מתכוין אלא להנאתו, אלא אגב דנקט לעיל שנשאת ברביעי תיהרג, דהתם מקפידים על קביעות כדי להעבירם על דתם, נקט ליה נמי הכא ברביעי. **ולדרוש** להו דאונס שרי. אין לפרש דפריך הכי: לדרוש כו' דשוב לא יהא אלא אונס, ואמאי קאמר ומסכנה ואילך, הוה ליה למימר ומן האונס ואילך! דא"כ – מאי משני משום פרוצות? דהא אפילו לא דרשינן להו דאונס שרי לא מסרי נפשייהו. דדוקא לצנועות אמרינן דמסרי נפשייהו. ועוד: וכי משום פרוצות יניחו להרוג הצנועות? אלא הכי פירושו: ולדרוש להו דאונס שרי, וכיון דליכא סכנה – אמאי לא מיחו בידם חכמים? ומשני: משום פרוצות לא מיחו בידם, אי נמי משום כהנות. **ותו** התם. בשלישי נהגו. ואמרינן בפ' בתרא דתענית (דף כו:): מאן דאמר נהגו – אורויי לא מורינן, והכא בשני – מותר לכתחלה. ופי' הקונטרס דפירש נהגו – רובא דעלמא, והכא מותר – יחידי, ולא גרסינן 'לכתחלה', אינו מיושב. **אי** דאתי וחליף ליעכב. פ"ה: חליף לאחר ד', וליעכב עד יום ד' של שבת הבא: וקשה לר"י: דאם כן מאי משני לא צריכא דאתי וקבע? אכתי ליעכב חדש או חדשים עד שילך! על כן נראה לר"י: שאם יתעכב כל יום ד' – אין לו לעכב עד יום ד' אחר, אלא יכנוס בג'. והכי פריך: אי אתי וחליף בד' גופיה – ליעכב עד דחליף! ומשני: דאתי וקבע כל יום ד'. **בשלישי** מיהא לכנום. ולא בעי למימר דאתי שר הצבא בג' – דא"כ יכנוס בד'. **איספרווא** דידיה בג' אתא. אין לתמוה: משום סעודה עקרינן תקנתא דרבנן ב' ימים, ומשום סכנה לא עקרינן אלא יום אחד?! דבעילת הגמון שכיח, שרגיל לבא ולבעול. ואי עקרינן שני ימים – אתא להשתכח. אבל אונס שר צבא – אינו אלא אקראי בעלמא: (לעיל) **תקנה** דרבנן מקמי גזרה לא עקרינן. כי פריך לעיל ליעקרוה לא משני תקנה דרבנן מקמי גזרה כו' כדמשני הכא משום דלעיל פריך וליעקרוה ויקבעו יום אחר כיון דאינו מתכוין אלא להעבירם על דת כשיקבעו יום אחר לא יחושו ולא מיעקרא תקנתא דרבנן הואיל ויהא יום אחד קבוע אבל הכא פריך וליעקרוה ולא יהא שום יום קבוע שאם יקבעו יום אתי ובעיל באותו יום ולהכי משני מקמי גזרה לא עקרינן תקנה דרבנן שלא יהא שום יום קבוע. (לעיל) **אי** הכי בשלישי נמי אתי ובעיל. פי' *אי אמרת בשלמא כדמעיקרא דאמרי בתולה שנשאת בד' תיהרג ואין (וע' תוס' שבת קכ:) מתכוונין אלא להעבירם לא יחושו אם יעשו ביום ג' אלא אי אמרת משום בעילת ההגמון כיון שמתכוין להנאתו בשלישי נמי אתי ובעיל.
בועל

תניא הרי שהיה פתו אפויה וטבחו טבוח ויינו מזוג ונתן מים ע"ג בשר ומת אביו של חתן או אמו של כלה מכניסין את המת לחדר ואת החתן ואת הכלה לחופה ובועל בעילת מצוה ופורש ונוהג ז' ימי משתה ואח"כ נוהג ז' ימי אבילות וכל אותן הימים הוא ישן בין האנשים והיא ישנה בין הנשים. וכן מי שפירסה אשתו נדה ואין מונעים תכשיטין מן הכלה כל ל'. פי' מכניסים את וכו'. שלא יקברוהו ותחול עליו האבילות בסתימות הגולל ושוב לא יוכל לכונסה עד שיעבור ז' ימי האבל. אלא כונס תחלה ואח"כ יקברו המת וכיון דחלה עליו חתונה הויא גביה כרגל שלא אתיא אבילות וחיילא עליה. ונוהג ז' ימי המשתה תחלה ואח"כ ז' ימי האבילות וכל אותן הימים אינו מתיחד עמה שמא יבעול. ואבל אסור בתשמיש המטה ואף בז' ימי המשתה שהן אצלו כרגל דברים של צנעה נוהג ואין מונעים וכו' ואע"פ שהיא אבילה שלא תתגנה על בעלה. ודוקא אביו של חתן הטורח בצרכי סעודה. ואמה של כלה המכינה לה לתכשיטין דליכא איניש דטרח להו. אבל איפכא לא:

וּבוֹעֵל בְּעִילַת מִצְוָה וּפוֹרֵשׁ, וְנוֹהֵג שִׁבְעַת יְמֵי הַמִּשְׁתֶּה, וְאַחַר כָּךְ נוֹהֵג שִׁבְעַת יְמֵי אֲבֵילוּת. וְכָל אוֹתָן הַיָּמִים הוּא יָשֵׁן בֵּין הָאֲנָשִׁים וְהִיא יְשֵׁנָה בֵּין הַנָּשִׁים. *וְאֵין מוֹנְעִין תַּכְשִׁיטִין מִן הַכַּלָּה כָּל שְׁלֹשִׁים יוֹם. אוְדַוְקָא אָבִיו שֶׁל חָתָן אוֹ אִמָּהּ שֶׁל כַּלָּה, דְּלֵיכָּא אִינִישׁ דְּטָרַח לְהוּ, אֲבָל אִיפְּכָא — לָא. אָמַר רַפְרָם בַּר פַּפָּא אָמַר רַב חִסְדָּא: לֹא שָׁנוּ אֶלָּא שֶׁנָּתַן מַיִם עַל גַּבֵּי בָשָׂר. אֲבָל לֹא נָתַן מַיִם עַל גַּבֵּי בָשָׂר — מִזְדַּבַּן. אָמַר רָבָא: וּבִכְרָךְ, אע"פ שֶׁנָּתַן מַיִם עַל גַּבֵּי בָשָׂר — מִזְדַּבַּן. אָמַר רַב פַּפָּא: וּבִכְפָר, אע"פ שֶׁלֹּא נָתַן מַיִם עַל גַּבֵּי בָשָׂר — לָא מִזְדַּבַּן. וְאֶלָּא, דְּרַב חִסְדָּא הֵיכִי מַשְׁכַּחַתְּ לָהּ? אָמַר רַב אַשִׁי: כְּגוֹן מָתָא מְחַסְיָא, דְּמַסְפְּקָא מִכְּרָךְ וּמַסְפְּקָא מִכְּפָר. תַּנְיָא כְּוָותֵיהּ דְּרַב חִסְדָּא: בהֲרֵי שֶׁהָיָה פִּתּוֹ אֲפוּיָה וְטִבְחוֹ טָבוּחַ וְיֵינוֹ מָזוּג, וְנָתַן מַיִם עַל גַּבֵּי בָשָׂר, וּמֵת אָבִיו שֶׁל חָתָן אוֹ אִמָּהּ שֶׁל כַּלָּה — מַכְנִיסִין אֶת הַמֵּת לַחֶדֶר וְאֶת הֶחָתָן וְאֶת הַכַּלָּה לַחוּפָּה, וּבוֹעֵל בְּעִילַת מִצְוָה וּפוֹרֵשׁ, וְנוֹהֵג שִׁבְעַת יְמֵי הַמִּשְׁתֶּה, וְאח"כ נוֹהֵג שִׁבְעַת יְמֵי אֲבֵילוּת. וְכָל אוֹתָן הַיָּמִים הוּא יָשֵׁן בֵּין הָאֲנָשִׁים וְאִשְׁתּוֹ יְשֵׁנָה בֵּין הַנָּשִׁים. וְכֵן *מִי שֶׁפֵּירְסָה אִשְׁתּוֹ נִדָּה — הוּא יָשֵׁן בֵּין הָאֲנָשִׁים וְהִיא יְשֵׁנָה בֵּין הַנָּשִׁים. *גוְאֵין מוֹנְעִין תַּכְשִׁיטִין מִן הַכַּלָּה כָּל ל' יוֹם. בֵּין כָּךְ וּבֵין כָּךְ לֹא יִבְעוֹל לֹא בְּעֶרֶב שַׁבָּת וְלֹא בְּמוֹצ"ש. אָמַר מָר: הוּא יָשֵׁן בֵּין הָאֲנָשִׁים וְהִיא יְשֵׁנָה בֵּין הַנָּשִׁים. מְסַיַּיע לֵיהּ לְרַבִּי יוֹחָנָן. דְּאָמַר רַבִּי יוֹחָנָן: דאע"פ שֶׁאָמְרוּ אֵין אֲבֵילוּת בַּמּוֹעֵד — אֲבָל דְּבָרִים שֶׁל צִינְעָא נוֹהֵג. דָּרַשׁ רַב יוֹסֵף בְּרֵיהּ דְּרָבָא מִשְּׁמֵיהּ דְּרָבָא: הל"ש אֶלָּא שֶׁלֹּא בָּעַל, אֲבָל בָּעַל — אִשְׁתּוֹ יְשֵׁנָה עִמּוֹ. וְהָא הָכָא, דִּבְבָעַל עָסְקִינַן, וְקָתָנֵי: הוּא יָשֵׁן בֵּין הָאֲנָשִׁים וְהִיא יְשֵׁנָה בֵּין הַנָּשִׁים! כִּי קָאָמַר — ואַפֵּירְסָה אִשְׁתּוֹ נִדָּה. הָא "וְכֵן" קָתָנֵי! הָכִי

רש"י

וּפוֹרֵשׁ. וְיִקְבְּרוּ אֶת הַמֵּת מִיָּד. דְּכֵיוָן דְּחָלָה עָלָיו חֲתוּנָּה — הָוְיָא לְגַבֵּיהּ כְּרֶגֶל, וְלָא חָיְיא אֲבֵילוּת וְחָיְילָא, וְנוֹהֵג שִׁבְעַת יְמֵי הַמִּשְׁתֶּה כו'. וְכָל אוֹתָן הַיָּמִים. שֶׁל יְמֵי הַמִּשְׁתֶּה וְשֶׁל אֲבֵילוּת. הוּא יָשֵׁן כו'. וְאֵין מִתְיַיחֲדִין זֶה עִם זֶה, שֶׁמָּא יִבְעוֹל, וְאָבֵל אָסוּר בְּתַשְׁמִישׁ הַמִּטָּה, כִּדְיָלְפִינַן בְּ"אֵלּוּ מְגַלְּחִין" (מו"ק דף טו:). וְאַף בְּשִׁבְעַת יְמֵי הַמִּשְׁתֶּה שֶׁהֵן כְּרֶגֶל נוֹהֵג הוּא אֲבֵילוּת שֶׁל דִּבְרֵי צִינְעָה, דְּהַיְינוּ אִיסּוּר תַּשְׁמִישׁ, כִּדְלְקַמָּן. וְאֵין מוֹנְעִין. בִּשְׁבִיל הָאֲבֵילוּת אֵין אוֹסְרִין עָלֶיהָ תַּכְשִׁיטֶיהָ, שֶׁלֹּא תִּתְגַּנֶּה עַל בַּעְלָהּ. כָּל שְׁלֹשִׁים יוֹם. וְאע"פ שֶׁהֵן יְמֵי אֲבֵילוּת לִשְׁאָר בְּנֵי אָדָם, וְכָל שֶׁכֵּן מִשְּׁלֹשִׁים וְאֵילָךְ. דְּלֵיכָּא אִינִישׁ דְּטָרַח. אִם יַפְסִידוּ מַה שֶּׁהֵכִינוּ. שֶׁנָּתַן מַיִם עַל גַּבֵּי בָשָׂר. שׁוּב אֵינוֹ רָאוּי לְמוֹכְרוֹ בְּמַקּוּלִין. בִּכְרָךְ. שְׁכִיחֵי אֱינָשֵׁי טוּבָא, וְיֵשׁ קוֹפְּלִים הַרְבֵּה. אֶלָּא דְּרַב חִסְדָּא. דְּמַפְלִיג בֵּין נָתַן לְלֹא נָתַן. הֵיכִי מַשְׁכַּחַתְּ לָהּ. לֹא בִּכְרָךְ וְלֹא בִּכְפָר. דְּמַסְפְּקָא מִכְּרָךְ וּמַסְפְּקָא מִכְּפָר. מוּפְלָאָה מִכְּלַל כְּרָךְ, וּמוּפְלָאָה מִכְּלַל כְּפָר. גְּדוֹלָה מִכְּפָר וּקְטַנָּה מִכְּרָךְ. תַּנְיָא כְּרַב חִסְדָּא. דְּמוֹקֵי לָהּ בְּנָתַן מַיִם עַל גַּבֵּי בָשָׂר. וְכֵן מִי שֶׁפֵּירְסָה אִשְׁתּוֹ נִדָּה. בִּכְנִיסָתָהּ לַחוּפָּה. הוּא יָשֵׁן כו'. וְאֵין נֶאֱמָנִין זֶה עִם זֶה. בֵּין כָּךְ וּבֵין כָּךְ. בֵּין יֵשׁ אוֹנֶס בֵּין אֵין אוֹנֶס. לֹא יִבְעוֹל. בְּעִילָה רִאשׁוֹנָה. לֹא בְּעֶרֶב שַׁבָּת כו'. בְּלֵיל שַׁבָּת, מִפְּנֵי שֶׁעוֹשֶׂה חַבּוּרָה. וְלֹא בְּמוֹצ"ש. לְקַמָּן מְפָרֵשׁ. מְסַיַּיע לֵיהּ. הָא דְּקָתָנֵי דְּאָסוּר בְּתַשְׁמִישׁ בְּשִׁבְעַת יְמֵי הַמִּשְׁתֶּה, שֶׁהֵן לוֹ כְּרֶגֶל. שֶׁל צִינְעָא. שֶׁאֵינוֹ נִיכָּר לַבְּרִיּוֹת שֶׁהוּא אָבֵל בְּכָךְ. לֹא שָׁנוּ. דְּאֵין נֶאֱמָנִין לְהִתְיַיחֵד. אֶלָּא שֶׁלֹּא בָּעַל. דְּתַקִּיף לֵיהּ יִצְרֵיהּ. דִּבְבָעַל עָסְקִינַן. דְּקָתָנֵי בּוֹעֵל בְּעִילַת מִצְוָה לִפְנֵי קְבוּרַת הַמֵּת. כִּי קָאָמַר. רָבָא לֹא שָׁנוּ, אַפֵּירְסָה אִשְׁתּוֹ נִדָּה קָאָמַר. דְּכֵיוָן דְּנִדָּה חֲמוּרָה, בַּעַל מְהֵימָן עֲלָהּ, דְּלָא אָתֵי לְזַלְזוּלֵי בְּאִיסּוּר כָּרֵת. הָא וְכֵן קָתָנֵי. קס"ד אַכּוּלָּהּ מִילְּתָא דַּאֲבֵילוּת מְדַמִּינַן לֵיהּ, וּבַאֲבֵילוּת דְּבַעַל עָסְקִינַן. ה"ק

תוספות

בועל בעילת מצוה ופורש. קודם שיקבר המת. אבל לאחר שנקבר — לא. כדאמרינן בסמוך: דברים של צינעא נוהג. ודייק לה מדקתני כל אותן הימים הוא ישן בין האנשים כו'. מיהו, מרישא דהכא לא ה"מ למידק דדוקא כשהמת בחדר הוא דשרי בעילת מצוה. דמצי לדחויי: דבועל בעילת מצוה — היינו אפי' לאחר שחל עליו אבילות. אבל קשה לרשב"א: אמאי לא דייק מדקתני "ופורש", מכלל דנוהג דברים של צינעא, מדלא התיר אלא בעילת מצוה דוקא! ואור"י: דהמ"ל פורש משום דם בתולים, כדאמרינן בפ' "תינוקת" (נדה דף סה:). אבל מ"הוא ישן בין האנשים" דייק שפיר דהוי משום אבילות, דאי משום נדות, כיון דבעיל — אשתו ישנה עמו, כדאמר רב יוסף בסמוך. ועוד: דכל אותן הימים משמע דכולהו הוי חד טעמא, דהיינו משום אבילות. והשתא מקילינן טפי באנינות דאורייתא מבאבילות דרבנן, מידי דהוה אנעילת סנדל ועטיפת הראש וכפיית המטה. **בעילת** מצוה. קרי לה בעילת מצוה משום דכתיב "כי בועליך עושיך" ואמרי' (סנהדרין דף כב:): אין אשה כורתת ברית אלא למי שעושה אותה כלי. וע"י כך מידבק בה, ובאין לידי פריה ורביה. ולהכי קרי לה לבעילה ראשונה בעילת מצוה. **אבל** איפכא לא. וה"ה אם אבלים מחמת שאר קרובים. תימה: דאמר בפ"ג דמועד קטן (דף כג. ושם): מתה אשתו — אסור לישא עד שיעברו ג' רגלים, ואם אין לו בנים — מותר לישא לאלתר משום פריה ורביה. הניחה לו בנים קטנים — מותר לישא לאלתר, משום פרנסתם. והכא אמר אבל איפכא לא, ומשמע דאין לו בנים עסקינן, מדקאמר דליכא דטרח להו, משמע דבבחור איירי! וי"ל: דלאלתר לאו דוקא, אלא כלומר מותר לאחר ז'. ומיהו, לבעול אסור עד לאחר ל', כדמוכח בתר הכי במעשה שמתה אשתו של יוסף הכהן, ואמר לאחותה בבית הקברות: לאי ופרנסי בני אחותיך, ואעפ"כ לא בא עליה עד זמן מרובה, מאי זמן מרובה — שלשים יום, מכלל דכנסה תוך ל'. ותוך שבעה ודאי אסור, כדמוכח הכא. ומה שאמר לה בבה"ק לא היה זה כניסה אלא שידוכין בעלמא. ונראה לר"י: דודאי אותו שיש לו בנים קטנים מותר לישא תוך ל', כדמשמע בעובדא דיוסף הכהן. אבל אותו שאין לו בנים כלל — אסור לישא עד לאחר שלשים, כיון שאין יכול לבעול תוך שלשים. וכן משמע במס' שמחות (פ"ז), דתניא: בד"א — כשיש לו בנים גדולים, אבל אין לו בנים או שיש לו בנים קטנים — מותר לישא אחרת לאחר ל'. משמע דאסור אפי' לישא תוך שלשים. ואע"ג דיש לו בנים קטנים מותר לישא תוך שלשים — מ"מ נקט אחר שלשים משום אין לו בנים. ור"ת ר"ל: דבאין לו בנים — אפי' לבעול שרי תוך שלשים אחר ז', משום פריה ורביה. וההיא דשמחות אינה מתיישבת כפי'. ונראה דביש לו בנים קטנים שרי לישא, ואפי' אם היא נמי אבילה — מפני שמפרנסת בניו. ואע"פ שאפשר באחרת, כדמוכח בעובדא דיוסף הכהן שהיתה אבילה מאחותה. ומיהו, אין כל כך ראיה, דשמא שאני התם לפי שהיא תרחם על בני אחותה יותר מאחרת. ואע"ג דתנן בפרק "החולץ" (יבמות דף מג. ושם): כל הנשים יתארסו חוץ מאלמנה, מפני האיבול, ולא מפליג מידי, משמע שאסורה אפי' למי שיש לו בנים קטנים כשהיא אבילה — התם משום דבלאו הכי אסורה, דצריכה להמתין ג' חדשים משום הבחנה. ואור"ת: דאפי' מתו אביו ואמו יכול לכנוס אחר ל'. והא דאמרי' במועד קטן (דף כב:): על כל המתים נכנס לבית המשתה אחר ל', על אביו ועל אמו אחר י"ב חדשים — ה"מ בשאר שמחות, אבל לישא אשה, שהיא מצוה יתירה — מותר, ואפי' יש לו בנים, משום שנאמר (קהלת יא) "בבקר זרע [את] זרעך ולערב אל תנח ידך". והביא ראיה מדתניא סתם כל ל' יום לנישואין, ולא מפליג בין אביו ואמו לשאר קרובים — משמע דכולהו לאחר ל' מותר. וה"ר יוסף הביא ראיה לדבריו, דתנן במסכת שמחות (פ"ט) בהדיא: על כל המתים אסור לילך לבית המשתה עד שישלימו ל' יום, ועל אביו ועל אמו אסור כל שנים עשר חדש, אא"כ היה של מצוה. אלמא שרי בכל משתה של מצוה. ול"ע אי קאי נמי ארישא, ושרי אפי' תוך ל' יום. **כגון** מתא מחסיא. תימה: רב חסדא מאי דוחקיה לאוקומי בנתן מים על גבי בשר? נוקמה בכפר, אע"פ שלא נתן מים על גבי בשר! ויש לומר: משום דניחא ליה לרב חסדא לאוקמה ברוב עיירות שהן בינוניות. וה"ק: כגון מתא מחסיא ורוב עיירות. ומש"ה נקט נמי בברייתא דמייתי "ונתן מים על גבי בשר", משום דאיירי ברוב עיירות. **מסייע** ליה לר' יוחנן כו'. מועד וחתן משוה אותן בכ"מ, כההיא דתניא בפ"ק דמועד קטן (דף ז: ושם): חתן שנולד בו נגע — נותנין לו ז' ימי המשתה לו ולאיצטליתו ולכסותו, וכן ברגל נותנין לו כל ימות הרגל. **אבל** דברים של צינעא נוהג. פי': חובה לעשות כן, ולא רשות. מדמייתי סייעתא מן הברייתא. וא"ת: רב ושמואל, דאמרי בפרק בתרא דמועד קטן (דף כד.): דתשמיש המטה בשבת של ז' ימי אבילות רשות, תיקשי להו ברייתא דהכא! ואין סברא לחלק בין מועד לשבת, ומקילין בשבת טפי. אלא נראה לר"י: דרב ושמואל מפלגי בין חתן למועד ושבת. אבל קשה: דכל אותן הימים הוא ישן בין האנשים — משמע אפי' בשבת! ופסקו ה"ג כר' יוחנן, ופירשו: אע"ג דקיימא לן כדברי המיקל באבל — ה"מ בתנאי, אבל באמוראי לא. ואור"י: דודאי נראה דהלכה כר' יוחנן, מדאמר התלמוד הכא מסייע ליה לר' יוחנן.
והלעת

עין משפט נר מצוה

ט א ב מיי' פי"א מהל' אבל הל' ח סמג עשין ב טוש"ע יו"ד סי' שמב וסי' שפג סעי' ב [רב אלפס כאן ובמ"ק פ"ג דף רלא.]

י ג מיי' וסמג שם טוש"ע שם סי' שפא סעי' ו:

יא ד מיי' פ"י שם הל' ג סמג שם טוש"ע שם סי' שלט סעי' ב [עי' כ"מ]:

יב ה ו מיי' פכ"ב מהל' איסורי ביאה הל"א סמג לאוין קכו טוש"ע אה"ע סי' כב סעי' א וטוש"ע יו"ד סי' שפג סעי' ב:

תוספות רי"ד

אמר רפרם בר פפא א"ר חסדא לא שנו אלא שניתן מים ע"ג בשר אבל לא ניתן מים ע"ג בשר מיזדבן. אמר רבא ובכרך אע"פ שניתן מים על גבי בשר מיזדבן. א"ר פפא ובכפר אע"פ שלא ניתן מים ע"ג בשר לא מיזדבן. ואלא דרב חסדא היכי משכחת לה כגון מתא מחסיא דמפקא מכפר ומפקא מכרך: אמר מר הוא ישן בין האנשים וכו'. מסייע ליה לר' יוחנן דאמר ר"י אע"פ שאמרו אין אבילות במועד אבל דברים שבצנעה נוהג. פי' ז' ימי חתונות כשבעת ימי הרגל הן לו. ומפני שתשמיש המטה הוי דבר של צנעה שאין בני העולם מרגישים אסור: דרש ר"י ברי' דרבא משמיה דרבא לא שנו אלא שלא בעל שיצרו תוקפו אבל בעל אשתו ישנה עמו בבית. והא הכא בבעל עסקינן וקתני הוא ישן בין האנשים וכו'. כי קאמר ר"י אפירסה נדה. והא וכן קתני ה"ק וכן מי שפירסה אשתו נדה ולא בעל הוא ישן בין האנשים ואשתו ישנה בין הנשים פי' אבל [בעל] כל נדה דעלמא מתקיים בעלה בבית וכשמת אביו של חתן או אמה של כלה צריכי שימור:

מסורת הש"ס

[יומא עח:]

[עי' תוס' יומא יח: ד"ה יחודי וכו' אריכות בסוגיא דהכא]

יומא דף עח:

גליון הש"ס

רש"י ד"ה כל ל' יום. ע' מג"א סי' תרי"ג ס"ק י"ב:

עין משפט נר מצוה

יג א מיי' פי"א מהל' איסורי ביאה הל' יט סמג לאוין קיא טוש"ע יו"ד סי' קצה סעי' י:

יד ב (מיי' פ"ב מהל' אבל) סמג עשין ב טוש"ע שם סי' שפג סעי' א:

טו ג [מיי' פ"ב מהל' אבל הל' ה] טוש"ע שם סי' שעד סעי' ו וסי' שפא סעי' ו:

טז ד מיי' פ"ב שם הל' ה סמג שם (טוש"ע יו"ד סי' שעד סעי' ו):

יז ה מיי' פ"י מהל' אישות הל' יד טוש"ע אה"ע סי' סד סעי' ג:

גמרא

הָכִי קָאָמַר: וְכֵן מִי שֶׁפֵּירְסָה אִשְׁתּוֹ נִדָּה וְלֹא בָּעַל – הוּא יָשֵׁן בֵּין הָאֲנָשִׁים, וְאִשְׁתּוֹ יְשֵׁנָה בֵּין הַנָּשִׁים. לְמֵימְרָא דַּאֲבֵילוּת קִילָּא לֵיהּ מִנִּדָּה? וְהָאָמַר רַבִּי יִצְחָק בַּר חֲנִינָא אָמַר רַב הוּנָא: *[א]כָּל מְלָאכוֹת שֶׁאִשָּׁה עוֹשָׂה לְבַעְלָהּ, נִדָּה עוֹשָׂה לְבַעְלָהּ, חוּץ מִמְּזִיגַת הַכּוֹס וְהַצָּעַת הַמִּטָּה וְהַרְחָצַת פָּנָיו יָדָיו וְרַגְלָיו. וְאִלּוּ גַּבֵּי אֲבֵילוּת תַּנְיָא: אע"פ שֶׁאָמְרוּ: אֵין אָדָם רַשַּׁאי לָכוֹף אֶת אִשְׁתּוֹ לִהְיוֹת כּוֹחֶלֶת וְלִהְיוֹת פּוֹקֶסֶת, [ב]בֶּאֱמֶת אָמְרוּ: מוֹזֶגֶת לוֹ הַכּוֹס, וּמַצַּעַת לוֹ הַמִּטָּה, וּמַרְחֶצֶת לוֹ פָּנָיו יָדָיו וְרַגְלָיו! לָא קַשְׁיָא, כָּאן – בַּאֲבֵילוּת דִּידֵיהּ, כָּאן – בַּאֲבֵילוּת דִּידָהּ. וְהָא אָבִיו שֶׁל חָתָן אוֹ אִמָּהּ שֶׁל כַּלָּה קָתָנֵי! כִּי קָתָנֵי – אַשְּׁאָרָא. וּמִי שָׁאנֵי בֵּין אֲבֵילוּת דִּידֵיהּ לַאֲבֵילוּת דִּידָהּ? וְהָתַנְיָא: *מִי שֶׁמֵּת חָמִיו אוֹ חֲמוֹתוֹ [ג]אֵינוֹ יָכוֹל לָכוֹף אֶת אִשְׁתּוֹ לִהְיוֹת כּוֹחֶלֶת וְלִהְיוֹת פּוֹקֶסֶת, אֶלָּא כּוֹפֶה מִטָּתוֹ וְנוֹהֵג עִמָּהּ אֲבֵילוּת. וְכֵן הִיא שֶׁמֵּת חָמִיהָ אוֹ חֲמוֹתָהּ אֵינָהּ רַשָּׁאָה לִהְיוֹת כּוֹחֶלֶת וְלִהְיוֹת פּוֹקֶסֶת, אֶלָּא כּוֹפָה מִטָּתָהּ וְנוֹהֶגֶת עִמּוֹ אֲבֵילוּת! תְּנֵי בַּאֲבֵילוּת דִּידֵיהּ: הוּא יָשֵׁן בֵּין הָאֲנָשִׁים וְאִשְׁתּוֹ יְשֵׁנָה בֵּין הַנָּשִׁים. הָא "וְכֵן" קָתָנֵי! כִּי קָתָנֵי – אַכִּיחוּל וְאַפִּירְכּוּס. וְהָא "עִמּוֹ" קָתָנֵי, מַאי לָאו עִמּוֹ בְּמִטָּה? לֹא, עִמּוֹ בְּבַיִת. *וּכְדַאֲמַר לֵיהּ רַב לְחִיָּיא בְּרֵיהּ: [ד]בְּאַפַּהּ – נְהוֹג אֲבֵילוּתָא, דְּלָא בְּאַפַּהּ – לָא תִּנְהוֹג אֲבֵילוּתָא. רַב אַשִׁי אָמַר: מִי קָמְדַמֵּית אֲבֵילוּתָא דְּהָכָא לַאֲבֵילוּתָא דְּעָלְמָא? *אֲבֵילוּתָא דְּעָלְמָא – חֲמִיר, וְלָא אָתֵי לְזַלְזוּלֵי בֵּיהּ. אֲבֵילוּת דְּהָכָא, כֵּיוָן דְּאַקִּילוּ רַבָּנַן – אָתֵי לְזַלְזוּלֵי בֵּיהּ. מַאי קוּלָּא? אִילֵימָא דְּקָתָנֵי בּוֹעֵל בְּעִילַת מִצְוָה וּפוֹרֵשׁ – הָתָם מִשּׁוּם דְּלָא חָל עָלָיו אֲבֵילוּתָא; אִי לְרַבִּי אֱלִיעֶזֶר – *עַד שֶׁיֵּצֵא מִפֶּתַח הַבַּיִת, אִי לְרַבִּי יְהוֹשֻׁעַ – עַד שֶׁיִּסָּתֵם הַגּוֹלֵל! אֶלָּא דְּקָתָנֵי: נוֹהֵג שִׁבְעַת יְמֵי הַמִּשְׁתֶּה, וְאַחַ"כ נוֹהֵג שִׁבְעַת יְמֵי אֲבֵילוּת. אֲמַר מָר: [ה]בֵּין כָּךְ וּבֵין כָּךְ לֹא יִבְעוֹל לֹא בְּעֶרֶב שַׁבָּת וְלֹא בְּמוֹצ"שׁ. בִּשְׁלָמָא בְּעֶרֶב שַׁבָּת – מִשּׁוּם חַבּוּרָה, אֶלָּא בְּמוֹצָאֵי שַׁבָּת אַמַּאי לֹא? אָמַר רַבִּי זֵירָא: מִשּׁוּם

רש"י

ה"ק כו'. כְּלוֹמַר, כִּי קָאָמַר 'וְכֵן' – אַהוּא יָשֵׁן בֵּין הָאֲנָשִׁים וְהִיא יְשֵׁנָה בֵּין הַנָּשִׁים קָאָמַר, וּלְעוֹלָם הָךְ דְּשֶׁלֹּא בָּעַל קָאֵי. קִילָּא לֵיהּ. לַעֲבוֹר עָלֶיהָ מִנִּדָּה, דְּאַאֲבֵילוּת לָא מְהֵימְנַתְּ לֵיהּ וְאַנִּדָּה מְהֵימְנַתְּ לֵיהּ. מְלָאכוֹת שֶׁהָאִשָּׁה עוֹשָׂה לְבַעְלָהּ. לְקַמָּן תָּנֵי לְהוּ בְּפֶרֶק "אַף עַל פִּי". חוּץ מִמְּזִיגַת הַכּוֹס. לְהוֹשִׁיט לוֹ. וְהַצָּעַת הַמִּטָּה וְהַרְחָצַת פָּנָיו כו'. שֶׁדֶּרֶךְ קֵירוּב וְחִיבָּה הֵן, וּבָאִין לִידֵי הֶרְגֵּל דָּבָר. אֵין אָדָם רַשַּׁאי לָכוֹף אֶת אִשְׁתּוֹ. בִּימֵי אֶבְלָהּ, כְּשֶׁמֵּת אָבִיהָ אוֹ אִמָּהּ. פּוֹקֶסֶת. מַעֲבֶרֶת סְרָק עַל פָּנֶיהָ. מוֹזֶגֶת לוֹ. וְלָא חָיְישִׁינַן לְהֶרְגֵּל דָּבָר. אַלְמָא: אֲבֵילוּת חֲמִירָא לֵיהּ. כָּאן בַּאֲבֵילוּת דִּידֵיהּ. לְעוֹלָם אֲבֵילוּת קִילָּא לֵיהּ מִנִּדָּה, וְהָנֵי מַתְנִיתָא הָכִי מִתָּרְצָן: הָא דְּקָתָנֵי לְעֵיל הוּא יָשֵׁן בֵּין הָאֲנָשִׁים כו' – בַּאֲבֵילוּת דִּידֵיהּ, וְהָךְ דְּקָתָנֵי מוֹזֶגֶת לוֹ כו' – בַּאֲבֵילוּת דִּידָהּ קָאֵי. דְּקָתָנֵי: אֵין אָדָם רַשַּׁאי לָכוֹף כו'. אַלְמָא בַּאֲבֵילוּת דִּידָהּ קָיְימִינַן, שֶׁאֵינָהּ רוֹצָה לִכְחוֹל וְלִפְקוֹס. וְהַיְינוּ טַעְמָא דְּמוֹזֶגֶת, דְּאִם יִתְגַּבֵּר יִצְרוֹ עָלָיו, כֵּיוָן דַּאֲבֵילוּת דִּידָהּ הוּא – אֵינָהּ שׁוֹמַעַת לוֹ. וְהָא אָבִיו שֶׁל חָתָן כו'. אַלְמָא בַּאֲבֵילוּת דִּידָהּ נַמִי אַחְמִיר תַּנָּא דִּלְעֵיל. כִּי קָתָנֵי. אִמָּהּ שֶׁל כַּלָּה – אַשְּׁאָרָא, אַ"מַכְנִיסִים הַמֵּת לְחֶדֶר". אֲבָל "הוּא יָשֵׁן בֵּין הָאֲנָשִׁים" – אַאֲבֵילוּת דְּחָתָן קָאֵי. וְנוֹהֶגֶת עִמּוֹ אֲבֵילוּת. אַלְמָא מִדְּלָא קָתָנֵי בַּאֲבֵילוּת דִּידֵיהּ הוּא יָשֵׁן בֵּין הָאֲנָשִׁים – שְׁמַע מִינָּהּ חֲמִיר לֵיהּ, וְלָא שָׁנֵי לָן. ה"ג: תְּנֵי בַּאֲבֵילוּת דִּידֵיהּ הוּא יָשֵׁן כו'. הָכִי גָּרְסִינַן. וְהָא עִמּוֹ קָתָנֵי מַאי לָאו עִמּוֹ בְּמִטָּה. אַלְמָא אֲבֵילוּת דִּידֵיהּ נַמִי מְהֵימָן. לֹא עִמּוֹ בְּבַיִת. וְטַעְמָא לָאו מִשּׁוּם דִּמְהֵימָן נָקֵט לָהּ, אֶלָּא לְאַשְׁמוֹעִינַן דְּאֵין אֲבֵילוּתוֹ מוּטָּל עָלֶיהָ אֶלָּא בְּפָנָיו מִשּׁוּם כְּבוֹדוֹ. וְכֵן הוּא אֵין אֲבֵילוּתָהּ מוּטָּל עָלָיו אֶלָּא לְפָנֶיהָ וְלִכְבוֹדָהּ. כְּדַאֲמַר לֵיהּ רַב לְחִיָּיא בְּרֵיהּ. כְּשֶׁמֵּת חָמִיו: בְּאַפַּהּ נְהוֹג אֲבֵילוּתָא כו'. פְּלוּגְתָּא דְּרַבִּי אֱלִיעֶזֶר וְרַבִּי יְהוֹשֻׁעַ בְּמוֹעֵד קָטָן. גּוֹלֵל. זֶהוּ כִּסּוּי שֶׁל אֲרוֹן הַמֵּת.

תוספות

והצעת המטה. נראה לר"י דהצעת המטה דהכא היינו פריסת סדינין, שהוא דבר של חיבה. אבל הצעת כרים וכסתות, שאינן דברים של חיבה – שרי לנדה. והביא ראיה מדתנן בפ' "אע"פ" (לקמן נט:): הכניסה לו ג' שפחות – אינה מצעת לו המטה ואינה עושה בצמר. ארבע – יושבת בקתדרא. ואמרינן בגמרא: אע"פ שאמרו ד' יושבת בקתדרא – אבל מוזגת לו כוס, ומצעת לו המטה, ומרחצת לו פניו ידיו ורגליו. ופי' בקונטרס: דהא דתנא ג' אינה מצעת לו המטה – היינו הצעת כרים וכסתות, דהוי דבר שיש טורח. אבל מצעת לו המטה – היינו פריסת סדין ולבדין, דמילי דחיבה נינהו שמתחבב עליו, ואין בו טורח. והויא הצעה של חיבה נראה דדוקא אסור. וכן משמע, דמזכירה בהדי מזיגת כוס והרחצת פניו ידיו ורגליו כי התם. מיהו, לספרים דל"ג במשנה אלא: ואינה מצעת המטה, ול"ג 'לו' ובגמרא גרסינן 'לו' – אין ראיה משם שיהו תרי גווני הצעה, דמתני' איירי בהצעת שאר מטות, ובגמרא איירי בהצעת מטה לבעלה לבדו.

פוקסת. פ"ה: מעברת סרק על פניה. ואין נראה, דאמר בפ"ב לקמן (דף יז.): לא סרק ולא פירכוס. משמע דתרי מילי נינהו. דפוקסת דהכא – היינו פירכוס, כדאמרי' בסמוך: כי קתני – אכיחול ואפירכוס. ובשילהי "המצניע" (שבת לה.) קתני: פוקסת ומעברת סרק על פניה. ולקמן בפ"ב פ"ה: פירכוס – קליעת שער. וקשה לר"י: דבשילהי "המצניע" (שם לד: ושם) קתני גודלת ופוקסת? אלא נראה דאחד מתיקוני נשים הוא.

ומי שאני בין אבילות דידיה לאבילות דידה. תימה: דבלאו מילתא דרב יוסף הוי מצי למיפרך ברייתות אהדדי! וי"ל: דאי לאו הוה מילתא דרב יוסף הוה מפלגינן בין שעת חופה לשלא בשעת חופה. דבשעת חופה – יצרו תוקפו אע"ג דבעל. אבל לרב יוסף לא מצי לפלוגי בהכי, דהא בבעל חשיב ליה כאשתו ישנה, דאפי' בשעת חופה אשתו ישנה עמו בנדה ובאבילות דידה, ואפילו הכי באבילות דידיה קתני: הוא ישן בין האנשים, ולהכי פריך שפיר. ולרשב"א נראה דאי לאו דרב יוסף – לא הוה קשה מידי. דעמו ועמה קתני בברייתא – לאו עמו במטה אלא עמה בבית, אבל לרב יוסף דבאבילות דידה אשתו ישנה עמו – א"כ הא דקתני נוהג עמה אבילות היינו עמה במטה, דומיא דהכא באבילות דידיה הוי עמו במטה. והא דמשני תני באבילות דידיה הוא ישן – אינו מגיה הברייתא, אלא מפרש ד'עמו' דקתני בברייתא דהכי הוא. ופריך: והא 'עמו' קתני, מאי לאו עמו במטה? פי': דומיא ד'עמה', ומשני: לא, עמו בבית, כדא"ל רב כו'.

עד שיסתם הגולל. בכמה מקומות פי' רש"י דגולל הוי כיסוי ארון, ודופק היינו קרשים שבצידי הארון. ונקרא דופק על שם שהגולל דופק עליו. וכעין זה פי' בערוך. וקשה לר"ת: דאמר בפרק "מי שמתו" (ברכות יט: ושם): מדלגין היינו על גבי ארונות. ואיך היו מדלגין? והלא הגולל והדופק מטמא באהל, כדאמרינן ב"העור והרוטב" (חולין קכו: ושם)! ועוד, דבפרק "בהמה המקשה" (שם עב:) דריש: "על פני השדה" – לרבות גולל ודופק. ולפ"ה הלא ארון אינו על פני השדה! ואומר ה"ר דוד מנלינבורק כי לפרש"י [דריש] לרבות גולל ודופק שפירש דלא מרבינן מעל פני השדה דמטמא אלא כשפירש, אבל בעוד שהוא טמון – בטל אגב קרקע, ולא מטמא באוהל. והשתא אתי נמי שפיר ההיא דמדלגים היינו על גבי ארונות. ועוד י"מ: אע"ג דגולל מטמא באהל – מ"מ יכולין לדלג ולטמאות עצמם בגולל, דתניא במס' שמחות (פ"ד): כל טומאה שאין נזיר מגלח עליה – אין כהן מוזהר עליה. ואר"ת: דמשובשת היא, דהא רביעית דם אין נזיר מגלח עליה, כדתנן בנזיר (דף נד. ושם) וכהן מוזהר עליה. ועוד הקשה: דתניא בעירובין (דף טו:): כל דבר שיש בו רוח חיים אין עושין ממנו לא גולל לקבר כו', ולפ"ה וכי דרך לעשות כסוי ארון מבעלי חיים? ויש לומר אע"ג דאין דרך לעשות כסוי ארון מבעלי חיים – מכל מקום כמה דברים אשכחן דלא שכיח, ומיירי בהן התלמוד לדרוש ולקבל שכר, כדאמרינן בפרק "המקשה" (חולין ע.): בלעתו חולדה והוציאתו והכניסתו והקיאתו ויצא מאליו מהו? הדביק שני רחמים ויצא מזה לזה מהו? אף על פי שלא יצא לעולם. ור"ת מפרש: דגולל היינו מצבה, שהיא אבן גדולה. ולשון גולל שייך על האבן, כדכתיב "וגללו את האבן" (בראשית כט). ודופק הן שתי אבנים, אחת לראשה ואחת לרגלה של מצבה. ופעמים כשאין המצבה מזומנת מעמידין שם בהמה או דבר אחר לסימן; וההיא דמדלגין לא היה שם מצבה. ומחמת המת לא היו מיטמאין, דרוב ארונות יש בהן פותח טפח. ולא תקשה לר' יהושע מאימת חל אבילות כשאין שם מצבה, די"ל: דכי מהדרי אפייהו דקוברין, כדאמרינן במועד קטן (דף כב.) דהנהו דלא אזלי בתר שכבא מכי מהדרי אפייהו. וקשה לר"י על פירוש רבינו תם: דתניא בתוספתא דאהלות בפרק ד': אמר רבי יהודה שתי אבנים גדולות של

תוספות רי"ד

למימרא דאבילות קילא [ליה] מנדה דהא בנדה [אינה] צריכה שימור אם בעל ואבילות (לא) מצרכינן שימור אע"פ שבעל. והא אר"י ב"ח א"ר פפא כל מלאכות שהאשה עושה לבעלה נדה עושה לבעלה חוץ ממזיגת הכוס והצעת המטה והרחצת פניו ידיו ורגליו ואילו גבי אבילות תניא אע"פ שאמרו אין אדם רשאי לכוף את אשתו לא להיות כוחלת ולא להיות פוקסת באמת אמרו מוזגת לו הכוס ומצעת לו המטה ורוחצת פניו ידיו ורגליו ומסיק ר"א מי קא מדמית אבילות דהכא לאבילות דעלמא. אבילות דעלמא חמירא ליה ולא אתי לזלזולי בה. אבל אבילות דהכא כיון דאקילי בה רבנן אתי לזלזולי בה ומאי קילותא דקתני נוהג ז' ימי המשתה ואח"כ נוהג ז' ימי אבילות: תניא מי שמת חמיו או חמותו אינו רשאי לכוף את אשתו להיות פוקסת אבל כופה מטתו ונוהג עמה אבילות ודוקא בפניה אבל שלא בפניה לא. כדא"ל רב לחייא בריה באפה נהוג אבילות שלא באפה לא תנהוג אבילות:

מסורת הש"ס

לקמן סא.

מ"ק כ: שמחות פי"א

ג"ז שם

מ"ק כז. סנהדרין מז: [שבת קנב:]

גליון הש"ס

גמ' אבילותא דעלמא חמיר. ע' סוטה ז ע"א תוס' ד"ה אמר:

מִשּׁוּם חֶשְׁבּוֹנוֹת. אֲמַר לֵיהּ אַבַּיֵי: וְחֶשְׁבּוֹנוֹת שֶׁל מִצְוָה מִי אֲסִירִי? וְהָא רַב חִסְדָּא וְרַב הַמְנוּנָא דְּאָמְרִי תַּרְוַיְיהוּ: *[א]חֶשְׁבּוֹנוֹת שֶׁל מִצְוָה מוּתָּר לְחַשְּׁבָן בְּשַׁבָּת! וְא"ר אֶלְעָזָר: [ב]פּוֹסְקִין צְדָקָה לַעֲנִיִּים בְּשַׁבָּת! וְאָמַר ר' יַעֲקֹב אָמַר ר' יוֹחָנָן: [ג]הוֹלְכִין לְבָתֵּי כְנֵסִיּוֹת וּלְבָתֵּי מִדְרָשׁוֹת לְפַקֵּחַ עַל עִסְקֵי רַבִּים בְּשַׁבָּת. וְאָמַר רַבִּי יַעֲקֹב בַּר אִידִי אָמַר רַבִּי יוֹחָנָן: מְפַקְּחִין פִּיקּוּחַ נֶפֶשׁ בְּשַׁבָּת. וְאָמַר רַב שְׁמוּאֵל בַּר נַחְמָנִי אָמַר רַבִּי יוֹנָתָן: הוֹלְכִין לְטַרְטִיָּיאוֹת וּלְקַרְקְיָיאוֹת לְפַקֵּחַ עַל עִסְקֵי רַבִּים בְּשַׁבָּת. וְתָנָא דְּבֵי מְנַשְּׁיָא: [ד]מְשַׁדְּכִין עַל הַתִּינוֹקֶת לֵיאָרֵס בְּשַׁבָּת, וְעַל הַתִּינוֹק לְלַמְּדוֹ סֵפֶר וּלְלַמְּדוֹ אוּמָּנוּת! אֶלָּא אָמַר רַבִּי זֵירָא: גְּזֵירָה שֶׁמָּא יִשְׁחוֹט בֶּן עוֹף. א"ל אַבַּיֵי: אֶלָּא מֵעַתָּה, יוֹם הַכִּפּוּרִים שֶׁחָל לִהְיוֹת בְּשֵׁנִי בְּשַׁבָּת יִדָּחֶה, גְּזֵירָה שֶׁמָּא יִשְׁחוֹט בֶּן עוֹף! הָתָם, דִּלְנַפְשֵׁיהּ, לָא טְרִיד, הָכָא דִּלְאַחֵרִים — טְרִיד. אִי נַמִי: הָתָם — אִית לֵיהּ רַוְוחָא, הָכָא — לֵית לֵיהּ רַוְוחָא. הַשְׁתָּא דְּאָתֵית לְהָכִי — עֶרֶב שַׁבָּת נַמִי, גְּזֵירָה שֶׁמָּא יִשְׁחוֹט בֶּן עוֹף. אִיבַּעְיָא לְהוּ: בְּתוּלָה נִשֵּׂאת בִּרְבִיעִי וְנִבְעֶלֶת בִּרְבִיעִי, וְלָא חָיְישִׁינַן לְאִיקְרוּרֵי דַּעְתָּא, אוֹ דִּלְמָא: בְּתוּלָה נִשֵּׂאת בִּרְבִיעִי וְנִבְעֶלֶת בַּחֲמִישִׁי, דְּחָיְישִׁינַן לְאִיקְרוּרֵי דַּעְתָּא? ת"ש, דְּתָנֵי בַּר קַפָּרָא: בְּתוּלָה נִשֵּׂאת בִּרְבִיעִי [ה]וְנִבְעֶלֶת בַּחֲמִישִׁי, הוֹאִיל וְנֶאֶמְרָה בּוֹ בְּרָכָה לַדָּגִים. אַלְמָנָה נִשֵּׂאת בַּחֲמִישִׁי וְנִבְעֶלֶת בְּשִׁשִּׁי, הוֹאִיל וְנֶאֶמְרָה בּוֹ בְּרָכָה לָאָדָם. טַעֲמָא — מִשּׁוּם בְּרָכָה, אֲבָל מִשּׁוּם אִיקְרוּרֵי דַּעְתָּא — לָא חָיְישִׁינַן. אִי הָכִי, אַלְמָנָה נַמִי תִּיבָּעֵל בַּחֲמִישִׁי, הוֹאִיל וְנֶאֶמְרָה בּוֹ בְּרָכָה לַדָּגִים! בְּרָכָה דְּאָדָם עֲדִיפָא לֵיהּ. וְאִי נַמִי — מִשּׁוּם שָׁקְדוּ. דְּתַנְיָא: מִפְּנֵי מָה אָמְרוּ אַלְמָנָה נִשֵּׂאת בַּחֲמִישִׁי וְנִבְעֶלֶת בְּשִׁשִּׁי? שֶׁאִם אַתָּה אוֹמֵר תִּיבָּעֵל בַּחֲמִישִׁי — לְמָחָר מַשְׁכִּים לְאוּמָּנְתּוֹ וְהוֹלֵךְ לוֹ, *שָׁקְדוּ חֲכָמִים עַל תַּקָּנַת בְּנוֹת יִשְׂרָאֵל, [ו]שֶׁיְּהֵא שָׂמֵחַ עִמָּהּ שְׁלֹשָׁה יָמִים: חֲמִישִׁי בְּשַׁבָּת, וְעֶרֶב שַׁבָּת, וְשַׁבָּת. מַאי אִיכָּא בֵּין "בְּרָכָה" לְ"שָׁקְדוּ"? אִיכָּא בֵּינַיְיהוּ אָדָם בָּטֵל, אִי נַמִי יוֹם טוֹב שֶׁחָל לִהְיוֹת בְּעֶרֶב שַׁבָּת. דָּרַשׁ בַּר קַפָּרָא: גְּדוֹלִים מַעֲשֵׂה צַדִּיקִים יוֹתֵר מִמַּעֲשֵׂה שָׁמַיִם וָאָרֶץ, דְּאִילּוּ בְּמַעֲשֵׂה שָׁמַיִם וָאָרֶץ כְּתִיב: °"אַף יָדִי יָסְדָה אֶרֶץ וִימִינִי טִפְּחָה שָׁמַיִם" וְאִילּוּ בְּמַעֲשֵׂה יְדֵיהֶם שֶׁל צַדִּיקִים כְּתִיב: °"מָכוֹן לְשִׁבְתְּךָ פָּעַלְתָּ ה' מִקְּדָשׁ אֲדֹנָי כּוֹנְנוּ יָדֶיךָ". הֵשִׁיב בַּבְלִי אֶחָד, וְר' חִיָּיא שְׁמוֹ: °"וְיַבֶּשֶׁת יָדָיו יָצָרוּ"! "יָדוֹ" כְּתִיב. וְהָכְתִיב "יָצְרוּ"! א"ר נַחְמָן בַּר יִצְחָק: יָצְרוּ אֶצְבְּעוֹתָיו, כִּדְכְתִיב: °"כִּי אֶרְאֶה שָׁמֶיךָ מַעֲשֵׂה אֶצְבְּעוֹתֶיךָ יָרֵחַ וְכוֹכָבִים אֲשֶׁר כּוֹנָנְתָּה". מֵיתִיבֵי: °"הַשָּׁמַיִם מְסַפְּרִים כְּבוֹד אֵל וּמַעֲשֵׂה יָדָיו מַגִּיד הָרָקִיעַ"! הָכִי קָאָמַר: מַעֲשֵׂה יְדֵיהֶם שֶׁל צַדִּיקִים מִי מַגִּיד — הָרָקִיעַ, וּמַאי נִיהוּ — מָטָר. דָּרַשׁ בַּר קַפָּרָא: מַאי דִּכְתִיב °"וְיָתֵד תִּהְיֶה לְךָ עַל אֲזֵנֶךָ" — אַל תִּקְרֵי "אֲזֵנֶךָ" אֶלָּא "עַל אָזְנֶךָ", שֶׁאִם יִשְׁמַע אָדָם דָּבָר שֶׁאֵינוֹ הָגוּן, יַנִּיחַ

רש"י

מִשּׁוּם חֶשְׁבּוֹנוֹת. שֶׁאִם יִכְנוֹס לְמוֹצָאֵי שַׁבָּת יַעֲשֶׂה סְעוּדָה בַּלַּיְלָה, וְיַחֲשׁוֹב בְּשַׁבָּת מַהוּ צָרִיךְ לְהוֹצִיא, וּכְתִיב "וְדַבֵּר דָּבָר" (ישעיה נח). מְפַקְּחִים. מוֹצִיאִין לָאוֹר. פִּיקּוּחַ. פושקונברמ"ש בְּלַעַ"ז. טַרְטִיָּאוֹת. פַּלְטֵי מְלָכִים וְשִׁלְטוֹנִים. לְלַמְּדוֹ אוּמָּנוּת. מִצְוָה הוּא, דִּכְתִיב (קהלת ט) "רְאֵה חַיִּים עִם אִשָּׁה אֲשֶׁר אָהַבְתָּ" — תורה אור לִמּוּד אוּמָּנוּת שֶׁתְּהֵא הֵימֶנּוּ עִם הַתּוֹרָה. וְאָמְרִינַן בְּקִידּוּשִׁין (דף כט.) שֶׁאָבִיו חַיָּיב לְלַמְּדוֹ אוּמָּנוּת. שֶׁמָּא יִשְׁחוֹט בֶּן עוֹף. בְּשַׁבָּת, לְצוֹרֶךְ מוֹצָאֵי שַׁבָּת. שֶׁיְּהֵא טָרוּד וְיִשְׁכַּח שֶׁהוּא שַׁבָּת. שֶׁחָל לִהְיוֹת בְּשֵׁנִי בְּשַׁבָּת. שֶׁצְּרִיכִין לְהַרְבּוֹת בִּסְעוּדָה אַחַר הַשַּׁבָּת, שֶׁהוּא עֶרֶב יוֹם כִּפּוּרִים. יִדָּחֶה. לִשְׁלִישִׁי בְּשַׁבָּת, שֶׁמָּא יִשְׁחוֹט בֶּן עוֹף לְצוֹרֶךְ סְעוּדַּת מָחָר. אִית לֵיהּ רַוְוחָא. לִשְׁחוֹט בַּלַּיְלָה, שֶׁהַסְּעוּדָה אֵינָהּ עַד לְמָחָר. הָכָא לֵית לֵיהּ רַוְוחָא. שֶׁהַסְּעוּדָה בַּלַּיְלָה אַחַר הַשַּׁבָּת מִשֶּׁחֲשֵׁיכָה מִיָּד. וְלָא חָיְישִׁינַן לְאִיקְרוּרֵי דַּעְתָּא. אִם לֹא יִמְצָא לָהּ בְּתוּלִים — לָא חָיְישִׁינַן שֶׁיִּתְקָרֵר כַּעֲסוֹ בְּהַאי פּוּרְתָּא. וְנִבְעֶלֶת בַּחֲמִישִׁי. מִשֶּׁתֶּחְשַׁךְ בִּרְבִיעִי וְתִיכָּנֵס לֵיל חֲמִישִׁי. בְּרָכָה לַדָּגִים. "פְּרוּ וּרְבוּ וּמִלְאוּ אֶת הַמַּיִם" כו' (בראשית א). הוֹאִיל וְנֶאֶמְרָה בּוֹ בְּרָכָה לָאָדָם. "פְּרוּ וּרְבוּ וּמִלְאוּ אֶת הָאָרֶץ" (שם). טַעֲמָא מִשּׁוּם בְּרָכָה. אֲבָל מַאן דְּלָא קָפֵיד אַבְּרָכָה, מִשּׁוּם אִיקְרוּרֵי דַּעְתָּא — לָא חָיְישִׁינַן מִשּׁוּם הַאי פּוּרְתָּא. בְּרָכָה דְּאָדָם עֲדִיפָא לֵיהּ. וּמִיהוּ, בְּשִׁשִּׁי לֹא תִּנָּשֵׂא בְּתוּלָה, דִּבְזִמַן אָרוֹךְ עַד שֵׁנִי בְּשַׁבָּת דְּאָתוּ דַּיָּינֵי חָיְישִׁינַן לְאִיקְרוּרֵי. אֲבָל מֵרְבִיעִי עַד חֲמִישִׁי — לָא חָיְישִׁינַן. לְמָחָר מַשְׁכִּים לְאוּמָּנוּתוֹ וְהוֹלֵךְ. שֶׁאֵין מִשְׁתֶּה אַלְמוֹן בְּאַלְמָנָה אֶלָּא יוֹם אֶחָד, כִּדְלְקַמָּן בְּפִירְקִין (דף ז.). חֲמִישִׁי בְּשַׁבָּת. יוֹם חוּפָּה. וְשִׁשִּׁי בְּשַׁבָּת. חִיבַּת בִּיאָה. אָדָם בָּטֵל. לְמ"ד בִּרְכָה דְּאָדָם עֲדִיפָא — אַף זוֹ תִּיבָּעֵל בְּשִׁשִּׁי, לְמ"ד מִשּׁוּם שָׁקְדוּ — נִבְעֶלֶת בַּחֲמִישִׁי, דְּהָא לֹא יַשְׁכִּים לְאוּמָּנְתּוֹ. גְּדוֹלִים מַעֲשֵׂה צַדִּיקִים מִמַּעֲשֵׂה יְצִירַת שָׁמַיִם וָאָרֶץ. וּמִשּׁוּם בַּר קַפָּרָא נָקַט לָהּ, דְּאַיְירֵי לְעֵיל בְּהַגָּדָה. אַף יָדִי. חֲדָא יָד. מִקְדָּשׁ מַעֲשֵׂה יְדֵי צַדִּיקִים הוּא. הָכִי קָאָמַר. הַאי "וּמַעֲשֵׂה יָדָיו" בְּמַעֲשֵׂה הַצַּדִּיקִים כְּתִיב, שֶׁקְּרוּיִן מַעֲשֵׂה שֶׁלָּהֶם מַעֲשֵׂה יָדָיו שֶׁל הקב"ה. וְה"ק: וּמַעֲשֵׂה יָדָיו, דְּהוּא מַעֲשֵׂה הַצַּדִּיקִים — מַגִּיד הָרָקִיעַ. שֶׁהָרָקִיעַ מֵעִיד עֲלֵיהֶם לַבְּרִיּוֹת שֶׁהֵם צַדִּיקִים, שֶׁמִּתְפַּלְּלִין עַל הַגְּשָׁמִים וּמָטָר יוֹרֵד. יָתֵד. קביל"י בְּלַעַ"ז.

תוספות

שֶׁל אַרְבָּעָה אַרְבָּעָה טְפָחִים, שֶׁעֲשָׂאָן גּוֹלֵל לְקֶבֶר הַמַּאֲהִיל עַל גַּבֵּי שְׁתֵּיהֶם — טָמֵא. נִיטְּלָה אַחַת מֵהֶן — הַמַּאֲהִיל עַל גַּבֵּי הַשְּׁנִיָּה טָהוֹר, מִפְּנֵי שֶׁיֵּשׁ לְטוּמְאָה דֶּרֶךְ שֶׁיֵּלֵא. מַה שַּׁיָּיךְ דֶּרֶךְ שֶׁיֵּלֵא לְפר"ת? וּבְתוֹסֶפְתָּא דְּאָהֳלוֹת ספ"ג תַּנְיָא: מַעֲשֶׂה בְּאֶחָד שֶׁמֵּת בְּעֶרֶב הַפֶּסַח וְלֹא רָצוּ לְקוֹבְרוֹ, וְנִכְנְסוּ הַנָּשִׁים וְקָשְׁרוּ הַחֶבֶל בַּגּוֹלֵל, מָשְׁכוּ הָאֲנָשִׁים מִבַּחוּץ וְקָבְרוּהוּ הַנָּשִׁים וְהָלְכוּ הָאֲנָשִׁים וְעָשׂוּ פִּסְחֵיהֶן לָעֶרֶב. מַשְׁמַע שֶׁלֹּא הָיוּ יְכוֹלִין הַנָּשִׁים לְקוֹבְרוֹ עַד שֶׁמָּשְׁכוּ הָאֲנָשִׁים מִבַּחוּץ אֶת הַגּוֹלֵל. וְאִם גּוֹלֵל הַוָּיא מַצֵּבָה — לָמָּה לֹא קְבָרוּהוּ בְּלֹא מַצֵּבָה עַד אַחַר הַפֶּסַח? אֶלָּא וַדַּאי הוּא כִּסּוּי אָרוֹן, כְּפֵירוּשׁ הַקּוּנְטְרֵס. וּלְפִי שֶׁהָיָה שֶׁל אֶבֶן הָיָה כָּבֵד כָּל כָּךְ*.

שמא יִשְׁחוֹט בֶּן עוֹף. יֵשׁ גּוֹרְסִים: בּוֹ עוֹף. אע"ג דְּשַׁבָּת לְשׁוֹן נְקֵבָה הִיא, דִּכְתִיב (שמות לא) "מְחַלְלֶיהָ מוֹת יוּמָת" — ה"נ הָוֵי לְשׁוֹן זָכָר "כָּל הָעוֹשֶׂה בוֹ מְלָאכָה" (שם לה), "שׁוֹמֵר שַׁבָּת מֵחַלְּלוֹ" (ישעיה נו). וְשַׁפִּיר גָּרְסִינַן נַמִי בֶּן עוֹף, דְּדֶרֶךְ בְּנֵי אָדָם לִשְׁחוֹט הָרַכִּין וְהַקְּטַנִּים, כִּדְכְתִיב (ויקרא ה) "שְׁנֵי בְנֵי יוֹנָה". וּבְפֶרֶק קַמָּא דְּקִידּוּשִׁין (דף לו: ושם) אָתְיָא מִבֶּן עוֹף, מַה לְּבֶן צֹאן שֶׁכֵּן קָבַע לוֹ כו'.

אלא מֵעַתָּה יוֹם הַכִּפּוּרִים שֶׁחָל לִהְיוֹת בְּשֵׁנִי כו'. תֵּימָה: אַמַּאי נָקַט יוֹם כִּפּוּרִים דְּלָא הָוֵי אֶלָּא לְרַבִּי יוֹסֵי הַגְּלִילִי? כִּדְתְנַן (חולין דף פג.): בְּד' פְּרָקִים בַּשָּׁנָה הַמּוֹכֵר בְּהֵמָה לַחֲבֵירוֹ צָרִיךְ לְהוֹדִיעוֹ: אִמָּהּ מָכַרְתִּי לִשְׁחוֹט כו', וְכְדִבְרֵי רַבִּי יוֹסֵי הַגְּלִילִי אַף עֶרֶב יוֹם הַכִּפּוּרִים בַּגָּלִיל. אַמַּאי לֹא נָקַט חַד מִד' פְּרָקִים דַּהֲוֵי לְכ"ע? וי"ל: דִּבְעֶרֶב יוֹם הַכִּפּוּרִים הָיוּ רְגִילִין לְהַרְבּוֹת בְּעוֹפוֹת וּבְדָגִים, כִּדְמַשְׁמַע בִּבְרֵאשִׁית רַבָּה (פי"א) גַּבֵּי הַהוּא חַיָּיטָא דִּזְבַן נוּנָא כו' מִשּׁוּם דַּהֲוֵי יוֹם סְלִיחָה וְכַפָּרָה. וּבְהָנְהוּ ד' פְּרָקִים הָיוּ מַרְבִּים בִּבְהֵמוֹת, דְּלֵיכָּא לְמִגְזַר שֶׁמָּא יִשְׁחוֹט.

אי הָכִי אַלְמָנָה נַמִי תִּיבָּעֵל בַּחֲמִישִׁי. פִּי': בִּשְׁלָמָא אִי הֲוָה תָּנֵי בַּבְּרַיְיתָא דִּבְתוּלָה נִבְעֶלֶת בַּחֲמִישִׁי מִשּׁוּם אִיקְרוּרֵי דַּעְתָּא, כִּדְקָמִיבַּעְיָא לַן, וְלֹא מִשּׁוּם בְּרָכָה לַדָּגִים דְּלָא חֲשִׁיבָא — הֲוֵי נִיחָא לַן בְּאַלְמָנָה דְּנִבְעֶלֶת בְּשִׁשִּׁי מִשּׁוּם בְּרָכָה. אֲבָל הַשְׁתָּא דְּטַעְמָא דִּבְתוּלָה מִשּׁוּם בְּרָכָה — אַלְמָנָה נַמִי תִּיבָּעֵל בַּחֲמִישִׁי!

אי נַמִי מִשּׁוּם שָׁקְדוּ. וא"ת: וְהֵיכִי מָצֵי לְמֵימַר מִשּׁוּם שָׁקְדוּ, הָא בַּבְּרַיְיתָא קָתָנֵי בְּהֶדְיָא מִשּׁוּם בְּרָכָה! וי"ל: דִּלְהַאי שִׁינּוּיָא הָוֵי פֵּירוּשׁ הַבְּרַיְיתָא הָכִי: אַלְמָנָה נִשֵּׂאת בַּחֲמִישִׁי וְנִבְעֶלֶת בְּשִׁשִּׁי. פִּי': מִשּׁוּם שָׁקְדוּ, כְּמוֹ שֶׁמְּפוֹרָשׁ בְּבְרַיְיתָא אַחֶרֶת, וא"ת: מִשּׁוּם בְּרָכָה דְּדָגִים הָיָה לָהֶם לְהָנִיחַ תַּקָּנַת שָׁקְדוּ — לֹא חָשׁוּ לְכָךְ, הוֹאִיל וּבְשִׁשִּׁי נַמִי נֶאֶמְרָה בְּרָכָה לָאָדָם.

מאי אִיכָּא בֵּין בְּרָכָה לְשָׁקְדוּ. אע"ג דְּמִשּׁוּם בְּרָכָה לֹא מִיקְּרֵי עִבַּרְיָינָא, מִכָּל מָקוֹם בָּעֵי לָמָּה לִי טַעְמָא דִּבְרָכָה. אִי נַמִי, בָּעֵי: מַאי אִיכָּא בֵּין לִישָּׁנָא דְּמְשַׁנֵּי בְּרָכָה דְּאָדָם עֲדִיפָא לֵיהּ, וּבֵין לִישָּׁנָא דְּאִי נַמִי מִשּׁוּם שָׁקְדוּ? וּמְשַׁנֵּי: דְּאִיכָּא בֵּינַיְיהוּ אָדָם בָּטֵל, אִי נַמִי י"ט שֶׁחָל לִהְיוֹת כו'. דְּלְלִישָּׁנָא דְּטַעְמָא דִּבְרַיְיתָא מִשּׁוּם שָׁקְדוּ וְלֹא מִשּׁוּם בְּרָכָה, הָכָא דְּלֵיכָּא שָׁקְדוּ — נִבְעֶלֶת אִם יִרְצֶה בַּחֲמִישִׁי. אֲבָל לְלִישָּׁנָא קַמָּא, דְּטַעְמָא דִּבְרַיְיתָא מִשּׁוּם בְּרָכָה, כִּדְמַשְׁמַע פְּשָׁטָא דִּבְרַיְיתָא — אֲפִילּוּ בְּאָדָם בָּטֵל אוֹ בְּיוֹ"ט שֶׁחָל לִהְיוֹת בְּעֶרֶב שַׁבָּת, דְּלֵיכָּא מִשּׁוּם שָׁקְדוּ, מִכָּל מָקוֹם מִשּׁוּם בְּרָכָה תִּבָּעֵל בְּשִׁשִּׁי. וַאֲפִילּוּ לְהַאי לִישָּׁנָא, אִי לָאו שֶׁתִּקְּנוּ מִשּׁוּם שָׁקְדוּ — מִשּׁוּם בְּרָכָה לְחוּדָהּ לֹא הָיוּ קוֹבְעִים יוֹם, כִּדְפְרִישִׁית לְעֵיל גַּבֵּי וְתִנָּשֵׂא בְּאֶחָד בְּשַׁבָּת.

דאילו בְּשָׁמַיִם וּבָאָרֶץ כְּתִיב אַף יָדִי וגו'. דְּמַשְׁמַע חֲדָא, אע"ג דִּמְסַיֵּים קְרָא "וִימִינִי טִפְּחָה שָׁמַיִם", וְאָמַר בְּשִׁילְהֵי "הַקּוֹמֵץ רַבָּה" (מנחות לו: ושם) יָד הַיְינוּ שְׂמֹאל, א"כ תַּרְתֵּי כְּתִיב — מ"מ בְּחַד מַעֲשֶׂה לֵיכָּא אֶלָּא חַד. אֲבָל בְּמַעֲשֶׂה צַדִּיקִים בְּחַד מַעֲשֶׂה, כְּמוֹ בֵּית הַמִּקְדָּשׁ, כְּתִיב תַּרְתֵּי יָדַיִם.

זה

עין משפט נר מצוה

יח א ב ג ד מיי' פכ"ד הל' שבת הל"ה סמג לאוין סה טוש"ע או"ח סי' שו סעי' ו:

יט ה טוא"ה"ע סי' סד:

כ ו מיי' פ"י מהל' אישות הל' יב סמג עשין מח טוש"ע אה"ע סי' (סג) [סד] סעי' ג:

[וע' בתוס' שבת קנב: וסוכה כג. ד"ה ולא ותוס' סנהדרין מז:]

תוספות רי"ד

ר"ח ורב המנונא דאמרי תרוייהו חשבונות של מצוה מותר לחשבן בשבת וא"ר אלעזר פוסקין צדקה לעניים בשבת. וא"ר יעקב ב"א אר"י מפקחין פקוח נפש בשבת והולכים לב"כ ולבתי מדרשות לפקח על עסקי רבים בשבת. ותנא דבי מנשה משדכין על התינוקת לארס בשבת ועל התינוק ללמדו ספר וללמדו אומניות בשבת. וא"ר שמואל בר נחמני אר"י הולכין לטרטראיות ולקרקסאות לפקח על עסקי רבים בשבת: תני בר קפרא בתולה נשאת בד' ונבעלת בה' הואיל ונאמרה בו ברכה לדגים ואלמנה נשאת בה' ונבעלת בששי הואיל ונאמרה בו ברכה לאדם ותניא מפני מה אמרו אלמנה נשאת בחמישי ונבעלת בו' שאם אתה אומר תבעל בחמישי למחר משכים הוא לאומנותו והולך. שקדו חכמים על תקנות בנות ישראל שיהא שמח עמה ג' ימים ה' בשבת וערב שבת ושבת:

שבת קנ.

[לעיל ב. ג. לקמן ז.]

ישעיה מח

שמות טו

תהלים צה

שם ח

שם יט

דברים כג

איבעיא להו מהו לבעול בתולה בשבת. ומסיק תלמודא והלכתא מותר לבעול בשבת:

יַנִּיחַ אֶצְבָּעוֹ בְּאָזְנָיו. וְהַיְינוּ דְּאָמַר ר' אֶלְעָזָר: מִפְּנֵי מָה אֶצְבְּעוֹתָיו שֶׁל אָדָם דּוֹמוֹת לִיתֵידוֹת? מַאי טַעֲמָא? אִילֵימָא מִשּׁוּם דִּמְחַלְּקָן — כָּל חֲדָא וַחֲדָא לְמִילְּתֵיהּ עֲבִידָא, דְּאָמַר מָר: *זוֹ זֶרֶת, זוֹ קְמִיצָה, זוֹ אַמָּה, זוֹ אֶצְבַּע, זֶה גּוּדָל! אֶלָּא: מַה טַּעַם מְשׁוּפּוֹת כִּיתֵידוֹת? שֶׁאִם יִשְׁמַע אָדָם דָּבָר שֶׁאֵינוֹ הָגוּן יַנִּיחַ אֶצְבְּעוֹתָיו בְּאָזְנָיו. תָּנָא דְּבֵי רַבִּי יִשְׁמָעֵאל: מִפְּנֵי מָה אוֹזֶן כּוּלָּהּ קָשָׁה וְהָאַלְיָה רַכָּה? שֶׁאִם יִשְׁמַע אָדָם דָּבָר שֶׁאֵינוֹ הָגוּן — יָכוֹף אַלְיָה לְתוֹכָהּ. ת"ר: *אַל יַשְׁמִיעַ אָדָם לְאָזְנָיו דְּבָרִים בְּטֵלִים מִפְּנֵי שֶׁהֵן נִכְווֹת תְּחִלָּה לָאֵיבָרִים. אִיבַּעְיָא לְהוּ: מַהוּ לִבְעוֹל בַּתְּחִלָּה בְּשַׁבָּת, דָּם מִיפְקַד פְּקִיד אוֹ חַבּוּרֵי מִיחַבַּר? וְאִם תִּימְצֵי לוֹמַר דָּם מִיפְקַד פְּקִיד, לְדָם הוּא צָרִיךְ — וְשָׁרֵי, אוֹ דִּלְמָא לְפֶתַח הוּא צָרִיךְ — וַאֲסִיר? וְאִם תִּימְצֵי לוֹמַר לְדָם הוּא צָרִיךְ, וּפֶתַח מִמֵּילָא קָאָתֵי, הֲלָכָה כְּר"ש *דְּאָמַר: דָּבָר שֶׁאֵין מִתְכַּוֵּין מוּתָּר, °אוֹ הֲלָכָה כְּרַבִּי יְהוּדָה דְּאָמַר: דָּבָר שֶׁאֵין מִתְכַּוֵּין אָסוּר? וְאִם תִּימְצֵי לוֹמַר הֲלָכָה כְּר' יְהוּדָה — מְקַלְקֵל הוּא אֵצֶל הַפֶּתַח אוֹ מְתַקֵּן הוּא אֵצֶל הַפֶּתַח? אִיכָּא דְּאָמְרִי: וְאִם תִּימְצֵי לוֹמַר דָּם חַבּוּרֵי מִיחַבַּר — לְדָם הוּא צָרִיךְ וְאָסוּר, אוֹ דִּלְמָא לַהֲנָאַת עַצְמוֹ הוּא צָרִיךְ וְשָׁרֵי? וְאִם תִּימְצֵי לוֹמַר לַהֲנָאַת עַצְמוֹ הוּא צָרִיךְ, וְדָם מִמֵּילָא קָאָתֵי — הֲלָכָה כְּרַבִּי יְהוּדָה אוֹ הֲלָכָה כְּר"ש? וְאִם תִּימְצֵי לוֹמַר הֲלָכָה כְּר' יְהוּדָה — מְקַלְקֵל בְּחַבּוּרָה אוֹ מְתַקֵּן בְּחַבּוּרָה הוּא? וְאִם תִּימְצֵי לוֹמַר מְקַלְקֵל בְּחַבּוּרָה הוּא — בִּמְקַלְקֵל הֲלָכָה כְּרַבִּי יְהוּדָה אוֹ

יַנִּיחַ אֶצְבָּעוֹ. שֶׁהִיא שְׁפוּיָה כְּיָתֵד. **מ"ט.** כְּלוֹמַר, בְּמַאי דּוֹמוֹת כִּיתֵידוֹת? **אִי נֵימָא דִּמְחַלְּקָן.** שֶׁמְּחוּלָּקוֹת זוֹ מִזּוֹ, וְאֵינָן מְחוּבָּרוֹת יַחַד. **חֲדָא חֲדָא לְמִילְּתֵיהּ.** קוּשְׁיָא הִיא: כָּל אַחַת יֵשׁ בָּהּ צוֹרֶךְ, וְאַף בְּצוֹרְכֵי גָבוֹהַּ. **זוֹ זֶרֶת.** מִן הַקְּטַנָּה מוֹדְדִין זֶרֶת שֶׁל חוֹשֶׁן. **זוֹ קְמִיצָה.** מֵאֶצְבַּע שֶׁאֵצֶל הַקְּטַנָּה מַתְחִילִין לִקְמוֹץ. חוֹפֶה שָׁלֹשׁ אֶצְבָּעוֹת עַל פַּס יָדוֹ, הַקְּמִיצָה וְהָאַמָּה וְהָאֶצְבַּע, וְקוֹמֵץ. **זוֹ אַמָּה.** מֵהַגְּדוֹלָה מוֹדְדִין אַמַּת בִּנְיָן וְאַמַּת כֵּלִים. **זוֹ אֶצְבַּע.** לְמַתַּן דָּמִים שֶׁל חַטָּאת, דִּכְתִיב בֵּיהּ "בְּאֶצְבָּעוֹ" (ויקרא ד). **זֶה גּוּדָל.** לְבֹהֶן יָד דְּאַהֲרֹן (שם ח) וְדִמְצוֹרָע (שם יד). **מְשׁוּפּוֹת.** אגויישי"ש בְּלַעַז. **אַלְיָה.** בָּשָׂר שֶׁבְּסוֹף הָאוֹזֶן. **נִכְוֵית תְּחִילָּה לָאֵבָרִים.** רַכּוֹת וְדַקּוֹת לִיכָּווֹת מִכּוּלָּם. וְהָכִי נַמִי אָמְרִינַן בְּמַסֶּכֶת ע"ז (דף לח.): הַאי גּוֹי דְּחָרֵיךְ רֵישָׁא — שָׁרֵי לְמֵיכַל אֲפִילּוּ מֵרֵישׁ אוּדְנֵיהּ, וְאע"פ שֶׁמְּמַהֵר לִיבָּשֵׁל. **מַהוּ לִבְעוֹל בַּתְּחִלָּה.** לָא שְׁמִיעַ לְהוּ הָךְ מַתְנִיתָא דִּלְעֵיל*. א"נ, שְׁמִיעַ לְהוּ, וּמִיבַּעְיָא לְהוּ: הֲלָכָה אוֹ אֵין הֲלָכָה. **מִיפְקַד פְּקִיד.** כְּמוֹ פִּקָּדוֹן, כָּנוּס וְעוֹמֵד וְאֵינוֹ נִבְלָע בְּדוֹפְנֵי הָרֶחֶם, לִהְיוֹת יְצִיאָתוֹ עַל יְדֵי חַבּוּרָה. אֶלָּא שֶׁהַפֶּתַח נָעוּל בְּפָנָיו, וּפוֹתְחִין לוֹ וְיוֹצֵא. **אוֹ חַבּוּרֵי מִיחַבַּר.** דַּם בְּתוּלִים הַיּוֹצֵא, עַל יְדֵי חַבּוּרָה הוּא בָּא, שֶׁהַדּוֹפֶן מִתְפָּרֵק מֵחֲבֵרוֹ. **אִם תִּימְצֵי לוֹמַר מִיפְקַד פְּקִיד.** וְאֵין בּוֹ מִשּׁוּם חַבּוּרָה, כַּוָּונַת הַמּוֹצִיאוֹ לְמַאי? לְדָם הוּא צָרִיךְ וּמִתְכַּוֵּין לְהוֹצִיאוֹ. **וְשָׁרֵי.** דְּהָא מִיפְקַד פְּקִיד. **אוֹ דִּלְמָא לְפֶתַח** מִתְכַּוֵּין. וַהֲרֵי הוּא כְּבוֹנֶה, וְאָסוּר. **וְאִם תִּימְצֵי לוֹמַר לְדָם הוּא מִתְכַּוֵּין.** וְלֹא לְפֶתַח, וּמִיהוּ עַל כָּרְחָךְ פִּיתְחָא מִמֵּילָא הָוֵי. **הֲלָכָה כְּרַבִּי יְהוּדָה.** בְּדָבָר שֶׁאֵין מִתְכַּוֵּין, וְאָסוּר. **אוֹ כְּר"ש.** וּמוּתָּר. וְא"ת: פְּסִיק רֵישֵׁיהּ וְלֹא יָמוּת הוּא! הָא פָּרְכִינַן לָהּ לְקַמָּן, וּמְשַׁנֵּינַן: יֵשׁ שֶׁבְּקִיאִין בְּהַטָּיָה, וְאֵין דָּם יוֹצֵא, וְאַף אֵין פֶּתַח נִפְתָּח. הִלְכָּךְ, לָאו פְּסִיק רֵישֵׁיהּ וְלֹא יָמוּת הוּא. **וְאת"ל הֲלָכָה כְּרַבִּי יְהוּדָה.** אַכַּתִּי אִיכָּא לְמִיבְּעֵי, דְּקַיְימָא לַן (שבת ד' קו.) כִּי אָמַר רַבִּי יְהוּדָה — בִּמְתַקֵּן, אֲבָל בִּמְקַלְקֵל — אֵינָהּ מְלָאכָה. וְיֵשׁ לִשְׁאוֹל עַל פֶּתַח זֶה, אִם תִּקּוּן הוּא אֶצְלָהּ אוֹ קִלְקוּל הוּא אֶצְלָהּ, שֶׁהַבְּתוּלָה חֲשׁוּבָה מִן הַבְּעוּלָה. וְאת"ל מְקַלְקֵל הוּא ל"ג, דְּאִי מְקַלְקֵל — לְדִבְרֵי הַכֹּל מוּתָּר, שֶׁאֵין לָךְ מְקַלְקֵל חַיָּיב אֶלָּא חוֹבֵל וּמַבְעִיר אַלִּיבָּא דְּרַבִּי שִׁמְעוֹן, וְהָכָא לָאו חוֹבֵל הוּא, דְּהָא בְּאת"ל דָּם מִיפְקַד פְּקִיד בָּעֵי לָהּ וְאָזֵיל. **וְדָם מִמֵּילָא קָא הָוֵי.** הוּא אֵינוֹ מִתְכַּוֵּין לְהוֹצִיאוֹ, אֲבָל הוּא יוֹצֵא, וְנִמְצֵאת חַבּוּרָה נַעֲשֵׂית שֶׁלֹּא בְּכַוָּונָה. **הֲלָכָה כְּרַבִּי יְהוּדָה.** בְּדָבָר שֶׁאֵינוֹ מִתְכַּוֵּין, וְשֶׁמָּא מְתַקֵּן הוּא וְאָסוּר. **אוֹ הֲלָכָה כְּר"ש.** דְּדָבָר שֶׁאֵין מִתְכַּוֵּין מוּתָּר. **וְאִם תִּימְצֵי לוֹמַר הֲלָכָה כְּרַבִּי יְהוּדָה.** קִלְקוּל הוּא וּמוּתָּר, אוֹ תִּקּוּן הוּא וְאָסוּר? וַאֲפִי' אִם קִלְקוּל הוּא יֵשׁ לִמְצוֹא צַד אִיסּוּר, אִם בְּדָבָר שֶׁאֵין מִתְכַּוֵּין סְבִירָא לַן כְּרַבִּי יְהוּדָה, וּבִמְקַלְקֵל בְּחַבּוּרָה סְבִירָא לַן כְּר"ש דִּמְחַיֵּיב. דְּאָמְרִינַן: כָּל הַמְקַלְקְלִין פְּטוּרִין חוּץ מֵחוֹבֵל וּמַבְעִיר, וְאוֹקִימְנָא כְּר"ש בְּפֶרֶק "הָאוֹרֵג" (שבת קו.). **הֲלָכָה כְּרַבִּי יְהוּדָה בִּמְקַלְקֵל.** וּמוּתָּר, דְּכִי אָמַר רַבִּי יְהוּדָה דָּבָר שֶׁאֵין מִתְכַּוֵּין אָסוּר — בִּמְתַקֵּן, אֲבָל בִּמְקַלְקֵל לֹא אָמַר. **אוֹ**

זה גודל. פי' בקונטרס לענין בהן יד דמצורע. ואין נראה, דאם כן הוה ליה למימר זה בהן! ועוד, דאפילו לא מחלק מלי משוי על בהן שהוא קצר מכולם. ונראה דלענין קמיצה קאמר, כדתנן (מנחות דף יא.): מוחק בגודל מלמעלה. אבל בידו אחרת לא יוכל לעשות, דבעינן עבודה בימין.

מהו לבעול בתחלה בשבת. אף על גב דתקנו שתהא בתולה נשאת ברביעי, בכל מקום אם אירע לו שלא בעל בליל חמישי – לא חייבוהו חכמים להמתין עד יום חמישי אחר, או עד יום ב', להכי בעי אם מותר לבעול בשבת אם לאו. אע"ג דתניא לעיל ומפרישין חתן מן הכלה לילי שבת תחלה מפני שהוא עושה חבורה, ותניא נמי באידך ברייתא: בין כך ובין כך לא יבעול לא בערב שבת ולא כו'. פי' בקונטרס דלא הוה ידע לה. א"נ ידע לה, ובעי היכי הלכתא. דאיכא למימר דפליגי בה ר' יהודה ור"ש. ומיהו, על כרחך נראה דלא ידע הברייתא דחיישינן שמא ישחוט בן עוף. דאי הוה ידע לה – מאי קמיבעיא ליה? הא בהא לא פליגי ר' יהודה ור"ש. והא דלא פשיט מינה לבסוף – משום דמשכח תנאי דפליגי עלה.

דם מיפקד פקיד או חבורי מיחבר. טעמא דחבורה לא כפרש"י דפירש בפרק "שמונה שרצים" (שבת קז:) דחייב משום צובע גבי ח' שרצים, דתנא התם: נצרר הדם אע"פ שלא יצא. וקשה לר"י: דב"אלו טריפות" (חולין מו:) בשמעתא דריאה תניא: ושאר שקצים ורמשים – עד שיצא מהם דם. והשתא התם מאי צובע איכא? הא לית להו עור! וה"נ, מאי צביעה איכא בהך חבורה? וכן גבי חבורה דמילה לא שייך צביעה! ועוד: דעל כרחך לשמואל איכא טעמא אחרינא, דבפרק "כלל גדול" (שבת עה. ושם) קאמר דשוחט לא מחייב משום צובע אלא משום נטילת נשמה. אלמא טעמא דחבורה הוי משום נטילת נשמה, כדקאמר שמואל התם. ורב דאמר התם משום צובע – אף משום צובע קאמר. ונטילת נשמה אין לפרש דטעמא משום הכאשה, שמחלישו ונוטל קצת נשמתו, דהכא אין צריך לחלישות האשה, ומיהו איסורא דקאמר הכא – איכא למימר דהויא דרבנן. אבל גבי מילה משמע דאיכא איסורא דאורייתא בהוצאת דם, דאמרינן בפרק "ר' אליעזר" (שם קלג:): האי אומנא דלא מייץ – סכנתא הוא, ומעברינן ליה. פשיטא מדקא מחללין שבת עליה! מהו דתימא: דם מיפקד פקיד, קמ"ל דחבורי מיחבר. ואי הוה משום החלשה – ליכא חילול שבת, דהויא מלאכה שאין צריכה לגופה, דאין צורך להחליש התינוק! ונראה לר"ת לפרש דהוצאת דם חשיבה נטילת נשמה, כי הדם הוא הנפש, וכשנוטל מקצתו נוטל מקצת נשמה. וקשה לר"י, דאמרי' בפרק "כלל גדול" (שם עה. ושם) גבי הצד חלזון והפוצעו: וליחייב נמי משום נטילת נשמה! ומשני: מתעסק הוא אצל נטילת נשמה, דכל כמה דאית ביה נשמה טפי ניחא ליה כו'. ולפי זה, אפילו הוא חי גמור – הרי יש כאן נטילת נשמה! ואומר ר"ת: כי דם חלזון שצובעין בו הוא מיפקד פקיד, ועל אותו אינו חייב משום נטילת נשמה, ועל שאר הדם שמחובר – חשיב ליה מתעסק.

לדם הוא צריך ושרי. וא"ת: והא פסיק רישיה הוא לענין הפתח! וי"ל: שיכול להוציא הדם בלא עשיית הפתח. פי' ר"ת: שצריך להוציא הדם שלא יתלכלך פעם אחרת כשיבעול. ולפירושו לקמן דקאמר: דם חבורי מיחבר, אי לדם הוא צריך ואסור. אף על גב דהויא מלאכה שאינה צריכה לגופה דשריא במקום צערא גבי מורסא, הכא גבי מצוה – אסור. ולקמן נפרש הא דפריך ממפיס מורסא לפירושו. ור"י מפרש: לדם הוא צריך – שצריך לראות אם היא בתולה.

אם תימצי לומר הלכה כרבי יהודה מקלקל הוא אצל הפתח ושרי. פי': דרבי יהודה אית ליה דמקלקל בחבורה פטור. אף על גב דפטור אבל אסור – מיהו הכא מותר לכתחלה, משום דאיכא תרתי: מקלקל בחבורה, ודבר שאינו מתכוין. וקשה, דבגרירה אסר ר' יהודה אע"ג דאיכא תרתי, דאין מתכוין ומקלקל נמי הוי, כדאמרינן בשילהי פ"ק דחגיגה (דף י.) דמוקי הך דחופר גומא ואין צריך אלא לעפרה דפטור אפי' כר' יהודה דמחייב מלאכה שאינה צריכה לגופה, וטעמא דפטור – משום דמקלקל הוי. ובפרק "י"ט" (ביצה כג. ושם) אסר רבי יהודה קירוד אף גב דאין מתכוין ומקלקל! ויש לומר: דהכא שרי טפי משום דאיכא נמי מצוה. א"נ, שלא במקום מצוה נמי היכא דאיכא תרתי – שרי. וגבי חריץ יש להעמיד כגון שאינו מקלקל לגמרי אלא מתקן קצת, דמשוי גומות מצד אחד. וגבי קירוד נמי, במה שמוציא דם – מיקל לבהמה קצת, כמו דם הקזה*.

את"ל הלכה כרבי יהודה מקלקל בחבורה הוא כו'. משמע דאי הלכה כרבי שמעון שרי אפילו הוא מתקן, כיון דאין מתכוין. וקשה: דבשילהי פרק "ספק אכל" (כריתות יט: ושם) *אמר: לרבי שמעון, הואיל ומקלקל בחבורה חייב – מתעסק נמי חייב. ומאי שנא דאין מתכוין פוטר רבי שמעון בחבורה טפי ממתעסק? וי"ל: דמתעסק שמתכוין למלאכה – לא מיפטר בשבת אלא משום דאין זה מלאכת מחשבת, ומשום הכי חייב לרבי שמעון מתעסק בחבורה כמו מקלקל בחבורה, דמחייב רבי שמעון אע"ג דאין זה מלאכת מחשבת. ולהכי תלינן במקלקל

גליון הש"ס

גמ' או הלכה כר"י דאמר דשא"מ אסור. ע' פסחים כה ע"ב תד"ה לא אפשר:

מנחות יח.

[מס' ד"א זוטא פ"ד]

[דף ג:]

ביצה כג. [שבת מח: וש"נ]

[ועי' תוס' בכורות כד: ד"ה והיינו]

ליתא בס הכי לישנא

או הֲלָכָה כְּר"ש? (אִיתְּמַר), בְּבֵי רַב אָמְרִי: רַב שָׁרֵי וּשְׁמוּאֵל אָסַר. בִּנְהַרְדְּעָא אָמְרִי: רַב אָסַר וּשְׁמוּאֵל שָׁרֵי. אָמַר רַב נַחְמָן בַּר יִצְחָק, וְסִימָנֵיךְ: אֵלּוּ מְקִילִין לְעַצְמָן וְאֵלּוּ מְקִילִין לְעַצְמָן. וְרַב שָׁרֵי?! *וְהָאָמַר רַב שִׁימִי בַּר חִזְקִיָּה מִשְּׁמֵיהּ דְּרַב: [א]הַאי מְסוֹכַרְיָא דְּנַזְיָיתָא אָסוּר לַהֲדוֹקָהּ בְּיוֹמָא טָבָא! בְּהַהוּא אֲפִילּוּ ר"ש מוֹדֶה. דְּאַבַּיֵי וְרָבָא דְּאָמְרִי תַּרְוַיְיהוּ: מוֹדֶה ר"ש *בִּפְסִיק רֵישֵׁיהּ וְלֹא יָמוּת. וְהָא אָמַר רַב חִיָּיא בַּר אַשִׁי אָמַר רַב: הֲלָכָה כְּרַבִּי יְהוּדָה, וְרַב חָנָן בַּר אַמִּי אָמַר שְׁמוּאֵל: הֲלָכָה כְּרַבִּי שִׁמְעוֹן. וְרַב חִיָּיא בַּר אָבִין מַתְנֵי לָהּ בְּלָא גַּבְרֵי, רַב אָמַר: הֲלָכָה כְּר' יְהוּדָה, וּשְׁמוּאֵל אָמַר: הֲלָכָה כְּרַבִּי שִׁמְעוֹן! לְעוֹלָם רַב כְּרַבִּי יְהוּדָה סְבִירָא לֵיהּ לְהָךְ לִישָּׁנָא דְּאָמַר דָּם מִיפְקַד פְּקִיד — מְקַלְקֵל הוּא אֵצֶל הַפֶּתַח. לְהָךְ לִישָּׁנָא דְּאָמַר דָּם חַבּוּרֵי מִיחַבַּר — מְקַלְקֵל בְּחַבּוּרָה הוּא. מְתִיב רַב חִסְדָּא: *תִּינוֹקֶת שֶׁלֹּא הִגִּיעַ זְמַנָּהּ לִרְאוֹת וְנִשֵּׂאת, ב"ש אוֹמְרִים: נוֹתְנִין לָהּ אַרְבָּעָה לֵילוֹת, וב"ה אוֹמְרִים: [ב]עַד שֶׁתִּתְחֶיה הַמַּכָּה. הִגִּיעַ זְמַנָּהּ לִרְאוֹת וְנִשֵּׂאת. בש"א: נוֹתְנִין לָהּ לַיְלָה הָרִאשׁוֹן. וּבֵית הִלֵּל אוֹמְרִים: עַד מוֹצָאֵי שַׁבָּת, [ג]אַרְבָּעָה לֵילוֹת.

מַאי

רש"י

או הֲלָכָה כְּר"ש. דִּמְקַלְקֵל בְּחַבּוּרָה חַיָּיב, כֵּיוָן דְּתִימְצֵי לוֹמַר הֲלָכָה כְּר' יְהוּדָה בְּדָבָר שֶׁאֵין מִתְכַּוֵּין דְּאָסוּר. **בִּנְהַרְדְּעָא.** מְקוֹמוֹ שֶׁל שְׁמוּאֵל. **וְסִימָנֵיךְ.** שֶׁלֹּא תִּטְעֶה לְהַחֲלִיף שְׁמַעְתְּתָא דְּבֵי רַב לִנְהַרְדְּעָא, וְדִנְהַרְדְּעָא לְדְבֵי רַב. **אֵלּוּ מְקִילִין לְעַצְמָן.** דְּבֵי רַב שֶׁצְּרִיכִים לַעֲשׂוֹת כְּדִבְרֵי רַבָּן, אוֹמְרִים שֶׁרַבָּן הִתִּיר. וּנְהַרְדְּעָא, הָעוֹשִׂים כִּשְׁמוּאֵל רַבָּן, אוֹמְרִים שְׁמוּאֵל הִתִּיר. **וְרַב שָׁרֵי.** בִּתְמִיָּה, אַלְמָא דָּבָר שֶׁאֵין מִתְכַּוֵּין מוּתָּר סְבִירָא לֵיהּ. **מְסוֹכַרְיָא דְּנַזְיָיתָא.** סְתִימַת נֶקֶב גִּיגִּית שֶׁמּוֹלִיכִין הַשֵּׁכָר דֶּרֶךְ הַנֶּקֶב וְסוֹתְמִין אוֹתוֹ בִּבְלָאֵי בְגָדִים. **אָסוּר לַהֲדוֹקָהּ.** מִשּׁוּם סְחִיטָה. **מוֹדֶה ר"ש כו'.** אֲבָל כָּאן יֵשׁ שֶׁבְּקִיאִים בְּהַטָּיָיה, כִּדְלְקַמָּן. **הֲלָכָה כְּרַבִּי יְהוּדָה.** בְּאֵין מִתְכַּוֵּין. **בְּלָא גַּבְרֵי.** בְּלָא אֲמוֹרָאֵי אַלִּיבָּא דְּרַב וְאַלִּיבָּא דִּשְׁמוּאֵל, אֶלָּא רַב וּשְׁמוּאֵל גּוּפַיְיהוּ. **לְהָךְ לִישָּׁנָא** דְּאָמְרַתְּ דָּם מִיפְקַד פְּקִיד. וְהָאִיסּוּר מִשּׁוּם פֶּתַח הוּא. **מְקַלְקֵל הוּא אֵצֶל הַפֶּתַח.** וּבִמְקַלְקֵל מוֹדֶה רַבִּי יְהוּדָה. **מְקַלְקֵל בְּחַבּוּרָה הוּא.** וְרַב סָבַר לָהּ כְּרַבִּי יְהוּדָה אַף בִּמְקַלְקֵל בְּחַבּוּרָה לְקוּלָּא, דְּקָא פָּטַר בָּהּ רַבִּי יְהוּדָה. **שֶׁלֹּא הִגִּיעַ זְמַנָּהּ לִרְאוֹת.** בְּמַסֶּכֶת נִדָּה אָמַר: אֵימָתַי הִגִּיעַ זְמַנָּהּ לִרְאוֹת — מִשֶּׁיַּגִּיעוּ יְמֵי הַנְּעוּרִים. **נוֹתְנִין לָהּ אַרְבָּעָה לֵילוֹת.** שֶׁכָּל דָּמִים שֶׁתִּרְאֶה בָּהֶן מֵחֲמַת תַּשְׁמִישׁ מַחְזְקִינַן לְהוּ כְּדַם בְּתוּלִים. **עַד שֶׁתִּתְחֶיה הַמַּכָּה.** כָּל זְמַן שֶׁאֵינָהּ מְשַׁמֶּשֶׁת בְּלֹא דָּם לֹא חָיְתָה הַמַּכָּה. **הִגִּיעַ זְמַנָּהּ לִרְאוֹת.** וְלֹא רָאֲתָה. **לַיְלָה הָרִאשׁוֹן.** אֲפִילּוּ לִבְעִילוֹת הַרְבֵּה.

מַאי

תוספות

במקלקל משום דטעם שניהם דפטורין בשאר מלאכות שבת הוי משום דבעינן מלאכת מחשבת, אבל שאינו מתכוין כלל למלאכה לא משום דבעינן מלאכת מחשבת מיפטר, דהא בשאר מקומות נמי מיפטר אין מתכוין, כגון גבי כלאים, דמוכרי כסות מוכרין כדרכן ובלבד שלא יתכוין כו' (כלאים פ"ט מ"ה), ותנן נמי: נזיר חופף ומפספס כו' (נזיר דף מב.), הילכך בחבורה נמי שרי.

האי מסוכרייתא דנזייתא אסור להדוקה כו'. פירש בקונטרס, וכן ר"ח ובערוך* בחד לישנא, וכן בסדר תנאים ואמוראים, דאסור משום סחיטה. וקשה לר"ת: דהא סחיטה משום ליבון, ולא שייכא בשאר משקים. דכל דבר המלכלך את בולעו, כגון יין ושכר ושמן – לא שייך ליבון בסחיטתו, אלא דוקא במים. וראיה לדבר – מדלא גזרינן בהו שמא יסחוט כמו גבי מים, כדאמרינן ב"אלו קשרים" (שבת דף קיג:): היה מהלך בשבת ופגע באמת המים כו' היכי ליעביד? לינחות במיא – אתי לידי סחיטה. ותניא נמי בפרק "חבית" (שם דף קמז: ושם): ומסתפג באלונטית ולא יביאה בידו, ומפרש בגמ' דאתי לידי סחיטה. ובפ"ב דבילה (דף יח. ושם) אומר דלכ"ע אין מטבילין את הכלים, ומפרש בגמרא גזירה משום סחיטה. ואילו בפרק "תולין" (שבת דף קלט:) תנן: מסננין את היין בסודרין. אלמא לגבי יין לא גזרינן משום סחיטה! ובריש "המביא" (ביצה דף ל.) נמי קאמר: ליפרוס סודרא עליה, ולא קאמר אתי לידי סחיטה, והיינו משום דלא שייך ליבון אלא גבי מים. והא דאמרינן בפרק "מפנין" (שבת דף קכח:): אם היתה צריכה שמן חבירתה מביאה לה בשערה. ופריך: והא אתי לידי סחיטה? ומשני: אין סחיטה בשער. משמע דשייך סחיטה בשמן. וכן בפ' "נוטל" (שם דף קמג.): ספוג, אם יש לו בית אחיזה – מקנחין בו, ואם לאו – אין מקנחין בו, משום דאתי לידי סחיטת שמן הנבלע בו! ההיא סחיטה אור"ת דהויא משום מפרק, ואסורה כמו סחיטת זיתים וענבים. והכא אומר ר"ת דליכא למימר דאסור משום מפרק, כיון שהנסחט הולך לאיבוד, *אע"ג דהוי פסיק רישיה. וכן פירש בערוך דכל פסיק רישיה דלא ניחא ליה שרי. ועיקר ראייתו מפרק "כל התדיר" (זבחים דף צא: ושם) אליבא דר"ש מזלפין יין על גבי האישים אע"ג דפסיק רישיה הוא, דודאי מכבה הוא, כיון דלא ניחא ליה בהאי כיבוי – שרי. ועוד מייתי ראיה מ"לולב הגזול" (סוכה דף לג: ושם) דקאמר ר"א בר"ש: ממעטים ענבים בי"ט, פי' ענבי הדס. ופריך: והא מתקן מנא! ומוקים לה במתכוון לאכילה, סבר לה כאבוה. ופריך: והא מודה ר"ש בפסיק רישיה כו'! ומשני: לא צריכא דאית ליה הושענא אחריתי. אלמא כיון דלא ניחא ליה, ולא חייש בהאי תיקון – שרי, אע"ג דפסיק רישיה הוא. ונראה לר"י דלא קשה מידי; דאיכא למימר דאסור לסחוט בשאר משקה משום ליבון כמו במים, ומ"מ לא חיישינן בהו שמא יסחוט, כיון שהטעם והריח נשארים בבגדים ומעט היה נהנה בסחיטתו. ומצינן למימר נמי דאסור משום מפרק. ואף ע"ג דהוי פסיק רישיה דלא ניחא ליה – אסור לכתחילה לר"ש, כמו במלאכה שאינה צריכה לגופה. וראיות הערוך אינן ראיות; דההיא דמתיר ר"ש לזלף יין על גבי האישים – איכא למימר דמצוה שאני. וכן ההיא דאית ליה הושענא אחריתי, איכא למימר דשרי משום מצוה. א"נ הכי פי': והא פסיק רישיה הוא! דאית ליה הושענא אחריתי, והואיל וכן – שרי לר"ש, דשמא לא יצטרך לה ונמצא שלא תיקן כלי, והלכך לאו פסיק רישיה הוא. אבל לר"י אסור, דשמא יצטרך לה ואגלאי מילתא דכלי עבד. ועל פי' הערוך קשה: דתנן בפרק "שמונה שרצים" (שבת דף קז.): המפיס מורסא בשבת, אם לעשות לה פה – חייב, ואם להוציא ממנה ליחה – פטור, ודוקא משום לצער פטור ומותר, אבל אי לאו משום לצער היה אסור, אע"ג דלא ניחא ליה בפה כלל, דאי ניחא ליה מן הפה – כי לא מתכוין נמי חייב! וכן מחט של יד ליטול בה את הקוץ דשרי – משום לצער, אבל אי לאו הכי – אסור, אע"ג דלא ניחא ליה כלל! אבל קצת קשה: אי פסיק רישיה דלא ניחא ליה אסור, אמאי קאמר רב בפרק "חבית" (שם קמה.) כבשים שסחטן לגופן פטור ומותר, הואיל וא"ל למים היוצאין, והשתא אע"ג דא"ל – היה להיות אסור! ואור"י: דמצינן למימר דדוקא כבשים שרי, דהוי הנסחט מהם כמו אוכלא דאיפרת, ואין שם משקה עליו, כדאמרינן דאפי' למימיהם פטור אבל אסור. ועוד י"ל: דכל דבר שאדם עושה במזיד, לא שייך למימר שמא יסחוט. דסברא הוא, כיון דלדעת כן הוא עושה. ולהכי, גבי מסננין את היין לא חיישינן שמא יסחוט. ואתיא שפיר האי דנדה מערמת וטובלת בבגדיה (ביצה דף יח.). וכן בפ"ח דיומא (דף עז:): ההולך להקביל פני רבו עובר עד צוארו במים, ולא גזרינן שמא יסחוט, לפי שלדעת כן הוא עושה. *ועוד איכא למימר התם דמצוה שאני. ובערוך פירש לשון אחר: מסוכרייא דנזייתא, סתימת גיגית של שכר אסור להדוקה, דשמא תבטל הסתימה אל הגיגית ויעשה כלי בשבת. ואין נראה לר"י, דהיכי דמי, דאם בדעתו לבטל שם בשעת הנחה – מאי פסיק רישיה שייך כאן? מיד הוא עושה כלי, דמתכוין לעשותו! ואם אין בדעתו לבטלה שם – א"כ לא הוי פסיק רישיה שיעשנה כלי! וי"ל בדוחק: שהוא מתכוין לבטלה ואינו מתכוין לעשות כלי, ושייך ביה פסיק רישיה הואיל ואינו מתכוין לגמרי לעשות כלי*. **לעולם** רב כר"י ס"ל כו'. לשמואל נמי איכא לשנויי לעולם כר"ש ס"ל, להך לישנא דאמר דם מיפקד פקיד – לפתח הוא צריך, ולהך לישנא דאמר חבורי מחבר – לדם הוא צריך: *מאי לאו דאי לא בעיל מצי בעיל. דלמאי נקט עד מוצאי שבת, אי לאו דאתא לאשמועינן דמצי בעיל בשבת, אע"ג דמשיר בתולים. דליכא למימר דנקט עד מוצ"ש לאשמועי' דבעינן רצופין – דהא לא בעינן שיהו רצופין, כדתניא בפרק בתרא דנדה (דף סד: ושם): מעשה ונתן לה ד' לילות מתוך י"ב חדש. והכי פי': נותנין לה ד' לילות עד מוצ"ש, שיבעול בכל לילה וישיר מקצת בתולים עד מוצ"ש. ואשמועינן דשרי להשיר בתולים בשבת! ומשני: לא, לבר משבת. ומוצאי שבת נקט לאשמועינן דבעינן רצופים. והוה מצי למיפרך מברייתא דפרק בתרא דנדה, דמוכח דאפי' מפוזרין, אלא דפריך ליה מגופה דברייתא: והא עד מוצאי שבת ארבעה לילות קתני! וא"ת: מעיקרא דמשני לבר משבת – מה עלה בדעתו? והא קתני בהדיא ד' לילות! וי"ל: דהוה ס"ד דהכי פירושו: נותנין לה עד מוצאי שבת לבר משבת, שהן בין הכל ד' לילות. ואיהו פריך: דמשמע דבעיל ד' לילות! ומשני: כשבעל. וקמ"ל כמו שמפרש בתר הכי: אע"ג דהוי פירצה דחוקה, דהא אי חזיא תלינן בדם בתולין, אפ"ה שרי.

מאי

תוספות רי"ד

האי מסוכרייתא דנזייתא אסור להדוקה ביומא טבא ואפילו ר"ש מודה בהא דאביי ורבא דאמרי תרוייהו מודה ר"ש בפסיק רישי' ולא ימות. פי' המורה סתימת נקב גיגית שמוציאים ממנו השכר וסותמים אותו בבלאי בגדים אסור להדוקה משום סחיטה. ואינו נראה כלל שמה שמשימים בנקב שמוציא ממנו מים או יין בלאי בגדים אין בו משום סחיטה שאינו מוכנין לא ללבנם ולא לקבל ממנו משקה ולאיבוד אזיל א"כ אמאי ליתסר. ור' נתן בעל הערוך פי' משום ר"ח ז"ל מטלית שמשימים על הגיגית לסתום פי' (ומפרקת) [ומהדקה] המטלית שם וזהו פתרון יפה. דודאי באותו המטלית קפיד אם תשרה. א) ומה שסוחט ממנו אסור משום מלבן שדומה לסוחט בגדים שרויים. וזה שאנו משימין בברזא של חביות מתיר ר' נתן בפירוש מפני שהולך לאיבוד:

א) עי' בערוך ערך סכר ה' לפירש שם לאסור משום סחיטה דניחא ליה שיזוב היין בתוך הכד ע"ש ואמשמע לאסור משום מפרק וצ"ע.

עין משפט נר מצוה

כא א טוש"ע א"ח סימן שכ סעיף יח:

כב ב ג מיי' פ"ה מהל' איסורי ביאה הל' יח יט סמג לאוין קיא (טוש"ע אה"ע סימן סג סעיף א וטוש"ע י"ד סימן קצג סעיף א):

מסורת הש"ס

ס"א ל"ג

שבת קיא. בכורות כה. [ע"ש]

שבת עה. קג. קיא: קיז. קכ: קלג. קמג. בכורות כה. סוכה לג: [ביצה לו.]

נדה יא: סד:

[אע"ג דמלאכה שא"צ לגופה אסור לר"ש היכא דלא ניחא ליה כלל שרי טפי כ"ה הנוסחא בתשובת רא"מ סי' לד]

[וע' תוס' שבת מח: ד"ה מיחסם]

[ועיין ערך סכר]

רש"ל גורס ומיהו

שייך לע"ב

כג א מיי' פ"ד מהל' ק"ש הל' א סמג עשין יח טוש"ע א"ח סי' ע סעי' ג:

כד ב מיי' פ"ד מהל' תפילין הל' יג ופ"ד מהל' אבילות הל' ט סמג עשין דרבנן ב טוש"ע א"ח סימן לח סעי' ה וטוש"ע יו"ד סי' שפח סעי' א:

כה ג מיי' פ"י מהל' שבת הל' יז סמג לאוין סה טוש"ע או"ח סי' שכח סעי' כח:

מַאי לָאו דְּאִי לָא בָּעַל מָצֵי בָּעֵיל אֲפִילּוּ בְּשַׁבָּת! אֲמַר רָבָא: לָא, לְבַר מִשַּׁבָּת. אֲמַר לֵיהּ אַבַּיֵי: וְהָא עַד מוֹצָאֵי שַׁבָּת אַרְבָּעָה לֵילוֹת קָתָנֵי! אֶלָּא אֲמַר רָבָא: כְּשֶׁבָּעַל. אִי כְּשֶׁבָּעַל — מַאי קמ"ל? קמ"ל דְּשָׁרֵי לְמִיבְעַל בְּשַׁבָּת, כִּדִשְׁמוּאֵל. דְּאָמַר שְׁמוּאֵל: *פִּירְצָה דְּחוּקָה מוּתָּר לִיכָּנֵס בָּהּ בְּשַׁבָּת, וְאע"פ שֶׁמַּשִּׁיר צְרוֹרוֹת. מְתִיב רַב יוֹסֵף: *[א]חָתָן פָּטוּר מִקְּרִיַּת שְׁמַע לַיְלָה הָרִאשׁוֹן עַד מוֹצָאֵי שַׁבָּת אִם לֹא עָשָׂה מַעֲשֶׂה. מַאי לָאו — דְּטָרִיד, דְּבָעֵי לְמִיבְעַל? אֲמַר לֵיהּ אַבַּיֵי: לָא, דְּטָרִיד דְּלָא בְּעֵיל. אֲמַר לֵיהּ רָבָא: וּמִשּׁוּם טִירְדָּא פָּטוּר?! אֶלָּא מֵעַתָּה טָבְעָה סְפִינָתוֹ בַּיָּם הָכִי נַמִי דְּפָטוּר?! וְכִי תֵּימָא ה"נ — וְהָאָמַר רַבִּי אַבָּא בַּר זַבְדָּא אָמַר רַב: *אָבֵל חַיָּיב בְּכָל הַמִּצְוֹת הָאֲמוּרוֹת בַּתּוֹרָה חוּץ מִן [ב]הַתְּפִילִּין, שֶׁנֶּאֱמַר בָּהֶן °"פְּאֵר"! אֶלָּא אֲמַר רָבָא: תַּנָּאֵי הִיא. דְּתָנְיָא חֲדָא: אִם לֹא עָשָׂה מַעֲשֶׂה בָּרִאשׁוֹן — פָּטוּר אַף בַּשֵּׁנִי, בַּשֵּׁנִי — פָּטוּר אַף בַּשְּׁלִישִׁי. וְתַנְיָא אִידָךְ: רִאשׁוֹן וְשֵׁנִי — פָּטוּר, שְׁלִישִׁי — חַיָּיב. וְאַבַּיֵי: הָתָם נַמִי בְּטִירְדָּא פְּלִיגִי. וְהָנֵי תַּנָּאֵי כִּי הָנֵי תַּנָּאֵי; דְּתַנְיָא: הַכּוֹנֵס אֶת הַבְּתוּלָה לֹא יִבְעוֹל בַּתְּחִלָּה בְּשַׁבָּת, וַחֲכָמִים מַתִּירִין. *מַאן חֲכָמִים? אֲמַר רַבָּה: רַבִּי שִׁמְעוֹן הִיא, *דְּאָמַר: דָּבָר שֶׁאֵין מִתְכַּוֵּין מוּתָּר. אֲמַר לֵיהּ אַבַּיֵי: וְהָא מוֹדֶה ר' שִׁמְעוֹן בִּפְסִיק רֵישֵׁיהּ וְלֹא יָמוּת! אֲמַר לֵיהּ: לֹא כְּהַלָּלוּ בַּבְלִיִּים שֶׁאֵין בְּקִיאִין בְּהַטָּיָה, אֶלָּא יֵשׁ בְּקִיאִין בְּהַטָּיָה. א"כ טוֹרֵד לָמָּה? לְשֶׁאֵינוֹ בָּקִי. יֹאמְרוּ: בָּקִי — מוּתָּר, שֶׁאֵינוֹ בָּקִי — אָסוּר! רוֹב בְּקִיאִין הֵן. אֲמַר לֵיהּ רָבָא בַּר רַב חָנָן לְאַבַּיֵי: אֶלָּא מֵעַתָּה שׁוֹשְׁבִינִין לָמָּה? מַפָּה לָמָּה? א"ל: הָתָם שֶׁמָּא יִרְאֶה וִיאַבֵּד. מְתִיב רַבִּי אַמִּי: *[ג]הַמֵּפִיס מוּרְסָא בְּשַׁבָּת, אִם לַעֲשׂוֹת לָהּ פֶּה — חַיָּיב. וְאִם לְהוֹצִיא מִמֶּנָּה לֵיחָה — פָּטוּר

יחזקאל כד

תורה אור

מאי קמ"ל. במאי דנקט עד מוצאי שבת, דלענין רצופים ליכא למימר, כדפרישית. **מאי** לאו דטריד דבעי למיבעל. הכא ליכא לשנויי לבר משבת כדלעיל — דא"כ אינו פטור עד מוצאי שבת, וקא משוית ליה לתנא טועה, דפטר ליה עד מוצאי שבת. אבל לעיל, אפילו כי אמרינן לבר משבת, ולא מצי למיבעל בשבת, מכל מקום דוקא נקט עד מוצאי שבת, משום דעד למוצאי שבת תולין בדם בתולים היכא דעבר ובעל. **והא** אמר ר' אבא אבל חייב בכל המצות כו'. ואביי סבר דטירדא דליכא מצוה כלל — מחייב, אבל טירדא דלא מצי בעיל — חשיב טירדא דמצוה, כיון שטרוד במה שאינו יכול לעשות מצוה.

חוץ מן התפילין שנאמר בהן פאר. ואמרינן בפרק בתרא דמועד קטן (דף טו.): מדאמר ליה רחמנא ליחזקאל "פארך חבוש עליך" מכלל דלעלמא אסור. ובקונטרס דפי' שנאמר בהן 'פאר', ואבל מעולל בעפר קרנו וראשו, היינו ליתן טעם דלא נילף שאר מצות מתפילין. וא"ת: ומאי שנא לגבי תפילין אמרינן דדוקא ליחזקאל נאמר, ולא לשאר אבלים, וגבי תלמוד תורה ילפינן שאר אבלים מיחזקאל, דאמרינן (שם): אבל אסור בתלמוד תורה, מדאמר ליה רחמנא ליחזקאל "האנק דום"! ויש לומר: דלאסור גמרינן, דמדאסר רחמנא ליחזקאל — לכ"ע נמי אסור. אבל להתיר — לא גמרינן, דליה לחודיה למשרי אתא. **והני** תנאי כי הני תנאי. אע"ג דפליגי תנאי בהדיא בהכי — מכל מקום דחיק אביי לעיל, דחשיב טירדא דמצוה הא דלא מצי בעיל, דניחא ליה לאקומי מתני' כשמואל דאסר לבעול. ומוקי נמי פלוגתא דברייתא אי חשיב טירדא הא דלא מצי בעיל, כדי לאוקמי כשמואל כל מה שיכול. **לא** כהללו בבליים שאין בקיאין בהטייה. פירוש: אינו פסיק רישיה, דכל העולם אינן כמו בבליים, אלא בקיאין הן. הילכך שרי להו למיבעל, ובלבד שלא יתכונו לבעול בעילה גמורה. ופריך: אם כן טורד למה? פירוש: בשבת אמאי פטר ליה לעיל מק"ש, כיון דבקיאין הן? בשלמא בחול איכא טירדא — לפי שמתכוין לבעול בעילה גמורה, ואף לבקיאין יש טירדא לבעול בעילה גמורה, כדאמר בפרק שני דברכות (דף טז. ושם) דר"ג היה פטור ומחמיר על עצמו, אע"ג דבקי היה, שלא היה בבלי. אבל בשבת שאינו מתכוין לבעול בעילה גמורה — טורד למה? ומשני: לשאינו בקי. פי': לפי שאינו בקי בשעת ק"ש, דאפי' הבקיאין בשעת מעשה — קודם מעשה יראים שלא יהיו בקיאין, הילכך טרודים כולם. **רוב** בקיאין הן. וכל חד וחד מספקינן ליה ברוב, וכולם מותרים. משמע הכא דרובן בקיאין בהטייה. וא"ת: דאמרינן בפ"ב דחגיגה (דף יד: ושם): בתולה שעיברה מהו לכהונה? כגון שבדקוה על פי חבית ולא היה ריאה נודף, מי חיישינן לדשמואל דאמר יכולני לבעול כמה בעילות בלא דם או דלמא באמבטי עיברה? ומסיק: דשמואל לא שכיח! ובפרק בתרא דנדה (דף סד: ושם) נמי קאמר: שאני שמואל דרב גובריה הוא. והא אמרינן הכא דרוב בקיאין הן! וי"ל: דשמואל היה יכול לבעול בעילה גמורה שאשה מתעברת בו, בלא דם. אבל בהטייה אין אשה מתעברת. ולהכי בההיא דחגיגה ליכא למיחש בהטייה אלא לדשמואל. **אלא** מעתה שושבינין למה מפה למה. פי' בקונטרס: כיון שהן בקיאין לבעול בלא דם — שמא יטה והיא לא תסיק אדעתה שהטה? ומשני: דשושבינין ומפה הם שאם לא יטה ויבעול בעילה גמורה, ויאבד המפה. ואם יטה ויאמר שלא מצא לה בתולים יכולה לומר עדיין בתולה אני. וקשה לר"י: דאינו מתרץ ממה שהקשה לו, דהוי ליה לשנויי דמסקא אדעתה לומר עדיין בתולה אני, ועיקר התירוץ חסר מן הספר! ונראה לר"י כפירוש ר"ת: דדוקא משבת קא פריך דמפה ושושבינין למה, דלריך לבעול בהטייה, דמעשה בכל יום שעושין שושבינין אפילו בשבת! ומשניך שמא יארע שלא יטה ויבעול בעילה גמורה ויאבד דם בתולים. והויא דומיא דטורד למה, דפריך נמי משבת. **אם** לעשות לה פה חייב. דפתח זה עשויה להכניס ולהוציא, להכנים אויר ולהוציא ליחה. **ואם** להוציא ממנה ליחה פטור. בפרק "שמונה שרצים" (שבת דף קז: ושם) מוקמינן לה כרבי שמעון. וסלקא דעתיה דרבי אמי דמותיב דדם מיפקד פקיד, ולדם הוא צריך ולא לפתח, ואפ"ה אסר שמואל כרבי שמעון, דהוי מלאכה שאינה צריכה לגופה. ולהכי פריך ממפיס מורסא, דכי היכי דלהוציא ממנה ליחה פטור, וקיימא לן דפטור ומותר כיון דאינו צריך לפתח, אף על גב דשאר מלאכה שאינה צריכה לגופה פטור אבל אסור — במורסא שרי משום צער. הכא נמי, משום מצוה הוי לן למשרי. ועוד: אפילו שרינן משום צערא טפי ממשום מצוה, כדפירש ר"ת לעיל, פריך שפיר; דהכא ודאי דהוי פסיק רישיה לענין פתח, אי לאו משום צערא היה אסור. אבל גבי

מַאי לָאו. הָנָךְ אַרְבָּעָה לֵילוֹת עַד מוֹצָאֵי שַׁבָּת דְּקָתָנֵי, לְהָכִי תָּנֵי לְהוּ: דְּאִי לֹא בָּעַל בְּעִילָה גְּמוּרָה — מָצֵי לְמִיבְעַל, וְכָל דָּם שֶׁהוּא מוֹצִיא תָּמִיד *כְּהַעֲרוֹתָיו הָוֵי דַּם בְּתוּלִים. וְשָׁמְעִינַן מִינָּהּ נַמִי, דְּמוּתָּר לִבְעוֹל בַּחֲבוּרָה בְּשַׁבָּת. וְהָא אַרְבָּעָה לֵילוֹת עַד מוֹצָאֵי שַׁבָּת קָתָנֵי. וְלָא מַשְׁכַּחַתְּ לֵיהּ לְבַר מִשַּׁבָּת, דְּהָא בָּרְבִיעִי נִיסֵּת, וְיֵשׁ כָּאן לֵילֵי חֲמִישִׁי וְשִׁשִּׁי וְשַׁבָּת וּמוֹצָאֵי שַׁבָּת. אִי כְּשֶׁבָּעַל. וְלָא אָתָא לְאוֹרוּיֵי לָן אֶלָּא הֶיתֵּר דַּם בְּתוּלִים, הַאי דְּנָקַט עַד מוֹצָאֵי שַׁבָּת מַאי קמ"ל? לִיתְנֵי: נוֹתְנִין לָהּ אַרְבָּעָה לֵילוֹת. עַל כָּרְחָךְ מִשּׁוּם בְּעִילַת שַׁבָּת נָקַט לָהּ. שֶׁמַּשִּׁיר צְרוֹרוֹת. וְהַאי נַמִי דִּלְמָא מְחַבֵּל פּוּרְתָּא, וּמְסַפֵּיקָא לָא אָסְרִינַן לֵיהּ. מַאי לָאו. הַאי דְּפָטַר לֵיהּ מִק"ש בְּלֵילֵי שַׁבָּת מִשּׁוּם דְּטָרִיד בְּמִצְוָה, דְּבָעֵי לְמִיבְעַל, וְהָעוֹסֵק בְּמִצְוָה פָּטוּר מִן הַמִּצְוָה. דְּטָרִיד דְּלָא בָּעַל. מִצְטַעֵר שֶׁלֹּא בָּעַל. מִשּׁוּם דְּטָרִיד פָּטוּר. בִּתְמִיָּה. וּמִשּׁוּם צַעַר פָּטוּר?! מֵאַחַר שֶׁאֵינוֹ מְחַשֵּׁב לַעֲסוֹק בְּמִצְוָה. שֶׁנֶּאֱמַר בָּהֶן פְּאֵר. "פְּאֵרְךָ חֲבוֹשׁ עָלֶיךָ" (יחזקאל כד), וְאָבֵל מְעוֹלֵל בְּעָפָר קַרְנוֹ וְרֹאשׁוֹ, וְאֵין זֶה פְּאֵר לִתְפִילִּין. [אֶלָּא אֲמַר רָבָא וַדַּאי לָא מָצֵית לְתָרוֹצֵי הָא דְּחָתָן פָּטוּר מק"ש מִשּׁוּם דְּלָא מָצֵי בָּעֵיל, דא"כ לָא הֲוָה פָּטוּר, דְּהָא לָא טָרִיד בִּדְבַר מִצְוָה. תַּנָּאֵי הִיא. בְּעִילַת חֲבוּרָה בְּשַׁבָּת, וּמַאן דְּאָסַר לִבְעוֹל בְּשַׁבָּת — כְּתַנָּאֵי אֲמָרָהּ לִשְׁמַעְתֵּיהּ, דְּאִיכָּא תַּנָּא אַחֲרִינָא דְּאָסַר לְמִיבְעַל. דְּתָנָא חֲדָא כו']. פָּטוּר. מִקְּרִיַּת שְׁמַע. שְׁלִישִׁי חַיָּיב. דְּשַׁבָּת הוּא, וְאָסוּר לִבְעוֹל. וְאַבַּיֵי. אָמַר לָךְ: הָנָךְ תַּנָּאֵי נַמִי בְּטִירְדָּא פְּלִיגִי, וְהַאי דְּפָטַר לֵיהּ מק"ש — לָאו מִשּׁוּם דְּשָׁרֵי לְמִיבְעַל, אֶלָּא קָסָבַר הַמִּצְטַעֵר לְצַעַר שֶׁל מִצְוָה פָּטוּר מִקְּרִיאַת שְׁמַע. וְלָא דָּמֵי לְאָבֵל דְּטָרִיד טִירְדָּא דִּרְשׁוּת, שֶׁאֵין לְצַעֲרוֹ מִצְוָה, אע"פ שֶׁאֲבֵילוּתוֹ מִצְוָה. וּמַאן דִּמְחַיֵּיב סָבַר: טִירְדָּא לָא פָּטַר. [וְרָבָא אֲמַר דְּבִמּוּתָּר לִבְעוֹל פְּלִיגִי, וְהָנֵי תַּנָּאֵי כְּהָנֵי תַּנָּאֵי]. בְּהַטָּיָה. שֶׁמַּטִּין לַצְּדָדִין, וְאֵין מוֹצִיאִים דָּם. אִם כֵּן. דִּבְקִיאִים. טוֹרֵד לָמָּה. מַהוּ טָרְדוֹ לְהִפָּטֵר מק"ש. בָּקִי מוּתָּר. לִבְעוֹל בְּשַׁבָּת, דְּלָא פְּסִיק רֵישֵׁיהּ וְלֹא יָמוּת הוּא. רוֹב בְּקִיאִין הֵן. הִילְכָּךְ סְתָמָא לָאו פְּסִיק רֵישֵׁיהּ וְלֹא יָמוּת הוּא. שׁוֹשְׁבִינִין לָמָּה. מֵאַחַר שֶׁיֵּשׁ בְּקִיאִין לִבְעוֹל בְּלֹא דָּם — הָא דְּתַנְיָא לְקַמָּן (דף יב.): הָיוּ מַעֲמִידִין לָהֶן שְׁנֵי שׁוֹשְׁבִינִין אֶחָד לוֹ וְאֶחָד לָהּ, כְּדֵי לְמַשְׁמֵשׁ אֶת הֶחָתָן וְאֶת הַכַּלָּה. כְּלוֹמַר, לְבַקֵּר אַחֲרֵיהֶם שֶׁלֹּא יִנְהֲגוּ בָּהּ רַמָּאוּת בְּטַעֲנַת בְּתוּלִים. וְאִי בְּקִיאִין בְּהַטָּיָה — מַה שׁוֹשְׁבִינִין מוֹעִילִין? מַפָּה לָמָּה. לְבָרֵר אֶת הַבְּתוּלִים. וְלִיטַעְמִיךְ ל"ג, אֶלָּא ה"ג: שׁוֹשְׁבִינִין לָמָּה? מַפָּה לָמָּה? אֲמַר לֵיהּ שֶׁמָּא יִרְאֶה וִיאַבֵּד. שֶׁמָּא לֹא יַטֶּה, וְיוֹצִיא דָּם וִיאַבְּדֶנּוּ, וְיֹאמַר לֹא מָצָאתִי דָּם, דְּאִילּוּ בְּהַטָּיָה, אִם בָּא לִטְעוֹן — תֹּאמַר לוֹ: עֲדַיִין בְּתוּלָה אֲנִי. הַמֵּפִיס מוּרְסָא. הַפּוֹתֵחַ פֶּה נֶפַח, שֶׁקּוֹרִין קלו"ג. אִם לַעֲשׂוֹת לָהּ פֶּה. שֶׁמִּתְכַּוֵּין לְיַפּוֹתָהּ וְלִהְיוֹת לָהּ פֶּתַח זֶה לְיוֹם מָחָר. חַיָּיב. שֶׁהוּא מְתַקֵּן פֶּתַח, וְחַיָּיב מִשּׁוּם בּוֹנֶה, °דְּאַשְׁכְּחַן בִּנְיָן בְּבַעֲלֵי חַיִּים, דִּכְתִיב "וַיִּבֶן אֶת הַצֵּלָע" (בראשית ב). פָּטוּר

גליון הש"ס

רש"י ד"ה חייב וכו' דאשכחן בנין בבע"ח. שבת צה ע"א.

מסורת הש"ס

נ"ל בהערלותיו. יעב"ץ

נדה סד.

ברכות טז.

סוכה כה. ברכות יא. טז: מו"ק טו. ע"ש [שמחות פ"ו]

[עירובין פג. וש"נ]

[לעיל ה: וש"נ]

נ"י כ"י

שבת קז. ושם: עדיות פ"ב מ"ה

פטור! התם פקיד ועקיר, הכא — פקיד ולא עקיר. רבי אמי שרא למיבעל בתחלה בשבת. אמרי ליה רבנן: והא לא כתיבא כתובתה! אמר להו: *אאתפסוה מטלטלין. רב זביד שרא למיבעל בתחלה בשבת. איכא דאמרי: רב זביד גופיה בעל בתחלה בשבת. רב יהודה שרא למיבעל בתחלה ביו"ט. אמר רב פפי משמיה דרבא: לא תימא ביו"ט דשרי, הא בשבת אסור — דהוא הדין דאפילו בשבת נמי שרי, *ומעשה שהיה כך היה. רב פפא משמיה דרבא אמר: ביו"ט — שרי, בשבת — אסור. א"ל רב פפי לרב פפא: מאי דעתיך, מתוך שהותרה חבורה לצורך הותרה נמי שלא לצורך? אלא מעתה מותר לעשות מוגמר ביו"ט, *דמתוך שהותרה הבערה לצורך — הותרה נמי שלא לצורך! אמר ליה: עליך אמר קרא °"אך אשר יאכל לכל נפש" דבר השוה לכל נפש. אמר ליה רב אחא בריה דרבא לרב אשי: אלא מעתה, נזדמן לו צבי ביו"ט, הואיל ואינו שוה לכל נפש — ה"נ דאסור למשחטיה?! אמר ליה: אנא דבר הצורך לכל נפש קאמינא, צבי צריך לכל נפש הוא. אמר רבי יעקב בר אידי: הורה רבי יוחנן בציידן: אסור לבעול בתחלה בשבת. ומי איכא הוראה לאיסור? אין. והתנן: *הורוה בית הלל בשתהא נזירה עוד שבע שנים אחרות, ואי נמי כי הא, דתניא: *גחוט השדרה שנפסק — ברובו, דברי רבי. ר' יעקב אומר: אפי' ניקב. הורה רבי כר' יעקב. אמר רב הונא: אין הלכה כר' יעקב. רב נחמן בר יצחק מתני הכי: אמר ר' אבהו שאל ר' ישמעאל בן יעקב דמן צור את רבי יוחנן בציידן, ואנא שמעי: מהו לבעול בתחלה בשבת? ואמר ליה: אסור. והלכתא: דמותר לבעול בתחלה בשבת.§ אמר רבי חלבו אמר רב הונא א"ר אבא בר זבדא אמר רב: אחת בתולה ואחת אלמנה טעונה ברכה. ומי אמר רב הונא הכי? והאמר רב הונא: אלמנה אינה טעונה ברכה! לא קשיא; כאן — בבחור שנשא אלמנה, כאן — באלמון שנשא אלמנה. ואלמון שנשא אלמנה לא? והאמר רב נחמן, אמר לי הונא בר נתן, תנא: מנין הלברכת חתנים בעשרה? שנאמר: °"ויקח עשרה אנשים מזקני העיר ויאמר שבו פה וישבו", ובועז אלמון שנשא אלמנה הוה! מאי אינה טעונה ברכה דאמר רב הונא — אינה טעונה ברכה כל ז' — ואבל יום אחד טעונה ברכה. אלא הא דתניא: *שקדו חכמים על תקנת בנות ישראל שיהא שמח עמה ג' ימים, במאי? אי בבחור — האמרת שבעה, אי באלמון — האמרת יום אחד! איבעית אימא: זבאלמון — יום אחד לברכה חושלשה לשמחה, ואיבעית אימא: טבבחור — שבעה לברכה ושלשה לשמחה. מיתיבי

שמות יב | רות ד

רש"י

פטור. וקיימא לן: פטור ומותר לכתחלה, ב"יציאות שבת" (דף ג.). קשיא למאן דאסר, דהאי נמי להוציא דם הוא. התם. גבי ליחה. פקיד. כנוס ביחד. ועקיר. כולו מן הבשר, ועומד לצאת. הכא. דם בתולים. פקיד הוא ולא עקיר. לגמרי, אלא נבלע קצת בכתלים, אע"פ שאינו מחובר כבשר דם החברים אלא כנוס. מיהו, דומה למחובר הוא, שאינו מוכן לצאת כליחה. אתפסוה מטלטלי. תנו לה מטלטלין תחת ידה במשכון לשיעבוד כתובתה, עד שיכתבו שטר כתובתה בשעבוד קרקעות. מאי דעתיך. למשרי יו"ט יותר מבשבת. לצורך. אוכל נפש, כגון שחיטה. מוגמר. בשמים על האש, לגמר את הכלים ואת הבגדים. עליך אמר קרא לכל נפש דבר השוה לכל נפש. מותר, ובעילה שוה לכל, אבל מוגמר אינו אלא למפונקים. ומי איכא הוראה לאיסור. ומי קרי איסור "הוראה"? משום דכל אדם רשאי להחמיר, והאוסר אין זה סמיכת דברים, שאפי' מן הספק, שאין ההלכה ברורה לו, הוא בא ואוסר. אבל המתיר סומך על שמועתו, או על סברת חכמתו, והיא "הוראה". הורוה ב"ה. משנה היא במסכת נזיר, בהילני המלכה שיצא בנה למלחמה, ונדרה שבע שנים בנזיר *כשיבוא לארץ, ועלתה לארץ, הורוה ב"ה שתהא נזירה עוד ז' שנים אחרות. חוט השדרה שנפסק ברובו. טעונה ברכה. ברכת חתנים. בועז אלמון הוה. דאמר מר: אבצן זה בועז, וכבר היו לו ל' בנים ושלשים בנות, בבבא בתרא (דף צא.). האמרת שבעה. דמדאיצטריך טעונה דקאמר רב הונא אוקימנא דאינה טעונה שבעה, מכלל דטעונה דקאמר רבי אבא — שבעה. מברכין

[עי' תוס' לקמן ט: ד"ה אין]
[עירובין סה. וש"נ]
[פסחים ה: ביצה יב:]
ומנתה בת"ל ועלתה לארץ כצ"ל. רש"ל
נזיר יט:
חולין מה.
[לעיל ה.]

תוספות

גבי בעילה אית לן למשרי אע"ג דליכא לצורך, כיון דלא הוי פסיק רישיה לענין פתח, כיון דאפשר להוציא דם בלא עשיית פתח כדמוכח לעיל (דף ה:). ומשני, הכא פקיד ולא עקיר, דקסבר דם חבורי מיחבר. והוא הדין דהוי מצי לשנויי דלפתח הוא צריך, אלא לפי מאי דקים ליה לדם הוא צריך משני ליה. ותימה: דהא שמואל במלאכה שאינה צריכה לגופה סבר לה כר' יהודה, כדאמרי' בפ' *"הכונס" (ד' פה. ושם) ובפ' "כל התדיר" (זבחים ד' צא:)! ועוד, דמדבר שאין מתכוין דשרי ר"ש ה"ל לאקשויי, ולא ממלאכה שאינה צריכה לגופה, כיון דרוב בקיאין ולא הוי פסיק רישיה.

מתוך שהותרה לצורך. פירוש: לצורך אוכל נפש, הותרה נמי שלא לצורך אוכל נפש, ובלבד שיהא צורך הנאת היום, או צורך קיום מצוה ביו"ט. כההיא דהוצאת קטן למולו, וספר תורה לקרות בו, ולולב לצאת בו (ביצה דף יב.). אבל שלא לצורך היום כלל — לא, כמו הוצאת אבנים דמיחייב, והאופה מיו"ט לחול לרב חסדא דאמר לוקה (שם דף כא.), משום דלית ליה "הואיל". ושחיטת עולת נדבה דשרי לב"ה (שם דף כ:) היינו משום שלא יהא שלחנך מלא ושלחן רבך חסר. ומוצא חמץ בתוך ביתו דאמרינן בפ"ק דפסחים (דף ו. ושם) דכופה עליו כלי ולא שרינן לשורפו — משום "מתוך", היינו: משום דאסור לשורפו מדרבנן משום מוקצה, דאסור לטלטלו. אבל אין לומר דאיירי כשביטלו, דמכל מקום מדרבנן מצוה לשורפו, והוי צורך היום, דבמצוה דרבנן נמי שרינן היכא דאיכא למימר "מתוך". והא דפליגי ב"ש וב"ה (ביצה דף יב:) במבשל גיד הנשה ביו"ט ואכלו, דלב"ש דלית להו "מתוך" לוקה, ולב"ה דאית להו "מתוך" — אינו לוקה, צריך לומר: אע"ג דלא חשיב אוכל נפש, משום איסור דרכיב עליה, מכל מקום צורך היום הוא, כיון דאכיל ליה. ונראה לר"י: דהוצאת תינוק לטייל — הוי צורך היום. ומיהו, הוצאה לצורך גוי נראה דאסור. ומה שנהגו עתה להוציא לצורך גוי היה נראה לרשב"א משום דרשות הרבים דידן לא הוי אלא כרמלית, דאין רחבין ט"ז אמה, וגבי יו"ט לא גזור רבנן, כי היכי דלא תקון רבנן עירובי חצירות ביו"ט, כדמשמע בריש פרק שני דביצה (דף טז:) דאמר: יו"ט שחל להיות ערב שבת כו' רבי אומר מערבין עירובי חצירות אבל לא עירובי תחומין, לפי שאתה אוסרו בדבר האסור לו ואי אתה אוסרו בדבר המותר לו. אלמא לא תקון עירובי חצירות ביו"ט. והוא הדין דלא גזרו בכרמלית. והא דקיימא לן בפרק "אמרו לו" (כריתות דף יד. ושם) ובפרק קמא דביצה (דף יב. ושם) דיש עירוב והוצאה ליו"ט — נראה דאיירי בעירובי תחומין. ושוב חזר בו, דמחצר שאינה מעורבת אין ללמוד ממנה לכרמלית, דחמיר טפי, כמו שפירשתי במסכת שבת (דף קיז.). ועוד נראה: דהא דקיימא לן דיש עירוב והוצאה ליו"ט — בעירובי חצירות מיירי, מדבעי למימר בפרק "אמרו לו" (כריתות דף יד. ושם) דאין עירוב והוצאה ליוה"כ, מדתנן התם: אם היתה שבת והוציאו בפיו — חייב, וכן בביצה (דף יב. ושם) בעי למידק דאין עירוב והוצאה ליו"ט מדשרו בית הלל להוציא קטן ולולב —והיינו עירובי חצרות, דהשתא מוכח לה שפיר מדשרו הוצאה, דלא גזרו רבנן אעירובי חצירות אלא משום הוצאה, אבל עירובי תחומין אין ענינה להוצאה. והא דקאמר ואי אתה אוסרו בדבר המותר לו — היינו משום דמותר להוציא לצורך. **אלא** מעתה יהא מותר לעשות מוגמר ביו"ט. ואם תאמר: לדידיה נמי תקשי, וכי לא סבר דאמרינן "מתוך"? הא טעמא דב"ה הכי הוא! ויש לומר: שהיה סובר דטעמא דבית הלל משום דאין עירוב והוצאה, כדקא ס"ד מעיקרא בביצה. אע"ג דהתם פריך עלה — דלמא לרב פפי לא שמיע לה. ועוי"ל: שהיה סובר הותרה שלא לצורך ובלבד שיהא דבר הרגיל. ולהכי פריך, דזה אינו רגיל טפי ממוגמר. **אמר** ליה **אנא** דבר הצריך לכל נפש **קאמינא** וצבי צריך לכל נפש. וקשה לר"י: דאמר בסוף פ"ב דביצה (דף כב.) מהו לכבות הנר מפני דבר אחר — ומסיק דאסור. הא הכא שרי, משום דצריך לכל נפש! וי"ל: דהכא דוקא בבעילה ראשונה, דמצוה היא, דהוי צורך מצות היום. אבל שאר בעילות — אין כל כך צורך היום. ועי"ל, דכיבוי הנר מפני דבר אחר הוי כמו מכשירין, דאפילו באוכל נפש אסור. וכן מוכח התם, דפריך עלה מהא דתניא דמכבין את הבקעת כדי שלא יתעשן הבית, ומשני: ההיא רבי יהודה היא דשרי מכשירי אוכל נפש, כי קאמינא לרבנן. **והלכתא** מותר לבעול בתחלה בשבת. ולא חיישינן שמא ישחוט בן עוף. ואהא סמכינן למיעבד סעודה בשבת.
במקהלות

עין משפט נר מצוה

כו א מיי' פ"י מהל' אישות הל' ט סמג עשין מח טוש"ע אה"ע סי' סו סעי' ב:
כז ב מיי' פ"ב מהל' נזירות הל' כא:
כח ג מיי' פ"ט מהל' שחיטה הל' א סמג עשין סג טוש"ע יו"ד סי' לב סעי' א:
[נ"ל בפ' כירה שבת מב.]
כט ד מיי' פ"ל מהל' שבת הל' יד סמג לאוין סה ועשין מח טוש"ע אה"ע סימן סב סעיף א וטוש"ע א"ח סי' רפ סעי' ב:
ל ה מיי' פ"ב מהל' ברכות הל' ט ומיי' פ"י מהל' אישות הל' ה סמג עשין מח טוש"ע אה"ע סי' סא סעי' ד:
לא ו ז מיי' פ"ב מהלכות ברכות הל' ט סמג שם טוש"ע שם סעי' ו:
לב ח מיי' פ"י מהלכ' אישות הל' י"ב סמג שם טוש"ע שם סי' סא סעי' ב [ועי' מ"מ]:
לג ט מיי' פ"ב מהל' ברכות ה"ט סמג שם טוש"ע שם סעי' ו:

תוספות רי"ד

א"ל והא לא כתיבא כתובה ואסרו חכמים לשהות אדם את אשתו שעה אחת בלא כתובה א"ל אתפסוה מטלטלי שיעור כתובתה. פי' שיהיה משכון בידה עד שיכתבו לה שטר כתובתה: א"ר חלבו א"ר אדא בר זבדא אמר רב א' בתולה וא' אלמנה טעונה ברכה [כל] שבעה. פי' טעונה ברכות כל ז' ימים ולקמן מוקי לה בדאיכא פנים חדשות: ומי אמר רב הכי והא"ר הונא אלמנה אינה טעונה ברכה כל ז' אלא יום א'. ל"ק כאן בבחור שנשא אלמנה כאן באלמון שנשא אלמנה. מיתיבי מברכים לבתולה ז' ולאלמנה יום א' מאי לאו לאלמנה שנשאת לבחור. לא לאלמון. אבל לבחור מאי ז'. א"ה ליתני מברכין לבתולה ז' ולאלמנה שנשאת לבחור ז' ולאלמנה שנשאת לאלמון יום א'. מילתא פסיקא קתני ליכא בתולה דבצירא מז' פי' ואפילו נשאת לאלמון. וליכא אלמנה דבצירא מיום א': אלא הא דתניא שקדו חכמים על תקנת בנות ישראל שיהא שמח עמה ג' ימים במאי אי בבחור הא אמרת ז' אם באלמון הא אמרת יום א'. איבעית אימא בבחור ז' לברכה וג' לשמחה איבע"א באלמון יום א' לברכה וג' לשמחה:

עין משפט נר מצוה

לד א מיי' פ"ח מהל' זכיה הל' ה סמג עשין פג טוש"ע חו"מ סי' רי סעי' א:

[בספר תהלים שלפנינו נדפס מלא]

לה ב מיי' פ"ב מהל' ברכות הל' ט ופ"י מהל' אישות הל' ג סמג עשין מח טוש"ע אה"ע סימן סא סעי' א:

לו ג מיי' פ"י מהל' אישות הל"ז טוש"ע שם סי' נה סעי' א:

לז ד ה מיי' פ"ג שם הל' כד סמג שם טוש"ע שם סי' לד סעי' א:

לח ו מיי' פ"ב מהל' ברכות הל' י סמג שם טוש"ע שם סימן סב סעי' ז ח [עי' כ"מ]:

גמרא

מיתיבי: מברכין לבתולה שבעה ולאלמנה יום אחד. מאי לאו — אפילו אלמנה שנשאת לבחור! לא, לאלמון. אבל לבחור מאי — שבעה, אי הכי ליתני: מברכין לבתולה שבעה, ולאלמנה שנשאת לבחור שבעה, ולאלמנה יום אחד! מילתא פסיקתא קתני, דליכא בתולה דבצרה משבעה, וליכא אלמנה דבצרה מיום אחד.§ גופא, אמר רב נחמן: אמר לי הונא בר נתן, תנא: מנין לברכת חתנים בעשרה — שנאמר: °"ויקח עשרה אנשים מזקני העיר ויאמר שבו פה". (רות ד) ורבי אבהו אמר מהכא: °"במקהלות ברכו אלהים ה' ממקור ישראל" (תהלים סח) ורב נחמן בהאי קרא דרבי אבהו מאי דריש ביה? מיבעי ליה לכדתניא, היה ר"מ אומר: *מנין שאפילו עוברים שבמעי אמן אמרו שירה על הים? שנאמר: "במקהלות ברכו אלהים ה' ממקור ישראל". ואידך — אם כן לימא קרא "מבטן", מאי "ממקור" על עסקי מקור. ורבי אבהו בהאי קרא דרב נחמן מאי דריש ביה? ההוא מיבעי ליה למידרש: *עמוני ולא עמונית, מואבי ולא מואבית. דאי סלקא דעתך לברכה — לא סגיא דלאו זקנים? ואידך: אי סלקא דעתך למידרש — לא סגיא דלאו עשרה? אין, לפרסומי מילתא. *וכדאמר ליה שמואל לרב חנא בגדתאה: פוק ואייתי לי בי עשרה, ואימא לך באנפייהו: המזכה לעובר — קנה. והלכתא: אהמזכה לעובר — לא קנה.§ תנו רבנן: מברכין ברכת חתנים בבבית חתנים. ר' יהודה אומר: אף בבית האירוסין מברכין אותה. אמר אביי: וביהודה שנו, גמפני שמתייחד עמה. תניא אידך: מברכין ברכת חתנים בבית חתנים, וברכת ארוסין בבית האירוסין, ברכת האירוסין מאי מברך? רבין בר רב אדא ורבה בר רב אדא, תרווייהו משמיה דרב יהודה אמרי: דבא"י אמ"ה אשר קדשנו במצותיו וצונו על העריות ואסר לנו את הארוסות והתיר לנו את הנשואות על ידי חופה וקידושין. רב אחא בריה דרבא מסיים בה משמיה דרב יהודה: הבא"י מקדש ישראל על ידי חופה וקידושין. מאן דלא חתים — מידי דהוה אברכת פרות ואברכת מצות, ומאן דחתים — מידי דהוה אקידושא.§ ת"ר: מברכין ברכת חתנים בעשרה כל שבעה. אמר רב יהודה: ווהוא שבאו פנים חדשות. מאי מברך? אמר רב יהודה: בא"י אמ"ה שהכל

רש"י

מברכין לבתולה שבעה. לקמן מפרש כשבאו פנים חדשות מברך כולן כל ימי המשתה, ואי לא — מברך חדא. במקהלות ברכו אלהים ה' ממקור ישראל. על ברכת מקור צריך קהל, והיינו עשרה כמו "הקהל את העדה" (במדבר כ), ואין הקהל בפחות מעדה, ועדה עשרה, כדילפינן (ברכות דף כא:) מעדת מרגלים "עד מתי לעדה הרעה" — יצאו יהושע וכלב. בגדתאה. עיר שבבבל ושמה בגדת. בפסק סדרו של רב שרירא גאון היא נזכרת. המזכה. מתנה על ידי אחר. לעובר. שבמעי אמו, קנה. בבית חתנים. כשנכנסה לחופת נישואין. אף בבית האירוסין. כשמקדשה, מברכין כל ברכת חתנים, כדמפרש. אמר אביי וביהודה שנו. [הא דר"י ביהודה שנו]. שמתייחד עמה. באירוסין, כדי שיהא לבו גס בה, כדלקמן (דף יב.). לפיכך מברכין ברכת חתנים מתחלה, דתניא במסכת כלה: כלה בלא ברכה אסורה לבעלה כנדה. ואסר לנו את הארוסות. מדרבנן, שגזרו על הייחוד של פנויה, ואף ארוסה לא התירו עד שתיכנס לחופה, ובברכה, כדפרישית: כלה בלא ברכה אסורה לבעלה כנדה. ואדרבנן נמי מברכין "וצונו", "ואסר לנו", כדאשכחן בנר חנוכה (שבת דף כג.). והתיר לנו. את נשותינו הנשואות לנו על ידי חופה וקידושין. אברכת פירות. בורא פרי העץ. ברכת מצות. על השחיטה, ועל המילה. דכיון דכולה חדא הודאה היא, ואין הפסק בקשה בינתיים — לא בעיא חתימה. כדאמר ב"ערבי פסחים" (פסחים דף קה.): ברכת המזון טעמא מאי — משום דהודאה היא, הא נמי — כולה הודאה היא. מידי דהוה אקידושא. כיון דבלשון קדושה היא כקידוש היום, חתמינן בה כי התם, דבההיא חתמינן משום דיש בה הפסק, כגון "כי הוא יום תחלה למקראי קודש". והוא שבאו. אל המשתה. פנים חדשות. בכל יום, שלא היו שם אתמול. מאי מברך אמר רב יהודה כו'. נראה בעיני: סדר ברכות שנסדרו על עסקי הזוג אינו אלא מ"אשר יצר" ואילך, שאותה ברכה מתחלת לדבר בשניהם; "אשר יצר את האדם" מדבר בזכר, והתקין

תוספות

במקהלות ברכו אלהים. אע"ג ד"מקהלות" — תרי קהלות משמע — אין סברא לחלק בין עשרה לעשרים לענין שום מילתא, ומקהלות דעלמא בעי למימר. ומיהו, בירושלמי דריש: "במקהלת" כתיב *חסר וי"ו.

המזכה לעובר קנה. אע"ג דשמואל גופיה פסיק כרבי יוחנן הסנדלר (לקמן דף נח:) דמקדיש מעשה ידי אשתו — המותר חולין, דאין אדם מקדיש דבר שלא בא לעולם, וכל שכן לדבר שלא בא לעולם, דגרע טפי; כדאמרינן בסוף פרק קמא דגיטין (דף יג: ושם) דקאמר: אפילו לרבי מאיר דאמר: אדם מקנה דבר שלא בא לעולם — הני מילי לדבר שבא לעולם, אבל לדבר שלא בא לעולם — לא אמר! מ"מ, שמואל חשיב עובר בא לעולם. אי נמי: שמואל אית ליה טפי אדם מקנה לדבר שלא בא לעולם. ממה שמקנה דבר שלא בא לעולם והויא סוגיא דבפרק קמא דגיטין (ג"ז שם) אתיא אליבא דרב הונא. וכן מצינו רב נחמן דבהדיא סברתו הפוכה מדרב הונא, דרב הונא אית ליה* בפירות דקל משבאו לעולם אין יכול לחזור בו, וגבי עובר קאמר* אף לכשתלד — לא קנה. ורב נחמן סבר לכשתלד קנה, ובפירות דקל קאמר אף משבאו לעולם יכול לחזור בו.

(שייך לע"א) **הורוה** בית הלל. גבי הילני המלכה. אע"ג דמבית חשמונאי היתה, שהרי אם מונבז המלך היתה, כדאמר ביומא (דף לז. ושם), ומלכות הורדוס מאה ושלש שנה בפני הבית, והלל לא נהג נשיאותו עד שלש שנים לאחר מלכות הורדוס, כדאמרינן (שבת טו.): הלל ושמעון, גמליאל ושמעון נהגו נשיאותן בפני הבית מאה שנה — מכל מקום כבר היו לו אז תלמידים שהורו.

(שייך לע"א) **והא** בועז אלמון שנשא אלמנה הוה. לאו דוקא אלמנה, דכשנשאת למחלון (וכליון) היתה גויה, אלא כיון דבעולה — היא כאלמנה חשיב לה.

(שייך לע"א) **באלמנה** שנשאת לבחור. דכיון שאין שניהם אלמונים — יש לברך כל שבעה.

שנאמר ויקח בועז עשרה אנשים. ובמסכת כלה דמייתי קרא ד"ויברכו את רבקה" (בראשית כד) איכא למימר דהתם ברכת אירוסין, והכא ברכת נישואין. ויש ללמוד משם שיש לברך ברכת אירוסין לאשה המתקדשת על ידי שליח, שהרי אליעזר שליח היה. ונראה דאסמכתא בעלמא היא, דעשרה לא מישתמע מהתם, ולא איירי פשטיה דקרא בברכת אירוסין.

רבי יהודה אומר אף בבית האירוסין מברכין אותה מפני שמתייחד עמה. ואמרי': כלה בלא ברכה אסורה לבעלה כנדה. ולפי שפעמים בא עליה שלא לשם חופה — עושין ברכה מתחלה, כדי שתבא כלה בברכה.

מאן דלא חתים מידי דהוה אברכת פירות. שאין בה אריכות. והאי נמי אינה ארוכה, ולא דמי לקידושא דאריך טפי. ומאן דחתים — מידי דהוה אקידושא דחתים ביה משום דאריך, והאי נמי חשיבא ארוכה. ומה שפירש בקונטרס דמשום דבלשון קדושה היא חתמי בה כמו בקידושא — אינו נראה. ק"ק: מאן דלא חתים בה, מאי שנא מברכת התורה דחתמינן בה ב"אשר בחר בנו" אע"ג דברכת אירוסין אריכא טפי מינה? ושמא לא היה חותם בה.

והוא שבאו פנים חדשות. אור"י: דפנים חדשות אין קורא אלא בבני אדם שמרבים בשבילם השמחה יותר. ושבת דחשבינן פנים חדשות, דאמרינן באגדה: מזמור שיר ליום השבת, אמר הקב"ה: פנים חדשות באו לכאן, נאמר שירה — התם נמי מרבין לכבוד השבת בשמחה ובסעודה.

שהכל

מסורת הש"ס

ברכות נ.

[יבמות סט. וש"נ]

יבמות סז. ב"ב קמב: [זבחים לב.]

[יבמות לג.]

[ב"ב קמב.]

גליון הש"ס

גמ' ברכת חתנים בבית חתנים. ע' סוכה כה ע"ב תד"ה אין שמחה:

תוספות רי"ד

א"ר נחמן א"ר הונא תנא מנין לברכת חתנים שהוא בעשרה שנאמר ויקח בועז עשרה אנשים וכו'. ור' אבהו אמר במקהלות ברכו אלהים ה' ממקור ישראל. פי' בה"ג בשעה שאתה מברך על המקור משום פריה ורביה עשה קהילה. א"ר יוסף הלוי הני ז' ברכות דמברכים בבית חתנים בין בשעת הכניסה בין בשעת המשתה בדאיכא פנים חדשות בין אשר ברא. בדליכא פנים חדשות לא מברכינן לה אלא בעשרה. דאר"י אר"י מברכין ברכת חתנים בעשרה כל ז' וחתנים מן המנין. ואשר ברא כיון דמברכת חתנים הוא לא מברכין לה בדליכא פנים חדשות אלא בעשרה. ואינו נ"ל דכל היכא דאמרי ברכת חתנים לא משמע אלא ז' ברכות ולא אשר ברא בלחוד דהכי אמרינן ברכת חתנים כל ז'. ואמר רב יהודה והוא שבאו פנים חדשות. אלמא לא מיקרייא ברכת חתנים אלא ז' ברכות. דהא אשר ברא בלחוד לא בעיא פנים חדשות. והלכך כי אר"י מברכין ברכת חתנים בעשרה כל ז' על ז' ברכות קאמר ובדאיכא פנים חדשות. אבל אשר ברא נ"ל כיון שהוא עיקר ברכת חתנות שחייב לברכה בכל יום אפילו אם אכל החתן יחיד חייב לאומרה. סגה"ס (והרב פוסק (כר') [בשם רבינו] יצחק הלוי ואפי' ברכת אשר ברא לבדו צריכה עשרה.) ת"ר מברכין ברכת חתנים בבית חתנים ר"י אומר אף בבית האירוסין מברכין אותן. אמר אביי ביהודה שנו מפני שמתיחד עמה. פי' ביהודה הי' מיחדים אותם משעת אירוסין כדי שיהא לבו גס בה. ולפיכך מברכים אותם ברכת חתנים תחלה ותניא במס' כלה כלה בלא ברכה אסורה לבעלה כנדה. ואע"ג דהוו מברכי להו משעת אירוסין דין ארוסה יש לה ולא דין נשואה ואינו זכאי לא במציאותי' ולא במעשה ידיה ולא בהפרת נדריה. ואם מתה אינה יורשה וכן הוא אינו חייב לה בשאר כסות ועונה ולא נקראת אשתו נשואה אלא כשמוסרים אותה לו לשם נשואין. דמסירה קונה שתהיה אשתו לכל דבר ולא ז' ברכות דז' ברכות לא עבדי אלא שיהא מותר להתיחד עמה. וכן דרך קהילות ממניאה שמברכים ז' ברכות משעת אירוסין ועומדים זמן הרבה. ואח"כ מוסרים אותה לו לחופה לשם נשואין. ומ"ה תנן בפירקין לקמן. חוץ מן הארוסה שביהודה. שאע"פ שהיו מברכים ברכות אירוסין אכתי ארוסה קרי לה עד שימסרנה לו לשם נשואין ונ"ל שכיון שבירך ז' ברכות משעת אירוסין אסור עוד לברכה בשעת נשואין דהוה להו ברכה לבטלה. א"נ י"ל משום אפושי שמחה. וכל מה שמברכין בתוך ז' ימי החתונה אין בם משום ברכה לבטלה והכי נמי עיקר חיתונים הנשואים הם שמה שבירך בשעת האירוסין לא בירך אלא להתיר היחוד ועיקר חתנותיה זו היא. הלכך מברכין אותם בשעת הנשואים: תניא אידך מברכין ברכות חתנים בבית חתנים וברכת האירוסין בבית האירוסין. ברכת האירוסין מאי מברך רבין בר אדא ורב' בר רב אדא תרווייהו משמיה דר"י אמרי. בא"י אמ"ה אקב"ו על העריות ואסר לנו את הארוסות והתיר לנו את הנשואות ע"י חופה וקידושין. רב אחא משמיה דרבא מסיים בא"י מקדש ישראל ע"י חופה וקידושין מאן דלא מסיים סבר מידי דהוי אברכת פירות וברכת מצות. ומאן דמסיים סבר מידי דהוי אקדושא דעלמא. פי' שמאריך בה דבריו צריך חתימה וכך הלכה. והאי ואסר לנו את הארוסות היא מדרבנן שאמרו כלה בלא ברכה אסורה לבעלה כנדה ואפ"ה מברך עליה מידי דהוה אנר חנוכה. וה"ל דאע"ג שכל המצות מברך עליהן עובר לעשייתן הכא ברישא מקדש והדר מברך. מפני שהוא תלוי ברעת אחרים ושמא יחזרו בהן והוו לבטלה: ת"ר מברכין ברכת חתנים כל ז'. אמר ר"י והיא שבאו פנים חדשות. פי' ברכות חתנים הוא ז' ברכות. ומ"ה צריך פנים חדשות אדם שעדיין

אשֶׁהַכֹּל בָּרָא לִכְבוֹדוֹ", וְ"יוֹצֵר הָאָדָם", וַ"אֲשֶׁר יָצַר אֶת הָאָדָם בְּצַלְמוֹ בְּצֶלֶם דְּמוּת תַּבְנִיתוֹ וְהִתְקִין לוֹ מִמֶּנּוּ בִּנְיַן עֲדֵי עַד בָּרוּךְ אַתָּה ה' יוֹצֵר הָאָדָם", "שׂוֹשׂ תָּשִׂישׂ וְתָגֵל הָעֲקָרָה בְּקִבּוּץ בָּנֶיהָ לְתוֹכָהּ בְּשִׂמְחָה בָּרוּךְ אַתָּה ה' מְשַׂמֵּחַ צִיּוֹן בְּבָנֶיהָ", "שַׂמֵּחַ תְּשַׂמַּח רֵיעִים הָאֲהוּבִים כְּשַׂמֵּחֲךָ יְצִירְךָ בְּגַן עֵדֶן מִקֶּדֶם בָּרוּךְ אַתָּה ה' מְשַׂמֵּחַ חָתָן וְכַלָּה", "בָּרוּךְ אַתָּה ה' אמ"ה אֲשֶׁר בָּרָא שָׂשׂוֹן וְשִׂמְחָה חָתָן וְכַלָּה גִּילָה רִינָּה דִּיצָה חֶדְוָה אַהֲבָה וְאַחֲוָה וְשָׁלוֹם וְרֵיעוּת, מְהֵרָה ה' אֱלֹהֵינוּ יִשָּׁמַע בְּעָרֵי יְהוּדָה וּבְחוּצוֹת יְרוּשָׁלַיִם קוֹל שָׂשׂוֹן וְקוֹל שִׂמְחָה קוֹל חָתָן וְקוֹל כַּלָּה קוֹל מִצְהֲלוֹת חֲתָנִים מֵחוּפָּתָם וּנְעָרִים מִמִּשְׁתֵּה נְגִינָתָם בא"י מְשַׂמֵּחַ חָתָן עִם הַכַּלָּה". לֵוִי אִיקְּלַע לְבֵי רַבִּי בְּהִלּוּלֵיהּ דְּר"ש בְּרֵיהּ, בְּרִיךְ חָמֵשׁ. רַב אַסִּי אִיקְּלַע לְבֵי רַב אַשִׁי בְּהִלּוּלֵיהּ דְּמָר בְּרֵיהּ, בְּרִיךְ שִׁית. לֵימָא בְּהָא קָמִיפַּלְגִי, דְּמ"ס חֲדָא יְצִירָה הֲוַאי, וּמ"ס: שְׁתֵּי יְצִירוֹת הֲוַאי? לָא, דְּכ"ע חֲדָא יְצִירָה הֲוַאי, מ"ס: בָּתַר מַחֲשָׁבָה אָזְלִינַן, וּמ"ס: בָּתַר מַעֲשֶׂה אָזְלִינַן. כִּי הָא *דְּרַב יְהוּדָה רָמֵי, כְּתִיב: °"וַיִּבְרָא אֱלֹהִים אֶת הָאָדָם בְּצַלְמוֹ" (בראשית א), וּכְתִיב: °"זָכָר וּנְקֵבָה בְּרָאָם" (שם ה), הָא כֵּיצַד? בַּתְּחִלָּה עָלָה בְּמַחֲשָׁבָה לִבְרָאוֹת שְׁנַיִם, וּלְבַסּוֹף נִבְרָא אֶחָד. רַב אַשִׁי אִיקְּלַע לְבֵי רַב כָּהֲנָא, יוֹמָא קַמָּא בְּרִיךְ כּוּלְּהוּ, מִכָּאן וְאֵילָךְ, באִי אִיכָּא פָּנִים חֲדָשׁוֹת — בְּרִיךְ כּוּלְּהוּ, וְאִי לָא — אַפּוּשֵׁי שִׂמְחָה בְּעָלְמָא הוּא, מְבָרֵךְ "שֶׁהַשִּׂמְחָה בִּמְעוֹנוֹ" וַ"אֲשֶׁר בָּרָא". מִשִּׁבְעָה וְעַד שְׁלֹשִׁים, בֵּין אֲמַר לְהוּ מֵחֲמַת הִלּוּלָא וּבֵין לָא אֲמַר לְהוּ מֵחֲמַת הִלּוּלָא — מְבָרֵךְ "שֶׁהַשִּׂמְחָה בִּמְעוֹנוֹ". מִכָּאן וְאֵילָךְ, אִי אֲמַר לְהוּ מֵחֲמַת הִלּוּלָא — מְבָרֵךְ "שֶׁהַשִּׂמְחָה בִּמְעוֹנוֹ", וְאִי לָא — לָא. וְכִי א"ל מֵחֲמַת הִלּוּלָא עַד אֵימַת? אָמַר רַב פַּפֵּי מִשְּׁמֵיהּ דְּרָבָא: געַד תְּרֵיסַר יַרְחֵי שַׁתָּא. וּמֵעִיקָּרָא מֵאֵימַת? *אָמַר רַב פַּפָּא: מִכִּי רָמוּ שַׂעֲרֵי בְּאַסִּינְתָּא. אִינִי? וְהָא רַב פַּפָּא אִיעֲסַק לְאַבָּא מָר בְּרֵיהּ, וּבְרִיךְ מִשְּׁעַת אֵירוּסִין! שָׁאנֵי רַב פַּפָּא דַּהֲוָה טְרִיחַ לֵיהּ. רָבִינָא אִיעֲסַק לֵיהּ לִבְרֵיהּ בֵּי רַב חֲבִיבָא, וּבְרִיךְ מִשְּׁעַת אֵירוּסִין. אֲמַר: קִים לִי בְּגַוַּויְיהוּ דְּלָא הָדְרִי בְּהוּ. לָא אִסְתַּיַּיע מִילְּתָא, וְהָדְרִי בְּהוּ. רַב תַּחְלִיפָא בַּר מַעַרְבָא אִיקְּלַע לְבָבֶל, בְּרִיךְ שִׁית אֲרִיכָתָא. וְלֵית הִלְכְתָא כְּוָותֵיהּ. רַב חֲבִיבָא אִיקְּלַע לְבֵי מְהוּלָא, בְּרִיךְ "שֶׁהַשִּׂמְחָה בִּמְעוֹנוֹ", וְלֵית הִלְכְתָא כְּוָותֵיהּ, מִשּׁוּם דִּטְרִידִי, דְּאִית לֵיהּ צַעֲרָא לְיָנוֹקָא. א"ר נַחְמָן אָמַר רַב: דחֲתָנִים מִן הַמִּנְיָן, *וְאֵין אֲבֵלִים מִן הַמִּנְיָן. מֵיתִיבֵי: חֲתָנִים וַאֲבֵלִים מִן הַמִּנְיָן! מַתְנִיתָא קָא רָמֵית עֲלֵיהּ דְּרַב?! *רַב תַּנָּא הוּא, וּפָלֵיג. אִיתְּמַר, *אָמַר ר' יִצְחָק א"ר יוֹחָנָן: חֲתָנִים מִן הַמִּנְיָן, וְאֵין אֲבֵלִים מִן הַמִּנְיָן. מֵיתִיבֵי: חֲתָנִים וַאֲבֵלִים מִן הַמִּנְיָן!

כי

וְהִתְקִין לוֹ מִמֶּנּוּ בִּנְיַן עֲדֵי עַד. הִיא הַנְּקֵבָה. שׂוֹשׂ תָּשִׂישׂ. לְפִי שֶׁאָנוּ צְרִיכִין לְהַעֲלוֹת זִכְרוֹן יְרוּשָׁלַיִם עַל רֹאשׁ שִׂמְחָתֵנוּ, שֶׁנֶּאֱמַר (תהלים קלז) "תִּדְבַּק לְשׁוֹנִי לְחִכִּי" וגו'. שַׂמֵּחַ תְּשַׂמַּח. בְּרָכָה לְחָתָן וְכַלָּה שֶׁיַּצְלִיחוּ בְּשִׂמְחָה וְטוּב לֵב. וַ"אֲשֶׁר בָּרָא" – לְשֵׁם כָּל יִשְׂרָאֵל. וּלְפִי שֶׁהַסֵּדֶר מַתְחִיל מֵ"אֲשֶׁר יָצַר", לְפִיכָךְ פָּתַח בָּהּ בְּבָרוּךְ וְחָתַם בָּהּ בְּבָרוּךְ, כְּדֶרֶךְ כָּל רָאשֵׁי סִדְרֵי בְרָכוֹת. וְ"שׂוֹשׂ תָּשִׂישׂ" וְ"שַׂמֵּחַ תְּשַׂמַּח" – מִפְּנֵי שֶׁהֵן בְּרָכָה הַסְּמוּכָה לַחֲבֶרְתָּהּ לֹא פָּתַח בָּהּ בְּבָרוּךְ, שֶׁכֵּן תִּיקְּנוּ לְכָל הַבְּרָכוֹת שֶׁסְּמוּכוֹת אַחַר הָרִאשׁוֹנָה עַל הַסֵּדֶר. וַ"אֲשֶׁר בָּרָא" מִפְּנֵי שֶׁהִיא נֶאֱמֶרֶת יְחִידִית בְּרוֹב יְמֵי הַמִּשְׁתֶּה, כְּשֶׁאֵין שָׁם פָּנִים חֲדָשׁוֹת – לְפִיכָךְ אֵינָהּ מִן הַסְּמוּכוֹת, וְהוּצְרַךְ לִפְתּוֹחַ בָּהּ בְּבָרוּךְ וּלְסַיֵּים בָּהּ בְּבָרוּךְ. אֲבָל "שֶׁהַכֹּל בָּרָא לִכְבוֹדוֹ" אֵינָהּ מִן הַסֵּדֶר, אֶלָּא לַאֲסִיפַת הָעָם הַנֶּאֱסָפִים שָׁם לִגְמוֹל חֶסֶד, זֵכֶר לַחֲסָדֵי הַמָּקוֹם שֶׁנָּהַג עִם אָדָם הָרִאשׁוֹן, שֶׁנַּעֲשָׂה לוֹ שׁוּשְׁבִין וְנִתְעַסֵּק בּוֹ. וַאֲסִיפָה זוֹ כְּבוֹד הַמָּקוֹם הִיא, וּבְרָכָה זוֹ לְכָךְ נִתְקְנָה. וּמִשְּׁעַת אֲסִיפָה הִיא רְאוּיָה לְבָרֵךְ, אֶלָּא מִכֵּיוָן שֶׁיֵּשׁ בְּרָכָה עַל הַכּוֹס הִזְקִיקוּהָ לְסַדְרָהּ עָלָיו, מִידֵּי דַּהֲוָה אַבִּרְכַּת בְּשָׂמִים וּבִרְכַּת עַל הָאוּר בְּמוֹצָאֵי שַׁבָּת, דְּאָמְרִי' *(ירושלמי *דפסחים פ"י): רַבִּי מְפַזְּרָן וְחוֹזֵר וְסוֹדְרָן עַל הַכּוֹס, וְרַבִּי חִיָּיא מְכַנְּסָן, הוֹאִיל וְיֵשׁ שָׁם כּוֹס. וּלְפִי שֶׁאֵינָהּ מִשְּׁאָר סֵדֶר הַבְּרָכוֹת, וְכוּלָּהּ הוֹדָאָה אַחַת – לֹא חָתְמוּ בָּהּ בְּבָרוּךְ, מִידֵּי דַּהֲוָה אַבִּרְכַּת פֵּירוֹת וּמִצְוֹת. וְכֵן בִּרְכַּת "יוֹצֵר הָאָדָם" שֶׁתִּיקְּנוּהָ לִיצִירָה רִאשׁוֹנָה שֶׁל אָדָם הָרִאשׁוֹן כִּדְלְקַמָּן, אִי לְמ"ד ב' יְצִירוֹת הֲווּ, אִי לְמ"ד ב' יְצִירוֹת עָלוּ בְּמַחֲשָׁבָה וּבָתַר מַחֲשָׁבָה אָזְלִינַן – מ"מ אֵינָהּ מִסֵּדֶר בִּרְכוֹת הַזִּוּוּג. דְּהָא בִּיצִירָה הָרִאשׁוֹנָה חֲכָתִּי נְקֵבָה לָא הֲוַאי. וְא"ת: לָמָּה הִיא בָּאָה? מִתּוֹךְ שֶׁאָנוּ מְבָרְכִין עַל יְצִירָה הַשְּׁנִיָּה, תִּקְּנוּ אַף עַל הָרִאשׁוֹנָה שֶׁהִיא עִיקָּר וּתְחִילָּתוֹ. וְהִתְקִין לוֹ מִמֶּנּוּ. מִגּוּפוֹ, מִצַּלְעוֹתָיו. בִּנְיַן עֲדֵי עַד. בִּנְיָן נוֹהֵג לְדוֹרוֹת. וְחַוָּה קָרֵי לָהּ בִּנְיָן עַל שֵׁם "וַיִּבֶן אֶת הַצֵּלָע" (בראשית ב). עֲקָרָה. יְרוּשָׁלַיִם. רֵיעִים הָאֲהוּבִים. הֶחָתָן וְהַכַּלָּה, שֶׁהֵן רֵיעִים הָאוֹהֲבִים זֶה אֶת זֶה. כְּשַׂמֵּחֲךָ יְצִירְךָ. כְּמוֹ שֶׁשִּׂמַּחְתָּ אֶת אָדָם הָרִאשׁוֹן. בְּגַן עֵדֶן מִקֶּדֶם. דִּכְתִיב "וַיִּטַּע גַּן בְּעֵדֶן מִקֶּדֶם, וַיָּשֶׂם שָׁם" וגו' (שם). מְשַׂמֵּחַ חָתָן וְכַלָּה. וּבָאַחֲרוֹנָה "מְשַׂמֵּחַ חָתָן עִם הַכַּלָּה". לְפִי שֶׁשִּׂמְחַת בְּרָכָה הָרִאשׁוֹנָה לֹא בְּשִׂמְחַת חֲתוּנָּה אָנוּ אוֹמְרִים, שֶׁהֲרֵי תְּפִלָּה הִיא שֶׁמִּתְפַּלְּלִים וּמְבָרְכִין שֶׁיִּהְיוּ שְׂמֵחִים בְּהַצְלָחָה כָּל יְמֵיהֶם, לְפִיכָךְ אֵין לַחְתּוֹם בָּהּ "מְשַׂמֵּחַ חָתָן עִם הַכַּלָּה", דְּמַשְׁמַע אִישׁ בְּאִשְׁתּוֹ, אֶלָּא בָּרוּךְ ה' מְשַׂמֵּחַ אֶת שְׁנֵיהֶם לְעוֹלָם, בְּסִיפּוּק מְזוֹנוֹת וְכָל טוּב. וּבָאַחֲרוֹנָה שֶׁבַח שֶׁמְּשַׁבֵּחַ לְהקב"ה שֶׁבָּרָא חֲתוּנַּת דִּיבּוּק אִישׁ בְּאִשָּׁה עַל יְדֵי שִׂמְחָה וְחֶדְוָה, לְפִיכָךְ יֵשׁ לַחְתּוֹם בָּהּ "מְשַׂמֵּחַ חָתָן עִם הַכַּלָּה", שֶׁהוּא לְשׁוֹן שִׂמְחַת אִישׁ בְּאִשָּׁה. בְּרִיךְ חָמֵשׁ. "שֶׁהַכֹּל" וַ"אֲשֶׁר יָצַר" וְ"שׂוֹשׂ תָּשִׂישׂ", "שַׂמֵּחַ תְּשַׂמַּח", "אֲשֶׁר בָּרָא". בְּרִיךְ שִׁית. "יוֹצֵר הָאָדָם" הוֹסִיף. חֲדָא יְצִירָה הֲוַאי. כְּמַאן דְּאָמַר בְּעֵירוּבִין (דף יח.) "וַיִּבֶן אֶת הַצֵּלָע" – פַּרְצוּף. שֶׁמִּתְּחִלַּת בְּרִיָּיתוֹ נִבְרָא שְׁנֵי פַרְצוּפִין, זָכָר מִלְּפָנָיו וּנְקֵבָה מֵאָחוֹר. שְׁתֵּי יְצִירוֹת. כְּמַאן דְּאָמַר זָנָב הָיָה, וּמִמֶּנּוּ נִבְרֵאת הָאִשָּׁה, וַהֲרֵי כָּאן שְׁתֵּי יְצִירוֹת. בָּתַר מַחֲשָׁבָה אָזְלִינַן. שֶׁשְּׁנַיִם עָלוּ בְּמַחֲשָׁבָה לְהִבָּרְאוֹת, וְנִבְרָא אֶחָד. בְּעֵירוּבִין בְּפֶ' "עוֹשִׂין פַּסִּין". מְבָרֵךְ שֶׁהַשִּׂמְחָה בִּמְעוֹנוֹ. בִּתְחִלַּת הַזִּימּוּן. בֵּין אָמַר לָהֶן. לַקְּרוּאִין. מֵחֲמַת הִלּוּלָא. קְרָאתִי לָכֶם הַלּוֹם לִסְעוּדָה. מֵעִיקָּרָא. קוֹדֶם הַחוּפָּה, אִם הִזְמִין קְרוּאִים, וְאָמַר לָהֶם: מֵחֲמַת שֶׁאֲנִי רוֹצֶה לְהַכְנִיס בְּנִי לַחוּפָּה. מֵאֵימָתַי. הָוְיָא הַתְחָלַת שִׂמְחַת חוּפָּה, לְבָרֵךְ "שֶׁהַשִּׂמְחָה בִּמְעוֹנוֹ". מִכִּי רָמוּ שַׂעֲרֵי בְּאַסִּינְתָּא. יֵשׁ שׁוֹרִין שְׂעוֹרִים בַּעֲרֵיבַת מַיִם *לְהָטִיל שֵׁכָר לְצוֹרֶךְ חוּפָּה. וְי"א: לְשֵׁם הֶחָתָן וְהַכַּלָּה זוֹרְעִין שְׂעוֹרִין בְּעָצִיץ, לוֹמַר: פְּרוּ וּרְבוּ וְצִמְחוּ כַּשְּׂעוֹרִים הַלָּלוּ. דַּהֲוָה טְרִיחַ לֵיהּ. מְתוּקָּנִים הָיוּ לוֹ כָּל צָרְכֵי חוּפָּה וּסְעוּדָה. אִיעֲסַק לִבְרֵיהּ. שִׁידֵּךְ לוֹ אִשָּׁה. וּבְרִיךְ מִשְּׁעַת אֵירוּסִין. שֶׁהַשִּׂמְחָה בִּמְעוֹנוֹ. וְהָדְרִי בְּהוּ. לֹא נָתְנוּ לוֹ הָאִשָּׁה. שִׁית אֲרִיכָתָא. הוֹסִיף דְּבָרִים עַל "שֶׁהַכֹּל" וְעַל בִּרְכַּת יְצִירָה רִאשׁוֹנָה, וְחָתַם בָּהֶם בְּבָרוּךְ. וְלֵית הִלְכְתָא כְּוָותֵיהּ. כִּדְפֵי' לְעֵיל. לְבֵי מְהוּלָא. לִסְעוּדַּת מִילָה. חֲתָנִים מִן הַמִּנְיָן. לְקַמָּן מְפָרֵשׁ לְמַאי הִלְכְתָא.

בְּבִרְכַּת

פסחים נג.

[עירובין יח. ע"ש היטב וע' גם ברכות סא. ומלוה לייבב. ושם איתא ר' אבהו וכ"א בשאילתות.]

[ע"ז ח:]

[סנהדרין יט.]

[עירובין כ: וש"נ]

[מגילה כג:]

[עיין תוס' ע"ז ח: ד"ה מכי וכו' השיגו על פירוש זה]

שהכל ברא לכבודו ויוצר האדם. פותחת בברוך אע"פ שכל אחת סמוכה לחבירתה, כיון דקלרות הן, אם לא היה פותח בברוך היה נראה הכל ברכה אחת. וכן "אשר יצר" אם לא היה פותח בברוך היה נראה שהיתה מתחלת מ"ברוך יוצר האדם אשר יצר". אבל "שוש תשיש" שהיא אחר ברכה ארוכה אין צריך לפתוח בברוך. ו"אשר ברא" פותחת בברוך, לפי שמברכים אותה בפני עצמה כשאין פנים חדשות, כדפירש בקונטרס. ועל "שהכל ברא לכבודו" ו"יוצר האדם" פי' בקונטרס טעם אחר. ור"ת פירש: ד"יוצר האדם" פותחת בברוך, לפי שיש שלא היו אומרים אותה, כדאמר בסמוך. ואור"ת דבפרק קמא דברכות (דף יא:), גבי ברכת התורה גרסי': ר' יוחנן מסיים בה הכי "והערב נא" דברכה אחת היא, דאי הוו שתי ברכות – היה צריך לפתוח בברוך, אע"ג דסמוכה לחברתה, כיון שאותה שלפניה היא קצרה. ובתר הכי גרסינן: הלכך נימרינהו לתרווייהו, ולא גרסינן "לכולהו" – דאם כן הוה משמע דשלש ברכות הן. **חדא** יצירה הואי. צריך לומר דהיינו כמאן דאמר פרצוף אחד, מדקאמר בתר הכי: דכולי עלמא חדא יצירה הואי, מר סבר בתר מחשבה אזלינן. וכריש פרק שני דעירובין (דף יח. ושם) משמע בהדיא דלמאן דאמר פרצוף אחד – הוה עלה במחשבה להבראות שנים. אבל למאן דאמר התם שני פרצופים – לא סבירא ליה הכי. כך פירש רשב"ם.

רב תנא הוא ופליג. לא בעי לשנויי כי תניא ההיא בברכת המזון כדמשני רבי יוחנן, דנראה לו דוחק להעמיד כן, ונוח לו טפי לומר דפליג. ומדלא קאמר ר' יוחנן *תנא ופליג – יש להוכיח דר"י אמורא היה, דאי הוה תנא – הוה משני כדמשני לרב. ואין להקשות: דאמאי לא משני רבי יוחנן הנא דאמרי כרב דתנא הוא? דרבי יוחנן לא היה מחזיק רב כתנא, דפליג עליו בכל דוכתא. ומיהו, איכא נמי רבי יוחנן שהיה תנא, דתניא בשילהי דנזיר (דף סה. ושם): וכמה שיעור תפיסה פירש רבי יוחנן כו'.

לט א מיי' פ"ב מהל' ברכות הל' יא ופ"י מהל' אישות הל' ג סמג עשין מח טוש"ע אה"ע סי' (סא) [סב] סעי' ה:
מ ב מיי' שם הל' י טוש"ע שם סעיף ד:
מא ג מיי' פ"י מהל' אישות ה"ו טוש"ע שם סעיף יג:
מב ד מיי' שם הל' ה ופ"ב מהל' ברכות ה"י טוש"ע שם סעיף ד:

תוספות רי"ד

שעדיין לא שמנן: מאי מברך אר"י שהכל ברא לכבודו. יוצר האדם. אשר יצר. שוש תשיש. שמח תשמח. אשר ברא. פי' תחלה מברך שהכל ברא לכבודו משום דברכת חתנים צריכה עשרה כדכתיב במקהלות ברכו ה' וכתיב ברוב עם הדרת מלך. וזו האסיפה היא על כבודו לברכו ברבים מ"ה מתחיל ומברך שהכל. אח"כ מברך יוצר האדם כנגד יצירה ראשונה שנברא לבדו. אח"כ מברך על יצירת שניהם האיך הפריד לו אשה מצלעותיו ומפני שמאריך דבריו חותם בה. אבל השתים הראשונות שהן קצרות אינו חותם בהן ואע"פ שהיא סמוכה לשלש ראשונות שבירך כבר פותח בה בברוך מפני שהשלש ראשונות פתיחה בברוך יש בהן. אבל חתימה אין בהם ואיזו נקרא ברכה הסמוכה לחברתה שאין פותחים בה בברוך כשמתחיל לאחרי' כגון ברכות י"ח וברכות ק"ש. אבל הסמוכה לברכה קטנה פותחים בה בברוך כמו שאנו עושים בק' ברכות שאותן שהם קצרות מברכין על כ"א וא' בפתיחה ולא יותר וכשמתחיל לברך ברכות הארוכות פותח בה בברוך. ואין סמיכות ברכות הקצרות פוטרת מלפתוח בה בברוך. וג"ל שטועים הם בני אדם שמתחילים מאה ברכות מאלהי נשמה מפני שלא מצינו בשום מקום שיתחיל בברכות בלא פתיחת ברוך. וכך ראוי להתחיל ברוך אשר יצר את האדם בחכמה. ויש בה פתיחה לפניה וחתימה לאחריה. ואח"כ אומר אלהי נשמה וחותם בה בברוך ואינו פותח בה בברוך מפני שהיא סמוכה להו. אח"כ אומר כל הקצרות. ואח"כ אומר המעביר שינה. ופותח בברוך. מפני שסמיכות ברכות הקטנות אינה פוטרתה. ובברכת התורה פותח בה בברוך מפני שלא נתקנה עם סדר ק' ברכות אלא כשצריך ללמוד הילכך יש בה פתיחה. אח"כ מברך שוש תשיש קודם שיברך על שמחת החתן דכתיב אם לא אעלה את ירושלים על ראש שמחתי. ומפני שהיא סמוכה לחתימת אשר יצר אינו פותח בה בברוך. אח"כ אומר שמח תשמח שישמח החתן והכלה כל ימיהם ואין זו שמחת הזיווג ומסיים בה משמח חתן וכלה ואינו פותח בה בברוך מפני שסמוכה היא לחתימת שוש תשש. אח"כ אומר אשר ברא שהוא שמחת הזיווג וחותם בה משמח חתן עם הכלה ששמחים כשמזדווגים זה עם זה ואע"פ שהיא סמוכה לחתימה הראשונה שלפניה ודין הוא שלא נפתח בה בברוך. אפ"ה מפני שמברכים אותה לבדה בדליכא פנים חדשות הוא פותח בה בברוך: רב אשי איקלע לבי רב כהנא יומא קמא בריך כולהו מכאן ואילך אמר אי איכא פנים חדשות נבריך כולהו. ואי לא אפושי שמחה בעלמא הוא. מברך שהשמחה במעונו ואשר ברא. פי' יומא קמא בין בשעת כניסתן לחופה בין בסעודה מברך כולהו ואין צריך פנים חדשות דהא מכאן ואילך לא הוי אלא בסעודה. א"כ יומא קמא אפילו בסעודה מברך ז' ברכות בלא פנים חדשות. ומכאן ואילך בלא פנים חדשות מברך שהשמחה במעונו בברהמ"ז ואשר ברא שהוא עיקר ברכת החתונות בסוף ברהמ"ז. מז' ועד ל' בין אמר מחמת הלולא בין לא אמר מחמת הילולא מברך שהשמחה במעונו. פי' אבל לא אשר ברא שהוא ברכת החתונות. וכיון שעברו ז' ימי חתונות אינו ראו לברכם. מכאן ואילך אי אמר מחמת הלולא מברך שהשמחה במעונו ואי לא לא. וכי אמר מחמת הלולא עד אימת. א"ר פפי משמיה דרבא עד תריסר ירחי שתא. מעיקרא מאימת א"ר פפא מכי רמו שערי באסותא פי' כיון שמשליך השעורים בגיגית לעשות מהן שכר לצורך הסעודה אבל לא משעת אירוסין: רבינא איעסיק ליה לבריה בי רב חביבא בריך משעת אירוסין. אמר קים לי בגווייהו דלא הדרי ביה ולא אסתעייא מילתא והדרי ביה: רב תחליפא איקלע לבבל בריך שית אריכתא. פי' הוסיף דברים על שהכל ועל יוצר האדם. והאריך בהן וחתם בהם ופסיק תלמודא ולית הלכתא (כפתם) [כוותיה]: רב חביבא איקלע לסעודת המילה בריך שהשמחה במעונו ופסיק תלמודא ולית הלכתא [כוותיה] משום דאית ליה צערא לינוקא. אר"י אמר ר"י מברכין ברכת חתנים בעשרה כל ז'. וחתנים מן המנין ברכת אבלים כל ז' ואין אבלים מן המנין. מאי ברכת אבלים ברכת רחבה פי' היו מברין את האבל ברחובה של עיר ומברכין שם כנגד השם וכנגד אבלים וכנגד המנחמים וכנגד כל ישראל כדמפרש בגמרא וצריכה עשרה ובאותן יו"ד אין אבלים מן המנין כברכת המזון כגון ג' לזימון ויו"ד לאלהינו:

מג א מיי' פ"ד מהלכות אבל הלכה ו טוש"ע יו"ד סי' שעט סעיף ה:
מד ב מיי' פי"ג שם הלכה א סמג עשין דרבנן ב:
מה ג מיי' שם הל"ח סמג שם:
מו ד מיי' פ"ד שם הל"א סמג שם טוש"ע יו"ד סי' שנב סעי' ב:

כי תניא ההיא בברכת המזון. פי' בקונטרס: להצטרף עם ג' לזימון, שהרי הוא חייב בכל המצות. ואין נראה לר"י, דא"כ לא אתא לאשמועינן אלא דחייב במצות – והוה ליה למימר בהדיא דחייב במצות! ועוד: דא"כ מאי פריך ליה מברכת אבלים בעשרה ואין אבלים מן המנין, דקאמר ברכה בשורה מי איכא? אלא ע"כ היינו ברכת המזון, והדרן קושיא לדוכתין, דקתני ואבלים מן המנין, ואוקמינן בברכת המזון. ולפירש הקונטרס לא קשיא מידי, דכי קתני ואבלים מן המנין – היינו להצטרף לזימון, לומר "נברך שאכלנו משלו", אבל ברכת אבלים שמברכים בברכת המזון – קאמר רבי יוחנן דאינו מן המנין. לכך צריך לפרש: כי תניא ההיא בברכת המזון – היינו ברכת אבלים שבברכת המזון. מכאן משמע שברכת אבלים שבברכת המזון לא הוי אלא בעשרה, מדסליק אדעתיה דמקשן דאיירי בברכת אבלים שבברכת המזון, וקאמר בעשרה, והוה ניחא ליה בהכי אי לאו משום דקתני לעיל בברייתא ואבלים מן המנין, אם כן צריך עשרה.

אלא כי קאמר ר' יוחנן ברחבה. אי גרסינן "אלא" משמע דההיא דלעיל נמי מעמיד ברחבה. ותימה: למה הוצרכו תרי מילי דר' יוחנן, ההיא דלעיל והך? וצריך לומר דחדא מכלל חברתה אתמר, ההיא דלעיל מכללא דהך. אבל אי ל"ג "אלא" – ניחא, דלעיל איירי בשורה והכא ברחבה בלא פנים חדשות. ומימרא שלישית של רבי יוחנן הוצרך להשמיענו דבפנים חדשות אין אבלים מן המנין. ואי נקט ההיא – ה"א איפכא דוקא מיום ראשון ואילך, אבל ביום ראשון שייכי טפי ומברכינן לה בלא י'.

תורה אור

כִּי תַּנְיָא הַהִיא — [א]בְּבִרְכַּת הַמָּזוֹן, כִּי קָאָמַר רַבִּי יוֹחָנָן — [ב]בְּשׁוּרָה. וְאֶלָּא הָא *דְּאָמַר רַבִּי יִצְחָק אָמַר רַבִּי יוֹחָנָן: *מְבָרְכִים בִּרְכַּת חֲתָנִים בַּעֲשָׂרָה — וַחֲתָנִים מִן הַמִּנְיָן, וּבִרְכַּת אֲבֵלִים בַּעֲשָׂרָה — וְאֵין אֲבֵלִים מִן הַמִּנְיָן. בְּרָכָה בְּשׁוּרָה מִי אִיכָּא? אֶלָּא, כִּי קָאָמַר רַבִּי יוֹחָנָן — בִּרְחָבָה. וְאֶלָּא הָא דְּאָמַר רַבִּי יִצְחָק אָמַר רַבִּי יוֹחָנָן: מְבָרְכִין בִּרְכַּת חֲתָנִים בַּעֲשָׂרָה כָּל שִׁבְעָה — וַחֲתָנִים מִן הַמִּנְיָן, וּבִרְכַּת אֲבֵלִים בַּעֲשָׂרָה כָּל שִׁבְעָה — וְאֵין אֲבֵלִים מִן הַמִּנְיָן, בִּרְכַּת רְחָבָה כָּל שִׁבְעָה מִי אִיכָּא? מַשְׁכַּחַתְּ לָהּ בְּפָנִים חֲדָשׁוֹת. כִּי הָא דְּרַב חִיָּיא בַּר אַבָּא מַקְרֵי בְּנֵיהּ דְּרֵישׁ לָקִישׁ הֲוָה, וְאָמְרִי לָהּ מַתְנֵי בְּרֵיהּ דְּרֵישׁ לָקִישׁ הֲוָה. שְׁכֵיב לֵיהּ יָנוֹקָא. יוֹמָא קַמָּא לָא אֲזַל לְגַבֵּיהּ, לְמָחָר דְּבָרֵיהּ לִיהוּדָה בַּר נַחְמָנִי מְתוּרְגְּמָנֵיהּ, אֲמַר לֵיהּ: קוּם אֵימָא מִלְּתָא כָּל קְבֵיל יָנוֹקָא. פְּתַח וַאֲמַר: °"וַיַּרְא ה' וַיִּנְאָץ מִכַּעַס בָּנָיו וּבְנוֹתָיו", דּוֹר שֶׁאָבוֹת מְנָאֲצִים לְהקב"ה — כּוֹעֵס עַל בְּנֵיהֶם וְעַל בְּנוֹתֵיהֶם, וּמֵתִים כְּשֶׁהֵם קְטַנִּים. וְאִיכָּא דְּאָמְרִי: בָּחוּר הֲוָה, וְהָכִי קָאָמַר לֵיהּ: °"עַל כֵּן עַל בַּחוּרָיו לֹא יִשְׂמַח ה' וְאֶת יְתוֹמָיו וְאֶת אַלְמְנוֹתָיו לֹא יְרַחֵם כִּי כֻלּוֹ חָנֵף וּמֵרַע וְכָל פֶּה דֹּבֵר נְבָלָה בְּכָל זֹאת לֹא שָׁב אַפּוֹ וְעוֹד יָדוֹ נְטוּיָה", *מַאי "וְעוֹד יָדוֹ נְטוּיָה"? אָמַר רַב חָנָן בַּר רַב: הַכֹּל יוֹדְעִין כַּלָּה לָמָּה נִכְנְסָה לַחוּפָּה, אֶלָּא °כָּל הַמְנַבֵּל פִּיו וּמוֹצִיא דְּבַר נְבָלָה מִפִּיו, אֲפִילּוּ נֶחְתַּם לוֹ גְּזַר דִּינוֹ שֶׁל שִׁבְעִים שָׁנָה לְטוֹבָה — נֶהְפָּךְ עָלָיו לְרָעָה. אֲתָא לְנַחוּמֵי, צַעוּרֵי קָמְצַעֵר לֵיהּ?! הָכִי קָאָמַר לֵיהּ: חָשֵׁיב אַתְּ לְאִתְפּוּסֵי אַדָּרָא. אֲמַר לֵיהּ: קוּם אֵימָא מִלְּתָא כְּנֶגֶד שִׁבְחוֹ שֶׁל הקב"ה. פְּתַח וַאֲמַר: הָאֵל הַגָּדוֹל בְּרוֹב גָּדְלוֹ, אַדִּיר וְחָזָק בְּרוֹב נוֹרָאוֹת, מְחַיֵּה מֵתִים בְּמַאֲמָרוֹ, עוֹשֶׂה גְּדוֹלוֹת עַד אֵין חֵקֶר וְנִפְלָאוֹת עַד אֵין מִסְפָּר, בא"י מְחַיֵּה הַמֵּתִים. א"ל: קוּם אֵימָא מִלְּתָא כְּנֶגֶד אֲבֵלִים. פְּתַח וַאֲמַר: אַחֵינוּ הַמְיוּגָּעִים הַמְדוּכָּאִין בָּאֵבֶל הַזֶּה, תְּנוּ לְבַבְכֶם לַחֲקוֹר אֶת זֹאת. זֹאת הִיא עוֹמֶדֶת לָעַד, נָתִיב הוּא מִשֵּׁשֶׁת יְמֵי בְרֵאשִׁית, רַבִּים שָׁתוּ רַבִּים יִשְׁתּוּ, כְּמִשְׁתֵּה רִאשׁוֹנִים כָּךְ מִשְׁתֵּה אַחֲרוֹנִים. אַחֵינוּ, בַּעַל נֶחָמוֹת יְנַחֵם אֶתְכֶם, בָּרוּךְ מְנַחֵם אֲבֵלִים. אָמַר אַבַּיֵי: "רַבִּים שָׁתוּ" — לֵימָא, "רַבִּים יִשְׁתּוּ" — לָא לֵימָא. "מִשְׁתֵּה רִאשׁוֹנִים" — לֵימָא, "מִשְׁתֵּה אַחֲרוֹנִים" — לָא לֵימָא. דְּאָמַר ר"ש בֶּן לָקִישׁ, וְכֵן תָּנָא מִשְּׁמֵיהּ דְּרַבִּי יוֹסֵי: *לְעוֹלָם אַל יִפְתַּח אָדָם פִּיו לַשָּׂטָן. אָמַר רַב יוֹסֵף: מַאי קְרָא — °"כִּסְדֹם הָיִינוּ לַעֲמוֹרָה דָּמִינוּ", מַאי אַהְדַר לֵיהּ — "שִׁמְעוּ דְבַר ה' קְצִינֵי סְדֹם וגו'". א"ל: קוּם אֵימָא מִלְּתָא כְּנֶגֶד מְנַחֲמֵי אֲבֵלִים. פְּתַח וַאֲמַר: אַחֵינוּ גּוֹמְלֵי חֲסָדִים בְּנֵי גּוֹמְלֵי חֲסָדִים, הַמַּחֲזִיקִים בִּבְרִיתוֹ שֶׁל אַבְרָהָם אָבִינוּ, (שֶׁנֶּאֱמַר: °"כִּי יְדַעְתִּיו לְמַעַן אֲשֶׁר יְצַוֶּה אֶת בָּנָיו וגו'"). אַחֵינוּ, בַּעַל הַגְּמוּל יְשַׁלֵּם לָכֶם גְּמוּלְכֶם, בָּרוּךְ אַתָּה מְשַׁלֵּם הַגְּמוּל. א"ל: קוּם אֵימָא מִלְּתָא כְּנֶגֶד כָּל יִשְׂרָאֵל. פְּתַח וַאֲמַר: רִבּוֹן הָעוֹלָמִים, פְּדֵה וְהַצֵּל מַלֵּט הוֹשַׁע עַמְּךָ יִשְׂרָאֵל מִן הַדֶּבֶר, וּמִן הַחֶרֶב, וּמִן הַבִּיזָּה, וּמִן הַשִּׁדָּפוֹן, וּמִן הַיֵּרָקוֹן, וּמִכָּל מִינֵי פוּרְעָנִיּוֹת הַמִּתְרַגְּשׁוֹת וּבָאוֹת לָעוֹלָם. טֶרֶם נִקְרָא וְאַתָּה תַעֲנֶה, בָּרוּךְ אַתָּה עוֹצֵר הַמַּגֵּפָה. אָמַר עוּלָּא, וְאָמְרִי לָהּ בְּמַתְנִיתָא תָּנָא: *[ג]עֲשָׂרָה כּוֹסוֹת תִּקְּנוּ חֲכָמִים בְּבֵית הָאֵבֶל; שְׁלֹשָׁה קוֹדֶם אֲכִילָה — כְּדֵי לִפְתּוֹחַ אֶת בְּנֵי מֵעָיו, שְׁלֹשָׁה בְּתוֹךְ אֲכִילָה — כְּדֵי לִשְׁרוֹת אֲכִילָה שֶׁבְּמֵעָיו, וְאַרְבָּעָה לְאַחַר אֲכִילָה — [א] אֶחָד כְּנֶגֶד "הַזָּן", וְאֶחָד כְּנֶגֶד בִּרְכַּת הָאָרֶץ, וְאֶחָד כְּנֶגֶד "בּוֹנֵה יְרוּשָׁלַיִם", וְאֶחָד כְּנֶגֶד "הַטּוֹב וְהַמֵּטִיב". הוֹסִיפוּ עֲלֵיהֶם אַרְבָּעָה: אֶחָד כְּנֶגֶד חַזָּנֵי הָעִיר, וְאֶחָד כְּנֶגֶד פַּרְנָסֵי הָעִיר, וְאֶחָד כְּנֶגֶד בֵּית הַמִּקְדָּשׁ, וְאֶחָד כְּנֶגֶד רַבָּן גַּמְלִיאֵל. הִתְחִילוּ, הָיוּ שׁוֹתִין וּמִשְׁתַּכְּרִין. הֶחֱזִירוּ הַדָּבָר לְיוֹשְׁנָהּ. מַאי רַבָּן גַּמְלִיאֵל? דְּתַנְיָא: *בָּרִאשׁוֹנָה הָיְתָה הוֹצָאַת הַמֵּת קָשָׁה לִקְרוֹבָיו יוֹתֵר מִמִּיתָתוֹ, עַד שֶׁהָיוּ מַנִּיחִים אוֹתוֹ וּבוֹרְחִין. עַד שֶׁבָּא רַבָּן גַּמְלִיאֵל וְנָהַג קַלּוּת בְּעַצְמוֹ, וְהוֹצִיאוּהוּ בִּכְלֵי פִשְׁתָּן. וְנָהֲגוּ [ד]כָּל הָעָם אַחֲרָיו לְהוֹצִיא בִּכְלֵי פִשְׁתָּן, אָמַר רַב פָּפָּא: וְהָאִידָּנָא נְהוּג עָלְמָא אֲפִילּוּ *בְּצַרְדָּא בַּר זוּזָא. § אָמַר רַבִּי אֶלְעָזָר

דברים לב | ישעיה ט | שם א | בראשית יח

בברכת המזון. להצטרף לג' לזמן עליו, שהרי הוא חייב בכל המצות. בשורה. כשהיו חוזרין מן הקבר היו עושין שורה סביב האבל לנחמו, ומושיבין אותו, והן עומדים סביב. ואמרי' בסנהדרין (דף יט.): אין שורה פחות מי'. ברחבה. כשמברין את האבל סעודה ראשונה משל אחרים, כדאמרינן במועד קטן (דף כז:), היו מברין אותו ברחבה ומברכין שם ברכת אבלים, כדמפרש לקמיה, "ברוך מנחם אבלים". אמר ליה. למתורגמניה. כל קביל ינוקא. לנגד המאורע, דברים ניחומים על מיתת הילד. וירא ה'. מה עשו אבות. וינאץ מכעס. שהכעיסוהו, וגרמו לו לפקוד על בניהם ובנותיהם. ואית דאמרי. לא תינוק היה המת אלא בחור היה, והך קרא אמר: "על בחוריו" וגו'. של ע' שנה. "ועוד" דריש כמו "ועד", עולמו של אדם, נטויה – נהפכת מטוב לרע. אתא לנחומי צעורי מצער ליה. בתמיה: מוכיח על פניו שבשביל עונו מת בנו?! חשיב את לאתפוסי אדרא. חשוב אתה למעלה לתופסך ואת בניך בעון הדור, דקי"ל: *בזמן שצדיקים בדור – צדיקים נתפסים על הדור, שנאמר "וממקדשי תחלו" (יחזקאל ט). האל הגדול ברוב גודלו. בברוך פתח בה, "ברוך אתה ה' אלהינו מלך העולם האל הגדול" וכו'. אחינו המיוגעים כו'. ברכה הסמוכה לחברתה היא, וכן סדורות על הסדר. באבל הזה תנו לבבכם לחקור זאת שזאת עומדת לעד. שהכל מתים, ולא תבכו יותר מדאי. משתה הראשונים לימא. משתה ראשונים הוא. בבריתו של אברהם. שגמל חסדים, דכתיב (בראשית כא) "ויטע אשל", ר"ת: אכילה שתיה לויה*. עשרה כוסות. להרבות לו בשתיה, כדכתיב (משלי לא) "תנו שכר לאובד, ויין למרי נפש". קודם אכילה. שהיו רגילין להמשיך פרפראות לפני סעודה, כגון כיסנין וסופגנין ואיסקריטין, ובאותם פרפראות משקין לאבל ג' כוסות. אחד כנגד הזן. על כל ברכה שותה הכוס, ומוזגין לו אחר. כנגד חזני העיר. תקנו להם ברכה עליו, לפי שהיו שמשי העיר להתעסק במתים ובשאר צרכי ציבור. פרנסי העיר. שהיו עשירים מבזבזים ממונם לקבורת עניים. כנגד בהמ"ק. תקנו עליו ברכת ניחומים, שינחמנו המקום בבניינו מאבלנו, שאנו מתאבלים עליו כבעל מת. כנגד ר"ג. לקמן מפרש. ליושנה. עשרה כוסות. הוצאת המת. שהיו קוברים אותו בכלים יקרים כגון שיראין וסרקות. בצרדא בר זוזא. בגד קנבוס שאינו שוה אלא דינר. האומר

מגילה כג:
[תוספתא מגילה פ"ג]
[שבת לג:]
שבת דף לג.
[וע"ע תוס' סוטה י. ד"ה פונדק]
ברכות יט. ס"ע
שמחות פי"ד [פסחים קי.]
מ"ק כז: [תוספתא נדה פ"ט]

הגהות הגר"א

[א] גמ' (אחד כנגד הזן כו' עד הטוב והמטיב) תא"מ (ואחד כנגד ד' ברכות האמורים למעלה פתח ואמר כו' ואולי על כל כוס אומר ברכה א'):

ס"א אינו

גליון הש"ס

גמ' כל המנבל פיו. עיין ט"ז יו"ד רסי' קכל:

[גי' הערוך צדרא ועיין ב"מ נא. דאיתא צדרייתא ופרש"י בגדי קנבוס אבל בשאלתות איתא בצרדא כדאיתא לפנינו]

הָאוֹמֵר "פֶּתַח פָּתוּחַ מָצָאתִי" — נֶאֱמָן לְאוֹסְרָהּ עָלָיו — וְאַמַּאי? [א]סָפֵק סְפֵיקָא הוּא: סָפֵק תַּחְתָּיו סָפֵק אֵין תַּחְתָּיו, וְאִם תִּמְצָא לוֹמַר תַּחְתָּיו — סָפֵק בְּאוֹנֶס סָפֵק בְּרָצוֹן! לָא צְרִיכָא [ב]בְּאֵשֶׁת כֹּהֵן. וְאִיבָּעֵית אֵימָא [ג]בְּאֵשֶׁת יִשְׂרָאֵל, וּכְגוֹן דְּקַבֵּיל בָּהּ אֲבוּהָ קִידּוּשִׁין פְּחוּתָה מִבַּת ג' שָׁנִים וְיוֹם אֶחָד. מַאי קמ"ל? תָּנֵינָא. *[ד]הָאוֹמֵר לְאִשָּׁה "קִדַּשְׁתִּיךְ". וְהִיא אוֹמֶרֶת "לֹא קִדַּשְׁתַּנִי" — הִיא מוּתֶּרֶת בִּקְרוֹבָיו, וְהוּא אָסוּר בִּקְרוֹבוֹתֶיהָ! מַהוּ דְּתֵימָא: הָתָם דְּוַדַּאי קִים לֵיהּ, אֲבָל הָכָא — מֵיקָם הוּא דְּלָא קִים לֵיהּ, קמ"ל. וּמִי אָמַר רַבִּי אֶלְעָזָר הָכִי? וְהָאָמַר רַבִּי אֶלְעָזָר: אֵין הָאִשָּׁה נֶאֱסֶרֶת עַל בַּעְלָהּ, אֶלָּא עַל עִסְקֵי קִינּוּי וּסְתִירָה, וּכְמַעֲשֶׂה שֶׁהָיָה! וְתִסְבְּרָא, מַעֲשֶׂה שֶׁהָיָה בְּקִינּוּי וּסְתִירָה הֲוָה?! וְעוֹד: מִי אֲסָרוּהָ? הָא לָא קַשְׁיָא; הָכִי קָאָמַר: אֵין הָאִשָּׁה נֶאֱסֶרֶת עַל בַּעְלָהּ אֶלָּא עַל עִסְקֵי קִינּוּי וּסְתִירָה, מִמַּעֲשֶׂה שֶׁהָיָה דְּלָא הֲוָה קִינּוּי וּסְתִירָה, וְלָא אִיתַּסְרָא. מִכׇּל מָקוֹם קַשְׁיָא: קִינּוּי וּסְתִירָה — אִין, פֶּתַח פָּתוּחַ — לָא! וּלְטַעֲמִיךְ, קִינּוּי וּסְתִירָה — אִין, עֵדִים — לָא?! אֶלָּא הָכִי קָאָמַר: [ה]אֵין הָאִשָּׁה נֶאֱסֶרֶת עַל בַּעְלָהּ בְּעֵד אֶחָד אֶלָּא בִּשְׁנֵי עֵדִים, [ו]וְקִינּוּי וּסְתִירָה — אֲפִילּוּ בְּעֵד אֶחָד נַמִי, וּפֶתַח פָּתוּחַ — כִּשְׁנֵי עֵדִים דָּמֵי. וְכִי תֵּימָא: מַעֲשֶׂה שֶׁהָיָה מִפְּנֵי מָה לֹא אֲסָרוּהָ — •הָתָם אוֹנֶס הֲוָה. וְאִיבָּעֵית אֵימָא, כִּי הָא דְּאָמַר רַבִּי שְׁמוּאֵל בַּר נַחְמָנִי אָמַר רַבִּי יוֹנָתָן: כׇּל

רש"י

הָאוֹמֵר פֶּתַח פָּתוּחַ מָצָאתִי. וְטַעֲנַת דָּמִים אֵין לוֹ, כְּגוֹן שֶׁהִיא מִמִּשְׁפַּחַת דּוֹרְקְטֵי שֶׁאֵין לָהֶם דַּם בְּתוּלִים, כִּדְלְקַמָּן (דף י'), אוֹ שֶׁנֶּאֶבְדָה מִמֶּנּוּ מַפָּה, וְלֹא יָדַע אִם הָיָה דָּם אִם לָאו. אֲבָל זֹאת בְּרוּרָה לוֹ, שֶׁפֶּתַח פָּתוּחַ מָצָא. נֶאֱמָן לְאוֹסְרָהּ עָלָיו. וְאַע"פ שֶׁאֵין הַדָּבָר הַזֶּה יָכוֹל לְהִתְבָּרֵר אֶלָּא עַל פִּיו, לְגַבֵּי נַפְשֵׁיהּ הָוֵי מְהֵימָן לְשַׁוּוֹיֵיהּ עֲלֵיהּ חֲתִיכָה דְּאִיסּוּרָא, אֲבָל לְהַפְסִידָהּ כְּתוּבָּתָהּ — לֹא מְהֵימָן. וְאַמַּאי. מִיתַּסְרָא עֲלֵיהּ, אֲפִי' אִי מְהֵימְנַת לֵיהּ דְּנִבְעֲלָה. סָפֵק תַּחְתָּיו. מִשֶּׁנִּתְאָרְסָה זִינְּתָה. סָפֵק אֵין תַּחְתָּיו. אֶלָּא קוֹדֶם שֶׁנִּתְאָרְסָה זִינְּתָה. סָפֵק בְּאוֹנֶס. וַאֲנוּסָה שָׁרְיָא בְּאֵשֶׁת יִשְׂרָאֵל, כִּדְלְקַמָּן (דף נא:) "וְהִיא לֹא נִתְפָּשָׂה". בְּאֵשֶׁת כֹּהֵן. שֶׁבְּאוֹנֶס אָסוּר בָּהּ. הִלְכָּךְ, חַד סָפֵק הוּא. פְּחוּתָה מִבַּת ג' שָׁנִים. וְעַכְשָׁיו הִיא גְּדוֹלָה, וּפִיתּוּיָהּ פִּיתּוּי וְאֵינוֹ אוֹנֶס. הִלְכָּךְ, חַד סָפֵק אִיכָּא — סָפֵק אוֹנֶס סָפֵק רָצוֹן. אֲבָל סָפֵק תַּחְתָּיו סָפֵק אֵין תַּחְתָּיו — לֵיכָּא, שֶׁאִילּוּ נִבְעֲלָה קוֹדֶם לָכֵן — הָיוּ בְּתוּלֶיהָ חוֹזְרִים, כִּדְתְנַן בְּמַסֶּכֶת נִדָּה (דף מד:): פְּחוּתָה מִכָּאן — כְּנוֹתֵן אֶצְבַּע בָּעַיִן, שֶׁהַדִּמְעָה יוֹצְאָה וְחוֹזֶרֶת. מַאי קמ"ל תָּנֵינָא. שֶׁאָדָם נֶאֱמָן עַל עַצְמוֹ לֶאֱסוֹר לוֹ אֶת הַמּוּתָּר עַל פִּיו. הוּא אָסוּר בִּקְרוֹבוֹתֶיהָ. בְּאִמָּהּ וּבִתָּהּ וַאֲחוֹתָהּ, דְּשַׁוְּיַהּ אַנַּפְשֵׁיהּ חֲתִיכָה דְּאִיסּוּרָא. וְהִיא מוּתֶּרֶת בִּקְרוֹבָיו. שֶׁהֲרֵי אֵינָהּ מוֹדָה בַּקִּידּוּשִׁין. וּבְמַסֶּכֶת קִידּוּשִׁין מוֹקְמִינַן לָהּ בְּאוֹמֵר: קִידַּשְׁתִּיהָ בִּפְנֵי עֵדִים, וְהָלְכוּ לָהֶם לִמְדִינַת הַיָּם. דְּוַדַּאי קִים לֵיהּ. שֶׁקִּידְּשָׁהּ. אֲבָל הָכָא. אֵימָא: מִתּוֹךְ שֶׁפָּנוּי הָיָה, וְאֵינוֹ בָּקִי — מֵיקַם הוּא דְּלָא קִים לֵיהּ. כְּסָבוּר שֶׁמָּצָא פֶּתַח פָּתוּחַ, וְאֵינוֹ כֵּן, וְלֹא אִיתְּסַר, קַמַשְׁמַע לָן. וּמִי אָמַר רַבִּי אֶלְעָזָר הָכִי. דְּאִשָּׁה מְזַנָּה נֶאֱסֶרֶת עַל פִּי בַּעְלָהּ. קִינּוּי. שֶׁאָמַר לָהּ: אַל תִּסָּתְרִי עִם פְּלוֹנִי. וּסְתִירָה. שֶׁבָּאוּ עֵדִים שֶׁנִּסְתְּרָה עִמּוֹ אַחַר קִינּוּי. וּכְמַעֲשֶׂה שֶׁהָיָה. דְּבַת שֶׁבַע. וְתִסְבְּרָא. דְּקָאֵי ר' אֶלְעָזָר? מַעֲשֶׂה שֶׁהָיָה מִי הֲוָה בֵּיהּ קִינּוּי? וְעוֹד מִי אֲסָרוּהָ. עַל אוּרִיָּה? דְּאִילּוּ נֶאֶסְרָה עַל אוּרִיָּה — נֶאֶסְרָה אַף עַל דָּוִד, דְּקַיְימָא לָן (סוטה דף כז:): כְּשֵׁם שֶׁאֲסוּרָה לַבַּעַל, כָּךְ אֲסוּרָה לַבּוֹעֵל. הָא לָא קַשְׁיָא. כְּלוֹמַר, מִשּׁוּם הָא קוּשְׁיָא לָא תִּדְחַיֵּיהּ לְרַבִּי אֶלְעָזָר. הָכִי קָאָמַר אֵין הָאִשָּׁה נֶאֱסֶרֶת עַל בַּעְלָהּ אֶלָּא עַל עִסְקֵי קִינּוּי וּסְתִירָה מִמַּעֲשֶׂה שֶׁהָיָה. מִמַּעֲשֶׂה דְּבַת שֶׁבַע אָנוּ לְמֵדִין כֵּן, שֶׁלֹּא הָיָה שָׁם קִינּוּי וּסְתִירָה, וְלֹא אֲסָרוּהָ. עֵדִים לָא. בִּתְמִיָּה: אֲפִי' יֵשׁ עֵדִים שֶׁזִּינְּתָה, שֶׁמָּא אֵינָהּ נֶאֱסֶרֶת בְּלֹא קִינּוּי?! וְהָא כְּתִיב (דברים כד) "כִּי מָצָא בָהּ עֶרְוַת דָּבָר". וְעוֹד, הָא לֹא נִתְפָּשָׂה אֲסוּרָה? אֵין הָאִשָּׁה נֶאֱסֶרֶת עַל בַּעְלָהּ בְּעֵד אֶחָד. דִּילִיף (סוטה דף ג:) "דָּבָר" "דָּבָר" מִמָּמוֹן. וְקִינּוּי וּסְתִירָה. אִם יֵשׁ עֵדִים שֶׁקִּינֵּא לָהּ, וְיֵשׁ עֵדִים שֶׁנִּסְתְּרָה אַחַר קִינּוּי. אֲפִי' בְּעֵד אֶחָד. אֲפִי' אֵין בְּטוּמְאָה אֶלָּא עֵד אֶחָד — נֶאֱמָן, דִּכְתִיב (במדבר ה) "וְעֵד אֵין בָּהּ", וְאָמַר מָר (סוטה ב:): כׇּל מָקוֹם שֶׁנֶּאֱמַר "עֵד" — הֲרֵי כָּאן שְׁנַיִם, וְקָאָמַר רַחֲמָנָא "עֵד אֵין בָּהּ" הֲרֵי, אֶלָּא חַד. "וְהִיא לֹא נִתְפָּשָׂה" — אֲסוּרָה, שֶׁרַגְלַיִם לַדָּבָר שֶׁזִּינְּתָה, שֶׁהֲרֵי קִינֵּא לָהּ וְנִסְתְּרָה, וְעֵד אֶחָד מְעִידָהּ שֶׁהִיא טְמֵאָה. וּמֵהַשְׁתָּא לָא תַּקְשֵׁי לָךְ דְּרַבִּי אֶלְעָזָר, דְּפֶתַח פָּתוּחַ לְאוֹסְרָהּ עַל עַצְמוֹ כִּבְנֵי עֵדִים דָּמֵי, שֶׁהֲרֵי דָּבָר בָּרוּר הוּא לוֹ שֶׁנִּבְעֲלָה. מִפְּנֵי מָה לֹא אֲסָרוּהָ. עַל דָּוִד, שֶׁהֲרֵי עֵדִים הַרְבֵּה יָדְעוּ.

גט

תוספות

האומר פתח פתוח מצאתי כו'. פירש בקונטרס דטענת דמים לא קאמר, כגון שנאבדה המפה או שהיא ממשפחת דורקטי שאין להם דמים. ור"ת מפרש: דבוגרת ומוכת עץ אין להם דמים, אבל אין פתחן פתוח ויכול לטעון טענת פתח פתוח. וקשה לפר"ת, דאמרי' ב"אלו נערות" (לקמן לו. ושם:): ובוגרת אין לה טענת בתולים? והאמר רב בוגרת נותנים לה לילה ראשונה. ומשני: אי דקא טעין טענת דמים — ה"נ, הב"ע — דקטעין טענת פתח פתוח. משמע דפתחה פתוח, ויש לה דמים! וי"ל: דר"ת גרים כגירסא ראשונה שהיתה בספרים; *אי דקא טעין טענת פתח פתוח — הכי נמי, הב"ע — דקא טעין טענת דמים. וה"פ: והאמר רב בוגרת נותנין לה לילה הראשונה, ומדתלינן כל הלילה בדם בתולים — משמע דאיכא בוגרת דאית לה דם בתולים טובא, אם כן אי אפשר לשום בוגרת שלא יהא פתחה סתום, אפילו אין לה דמים, וא"כ יש לה טענת בתולים בפתח פתוח! ומשני: אי דקטעין פתח פתוח — ה"נ דיש לה טענת בתולים. הב"ע דלית לה טענת בתולים — בטענת דמים, משום דאיכא בוגרת דדמיה כלין. ומיהו, בירושלמי משמע לא כפר"ת, דקאמר התם ר' יונה בשם ר' קריספא: בוגרת כחבית פתוחה של יין! ויש ליישב: דלענין דמים קאמר, משום דסתם חבית סתומה לעולם יש בה יין, שאין דרך לסתום חבית ריקנית. אבל חבית פתוחה — פעמים יש בה יין, פעמים אין בה יין. כך בוגרת, פעמים אין לה דמים פעמים יש לה. ומשום הכי אין לה טענת דמים כדפר"ת. וכדאמר בפרק "הבא על יבמתו" (יבמות נט. ושם): פרט לבוגרת שכלו בתוליה. **לא** צריכא באשת כהן. וא"ת: ונוקמה אחזקתה שהיא כשרה לכהונה, ונימא דלאו תחתיו זינתה! וי"ל: דלהדרבה, אית לן למימר דהשתא נבעלה, דלוקמה אחזקת הגוף שהיתה בתולה. **ואי** בעית אימא באשת ישראל דקביל בה אביה קידושין פחותה מבת ג' שנים. וא"ת: אכתי איכא ספק ספיקא; ספק באונס ספק ברצון, ואת"ל ברצון — ספק כשהיא קטנה, ופתוי קטנה אונס הוא, כדאמרינן ב"הבא על יבמתו" (שם סא:)! וי"ל: דסם אונס חד הוא. וא"ת: ונוקמה בחזקת היתר לבעלה! וי"ל: דאונסא קלא אית לה, כדאמרינן בירושלמי [אונסה יש לו קולן], והשתא דליכא קלא — הוי ליה רצון רובא ומיעוט אונס, ורובא וחזקה רובא עדיף. וא"ת: א"כ בספק ספיקא נמי תיאסר, דספק אונס כמאן דליתיה דמי, ולא נשאר אלא חד ספק; ספק תחתיו, והשתא לא שייך לאוקמה בחזקת היתר, כדפי'! [א] ואומר ר"י: דהאי רובא דברצון אינו רוב גמור, אלא הוי מדרבנן, והלכך במקום ספק ספיקא — שרי, ובמקום חד ספיקא — חשבי רבנן רצון לגבי אונס רובא. ואשכחן כי האי גוונא גבי תינוק שנמצא בצד העיסה (קדושין דף פ.), דלא הוי רובא אלא מדרבנן, ולהכי קאמר ר' יוחנן התם דאין שורפין עליו את התרומה. וא"ת: אכתי באשת כהן ובקיבל אביה קדושין פחותה מבת שלש לישראל איכא ספק ספיקא, דספק מוכת עץ ספק דרוסת איש, [באשת כהן אית לן למימר: את"ל דאינה מוכת עץ — מ"מ ספק תחתיו ספק אין תחתיו. אשת ישראל, את"ל דאינה מוכת עץ — ספק באונס ספק ברצון]. ואין לומר דמוכת עץ לא שכיח, דהא אמרינן ב"אלו נערות" (לקמן לו:) גבי סומא שאין לה טענת בתולין מפני שנחבטת על גבי קרקע. ופריך: כולהו נמי מיחבטן! א"כ שכיח! ולפירוש ר"ת דמוכת עץ עד פתחה סתום — אתי שפיר. וי"ל: דאם איתא דמוכת עץ היא — הויא טוענת, דאין גנאי בכך כמו בביאת אונס, ומדלא טענה — אין להסתפק בכך. **ומי** אמר ר' אלעזר הכי והאמר ר"א כו'. תימה: השתא דעדי לא מימר דלא מהימן אפי' לשוויה עליה חתיכה דאיסורא — תיקשי ליה מתני' דהאומר לאשה קידשתיך אסור בקרובותיה! וי"ל: דסבירא ליה למקשן דאין דבר שבערוה פחות משנים, ואפי' ראה אדם שזינתה אשתו, רק שלא היה שם עדים — לא היתה נאסרת עליו. והלכך, ממתני' לא קשיא ליה מידי, דקדשתיך בעדים קאמר, דמקדש אפי' בעד אחד — אין חוששין לקידושיו*. אבל הא דאמר ר' אלעזר דנאמן בלא עדים לומר מצאתי פתח פתוח — פריך שפיר. **קינוי** וסתירה אין עדים לא. הכי נמי דלא אתא למעוטי על פי עצמו, לכעדים דמי, כיון דקים ליה. **מפני** מה לא אסרוה. פירש הקונטרס: והלא אותו מעשה בעדים הוה. ואין נראה, דנהי דידעו לרבים הוה שהביאה לביתו — מ"מ לא ראו כמכחול בשפופרת, שבפני בני אדם לא שמשו! ונראה לר"י לפרש: וא"ת דפתח פתוח כשני עדים דמי — אמאי לא אסרוה לדוד? דדוד היה יודע בודאי שנבעלה, ואע"פ שעשה תשובה מכל מקום עיכבה. ואם היתה אסורה לו — לא היה אותו צדיק לוקחה לו לאשה.

כל

מסורת הש"ס

קדושין סה.

[כלאיתא קדושין סט.]

עין משפט נר מצוה

מז א ב ג מיי' פי"ח מהל' איסורי ביאה הל' י וא סמג לאוין קלח טוש"ע אה"ע סי' ו סעי' יד וסימן סח סעי' ז:

מח ד מיי' פ"ט מהל' אישות הל' טו טוש"ע שם סי' מח סעי' א:

מט ה מיי' פכ"ד מהל' אישות הל' יח סמג עשין מח טוש"ע אה"ע סי' קטו וטוש"ע שם סי' יא סעי' א [וברב אלפס קידושין פ"ג ד' רלח:].

[ועיין היטב ערוך ערך פתח א']

נ ו מיי' פ"א מהל' סוטה הל' טו סמג עשין נו טוש"ע אה"ע סי' קעח סעי' יד [וברב אלפס שם]:

תוספות רי"ד

אמר ר"א האומר פתח פתוח מצאתי נאמן לאוסרה עליו. פי' שלא טען טענות דמים לומר בעלתי ולא מצאתי דמים כגון שהיתה בוגרת או שהיתה ממשפחת דורקטי נאמן לאוסרה עליו. פי' המורה ואע"פ שאין הדבר הזה יכול להתברר אלא על פיו לגבי נפשיה הוי מהימן לשוויה עליה חתיכה דאיסורא אבל להפסיד כתובה לא מהימן. ואמאי ספק ספיקא הוא ספק תחתיו זינתה וספק לא זינתה תחתיו ואת"ל תחתיו זינתה ספק באונס ספק ברצון. ל"צ באשת כהן פי' דאפילו באונס אסורה לו הלכך חד ספק הוא ואבע"א באשת ישראל וכגון דקיבל [בה] אביה קידושין פחות מבת ג' שנים פי' שאין לומר קודם שאירסה זינתה שהרי בתוליה חוזרים ולא נשאר שם אלא חד ספק ומספיקא היא נאסרה לו: מאי קמ"ל תנינא פי' שאדם נאמן על עצמו לאסור לו את המותר לו. האומר לאשה קדשתיך והיא אומרת לא קדשתני הוא אסור בקרובותיה פי' באמה ובתה ואחותה דשוויהו אנפשיה חתיכה דאיסורא והיא מותרת בקרוביו שהרי אינה מודה בקדושיו ובמס' קידושין מוקי לה באומר לה קדשתיך בפני עדים והלכו להם למדינות הים. מהו דתימא התם הוא דודאי קים ליה פי' שקדשה אבל הכא מיקם הוא דלא קים ליה פי' מפני שהוא פנוי ויש לומר בהרצפא בעל וג"ל כי פתוח היה ואינו כן א"כ לא תיתסר קמ"ל וכ"ש אם טען בעלתי ולא מצאתי דם בנערה שלא בגרה ואינה ממשפחת דורקטי שהוא נאמן לאוסרה עליו שהוא טענה ודאית יותר מפתח פתוח: ומי א"ר אלעזר הכי פי' דאשה מזנה נאסרת ע"פ עצמו והא א"ר אלעזר אין האשה נאסרת על בעלה אלא על ידי קינוי וסתירה.

גליון הש"ס

גמ' התם אונס הוה. ע' יבמות לה ע"א תד"ה ואט"פ:

הגהות מהר"ב רנשבורג

א] תד"ה ואת"ל וכו' ואומר ר"י דהאי רובא דברצון אינו רוב גמור. עי' פ"י וש"ס הריב"ש סי' שע"ב ובסדרי טהרה בנדה יח ע"א בתוס' ד"ה שלוה וכו' ודו"ק:

ולטעמיך קינוי וסתירה אין עדים לא פי' אם יש עדים שזינתה שמא אינה נאסרת בלא קינוי והכתיב כי מצא בה ערות דבר. אלא הכי קאמר אין האשה נאסרת על בעלה בעד א' אלא בשני עדים. וקינוי וסתירה אפילו בע"א. ופתח פתוח מצאתי כב' עדים דמי. פי' אע"פ שעד אחד נאמן באיסורין. היכא דאמר ליה ע"א אשתך זינתה אינו נאמן שאין דבר שבערוה פחות משנים ואם קינא ונסתרה ובא ע"א (ואמר) [ואמר] נטמאת נאמן וקורעת כתובתה ויוצאה ואם רוצה לשתות אינה שותה. גם אם אמר פתח פתוח מצאתי נאמן על עצמו כשני עדים ושוי אנפשיה חתיכה דאיסורא:

*כָּל הַיּוֹצֵא לְמִלְחֶמֶת בֵּית דָּוִד גֵּט כְּרִיתוּת כּוֹתֵב לְאִשְׁתּוֹ, דִּכְתִיב: °"וְאֶת אַחֶיךָ תִּפְקֹד לְשָׁלוֹם וְאֶת עֲרֻבָּתָם תִּקָּח". מַאי "וְאֶת עֲרֻבָּתָם תִּקָּח" – תָּנֵי רַב יוֹסֵף: דְּבָרִים הַמְעוֹרָבִין בֵּינוֹ לְבֵינָהּ. אָמַר אַבַּיֵי: אַף אֲנַן נַמִי תָּנֵינָא, *בְּתוּלָה נִשֵּׂאת לְיוֹם הָרְבִיעִי. לְיוֹם רְבִיעִי – אִין, לְיוֹם חֲמִישִׁי – לָא, מַאי טַעֲמָא – מִשּׁוּם אִיקְרוּרֵי דַּעְתָּא. וּלְמַאי? אִי לְמֵיתַב לָהּ כְּתוּבָּה – נֵיתִיב לָהּ, אֶלָּא לְאוֹסְרָהּ עָלָיו, וּדְקָא טָעֵין טַעֲנָה. מַאי לָאו דְּקָטָעֵין טַעֲנַת "פֶּתַח פָּתוּחַ"! [א]לָא, דְּקָטָעֵין טַעֲנַת דָּמִים. אָמַר רַב יְהוּדָה אָמַר שְׁמוּאֵל: הָאוֹמֵר "פֶּתַח פָּתוּחַ מָצָאתִי" נֶאֱמָן לְהַפְסִידָהּ כְּתוּבָּתָהּ. אָמַר רַב יוֹסֵף: מַאי קמ"ל? תָּנֵינָא: *הָאוֹכֵל אֵצֶל חָמִיו בִּיהוּדָה שֶׁלֹּא בְּעֵדִים – אֵינוֹ יָכוֹל לִטְעוֹן טַעֲנַת בְּתוּלִים, מִפְּנֵי שֶׁמִּתְיַיחֵד עִמָּהּ. בִּיהוּדָה הוּא דְּלָא מָצֵי טָעֵין, הָא בַּגָּלִיל – מָצֵי טָעֵין. וּלְמַאי? אִי לְאוֹסְרָהּ עָלָיו – בִּיהוּדָה אַמַּאי לָא? אֶלָּא לָאו – לְהַפְסִידָהּ כְּתוּבָּתָהּ, וּדְקָא טָעֵין טַעֲנָה, *מַאי לָאו דְּקָא טָעֵין טַעֲנַת "פֶּתַח פָּתוּחַ"! לָא, דְּקָא טָעֵין טַעֲנַת דָּמִים. אִיתְּמַר

תורה אור: ש"א יז

גט כריתות כותב לאשתו. שאם ימות במלחמה יהא גט מיום כתיבתו. והרי מת אוריה במלחמה. דכתיב. במלחמת שאול "ואת אחיך" כו', ודוד למד מישי אביו להנהיג שאף היוצאין למלחמותיו עושין כן. **דברים המעורבים בינו לבינה.** אלו קדושין. **תקח.** תטול מביניהם על ידי גט. **אף אנן נמי תנינא.** דטוען "פתח פתוח מצאתי" אסרה עליו, ולא אמרינן לא קים ליה. **איקרורי דעתא.** עד שני בשבת הבאה. **ולמאי.** קפדי רבנן אי מקררא דעתיה. **ניתיב לה.** מה לנו להפסידה? והרי הוא נותן מדעת. **אלא לאו לאוסרה.** הוא דקפדינן, שלא יקרר דעתו ויקיים את האסורה לו. אלמא, כי אתי וטעין – אסרינן לה עליה. **טענת דמים.** דטענה מבוררת היא, וליכא למימר לא קים ליה. אבל בפתח פתוח – אימא לך לא קים ליה. **להפסידה כתובתה.** על פי עצמו, וטעמא לקמן מפרש: חזקה אין אדם טורח בסעודה ומפסידה. **האוכל אצל חמיו.** בימים שבין אירוסין לנשואין. **אין יכול לטעון טענת בתולים.** כשתכנס לחופה. **מפני שמתייחד עמה.** ביהודה היו מייחדין אותם כדי שיהא לבו גס בה. **ביהודה אמאי לא.** האומר פשיטא לי שלא באתי אליה, והא ודאי אחר זינתה – שוייה עליה חתיכה דאיסורא, מה לי גליל מה לי יהודה. **אלא לאו להפסידה כתובתה.** וביהודה לא מפסידה על פיו, דאמרינן הוא בא עליה באירוסין, ובגליל מצי טעין, דהא לא נתייחד. **מאי לאו דקטעין טענת פתח פתוח מצאתי.** דאע"ג דאין עדים בדבר זה ולא טענה מוכחת, אלא עליה סמכינן. דאמרינן: אי לאו דקושטא הוא – לא היה מפסיד סעודתו. ואם היה שונאה – מתחלה היה מגרשה, ולא טרח בסעודת נשואין. ומיהו, ביהודה לא מהימן, שמא בעל בימי אירוסין ושכח, או הערה בה מתוך חבתה, ולא ידע שנשבר בתוליה. **לא דקא טעין טענת דמים.** לעולם אימא לך: בדבר שאינו יכול לברר – אינו נאמן להפסיד כתובתה. ודיוקא דמתני', דדייקינן הא בגליל מצי טעין – דטעין טענת דמים. וכגון שהיו להם שושבינים שמשמשו אותן, ולא נעשית אונאה בדבר, ולא ראה ואיבד, וטענה ברורה היא. חכמים

כל היוצא למלחמת בית דוד גט כריתות כותב לאשתו. פי' בקונטרס: שאם ימות במלחמה – יהא גט מעת כתיבתו. וקשה לר"ת: דא"כ מאי כל היוצא, אם לא מהני אלא למי שאין לו בנים ויש לו יבם? ועוד: דתנן ב"מי שאחזו" (גיטין עג. ושם) מה היא באותן הימים? רבי יהודה אומר: הרי היא כאשת איש לכל דבריה, וקאי אמאי דקתני לעיל מינה: "הרי זה גיטך מהיום אם מתי". וכן משמע בתוספתא. אלמא, אע"ג דאמר "מהיום" – הויא אשת איש גמורה, כדמפרש בגמרא באומר "מעת שאני בעולם". פירוש: דהאי דאמר "מהיום" לא שיחול מיד, אלא דעתו שיחול שעה אחת קודם מיתתו, דהיינו מעת שהוא בעולם. ולא אמר "מהיום" אלא למעוטי לאחר מיתה, כלומר: מאותו יום שאני בעולם יהא גט. ומיהו, יש לחלק בין "מהיום" לפירש בהדיא שיחול מעת כתיבה – דע"כ מעת כתיבה קאמר שיהא גט. ועוד נראה: דאפי' אמר "מהיום" יש ליישב פי' הקונטרס, דלאו דוקא פירש שאם ימות במלחמה, אלא היו מתנים אם לא יחזור מן המלחמה. ואגב ריהטיה נקט בקונטרס אם ימות, דסתם מי שאינו חוזר מן המלחמה אינו חוזר לפי שמת. אלא ה"ה אם נשבה. והשתא "מהיום" דהכא אין שייך לומר "מעת שאני בעולם" כההוא ד"מי שאחזו", אלא "מהיום" – מיום כתיבה קאמר. ואם תאמר: והרי חזר אוריה ונתבטל הגט! ויש לומר: שהיה מתנה אם לא יחזור בסוף המלחמה, והרי לא חזר לבסוף. וניחא לפירוש זה הא דאמרינן בפרק "הזהב" (ב"מ נט. ושם): נוח לו לאדם שיבעול ספק אשת איש ואל ילבין פני חבירו ברבים. ומפיק ליה מהאי מעשה דבת שבע, דספק אשת איש הואי, דדלמא יחזור מן המלחמה. ור"ת מפרש: כותב גט כריתות לגמרי, בלא שום תנאי. ולפי' קשה: אמאי קרי לה ספק אשת איש? הא הואי גרושה גמורה! ואר"ת: דקרי לה ספק אשת איש לפי שהיו מגרשין בצינעא, שלא יהא נודע ויקפצו עליהם בני אדם לקדשם. ולפי' הקונטרס קשה קצת איך בא עליה? למה לא היה ירא שמא יחזור! **אי** למיתב לה כתובה כו'. משמע, אם היה בא לב"ד – היה נאמן להפסידה כתובתה, אע"פ שלאוסרה עליו לא היה נאמן, משום דאית לן למימר דשמא אינו בקי בפתח פתוח, ואוקמה בחזקת היתר. אבל מ"מ כתובתה הפסידה, אע"פ שיש לנו לומר שהוא טועה בפתח פתוח, דאית לן למימר אוקי ממונא בחזקת מריה. וקשה: דאמאי מפסידה כתובתה? והא הוה [א] ספק ספיקא; ספק אי הוא בקי בפתח פתוח אם לאו, ואם תמצא לומר פתח פתוח הוה – ספק באונס ספק ברצון, דאפי' אשת כהן באונס לא מפסדה כתובתה! ואין לומר דאפי' בספק ספיקא מפסדה כתובתה משום דמוקמינן ממונא בחזקתיה – דהא לקמן (דף יב:) גבי "משארסתני נאנסתי", והוא אומר "לא כי אלא עד שלא ארסתיך נאנסת והיה מקחי מקח טעות", ואיכא מאן דמפרש לקמן (דף יא:): מקח טעות ממאתים, אבל מנה אית לה. אלמא משום דבאותו מנה הוי ספק ספיקא – לא מפסדה; דספק קודם שנתארסה ספק אחר שנתארסה, ואם תמצא לומר אחר שנתארסה – אימור באונס הוה. דאי אמרת דאפי' בספק ספיקא מפסדה – אמאי אית לה אפי' מנה? וי"ל: דלא חשיב ספק ספיקא כהאי גוונא, משום דהאי ספיקא שמא באונס היא – לא חשיב ספיקא גמורה למיתב לה כתובה, דאימור קודם שנתארסה נאנסה. והשתא אתי שפיר הא דתנן במתני' (לקמן דף יג.): היא אומרת "מוכת עץ אני", והוא אומר "לא כי אלא דרוסת איש את" וקאמר ר' יהושע שאינה נאמנת ומפסדת כתובתה, אי לר' יוחנן – מנה, אי לר' אלעזר – ולא כלום. ואע"ג דהוי ספק ספיקא; ספק מוכת עץ ויש לה כתובה, ואפי' אם תמצא לומר דרוסת איש – אימור תחתיו נאנסה ונסתחפה שדהו ויש לה כתובה. אלא ודאי ספק באונס לא חשיב ספק, [ב] דאימור קודם שנתארסה נאנסה. ועוד אומר רבינו יצחק: דמוכת עץ לא שכיח, דהא דאמרינן (לקמן לו:): כולהו נמי חבוטי מיחבטן – היינו אליבא דר"ג, אבל רבי יהושע שמעינן דלית ליה טעמא דמיחבטן, דקאמר התם (לקמן לו.): חרשת ושוטה יש להן טענת בתולין, והיינו משום דס"ל דחבטא לא שכיחא. **מאי** לאו דקא טעין טענת פתח פתוח. נראה לפרש דקס"ד דבטענת דמים *ליכא למיחש לאיקרורי דעתא, דכיון דליכא דם לבו נוקפו ואין מתקרר. אבל בפתח פתוח – איכא למיחש שמא יתקרר. **נאמן** להפסידה כתובתה. אור"י: דשמואל מודה שפיר דנאמן לאוסרה עליו. ולהפסידה כתובתה אילטריך ליה לאשמעינן, דלא תימא דלא יהא נאמן, אע"ג דקים ליה בפתח פתוח דנימא במזיד משקר להפסידה כתובתה. ור"ח נמי מלי סבר דנאמן להפסידה, ונקט לאוסרה לרבותא, וכ"ש דנאמן להפסיד כתובתה, כדמוכח הסוגיא דלעיל. [ומיהו, בירושלמי משמע דלר"א אינו נאמן להפסיד כתובתה]. **אבל** בגליל מצי טעין. וא"ת: מנא ליה? דלמא ביהודה נאמנת לומר שבא עליה באירוסין ולא בגליל, אבל כשטוענת בתולה הייתי – בגליל נמי מהימנא? וי"ל: דמשמע ליה אינו יכול לטעון טענת בתולים בכל ענין, בין שאומרת שבא עליה מן האירוסין בין שאומרת פתח נעול מצא. דביהודה נאמנת במגו דאי בעיא אמרה באירוסין בא עליה. ולא בגליל, דליכא מגו. אבל קשה: דמייתי מדיוקא, והוה ליה לאתויי מרישא. דקתני (לקמן דף י:): בתולה אלמנה מן האירוסין כו' ויש להן טענת בתולין. וע"כ לענין כתובה איירי, דלאוסרה עליו – אפילו מן הנשואין נמי יש לה טענת בתולין, כיון דכנסה בחזקת בתולה, כדמוכח לקמן (דף יב.), דפריך: וניחוש שמא תחתיו זינתה! **מאי** לאו דקא טעין טענת פתח פתוח. וביהודה אע"ג דאיכא חזקה לא מהימן, כדפי' בקונטרס. א"נ: כיון דמתייחד עמה – ודאי בא עליה, דלא מוקי איניש אנפשיה. ואע"ג דגבי יבמה אמרינן (יבמות דף קיא:) דעד ל' יום מוקי אנפשיה – רוב פעמים לא מוקי אנפשיה אפי' שעה אחת, דעל דעת כן מתייחד *[עמה], ואיתרע חזקה. **לא** דקא טעין טענת דמים. דהויא טענה ברורה, מדאין סדינין מלוכלכים בדם. ונראה דבטענת פתח פתוח וטענת דמים דשמעתין, איירי שהיא טוענת שהוא בא עליה באירוסין, או אומרת בתולה הייתי. וא"ת: ונהימנא לדידה במגו דאי בעיא אמרה משארסתני נאנסתי דנאמנת לר"ג, דפסקינן לקמן (דף יג.) כוותיה! וי"ל: דאינה מודה ברצון שנבעלה מאחר. ועוד: דאין זה מגו, דמיפסלא נפשה מכהונה. אבל קשה: דליהמנה במגו דאי בעיא אמרה מוכת עץ אני, אפי' לרבנן דלקמן (דף יא:) דאמרי מוכת עץ כתובתה מנה, דאין זה מגו דאינה רוצה להפסיד כלום מכתובתה – מ"מ נאמנת במגו, דאי בעיא אמרה מוכת עץ אני תחתיך, ונסתחפה שדהו! לכך נראה דהוי מגו במקום חזקה, דאין אדם טורח בסעודה ומפסידה. אע"ג דבעי' היא בפ"ק דבבא בתרא (דף ה: ושם) אי אמרינן מגו במקום חזקה או לא, שמא חזקה דהכא עדיפא. ואי לא אמרינן מגו להוציא – אתי נמי שפיר: אמר

מסורת הש"ס: שבת נו. | [לעיל ב.] | לקמן יב.

[דטענת דמים מסתבר כשנתייחד עמה אם היו אז דמים בשעת תשמיש היתה מראה לאביה ולאמה או לבעלה כדי שלא יהא לו לב עליה כשישאנה וס"ד דטענת דמים אף ביהודה יכול לטעון אבל בפתח אינה מכרת אם פתחה נעול או לאו ואינה מגדת והשתא אתי שפיר דלא פריך מרישא דבפשיטות איכא לאוקמי בטענת דמים. ת"י עה"ג. ובתוס' הרשב"א מצאתי דפי' דבטענת דמים ביהודה נמי ס"ד דמהימן דליכא למימר שכח דאם איתא דהוה דם כשנתייחד עמה לא היה שוכח אבל בפתח פתוח איכא למימר דלא אסיק אדעתיה וא"ת מ"מ אם איתא דפתח לה פתח הוי דם וי"ל דאפשר למיפתח פתח בלא דם ולפי' ר"ח איכא לאוקמי בבוגרת שכלו דמיה שפתחה פתחא ולאו אדעתיה כיון דליכא דם ובכל בתולה אפשר לפותחה בלא דם כדשמואל מיהו ההיא דשמואל נמי משמע דפתחה נעול מדאין ריחה נודף ושמא יש לומר דמחמת דם נמי אין ריחה נודף. ע"כ:]

ב] [ולהאי שינויא לא מיתוקמא מתני' בפחות מג' שנים. ת"י עה"ג]

[*ולפי' ר"ח אתי שפיר דמיסתבר ליה לאוקמי מתני' בכל הנשים אפי' בבוגרת ומוכת עץ דאין להם דמים ועי"ל מאי לאו דקטעין אף פתח פתוח דאיירי מתני' בכל ענין שיטעון]

כ"ה בדפו"י

נא א מיי' פי"א מהל' אישות הלכה יב יג טוש"ע אה"ע סימן סח סעיף ג וסעיף ו

א] בת"י עה"ג וי"מ דהכא לא חשיב ספק ספיקא דאין יכולין להתהפך ולומר ברישא ספק באונס ספק ברצון ואת"ל ברצון ספק וכו' ולהכי לא חשיב אלא חדא ספיקא וה"נ י"ל בע"א דרוב בקיאין בפתח פתוח והוה ליה לענין כתובה רובא וחזקת ממונא ותו ליכא אלא חדא ספיקא אבל לענין לאוסרה איכא למימר סמוך מיעוטא דאין בקיאין לחזקה ואיתרע רובא והוי ליה פלגא ופלגא והוי ספק ספיקא ול"נ דה"פ אי למיתב לה כתובה ואיירי בטענת דמים דלענין כתובה איכא למיחש לאיקרורי דעתיה בטענת דמים

איתְּמַר, אָמַר רַב נַחְמָן אָמַר שְׁמוּאֵל מִשּׁוּם רַבִּי שִׁמְעוֹן בֶּן אֶלְעָזָר: א חֲכָמִים תִּקְּנוּ לָהֶם לִבְנוֹת יִשְׂרָאֵל, לִבְתוּלָה מָאתַיִם, וּלְאַלְמָנָה מָנֶה. וְהֵם הֶאֱמִינוּהוּ, שֶׁאִם אָמַר "פֶּתַח פָּתוּחַ מָצָאתִי" נֶאֱמָן. א"כ מַה הוֹעִילוּ חֲכָמִים בְּתַקָּנָתָם? אָמַר רָבָא: *חֲזָקָה, אֵין אָדָם טוֹרֵחַ בִּסְעוּדָה וּמַפְסִידָהּ. תָּנָא: הוֹאִיל וּקְנַס חֲכָמִים הוּא — לֹא תִּגְבֶּה אֶלָּא מִן הַזִּיבּוּרִית. קְנָסָא?! מַאי קְנָסָא? אֶלָּא אֵימָא: ב הוֹאִיל וְתַקָּנַת חֲכָמִים הוּא — לֹא תִּגְבֶּה אֶלָּא מִן הַזִּיבּוּרִית. רַבָּן שִׁמְעוֹן בֶּן גַּמְלִיאֵל אוֹמֵר: *כְּתוּבַּת אִשָּׁה מִן הַתּוֹרָה — וּמִי אָמַר רַבָּן שִׁמְעוֹן בֶּן גַּמְלִיאֵל הָכִי? *וְהָתַנְיָא: °"כֶּסֶף יִשְׁקֹל כְּמֹהַר הַבְּתוּלֹת" (שמות כב) שֶׁיְּהֵא זֶה כְּמוֹהַר הַבְּתוּלוֹת, וּמוֹהַר הַבְּתוּלוֹת כָּזֶה. ג מִכָּאן *סָמְכוּ חֲכָמִים לִכְתוּבַּת אִשָּׁה מִן הַתּוֹרָה. רַבָּן שִׁמְעוֹן בֶּן גַּמְלִיאֵל אוֹמֵר: כְּתוּבַּת אִשָּׁה אֵינָהּ מִדִּבְרֵי תוֹרָה, אֶלָּא מִדִּבְרֵי סוֹפְרִים! אֵיפוֹךְ. וּמַאי חָזֵית דְּאַפַּכְתְּ בַּתְרַיְיתָא? אֵיפוֹךְ קַמַּיְיתָא! הָא שָׁמְעִינָא לֵיהּ לְרַבָּן שִׁמְעוֹן בֶּן גַּמְלִיאֵל דְּאָמַר כְּתוּבַּת אִשָּׁה מִדְּאוֹרַיְיתָא, דִּתְנַן: *רַבָּן שִׁמְעוֹן בֶּן גַּמְלִיאֵל אוֹמֵר: נוֹתֵן לָהּ מִמְּעוֹת קַפּוֹטְקִיָּא. וְאִי בָּעֵית אֵימָא: כּוּלָּהּ רַבָּן שִׁמְעוֹן בֶּן גַּמְלִיאֵל הִיא, וְחַסּוֹרֵי מִיחַסְּרָא וְהָכִי קָתָנֵי: מִכָּאן סָמְכוּ חֲכָמִים לִכְתוּבַּת אִשָּׁה מִן הַתּוֹרָה. כְּתוּבַּת אַלְמָנָה אֵינָהּ מִדִּבְרֵי תוֹרָה אֶלָּא מִדִּבְרֵי סוֹפְרִים, שֶׁרַבָּן שִׁמְעוֹן בֶּן גַּמְלִיאֵל אוֹמֵר: כְּתוּבַּת אַלְמָנָה אֵינָהּ מִדִּבְרֵי תוֹרָה אֶלָּא מִדִּבְרֵי סוֹפְרִים. הַהוּא דַּאֲתָא לְקַמֵּיהּ דְּרַב נַחְמָן, אֲמַר לֵיהּ: פֶּתַח פָּתוּחַ מָצָאתִי. אֲמַר לֵיהּ רַב נַחְמָן: אַסְבּוּהוּ כּוּפְרֵי, מְבָרַכְתָּא חֲבִיטָא לֵיהּ. וְהָא רַב נַחְמָן הוּא דְּאָמַר מְהֵימָן! מְהֵימָן, וּמַסְבִּינַן לֵיהּ כּוּפְרֵי. רַב אַחַאי מְשַׁנֵּי: ד כָּאן — בְּבָחוּר, כָּאן — בְּנָשׂוּי. הַהוּא דַּאֲתָא לְקַמֵּיהּ דְּרַבָּן גַּמְלִיאֵל, אֲמַר לֵיהּ: פֶּתַח פָּתוּחַ מָצָאתִי. אֲמַר לֵיהּ: ה שֶׁמָּא הִטִּיתָה? אֶמְשׁוֹל לְךָ מָשָׁל, לְמָה הַדָּבָר דּוֹמֶה — לְאָדָם שֶׁהָיָה מְהַלֵּךְ בְּאִישׁוֹן לַיְלָה וַאֲפֵלָה, הִיטָּה — מְצָאוֹ פָּתוּחַ, לֹא הִיטָּה — מְצָאוֹ נָעוּל. אִיכָּא דְּאָמְרִי, הָכִי אֲמַר לֵיהּ: ו שֶׁמָּא בְּמֵזִיד הִטִּיתָה וְעָקַרְתָּ לְדַשָּׁא וְעִבְרָא? אֶמְשׁוֹל לְךָ מָשָׁל לְמָה הַדָּבָר דּוֹמֶה — לְאָדָם שֶׁהוּא מְהַלֵּךְ בְּאִישׁוֹן לַיְלָה וַאֲפֵלָה; הִיטָּה בְּמֵזִיד — מְצָאוֹ פָּתוּחַ. לֹא הִיטָּה בְּמֵזִיד — מְצָאוֹ נָעוּל. הַהוּא דַּאֲתָא לְקַמֵּיהּ דְּרַבָּן גַּמְלִיאֵל בַּר רַבִּי, אֲמַר לֵיהּ: רַבִּי, בָּעַלְתִּי וְלֹא מָצָאתִי דָּם. אָמְרָה לוֹ: רַבִּי, בְּתוּלָה הָיִיתִי. אָמַר לָהֶם: הָבִיאוּ לִי אוֹתוֹ סוּדָר. הֵבִיאוּ לוֹ הַסּוּדָר וּשְׁרָאוֹ בַּמַּיִם, וְכִבְּסוֹ, וּמָצָא עָלָיו כַּמָּה טִיפֵּי דָמִים. אָמַר לוֹ: לֵךְ זְכֵה בְּמִקָּחֶךָ. אֲמַר לֵיהּ הוּנָא מָר בְּרֵיהּ דְּרָבָא מִפַּרְזַקְיָא לְרַב אַשִׁי: אֲנַן נָמֵי נַעֲבֵיד הָכִי! אֲמַר לֵיהּ:

גִּיהוּץ

רש"י

חֲכָמִים תִּקְּנוּ לָאִשָּׁה כו'. כְּלוֹמַר: אִי הֲוַאי כְּתוּבָּתָהּ דְּאוֹרַיְיתָא, לָא הֲוֵי נֶאֱמָן לְהַפְקִיעָהּ אֶלָּא בְּעֵדוּת יְדוּעָה. אֲבָל כְּתוּבָּתָהּ — חֲכָמִים תִּיקְּנוּהָ, הֵם אָמְרוּ וְהֵם אָמְרוּ. הֵם שֶׁתִּיקְּנוּהָ אָמְרוּ שֶׁהוּא נֶאֱמָן לְהַפְסִידָהּ אַף בְּטַעֲנַת פֶּתַח פָּתוּחַ. א"כ. שֶׁבְּיָדוֹ לְהַפְקִיעָהּ. מַה הוֹעִילוּ חֲכָמִים בְּתַקָּנָתָן. שֶׁתִּקְּנוּ לָהּ כְּתוּבָּה. חֲזָקָה אֵין אָדָם טוֹרֵחַ בִּסְעוּדָה כו'. אֵין לָחוּשׁ שֶׁיִּטְעוֹן אָדָם כָּךְ אֶלָּא בֶּאֱמֶת. שֶׁאִם הָיָה שׂוֹנֵא אוֹתָהּ מִתְּחִילָּה — לֹא הָיָה טוֹרֵחַ בִּסְעוּדָה וְכוֹנְסָהּ וּמַפְסִיד סְעוּדָתוֹ חִנָּם, אֶלָּא הָיָה מְגָרְשָׁהּ מִתְּחִילָּה. אֶלָּא מִן הַזִּיבּוּרִית. אִם בָּאת לִגְבּוֹת כְּתוּבָּתָהּ, וְיֵשׁ לוֹ עִידִּית וְזִיבּוּרִית וּבֵינוֹנִית — אֵינָהּ יְכוֹלָה לוֹמַר תֵּן לִי עִידִּית אוֹ בֵּינוֹנִית בְּשָׁוְויָהּ; אֶלָּא אִם בָּא לִיתֵּן לָהּ זִיבּוּרִית בְּשָׁוְויָהּ — יִתֵּן. [מַאי קְנָסָא. כְּלוֹמַר מַאי פָּשַׁע דְּקָא קָנְסִינַן לֵיהּ]. מִן הַתּוֹרָה. מִ"כֶּסֶף יִשְׁקוֹל" כִּדִלְקַמָּן. כֶּסֶף יִשְׁקוֹל. בִּמְפַתֶּה נֶאֱמַר. כְּמוֹהַר הַבְּתוּלוֹת. הָאָמוּר בִּמְאַנֵּס אֶת הַבְּתוּלָה (דברים כב), קְנָסוֹ הַכָּתוּב נ' כֶּסֶף בִּשְׁבִיל מוֹהַר בְּתוּלֶיהָ. שֶׁיְּהֵא זֶה כְּמוֹהַר הַבְּתוּלוֹת. הִקִּישׁ הַכָּתוּב קְנַס הַמְפַתֶּה לִקְנַס הָאוֹנֵס: מַה לְּהַלָּן נ' — אַף כָּאן נ'. וּמַה כֶּסֶף הָאָמוּר כָּאן שְׁקָלִים, דִּכְתִיב "יִשְׁקוֹל" — אַף לְהַלָּן שְׁקָלִים, דְּלָא תֵּימָא מָעוֹת. מִכָּאן סָמְכוּ. מִדְּקָרֵי לָהּ מוֹהַר. נוֹתֵן לָהּ מִמְּעוֹת קַפּוֹטְקִיָּא. בְּפֶרֶק בַּתְרָא תְּנַן: נָשָׂא אִשָּׁה בא"י וְגֵירְשָׁהּ בְּקַפּוֹטְקִיָּא — נוֹתֵן לָהּ מִמְּעוֹת א"י, שֶׁהֵן קַלּוֹת. נָשָׂא אִשָּׁה בְּקַפּוֹטְקִיָּא וְגֵירְשָׁהּ בא"י — נוֹתֵן לָהּ מִמְּעוֹת א"י מִנְיָן הַכָּתוּב בַּכְּתוּבָּה, דְּאָזְלִינַן לְקוּלָּא. רשב"ג: נוֹתֵן לָהּ מִמְּעוֹת קַפּוֹטְקִיָּא, שֶׁנִּשְׁתַּעְבֵּד בָּהֶן, כִּשְׁאָר מִלְוֶה, דְּקָסָבַר: כְּתוּבָּה דְּאוֹרַיְיתָא. אַסְבּוּהוּ כּוּפְרֵי. הַלְקוּהוּ מַלְקִיּוֹת בְּמַקְלוֹת חֲרָיוֹת שֶׁל דֶּקֶל, שֶׁיֵּשׁ בָּהֶן עוֹקָצִין כְּמִין קוֹצִין, כִּדְאָמְרִינַן בְּסוּכָּה (דף לג.): וְאֵימָא כּוּפְרָא — "דְּרָכֶיהָ דַרְכֵי נוֹעַם" כְּתִיב. מְבָרַכְתָּא חֲבִיטָא לֵיהּ. זוֹנוֹת הָעִיר הַזֹּאת, שֶׁשְּׁמָהּ מְבָרַכְתָּא, חֲבוּטוֹת וּשְׁכוּבוֹת תָּמִיד לְפָנָיו לִזְנוּת, מֵאַחַר שֶׁהוּא בָּקִי בְּפֶתַח פָּתוּחַ. בָּחוּר — לָא מְהֵימָן, וּמַסְבִּינַן לֵיהּ כּוּפְרֵי עַל שֶׁמֵּעִיז פָּנָיו. נָשׂוּי — מְהֵימָן, וְלָא מַסְבִּינַן לֵיהּ כּוּפְרֵי. הִטָּה. כְּשֶׁהִגִּיעַ לְפֶתַח בֵּיתוֹ הַסָּגוּר וְיֵשׁ בּוֹ דָּבָר מְעַכְּבוֹ מִלִּפְתּוֹחַ, וּכְשֶׁמַּטִּין אוֹתוֹ לַצְּדָדִין — נִפְתָּח. אִיכָּא דְּאָמְרִי. בְּלֹא מִתְכַּוֵּין לָא שְׁכִיחַ הַטָּיָה, וְלָא אָמְרִי' שֶׁמָּא הִטָּה. אֶלָּא כָּךְ בְּדָקוֹ: שֶׁמָּא בְּמֵזִיד הִטִּיתָ וְעָקַרְתָּ לְדַשָּׁא וְעִבְּרָא = עָקַרְתָּ הַדֶּלֶת וְהַבְּרִיחַ. הִטָּה בְּמֵזִיד. בְּמִתְכַּוֵּין וּבְכֹחַ. וְכִבְּסוֹ. שֶׁהָיוּ טִיפֵּי הַדָּמִים מְכוּסִּים בְּשִׁכְבַת זֶרַע.

גִּיהוּץ

תוספות

אמר רב נחמן אמר שמואל חכמים תיקנו כו'. משמע דכתובה דרבנן. וכן ב"האשה רבה" (יבמות פט. ושם) גבי אין לה כתובה קאמר: מאי טעמא תקינו לה רבנן כתובה — שלא תהא קלה בעיניו להוציאה כו'. אלמא סתמא דהתלמוד סבר דכתובה דרבנן, וקשה: דנהגו לכתוב בכתובה "כסף זוזי מאתן דחזו ליכי מדאורייתא"! ואור"ת: דסמכינן ארשב"ג דמתני' דפרק בתרא (דף קי:) דמייתי לה נמי בסמוך, דאמר: נותן לה ממעות קפוטקיא, דקסבר כתובה דאורייתא. *וקי"ל כרשב"ג במשנתנו. ועוד אור"י: דלא קיימא לן כר"נ, דאשכחנא רב אשי דהוא בתראה דפליג עליה, כדמתרץ לקמן ברייתא (דף יב.) תני: כל שלא מושמש אינו יכול לטעון טענת בתולים. אלמא דחייש לשמא משקר, ולא אמרינן חזקה אין אדם טורח בסעודה ומפסידה. וכן פי' רבינו יצחק בן רבינו מאיר דרב אשי פליג אדרב נחמן. והא דאמרינן ב"האשה רבה" (יבמות פט. ושם): מ"ט תקינו רבנן כתובה — ה"פ: מ"ט תקינו רבנן כתובה היכא דתקינו, כגון באלמנה — שלא תהא קלה בעיניו להוציאה. ה"נ תקינו שלא יהא לה, כדי שתהא קלה בעיניו להוציאה.

חזקה אין אדם טורח כו'. תימה: תינח באשת כהן או בפחותה מג' דמיתסרא עליה, הילכך כיון דמפסידה — נאמן. ולמ"ד נמי לקמן כנסה בחזקת בתולה ונמצאת בעולה אין לה כתובה כלל — ניחא, דהשתא נמי מפסידה, שהרי מקח טעות הוא. אבל למ"ד יש לה כתובה מנה — לא מפסיד מידי, אלא שבא להפסידה מכתובתה מנה. אבל הסעודה לא מפסיד, ואמאי מהימן? ונראה דלא מהימן.

הואיל ותקנת חכמים היא לא תגבה כו'. תימה: דר"מ אית ליה לקמן בפרק "אע"פ" (נו: ושם) דכתובה דאורייתא, ובפ' "הניזקין" (גיטין מח: ושם) אמרי' דקסבר ר"מ דכתובת אשה בבינונית, משום חינא. וכיון דהויא דאורייתא — דינה בעידית, כדנפקא לן בריש ב"ק (דף ה.): וכולן כאבות לשלם ממיטב, דאתיא "תחת" "נתינה" "ישלם" "כסף", ואמאי הפקיעו דינה? ועוד, דלא מישתמיט תנא בשום מקום דאית ליה כתובת אשה ממטלטלי אלא לר"מ, כדאמרינן בכל דוכתין (יבמות לט.): הא מני — ר"מ היא, דאמר מטלטלי משתעבדי לכתובה. ולמ"ד דאורייתא — אמאי לא גבי ממטלטלי כמו ניזקין, כיון דמהתם ילפינן? וי"ל: דטעמא, שלא יפרשו מהן בני אדם אם יצטרכו למכור עידית או מטלטלים, וחשו כדי שיקפצו עליהן בני אדם.

נותן לה ממעות קפוטקיא. תימה לר"י: מה ריוח הוא לה שנותן לה מאותם המעות? מ"מ אינו נותן לה אלא שוה נ' שקלים! ואם היינו אומרים לעולם צריך ליתן לה שקלים שעומדין שם בקפוטקיא נ' שקלי קפוטקיא, ובארץ ישראל נ' שקלים של ארץ ישראל — הוה ניחא. כדאמרינן גבי ה' סלעים דפדיון בכור בפ' "יש בכור" (בכורות נ. ושם): ליסדר מר תילתא אחרינא דאוסיפו עלייהו, וסדר להו. מיהו אין נראה, דהתם כשהוסיפו — בכל מקום הוסיפו, אבל כשמוסיפין במקום אחד — אין נראה שבכך תשתנה מדה דאורייתא. ומיהו, בירושלמי דפירקין גרסינן אמתניתין דכתובה מאתים: רבי מונא בשם שמואל אמר: בשקל הקדש, רבי אבא בר בונא אמר: מטבע יוצא, וכן מסקי התם כמה אמוראי.

מברכתא חביטא ליה. פירוש: הלקוהו שמוציא ש"ר על בת ישראל, שהרי משקר. וכי זונות חבוטות לפניו שיהיה בקי? הלכך לא מהימן. והא אמר רב נחמן מהימן? ומשני: מהימן, ומסבינן ליה כופרי. ורב נחמן דאמר אסבוהו — לא משום שלא היה מאמינו, אלא היה מאמינו, ואמר להלקותו לפי שחשוד על הזנות. ורב אחא משני כדסבירא לן מעיקרא דלא מהימן, ואיירי בבחור. ועי"ל בניחותא: מברכתא חביטא ליה, אף על פי שהוא נאמן — הלקוהו, לפי שחשוד על הזנות. והאמר רב נחמן נאמן, ולא פירש להלקותו! ומשני: מהימן ומסבינן ליה, ורב נחמן לא איירי במלקות. רב אחא אמר: לעולם נאמן דאמר רב נחמן — היינו בלא מלקות, ובנשוי.

בתולה

תוספות רי"ד

אמר ר"נ אמר שמואל משום ר"ש ב"א חכמים תקנו להם לבנות ישראל לבתולה מאתים ולאלמנה מנה. והם הימנוהו שאם אמר פתח פתוח מצאתי נאמן א"כ מה הועילו חכמים בתקנתם. א"ר חזקה אין אדם טורח בסעודה ומפסידה. פי' המורה אין לחוש שיטעון כך אלא באמת שאם היה שונאה מתחילה לא היה טורח בסעודה לכונסה ומפסיד סעודתו חנם אלא מתחלה [היה] מגרשה והגאון פי' אימתי הבעל מהימן כששניהם טוענים ברי על הפתח הבעל אומר פתח פתוח מצאתי והיא טוענת לא כי אלא פתח נעול מצאת ותרווייהו טענו טענות ברי אז הבעל מהימן אבל אם היא מודה ליה אין פתח פתוח מצאת אבל תחתיך נאנסתי ונסתפחה שדך או מוכת עץ אני ואית לי כתובה ואיהו אמר שמא עד שלא ארסתיך והיה מקחי מקח טעות כיון דאיהי טוענת ודאי ואיהו ספק אינו נאמן כדאמר לקמן דפסק שמואל הלכתא כרבן גמליאל דאמר דאשה נאמנת ולא קשיא דשמואל אדשמואל דלא דמי תרתי טעניתא להדדי דהכא טענו ברי וברי והתם טענו ברי ושמא ואית לה מיגו וחזקה. פי' מיגו דאי בעי אמרה מוכת עץ אני תחתיך ולא פסלה נפשה מכהונה וכו' וחזקה דגופה דבתולה נולדה: וראיתי כתוב בה"ג דאי עביד בעל סעודה רבתי דינא הוא דשקיל אודינא מן האשה מטעם רבה ואינו נ"ל דעד כאן לא האמינוהו אלא להפסידה כתובתה שהוא מוחזק בה אבל להוציא ממון ממנה אינו נאמן בטענתו. וכתב רבינו יצחק ז"ל חזינן לגאון דקאמר ה"מ לענין מנה מאתים אבל לתוספת לא מהימן וטעמא דמסתבר הוא דלא תקינו רבנן אלא מנה מאתים אבל תוספת איהו כתב לה מנפשיה הלכך לא מהימן: תנא הואיל וכן דכתובתה תיקון חכמים היא לא תגבה אלא מן הזיבורית. פי' אם באת לגבות כתובתה ויש לו עידית בינונית וזיבורית אין יכולה לומר תן לי עידית או בינונית ובשויה אלא זיבורית נותן לה ובשויה: רשב"ג אומר כתובת אשה מן התורה. ומי ארשב"ג הכי והא תניא כסף ישקול כמוהר הבתולות מכאן סמכו חכמים לכתובת אשה מן התורה. רשב"ג אומר כתובת אשה אינה מה"ת אלא מדברי סופרים. איפוך ומאי חזית דאפכית בתרייתא איפוך קמייתא. דהא שמעינן ליה לרשב"ג דאמר כתובת אשה דאורייתא פי' דתנן בפ' בתרא דמכילתין נשא אשה בא"י וכו' רשב"ג אומר נותן לה ממעות קפוטקיא פי' נשתעבד בהן כשאר מלוה דקסבר כתובה דאורייתא. עי' בסו"פ: ההוא דאתא לקמיה דרב נחמן אמר פתח פתוח מצאתי אמר להו ר"נ אסבוהו כופרא. פי' הלקוהו בחריות של דקל שיש בהן עוקצין כמין קוצין: מברכתא חביטא ליה. פי' זונות מופקרות היו חבוטות לו שמכיר בפתח פתוח. והאר"נ האומר וכו' נאמן. נאמן ומספינן ליה כופרא. רב אחא משני כאן בבחור כאן בנשוי בחור לא מהימן ולא מספינן ליה כופרי נשוי מהימן ומספינן ליה כופרי: ההוא דאתא לקמיה דר"ג א"ל פ"פ מצאתי. א"ל שמא הטית אמשול לך משל למה הדבר דומה לאדם שמהלך באישון לילה ואפילה הטה מצאו פתוח לא הטה מצאו נעול. פי' בהגיעו לפתח ביתו הסגור ויש בו המעכבו מלפתוח. וכשמטין אותו לצדדין נפתח. ואי קשיא היכא שריא ליה. והא אמרן לעיל האומר פ"פ מצאתי מהימן לאוסרה עליו. תשובה אי הוה מהדר ליה ברי לי שלא הטיתי הוה אסורה עליו. אבל כיון דשתיק הרגיש ר"ג מתוך דבריו כמספקא ליה ואין טענתו טענה ברורה ולפיכך שריא עליה:

עין משפט נר מצוה

נב א מיי' פי"א מהל' אישות הל' א סמג עשין מח טוש"ע אה"ע סי' סח סעי' א וסעי' ח:

נג ב מיי' פט"ז שם הל' ג סמג שם טוש"ע שם סי' ק סעי' ב:

נד ג מיי' פ"י שם הל' ז טוש"ע שם סימן סו סעיף ו:

נה ד טוש"ע שם סי' סח סעי' ו בהגהה:

[וע' תוס' סוטה כז. ד"ה אין]

נו ה ו מיי' פי"א שם הל' יב טוש"ע שם:

מסורת הש"ס

קדושין מה: [יבמות קז.]

נ"י כ"י

[לקמן נו:]

לקמן לח: [כט:]

[ועי' תוס' סוטה כז. ד"ה אין]

לקמן קי:

גליון הש"ס

גמ' חכמים תקנו להם. עיין סנהדרין ח ע"א תד"ה מוליא שם רע:

נז א מיי' פ"א מהל' אישות הל' יב טוש"ע אה"ע סי' סח סעי' ד [עי' מ"מ]:
נח ב ג מיי' שם טור שו"ע שם סעיף ה:
נט ד מיי' פ"י שם הל' ט סמג עשין מח טוש"ע שם סי' סו סעי' ו:
ס ה מיי' פ"א שם הל' א והלכה ח סמג שם טוש"ע שם סימן סז סעיף א:
סא ו מיי' פ"א מהל' ביאת מקדש הל"ג (סמג לאוין ס) טוש"ע יו"ד סימן רמב סעיף יג בהגהה:

*גיהוץ שלנו ככבוס שלהם. ואי אמרת ניעבד גיהוץ — מעברא ליה חומרתא. ההוא דאתא לקמיה דרבן גמליאל ב"ר, אמר ליה: רבי, בעלתי ולא מצאתי דם. אמרה ליה: רבי, עדיין בתולה אני. [א]אמר להן: הביאו לי שתי שפחות, אחת בתולה ואחת בעולה. הביאו לו, והושיבן *על פי חבית של יין. בעולה — ריחה נודף, בתולה — אין ריחה נודף, אף זו הושיבה, ולא היה ריחה נודף, אמר לו: לך זכה במקחך. ונבדוק מעיקרא בגווה? גמרא הוה שמיע ליה, מעשה לא הוה חזי, וסבר דלמא לא קים ליה בגווה דמלתא שפיר, ולאו אורח ארעא לזלזולי בבנות ישראל. ההוא דאתא לקמיה דרבן גמליאל הזקן, אמר לו: רבי, בעלתי ולא מצאתי דם. [ב]אמרה לו: רבי, ממשפחת דורקטי אני, שאין להן לא דם נדה ולא דם בתולים. בדק רבן גמליאל בקרובותיה ומצא כדבריה. אמר לו: לך זכה במקחך, אשריך שזכית למשפחת דורקטי. *מאי דורקטי — דור קטוע.* אמר רבי חנינא: תנחומים של הבל ניחמו רבן גמליאל לאותו האיש. דתני רבי חייא: כשם *שהשאור יפה לעיסה כך דמים יפים לאשה. ותנא משום רבי מאיר: כל אשה שדמיה מרובין — בניה מרובים. איתמר, רבי ירמיה בר אבא אמר: "זכה במקחך" אמר ליה. ורבי יוסי בר אבין אמר: "נתחייב במקחך" אמר ליה. בשלמא למאן דאמר "נתחייב" — היינו דרבי חנינא, אלא למאן דאמר "זכה" — מאי זכותא? דלא אתי לידי ספק נדה. ההוא דאתא לקמיה דרבי, אמר ליה: רבי, בעלתי ולא מצאתי דם. [ג]אמרה לו: רבי, עדיין בתולה הייתי, ושני בצורת הוה. ראה רבי שפניהם שחורים, צוה עליהן והכניסום למרחץ, והאכילום והשקום, והכניסום לחדר, בעל ומצא דם. אמר לו: לך זכה במקחך. קרי רבי עליהם: "°צפד עורם על עצמם יבש היה כעץ". § **מתני'** [ד]בתולה כתובתה מאתים ואלמנה מנה. [ה]בתולה, אלמנה, גרושה, וחלוצה מן האירוסין — כתובתן מאתים, ויש להן טענת בתולים. § **גמ'** מאי אלמנה? אמר רב חנא בגדתאה: אלמנה — על שם מנה. אלמנה מן האירוסין מאי איכא למימר? איידי דהא קרי לה אלמנה — הא נמי קרי לה אלמנה. אלמנה דכתיבא באורייתא מאי איכא למימר? דעתידין רבנן דמתקני לה מנה. ומי כתב קרא לעתיד? אין, דכתיב: "°ושם הנהר השלישי חדקל הוא ההולך קדמת אשור", ותנא רב יוסף: *אשור זו סליקא. ומי הואי? אלא דעתידה, הכא נמי — דעתידה. ואמר רב חנא בגדתאה: מטר משקה, מרוה, ומזבל, ומעדן, וממשיך. אמר רבא בר רבי ישמעאל ואיתימא רב יימר בר שלמיא: מאי קרא — "°תלמיה רוה נחת גדודיה ברביבים תמוגגנה צמחה תברך". אמר רבי אלעזר: מזבח — מזיח, ומזין, מחבב, מכפר. היינו מכפר היינו מזיח! מזיח גזירות ומכפר עונות. ואמר רב חנא בגדתאה: *תמרי משחנן, משבען, משלשלן, מאשרן ולא מפנקן. אמר רב: אכל תמרים [ו]אל יורה. מיתיבי: תמרים, שחרית וערבית — יפות, במנחה — רעות, בצהרים — אין כמותן. ומבטלות שלשה דברים: מחשבה רעה, וחולי מעים, ותחתוניות! מי אמרינן דלא מעלו? עלויי מעלו, ולפי שעתא טרדא. מידי דהוה אחמרא, *דאמר מר *השותה רביעית יין אל יורה. ואיבעית אימא: לא קשיא; הא — מקמי נהמא, הא — לבתר נהמא. דאמר אביי, *אמרה לי אם: תמרי מקמי נהמא — כי נרגא לדיקולא, בתר נהמא — כי עברא לדשא. *דשא, אמר רבא: דרך שם. דרגא, אמר רבא: דרך גג. פוריא, א"ר פפא: שפרין ורבין עליה. אמר רב נחמן בר יצחק: אף

בתולה אלמנה גרושה וחלוצה. נראה לפרש דלרבותא נקט חלוצה. דסלקא דעתך אמינא: כיון דשומרת יבם לא מיתסרא כניסה לחופה, שהרי יבמה יבא עליה בעל כרחה, וה"א דכנשואה דמיא, קמ"ל. **אלמנה** דכתיבא באורייתא מאי איכא למימר. והא ליכא למימר דתפשוט מהכא דכתובת אלמנה מנה מדאורייתא — דהא מנה לא היה בימי משה, דלא הזכירה תורה אלא ככר. והא דאמרינן בבכורות (דף ה. ושם): משה רבינו נאמן היה ובקי בחשבונות, אלא שמנה של קודש כפול היה — לא שהיה מנה בימי משה, אלא כלומר: כמו שמנה של קודש בימי יחזקאל כפול היה — כך היה ככר של קודש כפול בימי משה. **ותנא** רב יוסף אשור זו סליקא ומי הואי. פי' בקונטרס: ומי הואי בבריאת עולם? ובלא רב יוסף מ"אשור" וכן מ"כוש" לא מצי למיפרך, דמצינן למימר דאשור וכוש שם המחוז ולא שם העיר, ומימות עולם היה שמם כך. אבל קשה: דמאי מייתי מאשור? דאשור, אע"ג דלא הוה בבריאת עולם, כיון דהוה בימי משה — שפיר הוה ליה למכתב, אבל מנה לא היה לו לכתוב, כיון שעדיין לא היה בדורו! ונראה לר"י לפרש: דסליקא בימי משה מי הואי? דקים ליה דסליקא לא היה בימי משה, וסבירא סליקא הולך חדקל, ולא אבל אשור שהיה בימי משה.

אמר רב אכל תמרים אל יורה. ואם תאמר: דבפ"ג דכריתות (דף יג: ושם) (אמר רב הונא) אמר רב: הלכה כר' אלעזר, דאינו מחייב על שאר משכרין אלא על היין בלבד! וי"ל: אע"ג דלא מחייב על ביאת מקדש — אסור להורות. *) וה"נ משמע בס"פ "אלו מומין" (בכורות מה:) דפסול לעבודה למאן דלא מחייב אשאר משכרין, אף על גב דעבודה לא אחיל — הוא הדין נמי דאל יורה.

מטבילין

*) [בכריתות תירצו דהתם מדאורייתא והכא מדרבנן הוא דאסור]

תורה אור
גיהוץ. לשיקיי"ר, כאבן הזכוכית. בכיבוס שלהן. שהיו מימיהם יפים לכבס, או סממנין יפים היו להן לכבס. ובכיבוס שלנו אין הבגד מלובן עד שיהיה מגוהץ. מעברא ליה חומרתא. שפשוף האבן מעביר את הדם. חומרתא. אבן, כדאמרינן בגיטין (דף סט:): ונזדהר בחומרתא דנפק מיניה, אבן המגלגלת בחמה מחמת חולי. ריחה נודף. מפיה מריחין ריח היין שנכנס לה דרך פתח הפתוח. גמרא הוה שמיע ליה. שעשו כן לבנות יבש גלעד, במסכת יבמות (דף ס:). דור קטוע. שאין להם לא דם נדה ולא דם בתולים. יפין לאשה. למהר לה הריון. נתחייב במקחך. על כרחך תקבל חופה הבאה לך במקחך, לשון: אין חבין לאדם (לקמן דף יא.) — דבר שהוא לרעתו קרוי חובה. שפניהם שחורים. מחמת רעבון. צפד עורם. דונש פירש: כמו דבק עורם על עצמם, ומנחם פירש: שחר עורם. **מתני'** בתולה אלמנה וגרושה. בין בתולה שהיא אלמנה, או גרושה או חלוצה מן האירוסין, וחזרה ונשאת. כתובתה. מן השני. מאתים. שהרי בחזקת בתולה היא נשאת לו. ויש להם טענת בתולים. אם לא נמצאה הב' בתולה — אבדה כל כתובתה, דמקח טעות היא לו. **גמ'** בגדתאה. דמן בגדת. על שם מנה. שאם נשאת משנתאלמנה — אין לה כתובה אלא מנה. דכתיבא באורייתא. ועדיין לא נתקנו כתובות. ומי כתיב קרא. לקרות על שם דבר העתיד. זו סליקא. שם עיר. ומי הואי. העיר בנויה בבריאת עולם, דכתיב "ההולך קדמת אשור". [מטר. ולא מאותיות דריש הכי, אלא לפום סברא]. מזבל. את הארץ. מעדן. נותן עדנה וזיו בפירות. תלמיה. של א"י. רוה נחת גדודיה כאשר ברביבים תמוגגנה. "רוה" — הרי משקה ומרוה. "תמוגגנה" — הרי מזבל, מעדן. וממשיך את הפירות — נפקא מ"צמחה תברך". תמוגגנה = דישטנפי"ר. מזיח. קס"ד: מזיח עונות. מזין. בזכות הקרבנות העולם ניזון, שהקרבנו' באין מן המזון וגורמין לו ברכה. מחבב. את ישראל אל אביהם. היינו מזיח היינו מכפר. הי ניהו מזיח, הי ניהו מכפר? מזיח גזירות. רעות מעל ישראל. משחנן. מחממות. משלשלן. שלשול. מאשרן. מחזיקות כח, כמו "אשרו חמוץ" (ישעיהו א). ולא מפנקן. אינן מרבות אסטניסא על הלב, וכלן לשבח. אל יורה. שוס הוראה, לפי שטורדות דעתו כשיכור. שחרית וערבית יפות. כללא דמילתא, לאחר אכילה — יפות. שחרית, דרכן של בני אדם כפת שחרית, כדאמר ב"המקבל" (ב"מ קז:) ערבית — לאחר אכילה. במנחה רעות. שהן קודם אכילה, לאחר שינת הצהרים. בצהרים. לאחר הסעודה, שאכל ושבע. אין כמותם. וטובות יותר מערבית. לפי שאינו מעוכב ביום מלילך לשדות לבית הכסא בכל עת שירצה, אבל בלילה טורח הוא לו. מבטלות מחשבה רעה. דאגה, לפי שמשמחות את הלב, והרהורים שעת אורה והגלה היא. כי עברא לדשא. מחזיקות את הגוף כבריח את הדלת.

אף

תוספות רי"ד

ההוא דאתא לקמיה דר"ג. א"ל בעלתי ולא מצאתי דם. אמרה לו רבי עדיין בתולה אני. אמר להן הביאו לי שתי שפחות א' בעולה וא' בתולה הביאו לו והושיבן על פי חבית של יין. בתולה אין ריחה נודף. בעולה ריחה נודף מפיה (כרימון) [כריח] בית היין. שנכנס לה דרך (הפגם הפגום) [פתח הפתוח] הושיבוה ולא היה ריחה נודף. אמר ליה לך זכי במקחך. ההוא דאתא לקמיה דר"ג הזקן א"ל רבי בעלתי ולא מצאתי דם. אמרה לו רבי בתולה שלימה נבעלתי אלא ממשפחת דורקטי אני שאין להם לא דם בתולות ולא דם נדה בדק ר"ג בקרובותי' ומצא כדבריה א"ל לך זכי במקחך: ההוא דאתא לקמיה דרבי. א"ל רבי בעלתי ולא מצאתי דם אמרה לו בתולה שלימה אני. אלא שני בצורת הם. ראה פניה מוריקות. פי' מושחרים מחמת רעבון. צוה עליהם והכניסם למרחץ והאכילם והשקם והכניסם לחופה ובעל ומצא דם. א"ל לך זכי במקחך. קרא עליהם צפד עורם על עצמם יבש היה כעץ. צפד פי' לשון דבק: **מתני'** בתולה כתובתה מאתים. ואלמנה מנה. בתולה אלמנה גרושה וחלוצה מן האירוסין כתובתן מאתים מן הנשואין כתובתן מנה. פי' בתולה שהיא אלמנה או גרושה וחלוצה מן האירוסין ונשאת. כתובתה מן השני מאתים שהרי בחזקת בתולה נשאת לו ויש לה טענות בתולים:

[תענית כט:]
[יבמות ס:]
[בערוך איתא מאי דורקטי תנא דור קטוע]
נדה ח: סד:
מו"ק יז. [מגילה ז.: ג"י קב"ל]
נ"י כ"י
איכה ד
בראשית ב
תהלים סה
יומא י
גיטין ע.
עירובין סה. [נזיר לח.]
[וע' תוס' סנהדרין מב. ד"ה העוסקים]
[קדושין לח: וש"נ]
[שבת עז:]

אַף אָנוּ נֹאמַר: אַיְילוֹנִית – דּוּכְרָנִית דְּלָא יָלְדָה.§ **מתני'** הַגִּיּוֹרֶת וְהַשְּׁבוּיָה וְהַשִּׁפְחָה, שֶׁנִּפְדּוּ וְשֶׁנִּתְגַּיְּירוּ וְשֶׁנִּשְׁתַּחְרְרוּ פְּחוּתוֹת מִבְּנוֹת שָׁלֹשׁ שָׁנִים וְיוֹם אֶחָד – כְּתוּבָּתָן מָאתַיִם, וְיֵשׁ לָהֶן טַעֲנַת בְּתוּלִין.§ **גמ'** אָמַר רַב הוּנָא: גֵּר קָטָן מַטְבִּילִין אוֹתוֹ עַל דַּעַת בֵּית דִּין. מַאי קמ"ל – *דִּזְכוּת הוּא לוֹ, וְזָכִין לְאָדָם שֶׁלֹּא בְּפָנָיו – תָּנֵינָא: *זָכִין לְאָדָם שֶׁלֹּא בְּפָנָיו, וְאֵין חָבִין לְאָדָם שֶׁלֹּא בְּפָנָיו! מַהוּ דְּתֵימָא: גּוֹי בְּהֶפְקֵירָא נִיחָא לֵיהּ, דְּהָא קַיְימָא לָן *דְּעֶבֶד וַדַּאי בְּהֶפְקֵירָא נִיחָא לֵיהּ, קמ"ל: דְּהָנֵי מִילֵּי – גָּדוֹל, דְּטָעַם טַעַם דְּאִיסּוּרָא. אֲבָל קָטָן – זְכוּת הוּא לוֹ. לֵימָא מְסַיַּיע לֵיהּ: הַגִּיּוֹרֶת וְהַשְּׁבוּיָה וְהַשִּׁפְחָה שֶׁנִּפְדּוּ וְשֶׁנִּתְגַּיְּירוּ וְשֶׁנִּשְׁתַּחְרְרוּ פְּחוּתוֹת מִבְּנוֹת שָׁלֹשׁ שָׁנִים וְיוֹם אֶחָד. מַאי לָאו – דְּאַטְבְּלִינְהוּ עַל דַּעַת בֵּית דִּין? לָא, הָכָא בְּמַאי עָסְקִינַן, בְּגֵר שֶׁנִּתְגַּיְּירוּ בָּנָיו וּבְנוֹתָיו עִמּוֹ, דְּנִיחָא לְהוּ בְּמַאי דְּעָבֵיד אֲבוּהוֹן. אָמַר רַב יוֹסֵף: הִגְדִּילוּ יְכוֹלִין לִמְחוֹת. אֵיתִיבֵיהּ אַבַּיֵּי: הַגִּיּוֹרֶת וְהַשְּׁבוּיָה וְהַשִּׁפְחָה שֶׁנִּפְדּוּ וְשֶׁנִּתְגַּיְּירוּ וְשֶׁנִּשְׁתַּחְרְרוּ פְּחוּתוֹת מִבְּנוֹת שָׁלֹשׁ שָׁנִים וְיוֹם אֶחָד – כְּתוּבָּתָן מָאתַיִם. וְאִי ס"ד הִגְדִּילוּ יְכוֹלִין לִמְחוֹת – יָהֲבִינַן לַהּ כְּתוּבָּה דְּאָזְלָה וְאָכְלָה בְּגֵיוּתָהּ?! לְכִי גָּדְלָה. לְכִי גָּדְלָה נַמִי, מְמַחְיָא וְנָפְקָא! כֵּיוָן שֶׁהִגְדִּילָה *שָׁעָה אַחַת וְלֹא מִיחֲתָה – שׁוּב אֵינָהּ יְכוֹלָה לִמְחוֹת. מְתִיב רָבָא: *אֵלּוּ נְעָרוֹת שֶׁיֵּשׁ לָהֶן קְנָס: הַבָּא עַל הַמַּמְזֶרֶת, וְעַל הַנְּתִינָה, וְעַל הַכּוּתִית, וְעַל הַגִּיּוֹרֶת, וְעַל הַשְּׁבוּיָה, וְעַל הַשִּׁפְחָה שֶׁנִּפְדּוּ וְשֶׁנִּתְגַּיְּירוּ וְשֶׁנִּשְׁתַּחְרְרוּ פְּחוּתוֹת מִבְּנוֹת שָׁלֹשׁ שָׁנִים וְיוֹם אֶחָד – יֵשׁ לָהֶן קְנָס. וְאִי אָמְרַתְּ הִגְדִּילוּ יְכוֹלִין לִמְחוֹת – יָהֲבִינַן לַהּ קְנָס דְּאָזְלָה וְאָכְלָה בְּגֵיוּתָהּ?! לְכִי גָּדְלָה. לְכִי גָּדְלָה נַמִי, מְמַחְיָא וְנָפְקָא! כֵּיוָן שֶׁהִגְדִּילָה שָׁעָה אַחַת וְלֹא מִיחֲתָה, שׁוּב אֵינָהּ יְכוֹלָה לִמְחוֹת. אַבַּיֵּי לֹא אָמַר כְּרָבָא – הָתָם קְנָסָא, הַיְינוּ טַעֲמָא *שֶׁלֹּא יְהֵא חוֹטֵא נִשְׂכָּר. רָבָא לֹא אָמַר כְּאַבַּיֵּי – *כְּתוּבָּה הַיְינוּ טַעֲמָא – שֶׁלֹּא תְּהֵא קַלָּה בְּעֵינָיו לְהוֹצִיאָהּ.§ **מתני'** הַגָּדוֹל שֶׁבָּא עַל הַקְּטַנָּה, וְקָטָן שֶׁבָּא עַל הַגְּדוֹלָה, וּמוּכַּת עֵץ – כְּתוּבָּתָן מָאתַיִם, דִּבְרֵי רַבִּי מֵאִיר. *וַחֲכָ"א: מוּכַּת עֵץ – כְּתוּבָּתָהּ מָנֶה. בְּתוּלָה, אַלְמָנָה, גְּרוּשָׁה וַחֲלוּצָה מִן הַנִּשּׂוּאִין – כְּתוּבָּתָן מָנֶה, וְאֵין

רש"י

אף אנו נאמר. אַף אָנוּ נִדְרוֹשׁ אֶת הַשֵּׁמוֹת, מַה לְּשׁוֹן אַיְילוֹנִית שֶׁקְּרָאוּהּ חֲכָמִים לְאִשָּׁה שֶׁאֵינָהּ רְאוּיָה לֵילֵד. דוכרנית. דְּמִתַּרְגְּמִינַן דְּכַר שְׁלִים (ויקרא ה) – הֲרֵי הִיא כְּאַיִל שֶׁאֵינוֹ יוֹלֵד.

גמ' (*על דעת ב"ד). אִם אֵין לוֹ אָב, וְאִמּוֹ הֱבִיאַתּוּ לְהִתְגַּיֵּיר. מטבילין. דְּאֵין לְךָ גֵּר בְּלֹא מִילָה וּטְבִילָה. על דעת בית דין. שְׁלֹשָׁה יְהוּ בִּטְבִילָתוֹ, כְּדִין כָּל טְבִילַת גֵּר שֶׁצְּרִיכִים ג'. וְהֵן נַעֲשִׂין לוֹ אָב, וַהֲרֵי הוּא גֵּר עַל יְדֵיהֶן, וּמַגָּעוֹ בְּיַיִן כָּשֵׁר. מהו דתימא גוי בהפקירא ניחא ליה. וְחוֹב הוּא לוֹ, וְאֵין אָדָם נַעֲשֶׂה שָׁלִיחַ לְאָדָם לְחוֹבָתוֹ שֶׁלֹּא בְּפָנָיו, כְּלוֹמַר שֶׁלֹּא מִדַּעְתּוֹ. וְקָטָן לָאו בַּר דֵּיעָה הוּא. דהא גבי עבד קי"ל. בְּפ"ק דְּגִיטִּין (דף יג.) דְּוַדַּאי בְּהֶפְקֵירָא נִיחָא לֵיהּ, נוֹחַ לוֹ לִהְיוֹת עֶבֶד וִיהֵא מוּתָּר בְּהֶפְקֵר זִימַּת הַשְּׁפָחוֹת, מִהְיוֹת בֶּן חוֹרִין לִהְיוֹת מוּתָּר בְּבַת יִשְׂרָאֵל, דְּלָא זִילָא לֵיהּ וְלָא שְׁכִיחָא לֵיהּ לְהֶפְקֵירָא. קמ"ל. הָכָא, דִּגְבֵי גּוֹי קָטָן לָא אָמְרִינַן הָכִי. דהני מילי. דְּנִיחָא לֵיהּ בְּהֶפְקֵירָא. גדול. שֶׁגָּדַל [בְּמִדּוֹת] הֶפְקֵירוּת, וְטָעִים לֵיהּ טַעְמָא דְּאִיסּוּרָא. הגדילו. קְטַנִּים שֶׁנִּתְגַּיְּירוּ, וַאֲפִי' עִם אֲבִיהֶן. יכולין למחות. וְלוֹמַר: אִי אֶפְשֵׁינוּ לִהְיוֹת גֵּרִים. וְחוֹזְרִין לְסוּרָן, וְאֵין לָנוּ לְעָנְשָׁן בְּבֵ"ד, וַאֲפִי' יָדֵינוּ תַּקִּיפָה. וְאִם קִידֵּשׁ אִשָּׁה מִשֶּׁמִּיחָה – אֵינָהּ צְרִיכָה גֵּט לִהְיוֹת כְּיִשְׂרָאֵל מוּמָר. לכי גדלה. לֹא יָהֲבִינַן לַהּ עַד שֶׁתַּגְדִּיל. שוב אינה יכולה למחות. וְאִם מִיחֲתָה – הֲרֵי הִיא כְּיִשְׂרָאֵל מוּמֶרֶת, לֵיעָנֵשׁ בְּכָל עוֹנְשֵׁי ב"ד. שיש להן קנס. נ' כֶּסֶף אִם יֶאֱנְסוּ. הבא על הממזרת. וְאַע"ג דְּלָא קָרֵינַן בֵּיהּ "וְלוֹ תִהְיֶה לְאִשָּׁה", שֶׁהֲרֵי אֵינָהּ רְאוּיָה לְקַיְּימָהּ – אֲפִילּוּ הָכִי יֵשׁ לָהּ קְנָס, כִּדְלְקַמָּן. אביי לא אמר כרבא. דְּמוֹתִיב מִקְּנָסָא, דְּקָסָבַר לָאו תְּיוּבְתָּא הִיא, דְּטַעְמָא דִּקְנָסָא – שֶׁלֹּא יְהֵא חוֹטֵא נִשְׂכָּר לְהִפָּטֵר. רבא לא אמר כאביי. דְּמוֹתִיב מִכְּתוּבָּה, דְּהָתָם טַעְמָא מַאי תַּקִּינוּ לַהּ רַבָּנַן כְּתוּבָּה – שֶׁלֹּא תְּהֵא קַלָּה בְּעֵינָיו לְהוֹצִיאָהּ, וְכָל זְמַן שֶׁלֹּא מִיחֲתָה – גִּיּוֹרֶת הִיא, וְעָבְדִינַן לַהּ תַּקַּנְתָּא.

מתני' הבא על הקטנה. פְּחוּתָה מִבַּת שָׁלֹשׁ, שֶׁאֵין בִּיאָתָהּ בִּיאָה, שֶׁהֲרֵי בְּתוּלֶיהָ חוֹזְרִין. וקטן. פָּחוֹת מִבֶּן תֵּשַׁע, שֶׁאָמְרוּ חֲכָמִים: אֵין בִּיאָתוֹ בִּיאָה, וּבָא עַל הַגְּדוֹלָה. ומוכת עץ. שֶׁנִּתְקַע לָהּ עֵץ בְּאוֹתוֹ מָקוֹם. כתובתן מאתים. אִם נִשְּׂאוּ לְאִישׁ אַחֲרֵי כֵן – לֹא אִבְּדוּ בְּכָךְ אֶת כְּתוּבָּתָן, אִם נְשָׂאָהּ סְתָם וְלֹא פֵּירֵשׁ לָהּ כְּלוּם. בתולה. שֶׁהִיא אַלְמָנָה אוֹ גְּרוּשָׁה אוֹ חֲלוּצָה. מן הנישואין. כְּגוֹן שֶׁנִּכְנְסָה לַחוּפָּה, וּמֵת בַּעְלָהּ בְּחֶזְקַת שֶׁלֹּא נִבְעֲלָה. כתובתה מנה. אִם נִיסֵּת לְאַחֵר סְתָם, כְּתוּבָּתָהּ מָנֶה, דִּבְחֶזְקַת בְּעוּלָה קָיְימָא מִשֶּׁנִּכְנְסָה לַחוּפָּה.

תוספות

מטבילין אותו על דעת ב"ד משום דזכות הוא. ותימה: דהא זכייה הוי מטעם שליחות, דכיון דזכות הוא לו – אנן סהדי דעביד ליה שליח, כדמוכח בפ"ק דב"מ (דף יב.) גבי חצר משום יד איתרבאי, ולא גרע משליחות. וא"כ היאך זכין לקטן? והלא אין שליחות לקטן, כדאמרינן ב"איזהו נשך" (שם עא:)! ועוד, דאכתי גוי הוא, ואמרי' התם: דקטן דאתי לכלל שליחות – אית ליה זכייה מדרבנן, גוי דלא אתי לכלל שליחות – אפילו זכייה מדרבנן לית ליה! ונראה לר"י: דהכא נמי דזכין לו – מדרבנן, כדאמרינן התם דקטן אית ליה זכייה מדרבנן. ואע"ג דאכתי גוי הוא – הא אתי לכלל שליחות. א"נ, כיון דבהך זכייה נעשה ישראל – הוה ליה כישראל גמור לענין זכייה. וא"ת: היכי הוי גר מדרבנן, ושרינן ליה בבת ישראל, וקידושיו קידושין, הא מן התורה גוי הוא! וי"ל: דקסבר כמ"ד ב"האשה רבה" (יבמות דף פט:) דיש כח ביד חכמים לעקור דבר מן התורה בקום ועשה. וכי פריך מאי קמ"ל – הוה מצי לשנויי קמ"ל דיש כח ביד חכמים לעקור דבר מן התורה בקום ועשה, וחד מתרי טעמי נקט. והא דאמרי' בריש "בן סורר" (סנהדרין דף סח: ושם) גבי גזל הגר "אם אין לאיש גואל", איש – אתה צריך לחזור אחריו אם יש לו גואל, אבל קטן – אי אתה צריך לחזור אחריו כו' – משכחת לה גר קטן מן התורה במעוברת שנתגיירה, *כדאמרי' בפרק "הערל" (יבמות דף עח. ושם): גויה מעוברת שנתגיירה – בנה אין צריך טבילה, והוי גר מן התורה, דישראל גמור הוא. ואית ליה ממון מן התורה – כגון שירש את אמו. ואי אתה צריך לחזור עליו – שאין לו יורשין, שאינו מוליד, ואחיו מן האם אין יורשין אותו. ולפי ספרים דגרסינן בב"מ (דף עא:): זכייה מיהא אית ליה, ולא גרס מדרבנן – ניחא, דמצי למימר דאית ליה זכייה מן התורה. וגוי קטן, כיון דבא להתגייר – חשבינן ליה כישראל קטן. ואע"ג דזכייה הוי מטעם שליחות, ואין לו שליחות מן התורה – ה"מ בדבר שיש בו קצת חובה, כגון להפריש תרומתו, דשמא היה רוצה לפוטרה בחטה אחת, או שמא היה רוצה להעדיף. אבל הכא, שזכות גמור הוא לו – יש לו שליחות. **מהו** דתימא גוי בהפקירא ניחא ליה. ואע"ג דרבנן פליגי אר' מאיר בפ' קמא דגיטין (דף יג. ושם), ולית להו טעמא דבהפקירא ניחא ליה – ה"מ גבי עבד שאינו חושש בהפקירא, שמפקיע עצמו מן השעבוד. אבל גבי גוי, שאינו משועבד – ניחא ליה בהפקירא. וכן נראה, דאי לא תימא הכי – היכי מייתי סייעתא מההוא דגיורת? דלמא רבנן היא, דאפילו בגדול לית להו בהפקירא ניחא ליה. **אבל** קטן זכות הוא לו. והא דתנן בפרק קמא דגיטין (ג"ז שם) האומר: תנו גט זה לאשתי ושיחרור זה לעבדי, רצה לחזור בשניהם – יחזור, דברי רבי מאיר. היינו בעבד גדול, דבקטן מודה רבי מאיר דזכות הוא לו, דלא ניחא ליה בהפקירא, כדאמרינן הכא, משום דלא טעים טעמא דאיסורא. א"נ, איירי אף בעבד קטן, וכגון שהוא של כהן, דחוב הוא לו שיצא לחירות, לפי שמפסידו מלאכול בתרומה. **לכי** גדלה. *וא"ת: והלא כבר גדולה היא; שהיא נערה כיון שהיא בת קנס! ומפרש ר"י: לכי גדלה ונהגה מנהג יהודית. **אביי** לא אמר כרבא שלא יהא חוטא נשכר. משמע דרבא לית ליה טעמא דשלא יהא חוטא נשכר. וקשה: דאמרי' בפ' "שור שנגח ד' וה'" (ב"ק דף לח: ושם): קסבר רבי מאיר כותים גירי אמת הן, וקנס הוא דקניס ר"מ בממונם לענין שור שנגח, שלא יטמעו בהן. ופריך: אלו נערות שיש להן קנס – הבא על הכותית. ואי קניס ר"מ בממונם – ה"נ ניקנוס! ומשני: דהכא לא בעי למקנס, שלא יהא חוטא נשכר. והשתא לרבא, דלית ליה הכא טעם דחוטא נשכר, היכי מצי משני התם? וי"ל: דהתם אית ליה שפיר האי טעמא, כיון דבדין יש להן קנס, דגרי אמת הן, אלא דבעי' למקנס להו. סברא הוא, דמשום טעמא שלא יהא חוטא נשכר מוקמינן לה אדינא. אבל הכא סבירא ליה לרבא, דמשום טעמא שלא יהא חוטא נשכר אין ליתן לה, כיון דמן הדין לית לה, שהרי גויה גמורה היא אם תמחה. ובפ' "אלו נערות" (לקמן דף לו:) דאית ליה לרבא שלא יהא חוטא נשכר גבי שבויה – משום דמוקמינן לה בקדושתה. ושמואל

עין משפט נר מצוה

סב א מיי' פי"א מהל' אישות הל' א' סמג עשין מח טוש"ע אה"ע סי' סז סעי' ג:

סג ב מיי' פי"ג מהל' איסורי ביאה הל' ז סמג לאוין קיז טוש"ע יו"ד סי' רסח סעי' ז:

סד ג מיי' פ"ד מהל' זכיה הל"ב סמג עשין פ"ב טוש"ע חו"מ סי' רמג סעי' א וטוש"ע יו"ד סי' רסח סעי' ז':

סה ד ה ו ז מיי' פ"י מהל' מלכים הל"ג טוש"ע יו"ד סי' רסח עי' ז':

סו ח מיי' פ"י מהל' אישות הל"ז טור אה"ע סי' סו:

סז ט מיי' פי"א מהל' אישות הל"ג סמג עשין מח טוש"ע שם סי' סז סעיף ד:

סח י מיי' שם טוש"ע שם סעיף ה:

סט כ מיי' שם הל' א טוש"ע שם סעי' ב:

מסורת הש"ס

[נ"ל גר קטן]

[ע' תוס' גיטין ה: ד"ה והא קי"ל] [עירובין פא: יבמות קיח: וש"נ]

[גיטין יג. ע' תוס' שם]

[קשה א"כ מתי תדע שעת המחאה דהא בקטנות אינה יכולה למחות כו' י"ל כגון שהתחילה מנהג גיות יום לפני גדלותה וכן נהגה יום או יומים לאחר גדלותה. ת"י עה"ג]

[יבמות נב: וש"נ]

[יבמות פט. לקמן לט: נד.]

[לקמן יג.]

(וע' תוס' ב"ק קט: ד"ה קטן ותוס' סנהדרין סח:)

(לקמן כט: ב"ק לח:)

תוספות רי"ד

הגיורת והשבויה והשפחה שנפדו ושנתגיירו ושנשתחררו פחותות מבנות ג' שנים ויום אחד כתובתן מאתים ויש להן טענת בתולים. פי' בחזקת בתולות הן. ואם נמצאת בעולה אומר לה מקחי מקח טעות ואבדה כל כתובתה. אמר ר"ה גר קטן מטבילין אותו ע"ד ב"ד. פי' אע"פ שאין לו אב ואם כגון תינוק שנמצא מושלך או ששבו ישראל קטני פלשתים ב"ד מלין אותם והם כישראל לכל דבר. והמורה פי' מטבילין אותו. דאינו גר עד שימול ויטבול. עיין פרק החולץ [דף מו] ובפ"ח דיבמות [דף ע"א]. מאי קמ"ל דזכין לאדם שלא בפניו תנינא זכין לאדם שלא בפניו ואין חבין לו לאדם אלא בפניו. מ"ד בהפקירא ניחא ליה וחוב הוא לו. פי' שאין אדם נעשה שליח לחובתו שלא בפניו כלומר שלא מדעת. קמ"ל דה"מ גדול דטעים טעמא דאיסורא אבל קטן זכות הוא [לו]. אמר ר"י ואם הגדילו. פי' הקטנים שנתגיירו ואפי' עם אביהן יכולין למחות. פי' יכולין לומר אי אפשינו להיות גרים ואין לנו לעונשם בב"ד. ואפילו ידינו תקיפה. ואם קידש אשה משמיחה אינה צריכה גט להיות כישראל מומר. ודוקא שלא הגיעו לכלל שתי שערות אבל אם הגדילו ולא מיחו אין יכולין למחות ואם מיחו הרי הן כישראל מומר וקדושי' קדושין. א) והגדילו דר"י לאו דוקא שבאו לכלל עונשין אלא שבאו לכלל דעת ועדיין לא באו לכלל עונשין: **מתני'** הגדול שבא על הקטנה וקטן שבא על הגדולה ומוכת עץ כתובתן מאתים. דברי ר"מ וחכ"א מוכת עץ כתובתן מנה. פי' קטנה פחותה מבת ג' שנים ויום אחד שאין ביאתה ביאה שהרי בתוליה חוזרין. וקטן פחות מבן ט' שאמרו חכמים אין ביאתו ביאה לקנות קנין גמור. כגון אם בא על יבמתו דהתם אמרי' אין ביאתו ביאה ב) חשובה לקנות לגמרי. פי' לא גרעה אותה ביאה ממאמר בגדול. שכמו שמאמר בגדול פוסלה על שאר האחין. כך ביאת [פחות] בן ט' פסלה על האחין. עיין בס"פ האשה רבה: מוכת עץ שנתקע לה עץ באותו מקום ויצאו בתוליה כתובתה מאתים. פי' לא הפסידו כתובתן אם נישאו סתם וחכ"א מוכת עץ כיון שאיבדה בתוליה כתובתה מנה: איתמר

א) ובדברי רבינו אלו נתיישב קושיית הת"י כאן בד"ה קשה וע"ש. ב) ע"ש ביבמות דף נ דמיירי שם בביאת בן תשע דעשו כמאמר בגדול אבל בפחות מבן תשע לא מיירי התם כלל וצ"ע.

גליון הש"ס

גמ' שלא יהא חוטא נשכר. ע"ב לקמן מ"ז נדה דף ד ע"ב: תוס' ד"ה לכי גדלה. ועיין נדה מד ע"ב תוס' ד"ה שלשים יום:

עין משפט
נר מצוה

ע א מיי׳ פי״א מהל׳ אישות הל״א טוש״ע אה״ע סי׳ סז סעי׳ ג:
עא ב מיי׳ שם הל״ג טוש״ע שם סעי׳ ד:
עב ג ד מיי׳ שם טוש״ע שם סעי׳ ה:
עג ה טוש״ע שם סעי׳ ב:

וְאֵין לָהֶן טַעֲנַת בְּתוּלִים. אהַגִּיּוֹרֶת וְהַשְּׁבוּיָה וְהַשִּׁפְחָה שֶׁנִּפְדּוּ וְשֶׁנִּתְגַּיְּירוּ וְשֶׁנִּשְׁתַּחְרְרוּ יְתֵירוֹת עַל בְּנוֹת שָׁלֹשׁ שָׁנִים וְיוֹם אֶחָד — כְּתוּבָּתָן מָנֶה, וְאֵין לָהֶן טַעֲנַת בְּתוּלִין.§ **גמ׳** אָמַר רַב יְהוּדָה אָמַר רַב: קָטָן הַבָּא עַל הַגְּדוֹלָה עֲשָׂאָהּ מוּכַּת עֵץ. כִּי אָמְרִיתַהּ קַמֵּיהּ דִּשְׁמוּאֵל, אֲמַר: באֵין מוּכַּת עֵץ בְּבָשָׂר. אִיכָּא דְּמַתְנֵי לְהָא שְׁמַעְתָּא בְּאַפֵּי נַפְשַׁהּ: קָטָן הַבָּא עַל הַגְּדוֹלָה, רַב אָמַר: עֲשָׂאָהּ מוּכַּת עֵץ, וּשְׁמוּאֵל אָמַר: אֵין מוּכַּת עֵץ בְּבָשָׂר. מֵתִיב רַב אוֹשַׁעְיָא: גָּדוֹל שֶׁבָּא עַל הַקְּטַנָּה, וְקָטָן הַבָּא עַל הַגְּדוֹלָה, וּמוּכַּת עֵץ — כְּתוּבָּתָן מָאתַיִם, דִּבְרֵי ר״מ. וַחֲכָמִים אוֹמְרִים: מוּכַּת עֵץ כְּתוּבָּתָהּ מָנֶה! אָמַר רָבָא: הָכִי קָאָמַר גָּדוֹל הַבָּא עַל הַקְּטַנָּה — וְלֹא כְלוּם, *דְּפָחוֹת מִכָּאן כְּנוֹתֵן אֶצְבַּע בָּעַיִן דָּמֵי. וְקָטָן הַבָּא עַל הַגְּדוֹלָה — עֲשָׂאָהּ מוּכַּת עֵץ, וּמוּכַּת עֵץ גּוּפָא — פְּלוּגְתָּא דְּר״מ וְרַבָּנַן. אָמַר רָמִי בַּר חָמָא: *מַחְלוֹקֶת כְּשֶׁהִכִּיר בָּהּ; דְּר״מ מְדַמֵּי לָהּ לְבוֹגֶרֶת, וְרַבָּנַן מְדַמּוּ לָהּ לִבְעוּלָה. אֲבָל לֹא הִכִּיר בָּהּ — דִּבְרֵי הַכֹּל וְלֹא כְלוּם. וְר״מ אַמַּאי מְדַמֵּי לָהּ לְבוֹגֶרֶת? נְדַמְּיֵיהּ לִבְעוּלָה! בְּעוּלָה אִיתְעֲבִיד בָּהּ מַעֲשֶׂה בִּידֵי אָדָם. הָא — לָא אִיתְעֲבִיד בָּהּ מַעֲשֶׂה בִּידֵי אָדָם. וְרַבָּנַן, אַדְּמַדְּמוּ לָהּ לִבְעוּלָה נְדַמְּיֵיהּ לְבוֹגֶרֶת! בּוֹגֶרֶת לָא אִיתְעֲבִיד בָּהּ מַעֲשֶׂה כְּלָל, הָא — אִיתְעֲבִיד בָּהּ מַעֲשֶׂה, אֲבָל לֹא הִכִּיר בָּהּ — לְדִבְרֵי הַכֹּל וְלֹא כְלוּם. מֵתִיב רַב נַחְמָן: *הִיא אוֹמֶרֶת "מוּכַּת עֵץ אֲנִי" וְהוּא אוֹמֵר "לֹא כִּי, אֶלָּא דְּרוּסַת אִישׁ אַתְּ". ר״ג וְר׳ אֱלִיעֶזֶר אוֹמְרִים: נֶאֱמֶנֶת! אֶלָּא אָמַר רָבָא: בֵּין הִכִּיר בָּהּ וּבֵין לֹא הִכִּיר בָּהּ, לְר״מ — מָאתַיִם, לְרַבָּנַן; הִכִּיר בָּהּ — מָנֶה, לֹא הִכִּיר בָּהּ — וְלֹא כְלוּם. וַהֲדַר בֵּיהּ רָבָא, דְּתַנְיָא: כֵּיצַד *הוֹצָאַת שֵׁם רַע? בָּא לְבֵית דִּין וְאָמַר: פְּלוֹנִי, לֹא מָצָאתִי לְבִתְּךָ בְּתוּלִים. אִם יֵשׁ עֵדִים שֶׁזִּינְּתָה תַּחְתָּיו — יֵשׁ לָהּ כְּתוּבָּה מָנֶה. אִם יֵשׁ עֵדִים שֶׁזִּינְּתָה תַּחְתָּיו?! בַּת סְקִילָה הִיא! הָכִי קָאָמַר: אִם יֵשׁ עֵדִים שֶׁזִּינְּתָה תַּחְתָּיו — בִּסְקִילָה, זִינְּתָה מֵעִיקָּרָא — יֵשׁ לָהּ כְּתוּבָּה מָנֶה. *וְאָמַר רַב חִיָּיא בַּר אָבִין אָמַר רַב שֵׁשֶׁת: זֹאת אוֹמֶרֶת כְּנָסָהּ בְּחֶזְקַת בְּתוּלָה וְנִמְצֵאת בְּעוּלָה — יֵשׁ לָהּ כְּתוּבָּה מָנֶה. וּמֵתִיב רַב נַחְמָן: *הַנּוֹשֵׂא אֶת הָאִשָּׁה וְלֹא מָצָא לָהּ בְּתוּלִים, הִיא אוֹמֶרֶת "מִשֶּׁאֵרַסְתַּנִי נֶאֱנַסְתִּי וְנִסְתַּחֲפָה שָׂדֵהוּ" וְהוּא אוֹמֵר "לֹא כִּי, אֶלָּא עַד שֶׁלֹּא אֵירַסְתִּיךְ, וְהָיָה מִקָּחִי מִקַּח טָעוּת", וְלֵית לָהּ כְּלָל? וַאֲמַר לְהוּ רַב חִיָּיא בַּר אָבִין: אֶפְשָׁר רַב עַמְרָם וְכָל גְּדוֹלֵי הַדּוֹר יָתְבִי כִּי אֲמַר רַב שֵׁשֶׁת לְהָא שְׁמַעְתָּא, וְקַשְׁיָא לְהוּ, וְשַׁנֵּי: מַאי מִקַּח טָעוּת — נַמִי מִמָּאתַיִם, אֲבָל מָנֶה — אִית לָהּ. וְאַתְּ אָמְרַתְּ לֵית לָהּ כְּלָל?! °וְאָמַר רָבָא: מַאן דְּקָא מוֹתִיב — שַׁפִּיר קָא מוֹתִיב, גמִקַּח טָעוּת — לְגַמְרֵי מַשְׁמַע. וְאֶלָּא קַשְׁיָא הַךְ! תְּרֵיץ וְאֵימָא הָכִי: אִם יֵשׁ עֵדִים שֶׁזִּינְּתָה תַּחְתָּיו — בִּסְקִילָה, זִינְּתָה מֵעִיקָּרָא — וְלֹא כְלוּם, דנִמְצֵאת מוּכַּת עֵץ — יֵשׁ לָהּ כְּתוּבָּה מָנֶה. וְהָא רָבָא הוּא דְּאָמַר לְרַבָּנַן לֹא הִכִּיר בָּהּ וְלֹא כְלוּם! אֶלָּא ש״מ: הֲדַר בֵּיהּ רָבָא מֵהַהִיא. ת״ר: כְּנָסָהּ רִאשׁוֹן לְשׁוּם נִישּׂוּאִין, הוְיֵשׁ לָהּ עֵדִים שֶׁלֹּא נִסְתְּרָה. אִי נַמִי, נִסְתְּרָה וְלֹא שָׁהֲתָה כְּדֵי בִּיאָה — אֵין הַשֵּׁנִי יָכוֹל לִטְעוֹן טַעֲנַת בְּתוּלִים, שֶׁהֲרֵי כְּנָסָהּ רִאשׁוֹן.

אָמַר

ושמואל אמר אין מוכת עץ בבשר. בלא הסיר בתולין איירי, דאי בהסיר — למה יש לה להיות פחותה ממוכת עץ.

לרבנן הכיר בה מנה לא הכיר בה ולא כלום. ומתני׳ ר״מ היא ולא רבנן. ואם תאמר: אמאי לא קאמר לרבנן בין הכיר בה בין לא הכיר בה מנה, כדקאמר במסקנא, ותיתי מתניתין לדברי הכל! וי״ל: דלא ניחא ליה למימר הכי, דכיון דרבנן מדמו לה לבעולה — הויא בלא הכיר בה כמו כנסה בחזקת בתולה ונמצאת בעולה, וסבירא ליה דלית לה ולא כלום. ובמסקנא סבר הא דמדמו לה לבעולה — היינו לענין מנה, אבל מקח טעות — לא הויא כמו בעולה, דאינו מקפיד כ״כ במוכת עץ שיהא מקח טעות.

הדר ביה רבא מההיא. אבל מהא לא בעי למימר דהדר ביה, משום דמקח טעות — לגמרי משמע. וא״ת: מנא לן דהדר ביה ממה שאמר לרבנן לא הכיר בה ולא כלום? נאמר שחזר בו ממה שאמר לא הכיר בה לר״מ מאתים, אלא נפרש לא הכיר בה — מנה, ונוקי ברייתא כרבי מאיר! וי״ל כדפי׳ לעיל בקונטרס: דאין זה סברא, דאי חשיב מקח טעות לא יהא לה כלום, ואי לא חשיב מקח טעות — למה לא יהא לה מאתים? כיון דמדמה לה לבוגרת, דאטו לבוגרת פוחתין לה מכתובתה*)!

אמר

*) ועוד נ״ל דניחא ליה טפי דלרבנן לא הכיר בה מנה דהשתא מיתוקמא מתני׳ וברייתא נמי כרבנן. ת״י עה״ג

וְאֵין לָהֶן טַעֲנַת בְּתוּלִין. אֵין יָכוֹל לְהַפְסִידָהּ אוֹתָהּ מָנֶה, וְלוֹמַר: בְּחֶזְקַת בְּתוּלָה נְשָׂאתִיךְ, וַהֲרֵי מִקָּחִי מִקַּח טָעוּת. **גמ׳** עֲשָׂאָהּ מוּכַּת עֵץ. נְהִי דְּאֵין בִּיאָתוֹ בִּיאָה, מִיהוּ לָא גָּרַע מֵעֵץ הַנִּתְקָע. וּלְרַבָּנַן דִּפְלִיגִי אַמּוּכַּת עֵץ כְּתוּבָּתָהּ מָנֶה, וְכֵן לְעִנְיַן כֹּהֵן גָּדוֹל, דִּתְנַן (יבמות דף נט.): לֹא יִשָּׂא אֶת מוּכַּת עֵץ — הָא נַמִי אֲסִירָא לֵיהּ. אֵין מוּכַּת עֵץ בִּבְשַׂר אָדָם. וְאִי בְּעוּלָה לָא הָוְיָא — מוּכַּת עֵץ נַמִי לֵיתָא. בְּאַפֵּי נַפְשָׁהּ. בְּלָא גַּבְרֵי. דְּלָא אֲמַר רַב יְהוּדָה מִשְּׁמֵיהּ דְּרַב וּמִשְּׁמֵיהּ דִּשְׁמוּאֵל, אֶלָּא אִינְהוּ גּוּפַיְיהוּ אִיפְּלוּג בָּהּ. וְקָטָן שֶׁבָּא עַל הַגְּדוֹלָה וּמוּכַּת עֵץ. וּמִדְּפַלְגִינְהוּ תַּנָּא לְתַרְתֵּי, וְלָא אִיפְּלוּג רַבָּנַן אֶלָּא בְּמוּכַּת עֵץ — שָׁמְעַתְּ מִינָּהּ: אֵין מוּכַּת עֵץ בְּבָשָׂר. הָכִי קָאָמַר גָּדוֹל הַבָּא עַל הַקְּטַנָּה וְלֹא כְלוּם. אֵינָהּ בִּיאָה לְדִבְרֵי הַכֹּל. הִלְכָּךְ, כְּתוּבָּתָהּ מָאתַיִם. וְלָא אִיפְּלוּג רַבָּנַן עֲלָהּ, דְּפָחוֹת מִכָּאן כְּנוֹתֵן אֶצְבַּע בָּעַיִן. דִּתְנַן בְּמַסֶּכֶת נִדָּה (דף מד) גַּבֵּי בַּת פְּחוּתָה מִג׳ שָׁנִים וְיוֹם אֶחָד: מָה הַדִּמְעָה הַיּוֹצְאָה ע״י אֶצְבַּע בָּאָה אַחֶרֶת תַּחְתֶּיהָ, אַף בְּתוּלִים שֶׁל פָּחוֹת מִכֵּן — חוֹזְרִין אֲחֵרִים תַּחְתֵּיהֶם. וְקָטָן שֶׁבָּא עַל הַגְּדוֹלָה. מוּכַּת עֵץ הִיא זוֹ, וּכְתוּבָּתָהּ מָאתַיִם, דִּבְרֵי רַבִּי מֵאִיר. וַחֲכָמִים אוֹמְרִים: כָּל מוּכַּת עֵץ כְּתוּבָּתָהּ מָנֶה. וְהָא נַמִי, דְּקָא מְשַׁוֵּית לָהּ מוּכַּת עֵץ — כְּתוּבָּתָהּ מָנֶה. כְּשֶׁהִכִּיר בָּהּ. כְּשֶׁכְּנָסָהּ וְכָתַב לָהּ כְּתוּבָּה, הָיָה יוֹדֵעַ שֶׁהִיא מוּכַּת עֵץ. מְדַמֵּי לָהּ לְבוֹגֶרֶת. דְּקַיְימָא לָן שֶׁכָּלוּ בְּתוּלֶיהָ, בְּמַסֶּ׳ יְבָמוֹת (דף נט.), דְּקָתָנֵי: "בִּבְתוּלֶיהָ" — פְּרָט לְבוֹגֶרֶת שֶׁכָּלוּ בְּתוּלֶיהָ, וַאֲפִי׳ הָכִי — כְּתוּבָּתָהּ מָאתַיִם. וְלֹא כְלוּם. דְּמִקַּח טָעוּת הוּא, וַאֲפִי׳ מָנֶה אֵין לָהּ. הִיא אוֹמֶרֶת מוּכַּת עֵץ אֲנִי. מִשֶּׁנִּתְאָרְסָה הָיְתָה. וְהוּא אוֹמֵר לֹא כִּי אֶלָּא דְּרוּסַת אִישׁ אַתְּ. הַנּוֹשֵׂא אֶת הָאִשָּׁה בְּחֶזְקַת בְּתוּלָה וְלֹא מָצָא לָהּ בְּתוּלִים, הִיא אוֹמֶרֶת מוּכַּת עֵץ אֲנִי כו׳. ש״מ אִית לָהּ כְּתוּבָּה, אוֹ מָנֶה אוֹ מָאתַיִם, דְּאִי לֵית לָהּ — מַאי נֶאֱמֶנֶת דְּקָאָמַר רַבָּן גַּמְלִיאֵל? אַלְמָא: מוּכַּת עֵץ שֶׁלֹּא הִכִּיר בָּהּ — יֵשׁ לָהּ כְּתוּבָּה, תְּיוּבְתָּא דְּרָמִי בַּר חָמָא דְּאָמַר לֹא הִכִּיר בָּהּ דִּבְרֵי הַכֹּל וְלֹא כְלוּם. אֶלָּא אָמַר רָבָא לְר״מ בֵּין הִכִּיר בָּהּ בֵּין לֹא הִכִּיר בָּהּ מָאתַיִם. וּמַתְנִי׳ דְּקָתָנֵי הִיא אוֹמֶרֶת מוּכַּת עֵץ אֲנִי, וְקָא תָּבְעָה מָאתַיִם — רַבִּי מֵאִיר הִיא. לְרַבָּנַן הִכִּיר בָּהּ מָנֶה. וּמַתְנִי׳ דְּהָכָא דְּקָתָנֵי: וַחֲכָמִים אוֹמְרִים מוּכַּת עֵץ מָנֶה — כְּשֶׁהִכִּיר בָּהּ. לֹא הִכִּיר בָּהּ וְלֹא כְלוּם. וְהָא לָא מָצֵינוּ לְמֵימַר: לְר׳ מֵאִיר הִכִּיר בָּהּ מָאתַיִם, לֹא הִכִּיר בָּהּ — מָנֶה. דְּאִי בְּמִקַּח טָעוּת מַחְזְקִינַן לֵיהּ מִשּׁוּם דְּלֹא הִכִּיר בָּהּ — לֵית לָהּ מִידֵי. וְאִי לָאו מִקַּח טָעוּת הוּא — אֵין חִילּוּק בֵּין הִכִּיר לְלֹא הִכִּיר. וַהֲדַר בֵּיהּ רָבָא גְּרַ׳. וְל״ג מֵהַהִיא. וַהֲדַר בֵּיהּ רָבָא מִמַּאי דַּאֲמַר לְרַבָּנַן לֹא הִכִּיר בָּהּ וְלֹא כְלוּם, אֶלָּא: בֵּין הִכִּיר בֵּין לֹא הִכִּיר — יֵשׁ לָהּ מָנֶה לְרַבָּנַן, וּמָאתַיִם לְר״מ. וּמַתְנִי׳ דְּהָתָם — דִּבְרֵי הַכֹּל. הוֹצָאַת שֵׁם רַע. לְיַעֲנֵשׁ מֵאָה כֶּסֶף אִם שִׁקֵּר, וְלִיסָּקֵל אִם אֱמֶת הָיָה. בָּא לְבֵ״ד. זָקוּק לָבוֹא לְבֵ״ד וְאוֹמֵר כו׳. וַאֲמַר רַב חִיָּיא גָּרְסִי׳. וּמוֹתִיב רַב נַחְמָן גְּרַ׳. נִסְתַּחֲפָה שָׂדֵהוּ. מַזָּלֵךְ גָּרַם, כְּאָדָם שֶׁהַמָּטָר בָּא וְסוֹחֵף אֶת זְרִיעָתוֹ וְעוֹקְרָהּ. מִקַּח טָעוּת לְגַמְרֵי מַשְׁמַע. וְאֵין לָהּ כְּלוּם. כִּי אָמְרָהּ רַב שֵׁשֶׁת לְהָא שְׁמַעְתָּא. לְהַאי זֹאת אוֹמֶרֶת דִּלְעֵיל, דְּיֵשׁ לָהּ כְּתוּבָּה מָנֶה. וְקַשְׁיָא לְהוּ. הָא דְּאוֹתְבִינַן. וַאֲמַר רָבָא גָּרְסִי׳. וְאֶלָּא קַשְׁיָא הַךְ. וְאַקְשִׁינַן לְרָבָא, אֶלָּא קַשְׁיָא הַךְ דִּלְעֵיל דְּקָתָנֵי זִינְּתָה מֵעִיקָּרָא יֵשׁ לָהּ כְּתוּבָּה מָנֶה. תְּרֵיץ. לְהַהִיא דִּלְעֵיל דְּכֵילַד הוֹצָאַת ש״ר, תֵּירוּצָא דְּתָרְלַתְּ לָהּ לָא תְּתָרְצָהּ הָכִי, אֶלָּא הָכִי: אִם יֵשׁ עֵדִים כו׳. נִמְצֵאת. לֹא הִכִּיר בָּהּ מַשְׁמַע. וְקָא מְתָרֵץ רָבָא: יֵשׁ לָהּ כְּתוּבָּה מָנֶה, אַלְמָא הֲדַר בֵּיהּ מֵהַהִיא דִּלְעֵיל, דְּהָא אִיהוּ אֲמַר: לְרַבָּנַן וְלֹא כְלוּם. וּכְרַבִּי מֵאִיר נַמִי לָא תּוֹקְמָהּ, דְּהָא רַבִּי מֵאִיר מָאתַיִם קָאָמַר. וְיֵשׁ לָהּ עֵדִים שֶׁלֹּא נִסְתְּרָה. רְבוּתָא אַשְׁמְעִינַן, דַּאֲפִי׳ הָכִי אֵין הַשֵּׁנִי יָכוֹל לִטְעוֹן טַעֲנַת בְּתוּלִים לְהַפְסִידָהּ כְּתוּבָּתָהּ, וְלֵימָא מִקַּח טָעוּת הוּא. שֶׁהֲרֵי כְּנָסָהּ רִאשׁוֹן. וְעָלָיו לָדַעַת שֶׁנִּבְעֲלָה.

זאת

תוספות רי״ד

איתמר קטן שבא על הגדולה רב אמר עשאה מוכת עץ. פי׳ דכיון שהוציא בתוליה אע״ג שאין ביאתו ביאה לא גרע מעץ הנתקע וכתובתה מנה לרבנן ושמואל אמר אין מוכת עץ בבשר פי׳ בבשר אדם. ואי בעולה לא הויא מוכת עץ נמי לא הויא והרי היא כאילו מיעכה היא באצבעה שהממעכת בתוליה באצבעה לא הפסידה מאתים דדוקא דרוסת איש ומוכת עץ לרבנן הפסידה המאתים אבל במיעוך לא הפסידה המאתים כיון שאין כוונתה אלא שלא להצטער תחת בעלה ובמוכת עץ דפליגי רבנן משום דהוי שלא לדעתה ומיסניא בהכי. אמרי׳ בפ׳ ד׳ אחין כל הני מיעכות של בית ר׳ תמר שמן וקי״ל כשמואל בדיני: אמר רמב״ח מחלוקת כשהכיר בה. פי׳ כשכונסה וכתב לה כתובה היה יודע שהיא מוכת עץ דר״מ מדמי לה לבוגרת פי׳ דקי״ל דכלו בתוליה ואפ״ה כתובתן מאתים ורבנן מדמו לה לבעולה ור״מ אדמדמי לה לבוגרת לדמו לה לבעולה בעולה איתעביד בה מעשה (בוגרת) [בידי אדם הא] לא איתעביד בה מעשה ורבנן אדמדמו לה לבעולה לדמו לה לבוגרת בוגרת לא איתעביד בה מעשה כלל הא איתעביד בה מעשה. אבל לא הכיר בה ד״ה ולא כלום פי׳ שמקח טעות הוא. ורבא אסיק דבין הכיר בה ובין לא הכיר בה לר״מ כתובתה מאתים לרבנן כתובתה מנה. וקי״ל כרבנן ולא כר״מ דיחיד ורבים הלכה כרבים: **מתני׳** בתולה אלמנה גרושה וחלוצה מן הנשואין כתובתן מנה ואין להן טענת בתולים. הגיורת והשבויה והשפחה שנפדו ושנתגיירו ושנשתחררו יתירות על ג׳ שנים ויום א׳ כתובתן מנה ואין להן טענת בתולים. פי׳ בתולה מן הנשואין וכגון שנכנסה לחופה ומת בעלה בחזקת בעולה קיימא משעה שנכנסה תחתיו וכתובתה מנה אם נשאת לאחר סתם ואין להם טענת בתולים להפסידה אותה מנה ולומר בחזקת בתולה נשאתיך והרי מקחי מקח טעות: תנו רבנן כנסה הראשון לשום נשואין ויש לה עדים שלא נסתרה או שנסתרה אלא שלא שהתה עמו כדי ביאה אין השני יכול לטעון טענת בתולים פי׳ להפסידה מנה הראוי לאלמנה מן הנשואין שהרי כנסה הראשון. ואע״פ שהעדים מעידין אינו יכול לטעון.

אמר

מסורת הש״ס

[נדה מד:]

[לקמן יג.]

לקמן יג. [טז.]

לקמן מו.

[לקמן יג.]

[לקמן יב: טז.]

גליון הש״ס

גמ׳ ואמר רבא מאן דקא מותיב שפיר. שבת קכג ע״א ר״ה ו ע״ב:

אָמַר רַבָּה: זֹאת אוֹמֶרֶת; כְּנָסָהּ בְּחֶזְקַת בְּתוּלָה וְנִמְצֵאת בְּעוּלָה יֵשׁ לָהּ כְּתוּבָּה מָנֶה. רַב אַשִׁי אָמַר: בְּעָלְמָא לְעוֹלָם אֵימָא לָךְ – לֵית לָהּ כְּלָל, וְשָׁאנֵי הָכָא – שֶׁהֲרֵי כְּנָסָהּ רִאשׁוֹן. וְנֵיחוּשׁ שֶׁמָּא תַּחְתָּיו זִינְּתָה! אָמַר רַב שֵׁרֵבְיָא: כְּגוֹן שֶׁקִּידֵּשׁ וּבָעַל לְאַלְתַּר. וְאִיכָּא דְּמַתְנֵי לָהּ אַמַּתְנִיתִין: בְּתוּלָה אַלְמָנָה, גְּרוּשָׁה, חֲלוּצָה, מִן הַנִּישּׂוּאִין – כְּתוּבָּתָן מָנֶה, וְאֵין לָהֶן טַעֲנַת בְּתוּלִין. בְּתוּלָה מִן הַנִּישּׂוּאִין הֵיכִי מַשְׁכַּחַתְּ לָהּ? כְּגוֹן שֶׁנִּכְנְסָה לַחוּפָּה וְלֹא נִבְעֲלָה. אָמַר רַבָּה: זֹאת אוֹמֶרֶת, כְּנָסָהּ בְּחֶזְקַת בְּתוּלָה וְנִמְצֵאת בְּעוּלָה – כְּתוּבָּתָהּ מָנֶה. רַב אַשִׁי אָמַר: לְעוֹלָם אֵימָא לָךְ בְּעָלְמָא לֵית לָהּ כְּלָל, וְשָׁאנֵי הָכָא שֶׁהֲרֵי נִכְנְסָה לַחוּפָּה. וְלֵיחוּשׁ שֶׁמָּא תַּחְתָּיו זִינְּתָה! אָמַר רַב שֵׁרֵבְיָא: כְּגוֹן שֶׁקִּידֵּשׁ וּבָעַל לְאַלְתַּר. מַאן דְּמַתְנֵי לָהּ אַבָּרַיְיתָא – כָּל שֶׁכֵּן אַמַּתְנִיתִין, וּמַאן דְּמַתְנֵי לָהּ אַמַּתְנִי' – אֲבָל אַבָּרַיְיתָא לָא, מִשּׁוּם דְּמָצֵי אָמַר לָהּ: אֲנָא אַעֵדִים סָמְכִי.§

מתני' *[א]הָאוֹכֵל אֵצֶל חָמִיו בִּיהוּדָה שֶׁלֹּא בְּעֵדִים – אֵינוֹ יָכוֹל לִטְעוֹן טַעֲנַת בְּתוּלִים, מִפְּנֵי שֶׁמִּתְיַיחֵד עִמָּהּ.§ **גמ'** מִדְּקָתָנֵי "הָאוֹכֵל" מִכְּלָל דְּאִיכָּא דּוּכְתָּא בִּיהוּדָה נַמִי דְּלָא אָכֵיל! אָמַר אַבַּיֵי: ש"מ בִּיהוּדָה נַמִי מְקוֹמוֹת מְקוֹמוֹת יֵשׁ. כִּדְתַנְיָא, א"ר יְהוּדָה: *בִּיהוּדָה, בָּרִאשׁוֹנָה הָיוּ מְיַיחֲדִין אֶת הֶחָתָן וְאֶת הַכַּלָּה שָׁעָה אַחַת קוֹדֶם כְּנִיסָתָן לַחוּפָּה, כְּדֵי שֶׁיְּהֵא לִבּוֹ גַּס בָּהּ. וּבַגָּלִיל לֹא הָיוּ עוֹשִׂין כֵּן. בִּיהוּדָה, בָּרִאשׁוֹנָה הָיוּ מַעֲמִידִין לָהֶם שְׁנֵי שׁוֹשְׁבִינִין, אֶחָד לוֹ וְאֶחָד לָהּ, כְּדֵי לְמַשְׁמֵשׁ אֶת הֶחָתָן וְאֶת הַכַּלָּה בִּשְׁעַת כְּנִיסָתָן לַחוּפָּה, וּבַגָּלִיל לֹא הָיוּ עוֹשִׂין כֵּן. בִּיהוּדָה, בָּרִאשׁוֹנָה הָיוּ שׁוֹשְׁבִינִין יְשֵׁנִים בַּבַּיִת שֶׁחָתָן וְכַלָּה יְשֵׁנִים בָּהּ, וּבַגָּלִיל לֹא הָיוּ עוֹשִׂין כֵּן. וְכָל שֶׁלֹּא נָהַג כַּמִּנְהָג הַזֶּה אֵינוֹ יָכוֹל לִטְעוֹן טַעֲנַת בְּתוּלִים. אַהַיָּיא? אִילֵימָא אַרֵישָׁא – "כָּל שֶׁנָּהַג" מִיבָּעֵי לֵיהּ! אֶלָּא אַסֵּיפָא – "כָּל שֶׁלֹּא מוּשְׁמַשׁ" מִיבָּעֵי לֵיהּ! אֲמַר אַבַּיֵי: לְעוֹלָם אַרֵישָׁא, וּתְנֵי: "כָּל שֶׁנָּהַג". אֲמַר לֵיהּ רָבָא: וְהָא "כָּל שֶׁלֹּא נָהַג" קָתָנֵי! אֶלָּא אֲמַר רָבָא, הָכִי קָאָמַר: כָּל שֶׁלֹּא נָהַג מִנְהַג גָּלִיל בַּגָּלִיל אֶלָּא מִנְהַג יְהוּדָה בַּגָּלִיל אֵינוֹ יָכוֹל לִטְעוֹן טַעֲנַת בְּתוּלִים. רַב אַשִׁי אָמַר: לְעוֹלָם [ב]אַסֵּיפָא, וּתְנֵי: "כָּל שֶׁלֹּא מוּשְׁמַשׁ".§

מתני' אַחַת אַלְמְנַת יִשְׂרָאֵל וְאַחַת אַלְמְנַת *כֹּהֲנִים כְּתוּבָּתָהּ מָנֶה. בֵּית דִּין שֶׁל כֹּהֲנִים הָיוּ גּוֹבִין לִבְתוּלָה אַרְבַּע מֵאוֹת זוּז, וְלֹא מִיחוּ בְּיָדָם חֲכָמִים.§ **גמ'** תָּנָא: וְאַלְמְנַת כֹּהֲנִים כְּתוּבָּתָהּ מָאתַיִם. וְהָאֲנַן תְּנַן: אַחַת אַלְמְנַת יִשְׂרָאֵל וְאַחַת אַלְמְנַת כֹּהֲנִים כְּתוּבָּתָן מָנֶה! אָמַר רַב אַשִׁי: שְׁתֵּי תַקָּנוֹת הָווּ; מֵעִיקָּרָא תַּקִּינוּ לִבְתוּלָה אַרְבַּע מֵאוֹת זוּז, וּלְאַלְמָנָה מָנֶה.

כֵּיוָן

רש"י

זֹאת אוֹמֶרֶת כו'. דְּהָא וַדַּאי בְּחֶזְקַת בְּתוּלָה כְּנָסָהּ, דְּסָמַךְ אַעֵדִים, וְקָאָמַר אֵין יָכוֹל לְהַפְסִידָהּ מָנֶה הָרָאוּי לְאַלְמָנָה מִן הַנִּישּׂוּאִין. **וְנֵיחוּשׁ שֶׁמָּא תַּחְתָּיו זִינְּתָה.** *אַמַּתְנִיתִין פָּרֵיךְ, דְּקָתָנֵי אֵין הַשֵּׁנִי יָכוֹל לִטְעוֹן טַעֲנַת בְּתוּלִים, וְלָא מַזְקִיקִינַן לֵיהּ לָבֹא לְבֵית דִּין, וְלֹא יִתְבָּרֵר הַדָּבָר אִם תַּחְתָּיו זִינְּתָה אִם לֹא, וְשֶׁמָּא אֲסוּרָה הִיא לוֹ? בִּשְׁלָמָא אַהָךְ דִּלְעֵיל, דַּאֲמַרַן כְּנָסָהּ בְּחֶזְקַת בְּתוּלָה וְנִמְצֵאת בְּעוּלָה יֵשׁ לָהּ כְּתוּבָּה – לָא מַקְשִׁינַן, דְּאִיכָּא לְמֵימַר כְּשֶׁבָּא לְבֵית דִּין וּבָאוּ עֵדִים שֶׁזִּינְּתָה קוֹדֶם לָכֵן. אֲבָל הָכָא קָתָנֵי: אֵין יָכוֹל לִטְעוֹן – מִתּוֹךְ כָּךְ לֹא יָבֹא לְבֵ"ד. **כְּשֶׁקִּידֵּשׁ וּבָעַל לְאַלְתַּר** גָּרְסִינַן, וְלָא גָּרְסִינַן כְּשֶׁקִּידֵּשׁ לְאַלְתַּר וּבָעַל לְאַלְתַּר – שֶׁלֹּא פֵּירַשׁ מִמֶּנָּה בֵּין קִידּוּשִׁין לִבְעִילָה, דְּוַדַּאי לֹא תַּחְתָּיו זִינְּתָה. **וְאִיכָּא דְּמַתְנֵי לָהּ.** לְהָא דְּרַבָּה וְרַב אַשִׁי וְרַב שֵׁרֵבְיָא אַמַּתְנִי'. **זֹאת אוֹמֶרֶת.** מִדְּקָתָנֵי מַתְנִי' אֵין לָהֶן טַעֲנַת בְּתוּלִים. **וְלֵיחוּשׁ שֶׁמָּא תַּחְתָּיו זִינְּתָה.** וְאַמַּאי תָּנֵי אֵין לָהֶן טַעֲנַת בְּתוּלִים. **מַאן דְּמַתְנֵי לָהּ.** לְהָא דְּרַבָּה וְרַב אַשִׁי אַבָּרַיְיתָא. **כ"ש אַמַּתְנִי'.** דְּכֵיוָן דְּאַבָּרַיְיתָא, אע"ג דְּאָמְרוּ עֵדִים לֹא נִסְתְּרָה לָרִאשׁוֹן, וְשֵׁנִי זֶה בְּחֶזְקַת בְּתוּלָה כְּנָסָהּ, וַאֲפִילּוּ הָכִי אַהֲדַר לֵיהּ רַב אַשִׁי לְרַבָּה: לְעוֹלָם לֹא תִּשְׁמַע כְּנָסָהּ בְּחֶזְקַת בְּתוּלָה וְנִמְצֵאת בְּעוּלָה יֵשׁ לָהּ כְּתוּבָּה, דְּשָׁאנֵי הָכָא שֶׁהֲרֵי כְּנָסָהּ רִאשׁוֹן. כָּל שֶׁכֵּן אַמַּתְנִיתִין, דְּלָא הִבְטִיחוּהוּ עֵדִים עַל כָּךְ, אִיכָּא לְמִתְנְיֵיהּ לִדְרַבָּה, וּמַאי דְּאַהֲדַר לֵיהּ רַב אַשִׁי. **וּמַאן דְּתָנֵי לָהּ.** דְּרַבָּה וְרַב אַשִׁי אַמַּתְנִיתִין. **אֲבָל אַבָּרַיְיתָא לָא.** מַתְנֵי לְהוּ, דְּמִבָּרַיְיתָא וַדַּאי שַׁפִּיר ש"מ זֹאת אוֹמֶרֶת דְּרַבָּה, וַעֲלָהּ לָא הֲוָה לְרַב אַשִׁי לְאַהֲדוּרֵי שָׁאנֵי הָכָא שֶׁהֲרֵי כְּנָסָהּ רִאשׁוֹן – דְּמָצֵי אָמַר: אֲנָא אַעֵדִים סָמֵכִי, וְכֵיוָן דְּקָתָנֵי אֵין הַשֵּׁנִי יָכוֹל לִטְעוֹן טַעֲנַת בְּתוּלִים – שָׁמְעִינַן וַדַּאי דְּזֹאת אוֹמֶרֶת: כְּנָסָהּ בְּחֶזְקַת בְּתוּלָה וְנִמְצֵאת בְּעוּלָה – יֵשׁ לָהּ כְּתוּבָּה. **מְקוֹמוֹת מְקוֹמוֹת יֵשׁ.** שֶׁחֲלוּקִין בְּמִנְהָגָם. וְנָפְקָא מִינָּהּ, דְּהֵיכָא דְּלָא נְהִיגֵי לְיַיחֵד – יָכוֹל לִטְעוֹן. **כִּדְתַנְיָא.** דִּמְקוֹמוֹת מְקוֹמוֹת יֵשׁ. **לְמַשְׁמֵשׁ.** לְפַשְׁפֵּשׁ וּלְמַשְׁמֵשׁ בְּמַעֲשֵׂיהֶן בְּאוֹתוֹ הַלַּיְלָה, שֶׁלֹּא יְקַלְקְלוּ זֶה אֶת זֶה בְּמַעֲשֵׂיהֶם בְּתַרְמִית. שֶׁלֹּא יִרְאֶה זֶה דַּם בְּתוּלִים וִיאַבֵּד, וְזוֹ לֹא תָּבִיא מַפָּה שֶׁיֵּשׁ עָלֶיהָ טִיפֵּי דָמִים. וּבְמָקוֹם שֶׁנָּהֲגוּ לְמַשְׁמֵשׁ לֹא נָהֲגוּ לְיַיחֵד. דְּאִילּוּ בְּמָקוֹם שֶׁנָּהֲגוּ לְיַיחֵד, מַאי מִישְׁמוּשׁ בָּעֵי? הֲרֵי אֵין שָׁם טַעֲנַת בְּתוּלִים. אַלְמָא בִּיהוּדָה מְקוֹמוֹת מְקוֹמוֹת יֵשׁ. **אִילֵימָא אַרֵישָׁא.** אַמִּנְהָג דִּמְיַיחֲדִין. **כָּל שֶׁנָּהַג לְהִתְיַיחֵד מִיבָּעֵי לֵיהּ.** דְּאֵין יָכוֹל לִטְעוֹן. **אֶלָּא אַסֵּיפָא.** אַמִּנְהָג דְּמִשְׁמוּשׁ שׁוּשְׁבִינִין. **כָּל שֶׁלֹּא מוּשְׁמַשׁ מִיבָּעֵי לֵיהּ.** דְּהַטּוֹעֵן טַעֲנַת בְּתוּלִים הוּא הַבַּעַל, וְהוּא אֵינוֹ נוֹהֵג מִישְׁמוּשׁ שֶׁבּוֹ [שֶׁאֵינוֹ תָּלוּי בַּבַּעַל], אֶלָּא עַל אֲבִי הַכַּלָּה לְמַשְׁמְשׁוֹ שֶׁלֹּא יְאַבֵּד אֶת בְּתוּלֶיהָ. וּמִשְׁמוּשׁ בַּכַּלָּה, שֶׁלֹּא תָּבִיא דָּם מִן הַחוּץ – תָּלוּי בַּבַּעַל. וְהֵיכִי תָּנֵי כָּל בַּעַל שֶׁלֹּא נָהַג מִישְׁמוּשׁ אֵינוֹ יָכוֹל לִטְעוֹן טַעֲנַת בְּתוּלִים? כ"ש דְּאִם לֹא נָהַג לְמַשְׁמֵשׁ וְהֵם מִישְׁמְשׁוּ אוֹתוֹ, דְּיָכוֹל לִטְעוֹן! הָכִי אִיבָּעֵי לֵיהּ לְמִתְנֵי: כָּל שֶׁלֹּא מוּשְׁמַשׁ אֵינוֹ יָכוֹל לִטְעוֹן, דְּשֶׁמָּא רָאָה וְאִבֵּד. **אֶלָּא אֲמַר רָבָא.** הַאי כָּל שֶׁלֹּא נָהַג – אַמִּנְהָג דְּגָלִיל קָאֵי, דְּתָנָא בְּבָרַיְיתָא: וּבַגָּלִיל לֹא הָיוּ עוֹשִׂין כֵּן, וַעֲלָהּ קָאֵי: כָּל שֶׁלֹּא נָהַג כַּמִּנְהָג הַזֶּה בַּגָּלִיל, אֶלָּא נִתְיַיחֵד כַּמִּנְהָג שֶׁבִּיהוּדָה – אֵינוֹ יָכוֹל לִטְעוֹן. **מתני' אַלְמְנַת כֹּהֲנִים.** אַלְמָנָה בַּת כֹּהֵן. **הָיוּ גּוֹבִין לִבְתוּלָה.** בַּת כֹּהֵן כְּשֶׁנִּישֵּׂאת לְכֹהֵן, וְכ"ש כְּשֶׁנִּישֵּׂאת לְיִשְׂרָאֵל. **גמ' שְׁתֵּי תַקָּנוֹת הָווּ.** לְאַלְמָנָה בַּת כֹּהֵן.

דִּמְזַלְזְלֵי

תוספות

אמר רבה זאת אומרת. נראה דהכא גרסינן רבה, דהא רבא קאמר לעיל דמקח טעות לגמרי משמע. ואי גרסינן הכא רבא – א"כ תיקשי מתניתין רישא לסיפא, דהא זאת אומרת איכא למידק נמי ממתניתין, כדאמרינן בסמוך. אלא ודאי נראה דהכא גרס רבה. דרבא דאמר לעיל מקח טעות לגמרי משמע, יפרש כמו רב אשי.

כנסה בחזקת בתולה ונמצאת בעולה יש לה מנה. והא דקתני שהרי כנסה ראשון – פירש ריב"ם דהכי משמע ליה: אין לשני טענת בתולין לחסרה מכתובתה כלום, שהרי כנסה ראשון וגרם להיות כתובתה מנה, ואינו יכול לחסרה כלום מאותה מנה, דלא מהניא טענת בתולין אלא ממנה דבתולין. **שאני** הכא שהרי כנסה ראשון. ואדעתא דבעולה נישאת. ואע"ג דעדים מעידים שלא נבעלה – אינו סומך על זה, מאחר שהיו נישואין, וסבר דלשכבה אומרים כן.

וניחוש שמא תחתיו זינתה. אין לומר דפריך אמאי אינו יכול לטעון טענת בתולים לאוסרה עליו, ניחוש באשת כהן שמא תחתיו זינתה, דליכא אלא חדא ספיקא; ספק תחתיו ספק אין תחתיו. דהא מצי לשנויי דהא דאינו יכול לטעון – היינו להפסידה מכתובתה, דאיכא ספק ספיקא: דאפי' תחתיו – אימור באונס הוה. ואין זה דוחק, דלעיל נמי מפרש אינו יכול לטעון טענת בתולים הכי. דקאמר: למאי? אי לאוסרה עליו – ביהודה אמאי לא כו', אלא אכתובה פריך, אמאי אינו מפסיד לה. ונראה לר"י דלרב אשי פריך: כיון דבעלמא אית ליה דאין לה כלום, והכא יש לה לפי שכנסה ראשון – א"כ יבא לידי איסור, שזה האיש סבור כיון שזו יש לה, אע"ג דבעלמא לית לה – אם כן מחזקין אותה ודאי בעולה מבעל ראשון, ואדעת כן רוצים לומר שנשאתי, ובחנם אטרח לבית דין, שודאי לא יאסרוה עלי. ולכך היה לנו להפסיד כתובתה, שיבא לב"ד ולא יטעה לומר שמותרת לו. ואפי' באשת ישראל יש לנו להפסידה, גזירה שיראה כהן שזו לא תאבד כתובתה, ויסבור אף בשלו כן, ולא יבא לב"ד. אבל לרבה לא פריך מידי, כיון דבעלמא נמי יש לה – ליכא למיטעי.

כגון שקידש ובעל לאלתר. וכן צריך נמי להעמיד שהראשון אחר שקידש כנסה לאלתר ומת מיד, ועדים מעידים שלא זינתה תחתיו. דאם נבעלה תחת הראשון – הרי נבעלה לפסול לה, ואסורה לכהונה.*)

שתי תקנות הוו. וליכא למימר דחדא תקנה הואי, ומתני' קודם תקנה וברייתא לאחר תקנה שתיקנו לאלמנה מאתים – דהא חזינן השתא דלית להו מאתים. וליכא למימר נמי דמעיקרא כי תקינו לבתולה ארבע מאות תקינו גם כן לאלמנה מאתים – דאין סברא לתקן לאלמנה מאתים אם לא אחר שראו צורך, [הילכך, מעיקרא לא רצו לשנותה משאר אלמנה, וכיון דחזו דקא מזלזלי בהו – ראו שהיה צורך, תקון להם מאתן. וכיון דחזו דפרשי מינייהו – אהדרינהו למילתייהו]. ולכך הוצרך לומר שתי תקנות הוו.

כיון

נ"ל אברייתא

[לעיל ט:]

[תוספתא פ"א]

[במשנה שבמשניות ליתא כהן]

עין משפט נר מצוה

עד א מיי' פי"א מהל' אישות הלכה ח סמג עשין מח טוש"ע אה"ע סימן סח סעיף ח:

עה ב טוש"ע שם ס"ב:

תוספות רי"ד

אמר רבא זאת אומרת כנסה בחזקת בתולה ונמצאת בעולה יש לה כתובה מנה. פי' כיון שהעדים מבררים ומעידים שלא בא עליה כשכנסה [ראשון] א"כ בחזקת בתולה כונסה וש"מ כנסה בחזקת בתולה ונמצאת בעולה כתובתה מנה. ר"א אמר בעלמא לעולם אימא לך דלית לה מידי ושאני הכא שכבר כנסה הראשון. פי' ואע"פ שמעידים העדים שלאחר שכנסה לא בא עליה יש לומר כיון שנתרצית לו לכונסה מאותה שעה היא נשאת לו. והל' כרב אשי דכנסה בחזקת בתולה ונמצאת בעולה אין לה כלום ורבא נמי הכי אמר לעיל במאי דתנן הנושא את האשה ולא מצא לה בתולים וכו' ואמר רבא מקח טעות לגמרי משמע ולית לה כלל. והכא דקאמר זאת אומרת דיוקא בעלמא סבר לדייק מינה ולמימר דתנא דהאי מתניתא ס"ל הכי וליתא אלא כדתרצה רב אשי. ומקשה וליחוש שמא תחתיו זינתה וא"ר שרביא כגון שקידש ובעל לאלתר. פי' כל היכא דהיא טענה טענת ברי ובעל טוען טענת שמא כגון תחתיך נאנסתי או מוכת עץ אני נאמנת ושקלא כתובה ושריא לבעלה כדלקמן ואפילו ר' יהושע דאמר לקמן בראוה מדברת חיישינן שמא נבעלה לנתין ולממזר דוקא להנשא לכהונה אבל לאוסרה על בעלה בייחוד בעלמא הא אמרי' לקמן דמודה ר"י דלא אסרה לה אפי' אם הוא כהן וה"נ אילו טענה האשה ואמרה שבעלי בא עלי קודם נשואין לא הוה מקשי' וליחוש שמא תחתיו זינתה דהיא נאמנת אלא התנא לא שנה טענת האשה אלמא לא טענה הכי ואפ"ה אומר' לו ב"ד שאינך יכול לטעון טענת בתולים שמא בא עליה קודם נשואין משעה ששניהם נאותו לכנוס ואע"פ שהאשה אינה יודעת לטעון. י"ל שלמפרע היה מערה בה והוציא בתוליה ולא הרגישה שלא עלו במטה כדרך חתן וכלה אלא עד אז היה מערה בה ולא שתה לבה ולא ידעה ומ"ה פריך וליחוש שמא תחתיו זינתה דהניחא שלא להפסידה כתובתה אמרי' שמא בעלה בא עליה ולא תפסיד כתובה מספק אבל מספקא תאסר עליו כיון שעדים מעידים שלאחר שכנסה לא בא עליה והיא נמי לא טענה טענה ודאית תאסר עליו מספק שמא תחתיו זינתה ולהכי איצטריך רב שרביא לומר שקידש ובעל לאלתר שיצאנו מזה הספק ויש כאן ספק שמא בעולה היתה מקודם לכן והרי מקחו מקח טעות בזה הספק אנו תולין כי בעלה בא עליה ואין כאן מקח טעות א) פי' המורה וניחוש שמא תחתיו זינתה אמתניתין פריך דקתני אין השני יכול לטעון טענת בתולים ולא מזקיקין ליה לבוא לב"ד ולא מתברר אם זינתה תחתיו אם לאו ושמא אסורה לו דבשלמא אהך דלעיל דאמרת כנסה בחזקת בתולה ונמצאת בעולה יש לה כתובה מנה לא מקשי' דא"ל כשבא לב"ד באו עדים שזינתה קודם לכן אבל הכא קתני אין יכול לטעון מתוך כך לא יבא לב"ד אמר רב שרביא כשקידש ובעל לאלתר. פי' שלא פירשה ממנו בין קידושין לבעילה דודאי לא ניחוש לזינתה: **מתני'** האוכל אצל חמיו ביהודה שלא בעדים אינו יכול לטעון טענת בתולים מפני שמתיחד עמה. אחד אלמנת ישראל ואחד אלמנת כהנים כתובתן מנה ב"ד של כהנים היה גובין לבתולה ד' מאות זוז ולא מיחו בידם חכמים: תניא א"ר יהודה בראשונה ביהודה (היה) [היו] מיחדים את החתן ואת הכלה שעה אחת קודם כניסתן לחופה כדי שיהיה לבו גס בה ובגליל לא היו עושים כן. ביהודה בראשונה (היה) [היו] מעמידים להם שני שושבינים אחד לו ואחד לה כדי למשמש את החתן ואת הכלה בשעת כניסתן לחופה פי' למשמש ולפשפש באותו הלילה במעשיהן שלא יקלקלו זה על זה שלא יראה זה דם בתולים ויאבד וזו תביא מפה שיש עלי' טפת דם ובגליל לא היו עושין כן. פי' גם ביהודה הי' מקומות שלא היו מיחדין. ושם היו מעמידים שושבינין דאי במקום שהיו מייחדים לא יועילו שושבינין שהרי אין שם טענת בתולים. ביהודה בראשונה היו שושבינים ישינים בבית שחתן וכלה ישינים בו ובגליל לא היו עושים כן. וכל שלא נהג כמנהג זה אינו יכול לטעון טענות בתולים. שהרי נתיחד עמה. אבל נהג מנהג גליל ולא נתייחד יכול לטעון ואע"פ שלא היו שם שושבינים יכול לטעון ומהימן ורב אשי פי' כל שלא משמש ביהודה אינו יכול לטעון פי' כיון שביהודה ממשמשים והוא לא משמש אמרי' לכתחלה עשה כדי להעליל עלילה עלי' אבל בגליל שלא נהגו מצי טעין אע"פ שלא משמש. ושמואל דאמר נאמן להפסידה כתובתה בטענת פתח פתוח דליכא למיקם עלה דמלתא להתברר ע"י שושבינים. וכגון שהיתה בוגרת שכלו בתוליה או אם היתה ממשפחת דורקטי אבל בטענות דמים אם נהגו למשמש ולא משמש אינו נאמן ובמקום שלא נהגו למשמש נאמן:

ב"ד

א) נ"ל והמורה פירש. ור"ל לרשי ז"ל פירש.

---

*) [רב אשי אומר תני כל שלא מושמש. אומר רבינו יצחק בן רבינו מאיר דרב אשי פליג ארב נחמן דלית לי' חזקה דאין אדם טורח כו' כדפי' לעיל. ור"ת אומר דלא פליג דדוקא ביהודה שנהגו למשמש ואירע שלא משמש אינו יכול לטעון דדומה לדבר שהוא כרמאות גילגל שלא מישמשוהו וכן משמע קצת דהא קתני ביהודה אינו יכול לטעון הא בגליל מצי טעין כדדייק לעיל אע"ג דבגליל לא היו ממשמשין כדקתני בברייתא ומיהו יש לפרש הא בגליל מצי טעין היינו אם אירע שמישמשוהו וע"כ צריך לפרש כן למאי דדחי לעיל לא דקא טעין טענת דמים ולא אמרי' חזקה דאין אדם טורח כו':]

עין משפט
נר מצוה

עו א טוש"ע אה"ע סי' סו סעיף ז:
עז ב מיי' פי"א מהל' אישות הל' יא סמג עשין מח טוש"ע שם סי' סח סעיף ט:
עח ג מיי' פ"א מהל' טוען ונטען הל' ט סמג עשין לה טוש"ע ח"מ סימן עה סעיף ט:

כיון דחזו דמזלזלי בהו – תקינו להו מאתן. כיון דחזו דקא פרשין מינייהו, דאמרי: עד דנסבינן אלמנת כהנים – ניזיל ניסיב בתולה בת ישראל, אהדרינהו למלתייהו.§ בית דין של כהנים כו'.§ אמר רב יהודה אמר שמואל: *לא ב"ד של כהנים בלבד אמרו, אלא אפי' משפחות המיוחסות בישראל, אם רצו לעשות כדרך שהכהנים עושין – עושין. מיתיבי: הרוצה לעשות כדרך שהכהנים עושין, כגון בת ישראל לכהן ובת כהן לישראל – עושין. בת ישראל לכהן, ובת כהן לישראל הוא דאיכא צד כהונה, אבל בת ישראל לישראל – לא! לא מבעיא קאמר; לא מבעיא בת ישראל לישראל, דלא מצי אמר לה עלויי קא מעלינן ליך, אבל בת ישראל לכהן, דמצי אמר לה עלויי קא מעלינן ליך, אימא לא, קמ"ל.§ **מתני'** *הנושא את האשה ולא מצא לה בתולים, היא אומרת: משארסתני נאנסתי, ונסתחפה שדהו. והוא אומר: לא כי, אלא עד שלא ארסתיך, והיה מקחי מקח טעות. *רבן גמליאל ורבי אליעזר אומרים: נאמנת. *רבי יהושע אומר: לא מפיה אנו חיין, אלא הרי זו בחזקת בעולה עד שלא תתארס והטעתו, עד שתביא ראיה לדבריה.§ **גמ'** *איתמר, "מנה לי בידך" והלה אומר "איני יודע". רב יהודה ורב הונא אמרי: חייב, ורב נחמן ורבי יוחנן אמרי: פטור. רב הונא ורב יהודה אמרי: חייב, ברי ושמא – ברי עדיף. רב נחמן ורבי יוחנן אמרי: פטור, *אוקי ממונא בחזקת מריה. א"ל אביי לרב יוסף: הא דרב הונא ורב יהודה – *דשמואל היא. דתנן: *היתה מעוברת, ואמרו לה: מה טיבו של עובר זה? מאיש פלוני, וכהן הוא. רבן גמליאל ורבי אליעזר אומרים: נאמנת. *ואמר רב יהודה אמר שמואל: הלכה כרבן גמליאל. ואמר ליה רב שמואל בר יהודה לרב יהודה: *שיננא, אמרת לן משמיה דשמואל הלכה כרבן גמליאל אף בראשונה. מאי "אף בראשונה"? אע"ג דאיכא למימר אוקי ממונא בחזקת מריה – אמר רבן גמליאל ברי עדיף. לימא רב יהודה ורב הונא דאמרי כר"ג, ורב נחמן ורבי יוחנן דאמרי כרבי יהושע? אמר לך רב נחמן: אנא דאמרי אפילו כרבן גמליאל; עד כאן לא קאמר ר"ג התם אלא דאיכא מגו, אבל הכא – מאי מגו איכא? אי נמי, עד כאן לא קאמר רבן גמליאל התם אלא דאמרינן אוקמה אחזקה, אבל הכא – מאי חזקה אית ליה להאי? הכי נמי מסתברא כדקא משנינן, דרב נחמן הוא דאמר כר"ג.
דאם

רש"י

דמזלזלי בהו. באלמנות, קלות בעיניהם להוציאן מפני שכתובתן מועטת, תקינו להו מאתן, דגנאי היה להן. ואע"פ שאלמנות ישראל נמי כתובתן מנה, מיהו כהנים חשידי טפי, וגנאי להם גירושי בנותיהן יותר מישראל. **מתני'** נאמנת. קא סלקא דעתך משום דברי ושמא ברי עדיף. הרי זו בחזקת. שנבעלה עד שלא תתארס, והטעתו. **גמ'** חייב. לשלם. פטור. מלשלם. ומכל מקום משביעין ליה שבועת היסת שכן הוא כדבריו, שאינו יודע שהוא חייב לו. וכהן הוא. כלומר מיוחס הוא. אף בראשונה. גבי תביעת כתובה. [אוקי כתובה אחזקתה. אחזקת הבעל. ה"נ גבי מנה לי בידך, איכא למימר נמי: אוקי ממונא בחזקת מריה, ופטור. אלא דאיכא מגו]. כגון "משארסתני נאנסתי", וכגון היא אומרת "מוכת עץ אני", דאמרינן מגו דאי בעיא טענה טענה מעלייתא מהך, כגון גבי "משארסתני נאנסתי" הוה טענה "מוכת עץ אני" [טענה מעלייתא], דלא פסלה נפשה מכהונה. וקאמרה "נאנסתי [משארסתני]", וקא מיפסלה נפשה, דאשת ישראל שנאנסה אסורה לכהן – ש"מ קושטא קאמרה. וגבי היא אומרת "מוכת עץ אני", אי בעיא אמרה "מוכת עץ אני תחתיך" ואית לה מאתן, וקא אמרה "מוכת עץ אני קודם לכן, ואין לי אלא מנה". אבל הכא. גבי האי תובע, מאי מגו איכא להימניה? הלכך אוקי ממונא בחזקת מריה. אוקמה אחזקה. מספקא לן שעת ארוסין, אי בתולה הואי ונשתעבד לה למאתים, אי בעולה הואי – העמד אשה על חזקתה ובתולה נולדה, והך השתא הוא דאיתניסה אחר אירוסין. מאי חזקה אית ליה להאי. תובע, דנוקמיה אחזקיה לגבות? הלכך זיל בתר חזקה דממונא. דא"כ

תוספות

כיון דחזו דמזלזלי בהו. פירש בקונטרס: שהיו קלות בעיניהן להוציאן, לפי שהיתה כתובתן מועטת. וקשה: דמעיקרא נמי הוו ידעי שקלות בעיניהן להוציאן כיון דמנה חשיב דבר מועט! ונראה לר"י לפרש: דמזלזלי בהו – שמקלת בני אדם היו נמנעים מלנושאם, לפי שהיו קלות בעיניהן, שאין לה כתובה אלא רביע ממה שיש לה לבתולה, ותקינו לה מאתן. כיון דחזו דפרשי מינייהו לגמרי, והיו קופצים קודם על בתולות ישראל, ולא היה שום אדם קופץ עליהם – אהדרינהו למילתייהו. היינו דנקט מעיקרא מזלזלי, שהיו נמנעים ולא לגמרי פורשים, ובתר הכי נקט "ופרשי". *בית דין של כהנים היו גובין כו' ולא מיחו בידם חכמים. אע"פ שלא כתב בלשון תוספת, אלא ארבע מאות דחזו ליכי. וקא ס"ד דלא תגבה, דלא חזו, ובלשון תוספת לא כתב – קא משמע לן דמנהג טוב מאד הוא, וראוי להיות בכהונה ובמשפחות המיוחסות. ושייך בהו למימר דחזו ליכי, ואפי' לא כתב לה כתובה – גובה ארבע מאות בתנאי ב"ד, כמו בבנות ישראל מאתים, דתקנה גמורה היא. **והוא** אומר לא כי כו'. אע"ג דבסוף "המניח" (ב"ק דף לה: ושם) דייק מדקתני "לא כי" דמיירי בברי, הכא דליכא למיטעי – קתני "לא כי" אע"ג דאיירי בשמא. **מנה** לי בידך והלה אומר איני יודע. פי': איני יודע אם הלויתני מעולם. אבל הלויתני ואיני יודע אם פרעתיך – תנן בהדיא ב"הגוזל בתרא" (שם קיח.) דחייב. **רב** הונא ורב יהודה אמרי חייב. לכאורה נראה דלית להו דרבי אבא דאמר: מתוך שאינו יכול לישבע משלם. דטעמיה דר' אבא משום דדריש (שבועות ד' מז.) "שבועת ה' תהיה בין שניהם" – ולא בין שני היורשין. כגון, אמר מנה לאבא ביד אביך, ואמר: חמשין ידענא, וחמשין לא ידענא. ואבוה כה"ג, מתוך שאין יכול לישבע – משלם. ואי מנה לי בידך והלה אומר איני יודע חייב – אין כאן שבועה, דאפי' הוא אומר אין יודע בכל – חייב. ותימה: דבפרק "יש נוחלין" (ב"ב דף קלה. ושם) גבי האומר זה אחי, משמע דאביי אית ליה מנה לי בידך והלה אומר איני יודע חייב. ובפ' "חזקת הבתים" (שם לד. ושם) משמע דאית ליה לדר' אבא! וי"ל: דאפי' למ"ד חייב, איכא למידרש "שבועת ה' תהיה בין שניהם" – ולא בין היורשין, דשניהם לא ידעי, אלא שעד אחד מעיד שאחד חייב לחבירו מנה. דבאבוה, מתוך שאינו יכול לישבע – משלם. תימה: דרב יהודה גופיה אית ליה בריש "הפרה" (ב"ק מו. ושם) אפילו ניזק אומר ברי ומזיק אומר שמא – המע"ה! ואין לומר דרב יהודה כסומכוס דאמר: ממון המוטל בספק חולקין, ולא אזיל בתר חזקת ממון, ולהכי כי איכא ברי ושמא – נוטל הכל, והתם דקאמר אמר רב יהודה אמר שמואל: זו דברי סומכוס, אבל חכמים אומרים: זה כלל גדול בדין כו' – אליבא דרבנן קאמר, וליה לא סבירא ליה. דהתם (בב"ב דף לב:) משמע דסבר כרבנן, גבי מוכר שור לחבירו ונמצא נגחן. ועוד, דתנן בפרק "השואל" (ב"מ לז. ושם): המשאיל אומר שאולה מתה והלה אומר איני יודע – חייב. וקאמר בגמרא: לימא תיהוי תיובתא דרב נחמן ור' יוחנן. ומאי קושיא? הא ע"כ מתני' כסומכוס אפי' לרב יהודה, דלרבנן מודה רב יהודה דפטור, ורב נחמן ורבי יוחנן ע"כ כרבנן, דלסומכוס לכל הפחות חולקין! אבל אי פליגי אליבא דרבנן, ולסומכוס לעולם חולקין, אפי' בברי ושמא – פריך שפיר ממתני', דכרבנן אתיא, דלסומכוס חולקין! וי"ל: דהתם ברי גרוע ושמא טוב, דלפי שהמזיק לא היה שם טוען זה ברי, ושמא דמזיק טוב – דלא הוה ליה למידע. אבל מנה לי בידך – הברי טוב והשמא גרוע, דהוה ליה לידע אם חייב אם לאו. אבל קשה: דבעי למימר הכא הא דרב יהודה דשמואל היא, דפסק כרבן גמליאל, והתם ברי גרוע ושמא טוב, שהבעל אינו יודע מתי נבעלה, ואם כן תיקשי דשמואל אדשמואל דפ' "הפרה" (ב"ק מו. ושם)! ויש לומר: דה"מ למימר וליטעמיך. ועוד יש לומר: דסוגיא דהכא סברה דזה כלל גדול בדין – לא לניזק אומר ברי ומזיק אומר שמא, אלא כדקאמר התם: אי נמי לכי הא. וקשה על זה דאפילו לפי אי נמי דהתם לא אתי שפיר, דהא בסוף "המניח" (שם דף לה: ושם) אית להו לרבנן בהדיא, דאפי' ניזק אומר ברי כו', ושמואל סובר כרבנן כדמוכח ב"המוכר שור לחברו"! **אלא** דאיכא מגו. האי שנויא לא אתיא אלא לרב נחמן, דלר' יוחנן בההיא דמוכת עץ ליכא מגו, כדמוכח לקמן. הקשה ה"ר יעקב מקורבי"ל: אכתי, ע"כ הא דרב יהודה דשמואל היא, דאי לשמואל פטור – תקשי ליה ממתניתין ד"השואל" (ב"מ ד' לז. ושם:): המשאיל אומר שאולה מתה, והלה אומר איני יודע – חייב, דלשמואל ליכא לשנויי כדמשני לרב נחמן ולרבי יוחנן כגון שיש עסק שבועה ביניהן, ומתוך שאינו יכול לישבע משלם, דשמואל אית ליה בהדיא בפ' "כל הנשבעין" (שבועות ד' מז. ושם) דחזרה שבועה לסיני, ולא משלם! וי"ל: דאיכא למימר דלעולם מנה לי בידך והלה אומר איני יודע – לשמואל פטור, ומוקי שמואל מתני' ד"השואל" כשיש עסק שבועה, וכההוא תנא דאית ליה מתוך שאינו יכול לישבע משלם, והוא סבר כאידך תנא, דפלוגתא דתנאי היא בפרק "כל הנשבעין" (שם). [ועי' ביתר ביאור תוס' ב"מ לז: סד"ה רב הונא].
רב

גליון הש"ס

גמ' הא דרב הונא ור"י דשמואל היא. עיין יבמות יח ע"ב תד"ה לאי לרב.

מסורת הש"ס

[ג"י כ"]
[לקמן לו.]
לקמן עה:
ב"ק קיח. בבא מציעא לז: ודף קטז: [ע' ב"ב קלה.]
[קדושין מה: וש"נ]
[עיין תוס' יבמות יח: ד"ה לאי לרב מאי]
[לקמן יג.]
לקמן יד.
[כתובות ט. וש"נ ועי' ע"ש חגיגה טו: פירוש על שיננא]

תוספות רי"ד

ב"ד של כהנים וכו'. אמר רב יהודה לא ב"ד של כהנים בלבד אמרו אלא אפילו משפחות המיוחסות שבישראל אם רצו לעשות כדרך שהכהנים עושין עושין ולא אמרי' דמחזי כעוקרים תיקון חכמים: **מתני'** הנושא את האשה ולא מצא לה בתולים היא אומרת משארסתני נאנסתי ונסתחפה שדך והוא אומר לא כי אלא עד שלא ארסתיך והיה מקחי מקח טעות ר"ג ור"א אומרי' נאמנת ור"י אומר לא מפיה אנו חיין אלא הרי היא בחזקת בעולה עד שלא תתארס והטעתו עד שתביא ראיה לדבריה היא אומרת וכו' מכאן מוכח שיש כתובה לארוסה ומשעת שאירסה נתחייב בכתובתה בתנאי ב"ד ומ"ה קאמרה ליה הכי דמקודם שנבעלה הוה משועבד לה ועכשיו שנאנסה לא הפסידה שעבודה דאי אמרת אין כתובה לארוסה עד שיכנסה וזאת כבר נבעלה קודם הנשואין אדרבה אומר הבעל לאשה נסתחפה שדך שהפסדת בתוליך ובעת הנשואין בעולה היית א"ו טעמא הוא משום דיש כתובה לארוסה ומשום אירוסין נתחייב לה: והוא אומר לא כי וכו'. פי' ואין לך כלום דהכי אוקמיה רבא לעיל מקח טעות לגמרי משמע דכנסה בחזקת בתולה ונמצאת בעולה א"ל כלום: ר"ג ור"א אומרים נאמנת. פי' ואפילו לבעלה מותרת אם היה ישראל א) דמאי דאמרן לעיל שהבעל נאמן לאוסרה עליו דוקא בברי וברי דהוא אומר פתח פתוח מצאתי והיא אומרת לא כי אלא פתח סתום היה ומכחשה ליה התם בעל נאמן לאוסרה עליו דשוייה אנפשיה חתיכה דאיסורא אבל הכא דאיהי טענה ברי ובעל שמא מותרת היא לו שהיא נאמנת בכל הן ליטול כתובתה והן להיות מותרת לו: ור"י אומר וכו'. פי' בהא פליגי דר"ג סבר אוקי איתתא אחזקתה ובחזקת בתולה הות קיימא ומספיקא לא מפקינן לה מחזקתה ור"י סבר אוקי ממוניה בחזקת מריה ומן ספיקא לא מפקינן ממונא עד שתביא ראיה לדבריה מר אזיל בתר חזקה דגופא. ומר אזיל בתר חזקה דממונא. ואמרי' לקמן דהיכא אזיל ר"ג בתר חזקה דגופא דוקא בברי ושמא דאיהי טענה ברי והבעל שמא התם אזיל ר"ג בתר חזקה דגופא ומפקינן ממונא מחזקת מריה אבל בשמא ושמא מודה ר"ג דלא אזלי' בתר חזקה דגופא אלא בתר חזקה דממונא והמע"ה: אר"י א"ש הלכה כר"ג ואי קשיא היכי פסיק שמואל הלכה כר"ג דאזיל בתר חזקה דגופא ומפיק ממונא מחזקת מרי' והתנן בב"ק שור שנגח את הפרה ונמצא עוברה בצידה ואין ידוע אם עד שלא ילדה נגחה ואם משילדה נגחה משלם חצי נזק לפרה ורביע נזק לולד ואמרי' עלה בגמרא אר"י א"ש זו דברי סומכוס דאמר ממון המוטל בספק חולקין אבל חכמים אומרים זה כלל גדול בדין המע"ה למה לי' למימר זה כלל גדול בדין ואפילו ניזק אומר ברי ומזיק אומר שמא והא במתני' איכא חזקה דגופא ואיכא חזקה דממונא דאוקי פרה אחזקתה ואימור מעוברת היתה בשעת נגיחה ומחמת נגיחת השור הפילה וחייב ליתן לו חצי נזק ולמזיק איכא חזקה דממונא וכיון דאית לניזק חוקה דגופא פליג ר"ג דאזיל בתר חזקה דגופא ומפיק ממונא מחזקת מריה ובשלמא אמתני' לא פליג ר"ג משום דהו"ל שמא ושמא דהכי אמרי' לקמן דבשמא ושמא לא אזיל ר"ג בתר חזקה דגופא אלא סבר המע"ה אלא במאי דאמרי' ואפילו ניזק אומר ברי ומזיק אומר שמא אמרי' המע"ה והא בהא מילתא פליג ר"ג דהיכא דתובע אומר ברי ונתבע אומר שמא אזלי' בתר חזקה דגופא ומפקינן ממונא מחזקת מריה והיכי אר"י משמיה דשמואל דחכמים פליגי על סומכוס ואמרי' [illegible]
[illegible] ושטר כתובה עליו והוא בא מספק לפטור א"ע ממה שהוא מחויב ועומד בו התם ודאי אר"ג אוקי אתתי' אחזקתה ואפיק ממונא מיני' דבעל כי היכי דהוה משועבד לה מעיקרא ור"י אפ"ה פליג עלי' ולא מפיק ממונא מחזקת מריה אבל הכא שהמזיק לא נתחייב ממון לניזק מקודם לכן (ואפילו) [ולא] בא לפטור עצמו [שנאמר] שנעמיד הניזק בחזקת הגוף ונוציא ממון ממנו אלא זה החיוב עכשיו יבוא עליו מספק וכיון שעכשיו רוצה לחול עליו מודה ר"ג דמספיקא לא מחייבינן לי' ואע"ג שיש לתובע חזקה דגופא אלא אמרי' המע"ה ולא ק' דשמואל אדשמואל: איתמר מנה לי בידך והלה אמר א"י ר"ה ור"י אמרי חייב ר"נ ור"י אמרי פטור מלשלם ר"ה ור"י אמרי חייב ברי ושמא ברי עדיף ר"נ ור"י אמרי פטור אוקי ממונא בחזקת מרי' פי' ומ"מ משבעי' לי' שבועת היסת שכן הוא כדבריו שא"י שחייב לו ונפטר: לימא ר"ה ור"י דאמרי כר"ג ור"נ ור"י דאמרי כר' יהושע. פי' דהכא נמי אשה אומרת ברי ובעל אומר שמא אמר לך ר"נ אנא דאמרי אפילו לר"ג ע"כ לא קאמר ר"ג התם אלא משום דא"ל אוקי איתתא אחזקתה פי' מספקא לן אשעת אירוסין אי בתולה הוה ואי בעולה הוה העמד אשה על חזקתה ובתולה היתה והשתא היא דאיתנס לאחר אירוסין אבל הכא מאי חזקה אית לי' להאי תובע דנוקמי' אחזקתה לגבות הלכך זיל בתר חזקת דממונא דאל"כ [אלא] דרב נחמן לא מתוקם כר"ג אלא כר' יהושע וק' הילכתא אהלכתא. והמורה גרים ע"כ לא קאמר ר"ג התם אלא משום דאיכא למימר מיגו. פי' מיגו דאי בעי' טענה טענה מעלייתא מהך כגון גבי משארסתני נאנסתי מיגו דאי בעיא אמרה מוכת עץ אני ולא פסלה נפשה מכהונה וקאמרה נאנסתי דקא פסלה נפשה מכהונה ש"מ קושטא קאמרה וגבי היא אומרת מוכת עץ אני מיגו דאי בעי' אמ' מוכ"ע אני תחתיך ואית לה מאתים וקאמרה מוכת עץ אני מקודם לכן ואין לה אלא מנה נאמנת אלא הכא גבי האי תובע מאי מיגו איכא וה"ה נמי דהוה מצי ר"ג למימר ע"כ לא קאמר ר"ג התם אלא משום דבעל הוה מחויב לה כתובה מעיקרא ועכשיו הוא בא לפטור עצמו מכתובה שנתחייב לו מקודם לכן אלא עכשיו אנו רוצים לחייבו לא אמר וכו' ודכתבינא לעיל אלא חד מתרי טעמא נקט. ה"נ מסתברא כדשנינן

א) נ"ל דאפי' אם קיבל בה קדושין פתוח [illegible]

דְּאִם כֵּן קַשְׁיָא הִלְכְתָא אַהִלְכְתָא, דְּקַיְימָא לָן *הִלְכְתָא כְּרַב נַחְמָן בְּדִינֵי, וּבְהָא אָמַר רַב יְהוּדָה אָמַר שְׁמוּאֵל הֲלָכָה כְּרַבָּן גַּמְלִיאֵל. אֶלָּא לָאו ש"מ כִּדְמְשַׁנֵּינַן, ש"מ.§ **מתני'** *הִיא אוֹמֶרֶת: "מוּכַּת עֵץ אֲנִי", וְהוּא אוֹמֵר: "לֹא כִּי, אֶלָּא דְּרוּסַת אִישׁ אַתְּ". ᵃרַבָּן גַּמְלִיאֵל וְרַבִּי אֱלִיעֶזֶר אוֹמְרִים: נֶאֱמֶנֶת, וְרַבִּי יְהוֹשֻׁעַ אוֹמֵר: לֹא מִפִּיהָ אָנוּ חַיִּין, אֶלָּא הֲרֵי זוֹ בְּחֶזְקַת דְּרוּסַת אִישׁ עַד שֶׁתָּבִיא רְאָיָה לִדְבָרֶיהָ.§ **גמ'** טַעֲנָתַיְיהוּ בְּמַאי? *רַבִּי יוֹחָנָן אָמַר: בְּמָאתַיִם וּמָנֶה, רַבִּי אֶלְעָזָר אָמַר: בְּמָנֶה וְלֹא כְלוּם. רַבִּי יוֹחָנָן אָמַר: בְּמָאתַיִם וּמָנֶה, סָבַר לָהּ *כְּר"מ, דְּאָמַר: בֵּין הִכִּיר בָּהּ וּבֵין לֹא הִכִּיר בָּהּ — מָאתַיִם. וְרַבִּי אֶלְעָזָר אוֹמֵר: בְּמָנֶה וְלֹא כְלוּם, סָבַר לָהּ כְּרַבָּנַן דְּאָמְרִי: בֵּין הִכִּיר בָּהּ בֵּין לֹא הִכִּיר בָּהּ — מָנֶה. בִּשְׁלָמָא ר' אֶלְעָזָר לָא קָאָמַר כְּר' יוֹחָנָן — דְּקָא מוֹקֵי לָהּ כְּרַבָּנַן, אֶלָּא רַבִּי יוֹחָנָן מ"ט לֹא אָמַר כְּר' אֶלְעָזָר? קָסָבַר: כְּנָסָהּ בְּחֶזְקַת בְּתוּלָה וְנִמְצֵאת בְּעוּלָה — יֵשׁ לָהּ כְּתוּבָּה מָנֶה. הָכָא, הוּא קָאָמַר מָנֶה וְהִיא קָאָמְרָה מָנֶה, מַאי אִיכָּא בֵּין טַעֲנָה דִּידֵיהּ לְטַעֲנָה דִּידָהּ? בִּשְׁלָמָא לְר' אֶלְעָזָר — הַיְינוּ דְּקָתָנֵי תַּרְתֵּי: חֲדָא — לְאַפּוּקֵי מִדְּרָמִי בַּר חָמָא, וַחֲדָא — לְאַפּוּקֵי מִדְּרַב חִיָּיא בַּר אָבִין א"ר שֵׁשֶׁת. אֶלָּא לְר' יוֹחָנָן, תַּרְתֵּי לָמָּה לִי? חֲדָא לְהוֹדִיעֲךָ כֹּחוֹ דְּרַבָּן גַּמְלִיאֵל, וַחֲדָא לְהוֹדִיעֲךָ כֹּחוֹ דְּרַבִּי יְהוֹשֻׁעַ. קַמַּיְיתָא לְהוֹדִיעֲךָ כֹּחוֹ דְּרַבִּי יְהוֹשֻׁעַ, דְּאַף עַל גַּב דְּאִיכָּא לְמֵימַר מִיגּוֹ — לָא מְהֵימְנָא, בָּתְרַיְיתָא לְהוֹדִיעֲךָ כֹּחוֹ דְּרַבָּן גַּמְלִיאֵל, דְּאע"ג דְּלֵיכָּא לְמֵימַר מִיגּוֹ — מְהֵימְנָא.§ **מתני'** *רָאוּהָ מְדַבֶּרֶת עִם אֶחָד, וְאָמְרוּ לָהּ: "מַה טִּיבוֹ שֶׁל אִישׁ זֶה?" — "אִישׁ פְּלוֹנִי, וְכֹהֵן הוּא". ᵇרַבָּן גַּמְלִיאֵל וְרַבִּי אֱלִיעֶזֶר אוֹמְרִים: נֶאֱמֶנֶת, וְר' יְהוֹשֻׁעַ אוֹמֵר: לֹא מִפִּיהָ אָנוּ חַיִּין, אֶלָּא הֲרֵי זוֹ בְּחֶזְקַת בְּעוּלָה ◦לְנָתִין וּלְמַמְזֵר, עַד שֶׁתָּבִיא רְאָיָה לִדְבָרֶיהָ. *הָיְתָה מְעוּבֶּרֶת, וְאָמְרוּ לָהּ: "מַה טִּיבוֹ שֶׁל עוּבָּר זֶה"? "מֵאִישׁ פְּלוֹנִי, וְכֹהֵן הוּא". ᶜרַבָּן גַּמְלִיאֵל וְרַבִּי אֱלִיעֶזֶר אוֹמְרִים: נֶאֱמֶנֶת, וְר' יְהוֹשֻׁעַ אוֹמֵר: לֹא מִפִּיהָ אָנוּ חַיִּין, אֶלָּא הֲרֵי זוֹ בְּחֶזְקַת מְעוּבֶּרֶת לְנָתִין וּלְמַמְזֵר, עַד שֶׁתָּבִיא רְאָיָה לִדְבָרֶיהָ.§ **גמ'** מַאי "מְדַבֶּרֶת"? *זְעֵירִי אָמַר: נִסְתְּרָה, רַב אַסִי אָמַר, ᵈנִבְעֲלָה. בִּשְׁלָמָא לִזְעֵירִי — הַיְינוּ דְּקָתָנֵי "מְדַבֶּרֶת", אֶלָּא לְרַב אַסִי מַאי "מְדַבֶּרֶת"? *לִישָּׁנָא מְעַלְיָא, כִּדְכְתִיב: °"אָכְלָה וּמָחֲתָה פִיהָ וְאָמְרָה לֹא פָעַלְתִּי אָוֶן". בִּשְׁלָמָא לִזְעֵירִי — הַיְינוּ דְּקָתָנֵי תַּרְתֵּי, "מְדַבֶּרֶת" וּ"מְעוּבֶּרֶת". אֶלָּא לְרַב אַסִי, תַּרְתֵּי לָמָּה לִי? ᵉחֲדָא לְהַכְשִׁיר בָּהּ, וַחֲדָא לְהַכְשִׁיר בְּבִתָּהּ. *הָנִיחָא לְמַאן דְּאָמַר: לְדִבְרֵי הַמַּכְשִׁיר בָּהּ מַכְשִׁיר בְּבִתָּהּ, אֶלָּא לְמ"ד: לְדִבְרֵי הַמַּכְשִׁיר בָּהּ פּוֹסֵל בְּבִתָּהּ, מַאי אִיכָּא לְמֵימַר? רַב אַסִי סָבַר כְּמ"ד לְדִבְרֵי הַמַּכְשִׁיר בָּהּ מַכְשִׁיר בְּבִתָּהּ. א"ל רַב פָּפָּא לְאַבַּיֵי: לִזְעֵירִי, דְּאָמַר מַאי "מְדַבֶּרֶת" נִסְתְּרָה, וְא"ר יְהוֹשֻׁעַ לָא מְהֵימְנָא — הָאָמַר רַב: *ᶠמַלְקִין עַל הַיִּחוּד וְאֵין אוֹסְרִין עַל הַיִּחוּד, לֵימָא דְּלָא כְּר"י! אֲפִי' תֵּימָא ר' יְהוֹשֻׁעַ, *מַעֲלָה עָשׂוּ בְּיוֹחֲסִין. מֵיתִיבֵי: רָאוּהָ שֶׁנִּכְנְסָה עִם אֶחָד לְסֵתֶר, אוֹ

תורה אור — משלי ל

דא"כ. דְּרַב נַחְמָן לָא מִיתוֹקַם כְּרַבָּן גַּמְלִיאֵל אֶלָּא כְּרַבִּי יְהוֹשֻׁעַ, קַשְׁיָא הִלְכְתָא אַהִלְכְתָא. **מתני'** דְּרוּסַת אִישׁ אַתְּ. קוֹדֶם שֶׁאֵרַסְתִּיךָ. **גמ'** טַעֲנָתַיְיהוּ בְּמַאי. מַה הִיא תּוֹבַעְתּוֹ, וּמַה הוּא רוֹצֶה לִיתֵּן? בְּמָאתַיִם וּמָנֶה. הִיא אוֹמֶרֶת: "מוּכַּת עֵץ אֲנִי, וְיֵשׁ לִי מָאתַיִם, וְאַע"פ שֶׁלֹּא הִכַּרְתָּ בִּי", וְהוּא אוֹמֵר: "דְּרוּסַת אִישׁ אַתְּ, וְאֵין לָךְ אֶלָּא מָנֶה". וְקָסָבַר: כְּנָסָהּ בְּחֶזְקַת בְּתוּלָה וְנִמְצֵאת בְּעוּלָה — יֵשׁ לָהּ כְּתוּבָּה מָנֶה. בְּמָנֶה וְלֹא כְלוּם. הִיא תּוֹבַעַת מָנֶה, וְהוּא אוֹמֵר: "אֵין לָךְ כְּלוּם". סָבַר לָהּ. תַּנָּא דְּמַתְנִי'. דְּאִילּוּ רַבִּי יוֹחָנָן לָא שָׁבֵיק רַבָּנַן וְעָבֵיד כְּר"מ. קָסָבַר. ר' יוֹחָנָן, כְּנָסָהּ בְּחֶזְקַת בְּתוּלָה וְנִמְצֵאת בְּעוּלָה — יֵשׁ לָהּ מָנֶה. הִלְכָּךְ, עַל כָּרְחָךְ מוּכַּת עֵץ דְּמַתְנִי' ר"מ הִיא, דְּאָמַר מָאתַיִם. וְהוּא אוֹמֵר: "דְּרוּסַת אִישׁ אַתְּ, וְיֵשׁ לִיךְ מָנֶה". דְּאִי רַבָּנַן הִיא — לֹא תָּבְעָה אֶלָּא מָנֶה, וְהוּא אוֹמֵר: "דְּרוּסַת אִישׁ אַתְּ וְיֵשׁ לָךְ מָנֶה" — מַאי אִיכָּא בֵּין טַעֲנָתָא דִּידֵיהּ לְטַעֲנָתָא דִּידָהּ? בִּשְׁלָמָא לְרַבִּי אֶלְעָזָר. דְּאָמַר דְּרוּסַת אִישׁ אֵין לָהּ כְּלוּם. הַיְינוּ דְּקָתָנֵי תַּרְתֵּי. בָּבֵי בְּמַתְנִי', גַּבֵּי פְּלוּגְתָּא דְּמָמוֹנָא: "הִיא אוֹמֶרֶת מִשֶּׁאֵרַסְתַּנִי נֶאֱנַסְתִּי" וְ"הִיא אוֹמֶרֶת מוּכַּת עֵץ אֲנִי". חֲדָא לְאַפּוּקֵי מִדְּרָמִי בַּר חָמָא וַחֲדָא לְאַפּוּקֵי כו'. "הִיא אוֹמֶרֶת מִשֶּׁאֵרַסְתַּנִי נֶאֱנַסְתִּי" תָּנָא לְמִיתְנֵי בָּהּ "וְהָיָה מִקָּחִי מִקַּח טָעוּת" — לְגַמְרֵי מַשְׁמַע, וְאֵין לָהּ כְּלוּם, לְאַפּוּקֵי מִדְּרַב חִיָּיא בַּר אָבִין דַּאֲמַר לְעֵיל (דף יא:): כְּנָסָהּ בְּחֶזְקַת בְּתוּלָה וְנִמְצֵאת בְּעוּלָה — יֵשׁ לָהּ כְּתוּבָּה מָנֶה. וְתָנָא הִיא אוֹמֶרֶת "מוּכַּת עֵץ אֲנִי" — לְאַפּוּקֵי מִדְּרָמִי בַּר חָמָא, דַּאֲמַר לְעֵיל גַּבֵּי מוּכַּת עֵץ: אֲבָל לֹא הִכִּיר בָּהּ — דִּבְרֵי הַכֹּל וְלֹא כְלוּם. אֶלָּא לְרַבִּי יוֹחָנָן. דְּאָמַר כְּנָסָהּ בְּחֶזְקַת בְּתוּלָה וְנִמְצֵאת בְּעוּלָה — יֵשׁ לָהּ כְּתוּבָּה מָנֶה. אִם כֵּן, מַאי מִקַּח טָעוּת דְּקָתָנֵי — מִמָּאתַיִם, אֲבָל מָנֶה — יֵשׁ לָהּ. לָמָּה לִי לְמִיתְנֵי כְּלָל לְהַהִיא? אִי לְאַשְׁמוּעִינַן פְּלוּגְתָּא דְּרַבָּן גַּמְלִיאֵל וְר' יְהוֹשֻׁעַ בְּבָרִי וְשֶׁמָּא, וְאוֹקֵי מָמוֹנָא בְּחֶזְקַת מָרֵיהּ, לִיתְנֵי חֲדָא לְאַפּוּקֵי מִדְּרָמִי בַּר חָמָא, וּלְאַשְׁמְעִינַן פְּלוּגְתַּיְיהוּ. דְּאִיכָּא לְמֵימַר מִגּוֹ. מִגּוֹ דְּאִי בָּעְיָא אָמְרָה "מוּכַּת עֵץ אֲנִי". בַּתְרַיְיתָא. לֵיכָּא לְמֵימַר מִגּוֹ לְר' יוֹחָנָן, דְּמוֹקֵי מַתְנִי' כְּרַבִּי מֵאִיר, דְּאָמַר: מוּכַּת עֵץ שֶׁלֹּא הִכִּיר בָּהּ — כְּתוּבָּתָהּ מָאתַיִם, לֵיכָּא שׁוּם מִגּוֹ, דְּמַה לִּי אוֹמֶרֶת "מוּכַּת עֵץ אֲנִי תַּחְתֶּיךָ", מַה לִּי אָמְרָה "מֵעִיקָּרָא". **מתני'** *[רָאוּהָ מְדַבֶּרֶת. בִּפְנוּיָה, וּמִשּׁוּם חֲשָׁשָׁא דִּפְסוּלִין לְנָתִין וּלְמַמְזֵר, וְכֵיוָן שֶׁנִּבְעֲלָה לְפָסוּל — פְּסָלָהּ מִן הַכְּהוּנָּה]. נֶאֱמֶנֶת. וּכְשֵׁרָה לִכְהוּנָּה, וְלָא מְסַפְּקִינַן לָהּ בְּנִבְעֲלָה לְפָסוּל לָהּ. הָיְתָה מְעוּבֶּרֶת כו'. בַּגְּמָ' מְפָרֵשׁ תַּרְתֵּי לָמָּה לִי. **גמ'** נִסְתְּרָה. וְאַע"פ שֶׁלֹּא רָאוּהָ שֶׁנִּבְעֲלָה — נִפְסְלָה לִכְהוּנָּה לְרַבִּי יְהוֹשֻׁעַ, כִּדְלְקַמָּן, דְּמַעֲלָה עָשׂוּ בְּיוֹחֲסִין. אָכְלָה וּמָחֲתָה פִיהָ. אַלְמָא נָקַט תַּשְׁמִישׁ בִּלְשׁוֹן אֲכִילָה. בִּשְׁלָמָא לִזְעֵירִי הַיְינוּ דְּקָתָנֵי תַּרְתֵּי. מְדַבֶּרֶת, לְהוֹדִיעֲךָ כֹּחוֹ דְּר' יְהוֹשֻׁעַ, דְּאע"ג דְּלָא רָאוּהָ שֶׁנִּבְעֲלָה – פְּסוּלָה. וּמְעוּבֶּרֶת – לְהוֹדִיעֲךָ כֹּחוֹ דְּרַבָּן גַּמְלִיאֵל. בְּבִתָּהּ. אִם הָעוּבָּר הַזֶּה נְקֵבָה תִּנָּשֵׂא לִכְהוּנָּה לְר"ג. דְּאִי אַשְׁמוּעִינַן בְּדִידַהּ – הֲוָה אָמֵינָא: אִיהִי, הוֹאִיל דַּהֲוָה לַהּ חֲזָקָה דְּכַשְׁרוּת מֵעִיקָּרָא – אָמְרִי' אוֹקְמַהּ אַחֲזָקָה וְאַל תַּפְסִילֶנָּה מִסָּפֵק. אֲבָל עוּבָּר, דְּלָא הֲוָה לֵיהּ חֲזָקָה דְּכַשְׁרוּת – אֵימָא לָא. הָנִיחָא לְמ"ד כו'. לְקַמָּן בִּשְׁמַעְתִּין. מַאי אִיכָּא לְמֵימַר. תַּרְתֵּי לְהַכְשִׁיר בָּהּ לָמָּה לִי? כֵּיוָן דִּמְדַבֶּרֶת דְּרָאוּהָ שֶׁנִּבְעֲלָה. מַלְקִין עַל הַיִּחוּד. מַכַּת מַרְדּוּת. וְאֵין אוֹסְרִין. אִשָּׁה עַל בַּעְלָהּ בִּשְׁבִיל יִחוּד בְּעָלְמָא. לֵימָא דְּלָא כְּרַבִּי יְהוֹשֻׁעַ. דְּמִשּׁוּם יִחוּד מַחֲזִיק לָהּ בְּנִבְעֶלֶת. בְּיוֹחֲסִין. בִּכְהוּנָּה. לְסֵתֶר. מַשְׁמַע יִחוּד בְּעָלְמָא. לְחוּרְבָּה

רב אסי אמר נבעלה. אבל נסתרה, מודה ר' יהושע דנאמנת לומר לכשר נבעלתי, במגו דאי בעיא אמרה לא נבעלתי. וא"ת: והא רבי יהושע לית ליה מגו גבי משארסתני נאנסתי! ויש לומר: דהתם לא הוי מגו גמור, דהא אפילו אמרה מוכת עץ אני – אינה נאמנת לרבי יהושע. כדתנן במתני'. ולא קרי ליה מגו אלא לפי שהיא ◦טענה מעולה ביותר. **חדא** להכשיר בה וחדא להכשיר בבתה. ולריכי תרווייהו: חדא להודיעך כחו דרבן גמליאל, וחדא להודיעך כחו דרבי יהושע. **לדברי** המכשיר בה פוסל בבתה. ומעוברת דנקט – משום ליסנא מעליא. **ואין** אוסרין על היחוד לימא דלא כרבי יהושע. תימה לרשב"א: דלזעירי (נמי) דאמר נסתרה, איירי כגון דמודה היא שנבעלה. דאי אמרה לא נבעלתי – אם כן הוי ספק ספיקא, דמכשיר רבי יהושע, כדאמר לקמן: התם – ספק ספיקא! ויש לומר: דלעולם איירי דקאמרה לא נבעלה, וחשיב ליה חדא ספיקא, משום דאין אפוטרופוס לעריות. אבל קשה! דבהדי' משמע בריש פרק שני (לקמן טו.) דאיירי בנבעלת, דקאמר: הניחא לזעירי דאמר מאי מדברת נסתרה, דמגו דאי בעיא אמרה לא נבעלתי – מהימנא כו'! לכך נראה דפריך לזעירי, דבספיקא חדא אסרינן לה, והא יחוד דאשת איש דספיקא חדא היא, ואין אוסרים על היחוד! וק"ק: דלכאורה נראה דיחוד איחוד פריך, מדפריך לזעירי ולא לרב אסי! **מעלה** עשו ביוחסין. תימה: דמשמע דאין אוסרין על היחוד איירי באשת איש, ולא בפנויה. ובסוף קדושין (דף פא. ושם) מוקי מלקין על היחוד – דוקא בפנויה, אבל באשת איש – לא, דאתה מוליא לעז על בניה. ואפי' למר זוטרא דמלקין ומכריז באשת איש, מודה דבפנויה נמי איירי! ואור"ת: דאף על גב דמלקין על היחוד איירי בפנויה, אין אוסרין על היחוד – לא איירי אלא באשת איש. *וא"ת: והא אמרינן בפ' בתרא דנדרים (דף נא:) גבי ההוא נואף דעייל לגבה דההיא איתתא, אמר ליה נואף: לא תיכול מינהון, דטעמינהו חויא. אמר רבא: איתתא שריא, אם איתא דעבד איסורא – ניחא ליה דלימות. משמע דאי לאו האי טעמא – היתה נאסרת על ידי יחוד! ויש לומר דנואף שאני. וה"ר יוסף דשליטן תירץ: דאין אוסרים על היחוד – איירי בפנויה, כמו מלקין על היחוד. ולא איירי לכהונה, אלא אין אוסרין אותה לבנו כשתתייחד עם אביו, לרבי יהודה דאסר באנוסת אביו (יבמות דף צז.).

השכנתו

[מיהו קשה לאפריך מרב דאמר אין אוסרין על היחוד הוה ליה למיפרך מהא דקי"ל בכולי תלמודא וסתם משניות דאין אשה נאסרת על בעלה אלא על ידי קינוי וסתירה לכך נ"ל דרב איירי בפנויה דוקא וה"פ דמעלה עשו ביוחסין לאסור היכא דאמרה לכשר נבעלתי דמודה מיהא ולא מהימנינן לה במגו אבל אי אמרה לא נבעלתי בהא לא עשו מעלה ובהא איירי רב. ת"י]

עין משפט נר מצוה

עט א מיי' פי"א מהל' אישות הלכה י טוש"ע אה"ע סימן סח סעיף ט:
פ ב ג ד ה מיי' פט"ו מהלכות איסורי ביאה הלכה יא ופי"ח הלכה יג יד סמג לאוין קכא טור שו"ע שם סי' ו סעיף יז:
פא ו מיי' פכ"ב שם הל' ג סמג לאוין קכו טוש"ע שם סימן כב סעיף ב:

גליון הש"ס

מתני' לנתין ולממזר עי' גיטין פט ע"א תוס' ד"ה בעולה ובמהרש"א שם: **תוס'** ד"ה רב אסי וכו' טענה מעולה ביותר. וכ"כ הרשב"א קדושין דף נ ע"א ד"ה הא:

[קדושין עט: ב"מ קי.] [לעיל יא: לקמן טז.] [לקמן טז.] [לעיל יא.] [לקמן טז.] שם קדושין עד. [עה.] ג"י כ"י [לקמן טז. יבמות יח:] [פסחים ג. וש"נ] [קדושין עד.] שם פא. [קדושין עג. לקמן טו.]

תוספות רי"ד

דא"כ קשה הלכתא אהלכתא דקיי"ל הלכה כר"נ בדיני. ובהא אמר ר"י אמר שמואל הלכה כר"ג ש"מ: **מתני'** היא אומרת מוכת עץ אני והוא אומר לא כי אלא דרוסת איש את ר"ג ור"א אומרים נאמנת ור"י אומר לא מפיה אנו חיין אלא ה"ז בחזקת דרוסת איש עד שתביא ראיה לדבריה: טענתייהו במאי. פי' מה היא תובעתו ומה הוא רוצה ליתן ר' יוחנן אמר במאתים ומנה פי' היא אומרת מוכת עץ אני ויש לי מאתים ואע"פ שלא הכרת בי והוא אומר דרוסת איש את ואין לך אלא מנה וכנסה בחזקת בתולה ונמצאת בעולה יש לה כתובה מנה וסבר לה כר"מ דאמר מוכת עץ בין הכיר בה בין לא הכיר בה כתובתה מאתים וכנסה בחזקת בתולה ונמצאת בעולה כתובתה מנה הלכך ע"כ מוכת עץ דמתני' ר"מ היא דאמר מאתים והוא אומר דרוסת איש את ואין לך אלא מנה ואי רבנן היא לא טענה אלא מנה מאי איכא בין טענה דידיה לטענה דידה במנה טענה לו ומנה מודה לה ופי' [המורה] סבר לה דלעיל סבר לה תנא דמתני' דאילו ר' יוחנן לא שביק רבנן ועביד כר"מ ור"א סבר במנה ולא כלום סבר לה כרבנן דאמרי בין הכיר בה בין לא הכיר בה כתובתה מנה וכנסה בחזקת בתולה ונמצאת בעולה אין לה כלום בשלמא ר"א לא אמר כר"י דקא מוקי לה כרבנן פי' במנה ולא כלום: היינו דקתני תרי בבא במתני' גבי פלוגתא דממונא היא אומרת משארסתני נאנסתי וכו' והוא אומר לא כי והיה מקחי מקח טעות ומקח טעות לגמרי משמע ואין לה כלום אלא ר"י מ"ט לא אמר כר"א קסבר כנסה בחזקת בתולה ונמצאת בעולה יש לה כתובה מנה הכא הוא אומר מנה והיא אומרת מנה מאי איכא בין טענתה לטענתיה והלכתא כר"א דקיימי רבא ורב אשי כוותיה דכנסה בחזקת בתולה ונמצאת בעולה אין לה כלום כדכתיבנא לעיל ובמוכת עץ נמי הלכתא כרבנן דאמרי מנה: **מתני'** ראוה מדברת עם א' מה טיבו של זה איש פלוני וכהן הוא ר"ג ור"א אומרים נאמנת ור"י אומר לא מפיה אנו חיין אלא ה"ז בחזקת בעולה לנתין ולממזר עד שתביא ראיה לדבריה היתה מעוברת מה טיבו של עובר זה מאיש פלוני וכהן הוא ר"ג ור"א אומרים נאמנת ור"י אומר לא מפיה אנו חיין אלא ה"ז בחזקת מעוברת מנתין וממזר עד שתביא ראיה לדבריה: וכהן הוא פי' מיוחס ולא כהן ממש שאינה נאמנת להחזיק העובר בחזקת כהן אלא בחזקת כשר שאם הוא בת תנשא לכהונה: מאי מדברת זעירא אמר נסתרה ואע"פ שלא ראוה שנבעלה פסולה לכהונה לר"י כדלקמן שמעלה עשו ביוחסין ור"א אמר נבעלה בשלמא לזעירא היינו דקתני מדברת אלא לר"א מאי מדברת לישנא מעליא כדכתיב אכלה ומחתה פיה וגו' פי' נקט תשמיש בלשון אכילה בשלמא לזעירי היינו דקתני תרתי מדברת ומעוברת פי' מדברת להודיעך כחו דר"י דאפילו בעדי יחוד בלבד אסורה היא לכהן משום דמעלה עשו ביוחסין ומעוברת להודיעך כחו דר"ג אלא לר"א תרתי למה לי פי' לתני מדברת וכ"ש מעוברת. חדא להכשיר בה וחדא להכשיר בבתה דאתמר ר"י אמר לדברי המכשיר בה מכשיר בבתה לדברי הפוסל בה פוסל בבתה ור"א אומר אף לדברי המכשיר בה פוסל בבתה דבשלמא איהי אית לה חזקה דכשרות פי' מעיקרא ואוקמה אחזקה ולא תפסלנה מספק אבל בתה לית לה חזקה דכשרות והלכתא כר' יוחנן דהוא רביה דר"א שאין הלכה כתלמיד במקום הרב ותו דקאי כאבא שאול דתנן בעשרה יוחסין אבא שאול היה קורא לשתוקי בדוקי ואמרי' בגמ' מאי בדוקי שבודקין את אמו ואי אמרה לכשר נבעלתי נאמנת ואע"ג דאיכא רוב פסולים אצלה וא"ר הל' כאבא שאול: א"ל ר"פ לאביי לזעירי דאמר נסתרה ואר"י דלא מהימנא הא דאמר רב מלקין על היחוד

פב א מיי' פי"ח מהל' איסורי ביאה הלכה כא סמג לאוין קכא טור ש"ע אה"ע סימן ז ס"ד:

פג ב מיי' פט"ו שם הלכה יא סמג שם טוש"ע שם סי' ו סעיף יז:

ואע"ג דמיעוט שובדי כוכבים אין פרוצים מ"מ חשבינן לה ודאי בעולה מן הרוב הפרוצים. ת"י:

פד ג מיי' פ"כ שם הל' כ סמג לאוין קכב טוש"ע שם סימן ג סעיף ט:

פה ד מיי' פט"ו שם הלכה יז טוש"ע שם סימן ד סעיף כז [וברב אלפס עוד ביבמות פ"ז דף כז ע"א]:

השבתנו על המעוברת. פי': לדידן ניחא, דאשה מזנה בודקת ומזנה, ולא דמיא לשבויה. אלא לדידך, דלית לך הך סברא – תינח מעוברת, אבל מדברת אפילו לפי דבריך יש הפרש, דלזו יש עדים ולזו אין עדים, ואיכא מיגו! אמר להם: מדברת היינו שבויה, וכמו ששבויה אין נאמנת לומר לא נבעלתי – ה"נ מדברת, כדמסיק: לפי שאין אפוטרופוס לעריות. ומיהו, פי' זה לא יתכן למאי דפרישית לעיל, דלר' יהושע נאמנת לומר לא נבעלתי. ופר"י בדוחק: מדברת היינו שבויה, דכמו *ששבויה בחזקת בעולה – כך מדברת בחזקת בעולה, לענין שאם אמרה לכשר נבעלתי שאינה נאמנת במיגו, לפי שירא לומר לא נבעלתי. ולהכי אהני דאין אפוטרופוס לעריות דלא חשבינן ליה מיגו. **מסייע** ליה לר' יהושע בן לוי. הקשה ר"ת: אכתי תיפוק ליה, דהתם בשבויה – כל פסולים, והכא בחורבה דדברא – רובו! ותירץ: דרוב ככל. וליכא למימר, במדברת דליכא אלא רוב איכא למימר סמוך מיעוטא לחזקה, ואיתרע לה רובא, דאפילו אית להו סמוך מיעוטא לחזקה לר"ג ור' יהושע – מ"מ לא הוי אלא פלגא ופלגא, ודין הוא שתאסר מספק, דספק איסורא לחומרא. ולא דמי לתינוק שנמצא בצד העיסה בפרק "עשרה יוחסין" (קדושין דף פ. ושם) דמטהרין מטעם סמוך מיעוטא לחזקה, דאם אמרו ספק טומאה לטהר יאמרו ספק איסור להתיר?! כדאמרינן פרק "כיסוי הדם" (חולין דף פו:). **מכשיר** אפילו ברוב פסולים. והא דקאמרינן בפ' "עשרה יוחסין" (קידושין עד. ושם) גבי אבא שאול היה קורא לשתוקי בדוקי, ומפרש בגמרא שבודקין אמו, ואומרת: לכשר נבעלתי. ופריך: כמאן – כר"ג, תנינא חדא זימנא: היתה מעוברת כו', פי': והוה ליה למתני וכן אמר אבא שאול? וכן פי' שם בקונטרס. ומשני: דאבא שאול עדיפא מר"ג, דאי מהתם – הוה אמינא ברוב כשרים אבלה כו', אע"ג דאמרי' הכא דר"ג מכשיר אפילו ברוב פסולין – אבא שאול קאי אמתני', וממתני' לא משמע מידי דאיירי ברוב פסולין. והא דפריך התם לעיל, למאי דהוה בעי למימר דאבא שאול אתא להכשיר בבתה: הניחא למ"ד לדברי המכשיר בה פוסל בבתה, אבל למ"ד מכשיר בבתה – מאי איכא למימר? התם פריך שפיר, דאפי' לזעירי לשון המשנה דקתני: מה טיבו של עובר זה, משמע דאתא להכשיר בבתה. **פשיטא** מי ידעינן אבוה מנו. הכא לא בעי לשנויי לא צריכא דאי תפס, כדמשני בפרק "עשרה יוחסין" (שם דף עה. ושם) גבי ארוסה שעיברה. דהתם רגלים לדבר דמארוס נתעברה, ואיכא למיתלי ביה טפי מבאינש דעלמא. **בעינן** זרעו מיוחס אחריו. והא דאמר ב"החולץ" (יבמות דף לז.): ראשון ראוי להיות כ"ג, גבי ספק בן תשע לראשון – בפרק "נושאין על האנוסה" (שם דף ק:) פריך לה, ומשני: זרעו מיוחס אחריו – דרבנן, וקרא אסמכתא בעלמא הוא, וכי גזור רבנן – בזנות, בנישואין לא גזור.

[ההוא ארוס וארוסתו. והא דאמר ב"עשרה יוחסין" (קדושין דף עה.), איתמר: הבא על ארוסתו בבית חמיו, רב אמר: הולד ממזר, ושמואל אמר: הולד שתוקי – כשלא בדקו את אמו. דאי בשבדקו – קשיא דשמואל אדשמואל. דהכא אמר שמואל דנאמנת, דהלכה כרבן גמליאל דנאמנת, והתם קאמר איפוך, שמואל אמר: הולד ממזר. וכן משמע, דבמסקנא משני התם: לעולם לא תיפוך כו'. ומפרש: מאי שתוקי – שבודקין את אמו, ואומרת לכשר נבעלתי. ואם תאמר: אכתי לשמואל, דהתם משמע דוקא בבא על ארוסתו בבית חמיו מהני בדיקה, והכא משמע אפילו כי לא מודה אמר שמואל דנאמנת, כרבן גמליאל! ויש לומר: דהא דנקט בא – היינו משום רבותא דרב נקטיה, דאפילו הכי אמר הולד ממזר. אי נמי, התם הוא דבעינן בא – משום דאיירי בדדיימא מעלמא, כדאמר רבא ביבמות בשלהי "אלמנה לכהן גדול": מסתברא מילתא דרב בדדיימא מעלמא, והכא בדלא דיימא מעלמא מיירי. ועוד: דבכל הספרים גרס בקדושין: ארוסה שעיברה, והשיא דוקא קאמר שבודקין. אבל בבא – א"צ בדיקה. ומיהו, קשה ללישנא קמא ביבמות בסוף פ' "אלמנה", דפליגי רב ושמואל בבא, ומסיק התם אביי דאע"ג דלא דיימא מעלמא פליגי, דדלמא מדאפקרה נפשה לגבי ארוס מפקרה נפשה לגבי עלמא, הא אמר הכא חדא דקא מודה, ומשמע דכשר אפילו לר' יהושע, ובא כמודה דמי

או לחורבה, ואמרו לה: "מה טיבו של איש זה"? "כהן הוא, ובן אחי אבא הוא". רבן גמליאל ור"א אומרים: נאמנת. רבי יהושע אומר: לא מפיה אנו חיין, אלא הרי זו בחזקת בעולה לנתין ולממזר, עד שתביא ראיה לדבריה. בשלמא לזעירי – היינו דקתני תרתי, "לסתר או לחורבה". אלא לרב אסי, דאמר נבעלה – תרתי למה לי? חדא קתני, לסתר דחורבה. והא "לסתר או לחורבה" קתני! חדא לחורבה דמתא, וחדא לחורבה דדברא. וצריכי, דאי אשמעינן חורבה דמתא – בהא קמכשר רבן גמליאל, משום דרוב כשרים אצלה. אבל לחורבה דדברא, דרוב פסולין אצלה – אימא מודה ליה לרבי יהושע. ואי אשמעינן בההיא – בההיא קאמר רבי יהושע, אבל בהא – אימא מודה לר"ג, צריכא. מיתיבי: *זו עדות שהאשה כשרה לה, ורבי יהושע אומר: אינה נאמנת. אמר להם ר"י: אי אתם מודים [א]בשבויה שנשבית ויש לה עדים שנשבית והיא אומרת "טהורה אני", שאינה נאמנת? אמרו לו: אבל. ומה הפרש יש בין זו לזו? לזו – יש עדים, ולזו – אין לה עדים. אמר להם: אף לזו יש עדים, שהרי כריסה בין שיניה! אמרו לו: רוב גוים פרוצים בעריות הם. אמר להן: *אין אפוטרופוס לעריות. בד"א – בעדות אשה בגופה, אבל עדות אשה בבתה – דברי הכל הולד שתוקי. מאי קאמר להו ומאי קמהדרי ליה? הכי קאמרי ליה: השבתנו על המעוברת, מה תשיבנו על המדברת? אמר להם: מדברת היינו שבויה. אמרו לו: שאני שבויה דרוב גוים פרוצים בעריות הם. אמר להם: הא נמי, כיון דאיסתתר – אין אפוטרופוס לעריות. קתני מיהת תרתי, מדברת ומעוברת, תיובתא דרב אסי! תיובתא. ותיפוק ליה דהתם רוב פסולין אצלה, והכא רוב כשרין אצלה! מסייע ליה לרבי יהושע בן לוי, דאמר רבי יהושע בן לוי: לדברי המכשיר – מכשיר אפילו ברוב פסולין, לדברי הפוסל – פוסל אפילו ברוב כשרים. א"ר יוחנן: *[ב]לדברי המכשיר בה – מכשיר בבתה, לדברי הפוסל בה – פוסל בבתה. ורבי אלעזר אומר: לדברי המכשיר בה – פוסל בבתה. אמר רבה: מ"ט דר"א? בשלמא איהי – אית לה חזקה דכשרות, בתה – לית לה חזקה דכשרות. איתיביה ר"א לרבי יוחנן: בד"א – בעדות אשה בגופה. אבל עדות אשה בבתה – דברי הכל הולד שתוקי. מאי לאו – שתוקי ופסול? לא, שתוקי וכשר. ומי איכא שתוקי כשר? אין, כדשמואל, דאמר שמואל: *עשרה כהנים עומדים, ופירש אחד מהם ובעל – הולד שתוקי. מאי שתוקי? אילימא שמשתיקין אותו מנכסי אביו – פשיטא, ומי ידעינן אבוה מנו? [ג]אלא שמשתיקין אותו מדין כהונה, דכתיב: "°והיתה לו ולזרעו אחריו ברית כהנת עולם" – מי שזרעו מיוחס אחריו, יצא זה שאין זרעו מיוחס אחריו. [ד]ההוא ארוס וארוסתו דאתו לקמיה דרב יוסף, היא אמרה: מיניה, והוא אמר: אין

תורה אור

במדבר כה

לחורבה. סתמא לבעילה, שהוא מקום לזנות. **חורבה דמתא.** סתם בעילתה מאחד מבני העיר. ואיכא למימר בעיר שרובה ישראל כשרים קאמר. **דדברא.** ספק אחד מסוף העולם בא לכאן. ורוב העולם גוים הם, ופוסלים אשה בביאתם לכהונה, כדאמר ביבמות (דף מה.) ובקדושין (דף עה:): יבוא גוי ועבד שאין לו אלמנות וגירושין בה. **זו עדות שהאשה.** עצמה כשרה לומר: לכשר נבעלתי. **אינה נאמנת.** ליגשא לכהן. **אמרו לו אבל.** הן, כמו "אבל שרה אשתך" (בראשית יז) דמתרגמינן: בקושטא. **ומה הפרש בין זו לזו.** ר' יהושע קאמר לה. **לזו יש עדים.** שנבעלה, דכיון דנשבית לבין הגוים, והם פרוצים בעריות, כולנו עדים שנבעלה. **ולזו אין עדים.** שנבעלה, שלא ראוה אלא מדברת, ומיגו דאי בעיא אמרה לא נבעלתי, כי אמרה נמי לכשר נבעלתי – מהימנא. **אף לזו.** כלומר, אף כאן יש אחת שיש לה עדים, ואתם חולקים עלי, בהיותה מעוברת. **אמרו ליה כו'.** לקמיה מפרש מאי קא מהדרי ליה על מאי דקאמר להו. **אין אפוטרופוס כו'.** לקמן מפרש. **בד"א.** דנאמנת לר"ג. **בעדות אשה בגופה.** כלומר, להכשיר את עצמה לכהונה, דלא מחזקינן לה כנבעלה לפסול. **מאי קאמר להו כו'.** כלומר, מאי קאמר להו איהו, דקא מהדרי ליה איניהו רוב גוים פרוצים בעריות. כלום תשובה היא זו על מה שאמר להם אף לזו יש לה עדים? אין לך פרוץ גדול מזה, דקחזינן דנתעברה ממנו. **השבתנו על המעוברת.** תשובה גמורה ונצחת. **מדברת היינו שבויה.** מה מדברת אין לה עדים – אף שבויה אין לה עדים בבעילה, ואתם מחזיקים אותה כנבעלה. **פרוצים בעריות.** והא ודאי נבעלה. **אין אפוטרופוס לעריות.** אין אתם יכולים להיות לה אפוטרופוס, לומר: לא נבעלה. **ותיפוק ליה וכו'.** לרבי יהושע פריך: נהי נמי דאין אפוטרופוס לעריות, תיפוק ליה דלא דמי לשבויה, דהתם רוב פסולין כו'. **מכשיר אפי' ברוב פסולים.** דאמרינן: אוקמה אחזקה. ועל רוב פסולים, שהיו מכשירים אותה, הביא הוא להם ראיה מן השבויה. **אית לה חזקה דכשרות.** וי"ל: אשה זו בחזקת כשרות עומדת, ומספק אתה בא לפוסלה – אל תפסילנה מספק. **לא שתוקי וכשר.** כלומר, שתוקי הוא במקצת, שאם כהן היה הבועל והעובר יהיה זכר – משתקין אותו מדין כהונה, כדלקמן. אבל כשר הוא ליוחסין, שאם נקבה היא – תינשא לכהונה, ואם זכר הוא – בתו ואלמנתו כשרות לכהונה. **ופירש אחד מהן.** ואין ידוע איזה הוא. **הולד שתוקי.** ואע"פ שברור לנו שמכהן כשר בא. והאי שתוקי על כרחך כשר ליוחסין, ואם נקבה היא – ראויה לכהן, וקרי ליה שתוקי. **מדין כהונה.** שלא יעבוד עבודה, ולא יאכל תרומה. **מיוחס אחריו.** שאנו יודעין מי אביו.

[תוספתא סוף פרק א]

[חולין יא: נדה ל:]

[קדושין עד.]

יבמות ק:

תוספות רי"ד

היחוד ואין אוסרים על היחוד ליוזא דלא רר"י פי' דמשום יחוד מחזיק לה כנבעלה פי' מלקין מכות מרדות לאשת איש שנתייחדה עם א' אבל אין אוסרין אותה על בעלה בעדי יחוד אלא היכא דקינא לה מעיקרא בפני שנים ואמר לה אל תסתרי עם איש פלוני אם נסתרה עמו היא סוטה האמורה בתורה והיא אסורה לו עד שתובדר במים המאררים אבל בלא קינוי מעיקרא אינה נאסרת לו בסתירה בלחוד. ומהדר מעלה עשו ביוחסין פי' דלא אסרה ר"י אלא אם היתה פנויה שלא תנשא לכהן דאמרינן דלמא נבעלה לפסול לה אבל לבעלה לא אסרה ואפי' אם היה בעלה כהן. אר"י א"ש הלכה כר"ג אריב"ל לדברי המכשיר מכשיר אפילו ברוב פסולים לדברי הפוסל פוסל אפי' ברוב כשרים: ההוא ארום וארוסתו דאתו לקמיה דר"י היא אומרת מיני' והוא אומר

גמרא

אין, מינאי. אמר רב יוסף: למאי ניחוש לה? חדא – דהא קא מודה, ועוד: הא *אמר רב יהודה אמר שמואל: הלכה כרבן גמליאל. א]אמר ליה אביי: *ובהא, כי לא מודה מכשר רבן גמליאל? והאמר ליה שמואל לרב יהודה: שיננא! אהלכה כר"ג, ואת לא תעביד עובדא עד דאיכא רוב כשרין אצלה. והכא – רוב פסולין אצלה! וליטעמיך, תקשי לך היא גופא: הלכה – ואת לא תעביד עובדא?! אלא מאי אית לך למימר: בהא – לכתחלה, הא – דיעבד, והא נמי, כדיעבד דמי. רמי ליה אביי *לרבא: ומי אמר רבי יהושע אינה נאמנת? ורמינהו: *העיד ר' יהושע ורבי יהודה בן בתירא געל אלמנת עיסה שהיא כשרה לכהונה! א"ל: הכי השתא! התם – אשה נישאת – בודקת ונישאת, הכא – אשה מזנה – בודקת ומזנה?! אמר רבא: דרבי יהושע אדרבי יהושע קשיא, דרבן גמליאל אדרבן גמליאל לא קשיא? והא קתני סיפא, אמר להן רבן גמליאל: קבלנו עדותכם, ואבל מה נעשה שהרי גזר רבן יוחנן בן זכאי שלא להושיב בית דין על כך, שהכהנים שומעין לכם לרחק אבל לא לקרב! אלא אמר רבא: דרבן גמליאל אדרבן גמליאל לא קשיא; התם – ברי, הכא – שמא. דר' יהושע אדר' יהושע נמי לא קשיא; התם – חד ספיקא, הכא – תרי ספיקי. הלכך, לרבן גמליאל – אלים ליה ברי, דאפילו בחד ספיקא נמי מכשיר. וקיל ליה שמא, דאפילו בספק ספיקא – נמי פסיל. לרבי יהושע אלים ליה חד ספיקא, דאפילו בברי נמי פסיל וקיל ליה ספק ספיקא, דאפילו בשמא – נמי מכשיר. תנו רבנן: *איזוהי אלמנת עיסה – הכל שאין בה לא משום ממזרות, ולא משום נתינות, ולא משום עבדי מלכים. אמר רבי מאיר: שמעתי

רש"י

אין מינאי. אמת, ממני הוא. ובהא כי לא מודי כו'. דקא אמרת ועוד. ארוסה הכל פסולין אצלה חוץ מן הארוס. הא לכתחלה. אם בא כהן לימלך לבית דין, לא שרינן ליה לכונסה אא"כ היו רוב כשרים אצלה. דיעבד. אם נשאה כהן ולא נמלך, לא מפקינן לה מיניה. והא נמי כדיעבד דמי. שנתעברה ואתה בא לפסול העובר ולאוסרה על הארוס, דאם אין אתה מאמינה הרי אתה מוציאה מבעלה. מי אמר רבי יהושע אינה נאמנת. אלמא לא מוקמינן לה אחזקה. עיסה. לשון ספק. על אלמנת עיסה. שהיא באה מכח ספק חלל, כדלקמן, שנטמע בה ספק חלל, כגון שנזרק בעל אמו הראשון לה גט, ספק קרוב לו ספק קרוב לה, ומת. ונמצאת זו ספק גרושה ספק אלמנה, ונשאה כהן והוליד ממנה בן – זהו ספק חלל. והעיד ר"י על אלמנתו של זה שהיא כשרה. אלמא מוקמינן לה אחזקה, ואמרינן: אל תפסילנה לזו מספק, כלומר שמא בעלה חלל היה. בודקת ונישאת. וי"ל שבדקה אחר אותן גירושין, והוגד לה שקרוב לו היו, ולא נתגרשה כלל, ואלמנה היתה, וכשרה לכהן. בודקת ומזנה. בתמיה. דרבן גמליאל אדרבן גמליאל לא קשיא. בתמיה, דלא חיישת לתרוייהו. הא קתני סיפא. דהיא אמר להן כו'. קבלנו עדותכם. נאמנים אתם לנו שכך שמעתם. על כך. להתירה לכהונה, דודאי אסורה. שהכהנים שומעין לכם. אם תאמרו אסורה. אבל לא לקרב. אם תאמרו מותרת. התם ברי. מתניתין, היא אומרת: ברי לי שלכשר נבעלתי. הכא. גבי אלמנת עיסה, כי היכי דלדידן מספקא לן, לדידה נמי מספקא לה, וליכא למימר בה: ברי ושמא – ברי עדיף. חד ספיקא. מתניתין חד ספיקא היא – ספק נבעלה לכשר, ספק נבעלה לפסול; שהרי לא בא זה לפנינו, ואילו בא – שמא היינו מכירים בו שהוא פסול. הכא. גבי אלמנת עיסה. תרי ספיקי. אמו של ספק חלל זה – בה נולד הספק, והיא עצמה לא נאסרה אלא מספק. וזו שבאה מחמת בנה קרי לה ספק ספיקא. ומדברי רבי יוסף טוב עלם מצאתי: [אלמנת עיסה] – אשה שהיה בעלה ספק ספיקא, כגון שנתגרשה אמו מבעלה הראשון, ספק קרוב לו ספק קרוב לה, ומת בתוך שלשה חדשים, ונשאת לכהן תוך שלשה חדשים, וילדה את זה; ספק שהוא בן תשעה לראשון וכשר, ואפילו היתה מגורשת, שהרי קודם לגט נתעברה, או אפילו אחר הגט – והוא ישראל ולא כהן. וספק בן שבעה לאחרון, ובנו של כהן הוא, והרי הוא ספק חלל. הרי ספק ספיקא: שמא אינו בנו של כהן, ואת"ל בנו הוא – שמא לא היתה אמו גרושה אלא אלמנה. ולהכי קרי לה עיסה, שיש בה עירובי ספיקות הרבה, כעיסה זו שהיא בלוסה. והא דאמרינן לקמן "כל שנטמע בה ספק חלל" – היינו פירושה: כל שנטמעו בה ספק עירובי חלל. נטמע. נתערב. איזוהי אלמנת עיסה. שהעידו עליה שהיא כשרה. כל שאין. בעירובי ספקותיה לא ספק ממזרות ולא ספק נתינות ולא ספק עבדי מלכים, אלא ספק חלל לבדו. מש"ה נקט עבדי מלכים, משום עבדי שלמה *שהיו עשירים ובעלי זרוע ונשאו להם בנות ישראל. וכגון זרעו של הורדוס שהי' עבד לבית חשמונאי, וגברה ידו ומלך.

תוספות

דמי, דהא מודה דהכא אינו אלא שהיה אומר שבא עליה, דפשיטא שלא היה מזנב אחריה לאורבה שלא תזנה, ובין לרב ובין לשמואל אסור הוא בבת ישראל, דשתוקי דקאמר לשמואל היינו – דאסור בבת ישראל לכולהו לישני דבפרק בתרא דקדושין! וללישנא דבדוקי נמי קשה טפי, דמשמע דאפילו ע"י בדיקת האם לא מיתכשר אלא לר"ג, אבל לרבי יהושע לא, והכא אמר דהא קא מודה, וכשר לכ"ע! ושמא יש לחלק: דבא דהתם – היינו שפעם אחת בא עליה, אבל מודה דהכא דקאמר מיניה – היינו שבא עליה ביאות הרבה, והיה רגיל אצלה תמיד, וכדאמרינן: רוב בעילות הלך אחר הבעל. **חדא** דקא מודה. וללישנא קמא דיבמות – דלא דיימא מעלמא, ולאיכא דאמרי – דאפילו דיימא מעלמא, כיון דקא מודה – בתריה דידיה שדינן ליה. **חדא** דקא מודה. מלינן לפרש דאיירי לענין לאוסרה על הארוס, וה"פ: חדא דקא מודה – הלכך אינה נאסרת עליו, ועוד הא רב יהודה כו', לא קאמר ועוד אפילו לא מודה, דאם אינו מודה – פשיטא דנאסרת עליו. אלא כלומר, אפילו כי ליכא טעמא דמודה, כגון לאביי דס"פ "אלמנה": מדאפקרה נפשה לגבי ארוס מפקרה נפשה נמי לגבי עלמא – אפ"ה אינה נאסרת עליו משום דנאמנת כר"ג, כן פי' לנו ר"י. ואי אפשר להעמידה. דלפי דבריו, אם כן הא דאמר אביי "מדאפקרה נפשה" – היינו בשלא בדקו את אמו. וזה אינו, דהא אפלוגתא דרב ושמואל קאי, דמוקמי בקדושין מאי שתוקי – בדוקי! ולמאי דגרסינן בקדושין: ארוסה שעיברה – לא קשה מידי. על כן צריך לפרש דהכא לא איירי לאוסרה עליו, אלא לענין להכשיר את הולד. והשתא הוי "ועוד" כפשוטו: ועוד, דאפילו לא יודה. ולאו דקאמר דלאו מיניה – דבהא לא מכשיר ר"ג כיון דהוי ברי וברי, כדאמר ברפ"ב, אלא כגון שמת או דליתיה קמן דלישייליה. והא דחשיב ליה בסמוך דיעבד – לפי שלא היה יכול הולד להינשא לבת ישראל, ואפילו לממזרת אסור, דמדאורייתא כשר הוא, דהאי הוי כדיעבד, הלכה כר"ג]: (מן ד"ה ההוא ארוס ע"כ היה חסר מהתוספות). **אלמנת** עיסה. פירש בקונטרס שני פירושין, ושניהם דחוקים. דהא אמרינן לקמן: איזו היא אלמנת עיסה – כל שנטמע בה ספק חלל. *) ומה טימוע שייך במה שנישאת לספק חלל? ועוד: דאין לשון עיסה נופל על אדם אחד, אלא על משפחה שייך לשון עיסה, כדאמרינן (קידושין דף סט:): כל הארצות עיסה לארץ ישראל, וא"י עיסה לבבל. ובתוספתא תניא: מפני מה אמרו עיסה פסולה – מפני ספיקי חללין. ומה ספיקי חללין שייך לאלו הפירושין?! ונראה לר"י ולריב"א: דעיסה קורא המשפחה שנטמע בהם ספק חלל אחד, או הרבה ספיקי חללים. ולהכי חשיב ליה לקמן ספק ספיקא, דכל אחד מבני המשפחה ספק אם הוא אותו ספק שנתערב בהן, אם לאו. ולקמן גרסינן: איזהו עיסה – כל שנטמע בה כו', ולא גרסינן אלמנת. והכי איתא בירושלמי. ואפילו גרסינן אלמנת, כל שנטמע בה – קאי אעיסה. ואם תאמר: דבפרק "עשרה יוחסין" (שם דף עה.) משמע דאפילו מאן דמכשר אלמנת עיסה מודה בבת דפסולה, גבי הא דאמר רב חסדא: הכל מודים באלמנת עיסה שפסולה לכהונה כו', ולאפוקי מהני תנאי, דתנן: העיד רבי יהושע כו', ומה לי אלמנה מה לי בת, דבת נמי הוי ספק ספיקא כמו באלמנה! וי"ל: דבת העיסה אין לה חזקה דכשרות, ואע"ג דבעלמא מקילין בספק ספיקא – הכא מעלה עשו ביוחסין, כי היכי דמצריך לקמן תרי רובי להכשיר אף על גב דבעלמא סגי בחד רובא. **דרבי** יהושע אדר"י לא קשיא. והשתא לא מצי לשנויי דבודקת ונישאת כדמשני לעיל, כיון דהשתא אוקימנא באומרת שמא. **תנו** רבנן איזו היא אלמנת עיסה. קשה לרבינו תם על גרסת הספרים דגרסי אלמנת עיסה, דאם כן אית ליה לרבי יוסי דאלמנת עיסה כשרה, דהא מכשר לקמן שתוק ממזר, וכל שכן דמכשר באלמנת עיסה, כדמוכח הסוגיא. ובפרק "עשרה יוחסין" (ג"ז שם) אמר בהדיא דלרבי יוסי אלמנת עיסה פסולה! לכך מוחק רבינו תם "אלמנת", וגרים: איזוהי עיסה. ולענין בת קתני, וקאי אהאי דתנא בשילהי עדיות: העיסה נאמנת לטהר ולטמא, לרחק ולקרב, לאסור ולהתיר. וה"פ: נאמנת לטהר עצמה בלויתה או בשתיקה, למר כדאית ליה ולמר כדאית ליה. לטמא ולטהר – שייך לענין ממזרות ונתינות, כדתנן (קדושין דף עב:): ממזרים ונתינים עתידין ליטהר. לרחק ולקרב – שייך אחללות, כדתנן: הכהנים שומעים לכם לרחק ולא לקרב, וכן לקמן (דף כח.) "וריחקום בני משפחה". ולאסור ולהתיר – שייך אעבדים. והא דפריך בפ"ב (לקמן דף כח:) טמאה וטהורה ס"ד – התם דכייל כל פסולי בחד לישנא, הוה ליה למיתני: משפחה זו כשרה וזו פסולה, אבל אממזרות ונתינות לחודא – שייך שפיר לשון טומאה וטהרה. ונאמנת נקט – משום לטהר לקרב ולהתיר, אע"ג דלטמא ולרחק ולאסור בלויתה או בשתיקה לא שייך נאמנות, ועלה קתני בברייתא דהכא: איזו היא עיסה שנאמנת בלויתה או בשתיקה ולטהר את הבת – כל שאין בה כו', והכי משמע בתוספתא, דקתני: נאמנת עיסה לטהר ולטמא, לאסור ולהתיר, לרחק ולקרב, ובאלמנת עיסה לא נגעו. והשתא לא קשה דרבי יוסי אדרבי יוסי, דהא דאכשר רבי יוסי בשתוק ממזר – אגוף העיסה קאי, להכשיר את הבת, אבל במקום שמזכיר אלמנת עיסה להכשיר – דוקא אלמנה, ולא הבת, כדמוכח בקדושין (דף עה.) ושם ודאי פוסל רבי יוסי אפילו את האלמנה, כדמוכח נמי בקדושין. וכדברי ר"ת משמע בירושלמי, דקתני: איזהו עיסה – כל שאין בה לא ממזר ולא נתין ולא עבדי מלכים. רבי מאיר אומר: כל שאין בה אחד מכל אלו בתה כשרה, אלמא דבכשרות דבת מיירי, ולא באלמנה. ומיהו קשה לרשב"א: כיון דהך ברייתא קיימא לפרושי ההיא דסוף עדיות, אם כן רבי מאיר דסבר דחלל בין צווח בין שתק כשר, א"כ היכי מפרש הא דקתני לרחק? ואור"י: הא דמכשר ר"מ חלל שותק – הני מילי כשאחרי כן שואלין ממנו אם הוא חלל אם לאו, וצווח, אבל אם לעולם שותק – פשיטא דפסול. והא דקתני דנאמנת לרחק – אם לעולם שותק. לא

*) [וגם על חלל עצמו אין שייך לשון טימוע]

תוספות רי"ד

אין מינאי הוא אר"י למאי ניחוש לה חדא דהא קא מודי ותו האר"י אמר שמואל הל' כר"ג פי' דכי אומרת מאיש פלוני וכהן הוא נאמנת ואע"ג דאתי ההוא פלוני ומכחיש לה ואמר לא באתי עלי' מעולם היא נאמנת דאי איתא דהיכא דקא מכחיש לה לא מהימנא א"כ אמאי מהימן לה ר"ג מסתמא יבוא אותו פלוני ויאמר אם בא עליה אם לאו אלא ודאי דאע"ג דהוה אתי ומכחיש לה היא נאמנת בין להכשיר בה בין להכשיר בתה והכא נמי אע"ג דאתי ארוס ואמר מעולם לא באתי עליה היא נאמנת להכשיר העובר ולהכשיר עצמה אם תתאלמן אבל לארום ודאי אסורה דשויא אנפשיה חתיכה דאיסו' א"ל אביי ובהא כי לא מודה מי מכשיר ר"ג והא"ל שמואל לר"י שיננא הלכתא כר"ג ואת לא תעביד עובדא [עד] דאיכא רוב כשרים אצלה והכא רוב פסולים אצלה פי' ארוסה הכל פסולין אצלה חוץ מן הארום וליטעמך תיקשי לך היא גופא הלכה ואת לא תעביד עובדא. אלא הא לכתחלה הא דיעבד והכא נמי כדיעבד דמי פי' אם בא כהן לימלך לב"ד לא שרינן ליה לכתחלה אלא א"כ הוי רוב כשרים אצלה והא דיעבד פי' המורה אם נשאה כהן ולא נמלך לא מפקינן לה מיניה והא נמי כדיעבד דמי שנתעברה ואתה בא לפסול העובר ולאסרה על הארום אם אין אתה מאמינה הרי אתה מוציאה מבעלה. ואינו נ"ל דאפי' אם מהימנינן לה ה"מ להכשיר גופה ובתה לכהונה אבל על בעלה לא ומשום דשויתה אנפשיה חתיכה דאיסורא אלא נ"ל כך [פירושו] אי לא מהימנינן לה משוינן לבתה ממזרת ואסורה לבא בקהל ולא דמיא לפנויה שנתעברה דאע"ג דפסיל לה לכהונה לא פסיל לה לקהל דאימר לחלל נבעלה ואסורה לכהן ומותרת לישראל אבל הכא אי מספקת לה דנתעברה מאחר הויא לה ממזרת ומה לי לאפוקי מקהל ומה לי לאפקה מבעלה וכי היכי דדיעבד דהתם אמרת נאמנת הכא נמי נאמנת ומותרת בתה לכהן כדי שלא תוציאנה מקהל והא דר"י אתיא כשמואל דבפרק אלמנה לכ"ג פליגי רב ושמואל בארוסה שעיברה דרב אמר הולד ממזר ושמואל אמר הולד שתוקי ובפרק עשרה יוחסין מפרש' אמילתא דשמואל מאי שתוקי בדוקי כאבא שאול דבדק' לי' לאימ' ואי אמרה מארוסה נתעברה

עין משפט נר מצוה

פו א ב מיי' פט"ו מהל' איסורי ביאה הלכה יא ופי"ח הלכה יג יד סמג לאוין קכא טוש"ע אה"ע סימן ו סעיף יז [וברב אלפס עוד ביבמות פ"ז דף כ"ז]:

פז ג ד ה מיי' פי"ט שם הלכה ט טור אה"ע סימן ו וש"ע אה"ע סימן ב סעיף ה.

מסורת הש"ס

[לעיל יב:]

[עי' תוס' יבמות קטו: ד"ה וכן הוין ותוס' ב"מ ע. סד"ה אתא ותוס' לקמן פה: ד"ה ועוד]

[נ"ל לרבה]

קדושין עה. עדיות פ"ח מ"ג

[תוספתא קדושין פ"ה]

[יבמות טז:]

הגהות מהר"ב רנשבורג

א] גמ' א"ל אביי ובהא כי לא מודה מי מכשיר ר"ג. עיין ב"מ ע ע"א תד"ה אתא מריה וכו':

עין משפט נר מצוה

פח א מיי' פי"ט מהל' איסורי ביאה הלכה כב טוש"ע אה"ע סימן ב סעיף ז:

שמעתי כל שאין בה אחד מכל אלו – משיאין לכהונה. ר"ש בן אלעזר אומר משום ר"מ, וכן היה ר"ש בן מנסיא אומר כדבריו: איזוהי אלמנת עיסה – כל שנשתמע בה ספק חלל. מכירין ישראל ממזרים שביניהם, ואין מכירין חללין שביניהם. אמר מר: איזוהי אלמנת עיסה – כל שאין בה לא משום ממזרות, ולא משום נתינות, ולא משום עבדי מלכים. הא חלל – כשר. מאי שנא הנך – דאורייתא, חלל נמי דאורייתא! ותו, אמר רבי מאיר: שמעתי כל שאין בה אחד מכל אלו משיאין לכהונה, היינו תנא קמא! ותו, ר"ש בן אלעזר אומר משום ר' מאיר, וכן היה ר"ש בן מנסיא אומר כדבריו: איזוהי אלמנת עיסה – כל שנשתמע בה ספק חלל, מכירין ישראל ממזרים שביניהן ואין מכירין חללין שביניהן, והא אמרת רישא חלל כשר! א"ר יוחנן: "ממזר" – צווח, ו"חלל" – שותק, איכא בינייהו. תנא קמא סבר: [א]כל פסול דקרו ליה ושתיק – פסול. והכי קאמר ת"ק: איזוהי אלמנת עיסה – כל שאין בה לא שתוק ממזרות, ולא שתוק נתינות, ולא שתוק עבדי מלכים, ולא שתוק חלל. וקאמר ליה ר"מ: הנך הוא – דקא פסיל ליה בקהל, אבל שתוק חלל – כשר, והא דשתיק – משום דלא איכפת ליה. וקאמר ליה ר"ש בן אלעזר לתנא קמא דר' מאיר: אי שמיע לך דמכשר ר"מ בשתיקה – לא דקרו ליה חלל ושתיק, אלא דקרו ליה ממזר ושתיק, והאי דשתיק – סבר: ממזר קלא אית ליה. אבל "ממזר" וצווח, "חלל" ושותק, פסול, והאי דאשתיק – סבר: מיסתייה דלא מפקי ליה מקהל. תני חדא: ר' יוסי אומר שתוק ממזר – כשר, שתוק חלל – פסול. ותניא אידך: שתוק חלל – כשר, שתוק ממזר – פסול! לא קשיא; הא – ת"ק אליבא דר"מ, הא – דר"ש בן אלעזר אליבא דר"מ.§

מתני' א"ר יוסי: מעשה בתינוקת שירדה למלאות מים מן העין, ונאנסה, אמר רבי יוחנן בן נורי: אם רוב אנשי העיר משיאין לכהונה – הרי זו תינשא לכהונה.§

גמ' אמר ליה רבא לרב נחמן: ר' יוחנן בן נורי דאמר כמאן? אי כרבן גמליאל – אפילו ברוב פסולין נמי מכשר, אי כרבי יהושע – אפילו ברוב כשרים נמי פסיל! אמר ליה: הכי אמר רב יהודה אמר רב:

בקרונות

שמעתי כו'. לקמיה פריך: היינו תנא קמא, דתנא קמא נמי הכי אמר, דמשום דאין בה אחד מכל אלו העידו עליה להכשיר. מכירין ישראל ממזרין שביניהן. וספק ממזר יש לך להכשיר, דאי ממזר הוה – מידע הוו ידעי ביה. ואין מכירין חללין שביניהן. וספק חלל יש לך לפסול. ולקמיה פריך: הא אמרת רישא: איזוהי אלמנת עיסה – כל שנשתמע בה ספק חלל, אלמא ספק חלל כשר. הא חלל כשר. משום ספק חלל לא פסיל לה. מאי שנא הנך. דפסיל לה ספק דידהו. דאורייתא. משום דוודאן פוסלין מן התורה בביאה, דנפקא לן ביבמות (דף סח.) מ"כי תהיה לאיש זר", כיון שנבעלה לפסול לה – פסלה. חלל נמי. ודאי פסול מדאורייתא, דילפינן לה התם מ"לא יחלל זרעו", מקיש זרעו לו, מה הוא פוסל בביאתו – אף זרעו פוסל. והוא גופיה נפקא לן מ"לא יחלל", שני חילולין במשמע, אחד לזרעו ואחד לאשתו. ר"ש בן אלעזר כו'. סיפא דמילתיה ארישא דמילתיה פריך, דקתני סיפא: אין מכירין חללין שביניהן, משמע אפשר שהיה חלל אבל לא היו מכירין בו, אלמא אית ליה דפסיל. ורישא אמר: איזוהי אלמנת עיסה, והכשיר כל שנשתמע בה ספק חלל. אמר ר' יוחנן ממזר צווח וחלל שותק איכא בינייהו. אדם שכשקורין אותו ממזר הוא צווח, וכשקורין אותו חלל – שותק, איכא בין ר"מ לת"ק ובין תנא קמא, דברייתא אליבא דר"מ ור"ש בן אלעזר אליבא דר"מ. תנא קמא סבר כל פסול דקרו ליה ושתיק פסול. דהודאה היא. וכל שאין בה לא משום ממזרות כו' דקאמר – אשתיקות קאי. והכי קאמר איזוהי אלמנה עיסה. להכשיר. כל שאין בה לא שתוק ממזרות ולא שתוק נתינות. וכיון דתלה טעמא בשתיקה, הוא הדין לכל שתוקי פסול, ולא הוצרך למנות את כולם. ובאיזו הכשירו – באשת ספק חלל שאנו מכירין את ספיקו, שנתגרשה אמו ספק. אבל מי שאין מכירין בו, ושמענו שפוסלין אותו ושותק – פסול. וקאמר ליה ר"מ. דווקא הני, אבל שתוק חלל לא פסול. והא דשתיק. לאו משום דאודי, אלא משום דלא איכפת ליה, הואיל ולאו פסול קהל הוא. והיינו דקאמר כל שאין בה אחד מכל אלו שתיקות – משיאין בנותיהן לכהונה, ואפי' יש בו שתוק חלל. וקאמר ליה ר"ש לתנא קמא. לאו לתנא קמא דברייתא קאמר, דההיא רבנן היא. אלא לתנא ששנה דברי ר"מ בבית המדרש, ואמר בשם ר"מ שמעתי כל שאין בה כו'. אי שמיע לך כו'. והכי קאמר: איזו היא אלמנת עיסה – כל שנשתמע בה ספק חלל שאנו מכירין את פסולו, שהיתה אמו ספק גרושה. אבל שתוק חלל ואין אנו מכירין בו – פסול, כתנא קמא. ומיהו, בהא פליג רבי מאיר אתנא קמא: דאיהו כל פסול דשתיק ביה פסיל, ולרבי מאיר חלל שתוק הוא דפסול, דסבר מסתייה דלא מפקי ליה מקהל, ואם אני צווח – יכריזו עלי, ויודע פסולי בבירור. ועכשיו אין מכירין ישראל חללין שביניהם. אבל שתוק ממזר – כשר, דהאי דשתיק, סבר: הכל יודעין שאיני ממזר, דמכירין ישראל ממזרין שביניהן. **מתני'** מן העין. מן המעיין. אם רוב העיר. כשרין להשיא בנותיהן ואלמנותיהן לכהונה, שאין רוב בני העיר מן הפוסלין אשה לכהונה בביאתן – אף זו תינשא לכהונה. **גמ'** דאמר כמאן. דבעי רוב כשרין. אפילו ברוב פסולין נמי מכשר. דאית ליה: העמד אשה על חזקתה. אמר ליה הכי אמר כו'. לעולם כרבי יהושע, והכא משום דאיכא תרי רובי לכשרות – אכשרה, וכדרב יהודה. ולקמן מפרש טעמא ואזיל מאי שנא תרי רובי מחד רובא.

בקרונות

לא משום ממזרות כו'. הא דלא חשיב עמוני ומואבי – משום דלא פסיקא, דזכרים אסורין ונקבות מותרות. ומצרי ואדומי לא חשיב, דאינן אסורין אלא עד דור שלישי. **ותו** ר"ש בן אלעזר אומר איזוהי עיסה כל שנשמע בה ספק חלל והאמרת רישא חלל כשר. ה"ג בכל הספרים, ובפירוש ר"ת. ומפרש: כל שנשמע בה ספק חלל, הא ודאי חלל – פסול. והא אמרת רישא חלל כשר, והיינו ודאי חלל! ואין נראה, דמאי פריך מתנא קמא? דלמא ת"ק פליג עליה! ופירוש הקונטרס וגרסתו עיקר. **ממזר** צווח וחלל שותק איכא בינייהו. תימה: דהוה ליה למימר ממזר צווח ושותק וחלל שותק איכא בינייהו! דבממזר שותק נמי פליגי, דהא מכשר ליה ר"ש בן אלעזר*! **אבל** ממזר צווח וחלל שותק פסול. וא"ת: ממזר צווח מנא ליה דפסל ר"ש בן אלעזר? ואומר ר"י: מדקתני במילתיה איזוהי עיסה – כל שנשמע בה ספק חלל. דלא הוה ליה למימר אלא מכירין ישראל ממזרים שביניהם, ואין מכירין חללין שביניהם, דמינה שמעינן בחלל צווח דכשר, כי היכי דלא הוצרך להשמיענו כל שנשמע בה ספק ממזר. אלא ודאי אתא למידק דחלל צווח דוקא כשר, הא ממזר צווח – פסול. **מסתייה** דלא מפקינן ליה מקהל. וא"ת: מה צריך להאי טעמא? לימא: הא דשתיק – משום דאודויי קא מודי, דהא ממזר שותק פסול לת"ק משום דשתיקה כהודאה, וה"ה דחלל שותק לר"ש, דפסול מהאי טעמא! ואע"ג דגבי ממזר שותק לדידיה לא הוי שתיקה כהודאה – היינו משום דסבר דממזר קלא אית ליה. וי"ל: דהכי פירושא: סבר מסתייה דלא מפקינן ליה מקהל (כהונה). פי': אפי' מקהל כהונה, אע"פ שזה מחרפו וקוראו חלל – סבור דאין מוציאין אותו מקהל כהונה, וסבור אם יצווח יחזרו לברר הדבר ויפסלוהו, וטעם זה שייך גם בממזר שותק לת"ק, ולא נאמר דשתיקה כהודאה. וכן פירש בקונטרס. **כמאן** אי כר"ג אפילו ברוב פסולין נמי מכשר. וא"ת: והא לא מכשר ברוב פסולין אלא כשטוענת ברי, ואית לה מיגו דאי בעיא אמרה לא נבעלתי, או בלא מגו היכא דאיכא למימר בודקת ומזנה. אבל הכא, אפילו טוענת ברי – הא לית לה מגו. וליכא למימר בודקת ומזנה, דהא נאנסה! ואפי' אם נאמר דהכא לא ראוה שנאנסה, אלא היא אמרה כן, דאית לה מגו – א"כ תקשי הלכתא אהלכתא, דלקמן פסיק רב הלכה כר' יוסי, ולעיל פסיק רב יהודה אמר שמואל הלכה כר"ג! ואין נראה לומר דפליגי, דא"כ מאי מייתי אעובדא דארוס וארוסתו מרב יהודה אמר שמואל, וכן לעיל (דף יג.) פריך הלכתא אהלכתא, קי"ל כרב נחמן בדיני כו' ואדרבה הא רב פסיק כר' יהושע וקי"ל כרב באיסורי! ויש לומר, דהכי פירושו: כמאן, אי כר"ג ובטוענת ברי, ובלא ראוה שנאנסה, דאיכא מגו – אפילו ברוב פסולים נמי מכשר, ואיירי נמי כשראוה מדברת, דאי לא ראוה מדברת – מאי פריך אי כרבי יהושע אפילו ברוב כשרים נמי פסול? ומשני אמר

[ושמא לא נקיט אלא מאי לאכשר ר"מ ור"ש בן אלעזר פוסל. ת"י.]

תוספות רי"ד

נאמנת: **מתני'** א"ר יוסי מעשה בתינוקת שירדה למלאות מים מן המעיין ונאנסה וא"ר בן נורי אם רוב העיר משיאים לכהונה ה"ז תנשא [לכהונה] אר"י אמר רב

גליון הש"ס

מתני' א"ר יוסי מעשה בתינוקת. עיין יבמות דף סז ע"ב תוס' ד"ה אין חוששין:

בְּקְרוֹנוֹת שֶׁל צִיפּוֹרִי הָיָה מַעֲשֶׂה, וְכִדְרַבִּי אַמִּי, דְּאָמַר רַבִּי אַמִּי: וְהוּא שֶׁהָיְתָה סִיעָה שֶׁל בְּנֵי אָדָם כְּשֵׁרִין עוֹבֶרֶת לְשָׁם, וְכִדְר' יַנַּאי. דְּאָמַר ר' יַנַּאי: נִבְעֶלֶת בִּקְרוֹנוֹת — כְּשֵׁרָה לִכְהוּנָּה. בִּקְרוֹנוֹת סָלְקָא דַּעְתָּךְ?! אֶלָּא: נִבְעֶלֶת בִּשְׁעַת קְרוֹנוֹת — כְּשֵׁרָה לִכְהוּנָּה. אֲבָל פֵּירַשׁ אֶחָד מִצִּיפּוֹרִי וּבָעַל — הַוָּלָד שְׁתוּקִי. כִּי הָא דְּכִי אֲתָא רַב דִּימִי אֲמַר זְעֵירִי א"ר חֲנִינָא, וְאָמְרִי לָהּ אֲמַר זְעֵירִי אֲמַר ר' חֲנִינָא: הוֹלְכִין אַחַר רוֹב הָעִיר, וְאֵין הוֹלְכִין אַחַר רוֹב סִיעָה. כְּלַפֵּי לַיָּיא?! הָנֵי נָיְידִי וְהָנֵי קְבִיעִי וְקַיְימִי! אֶלָּא: א הוֹלְכִין אַחַר רוֹב הָעִיר וְהוּא דְּאִיכָּא רוֹב סִיעָה בַּהֲדָהּ. וְאֵין הוֹלְכִין אַחַר רוֹב הָעִיר גְּרֵידְתָּא וְלֹא אַחַר רוֹב סִיעָה גְּרֵידְתָּא. מ"ט — גְּזֵרָה רוֹב סִיעָה אַטּוּ רוֹב הָעִיר. וְרוֹב הָעִיר נַמִי, *אִי דְּקָא אָזְלֵי אִינְהוּ לְגַבָּהּ — כָּל דְּפָרֵישׁ *מֵרוּבָּא פָּרֵישׁ! ב*לָא צְרִיכָא, דְּקָא אָזְלָא אִיהִי לְגַבַּיְיהוּ, דַּהֲוָה לֵיהּ קָבוּעַ, וְא"ר זֵירָא: כָּל קָבוּעַ כְּמֶחֱצָה עַל מֶחֱצָה דָּמֵי. וּמִי בָּעֵינַן תְּרֵי רוּבֵּי? וְהָתַנְיָא: *ג תֵּשַׁע חֲנוּיוֹת, כּוּלָּן מוֹכְרוֹת בְּשַׂר שְׁחוּטָה, וְאַחַת מוֹכֶרֶת בְּשַׂר נְבֵלָה, וְלָקַח מֵאַחַת מֵהֶן וְאֵינוֹ יוֹדֵעַ מֵאֵי זֶה מֵהֶן לָקַח — סְפֵיקוֹ אָסוּר. ד וּבַנִּמְצָא — הַלֵּךְ אַחַר הָרוֹב! וְכִי תֵּימָא בְּשֶׁאֵין דַּלְתוֹת מְדִינָה נְעוּלוֹת, דְּקָא אָתֵי לַהּ רוּבָּא מֵעָלְמָא — וְהָא א"ר זֵירָא: *אע"פ שֶׁדַּלְתוֹת מְדִינָה נְעוּלוֹת! *מַעֲלָה עָשׂוּ בְּיוּחֲסִין. גּוּפָא, א"ר זֵירָא: כָּל קָבוּעַ כְּמֶחֱצָה עַל מֶחֱצָה דָּמֵי, בֵּין לְקוּלָּא בֵּין לְחוּמְרָא. מְנָא לֵיהּ לְר' זֵירָא הָא? אִילֵימָא מִתֵּשַׁע חֲנוּיוֹת כּוּלָּן מוֹכְרוֹת בְּשַׂר שְׁחוּטָה וְאַחַת בְּשַׂר נְבֵלָה, וְלָקַח מֵאַחַת מֵהֶן, וְאֵינוֹ יוֹדֵעַ מֵאֵיזֶה מֵהֶן לָקַח — סְפֵיקוֹ אָסוּר, וּבַנִּמְצָא — הַלֵּךְ אַחַר הָרוֹב, הָתָם לְחוּמְרָא! אֶלָּא, *ה מִתִּשְׁעָה צְפַרְדְּעִים וְשֶׁרֶץ אֶחָד בֵּינֵיהֶם, וְנָגַע בְּאֶחָד מֵהֶן וְאֵינוֹ יוֹדֵעַ בְּאֵיזֶה מֵהֶן נָגַע, סְפֵיקוֹ טָמֵא. הָתָם נַמִי לְחוּמְרָא! אֶלָּא ו מִתִּשְׁעָה שְׁרָצִים וּצְפַרְדֵּעַ אֶחָד בֵּינֵיהֶם, וְנָגַע בְּאֶחָד מֵהֶן, וְאֵינוֹ יוֹדֵעַ בְּאֵיזֶה מֵהֶן נָגַע, בְּרה"י סְפֵיקוֹ טָמֵא, בִּרְשׁוּת הָרַבִּ' סְפֵיקוֹ טָהוֹר. וּמִדְּאוֹרָיְיתָא מְנָא לָן? *אָמַר קְרָא: ° "וְאָרַב לוֹ וְקָם עָלָיו" — ז עַד שֶׁיִּתְכַּוֵּין לוֹ. וְרַבָּנָן? אָמְרִי דְּבֵי ר' יַנַּאי: פְּרָט לְזוֹרֵק אֶבֶן לְגוֹ. *הֵיכִי דָּמֵי? אִילֵימָא דְּאִיכָּא תִּשְׁעָה גּוֹיִם וְאֶחָד יִשְׂרָאֵל בֵּינֵיהֶם — וְתֵיפּוֹק לֵיהּ דְּרוּבָּא גּוֹיִם נִינְהוּ! אִי נַמִי פַּלְגָא וּפַלְגָא — *סְפֵק נְפָשׁוֹת לְהָקֵל! לָא צְרִיכָא, דְּאִיכָּא תִּשְׁעָה יִשְׂרְאֵלִים וְגוֹי אֶחָד בֵּינֵיהֶם, דַּהֲוָה לֵיהּ גּוֹי קָבוּעַ, וְכָל קָבוּעַ כְּמֶחֱצָה עַל מֶחֱצָה דָּמֵי. אִיתְּמַר רַב חִיָּיא בַּר אַשִׁי אָמַר רַב: הֲלָכָה כְּרַבִּי יוֹסֵי, וְרַב חָנָן בַּר רָבָא אָמַר רַב: הוֹרָאַת שָׁעָה הָיְתָה. מְתִיב רַבִּי יִרְמְיָה: וּלְיוּחֲסִין לָא בָּעֵינַן תְּרֵי רוּבֵּי? וְהָתְנַן: מָצָא

דברים יט

רש"י

בִּקְרוֹנוֹת שֶׁל צִיפּוֹרִי. בְּיוֹם הַשּׁוּק, שֶׁסִּיעוֹת וְשַׁיָּירוֹת מִמָּקוֹם אַחֵר בָּאוֹת שָׁם. וְכִדְרַבִּי אַמִּי. דְּהַשְׁתָּא אִיכָּא רוֹב סִיעָה וְרוֹב הָעִיר. נִבְעֶלֶת בִּקְרוֹנוֹת. מַשְׁמַע עַל הַקָּרוֹן. בִּשְׁעַת קְרוֹנוֹת. שֶׁהַשַּׁיָּירוֹת בָּאוֹת לָעִיר. כְּשֵׁרָה לִכְהוּנָּה. כִּדְקָאָמַר: וְהוּא שֶׁהָיְתָה סִיעָה שֶׁל בְּנֵי אָדָם כְּשֵׁרִים עוֹבֶרֶת שָׁם, דְּאִיכָּא לְמֵימַר שֶׁמֵּהֶם הָיָה. אֲבָל פֵּירַשׁ אֶחָד מִצִּיפּוֹרִי. דְּיָדְעִינַן וַדַּאי דְּמִן הָעִיר הָיָה, אע"פ שֶׁצִּיפּוֹרִי עִיר שֶׁרוּבָּהּ מְשִׂיאִין לִכְהוּנָּה. הַוָּלָד שְׁתוּקִי. דְּבַחַד רוּבָּא לָא מַכְשַׁר. וְכִי הָא דְּכִי אֲתָא רַב דִּימִי אֲמַר זְעֵירִי אֲמַר רַבִּי חֲנִינָא וְאָמְרִי לָהּ. שֶׁלֹּא הוּזְכַּר רַב דִּימִי כָּאן, אֶלָּא זְעֵירִי אֲמַר רַבִּי חֲנִינָא, דְּבָעֵינַן תְּרֵי רוּבֵּי. וּכְדִמְפָרֵשׁ טַעְמָא. הוֹלְכִין אַחַר רוֹב הָעִיר. לְהַכְשִׁיר. וְאֵין הוֹלְכִין אַחַר רוֹב סִיעָה. כְּגוֹן בְּמָקוֹם רָחוֹק מִן הָעִיר, דְּבְוַדַּאי מֵאַנְשֵׁי הַסִּיעָה הֲוָה — אֵין מַכְשִׁירִין אוֹתָהּ, וַאֲפִילּוּ רוּבָּן כְּשֵׁרִין. וְקַשְׁיָא לָן כְּלַפֵּי לַיָּיא. כְּנֶגֶד אֵיפוֹא הַדָּבָר הַזֶּה סוֹבֵב?! הָנֵי נָיְידִי. רוֹב סִיעָה נָיְידִי, וְיֵשׁ לְהַלֵּךְ בָּהֶן אַחַר הָרוֹב. וְהָנֵי. שֶׁל עִיר. קְבִיעִי. וַאֲמְרִינַן לְקַמָּן: כָּל קָבוּעַ כְּמֶחֱצָה עַל מֶחֱצָה דָּמֵי, וַאֲפִילּוּ אֵין שָׁם אֶלָּא אֶחָד — פְּסוּלָה. וְלֹא אַחַר רוֹב סִיעָה גְּרֵידְתָּא. וְהָכִי קָאָמַר: אֵין הוֹלְכִין אַחַר רוֹב סִיעָה לְבַדָּהּ, וְכָל שֶׁכֵּן אַחַר רוֹב הָעִיר לְבַדָּהּ. מ"ט. אַחַר רוֹב סִיעָה לָא. גְּזֵרָה אַטּוּ רוֹב הָעִיר. דִּקְבִיעִי. וּפָרְכִינַן. רוֹב הָעִיר נַמִי. אִי עָקַר הַבּוֹעֵל מִבֵּיתוֹ וְאָזַל לְגַבָּהּ — הֲוָה נָייד, וְקי"ל: כָּל דְּפָרֵישׁ מֵרוּבָּא פָּרֵישׁ! וּמְשַׁנֵּי. אִיכָּא דְּקָאָזְלָא לְגַבַּיְיהוּ כו', וְלָא גָּרְסִינַן *מַאי אִיכָּא, יֵשׁ שֶׁהוֹלֶכֶת הִיא אֶצְלוֹ וְהָוֵה לֵיהּ קָבוּעַ. הִלְכָּךְ, אֲפִילּוּ בְּרוֹב כְּשֵׁרִים, אוֹ רוֹב הָעִיר אוֹ רוֹב סִיעָה — פָּסוּל, כְּרַבִּי יְהוֹשֻׁעַ. וּמִשּׁוּם תְּרֵי רוּבֵּי אַכְשְׁרָהּ, דְּלֵיכָּא לְמִיגְזַר מִידֵּי. וְלָקַח בָּשָׂר מֵאַחַת מֵהֶן. בְּמָקוֹם קְבִיעוּת. סְפֵיקוֹ אָסוּר. דְּכָל קָבוּעַ כְּמֶחֱצָה עַל מֶחֱצָה דָּמֵי. וּבַנִּמְצָא. בָּשָׂר הַנִּמְצָא בַּשּׁוּק, וְלָא יָדְעִינַן מֵאֵיזֶה פֵּירַשׁ. הַלֵּךְ אַחַר הָרוֹב. הוֹאִיל וְהַבָּא לְפָנֵינוּ לֹא בִּמְקוֹם קְבִיעוּת לְקָחָהּ, וּכְבָר פֵּירְשָׁה עַל יְדֵי אַחֵר, וְכָל דְּפָרֵישׁ מֵרוּבָּא פָּרֵישׁ. דְּקָאָתֵי לָהּ רוּבָּא מֵעָלְמָא. וּכְגוֹן שֶׁרוֹב סִיעַת טַבָּחֵי יִשְׂרָאֵל כְּשֵׁרִים בָּאוּ לְכָאן, דְּאִיכָּא תְּרֵי רוּבֵּי. אוֹ שֶׁרוֹב טַבָּחֵי כָּל הַמְּדִינָה יִשְׂרָאֵל, דְּאִיכָּא תְּרֵי רוּבֵּי: רוֹב הָעִיר, וְרוֹב הַמְּדִינָה דְּנָיְידִי. אֶלָּא מִתִּשְׁעָה צְפַרְדְּעִים כו'. תּוֹסֶפְתָּא הִיא בְּמַסֶּ' טְהָרוֹת: תִּשְׁעָה לְפַרְדְּעִים מֵתִים בִּרְשׁוּת הַיָּחִיד, וְשֶׁרֶץ אֶחָד כְּגוֹן צָב שֶׁהוּא דּוֹמֶה לִצְפַרְדֵּעַ, בֵּינֵיהֶם, וְנָגַע בְּאֶחָד מֵהֶן — סְפֵיקוֹ טָמֵא. אֶלָּא מִתִּשְׁעָה שְׁרָצִים כו'. אַף הִיא תּוֹסֶפְתָּא בְּמַסֶּ' טְהָרוֹת, וְקָתָנֵי: בְּרה"י סְפֵיקוֹ טָמֵא, בִּרה"ר סְפֵיקוֹ טָהוֹר, אַלְמָא כְּמֶחֱצָה דָּמֵי וּלְקוּלָּא. דְּאִי לָאו כְּמֶחֱצָה דָּמֵי — אֵין כָּאן סְפֵק טוּמְאָה אֶלָּא וַדַּאי טוּמְאָה, דְּהָא רוּבָּא שְׁרָצִים. אָמַר קְרָא וְאָרַב לוֹ עַד שֶׁיְּהֵא מִתְכַּוֵּין לוֹ. פְּרָט לְמִתְכַּוֵּין לַהֲרוֹג אֶת זֶה וְהָרַג אֶת זֶה. הָכִי דָּרֵישׁ לֵיהּ ר"ש בְּסַנְהֶדְרִין. וְאָמְרִינַן הָתָם: וְרַבָּנָן הֵיכִי דָּרְשֵׁי לֵיהּ? אָמְרֵי דְּבֵי ר' יַנַּאי פְּרָט לַזּוֹרֵק אֶבֶן לְגוֹ. לְתוֹךְ חֲבוּרַת בְּנֵי אָדָם גּוֹיִם וְיִשְׂרְאֵלִים. אֲבָל שְׁנֵי יִשְׂרְאֵלִים עוֹמְדִין, וְנִתְכַּוֵּין לַהֲרוֹג (א) זֶה (וְהָרַג זֶה) וְהִתְרוּ בּוֹ וְקִבֵּל הַתְרָאָה, וְנָפְלָה הַכָּאָה עַל חֲבֵירוֹ — חַיָּיב. וְהַיְינוּ טַעְמָא דְּקָאָמַר הָכָא וְרַבָּנָן, מִשּׁוּם דִּבְסַנְהֶדְרִין הָכִי אִיתָא. תֵּיפּוֹק לֵיהּ דְּרוּבָּא גּוֹיִם נִינְהוּ. וְלָמָּה לִי קְרָא? וְאִי נַמִי פַּלְגָא וּפַלְגָא, אַכַּתִּי לָא אִיצְטְרִיךְ קְרָא, דְּמֵהֵיכָא תֵּיתֵי דְּנִיקְטְלֵיהּ? סְפֵק נְפָשׁוֹת. דִּינֵי נְפָשׁוֹת לְהָקֵל, דְּהָא "וְהִצִּילוּ הָעֵדָה" כְּתִיב (במדבר לה). דַּהֲוָה לֵיהּ גּוֹי קָבוּעַ בֵּינֵיהֶם. וְאַשְׁמוּעִינַן הַאי קְרָא דְּכָל קָבוּעַ כְּמֶחֱצָה עַל מֶחֱצָה דָּמֵי. הוֹרָאַת שָׁעָה הָיְתָה. הָךְ דְּרִיב"נ לוֹרֶךְ שָׁעָה הָיְתָה, אוֹ רָאוּ שָׁם שֶׁאָמַר לִידֵי הֶיכֵּר דְּבָרִים לְהַתִּיר, אֲבָל לְדוֹרוֹת — תְּרֵי רוּבֵּי בָּעֵינַן. קס"ד דְּמִשּׁוּם רוֹב הָעִיר גְּרֵידְתָּא אַכְשְׁרוּהָ, וַאֲמַר רַב הֲלָכָה כְּרַבִּי יוֹסֵי. מַתִּיב רַבִּי יִרְמְיָה כו'. מָצָא

תוספות

אמר רב בקרונות של לפורי היה מעשה כו' – פי': לעולם דלא טענה ברי. ור' יוחנן בן נורי בתרווייהו היכא דלא טענה ברי – לכ"ע בעינן תרי רובי. והא דלא קאמר בשניה לעולם דלא טענה ברי, משום דלאתקפתא לא קאמר אי בטוענת ברי כו'. אי נמי יוכל לפרש, דבשניה נמי איירי בברי, ודאיכא מגו. ולא תקשי הלכתא אהלכתא, דדוקא דיעבד פסיק שמואל כר"ג כדאמר לעיל: ואת לא תעביד עובדא עד דאיכא רוב כשרין. אף על גב דלעיל משמע דברוב אחד שרי לכתחלה, רב חייא בר אשי סבר דלכתחלה בעינן תרי, רובי ומתני' קתני הרי זו תנשא – דמשמע לכתחלה.

דלמא אזלא איהי לגבייהו. פי' לתוך ביתם, דאפילו בתוך העיר לא חשיב קבוע, דדמי לנמלא בין החנויות, דלא חשיב קבוע. וכן גבי תינוק מושלך בעיר לא חשיב קבוע, הואיל ולא נמלא בבית. ולכך פירש בקונטרס שפירש בועל מביתו. וא"ת: דבנזיר פ"ב (דף יב. ושם) פריך אהא דאמר: האומר לשלוחו "לא וקדש לי אשה סתם" – אסור בכל הנשים, שבעולם מקן סתומה, ומסיק: אמינא לך אנא אשה דלא ניידא, ואת אמרת לי איסורא דנייד? וכי תימא ה"נ בשוקא אשכחה וקדיש – התם הדרא לניחותא. משמע לגבי אדם לא שייך כל דפריש מרובא פריש משום דהדר לניחותיה! ולאו פירכא היא, דהתם בשעת האיסור כשזה בא על שום אשה הדרא לניחותא האשה שקידש השליח. אבל הכא, כי אזלי אינהו לגבה בשעה שאוסרה הרי הוא נייד.

פרט לזורק אבן לגו. תימה: דלר' שמעון קבוע מנא ליה? ואין לומר דמסקינן בפ' "הנשרפין" (סנהדרין דף עט. ושם) דר"ש סבר כרבי דיליף "נתינה" "נתינה" ואייתר ליה "וארב לו" לקבוע – דאכתי לתנא דבי חזקיה מנא ליה קבוע? דלית ליה דרבי, דהא באין מתכוין פטור ממונו*.

וספק נפשות להקל. תימה: למ"ד: התראת ספק לא שמה התראה, אפילו ספק נפשות להחמיר – פטור, משום דהתראת ספק היא! ואי למ"ד שמה התראה – היכי פטרינן ליה כשנמצא שישראל הרג? הא מיחייב בהכה את זה וחזר והכה את זה*, ובנותר כשאמרו לו אל תותיר, אע"ג דספק הוא! וי"ל: דשאני התם שיודע בודאי שיבא לידי איסור אם יותיר או יכה שניהם – מש"ה שמה התראה, אבל הכא – אינו יודע שודאי יבוא לידי איסור, שאינו יודע את מי יכה.

וליוחסין לא בעינן תרי רובי ורמינהי כו'. הוה מצי לשנויי: שאני תינוק דלית לי' חזק' דכשרו'. ולרב

תוספות רי"ד

בקרונות של צפורי היה מעשה וכדר' ינאי דאמר נבעלה בשעת קרונות כשירה לכהונה פי' קרוניות הבאים ממקום אחר ומתקבצים שם ליום השוק והוא שהיתה סיעה של בני אדם כשרים עוברים שם דהוה תרי רובא לכשרות רוב העיר ורוב סיעה. פי' כל זה מפני שלא ידעה למי נבעלה אבל אי ידעה ואמרה לכשר נבעלתי הלכה כר"ג ונאמנת אפילו ברוב פסולים: ומקשי' ומי בעי תרי רובי והתניא ט' חנויות כולן מוכרות בשר שחוטה ואחת מוכרת בשר נבילה ולקח מאחת מהן ואינו יודע מאיזה מהן לקח ספיקו אסור שכל קבוע כמחצה על מחצה דמי ובנמצא הלך אחר הרוב דכל דפריש מרובא פריש. ומהדר מעלה עשו ביוחסין: איתמר אר"ח אמר רב הלכה כר' יוסי פי' דבעי' תרי רובי: א"ר זירא כל קבוע כמחצה על מחצה דמי בין לקולא בין לחומרא לחומרא כגון ט' חנויות דאמרן. א"נ ט' צפרדעים ושרץ א' ביניהם ברה"י ונגע באח' מהן ואינו יודע באיזה מהן נגע ספיקו טמא. לקולא כגון ט' שרצים וצפרדע א' ביניהן ברה"ר ונגע באח' מהן וא"י באיזה מהן נגע ספיקו טהור אלא כמחצה על מחצה דמי ולקולא. דאי לאו כמחצה על מחצה דמי אין כאן ספק טומאה אלא ודאי טומאה דהא רובא שרצים: האשה

עין משפט נר מצוה

פט א ב מיי' פי"ח מהלכות איסורי ביאה הל' יד סמג לאוין קכא טוש"ע אה"ע סימן ו סעיף יז יח:

צ ג מיי' פ"ח מהלכות מאכלות אסורות הל' יא סמג לאוין קמא טור ש"ע י"ד סימן קי סע"ג:

צא ד מיי' שם וטוש"ע שם ובסי' סג ס"א:

צב ה ו מיי' פי"ח מהלכות אבות הטומאות הלכה ב:

צג ז מיי' פ"ד מהל' רוצח הלכה א סמג לאוין קמג.

מסורת הש"ס

[קדושין עג.]

[ברכות כח. וש"נ]

פסחים ט: חולין לה. נדה יח.

נ"ל מאי רוב העיר איכא כו' רש"ל

נדה יח. ע"ש תוספתא טהרות פ"ו

ב"ק מד: סנהדרין עט.

[יומא פד.]

[שבת קכט. וש"נ]

[רש"ל מוחק וג"ב גירסת רש"י איכא דקאזלא לגבייהו ועי' ב' גירסות בב"י אה"ע סימן ו]

[לעיל יג. וש"נ]

[ובסנהדרין עט. ד"ה וכל כתבו תוס' תירוץ אחר ועי"ל בב"ק מד: ד"ה כל ועי' תוספות נדה יח. ד"ה ספיקא]

יבמות קח.

הגהות הב"ח

(א) רש"י ד"ה אמרי וכו' להרוג את זה והרג את זה:

*מָצָא בָּהּ תִּינוֹק מוּשְׁלָךְ, אִם רוֹב גּוֹיִם — גּוֹי, אִם רוֹב יִשְׂרָאֵל — יִשְׂרָאֵל, מֶחֱצָה עַל מֶחֱצָה — יִשְׂרָאֵל. וְאָמַר רַב: לֹא שָׁנוּ אֶלָּא לְהַחֲיוֹתוֹ, [א]אֲבָל לְיוֹחֲסִין — לֹא, וּשְׁמוּאֵל אָמַר: לְפַקֵּחַ עָלָיו אֶת הַגַּל! אִשְׁתַּמִּיטְתֵּיהּ הָא דְּא"ר יְהוּדָה אָמַר רַב: בִּקְרוֹנוֹת שֶׁל צִפּוֹרִי הֲוָה מַעֲשֶׂה. וּלְרַב חָנָן בַּר רָבָא דְּאָמַר: הוֹרָאַת שָׁעָה הָיְתָה, קַשְׁיָא הָא! מַאן דְּמַתְנֵי הָא לָא מַתְנֵי הָא. גּוּפָא, מָצָא בָּהּ תִּינוֹק מוּשְׁלָךְ, אִם רוֹב גּוֹיִם — גּוֹי, אִם רוֹב יִשְׂרָאֵל — יִשְׂרָאֵל, מֶחֱצָה עַל מֶחֱצָה — יִשְׂרָאֵל, אָמַר רַב: לֹא שָׁנוּ אֶלָּא לְהַחֲיוֹתוֹ, אֲבָל לְיוֹחֲסִין — לֹא, וּשְׁמוּאֵל אָמַר: לְפַקֵּחַ עָלָיו אֶת הַגַּל. וּמִי אָמַר שְׁמוּאֵל הָכִי? וְהָאָמַר רַב יוֹסֵף אָמַר רַב יְהוּדָה אָמַר שְׁמוּאֵל: אֵין הוֹלְכִין בְּפִיקּוּחַ נֶפֶשׁ אַחַר הָרוֹב! אֶלָּא, כִּי אִיתְּמַר דִּשְׁמוּאֵל — אַרֵישָׁא אִתְּמַר: אִם רוֹב גּוֹיִם — גּוֹי, אָמַר שְׁמוּאֵל: *[ב]וּלְפַקֵּחַ עָלָיו אֶת הַגַּל — אֵינוֹ כֵּן. "אִם רוֹב גּוֹיִם — גּוֹי". לְמַאי הִלְכְתָא? אָמַר רַב פַּפָּא: [ג]לְהַאֲכִילוֹ נְבֵילוֹת. "אִם רוֹב יִשְׂרָאֵל — יִשְׂרָאֵל", לְמַאי הִלְכְתָא? אָמַר רַב פַּפָּא: [ד]לְהַחֲזִיר לוֹ אֲבֵידָה. "מֶחֱצָה עַל מֶחֱצָה — יִשְׂרָאֵל" לְמַאי הִלְכְתָא? אָמַר רֵישׁ לָקִישׁ: [ה]לִנְזָקִין. ה"ד? אִי נֵימָא דִּנְגָחֵיהּ תּוֹרָא דִּידָן לְתוֹרָא דִּידֵיהּ — לֵימָא לֵיהּ: אַיְיתֵי רְאָיָה דְּיִשְׂרָאֵל אַתְּ וּשְׁקוֹל! לָא צְרִיכָא, דִּנְגָחֵיהּ תּוֹרָא דִּידֵיהּ לְתוֹרָא דִּידָן. פַּלְגָּא — מְשַׁלֵּם, וְאִידָךְ פַּלְגָּא — אָמַר לְהוּ: אַיְיתֵי רְאָיָה דְּלָאו יִשְׂרָאֵל אֲנָא, וְאֶתֵּן לְכוֹן.§

הדרן עלך בתולה נשאת

מָצָא בָּהּ תִּינוֹק מוּשְׁלָךְ. מִשְׁנָה הִיא בְּסֵדֶר טָהֳרוֹת גַּבֵּי עִיר שֶׁיִּשְׂרָאֵלִים וְגוֹיִם דָּרִים בָּהּ. מֶחֱצָה עַל מֶחֱצָה יִשְׂרָאֵל. לְקַמֵּיהּ מְפָרֵשׁ מַאי אִיכָּא בֵּין רוֹב יִשְׂרָאֵל לְמֶחֱצָה עַל מֶחֱצָה, דְּפָלֵיג לְהוּ בִּתְרֵי. לֹא שָׁנוּ. דְּאִם רוֹב יִשְׂרָאֵל יִשְׂרָאֵל. אֶלָּא לְהַחֲיוֹתוֹ. ב"ד מְצוּוִּין לְפַרְנְסוֹ, מִשּׁוּם "וְחֵי אָחִיךָ עִמָּךְ" (ויקרא כה). אֲבָל לְיוֹחֲסִין לֹא. דְּאִם בַּת הִיא — אֲסוּרָה לְכֹהֵן, וַאֲפִי' לֵיכָּא לְמֵיחַשׁ מִשּׁוּם אֲסוּפִי, כְּגוֹן הָנָךְ דְּאָמְרִינַן בְּ"עֲשָׂרָה יוֹחֲסִין" (קדושין עג:): *מְשַׁלְּטֵי הַדָּמֵיהּ, תָּלֵי פִּיתְקָא, תָּלֵי קְמֵיעָא — מֵיהוּ חָיְישִׁינַן שֶׁמָּא בַּת גּוֹי הִיא. (א) וּלְמ"ד גִּיּוֹרֶת פְּסוּלָה לִכְהוּנָּה — אֲפִילּוּ קְטַנָּה זוֹ אֲסוּרָה לְכֹהֵן, דִּתְרֵי רוּבֵּי בָּעֵינַן לְיוֹחֲסִין. וּשְׁמוּאֵל אָמַר אַף לְפַקֵּחַ עָלָיו אֶת הַגַּל. בְּשַׁבָּת, חָשְׁבִינַן לֵיהּ לְיִשְׂרָאֵל. אִשְׁתַּמִּיטְתֵּיהּ. לְרַבִּי יִרְמְיָה. הָא דַּאֲמַר רַב יְהוּדָה. דְּהָכָא נַמִי תְּרֵי רוּבֵּי הָווּ. וּלְרַב חָנָן בַּר רָבָא דַּאֲמַר. מִשְּׁמֵיהּ דְּרַב. הוֹרָאַת שָׁעָה הָיְתָה. וְהָתָם תְּרֵי רוּבֵּי הָווּ, וְקָאָמַר: הוֹרָאַת שָׁעָה הָיְתָה, אֲבָל לְדוֹרוֹת – לָא בָּעֵינַן תְּרֵי רוּבֵּי. קַשְׁיָא הָא. דְּרַב, דְּאָמַר: אֲבָל לְיוֹחֲסִין לֹא. אַלְמָא רַב תְּרֵי רוּבֵּי בָּעֵי. לָא מַתְנֵי הָא. דְּאָמַר רַב יְהוּדָה אָמַר רַב בִּקְרוֹנוֹת שֶׁל צִפּוֹרִי הֲוָה מַעֲשֶׂה, וְחַד רוּבָּא הֲוָה. הִלְכָּךְ, הוֹרָאַת שָׁעָה הָיְתָה. מִי אָמַר שְׁמוּאֵל הָכִי. דִּלְעִנְיַן פִּיקּוּחַ נֶפֶשׁ בָּעֵינַן רוּבָּא. אֵין הוֹלְכִין כּוּ'. דַּאֲפִילּוּ בְּסָפֵק גּוֹי סָפֵק יִשְׂרָאֵל, בְּרוֹב גּוֹיִם — מְפַקְּחִין. וּלְעִנְיַן פִּיקּוּחַ נֶפֶשׁ אֵינוֹ כֵּן. דַּאֲפִילּוּ בְּרוֹב גּוֹיִם מְפַקְּחִין, דְּאֵין הוֹלְכִין בָּהּ אַחַר הָרוֹב. לְמַאי הִלְכְתָא. כֵּיוָן דְּאָמַר שְׁמוּאֵל מְפַקְּחִין עָלָיו אֶת הַגַּל — אַלְמָא לָאו גּוֹי הוּא לְכָל מִילֵּי, וּלְמַאי הִלְכְתָא חָשֵׁיב לֵיהּ גּוֹי? לְהַאֲכִילוֹ נְבֵלוֹת. בְּיָדַיִם, וְכ"ש שֶׁלֹּא יַחֲזִירוּ לוֹ אֲבֵידָה וְלִנְזָקִין. לְהַחֲזִיר לוֹ אֲבֵידָה. רְטוּשָׁא הִיא, דְּמוֹלִיכִין מִיַּד יִשְׂרָאֵל הַזּוֹכֶה בָּהּ. וְעוֹד, דַּאֲמוּר רַבָּנַן (סנהדרין דף עו:): הַמַּחֲזִיר אֲבֵידָה לְגוֹי, עָלָיו הַכָּתוּב אוֹמֵר "לְמַעַן סְפוֹת הָרָוָה אֶת הַצְּמֵאָה", שֶׁהַשֵּׁם מְוַותֵּר לַחֲטָאתָן שֶׁל יִשְׂרָאֵל, וְנֶאֱמַר "לֹא יֹאבֶה ה' סְלוֹחַ לוֹ". מֶחֱצָה עַל מֶחֱצָה יִשְׂרָאֵל לְמַאי הִלְכְתָא. לְהַחֲזִיר לוֹ אֲבֵידָה לָא מָצֵית אָמְרַתְּ דְּא"כ לְמַאי הִלְכְתָא פַּלְגִינְהוּ מֵהֲדָדֵי. לִנְזָקִין. דִּתְנַן בּ"ק (דף לז:) שׁוֹר שֶׁל יִשְׂרָאֵל שֶׁנָּגַח לְשׁוֹר שֶׁל גּוֹי פָּטוּר וְשׁוֹר שֶׁל גּוֹי שֶׁנָּגַח לְשׁוֹר שֶׁל יִשְׂרָאֵל בֵּין תָּם בֵּין מוּעָד מְשַׁלֵּם נֶזֶק שָׁלֵם וְיִשְׂרָאֵל לְיִשְׂרָאֵל תָּם מְשַׁלֵּם חֲצִי נֶזֶק וּמוּעָד מְשַׁלֵּם נֶזֶק שָׁלֵם. אִילֵימָא כּוּ'. וְקָאָמְרַתְּ דְּדָיְינִינַן לֵיהּ כְּיִשְׂרָאֵל וּמְחַיְּיבַתְּ לֵיהּ לְשַׁלֵּם לוֹ חֲצִי נִזְקוֹ. לֵימָא לֵיהּ. יִשְׂרָאֵל אַיְיתִי רְאָיָה דְּהָא מֶחֱצָה עַל מֶחֱצָה הוּא וּסְפֵיקָא הוּא. לָא צְרִיכָא כּוּ'. וְקָא תָּבַע לֵיהּ יִשְׂרָאֵל נֶזֶק שָׁלֵם לְתָם כְּדִין גּוֹי וְאַשְׁמְעִינַן תַּנָּא דְּכְיִשְׂרָאֵל דָּיְינִינַן לֵיהּ וְלֹא מְשַׁלֵּם אֶלָּא חֲצִי נֶזֶק דְּא"ל אַיְיתִי רְאָיָה.

הדרן עלך בתולה נשאת

ולרב חנן דאמר הוראת שעה היתה. ולדורות סגי בחד רובא – קשיא הך. ולא מיסתברא ליה למימר דהוראת שעה היתה שהתיר בתרי רובי. אבל לדורות לא סגי אפילו בתרי רובי. **מאן** דמתני הא לא מתני הא. פי' בקונטרס: דרב חנן לא מתני דבקרונות של צפורי היה מעשה, ולא הוה אלא חד רובא. ולפירושו לא פליגי דלדורות לכ"ע בעינן תרי רובי, ולא פליגי אלא במעשה היכי הוה. ור"ת פי': דרב חנן לא מתני אבל ליוחסין לא, וסגי לדידיה לדורות בחד רובא. אבל קשה לפירושו: לרב חנן תקשי ר' יוחנן בן נורי דאמר כמאן דסגי בחד רובא, כדפריך לעיל! ועוד: דלא מיסתבר דשום אמורא יחלוק אההיא דאבל ליוחסין לא, דרב גופיה קאמר לה בלא אמורא. ולהכי אפירכא דרבי ירמיה לא משני מאן דמתני הא לא מתני הא. **אם** רוב גוים גוי למאי הלכתא. לא מצי למימר לענין שלא להחיותו, דמאי איריא רוב גוים — אפילו מחצה נמי, דדוקא ברוב ישראל קאמר רב דהוי ישראל להחיותו. **להחזיר** לו אבדה. הוה מצי למימר להחיותו, כדאמר רב. אלא נקט להחזיר לו אבדה דהוי רבותא טפי, דאיסור גדול הוא *משום "למען ספות הרוה וגו'". אבל להחיותו לא הוי רבותא כל כך, דהא *מפרנסין עניי גוים עם עניי ישראל. ואפי' לשמואל דאמר *אין הולכין בממון אחר הרוב, היינו, *במוכר שור לחבירו ונמצא נגחן, שבהיתר באו המעות לידו, ומדעתו נתנם לו הלוקח, אבל הכא מודי דאזלינן בתר רובא. **לא** צריכא דנגחיה תורא דידיה כו'. תימה: דהכי נמי הוה מצי למימר מחצה על מחצה גוי, ומנגח תורא דידן לתורה דידיה, [כולה מילתא הוי מצי למימר לענין נגיחה. אלא ניחא בכל חד למצוא דבר חדש. מהר"ס].

הדרן עלך בתולה נשאת

צד א מיי' פט"ו מהל' איסורי ביאה הלכה כה טוש"ע אה"ע סימן ד סעיף לג:

צה ב ג ד ה מיי' שם הל' כו וטור שו"ע שם סעיף לד:

כדאיתא סנהדרין עו:

כדאיתא גיטין סא.

[ב"ק מו: וב"ב נב:]

[עי' תוס' ב"ק מו: ותוס' ב"מ כ: ד"ה איסורא ותוס' סנהדרין ג: ד"ה דיני ותוס' יומא פה.]

מכשירין פ"ב מ"ז יומא פד:

הגה"ה פי' משלטי הדמיה. מתוקנין אבריו. פיתקא. קמיע של כתב. קמיעא. קמיע של עיקרין דהא חסה על חייו והוכיח מתלתו שאוהבת אותו ולא השליכתו למות:

[נראה לר"י דמשום דהפיק וחי בהם ולא שימות בהם ומשמע שלא יבוא לידי מיתה בשום ענין לכך יש לחוש למיעוט ישראל. ת"י]

הגהות הב"ח

(א) רש"י ד"ה אבל כו' ולמ"ד גיורת. נ"ב בפרק הבא על יבמתו דף ס ע"ב: